The Real Paradise

The Real Paradise

Memories of Africa 1950-1963

Ann M. Davidson

The Pentland Press Limited
Edinburgh · Cambridge · Durham

First published in 1993 by
The Pentland Press Ltd.
1 Hutton Close
South Church
Bishop Auckland
Durham

ISBN 1 85821 044 5

Typeset by Elite Typesetting Techniques, Southampton.
Printed and bound by Antony Rowe Ltd., Chippenham.

"The real paradise is the paradise we have lost": Marcel Proust

This account of my life as the wife of an administrative officer in the last years of the British Raj in Central Africa is dedicated in general to that gallant sisterhood, the wives of the men who served in the Colonial Service throughout its span in Africa: in particular to four who shared the Nyasaland years with me:

Iris, Hazel, Jean and the memory of Chris

Chapter 1

In my mother's family was a tradition of service in far-away places. Geography was my weakest subject at school – I like to think this was because it was boringly taught – but the fascination and influence of foreign lands were a constant element in my childhood.

A great-uncle and aunt worked in India, both as medical missionaries. He was the second youngest son of a Victorian family of eight, and his children were nearer in age to my generation than to my mother's, whose cousins they were. Great-Uncle Jim Macphail's name was to become legendary among his people. He established a hospital in the 1890s at Bamdah in north east India where, over a lifetime's work, he restored or saved the sight of thousands of Indians suffering from cataract. His wife Jennie was one of the first Scottish woman doctors. In her day women students were not admitted to the more advanced medical classes in Britain and she had gone to Brussels to complete her degree.

We three sisters envied their family of four boys and a girl who, as they grew up, worked their passage home and to other parts of the world they wanted to explore. Safe in our small world we judged this to be a terrifying achievement. Occasionally, one or more turned up to stay with us: dark-haired, dark-eyed, very thin, brown and *good*. This virtue I and my elder sisters firmly assumed on their behalf: missionaries' children must be good. We learned with awe that at our age they were given a drink of water and a piece of dry bread for elevenses and during their visits suffered pangs of guilt over our glass of milk and digestive biscuits.

They brought rare presents: a set of tiny brass cooking utensils, even tinier ivory elephants and smooth wooden boxes which opened to reveal another and yet another inside, until at last was the smallest, the size of a pea. When I discovered *The Jungle Book* I pictured Mowgli as a mixture of the Indian cousins, as we called them. The story of Rikki-Tikki-Tavi and Nag, read and reread with frissons of horror, took place, in my imagination, in and around the long low bungalow familiar from descriptions and photographs. These old-fashioned prints, sepia-tinted, gave a wonderful impression of the brownness of India, more authentic than black and white, more mysterious than present day colour.

An exciting and sophisticated contrast to the spartan conditions of life on a mission station was provided by an uncle and aunt who lived in North China, where Uncle Teddie was General Manager of the Kailan Mines in Tientsin. They sent home photographs of their splendid town house. It had a projecting roof, elaborately ornamented, like the first storey of a pagoda. In the hot weather the family moved to Chinwangtao, to a cottage by the sea with a garden fit for a fairy tale. We were enthralled by letters telling of lavish entertaining, picnics, race meetings, the leisured ritual of the English colony. There were also photographs of their two daughters, a few years younger than we. To our countrified eyes they were always dressed in party frocks. They were sometimes flanked by large, bland-faced servants with the intriguing names of Number One, Number Two and so on, down a long line, we glumly surmised, feeling inadequate – we only had a cook and maid, at best.

The arrival of the box from China at Christmas was one of the unforgettable marvels of childhood. From heaps of wood shavings emanating a thrilling fragrance there emerged dainty heelless slippers gleaming with beadwork, traditionally dressed Chinese dolls with real hair and a supply of fashionable wigs for all occasions. There were always three ravishing, brilliant silk kimonos which we wore as summer dressing-gowns, beginning for me a lifelong love affair with exotic colours. There were Japanese parasols, three inches long, made of bamboo and paper, gorgeous fans like giant butterflies which opened with a delicious 'whirr', and small human figurines of peasants, fishermen and artisans, all exquisitely formed and finished, standing in individual boxes of satinwood with a sliding glass panel as a lid. Some of these toys were too precious for everyday use and, along with Mother's jewel box, were produced as a special treat during wet holidays and illness. I remember sitting up in bed, making mountains and valleys of the quilt, rivers of necklaces, lakes of brooches and gardens of rings. The satinwood boxes were cottages and the little figurines were carefully moved about the scene.

Only once was I let down by this fabulous family. When they came home on leave for the first time in my life, it was a shock to me that the Chinese cousins had not the slightest trace of slanting eyes or inscrutable mien. (The Indian cousins had not failed in this respect: they really looked Indian.) However, my first sight of their mother, Mother's youngest sister, swept away all reservations. Aunt Isabel was simply the most glamorous creature I had ever set eyes on – I was six – and she remained the most beautiful woman I have known. My hands sank into the soft depths of her furs and the fine textures of her clothes were infinitely strokeable. Her perfume made me feel faint with pleasure. She presented Mother with a very long string of glittering Chinese crystal beads and, claiming they were unbreakable, challenged her to cast them down on the old stone flags of our kitchen; but Mother would not hear of it. I was deeply impressed by this refusal and thereafter tempered my tendency to fawn. Throughout my childhood and adolescence, subtleties in Mother's behaviour toward people never failed to cast light on them, so that I saw them with clearer eyes.

Wider and more intimate contacts were nearer to home. Mother's middle sister, Katherine Macphail, worked as a doctor in Serbia during the 1914–18 war. She returned home from that experience with a legacy of gradually increasing deafness, the result of contracting typhus in a severe epidemic from which she was fortunate to emerge alive, and a passionate dedication to sick children. She went back to Yugoslavia to work with children suffering from tuberculosis of the bones. In time she built her own hospital not far from Belgrade, at Kamenica, overlooking the Danube, where she lived and worked until the second world war engulfed Europe. Photographs showed a dazzling white building surrounded by olive groves and vineyards. On long open verandahs sunburnt children, their eyes dark and luscious in their thin faces, lay in rows of beds, some with their limbs encased in frames or attached to pulleys. The figure of the bambino was carved above the entrance and inside in the narrow hall there was a mosaic of the Scottish lion set into the centre of the floor. (The heart-breaking time came when she had to arrange for the evacuation of the children and her own flight from the approaching enemy. The Germans took over the building for their own purposes, and though they stripped the place of everything which could be stolen or destroyed, they could do nothing about the defiant figure rampant in the floor, short of blowing up the foundations. The lion is still there.)

Aunt Kathie came home on leave regularly in the '20s and '30s and always spent some time with us, at home and on holiday in the Highlands. She brought an almost tangible quality of light into the house. She was a great tease and filled our days with laughter. We followed her about like puppies, game for anything. There were gifts of intricately beaded bracelets, cross-stitched linen for Mother, dresses for us, vividly embroidered slippers and brightly painted wooden dolls from Russia which, like the Indian boxes, opened to reveal a whole family in diminishing sizes. She had expressive, sun-freckled hands and was habitually enveloped in the blue haze of the chain smoker. We thought this terribly 'chic' (a word I had adopted instantly from Aunt Isabel – I was already in love with words, another life-long affair) and experimented on our dolls, plying them with tiny pieces of lighted string. Our cheeks ached with our efforts to keep them alight for our precocious pupils. I think it was a significant sign of the times that it never entered our heads to have a go at the real thing.

She held us spellbound with tales of grape harvest, feast days and festivals, foreign royalty, ambassadors, journalists and artists. She kept a tame fox and there were always dogs, among them a poodle called Josephine whose coat clippings were knitted by a friend into the inevitable sweater. One year she went on a riding holiday in the Balkans with several friends who shared her Bohemian outlook and craving for adventure. They visited villages high in the mountains whose inhabitants gathered in wonder to gaze at the group of cropped-haired, breeched women. When they reached the banks of the Danube they handed over their horses and floated on a raft to their journey's end. Her villa at Kamenica was a meeting place for a cosmopolitan collection of friends and visitors of many nationalities. She was a born raconteur and we children recognised the gift and listened totally. She certainly was responsible for filling my mind with visions of people and places which I cherish to this day.

An English friend of hers, Flora Sands, was caught up in the retreat from Serbia in the first world war. She cut off her long hair, donned a uniform and fought as a man. She rose to the rank of sergeant, was decorated several times and later happily married a corporal in the Serbian army. One of her closest friends, Draga Surditch, lived on her own beautiful little island, with just enough land to contain her farm. There was a Scottish-Serbian family who interested us enormously. The children were contemporary with us and had names which charmed us – Laga, Tinkle, Dana and Ivan. Their Scottish mother, Con Duchmanitch, visited us once with Aunt Kathie. She was tall, fair, elegant and the only person I have met who wore a monocle; ineffably stylish. The Duchmanitches lived on the Dalmatian coast in a house built out over the water on three sides, a paradise where they lived like gypsies. It haunted my imagination for years and took its final form from a postcard of the Castle of Chillon someone sent me in my teens. They kept an astonishing medley of pets, their greatest extravagance being white mice, which multiplied to one hundred and twenty, all with name and pedigree, housed in neat tiers of cages. We kept up a long-distance, passionate friendship, through Aunt Kathie, with these children, and when I finally met them, many years later, we confessed delightedly to a feeling of having known each other all our lives.

There was the unique Miss Murphy, secretary of the hospital, who more than once came on leave with Aunt Kathie. She had bright red hair which never dimmed with the years, and she spoke in a mixture of languages which lent drama to her simplest utterance and kept us in an ecstasy of anticipation. She was half Irish, half Russian, and had escaped at the beginning of the Revolution with her brother, after much adversity. She had a passion for collecting local herbs and fungi and would invade her hostess's kitchen to concoct delicious dishes which Mother served with a worried expression. However, nobody was ever any the worse. It was a Russian friend of Miss Murphy's who took me as a school girl to see Chekov's *The Seagull* in Glasgow. It was my first grown-up evening at the theatre, ending with supper in a restaurant, the height of sophistication. Exhausted with excitement I wondered aloud if the violence and emotions of the characters were perhaps a bit exaggerated. My companion replied, 'No, no, I assure you. In these houses away in the country it could be very boring, and people got on each other's nerves.' She rolled back the loose sleeve of her dress and showed me a thin scar which ran from wrist to elbow, saying calmly, 'My brother did that with a sword. He was just terribly bored.' She added as an afterthought 'That is why I always wear long sleeves.'

Among the many guests who arrived at the house with a letter of introduction from Aunt Kathie, our greatest friend was Dr Milan Sokolovitch, a stunningly handsome young Serb who was, at Aunt Kathie's instigation, studying children's diseases in Glasgow. He loved children and spent many enchanted times with us. Our house stood by itself on a hill, surrounded by fields. On summer nights the silence was absolute, and one heard one's blood pulsing in one's head. On still winter nights the only sound was the telephone wires humming in the frosty air. One rainy afternoon in the nursery he patiently baked miniature loaves of real bread for the dolls which we later nibbled for tea. At night he would prowl in a specially fearful version of hide-and-seek. Every light was put out and the doors of the downstairs rooms opened, so that their firelight was our only guide as we crept about the house. Mother sat with her knitting by the flickering glow of the drawingroom fire, smiling to herself as tension mounted. We did not always find him and the game would collapse in nerve failure; we put on all the lights and shrieked with relief at the dénouement. When he left to go back by bus to Glasgow, we walked with him to the end of the lane while he counted the stars for us in eight languages.

He also had a genius for finding good hiding places in the garden. None of us ever forgot the day we stood in the front garden calling, 'Come out, come out, wherever you are,' and that sleek head, with its olive face and flashing teeth, rose in triumph right up through the middle of the foaming blossoms in Mother's precious spiraea bush. Not a petal suffered. I still remember the heady sound of his feet behind me sending the gravel of the drive flying as I ran like the wind, certain of capture. In those days the tennis court was merely a glorified playground, with a swing and a large see-saw. In summer it was the scene of many an epic game of rounders, in which sometimes three generations joined. My paternal grandfather, a dapper, precise little man, invariably resigned before the end of the game, shocked and infuriated by the rules which according to Dr Sokolovitch's flair for improvisation governed Serbian sport.

The war put an end to this kind of life forever. Dr Sokolovitch was killed in an air raid on Mish. In the following years news reached us of the fate of other friends, some of whom we were never to see again. As for Aunt Kathie, her heroic story deserves a book to itself.

On 14th January 1950, I stood at the rail of a Union Castle ship and watched for the first time the cliffs of Dover recede over a wintry sea. I had been married for just over a year. My husband was a newly recruited Administrative Officer in His Majesty's Colonial Service. So, in my small way, I was about to carry on the Macphail tradition. I was destined for Africa.

Chapter 2

Before World War II, a university degree was the essential qualification for entry into the administrative branch of the Colonial Service. After the war, for obvious reasons, a different approach to recruitment had to be devised for candidates, most of whom had been in one of the armed services, some with five years' war service behind them. Ron, whom I was to marry in December 1948, was fortunate to be granted an early release from the RAF, on condition that he return to St. Andrews University to complete the B Sc. degree he had begun four years earlier when he was attached to the University as a member of the Initial Training Wing. He graduated in the summer of 1948 and immediately applied to join the Colonial Service. His appointment was dependent upon the results of three interviews, preceded by the customary deluge of testimonials. The interviews were conducted in a friendly, relaxed atmosphere quite unlike the taxing ordeal he had expected. The only topics which remained highlighted in his memory later were the various systems used in contract bridge and the novels of Jane Austen. However, there must have been method in the madness, for out of the eighty successful candidates, only one on the training course for administrative cadets which followed was found to have been an unsuitable choice.

Later that summer, while Ron was staying with my family, the momentous telegram from the Colonial Office arrived. He had been accepted. He was posted to Nyasaland, in Central Africa. None of us knew precisely where it was; only that it was David Livingstone country. Out came the atlas and I felt a sudden frisson of desolation, shared, I sensed, by my mother, as Ron's finger on the map traced the immense distances of sea and land beyond which it lay. In October he went up to Oxford, where he was to spend the academic year undertaking colonial studies on what was known as the Devonshire Course, initiated in 1946 by a statesman of that name (I think an ex-Colonial Secretary.) Subjects included constitutional and colonial history, criminal law and law of evidence, anthropology, local government and land utilisation. For the Michaelmas term Ron lived in college rooms at St. Peter's Hall.

We were married during the Christmas vacation and in January I accompanied him to Oxford, where we started married life at 38 Banbury Road. We had a sunny bed-sittingroom on the first floor and shared a tiny kitchen in the basement. There were two beautiful and wilful Siamese cats with brilliant sapphire eyes who had the run of the house and became faithful fireside companions. With a mixture of inspired desperation and ingenuity I transformed our somewhat spartan room into a bright, attractive haven: the first in a long line of 'havens' I was to create over the years out of equally unprepossessing materials. We had very little money, but with few exceptions we found everyone in the same boat. Yet despite lean times and rationing, there was a constant flow of modest hospitality given and received, an embryo of the traditional open house of Colonial hospitality we would later experience. We soon made friends with other married couples on the Course and for the next six months led a fairly hectic and carefree life of hard work and play.

There were three or four classes a day and often an evening lecture by an outside speaker, either a distinguished scholar in some specialised field or a retired colonial servant. All the men were mad keen, impatient to put the book work behind them and get out into the field: they talked shop incessantly. It took me only the few days before term started to realise that here was a cut and dried case of sink or swim and I opted without hesitation for attending all classes and lectures with Ron. I was only a year away from my own graduation in Honours English Literature and Language at St. Andrews and was about to find myself swimming, without a life belt I sometimes felt, in very different waters.

Excerpts from weekly letters to my mother give the tenor of our days.

9th January:

We have adopted the British Restaurant for lunch, without pride! The food is good and plentiful and I certainly could not produce anything better for 2s 6d. The decor is rather hideous. Oxford is a delightful place – you find labourers and very county ladies sitting at the same table. Ron is being wonderfully helpful, comes on all shopping expeditions and every morning cleans out and lights the fire.

16th January:

Lectures begin tomorrow and I am going along too. I shall take my own notes which will be a help to Ron, as he found it very difficult last term. His scientific background has not prepared him for the type of class where there is a constant flow of information to be taken down quickly. His special subject this term is anthropology and I am reading a book called *Human Types* and summarising it for him – whatever next?

We have a little side window which at night gives a view of Banbury Road exactly like one of the illustrations from *The Silent Traveller*. There is a row of tall, spidery trees along the pavement and the street lamps, their posts invisible, shine through the branches like Chinese lanterns. The garden has pines, larches and a willow.

23rd January:

It has felt good to start attending classes and lectures. I find I relax, the academic atmosphere being familiar in a whirl of days filled with the un-familiar! All the 'students' are very quiet and courteous and never stamp or shuffle their feet as we did. But of course these men are far more mature, nearly one hundred per cent ex-Services. I love the sophistication of their humour. Quiet laughter ripples round the room, sometimes surprising and gratifying the lecturer. Very few wives turn up during the day but a lot go in the evening. There are one or two expectant mothers among them and I know some of them have jobs. The classes and lectures are held in Rhodes House, a mag-nificent building, all marble and parquet floors, high ceilings and book-lined walls.

29th January:

On Wednesday afternoon a Lady Bourdillon, whose husband has had a distinguished career in India and West Africa, came to the Colonial Service Club at Park Grange – the residence available for people on the Course who can afford it – to give a talk to the wives on 'The role of women in the Colonial Service'. We all had tea at long tables and it was to me quite an ordeal – about thirty women surreptitiously looking each other over most of the time! I in-dulged in it too, of course, and picked out perhaps six congenial-looking souls. Lady Bourdillon was about sixty, exquisitely groomed, slim, vivacious and so charming everyone was fascinated. She spoke most enthrallingly and infor-mally for over an hour with only a small card of notes. I was thrilled, and walking back alone – and how I appreciate being alone these days – I felt for the first time *I* had something to contribute to the Colonial Service and began to see dimly the possibilities of the life we shall lead from the first humble level upwards. What a challenge!

We went one evening to a lecture entitled 'Village Betterment' by a Major Brayne, who has worked in India for more than thirty years. He was a lively, youthful-elderly man, vigorous and vivid with enthusiasm for his work. Our very first outside speaker was a magnificent looking man whose subject was 'The District Officer and the Missionary' . Heady stuff! I have yet to discern in the overseas speakers who have lived in the Colonies for ages any signs of physical or mental deterioration – what a prig I sound – I just mean it is reassuring and gives one hope!

I have another anthropology book to summarise – *'Hunger and Work in a Savage Tribe'* forsooth! I enjoy criminal law and colonial history most.

1st February:

At last Ron took me round to St. Peter's Hall and introduced me to his Canadian friend, Al Scarth, a stunning young man reading law. Very civilised. He had spent the Christmas vacation touring Europe as a member of the Oxford ice-hockey team and had some interesting comments to make on the spirit of sportsmanship shown by different nationalities – he thought the French had the poorest!

One afternoon we walked down by the river, my first sight. It was like being in another world. The town seemed far away, shrouded in mist. All along the banks huge willows and oaks grew over the water and the river twisted and turned for miles, sometimes almost at right angles, so that a small sailing boat would suddenly appear ahead, apparently moving magically over dry land, until we came to a bend and saw the water. We passed the famous 'Trout', a wonderful old inn with a sluice and very formal garden, and ended up in a little village called Wolvercote, where we had a delicious country tea of bread and jam and home made tart in a pub called 'The White Hart'. It cost 4s, so no cinema this week!

6th February:

Although I am so happy and busy here, I am very aware of not being in my own country – good practice, I know. It is odd how strongly I feel the difference in nationality, and no matter how friendly people are here, and they most certainly are, I quite definitely sense that I am different from them and something of an alien in their midst, though they seem interested enough in that something!

One afternoon as we were going into St. Peter's Hall, Ron introduced me to an Indian student he knows there. For something to say I asked him if he had ever come across the name Macphail in India. His reaction was immediate – 'James Russell Macphail!' he intoned joyfully. 'My cousin,' I murmured modestly. On he went in great excitement. 'He was my tutor in English at Madras College and taught me for three years – a brilliant man. You must write him my good wishes. My name is Aboubackar.' He wrote it down for me, laughing and waving his arms about. So I shall have to write to Russell. We were on our way to tea with Gil, who was Ron's neighbour last term. He is a large, genial rowing man, ex-Navy and one of the nicest men I have met here. Al Scarth was there and another Canadian called Freddie drifted in and said, 'I just called in to look you over and see if you are OK for Ron. Hmmmm, you'll do, I guess', and drifted out again! I love going to St. Peter's – the talk is always stimulating and so different and so far from all things colonial!

Yesterday our three nicest married couples came to tea. I gave them apple and ginger brown bread sandwiches, wedding cake (the last of it, alas), home-made apple cake and chocolate biscuits. It was awful to see everything vanish but also rather satisfactory. I sometimes wonder if any of us really has enough to eat!

This evening we are having four huge men from St. Peter's round after dinner. I have made masses of apple cake (so far my only baking skill) and there will be plenty of coffee. The Canadians praise my coffee brewing, which encourages me.

If there are things you want to know which I have not thought to tell you, do ask, though I think I give you a fairly comprehensive account of everything here. I am afraid I still think of home a hundred times a day!

13th February:

Thank you for the cushion covers – lovely. My eyes speed to them the moment I enter the room. It really does have a special atmosphere now – Al says it is a triumph over poverty!

The parcel has just arrived and is wonderful – my favourite kind of oatcakes, some welcome butter and our first fresh eggs – we shall have a boiled one each. The others are leaky, so they go into an omelette and a *sponge cake* – clever Ann!

Yesterday we had Joan and Mike Saunders for tea. They are on the Second Devonshire Course, given for men who have already done a tour of service. They go back to Nyasaland for their second tour in March. They were enormously helpful, easily and amusingly answering the list of earnest questions we had prepared for them. They also went over a huge, ominously expensive list of equipment which one of the big London firms has sent everyone, and laughed away most of the items as quite unnecessary. They obviously love the life out there and left us much relieved and cheered by their enthusiasm. I have been very impressed by the Second Course men. They have attended some classes and lectures and get up and express themselves very well indeed, relating their experiences. They have poise and always look immaculate. One of the great pleasures here is the really beautiful, cultured voices one hears all round, all the time.

20th February:

It is Torpids week. Ron and I went to the river on Thursday and Saturday afternoon and watched in brilliant sunshine. I was more interested in the fascinating variety of people, hundreds of them crowding the towpath, running or cycling along, following their favourite boat and shouting lustily. We did not see an actual bump but saw several exceedingly close boats. I do not enjoy it all that much, as the men go all out and look all in! Needless to say I do not broadcast my very unsporting and unOxford reaction!

27th February:

Ron was set an essay on Animal Husbandry – something rich and rare to tackle! He left it rather late and we have had a tremendous rush to get it into its final form. He made copious factual notes and I managed to write them into a reasonable form of essay. We worked late over cows, sheep, goats and pigs and found ourselves around midnight hysterically mirthful, arguing about the nomenclature of cattle's 'relatives'! He did not read it over till breakfast next morning – he had to read it to twelve men at the 9.15 seminar! I gather it went off all right!

I should love to accept your offer of my fare north at Easter. I shall talk it over with Ron and see what we think. He has to go up to London on 16th March for two days to attend a Magistrate's Court. He is to sit in with the clerk and see how things are done. He is to get 8*s*. 6*d*. a day for expenses. Tom [Ron's guardian] has kindly said we can stay at the Langham Place flat. We are hoping for a night at the ballet. It would be very wonderful to have that and then visit you as well – Ron will be most envious, hard-worked soul that he is.

8th March:

I am, of course, coming home! We go up to London on 16th March and I think I shall travel up by day on Sunday 18th. Tom has booked our seats for the ballet, and the programme is quite perfect: *Les Sylphides, Symphonic Variations* and *La Boutique Fantastique.*

14th March:

Ron has finished his essay 'Magic and Religion' and I have written it out for him – an extremely sane and scientific piece of work, based on Dr Murphy's *Lamps of Anthropology* and *Primitive Man.* [Two books written by a family friend.] God bless dear Dr Murphy! I should really write to him.

The end of term ball was all I had hoped. My dress arrived, bless you, lovelier than I remembered and miraculously white. You have sewn up the train beautifully. There were eleven in our party and after drinks at the Colonial Club we went to the George Hotel and enjoyed an excellent dinner. Then we all went on to Rhodes House which was quite transformed for the festivities. I had a great evening's dancing – hardly saw Ron! Champagne flowed and there was a late buffet. Afterwards we were borne back to Park Grange with other revellers and continued to celebrate till 3.30. Someone produced a gramophone and we danced in the corridors – such fun and well deserved after a jolly hard term.

6th April:

I received an ecstatic welcome back from Ron. Al says he has never seen a man so much influenced by a woman! Do not regret my somewhat flu'ey visit. I loved every minute.

25th April:

Our week at West Coker was sheerest luxury and we wallowed in it. Ron was greatly taken with the house, especially the minstrels' gallery and the marvellous library: shelves to the high ceiling and ladders, and an enormous section on Empire! Whenever he vanished, I knew where he would be found! We had the 'ghost' bedroom, which has a sweet little stair up into a very modern bathroom. The weather was perfect and we have come back bleached and bronzed and relaxed. Uncle Teddie is a marvellous, generous host. Aunt Isabel looked beautiful as ever but tired, and her vagueness has definitely worsened, but I think she was happy to see me and to get to know Ron. We shared two lovely evenings of music with her in her little sittingroom. We drove to the sea one day – magnificent views of rolling downs, ending up for tea at Dorchester where we saw Hardy's statue – exciting for no one but me! We cycled with a picnic lunch to Ham Hill and heard our first cuckoo, and we walked over to East Coker one gorgeous hot morning to let Ron see the house. The countryside is so luxuriant and beautiful in Somerset. I had forgotten. We only went riding once, but I began to get the feel of it and the 'feel' of it remained, quite painfully, for two days! There were two lunch parties for friends from China days – very sophisticated! I felt all thumbs but it was all grist for my mill! They asked local friends in to meet us for drinks most evenings, which was pleasant. The pace of life at Coker is always so blissfully leisurely. I felt spoilt and pampered and mightily loth to leave, Ron too.

We arrived back here to find everyone talking about learning to punt, successes and disasters.

2nd May:

Oxford is a mass of pink and white blossom which drifts down like snowflakes on the breeze and at night against the stars, the trees' branches look as if they are laden with frozen snow. There is a magnificent chestnut tree opposite us and lovely laburnum trees have revealed themselves in the back garden, wearing yellow pony tails tied with green ribbons. Work now hangs heavily over the days – and over the wives!

10th May:

Everything is extremely quiet, as all the men are working hard. There are still morning classes but that is all. Ron does take time off for tennis and we make up a four most afternoons. He got Beta Plus for his essay on 'Magic and Religion' and was complimented on its interest by his tutor – madly bucked!

16th May:

Everyone found the exams very trying. I think it is hard on these men who have been away from academic work for so long. From what they tell me, they all seem to have read too many books and found the questions difficult to tackle as there was so little time to condense their knowledge. I reckon Ron has done well enough.

Sunday was a heavenly day and after an early lunch, a large party of us went on the river, including the specially lovely baby I told you about. They tied three punts together, into which twelve of us were packed. The pram was tied onto the middle punt and off we went from 2.30 till 6.00, stopping under willow trees by the bank for tea. It was quite perfect, drifting along past wonderful gardens and under little bridges. There were dozens and dozens of punts and canoes, and we had the benefit of the Sunday afternoon concert from at least six radios, including one in our punt. The men took turns at punting, some very nervously. People stared at our strange little flotilla and laughed delightedly when they saw the pram. I lay back in the sun thinking of all the famous ghosts who must have done this over the centuries and I smelt the river smell, even if it was not the Cam!

Today classes are back to normal and Ron and I started on law of evidence this afternoon. I enjoy law enormously – it reminds me of a mixture of logic and crosswords!

23rd May:

We spent two afternoons by the river, watching the bumps of Eights week. On Saturday, a lovely day, there were thousands of people milling about on every available inch of space on the tow path, the barges, the jetties and the pavilions. There were some extremely pukka fathers and mothers trying not to look too proud of their great perspiring sons who were taking part, and there were some wonderful sisters, fiancées and hangers-on in very chic outfits – all picture hats and parasols!

St. Peter's Hall ball is this Friday and two very charming friends of ours there, Tony and Gordon, have no partners, so they are to 'inspect' Elspeth [my sister who had a job in Oxford] this evening here, over coffee, and then, presumably, toss for her! The tickets cost £2, so we have decided to give it a miss. It is really rather a shame, for I like the St. Peter's men and feel much more at home with them than with the Colonial Service set, but it is an awful lot of money at this stage of the term. I have not yet dared tell Elspeth we are not going, in case she panics and refuses to turn up. It will give her a lovely evening and no doubt some new contacts! I am willing to bet Tony will somehow win the toss. He is from Tanganyika and very much the life of the party. Gordon is big, a rowing man, with great charm and a very bad stutter which he simply ignores! He broke an oar (excuse me, a BLADE) on Saturday and arrived back at the pavilion clutching the pieces to the accompaniment of boos and other rude noises from the balcony.

31st May:

The exam results came out last Wednesday and Ron has passed. Only two failed and three got distinction (one a St. Andrews man – hurrah!). That evening there was a lecture at Rhodes House to which everyone went rather reluctantly as we were all in a mood to celebrate. After fifteen minutes the speaker had not turned up, so out we trooped, heading for the Colonial Club. Just as we left the building a man in a hurry dashed past us and went in – obviously the unfortunate speaker. I have never seen ten people walk away so quickly, deaf to the cries of an unlucky victim who had been caught by Authority, vainly endeavouring to rope us in. We all enjoyed a splendid evening of relaxation.

The evening with Elspeth, Gordon and Tony was most successful. Tony had found a partner, so Elspeth was asked by Gordon. He got into great difficulties with his stutter while poor Elspeth had to wait for the outcome unhelpfully, as she was not supposed to know what he was trying to say! They were all three horrified when they discovered we were not going and immediately swept away all doubts, protests and excuses, promising instant procurement of a dress suit for Ron, and of course we were persuaded to change our minds. I am so glad we did, for it was a glorious evening, going on till daylight. There is something unique about these balls which I think will be memorable forever.

A thousand thanks for the cheque. We really were about to start living on air! How did you know?

7th June:

The honey was most welcome. Thank you very much indeed. It arrived at a time when we had absolutely nothing to brighten up teatime. I do not know why, but food seems to be getting more and more difficult to manage in Oxford – perhaps I am too tired to cope with it. We have been working terribly hard and will be thankful when term ends on 20th June. Then HOME!

Chapter 3

We spent the summer in Scotland, staying at my parents' house. I found plenty to do, going through all my possessions and our wedding presents and gradually packing tea-chests, trunks, linen chest and a huge wooden box which weighed a ton and exactly contained my five hundred-strong collection of books. Ron, being a bit of a wanderer, had accumulated very little. Mother was a born packer and I benefited from her supervision. I think I must have inherited her expertise. It is almost a creative process. After a gestation period of dread, reluctance and procrastination, a sudden urge would release me into therapeutic activity and slowly but surely our precious belongings vanished in methodical fashion into well cushioned layers of tightly wrapped security. It is a tribute to her to record that I never, in the next twenty years, unpacked a single broken or damaged article: that was the province of servants and the ravages of the tropical climates we lived in, particularly hard on books. Ron spent most of his summer travelling by bus every weekday to Airdrie, our nearest town, where, under the guidance of various departments of the Town Council, he learned the practical side of local government.

In early October we took off for the south again, London this time, all our heavy luggage crated, labelled and ready for the ship's hold. We were lucky enough to be able to store it with friends. We were launching into a three months' intensive course in Chinyanja, held at the London School of Oriental and African Studies. Our teacher was Dr Guy Aitkens, who had spent some time in Nyasaland studying the language prior to setting it down on paper for the first time in a systematic form, with its own syntax, grammar and orthography, a basic vocabulary for domestic and field communication, and a very interesting collection of verbal sayings and folk lore. We were his first pupils: 'my guinea pigs', he called us. Six cadets and two wives attended the classes. The wives were encouraged to sit the exams at the end of the course – and were paid ten pounds, in those days a princely sum, if they passed. [We did.] Two young Nyasalanders studying in London were roped in to give us conversation classes. There were also rather dreary classes twice a week at the London School of Economics, on anthropology and economic aspects of colonial affairs. It was all very different from the relaxed atmosphere of Oxford. We lived on the outskirts of Barnes in a small, pleasant guest house, the only other guests

15

being a married couple we had known well in Oxford, bound for Northern Rhodesia. There was practically no social life, as we all scattered at the end of the day laden with homework. I was thankful not to have to cope with domestic chores. We occasionally had a meal with friends old and new living in London. None of us could afford more. The daily journey into town by bus and under-ground took only twenty-five minutes and our last class finished at three, which meant we got back before the rush hour. But it was a punishing taste of commuter life and we all longed for the time when we would turn our backs on it forever – or so we thought in those heady days of certainty.

The tone of my letters reflects the change of tempo in our life.

8th October:

There are eight of us learning Chinyanja and what a shattering experience it is proving to be! We already have, or rather are expected to have, a vocabulary of one hundred and twenty words. I have found this first week appallingly difficult but I think I have got things straightened out in my mind over the weekend. A background of Latin and French helps not one whit, in fact it is a positive disadvantage. Ron, the scientist and self-confessed ignoramus linguis-tically, copes imperturbably from scratch, as it were – maddening! I have to forget all about Indo-European languages, just forget. Basic changes are made in the prefix, not the suffix, so I have to turn my brain back to front. At least the pronunciation is easy – every syllable sounded and given equal stress. It sounds lovely, rather like Italian. There is no doubt we shall have to work very hard to keep up with each day's material.

We lunch at the School of Oriental and African Studies where we see all the nice, familiar Oxford faces (none, of course, from St. Peter's, alas), and we meet friends and acquaintances as confused as ourselves, especially those bound for West Africa, who explode and implode strange sounds, wrap their tongues round their palates and waggle their jaws to produce the desired effect. It is very funny and not funny at all! At lunch on Friday there was a gloomy silence at one point and I was suddenly inspired to tell the long tableful Aunt Kathie's story about the foreigner with basic English who arrived in London and the first thing he saw was a placard outside a newsagents with the headline 'Exhibition Pronounced Success'. Collapse in hysterical laughter all round. Good!

Yesterday afternoon we went to Kew Gardens, an enchanting place. The autumn colours of the trees contrasted with the gorgeous magentas, pinks and oranges of the exotic plants in the hot-houses. My eyes felt positively dazzled and mesmerised. Going back in the bus I planned and landscaped flaming visionary gardens which cheered me enormously. So, another aspect of the prospect before us, another widening of horizons!

16th October:

The brain-battering continues apace and our vocabulary is up to two hundred and fifty words – we hope. At least I have stopped dreaming in Chinyanja. On Wednesday we were divided into four pairs and given a dialogue to record, which was then played back. So cruel! The African women apparently pitch their voices very high. I am prepared to do this to pander to Dr Aitken's expectations of me – he thinks I am quite good – but once away I shall descend to my normal tone, so there. The latest word we have been practising means 'I'm only joking', and, take a deep breath, goes like this: *ngkhamwabakhamwa*. Roll on the day when I can feel jokey in Chinyanja.

On Thursday afternoon we met Ron's Nyasalander, Mathias Kantiki. Each cadet is allocated an African who meets him socially and converses in Chinyanja as much as possible. We had tea with him at his hostel, which was full of huge, grinning, blue-black Africans discussing their day's lectures in loud, pukka voices – Nigerian law students, I gather. Mathias is nice, a dapper young man, friendly and at ease. We felt at home with him at once and found so much to talk about that the rule about Chinyanja was totally ignored. His English is excellent.

Yesterday afternoon Ron and I went for a sunny, windy walk on Barnes Common. Our main relaxation at weekends is bridge. I find it a great, soothing escape. There is a wonderful collection of records in the lounge and we are allowed full use of them, so we have enjoyed some lovely evenings.

22nd October:

Please thank Daddy for selling the picture for me. I am greatly relieved to have the money, as Ron's shoes are a disgrace and now I can buy him a new pair for his birthday.

We are trying to speak Chinyanja to each other as much as possible, to gain fluency and lose self-consciousness, a real stumbling block with Ron, but speak it he must! There are lots of everyday phrases we can use. Being in the oral tradition, it is fairly repetitive, which helps.

Yesterday morning we went to Bakers to place our humble order. We bought a card table, a large thermos, three Tilly lamps, and basic camping equipment: beds, canvas bath and basin in wooden frames, and folding chairs. It is an amazing shop, with every possible necessity and luxury for life in the tropics. We had to restrain ourselves. I was depressed for the rest of the day, having had to walk away from a beautiful, elegant pair of soft leather mosquito boots. They would have made anything in my meagre wardrobe look great. We went on to a less expensive shop and bought china. All these purchases go direct to the ship.

31st October:

The weather has been fearfully wet and blustery, though some of the mornings were beautifully rosy and misty, and the river and embankment from Hammersmith Bridge look lovely, almost foreign to me, in the early haze. Today there is a real pea-souper.

Yesterday afternoon Ron played squash with Dr Aitkens, and after tea with him, he insisted on taking us (screaming silently in protest – our precious Saturday!) to an Anthropological Society lecture which turned out to be excruciatingly boring, given by a gaunt man who had grown thin in Kenya for twenty-five years, studying an obscure tribe with rather obscure results. I just switched off and observed the audience, full, no doubt, of distinguished scholars. They all had craggy, jutting bone structures. Surprisingly, while all the men looked slightly dusty and dishevelled, their wives looked alert and very smart. Perhaps some day someone will make an anthropological study of that!

6th November:

Last Monday we were given a turntable, a pair of earphones and a record in Chinyanja and asked to write down what we heard. I had just washed my hair, consequently silk-slippery, and the earphones kept sliding off up to the top of my head, leaving my ears bare. Also, as you know, it takes me a little time to master things mechanical, and I got all tied up with my pen and the little gadget which turns back the record for replay. I found out later I had fared no worse than anyone else. I am fed up with being made to feel flustered!

14th November:

We both have dreadful, heavy colds, but it has been a good week. Quite suddenly the difficulties with the language have vanished. I have beaten the brute and taken off, but definitely and effortlessly off! The relief is indescribable. On Friday evening we had dinner in London at the flat of our favourite Colonial Service people, Dick and Peggy Turpin. We ate a delicious dinner, had a great talk and then some very good bridge. They are posted to Fiji and know their sailing date, so we should hear any day now. I went to bed feeling really human for the first time since we came south.

There is a charming young bachelor in the Chinyanja group, David Baxster, who took the Devonshire Course at Cambridge. We have become good friends and he always sits with us. On several occasions Dr Aitkens, who is very absent-minded, has called me 'Mrs Baxster'. The faces of my two 'husbands' are a study. David goes very pink and bridles slightly. Ron's nostrils whiten round the edges, a sure sign he is not amused.

21st November:

On Friday we had our yellow fever and TAB inoculations. Next morning we had high temperatures and our arms were swollen and sickeningly sore, so we have lain very low over the weekend. I dread the journey into town tomorrow, as one wants to scream if anyone bumps one's arm. We shall get the second TAB and vaccination before we come north. Everyone loathes the injections and several strong men among us actually fainted. It is all pretty brutal – there is a long queue and the trouble is you can see what is being done long before it is your turn – horrible!

27th November:

On Friday we met Tisha and gave her a farewell lunch. She is off to Malta for another six months of hospital work. Ron felt we should give her a good send-off, and so we had a devastatingly expensive lunch at Fortnum's. Of course the food was delicious but it spoils one for anything less and I foresee lunches of coffee and buns for a week.

On Thursday after tea, we went round and spent the evening with Mathias. We had dinner in his hostel, in a room full of black faces, white teeth and bubbly voices. Lester Nkomba, who takes us for conversation, joined us and we all went to a News Theatre. Among other items we saw President Truman with the Shah of Iran, and Lester asked me which was which! We all got the giggles – they are marvellous at laughing at themselves. The moment they see they have said or done something funny in our eyes, they start to laugh. I love it and the way they never take umbrage.

We have short, informal language exams almost every day from now until the end of term. Clever Dr Aitkens makes it all very relaxed. No one is really worried except for the oral, which we all dread, but I feel certain we shall all pass. I would never have believed three months ago I could be so calm and blasé.

Tom phoned last night to ask us to go with him to *Peter Grimes* next Thursday. It is a little frustrating, as there are several shows I would rather see, but it will be interesting and one must move with the times!

4th December:

We went round to Tom's flat about six and had sherry and little sandwiches of smoked salmon which I would have gladly eaten twice as many twice as quickly (sorry, bad grammar). I seem to be always hungry. We raced by taxi to Covent Garden, got there just in time and found we had wonderful seats in the first tier above the stalls, which is quite low down. *Peter Grimes* was very odd, musically, but it grew on me. It has drama, and the setting and atmosphere were wonderfully authentic. Joan Cross, vast and oh, so plain, sang clearly and beautifully and Peter Pears, a great bear of a man, has a golden voice. The drop curtain between the acts was a long tunnel under the sea with bones lying about, very evocative of 'full fathom five, etc'. By the end we were all completely gripped. Covent Garden looked simply lovely. There were lots of people in evening dress, including young people, all very earnest and intense. At the intervals we went upstairs for a drink and I devoured more small delicacies. We had a late supper in a nearby café afterwards and got back, half dead, about midnight.

13th December:

The weather has become freezing cold, which pulls one down by the end of the day and everyone has the jaded, end of term feeling. I think we have all outgrown student life! Exams, thank goodness, finish tomorrow with the beastly oral, and then we all, including the two Africans, go to lunch with Dr Aitkens and his wife, and for tea with Dr Hastings Banda, an African doctor from Nyasaland who has practised in London for many years. We gather he is a sort of self-exiled leader of his people.

The great event last week was the farewell dance, a tremendous success. The Hyde Park Hotel is positively luscious, with thick, soundless carpets, pillars, hundreds of mirrors, vast ceilings and magnificent chandeliers. We made up a party of eight with our best Oxford friends and enjoyed ourselves thoroughly. There were some wonderful dresses, the outstanding one being flame-coloured velvet. With a sudden premonitory pang, I wondered where on earth it would end up!

There were no classes in the afternoon next day, in honour of the match at Twickenham. Instead of being loyal to Oxford, Ron and I slipped away and saw *Les Enfants du Paradis* for the third time – enchanting as ever.

On Friday we have our final inoculations, but no matter how ill we feel, we shall turn our faces towards the north, praise be. I do not remember a longer three months in all my life.

Chapter 4

The French have a saying: *'Partir c'est mourir un peu.'* I went through the first of many harrowing farewells which were to haunt my life henceforth. I was leaving my mother a semi-invalid, my father on the verge of retirement and the whole family preparing to leave our beloved 'Dunalastair', the country home where my sisters and I had spent a childhood and adolescence of unforgettable stability and happiness. A state of shock suspended me in a void and produced a heightened clarity of vision and reaction during a journey rich in interest and novelty, an experience which in retrospect was a kaleidoscopic space of time between the two worlds of my past and future.

Ron and I sailed from Tilbury on the *Llandovery Castle*. His terms of service entitled us to paid first class passages. The majority of the passengers were middle-aged couples escaping from the English winter on business trips to warmer climes and wealthy South Africans returning home from holidays in Europe. They set the financial tone of the ship, which meant generous tipping and high stakes at bridge and betting games. We had very little spending money and expensive shore excursions had to be shunned. Fortunately we made up a group with other young people who were likewise starting out on a Colonial Service career.

My first long voyage unveiled a new dimension in my life: I discovered that I loved the sea. For the first few days January gales ensured stormy weather. In the black nights the cabin creaked and groaned and I snuggled down in my blanket-piled bunk to enjoy, with each slow roll of the ship, the sensation in my body like mercury being rolled in the palm of a hand. We passed through the Bay of Biscay on a Homeric day of pale sun and racing cloud shadows, the sea an inky blue flecked with white to the horizon. With heady exhilaration we paced unsteadily round and round the heaving decks, our faces stiff and salty, our ears battered by the mighty thud and sluice of the ship's steady plough through huge waves breaking green as they surged along her sides. The shrieking wind tore the words thinly from our lips. At night the sea was a dark presence, darker than the sky, where no stars shone.

In calm weather we reached our first port, Las Palmas in the Canary Islands, on an overcast, sultry day, a sticky, smelly land breeze blowing. We struggled through the crowd of importunate vendors of dolls, bracelets, pens and watches, escaped in a horse-drawn open vehicle through the main thoroughfare and took a quiet drive round a residential district where I had my first glimpse of exotic architecture: houses with interiors shadowy behind trellised balconies, white, cream or lavender walls ablaze with tumbling bougainvillaea, roofs edged with a decorative filigree finish which gave them the appearance of elaborately iced wedding cakes standing in neat rows.

We sailed late that night and spent the next seven days at sea, during which we crossed the Equator and took part, mercifully as spectators, in the rather tedious ceremonies. We turned out one morning to find a transformation scene. The ship's officers had shed their navy blue and donned 'whites' for the hot weather. At mid-morning the stewards served ice cream instead of beef tea, the pool had been filled and deck games went into full swing. There were dances and film shows on deck in the evenings. There was no air conditioning in those days and we lived at ease on the spacious, airy decks. The portholes stood open and in the great heat metal fixtures were fitted to them which caught the outer air and funnelled it into the cabins.

Seen from a distance Ascension Island reminded me of the Hebridean Island of Rhum, with a long cloud lying just below the peaks. We lay off-shore while a boat went in with mail and supplies. It was, even then, a 'hush-hush' place and we were not permitted ashore. On closer inspection, as the ship swung to her anchor and the engines were muted to a mere vibration, it was a bleak, bare island, with a small settlement of buildings huddled together. The only sounds were the wind gusting, the distant roar of the heavy swell pounding itself into white surf up a golden beach and the wild cries of frigate birds which wheeled overhead and perched on the masts. It was difficult to imagine the isolation of the men stationed there.

Three days later we anchored off St. Helena, which smelt sweet on the wind. There was a tremendous swell running, and from our dining room porthole there were glimpses of spray on rocks, an upsurge of dark cliff face, the sky, then a swoop down to rocks again. Breakfast was a little tremulous. In the narrow rowing boat which took us in, we seemed to be dropping from one long green shelf to another as we moved towards the jetty. A motley collection of venerable cars stood in the little town square, presided over by competitive owners. Our group settled for a yellow open eight-seater. We were borne through the main street at high speed and immediately began to climb. Escarpment roads were new to me and I was appalled as we swung up round one hairpin bend after another on a surface tilted between towering rock face radiating heat and a precipitous drop. This experience was a baptism of fire which cured me forever of nerves and I was able to take in my stride the hundreds of miles of escarpment travel which lay in store for me. I concentrated my attention on the rapidly expanding view of the green countryside and, venturing a look back, saw the ship like a toy steamer in a basin of water far below. Once on top we followed a rough track, passing docile-faced donkeys and thin children who ran along by the car begging irresistibly for pennies. The people of the island seemed gentle and hardworking, a mainly peasant community who, we learned, observed the religious teachings of the Salvation Army. We walked down a steep path to Napoleon's tomb, set in a little glade of tall, feathery trees with tended flower beds and nearby a spring of very cold water from which, a notice informed us, the royal exile used to drink. We went on to his house, Longwood, walked in the garden beside the tricorne-shaped pool and looked through the windows into stark, ghostly rooms. Belated structural repairs had been started, and there was sad evidence of the ravages of time and termites. Despite the organised trips and tourist notices, the island had retained its dignity and its sombre history touched the imagination.

During the next week's run down to Cape Town the weather was very hot. We lazed on deck by the pool for hours. Flying fish sparkled and spun in briefly airborne shoals and schools of porpoises rolled and dipped sleekly in and out of a sea so still it parted before the ship's bows like folds of blue silk, with just a little fizz of bubbles. Nights were magical, the air velvety soft and cool on sun-warmed skin. Phosphorescence shone and glimmered like a pale reflection of the piercing stars which in their billions seemed to be trying to crowd each other out of the sky.

As we approached Cape Town, reality began to impinge on this sea-dream. The notorious Cape rollers made packing a difficult and bruising task. There was mail from home which I read avidly, oblivious to the bustle and confusion around me. We went without delay through Customs, took a taxi to the Overseas League where we booked in for the night and sallied forth to explore. The hot morning sun bathed the streets and buildings in dazzling light, making shade and shadows dramatically dense, and always, everywhere, the splendour of Table Mountain dominated the town, looming far above the highest roof lines and at the end of every vista. A bus took us part of the way up the foothills of the mountain, then we walked through pinewoods to the cable house where we boarded the small, cage-like car and moved smoothly up the steep cable. Having a good head for heights was an advantage but it still was a hair-raising ascent of over 3,500 feet. We stepped out onto a flat, rocky platform and stood in wonder surveying the enormous expanse which stretched below, like a relief map. It was my first breathtaking sight of an aspect of Africa which captured my spirit forever: the immense panoramic landscapes of mountains, valleys and plains, all suffused with light of a golden quality peculiar to Africa. I always felt alien and vulnerable amid such vastness. It set up a tension in daily life which simply does not exist on home ground and produced a sense of being extraordinarily alive and an urge to live life well, thus presenting a constant challenge to my courage. Be it in a tent, a hut, a house, garden or village, I was always aware of this great, testing presence in the background.

The return down the cable was exciting, as we realised fully from the overwhelming view we had just left how adventurous the undertaking was. In the relative cool of evening we walked through the brightly lit streets, garish to our sea-bemused eyes. Down a quiet side street I heard for the first time a sound which would become part of everyday life: the shrill chorus of cicadas.

Next morning we saw the famous tablecloth effect on the mountain as a cloud crept up and over the crest and poured down into the gullies. We took a bus to a bathing pool by the sea and spent the day there. After dark we boarded the first of three trains for the overland journey to Central Africa. Our compartment was tiny, containing two bunks, one above the other, and a wash-basin ten inches in diameter which unfolded from the wall. We sat on the lower bunk and had about two feet in which to stretch our legs. There was a pleasant diningcar; the lavatories were kept impressively clean. All the stewards were Coloureds, polite and unobtrusive. The train left at nine o'clock and we settled ourselves for an uneasy night. In the morning we got up to the astonishing sight of the Great Karroo desert. All day the long train chugged its way across a grotesque landscape of high hills of bright red rock extending endlessly over red sand. From dawn till dusk the sun blazed down and by noon the atmosphere was barely tolerable. Sand and smuts clung to our moist faces and limbs and settled on our sweat-soaked clothes. It was impossible to read. We sat in a stupor of endurance, talking weakly to keep up our spirits. Only after dark was it possible to breathe freely. Next morning the scenery had changed to flat vermilion plain sparsely dotted with low scrub, and by afternoon we were in green bush country. On the third day the train began to climb steadily and during the night we crossed the Limpopo into Southern Rhodesia. After breakfast we arrived at Bulawayo and went straight to a hotel to have a bath, an indescribable relief. The town, at 6,000 feet, was refreshingly cool, the sky overcast with a high, closely packed cloud ceiling restful to the eye. The strikingly wide streets had been built to accommodate a U-turn by the early settlers' wagons with their long teams of oxen. We had no energy to go sight-seeing. After dark we boarded the train in which we were to spend the next three nights, travelling to Beira on the Mozambique coast.

We had the same type of compartment, much more acceptable in the cool weather. There was no dining-car, meals being provided at stations *en route*; this gave us the chance to stretch our legs. We were travelling continuously down among folds of hills which rolled back towards rugged mountain ranges. During the last night the train seemed to rush towards sea level and in the morning arrived at Beira, an unattractive port teeming with a myriad assortment of dark faces. The day was hot and sticky and we spent most of our time on the verandah of an hotel. Darkness came with the tropical abruptness that still took me by surprise, and we made our way to the station, a clammy wind blowing off the sea. Here we boarded the small train which would take us on the final lap of this marathon journey to our destination, the British Protectorate of Nyasaland.

Our compartment had bunk beds on either side, which was more comfortable, and we sat looking out at the Southern Cross tilted low on the horizon and marvelled at the cacophonous night sounds of insects and frogs which could be heard above the noise of the train and rose to a crescendo at stations. During dinner a locust-like insect about six inches long blundered into the dining-car and flopped about. At the next table a woman screamed, curling herself up on her seat to avoid it, and went on screaming until a Portuguese steward, with a look of contempt on his swarthy face, gathered it into a napkin and shook it out of a window. Ah, I thought, trembling, things to come: there will be no screaming.

During breakfast we crossed the Lower Zambezi Bridge, 12,064 feet in length, the longest single-line bridge in the world, and soon after, crossed the border into Nyasaland. With mounting excitement we feasted our eyes on scenery freshly washed in radiant morning light. We were arriving towards the middle of the wet season, so our first impression was of a green, luxuriant landscape, everything on a scale of awesome grandeur. There were great plains scattered with thousands of trees, wide brown rivers and all around the horizon at intervals, clear-cut, soaring blue mountains, long diaphanous waterfalls shimmering in their gullies. Majestic clouds hung aloft in the sky at different levels, throwing purple shadows over the whole scene. Already the spell was being cast. We did not turn away until a brief, flaming sunset had died into darkness. Shortly afterwards the train drew up for the last time and we stumbled off, stiff and weary, at Limbe station. A taxi took us the few miles to our hotel in Blantyre, the commercial capital. I had a vague impression of tall trees in the headlights and a refreshing scent of eucalyptus. Through mists of exhaustion a bath was achieved and I crawled under the unfamiliar pall of a mosquito net, first looking in and under the bed for snakes, a ritual I was to observe every night I spent in Africa for the next fourteen years.

Chapter 5

No whiff of the portentous wind of change which was building up over imperial horizons like a cyclone beyond a fair sea had raised a ripple on the surface of life in Nyasaland when we arrived in early 1950. It was known in the Colonial Service as the Cinderella of the British territories in Africa; there was as yet no sign that the clock would ever strike midnight and we were quite unaware that we were about to participate in the last of the halcyon years. Nyasaland had not fallen under British influence by conquest or annexation. It was led under the protection of the Crown by British missionaries and traders with 'the consent and desire of the Chiefs and people', as the first Proclamation put it, on 21st September 1889, almost exactly thirty years after Livingstone first set foot on the shores of Lake Nyasa.

Situated in south-east central Africa, Nyasaland is some 520 miles in length and varies in width from 50 to 100 miles. The area is 46,066 square miles (i.e. 36,686 square miles of land, 8,682 square miles of Lake Nyasa and 698 square miles of other lake water), nearly three quarters of the area of England. It is completely landlocked, its nearest point to the sea being 130 miles inland. Lake Nyasa is the third largest lake in Africa and among the first twelve great lakes in the world, some 355 miles in length and varying in width from 10 to 50 miles. The dominant feature in the physiography of Nyasaland is the deep trough-like depression, forming part of the Great Rift Valley that traverses it from north to south. The greater part of this trough is occupied by Lake Nyasa, the remainder by the Lake's only outlet, the Shire River. The difference in altitude to be found is extensive in range, and both the highest and the lowest points occur in the southern part of the country. On a clear day one may stand at the lowest point, 120 feet above sea level near Port Herald, and look northwards to the highest point of nearly 10,000 feet on Mlanje mountain.

There are two main seasons in the year, the wet and the dry. The wet season occurs between November and May; for the remainder of the year it is dry, with increasing temperatures in October and November just prior to the rains. (October, in particular, was known as 'suicide month', with good reason.) At the onset of the dry season, the south-east trade wind becomes established, and in June and July this wind brings with it a moist maritime air from the Mozambique channel which precipitates in the form of light rain and mist. This depressing phenomenon is known as a *chiperoni* and usually lasts about three days. (We used to say it tended to happen at weekends.) It takes its name from a mountain lying in Portuguese territory whence the wind appears to come.

The main food crops of Nyasaland were maize, the staple food of the plateau areas of dry, open woodland, and cassava, the staple food of the Lake-shore. Where climate and soil conditions were suited, a wide variety of crops were grown. Tobacco, tung, tea, coffee, rice, rubber, cotton and groundnuts were grown on plantations or smallholdings as cash crops, and in addition to the food crops, potatoes, beans, pigeon peas, pumpkins and millet were also grown.

For administrative purposes the Protectorate was divided into three provinces; Northern, Central and Southern, each under the aegis of a Provincial Commissioner who was responsible to the Governor. Each province was divided into districts, eighteen in all, which were the responsibility of District Commissioners, assisted by one, two or three Assistant District Commissioners, depending on the size and complexity of the district. There were a few sub-districts in the charge of an Assistant District Commissioner. The district headquarters were called the 'Boma', a Swahili word meaning a protective enclosure. Much of each month was spent by the DCs and their ADCs in travelling through the district by car, bicycle or on foot, liaising with the chiefs, keeping in contact with the people, interpreting Government policy and supervising the work of the African courts and the sub-treasuries of local authorities. This touring of the district was known as *ulendo*, from the Chinyanja verb, *kulendo*, to go. Chinyanja was the principal Bantu language of the country, the others being Yao and Tumbuka.

The Administrative capital of Nyasaland was Zomba, in the Southern Province, said to be the most beautiful seat of Government in the British Empire. In Holinshed's *Chronicles*, he records a saying by Mary, Queen of Scots: 'When I am dead and opened, you shall find "Calais" lying in my heart.' I know what lies in mine: an image of the sweep and surge of Zomba mountain along the sky, high above the little town, rising to the rare, heady air of 7,000 feet, where to draw breath was like drinking champagne.

Chapter 6

Excerpts from my letters take up the story of our arrival in Nyasaland.

13th February:

The hotel, known throughout Nyasaland as simply 'Ryall's', is comfortable.
We have the heavenly luxury of a private bathroom and *khonde* (verandah). It
took us a day to pull ourselves together; I have never felt so utterly weary, dirty
and dazed.

Life is taken at a leisurely pace here and we are going to be kept hanging
about, which is tiresome, as there is little to do in Blantyre, which is what I imagine a pioneer town in the mid-West was like! Ryall's is obviously the focal
meeting point in town and we entertain ourselves by observing the comings and
goings. The regulars are local business men, tanned and spruce, uniformly
dressed in dark trousers, long-sleeved shirt and tie, and carrying a jacket or
blazer; and men from outlying farms and plantations in town for the day. They
are deeply sunburnt, their teeth and eyes flashing in their dark faces. Their hair
is longer than is the fashion and their clothes noticeable for their age and style!
They drive big American cars or station wagons and there are usually several
large dogs sitting profiled in the back seat. There are also Government people in
from the districts on business or passing through. They all have the intense,
aloof look of men completely absorbed in their work. It is familiar to me. I saw
it on the faces of the Second Devonshire Course men at Oxford. It makes me
quail slightly, as something tells me Ron's face is about to assume the same
dedicated look! [It did.]

He is very keyed up and raring to go. He reported to the PC's office this
morning. We are posted in the Southern Province, to Kasupi, a sub-Boma about
twenty miles from Zomba, and he will work for the DC Zomba. We have
arrived at the tail-end of a famine and Ron will be on famine relief work for two
months, which will involve considerable travelling in the district: good experience for him. He was also briskly told to go away and buy himself a car, as it is
impossible to do his work properly without one. (They might have told us.)
What a panic! We were rather shattered, as we have *no savings*. However, there
is a Government loan scheme which works very well and everyone makes use

of it, even those with private means. They certainly do things in the grand manner here. I think Ron is secretly delighted at the prospect of owning a car, but dares not say so, as he knows my Scottish soul revolts against being in debt! We spent the afternoon shopping for a vast store of provisions, and tomorrow we go shopping for a car, heaven help us.

18th February:

Yesterday we thankfully left Blantyre behind us and drove over to Zomba, where we are staying with the DC and his wife till Monday. Our car is a Peugeot 203, 14 HP, dark grey, brown upholstery, with the streamlined look French cars have. It was the best of a very limited choice and Ron is very pleased with it. He drives as naturally as he breathes. (Too fast, I think, but that is probably the RAF!) It cost £599 and there is a monthly deduction from his salary over four years.

We have engaged a head boy, whose name is Aflike. He has good references so we hope for the best. He is going to find a second house boy and a cook from among his numerous relatives. He calls Ron 'bwana', me 'madam'. The DC says firmly three is the minimum number of servants we can have – any fewer and they refuse to work.

The DC's house stands about 4,000 feet up the 7,000 feet plateau of Zomba mountain. All the senior officers' houses are built on the terraced slopes and the roads wind up steeply in twisting hairpin bends. The lesser fry live in the township below. The house has French windows opening onto a wide *khonde* which overlooks flowerbeds and lawns, immaculately kept, and beyond to the most spectacular view imaginable. My eyes cannot have their fill of it. I look over the tops of trees, layer on descending layer, to the houses spread out far below, and on the edge of town the police camp and the barracks of the KAR (King's African Rifles). I can hear their buglers sounding duties of the day. Beyond lies a huge plain, scattered with trees and little conical hills, stretching for some forty miles till it meets the majestic massif of Mlanje mountain. I am entranced by its changing aspects as the sun moves over the great blue vault of the sky. At dawn it is invisible behind impenetrable cloud across a snow-white ocean of mist. During the day it dominates the landscape, its gullies, contours and peaks literally coming to light as the hours pass. After sunset it loses all depth and its silhouette against the pale green sky has the texture of those black velvet paper transfers we used to stick on the walls of the nursery.

I am writing this in blissful peace and quiet at mid-morning. It is so tiring staying with strangers in a strange environment with which they are familiar. Ron is down at the Boma with the DC, John Watson. His wife Dorothy is a doctor, and works every day on medical famine relief at the African hospital. Coffee has just been brought in by a tall, silent African wearing a red fez and long white robe, obviously a Muslim. I am still rather taken aback when this happens! The natives look happy and friendly and are absolutely delighted when we venture to try out our careful, academic Chinyanja. The old hands use a very basic form. For example, when they call for meals they say *tenga kudya* which means 'bring food'; or simply, *kudya*, 'food'. We were taught to say *tengani zakudya*, using the polite imperative plural and the plural noun, which is more accurate. I am not quite sure if Dr Aitkens was very popular out here! Nor if his 'guinea pigs' will be, either!

Things are done in a very casual, relaxed way. When Ron suggested on the phone he would get hold of a lorry to bring our luggage over on Thursday and drive over himself with me, to begin work on Friday, the DC said, 'Oh, I say, be a good chap and make it Friday and then we can start you off on Monday'! Naturally Ron and I are simply bursting to get to Kasupi and spread ourselves after this eternity of living out of suitcases.

The subject of servants among white women in Africa was an inexhaustible and painful one. Ron and I were very soon to realise that in Aflike we had found the equivalent of the European 'treasure', that almost extinct species. During his working life (begun as a tennis ball-boy at Government House), he had been excellently trained by an accomplished housewife and he had a far more efficient idea of how to run a house than I had yet acquired. We found him through the head boy in the dining room at Ryall's, who was his cousin. The reason for his availability to us I only found out from him months later. He had worked for years in the service of a tobacco planter. Shortly before our arrival, there had been a theft in the house of some jewellery belonging to the wife, who was convinced one of the servants was the culprit, and when none of them would own up, she sacked them all.

There was nothing to tell us there was anything momentous about the first encounter outside Ryall's the day before we left. Indeed, my heart sank at the sight of him, thin to the point of gauntness, clad in clean but ragged khaki shorts and shirt, his voice low and his manner cowed. However, the testimonials in his work book were good: no mention of suspected theft. So, when we drove off from Ryall's, Aflike was sitting in the back seat, almost buried in luggage, smiling shyly each time I looked round to see how he was faring. Little did we know that we had acquired the greatest bonus Africa could offer: a good and faithful servant; much more, a spirit and a presence in our home essential to the creation of a certain quality of domestic life I had promised myself I would achieve. Another 'haven' was about to be born.

28th February:

I have been longing to write to you for a week now, because *at last* we are on our own and our life here has really begun. We left Zomba on Tuesday morning and drove out to Kasupi, following the DC's car. Dorothy very kindly provided us with a picnic lunch to tide us over.

Our house stands on its own little hill high above the main road north. It used to be sub-Boma offices but has stood empty for some years. This is the first time it becomes a private dwelling, though one of its three rooms houses the local Post Office, which has basic facilities and a telephone which works for half an hour in the morning and again in the evening. The post-master is an Indian, and has a splendid time checking the lines and chatting with his contacts each morning as we sleepily sip our morning tea next door! The DC has had everything cleaned up for us and PWD (Public Works Department) workers are putting the finishing touches on a bamboo garage and huts for our servants. There is a roughly terraced garden at present buried in weeds. At its edge is a precipitous drop down through trees to a long, widening plain flanked by wooded mountains and terminating in another dim range across the horizon. The plain is thinly dotted with trees, round which cluster villages of huts with mud walls and grass roofs, beside long stretches of maize gardens. In the daytime smoke hangs in tall, motionless columns. When there is a baboon scare on, we hear the excitement. The baboons come in gangs and raid the crops in broad daylight. The villagers have built watch towers, glass platforms raised on poles in the fields, where they post a look-out, and when he gives the alarm, the entire population rushes out with sticks and stones to drive off the thieves, the women uttering a concerted, ululating cry which carries for miles in the still air. The silences of Africa are wonderful.

At the back of the house a steep path leads down to a small native village in a valley, so we need never feel isolated. The homely sounds of daily life – wood chopping, maize pounding, children calling and laughter – drift up to us, and at night we can see the cooking fires glowing and hear voices, sometimes singing. There is always the scent of wood smoke.

The house is brick, with a straw thatched roof, whitewashed walls and a rickety, roofed *khonde* along the front. We have two big rooms with double French windows back and front and two smaller windows. The floors are of red stone and polish beautifully. I have bought large, locally woven floor mats for 1s. 6d. each. The furniture is Government stock, heavy and unimaginative, but made of a local wood which also polishes well, and with our books, pictures and ornaments our diningroom/sittingroom looks airy and uncluttered. The curtains are a cool blue with white flowers. I got the materials in a Greek shop for 2s. 11d. a yard, and they made them up for me in a morning, charging 6d. per curtain! The ones in the bedroom are golden yellow with the same white design. It contains two mosquito-netted beds, two wardrobes, two dressing tables, a dresser with a wash basin and jug, and in a corner stands a full sized tin bath. All these are provided. Water is carried from a nearby spring *(kasupi* means a spring) in big petrol tins and heated on the kitchen fire. The *chimbudzi* (lavatory) is outside at the back down some roughly hewn steps, very precarious in the rain. It is a bamboo hut with a brick floor. The seat is wooden and placed over a tin container. A large box of sand and small shovel complete the scene. It is known among Europeans as 'the thunderbox'.

The kitchen is a separate hut at the end of the house at the back, usually full of smoke, the strict domain of the cook, I am glad to say. The Post Office is the room next to our bedroom; the back half is partitioned off and is our store. We have put all our crates and boxes there, and it also contains shelves for the food stores, the meat safe – a small square cupboard made of fine mesh – and the water filter, which is kept filled up with boiled water.

We have two outside workers supplied free: *machila* men. This is a tradition maintained from the old days when every Boma was supplied with a *machila*, a kind of rickshaw with shafts fore and aft, in which the DC travelled when on *ulendo*, carried by two porters. On the larger outstations there is also a Government-employed carpenter, who makes and mends for the householders, and charges only for his materials.

Ron's office, which he shares with his African clerk, is a big hut just beyond the house. The whole place is rather tumbledown and decrepit, and the DC has waived the usual 10% of salary deducted for rent. I think he was apprehensive about my reaction to the primitive conditions but quite honestly, I made up my mind at Oxford to tackle whatever problem presented itself out here, so I am ready for anything in the way of housing as long as it is ours!

Ron's clerk, Willis, who is also his interpreter, lives down in the village and sells us fruit and vegetables from his garden. A big bunch of bananas costs 4*d*. and a grapefruit is 1*d*. We have a very fruitful lemon tree in the garden. The Kasupi villagers seem to have taken us under their wing, as it were, and each morning someone turns up, eager to sell eggs at 1*d*. each, and chickens, alive and kicking, at 9*d*. each. I have even been able to buy kapok, locally grown, with which to stuff my cushion covers. We use powdered milk, more acceptable than the fresh milk in Zomba which has to be boiled and tastes disgusting. Aflike bakes excellent bread and works miracles in that wretched kitchen. We expect the house boy and cook any day, nephew and uncle respectively. One of the *machila* men goes into Zomba twice a week for our meat (8*d*. a pound!), travelling on the local bus which plies between Zomba and Liwonde ferry, twelve miles north of us. I felt guiltily it was a bit much to ask, so on the first occasion I walked down the drive to the main road to see for myself . . .

The bus looks as if it is about to burst at the seams, the roof piled with bicycles, bundles and baskets, the wooden seats crammed with humanity: spitting elders, nursing mothers, live cocks and hens, a goat. Heads and arms overflow out of the windows. The *machila* man squeezes himself on board somehow, calling out in an important voice that the *dona* (white woman) has come with her husband, a new ADC, to live at Kasupi. The bus explodes at this bombshell. Everyone cranes forward, stares, exclaims, smiles, points, makes comments. Babies start to cry, old crones cackle with laughter, hens squawk and the goat bleats. We are news! The bus lurches forward and the little *machila* man, eyes rolling with reflected glory, sinks instantly from sight. There will be much prestigious gossip on the way to Zomba. Perhaps there is something to be said for feudalism after all!

Chapter 7

We arrived in Nyasaland in time to take part in the last weeks of relief work, organised by the Government to deal with famine conditions caused by a drought which had struck the country a year before and was now almost at an end, as there had since been enough rain to ensure that this year's maize crop would be normal. Because of shortage of staff and the vast areas to be covered, it was impossible to distribute maize in every village, so selling centres were set up at focal points in the districts, and people from surrounding villages went once a week to buy maize which Government imported and sold to them at 2*d.* a pound. During the critical months, men from all departments were roped in to help, and some of the wives joined in the work, but now the emergency was nearly over and the Administration was doing most of the selling. We spent our first six weeks travelling round the centres of Zomba district. In this way Ron learned the whereabouts of many villages, met the chiefs and village headmen, and became known among the people more quickly than would have been possible in normal times.

The work involved a three-day circular tour and local trips for the rest of the week. The DC started us off on our first *ulendo*. He picked us up early in the morning and drove us down the escarpment into the long valley leading to Liwonde ferry. The road, though ravaged by recent heavy rain, was cracked and dry; fine dust filtered into the car through every crevice, seam and hinge. In our wake it rose up in a swirling double red funnel. Africans walking along the verges stood aside, pulling pieces of clothing across their faces, waiting patiently for the dust to settle. The DC told us that by noon the wind caused by the speed of the car was scorching hot, almost unendurable on one's face and arms; it was less uncomfortable to drive with the windows closed. (We soon learned this for ourselves.) We knew we were approaching water by the smell of damp vegetation and a change in the air, not coolness but a thinner quality of heat. A final bend brought us suddenly within a few yards of the river Shire, broad between banks dense to the water's edge with trees and long reeds. The water lay muddy and swollen, with as yet only a slight shimmer of heat over it. The clarity of the morning light was so brilliant it turned the green of the trees blue against the deeper blue of the sky, and sunlight and shadow merged into delicate, smudged detail. A solitary African sat on the near bank, wearing a white robe and a bright red turban. In the flash of first impression, the scene looked like one of Corot's sundrenched landscapes.

The ferry was a broad platform built over a deep keel, and was drawn across by six men pulling on a heavy steel cable stretched between the banks. We were to make the crossing many times. The ferrymen got to know the hoot of our horn in the distance, and if they were on the opposite side they gave answering shouts and made a great fuss and commotion on their way over. With us, they sang as they pulled, one man singing a line, the others joining in. Sometimes it was an old song, more often it was a spontaneous improvisation for our benefit, describing us and our *ulendos* in flattering terms, then lightly touching on their own hard work, with just a hint of anticipated reward.

(Only once did we cross at night, on our way home to Kasupi: the water so still and the stars so brightly burning that sky and river formed an encircling world through which we glided suspended among myriadfold diamonds floating in the darkness above, around and below. Even the ferrymen fell silent. I might wish and wish we had done it again, but then the impact of that unique occasion is what makes it possible for me, at will, to take the ferry at night across the river to Liwonde.)

On the far side of the Shire the country opened out into flat grassland, well populated with villages, blue mountains here and there on the horizon. There never was a horizon without its share of mountains, wherever we went. We were in bush country now and the surface of the road was appalling: it looked and felt like corrugated iron. The DC said it was very hard on the car and the way to tackle it was to grit your teeth, put your foot down and get it over as soon as possible, which he proceeded to do, while we vibrated all over and I thought with dismay of our lovely new car. As we got to know the district, so we got to know where the worst stretches of corrugation lay. His advice was correct; the car could skid badly if one took it slowly.

About forty miles on, we came to the maize market at Balaka. The heat was oppressive and I was feeling carsick, so I did not really take in the details of a scene which was to become familiar in the next weeks. I was aware of a great crowd of Africans milling around a fenced-off compound, of heat, flies, dust and an alien, overwhelming reek of perspiring bodies. The European in charge, a young agricultural officer, came over and introduced himself as John Brill. He was to be our host for the night. He suggested I make my way (*what* way, I thought in bewilderment. I was to get used to being faced with having to simply take off into the bush on foot for an unmeasured, unknown destination. I have dreamt intermittently of this ever since, always with a haunting sense of foreboding that my strength may fail me before some vague goal is reached) to the Government farm where I would find his wife, who would be glad of my company, as she saw very few white women. I felt a trickle of sweat run down my back. Brill went on to explain that the normal road to the house was impassable at this stage of the rains. The only way to reach it was to walk about a mile till I came to a railway bridge over a river, cross it and walk two miles beyond that. I looked at him without a word, thinking: no wonder your wife hardly ever sees a white woman. The DC, one of the kindest men I have known, stepped in and said firmly he was coming with me as far as the bridge. So off we went, Ron remaining behind to learn the ropes of maize selling.

It was my first walk through the bush and it was nearly noon. The narrow path lay beneath fields of tall – taller than I – dusty maize stalks with untidy leaves hanging like torn wallpaper, which rustled, flapped and fanned waves of hot air into my face. Heat also rose from the baked ground. For the first time I became aware of the characteristic smell, acrid, slightly reminiscent of vomit, which emanated from the soil of village maize gardens. One's sense of smell seemed to become more acute in the bush, as indeed was the case with all one's senses. As we walked along in single file, the DC leading the way, he remarked in a worried voice, 'The bridge may be a bit unpleasant for you. Have you a good head for heights?' My inside tied itself into a knot for the second time this awful day but I answered, truthfully, that yes, I did have a good head for heights. The path came to an end at a single track of railway, and, stepping onto the line, my companion cleared his throat nervously and pointing ahead said, 'There's your bridge. Do you think you can manage it all right?' He added abruptly, 'I shall see you over.' My heart thumping with exertion and my eyelids damp with sweat, I pushed aside the last of the maize and looked about me. We were on the steep bank of a swiftly running river and 'my bridge' was simply the continuation of the railway line across the gap between the banks of about fifty yards, the line being supported on concrete posts standing some sixty feet above the muddy, turbulent water. I looked bleakly at the DC and said, 'Oh yes, I can manage it perfectly well.' The look of concern on his nice brown face inspired me to give him a reckless grin. 'Pride goes before a fall, but here goes,' I said, and stepped in front of him onto the line. I walked dead centre between the rails and put my feet down firmly on each sleeper. A pattern of sleeper-space-sleeper-space-sleeper flowed steadily past my lowered eyes and I tried not to notice the movement of the water below at right angles to my pattern. Suddenly I heard a polite cough ahead and, looking up, I found myself, unbelievably, face to face with an African wheeling a bicycle. I stopped petrified astride two sleepers; he showed no sign of alarm. With an apologetic smile and a murmured greeting of *'Zikomo'* (thank you/excuse me) he picked up his bicycle and stepped carefully over the rail onto the twelve inches or so of projecting sleeper, holding the bicycle out over space in a perfect act of balance while I reassembled my reflexes and moved past him. Neither I nor the DC uttered one word till we reached the other side and then not many. A Government lorry was drawn up on the rough track nearby, into which he promptly handed me (he had the true field instinct for seizing opportunities as they presented themselves), peremptorily ordering the sleepy, surprised African driver to take me to the farm. He then turned back, gallant man, to recross the bridge.

Shut up in the stuffy cab with the driver who, in a fit of pique, was taking it out on the gears, I wedged myself into my corner, fixed my eyes on the filthy radiator and wondered if I would ever stop shaking. After a timeless interval of pitching and crashing over pot-holes we stopped, the driver and I looked at each other blankly, then he indicated with an abrupt gesture that we had arrived. I climbed down into a small compound, nearly forgot to thank him and walked through a neat garden and onto the *khonde* of a brick bungalow. In the bush life of open doors and windows and no electricity, we all announced ourselves and were received, in African fashion. A visitor stands at the doorway and calls *'Odi '*(I am here), and the host within calls *'Odini'* (I too am here), and there is welcome. Mrs Brill took me into a room curtained against the glare outside and to the accompaniment of a lonely woman's chatter I privately pulled myself together. The men arrived just before dark, tired, dirty and thirsty. Ron and I greeted each other as if we had been parted for days, not hours. (He had not relished the bridge either, but at least he had not met a man with a bicycle!) At dinner we tasted our first guineafowl. I went to sleep that night comforted by the totally false conviction that nothing could ever be worse than this first day's *ulendo*.

Next morning, after a breakfast including a slice of paw-paw sprinkled with lemon juice, both from the garden, we said good-bye to the Brills and walked across country for a mile to the railway line where we were to board a goods train which would take us to Utale, the next market place. Brill had arranged for a messenger to be posted further up the line to stop the train and tell the driver to look out for two Europeans on famine relief work and pick them up. We sat down at the top of the embankment under an umbrella (acacia) tree to wait. We did not sit for long; the ants always saw to that. So we leaned on the trunk, and we were to lean for two hours. Looking back, it seems to me that an incredible amount of time during our first tour was spent in waiting. In the district we had to learn a new concept of time, in which a day's well-planned schedule played no part. The pace of life quickened and slowed, things happened in their own time, not ours; when they happened we acted, when they failed to happen we compromised. Delays and abandoned plans had a snowballing effect and un-fulfilled commitments grew to exhausting proportions, so that the work was very hard in a long-drawn-out way. There was no such thing as a sense of urgency, and it was futile either to expect it or to try to impose it. Only now did I realise that there was no word for 'must' in Chinyanja.

At last the train laboured into view, the Indian guard hanging out of his van in the rear, waving to us. We sprang to life and slithered down the embankment. The train clanked to a standstill in a blast of heat and we hauled ourselves up into the van, where the guard, a Mr Patel, produced two wooden boxes for us to sit on. He smiled politely when we (foolishly) commented on the lateness of the train, and retreated into a taciturnity which we were to discover was natural to him. The train moved on again, slowly. There was nothing to see but the steep brown banks on either side. The roof and walls of the van were hot to the touch and the air blowing in at the open doors was like the rush of heat from an oven. One's body felt as if it might suddenly burst into flames. About an hour later we reached Utale station, a bare sandy clearing with a small hut for officialdom. There was no platform and we had to make a long jump down to the track, where we hastily moved away from the side of the train; its entire outline wobbled in the searing air that radiated from it.

Here once more under a group of dark green mango trees was a surging crowd of Africans fenced off from a bamboo shelter where two Europeans sat at a table. One of them rose and came forward to welcome us: a bearded Frenchman in a long white robe tied with a black cord, Father Craine from the Roman Catholic Mission three miles away, where we would sleep that night. Ron was to relieve him at the maize market. Here once more matters were taken out of my hands. The good Father proudly produced an ancient *machila* and two African boys from the Mission, shifting and shuffling in the shafts like fresh horses eager to go. I was inwardly outraged by this anachronistic arrangement on my behalf and said I would much prefer to walk, but my host simply shook his head eloquently and to avoid offending him I climbed in and the boys set off at a brisk trot. It was a most uncomfortable way of travelling, I soon discovered, as my steeds did not synchronise their movements and I was jolted and pitched about. The smell literally rising from their energetic efforts engulfed me.

The scenery and atmosphere were jungle-like. Huge baobab trees festooned with creepers and lianas rose above thick undergrowth. A bird invisible among them occasionally made a sound like the clear note of woodwind, which seemed to probe the silence cautiously and then withdraw. (Its local name was the rain bird, as it called only in the wet season, foretelling more rain. I never set eyes on one but I must have heard it thousands of times.) Long, tawny grasses growing right up to the edge of the path shook and rippled mysteriously in the still, heavy air and I felt the hairs on my arms stiffen and half-expected to see a lion step out on the path. I suppose all fear is primitive. I do know that during that three-mile journey I suffered a kind of dark terror, unimaginable until now. It left me as suddenly as it had seized me; a reassuring avenue of acacia trees appeared ahead, beyond it a long garden and a red brick two-storied building beside which grew a tall palm tree, lending an incongruously luxurious aspect to the scene, presumably, I thought savagely, because palm trees are connected in one's mind with the pleasures of the tropics. The *machila* stopped in a steam of achievement at a small side building. As I shakily disentangled myself, a very old nun came out and led me into a bare, blessedly cool room where we sat down on two hard chairs. To my dismay, she spoke no English, only French and Chinyanja, and as she had not been home since 1911 her French, she gave me to understand, was rusty. She had a gentle, tired face and was very polite but was clearly not expecting me; all visitors, she said anxiously, were always entertained by the Father in the main building. She brought me a glass of water and for over half an hour we held a stumbling conversation, I resurrecting my basic French and using my hesitant Chinyanja. The arrival of Father Craine by bicycle put an end to our mutual ordeal. He took me over to the main building where at about three in the afternoon I sat down to lunch with him and two African Brothers, wearing long, brown robes. They were friendly and very interested to hear about the Chinyanja course in London. I rallied my wits to entertain them. They sat wide-eyed and open-mouthed when I suddenly reeled off a folklore story I had learned by heart as part of the oral exam, to let them hear my accent, and when I had finished went into gales of astonished laughter – that uniquely African laughter, high-pitched yet melodious – in which I joined, more hysterically than they knew, while Father Craine pursed his lips and smiled primly. I began to feel better. Ron arrived as we were having coffee, looking very weary. He would eat nothing, and sat drinking bottles of water.

(For some months I fought against the inevitable irregularity of meals which field work entailed, but there seemed to be no solution to the problem. When you had travelled a long distance to carry out some task, you wanted to see it through without interruption in order to complete it by the end of the day. Also, as I myself discovered, one gets very thirsty walking in the bush, but hardly ever hungry. At first when we were out walking for the day among the villages, we took a picnic lunch with us, but when the time came to eat, we found we had no appetite for food. We were far more interested in having a rest in the shade and a drink or a refreshing mango straight from the tree. When we got back to camp we never wanted to eat at once though we might feel weak and empty.)

Soon afterwards, Father Craine showed us to a bedroom on the upper floor and told us we could have a bath in the room immediately below, where a tin bath filled with cold water was the only furniture. The windows were uncurtained so I bathed in record time. All the rooms were permeated by the musty smell of bats. It clung to the bed linen and mosquito nets and even tainted the food. We changed into slacks and long-sleeved shirts in a vain endeavour to ward off the mosquitoes drifting in clouds from the river, which was very near. 'They always make for the newcomers,' Father Craine was to say, cheerfully. 'They like your good red blood.' (Neither of us ever got malaria, which was exceptional, considering our life style. We never failed to take our daily Paludrine; people said it damaged one's memory but I never found this to be so.) At sunset we went out on the *khonde* and, leaning on the rail, looked down over the garden. Below us two water carriers passed by with a large bucket slung between shoulder poles. They were singing a Latin hymn in clear boys' voices. It was moving to hear the ancient, formal words, while the tall palm and exotic shrubs in the garden stirred their dark branches against the crimson sky and drums from a nearby village beat out a very different language. We made our way to the back *khonde* where, in a pool of lamplight, chairs and a table with a tray of drinks were set out and Father Craine and a newly arrived guest were already seated. I was introduced to Derek Arnall, whom Ron had met at the market, also a Government employee. He had misjudged his timing and had had to cycle the last mile in the brief twilight. Father Craine clicked his tongue and said it was not safe to use the path after dark. (What about during the day, I pleaded silently, stricken by memory.) He went on to tell us that one day towards sunset he was hurrying back to the Mission on foot when he felt a sudden compulsion to look behind him. He turned and there on the path about ten yards away was a lion standing watching him. He took a few involuntary paces back and it immediately moved forward, then stopped as he did. In desperation, he took off his jacket and, waving it in front of him, he walked slowly backwards for about a quarter of a mile. The lion followed him, keeping its distance, until the trembling Father stepped back through the Mission door to safety.

(Most of us eventually acquired our own story about a lion; mine was about a leopard. One of my favourites was told by the wife of a senior Administrative Officer in the Secretariat. She and her husband were driving to the Lake on local leave. It was very hot and she drank a whole flask of tea as they crossed Liwonde ferry. It was now just after sunset and she had been aware for some time that she had a full bladder. Realising she could not wait till they arrived at their destination, she asked her husband to stop so that she could slip out and go behind a bush. The sky was lit by the afterglow of the sunset and dusk had not yet thickened into darkness. They were in open savanna on a deserted road which gradually climbed a hill to the horizon. There were no bushes and she was by the back of the car when her husband suddenly called out, 'You'll have to hurry! There's a lion coming.' She peered round and saw, silhouetted against the sky on the crest of the hill, the distinct outline of a large lion. He paused for a moment and then moved off the skyline and into the dusk where he became a shadowy object moving steadily down the hill towards them. Having waited till she was in dire need, there was no way she could control herself now and she just had to go on with what she was doing, which seemed endless, while her husband, swearing under his breath, watched the progress of the lion. At last she scrambled back into the car and slammed the door. Less than ten seconds later the lion materialised out of the gloom, drew level and, swinging his great head momentarily in their direction, padded past, while they sat motionless with bated breath.)

There was no market next morning and we were free until the afternoon when, along with Derek Arnall, we were to start our return journey. At break-fast Father Craine suggested that we three might like to accompany him on a visit to the leper colony across the river. None of us welcomed the idea but to refuse was unthinkable. As we set out, images of leprosy from a short story by Kipling read years ago began to sustain my unquenchable imagination, in-creasing a general feeling of unease caused by high humidity, the rank smell of the riverside vegetation and the unfamiliar sights of the awesome prodigality of nature: a long sinister line of soldier ants pouring like a stream of oil across the path; writhing heaps of tan-coloured slugs which lay under the trees, looking from a distance like mounds of swept up leaves. One felt that any creature that could lay a single egg in a temperate climate would produce a thousand here. The river proved to be a narrow flow of water between an expanse of shiny brown mud, over which we slithered to a crude canoe made of a tree-trunk hollowed out by fire, its sides curving in, so that there was only room for our feet in the narrow bottom, while we perched on the edge. A skinny African boy wielding a long pole pushed us across.

A steep path brought us to the settlement's dispensary, where a French nun came out to greet us. She had a quick, strained smile and beautiful wide-set eyes. Her face was damp and grey against her white, tightly-bound wimple and long starched habit. I felt guiltily cool in my cotton open-necked blouse and skirt. The colony housed about six hundred lepers and owing to lack of funds was one of only a few in the Protectorate, though there were a number of dispensaries where people could go for treatment. Row upon row of huts filled two big compounds. The first housed those suffering from the early stages of the disease. People were moving about freely in an atmosphere of normal village life. The Sister called over a child and showed us an early symptom, a patchy whiteness on the skin of the forehead and cheeks. The further compound was very different. There was a stillness, a sense of ebbing life. Many of the sufferers lay by their huts, ragged bundles of rotting flesh. We saw limbs which ended brutally in a rounded stump. Here and there a head lifted and a face turned towards us, so ravaged that apart from the eyes it was almost featureless. When it was time to leave, the Sister stood at the door of her dispensary and watched us walk away, returning our farewell wave from the first bend in the path. On the way back I was silent, thinking about what I had seen, but mostly about the Sister. I felt sick, humble, shocked and angry, though I am sure she would have wanted none of these reactions from me. It outraged me to think of her working there probably for the rest of her life.

The train left Utale at 2.00 p.m. and never took less than four hours to reach Limbe, some sixty miles away. We did this three-day trip weekly for the next five weeks and came to dread the train journey. There would be an inexplicable delay of up to an hour at Utale; we soon learned the futility of questioning the timetable. We discovered that the engine driver's village was near the line, about twenty-five miles from Utale, and we usually passed there during the hottest part of the afternoon. He simply stopped the train and slipped away to his village for refreshment while we stifled in the guard's van and Mr Patel withdrew into one of his self-protective silences.

On this first trip we took a taxi from Limbe station and spent the night at Ryall's, rejoicing in its comforts. Derek Arnall, who had left his car in Blantyre to be serviced, drove us to Kasupi on his way back up-country. These famine relief *ulendos* were always meticulously organised beforehand but were subject to an infinite variety of mishap. Derek and I quickly discovered a shared passion for cinema. This mutual interest was the foundation of a friendship which has lasted to this day. He was the first friend I made in Nyasaland and has always had a special place in my affections; he is also the only friend still living there, in what became in 1964 the independent state of Malawi.

We did this trip once from the opposite direction, which meant setting out from Kasupi at 4.00 a.m. and driving seventy miles to Limbe to catch the train. It was our first experience of being out and about before sunrise. We left the house in the dark and a soft, wild wind was tossing the trees so that the stars seemed to sway in the sky. As dawn came, the darkness slowly lifted like a lid from the horizon, revealing a thin lemon line which as it broadened turned to orange, to red. Then the lid was off, light leapt across the sky, the sun was up and all at once the road was alive with Africans walking and cycling on their way to market or work in Zomba. The air was deliciously cool and fresh and the sun's long, low rays seemed to spill over the scene, drenching everything in golden light. Black skins gleamed, teeth flashed, eyes glistened. The women swayed gracefully under their head-loads, one hand holding a banana leaf over their shoulders to shade the sleeping baby on their backs. One man was eating a stalk of sugar cane, effortlessly tearing away the tough outer bark with his teeth – a daunting sight to European eyes. Smoke from village fires spiralled lazily upwards above the maize gardens by the roadside. It was an hour in the African day which came to hold a special enchantment for me, when all was pristine, promiseless of the dust and heat to come.

Chapter 8

At the beginning of the famine the people were allowed to buy as much maize as they could pay for. Then it was discovered that some of the more prosperous Africans were buying it in bulk and transporting it to the towns, where they sold it at a considerable profit. No maize was sold officially in towns, as other foods were available, whereas in the villages, if there was no maize there was starvation. As a result of this illegal practice – ironically, it was one of the few signs of private enterprise we ever came across – a rule was made that seven pounds of maize per head, at 2*d*. a pound, could be bought each week, providing every individual with a ration of a pound a day. The village headmen, who knew their own people, always came to the market and stood by to see that only the correct amount was bought for each family.

By the time Ron and I did famine relief work, the worst cases had died or been taken to hospital, but in some villages there were still people becoming desperately ill, mostly young women with babies and small children, who somehow managed to struggle to the markets. Before the day's selling began, they were helped onto the supply lorry, to be driven to hospital over miles of dirt road. The children had big bloated bellies which seemed almost too much of a burden for their thin legs, and the babies looked scarcely human, clutching their mothers like sick monkeys, their feverish eyes monopolising their tiny shrunken faces. The mothers were mere skeletons, their breasts hanging emptied and shrivelled, their skin clinging to their bones like wet brown cloth. They could barely walk and one marvelled to see them breathe. The old and sick who were too weak to walk from the villages were left to die in their huts. In 1950 there were no TV cameras to record these harrowing sights.

Now that the worst famine conditions were over, the Africans took an entirely different view of the matter. By the time we reached the selling point, accompanied by a lorry loaded with bags of maize, a huge crowd would have gathered, prepared to stay as long as there was anything going on and to make a social occasion of the day. They pressed close against a bamboo fence set up round a square compound. There was a narrow entrance at one corner guarded by two men dressed in khaki shorts and shirt and tall red fez, the uniform of the African government messengers who carried out errands in the Boma and in the field. They allowed a single queue of buyers to file through and come up to a table, placed under a tree, if possible, where we sat facing the compound. The procedure was simple. I received the money, piled it up in denominations and gave change. Ron wrote the required number of pounds on a slip of paper which was handed on by the buyer to Ron's office clerk, Willis, who stood beyond the table ankle-deep in grain. With a pound measure he scooped the maize up into the basket, basin or piece of cloth which was held out to receive it, counting aloud breathlessly in a reassuring voice. Willis was a young man, the son of a chief and Mission educated, with high hopes for himself in the future, not, alas, fulfilled. (He became a thief.) He had a magnificent physique, of which he was well aware, and he worked unruffled and tireless for hours, bent double over straight knees, sending the maize flying in a steady shower into the containers, while the buyers rolled anxious eyes at the grains which fell beyond their mark, each one of which was meticulously sought out and gathered in a carefully cupped hand.

In theory the whole process should have gone like clockwork; the villagers had been coming to buy every week for months and knew the routine, but they continued to behave like an unruly mob being put through their paces for the first time.

They had to be constantly reorganised and kept in order and they enjoyed it all enormously, laughing, jostling and cheating each other for a place in the queue. Sometimes pandemonium broke loose and proceedings were held up while Ron charged at the fence, rattling his stick along it and shouting orders in mock fury. They loved these little diversions and settled down again good-humouredly. The buyers, mostly women, took their time. Their money was always kept out of sight. Slowly they would fumble about in their clothing and eventually produce a small bundle of coins tied up in a rag, or unwind an elaborate turban of unsuspected length which revealed the money tied up in an inside corner. Meanwhile we drooped at the table and Willis stood waiting, glistening with sweat, maize dust powdering his eyebrows, eyelashes and tight curls, so that he looked like a handsome old man. As the sun moved up the sky we were gradually robbed of whatever shade there was and in the fierce heat the flies buzzed, the dust thickened and the choking, alien smells intensified. Tempers could fray. One day about noon, when there was a particularly large and obstreperous crowd, Ron's control snapped and he suddenly leapt into the middle of the compound, dragging with him the surprised Willis, who acted as interpreter. In a grim voice, almost beside himself, he addressed his startled audience. 'Now listen to me! I am not here for fun. I'm here to sell maize and you're here to buy it. It can be done quietly and in good order. I know what I'm talking about. In England during the war everyone had to queue for food and we had to behave properly and wait our turn or be flung out. Now, either you do the same or I pack up and go home and *you* go hungry.' Willis, an actor manqué if ever there was one, had been following this tirade with rapt attention, a wide grin on his face. He now stepped forward and did full justice to his soliloquy. (We both understood enough Chinyanja to realise that he embellished in translation whenever possible, but let him have his fling.) When he finished there was a moment's stunned silence. Then everyone began to clap politely and with appreciation, a sure sign that the voice of authority had been recognised.

As soon as we got back to Kasupi we counted the money, which had been put into bags and loaded into the car. It was mostly in pennies and small silver, and varied in amount between one and two hundred pounds worth. It felt and smelt disgusting, and we used pints of disinfectant in the bath water which Aflike started heating the moment he heard the car coming up our hill.

My letters give details of our life at Kasupi.

3rd March:

We have now received three *Observers*, three *Spectators* and three *Illustrated London News*, all of which I have devoured from cover to cover – and how wonderful of you to do the crosswords in pencil and rub them out! This kind of reading matter makes me very homesick. Ron says he almost dreads the arrival of the mail, as I seem to go very far away from him for the rest of the day. Having been such a wanderer he really has no pulled-up roots with exposed nerve ends to deal with.

Our cook and second houseboy have arrived, Hassani and Kidney, respectively, the former quite an old man, the latter a boy in his early teens, untrained but willing. He sweated so pungently with nerves when introduced that I presented him with a bar of soap and sent him to an Indian shop to buy two pairs of khaki shorts and shirts, with money I badly wanted for something else, but it had to be done. My heart quails a little but I must be patient. On his first morning Hassani, also a bundle of nerves, produced cornflakes *heated up* in orange juice, and when we had our first guest, the DC, to lunch today, the biscuits and cheese arrived at the table cooked in a pie dish. I gritted my teeth and called for mustard! The DC cleared his plate without turning a hair, declaring it was a 'jolly good savoury'. He is an angel. These two culinary disasters were served by an impassive Aflike – who surely knows better – I presume out of loyalty to his uncle, though I suspect he felt as mortified as I. Well, I will not tolerate nepotism in my household, so in a stern but tactful interview with Aflike later, I made it clear that he is in charge and has the final say in all domestic affairs, backed, of course, by me.

This morning I began my first official day's work, for which I am paid £1 per day. The market was about twelve miles away and we sold from 8.30 a.m. till 1.30 p.m., getting back shortly before 2 o'clock, to find the DC unexpectedly on our doorstep, so of course he stayed to lunch. I will write more fully about it later. I simply must go to bed as it is 10.30 and we get up at 5.30.

9th March:

Our timetable has been rather upset, because Ron has had a feverish cold with an alarmingly fluctuating temperature. I think he has been driving himself too hard. Last Wednesday, the day after I wrote to you, we sold maize at Kasupi, in the village at the foot of the hill behind the house. We began at 8.30 a.m. and worked without a break till 4.00 p.m. The people are desperate for maize, and most of them come a long way and have to get back to their villages afterwards, so we felt we must get on with it. Aflike carried trays of tea down from the house, looking very clean and aloof among the rags and rabble! The maize sells at 2*d*. a pound, so you will realise how much work we got through when I tell you we collected £188. Next morning we drove about twenty miles to a turn-off where Ron had to inspect a road and report back to the DC whether it was passable after recent heavy rainfall. It was just a dirt track and as we drove cautiously along it, quite suddenly the car was slithering in deep, black mud and before Ron could get control it became completely bogged down. Fortunately for us, Africans materialised as if by magic from the bush [they invariably did in an emergency] and helped us extricate it amidst shouts and bursts of laughter. (Ron was not amused.) We were all covered in thick mud. Then Ron had to set to and clean the car's innards sufficiently to persuade the engine to start, all under the blazing sun. It was just inexperience. I learned a lesson too: from now on there will be a bottle of drinking water in the car, always, however short the journey. By evening Ron's temperature was 103° F! We were supposed to get up at 4.00 a.m. next morning to reach Utale in time to sell maize at 10.00 a.m., but I sent a telegram to the DC in the morning. For once I blessed the presence of the Post Office. I usually curse it, as the Africans are so used to the house being empty they wander about the garden and then hover, staring into the house inquisitively when they realise it is occupied. All the doors and windows are wide open, of course, and I find the lack of privacy very trying indeed.

Ron spent the day on his bed, which was moved over by the windows. One of the ADCs arrived from Zomba with pills and quinine and stayed to lunch – no further disasters! Ron felt a bit better on Saturday and we drove into Zomba to hand over the vast sum of money we had accumulated. Yesterday we sold maize at Liwonde and had a gruelling morning without ill effects and today he seems fully recovered, so we sold maize at Kasupi. I insisted we had an hour's break for lunch up at the house and we finished for the day at 4.00 p.m. We have been told that temperatures soar very easily here but that we should never take risks.

Our house is gradually acquiring a nice, lived-in look and we love coming back to it. There is a waterfall on the hillside beyond Ron's office. It is invisible but we are constantly aware of it. I have not yet had the courage to suggest we go and find it, as the approach is through dense bush. So far we have seen monkeys; troops and troops of baboons, ugly creatures; a large kind of wild cat – seen from the car –

and two very long snakes, also seen from the car. The DC warned us to be careful about driving over snakes but this is sometimes unavoidable. They have been known to survive, entangled in the wheel spokes and ready for revenge as one steps out of the car! I learned today from Aflike that Kasupi has a reputation for leopards, so as far as I am concerned that waterfall will be forever unseen and unsung!

15th March:

We have been lent a carpenter from Zomba for as long as we need him. He stays with a friend in the village. He has made two towel rails, two small side tables and, to my intense pleasure, a good substantial bookcase built on a base of cupboards. He is now making some utilitarian bits and pieces for Ron's office and then we must call a halt.

This Saturday is a great occasion in Zomba, as the Dramatic Society is putting on *Quiet Wedding*. Everybody gives dinner parties, and evening dress is *de rigeur*. I was wistfully wishing we could go but saying nothing as our weekends at Kasupi are so precious. However, to my delight, we have been invited to go to the play and stay overnight on Saturday, and we would not dream of refusing. Our invitation comes from a Mr and Mrs Littlewood. He works in Establishments in the Secretariat and was supervisor of the Cambridge Devonshire Course when we were at Oxford. When we went on a sports day to Cambridge we were introduced to him. He wrote me such a charming letter saying we must not miss one of the social 'do's' of the year. It is pleasing that people in the big city think kindly of two new bush babies! We have joined Zomba Club as country members, and this will make a marvellous introduction to it.

23rd March:

The famine is drawing to a close and we stop selling in a fortnight. Ron is thankful, as he is longing to get down to the proper field duties of an ADC at last. I shall miss the money, such as it is. Earning even pocket money is good for the morale.

Our weekend in Zomba was a great success. We drove in on Saturday morning early as Ron had a lot of business to do at the Boma. I am afraid we blotted our copybooks by being late for lunch at the Littlewoods. There are so many winding roads along the terraces on the mountain slopes and the houses are all set well back in large gardens behind trees and shrubs, without numbers or names. It was made plain that junior officers and their wives are expected to be punctual. I felt awful. They had started lunch, as they have two small daughters who lunch with them and there is a strict routine. They are a very quiet, private couple, and we both felt they were making a special effort to entertain us. They spent nine years in Accra where the social life was hectic and I think they feel they have done their stint and want to settle down to enjoy family life. We all retired for a rest in the afternoon but things brightened up after a bath and change into evening dress, when we gathered for drinks before dinner. Littlewood is tall and good looking and was wearing black evening trousers, white mess jacket and a gold cummerbund, the Gold Coast's 'badge' colour, as it were. After dinner – no other guests – we joined in the procession of cars which were bumping and twinkling their way down the mountain roads to the Club. It was great fun being in a well dressed, lively audience, and what a lot of handsome men and pretty women! The theatre, which is also used as a cinema, is really a big ballroom with a stage at the far end. Everyone has to be in their seats at a stated time. Then the KAR band played the National Anthem at the front entrance and we all stood up as His Excellency the Governor (always referred to as HE), his wife and their party came in and made their way to seats at the front. He is a large, ugly man with a charming manner, she is fair and slim. She was wearing an elegant fitted gown of honey-coloured satin with matching long gloves and jewels in her hair. Their presence really did add excitement to the occasion.

The play was amusing and very well acted, with professional-looking sets. The audience enjoyed their own 'in' jokes. When one of the characters spoke the line 'I *hate* whisky', there was a ripple of laughter, as apparently this is far from being the case. At the intervals we had a drink and ran the gauntlet of discreetly appraising eyes, feeling very conspicuous as newcomers, but the atmosphere was intimate and friendly.

On Sunday morning we did what I have been longing to do ever since I first set eyes on it. We went up Zomba mountain! Littlewood drove us up in his big, comfortable car. You go up and down by a clock system, which has to be strictly observed: up on the hour, down on the half hour. The dirt road is very narrow, set close against the mountainside with a very steep drop on the outer edge, hair-raising, but then most of the roads are. The plateau is thrilling, it is so beautiful, as I sensed it would be. The air is divinely clean and thin; it is exciting just to breathe it. There are weekend cottages owned mostly by wealthy settlers scattered about in beautiful settings. (Some can be rented for local leave.) There is a splendid river with falls and deep pools and a little dam where people fish. The undulating slopes of the plateau are well afforested and there are many good walks. The views are breathstopping and I reckon overlook about three-quarters of the Southern Province. It is like looking at a relief map – you see round and over mountains. Even Mlanje loses a little of its grandeur. On the drive down I felt intoxicated, light-headed, and the blood was singing in my ears. I longed to get away by myself to think about it, privately, it so moved me. We left after tea and drove at high speed back to Kasupi through the golden light of late afternoon, the low sun's rays shining straight into our eyes.

We have started to clear the garden: quite a task. We have discovered, indeed laid bare, three lemon trees, a rose bush, a bush of jasmine and a small hedge of plumbago, which has sweet smelling, pale blue flowers. Dorothy (the DC's wife) kindly gave us a packet of zinnia seeds, which she says come up very quickly. We put them in three days ago and I have on more than one occasion caught Ron stealing out to gaze hopefully at their pristine flower bed!

Chapter 9

For a short time after our arrival in Nyasaland, all the black faces looked very much alike, and if Aflike mingled with a crowd of Africans, I had difficulty in singling him out, but I soon learned to discriminate. The predominant tribe in the Southern Province was the Chewa; Willis, the Clerk, was a typical example, with his well built body, flaring nostrils and thick lips. Aflike was a member of the Yao tribe, which has Arab blood in its veins. This influence gave his body its fine bones and lean suppleness and his features a more delicate modelling. I came to realise his slight form belied a lithe strength and staying power. His wife Aleni had the same fine bone structure. She had a still, enigmatic face which could be suddenly irradiated by a dazzling smile. Aflike was a Muslim and could therefore have four wives but in the years I knew him there was only Aleni, who was childless. He had divorced his first wife, by whom he had a son, Lajeb, who later joined our household. Aflike's voice had a special note in it when he spoke to Aleni and she would answer him in the same soft tone. She kept very much in the background but almost at once we established a kind of private bond between us. She liked to sit by the kitchen door sunning herself. Always when I caught her eye, she gave me her radiant smile, and by a tiny shrug of her shoulders or some subtle change of expression, silently convey to me that she knew how the day was going with me, and I would respond with a smile or a shrug, before turning away with a sudden pang of homesickness. It was very much a man's world I was living in then.

Although Aleni was one of the few really beautiful African women I came across in the country, all the women were a pleasure to see. They carried themselves well, having been in the habit from an early age of balancing loads on their heads. I never ceased to marvel at the sight of a woman walking along a path or the main road, usually with a baby strapped to her back, while on her head, set at an angle which was obviously exactly right but which always looked precarious, she carried with easy nonchalance a tall crock of water or a basin tied up in cloth containing her market produce, or even a single egg. In the more remote areas, where white people were seldom seen, when we met or overtook a woman on a path in the bush, she would return our greeting in a high, faint voice, step aside off the path and sink in one supple movement to her knees, her load still balanced, to let us pass. It was a custom which dismayed me but there was nothing I could do about it.

50

I liked to watch a group of village women sitting under a tree. I found something very soothing in the sound of their singsong voices, muted in the heat, and the clink of their bright bracelets endlessly sliding along their languid arms. Their bodies, so often prematurely thickened by child-bearing and heavy manual work, never lost that peculiarly feminine ability to look graceful and at ease seated on the ground. Their most typical and recurrent movement was the slow unwinding and rewinding of the length of cloth which they wore wrapped round the body and tucked into itself under the armpits. Even the tiny girl children wore their little piece of cloth and they took on a charming air of sophistication as they imitated in miniature this ritual gesture of their mothers and grandmothers.

Aflike was impressed by the fact that we could communicate with him, however basically, in Chinyanja, and on *ulendo* I often heard him explaining with pride to the villagers that his new bwana and dona had learned Chinyanja 'at school in England'. This statement always produced a long-drawn-out 'ehhhhh' with which the Africans politely acknowledged an interesting piece of information. This was an echo of the traditional reaction to a storyteller, when the listeners punctuated his narrative with 'ahs' and 'ehs' to show their appreciation and attention. Sometimes we were so busy and preoccupied with settling down and adapting to our new life that we had neither patience nor energy to struggle with Chinyanja. These lapses did not go unnoticed by Aflike, whose face discreetly registered his disapproval. Eventually he and I evolved a mutually satisfactory medium of communication. When giving him instructions I spoke Chinyanja but when I talked to him as a private person I spoke in a mixture of English and Chinyanja. He tended to speak to me in Chinyanja but would sometimes break into English to help me understand. He had a good ear and was quick to learn new words and phrases which he would use with precisely my intonation. One morning, standing beside him on the *khonde*, companionably surveying our domain before the day's work began, I said, more to myself than to him, 'This garden is as dry as a bone.' He was off at once to fetch a garden boy, shaking his head, chuckling – he always chuckled at anything new, as a kind of safeguard until he got used to it – and repeating over and over: '*Dry* as a bone, *dry* as a bone.'

Aflike was not talkative by nature nor, clearly, was he accustomed to communicating in a personal way with his employers. However, we gradually won his confidence. He was in early middle age, had seen many changes, and possessed memories of great interest which he began to share with us as time went on. He once said to me, 'When my grandfather was young' – he always indicated age by height and in this instance put his hand at the level of his knees – 'the paths were not safe to walk upon. Then the DCs came and made the paths safe.' To this day I cherish these words. Often alone for hours, I was glad of his friendly presence about the place and we were soon sharing little domestic jokes, which he would go off and recount to his wife. The interest we showed in him was not long in taking effect. His spirits and appearance improved so much he hardly looked the same person we had taken into employment. His face in repose never lost its look of melancholy, but he began to comport himself as a man of definite personality and character.

It simply did not occur to us that Aflike could not read or write. He and I would discuss what fruit and vegetables I wanted from the Kasupi market and I would unthinkingly write down the list and give it him. He always brought back what I had ordered. When I asked him for a tin or jar from the store, he produced the right one, presumably because he knew by heart the colour and shape of the labels. Then, early one evening, Ron was reading the local paper and came across an item of news he thought would be of interest to discuss with Aflike. He went out to the back but returned almost at once, looking very much put out. He had tried to give the paper to Aflike, who just stood rooted to the spot with hanging head, his pride deeply wounded. A few days later, after careful thought, I remarked casually to Aflike as he was removing the tea tray that I thought it would be a good thing for him and for me if I taught him to read and write. The china rattled on the tray as, with a slight bow, he gravely agreed it would be a good thing. I told him we would start the next day, after tea, with an hour's lesson. He hurried from the room and presently I heard his voice, raised in excitement, repeating our exchange to Aleni, and her 'ehhhs' at the news. Wondering what I had let myself in for, I spent the evening working out the first lesson, drawing on my Chinyanja notebooks for guidelines.

He learned quickly, squatting by my chair, curling and uncurling his toes, like a cat its claws, in mental effort. As we progressed, he relaxed, hugged himself with wonder at the unfolding miracle and shook with silent laughter. Never was there a more lighthearted schoolroom. When he was off duty in the afternoons, I would hear the drone of his voice repeating the alphabet and catch glimpses of him at odd moments laboriously copying letters into the exercise book I had given him. It was moving to see this middle-aged man toiling at something I had done when I was about five, especially as I knew he had a working knowledge of English, Portuguese, Swahili, Yao and Chinyanja.

It was difficult for me to comprehend how few possessions Aflike and his wife had, and I was shaken to realise that every scrap of anything I threw away was put to some use whenever possible and that my wastepaper basket must sometimes seem like a treasure chest to them. Every morning when I did the flowers – before the garden was established I used mainly the many and various beautiful grasses that grew on the verge of the drive – I wrapped the withered blooms in an old newspaper and put the bundle in the dustbin which stood by the kitchen door. As soon as my back was turned I would hear the lid being removed, and Aflike would shake out the paper and drape it carefully on a rock to dry. He would later use it for rolling cigarettes or barter it among the villagers for eggs. I saw a red ribbon which I had thrown away adorning his waist the next day as a belt for his trousers. I gave him an old shirt to use for polishing the car and later recognised it, minutely patched and darned, on his back. In time I gave him his own supply of papers and offered him our old clothes for himself and his wife, which he always accepted with his little dignified bow. We, of course, supplied his uniforms.

My mother sent us a regular supply of newspapers and weeklies which I would settle down to read after lunch. I became aware that Aflike tended to hover in the vicinity, watching me with eyes hungry for knowledge. So I got into the habit of opening *The Illustrated London News* first and picking out suitable pictures to show him; no easy task, as some of the outward trappings of Western civilisation conveyed nothing to him. He had served in the KAR during the war and like all Africans loved parades and ceremonies, so photos of Trooping the Colour went down very well. I made mistakes. An exciting, to me, photo of Broadway skyscrapers lit up at night, painstakingly explained, produced dead silence and then a short spasm of giggling and repeating under his breath the small exclamation '*ai, ai*', the equivalent of 'well, well'. The African reaction of hilarity at the inexplicable showed itself on many occasions.

Someone had given me a present of two unbreakable glasses which looked like ordinary crystal. (We used them on *ulendo*.) Now glassware was a delicate subject in more ways than one in most households. A slap-dash approach to washing-up made sad inroads on treasured wedding presents. As I unpacked them I had an idea. I summoned Aflike, Hassani and Kidney, showed them the glasses and with studied nonchalance hurled them violently across the room. They struck the wall and fell noisily to the stone floor, where they lay intact. The reaction of my audience was all that I could have desired. Their breath left them with a concerted hiss of horror and they sprang back, each trying to get behind the other, like shuffled cards. Then came a prolonged moment of silence followed by convulsions of laughter. When I made to repeat the performance they begged me not to and fled from the room, still laughing and clutching each other. There were occasional mild earth tremors which gave warning of their approach with a low rumble which increased in volume till the climax of rattling doors and windows and sometimes a slight movement of the walls. They usually lasted for only a matter of seconds, but it was an uncanny experience. After the stillness which always fell when the last rumble had died away, Ron and I would smile at each other and wait for the inevitable peals of mirth from the kitchen, and then Aflike would look in, breathless and grinning, to assure himself that all was well. At one such aftermath, the scientifically-minded Ron was misguidedly moved to explain this phenomenon to Aflike. He listened courteously with downcast eyes until the strain became too much for him and he dissolved into helpless giggling.

The only time when Aflike was unpredictable and caused me vexation was during Ramadan, a period of thirty days in the ninth month of the Muslim year, during which strict fasting is observed from sunrise to sunset. Ramadan was dreaded by all householders, as the Muslim servants, whether from sheer faintness caused by their fast or from some spiritual upheaval, became erratic in manner and behaviour. (They also hawked and spat all day.) Hostesses tried to avoid entertaining on any scale during this time and frankly gave their reasons. The effect was cumulative, so that towards the end of the four weeks there was an unnerving atmosphere of feyness in the air, which could develop into dangerous tension if there were discontent and unrest in the colony; it was the most likely time for trouble to break out. Aflike worked as well as ever, but there was something distrait in his manner and his eyes had a feverish glitter. He withdrew into himself and avoided my company as much as he could. He also adopted an oblique approach to a problem, which I had to learn how to handle. One example is sufficient. After breakfast one morning he confronted me abruptly with, 'Sorry, Madam, *very* bad dinner last night.' He knew, and he knew I knew, that there had been absolutely nothing wrong with last night's dinner. It was nearing the end of Ramadan and I felt exasperation rising but managed to say in a neutral voice, 'Yes, Aflike. What went wrong?' He flinched at this uncouth lack of subtlety in my tactics. We eyed each other wearily, then, fanning out his hands in a gracious gesture of capitulation Aflike came to the point. 'Madam,' he said, 'The kitchen boy broke a glass when he was washing up.'

Chapter 10

I never tired of looking out over the grand panoramic landscape lying spread below Kasupi. Like the sea, it was always changing. On a serene, sunny day a small innocent puff of cloud would detach itself from a high mass and float lower and lower, hovering over the plain. Suddenly it sent what looked like a solid shaft down into the ground, growing smaller and smaller as it poured itself down the shaft until the shaft itself sank from sight and the rush of rain was over, while all around, the plain lay shimmering in the heat. Sometimes several of these small cloudbursts broke at the same time, setting up a muffled roar, and I would wait for the sharp smell of rain to come drifting across the dusty miles to me.

Towards the end of the rains there were swift changes in the weather. In the morning it was often impossible to imagine that it could rain that day, when the sky presented a flawless arc of deepest blue and the sun felt like a solid touch on the skin. Then, unobtrusively, the clouds were there, puffing themselves up beyond the high ridges, swelling and surging over the sky, and soon, down crashed the rain. The ground became wet so quickly the water appeared to have welled up from underneath and submerged the earth rather than descended upon it. Our short flight of steps produced a series of splashing waterfalls and from the overhanging roof of the *khonde* the water fell in an unbroken transparent sheet. The effect under a corrugated iron roof was even more startling, but more mundane. The noise was so loud one had to shout to be heard, and each hollow in the iron acted as a runway, so that from inside it looked as if dozens of taps in a row along the edge of the roof had been turned fully on. As suddenly as it began, the rain stopped, and a cool cacophony of dripping, gurgling and plopping filled the air, while the steam rose as the sun with burning intensity sucked up the moisture. Gradually the sounds died away, the mud ruts in the roads began to harden, and the soil in the garden cracked once more.

Another feature of this time of year was the thunderstorms. These came mostly at night, after a breathless day of searing heat. In the darkness, lightning travelled fitfully round the horizon like intermittent gun flashes, silently silhouetting the shoulder of a mountain for a flickering moment or revealing the presence of huge clouds hanging unseen in the night. Gradually the storm gathered momentum. Twisted rods of lightning plummeted down the sky with a noise like fireworks bursting and earthed themselves with a thump, thunder hurtled across the firmament and the mountains caught the sound and flung it back and forth till thunder and echo mingled in a thought-obliterating crescendo. It always felt as if our little hilltop was at the centre of the climax overhead.

It was a weird experience to be overtaken by a thunderstorm. As we drove through thick darkness with the rain slanting across the headlights like thin bands of steel – when I belatedly saw Olivier's film of *Henry V*, the flight of arrows at Agincourt instantly restored this image of Africa to my inner eye – the landscape from horizon to horizon would suddenly spring to life, every detail as clear as in daylight, in a long livid waver of pale lavender light, then vanish into pitch blackness again, leaving us momentarily blinded.

One beautiful day, standing in the DC's garden, I actually heard a great thunder cloud emit a deep 'whouff' as it billowed up the sky like smoke exploding from a giant chimney in a seething mass of dazzling white. I had anticipated being afraid in these tremendous tropical storms, but they were so much larger than life, extravagantly unreal, that my reaction was one of sheer exhilaration with, perhaps, a dash of fatalism.

The rainy season brought out the insects and the creepy crawlies, though in memory I seem to have waged an everlasting war on most of them throughout the year, certainly the snakes. (At the beginning of each tour I got the garden boy to cut me a hefty stick which never left my side and was used, more times than I care to remember, with a repetitive, messy but deadly accuracy born of stark terror.) We got into the habit of shaking out our shoes in the morning: a favourite hiding place for small, inch-long scorpions, which also lurked in the pages and spines of my books. Harmless, sinister-looking black centipedes, as thick and long as a long, thick finger, glided smoothly as if on wheels across the stone floors and fell headlong down the steps. '*Bongololo,*' Aflike pronounced with distaste when I first drew his attention to one. He picked up my stick and before I could stop him dealt instant annihilation from which I averted my eyes.

Flying ants abounded. They bred underground and emerged in silver-winged streams into the air in their thousands. Clouds of them would suddenly invade the room in the evening, attracted by the lamplight, and hurl themselves to death against the hot funnels. Aflike swept up their discarded wings in rustling heaps next morning. The Africans considered them a great delicacy. One evening on *ulendo* as we sat by the tent with our sundowners, looking from a high ridge down over the plain towards Mlanje, we saw many tiny flickering lights like a distant metropolis. We called Aflike, who explained that villagers must have found flying ants' breeding grounds over a wide area and were attracting them with fire as they came out of the ground.

Cockroaches were a constant menace in even the most fastidious households. I pursued them to inflict a lingering death with a spray, or stamped on them if taken by surprise. I always held my ears as I did so, as I could not bear to hear the crackle and squelch of their demise. In the towns, a team from the Department of Health was available to spray emptied food stores and pantries. The doors were then shut till next morning, when a dreadful scene of dying and dead bodies in awesome numbers was laid bare to the cringing mistress of the house. They were swept up and thrown into the fire.

We were always on the watch for the destructive white ants, which could damage the fabric of the house, but it was the minute, scavenging red ants with which I became most familiar. They would swarm in their hundreds, suddenly, from nowhere, should a crumb or morsel of food, or a dead insect, be inadvertently left lying about. Sometimes the insect was not dead, and a frenzied drama was enacted as the struggling victim was handed along the moving line of attackers till finally exhausted and overcome.

The only living creatures I welcomed in the house were the delicate praying mantis and the companionable geckos which darted about the walls flicking out their tongues in pursuit of food and remained for hours splayed motionless on the ceiling, their hearts throbbing in their semi-transparent bodies. If caught by the tail by a cat, they simply discarded the tail and darted off, a shorter version of their previous selves. It did the cats no good at all to eat lizards. They sickened, shivered and shook, and took a long time to recover. Sometimes they wasted away.

Chapter 11

When the maize markets were closed down, the normal routine of life in the district gradually unfolded. At least half of every month was spent under canvas; packing and unpacking became an automatic exercise. The wear and tear on good suitcases, china and glass were quickly apparent, so I visited the carpenter attached to Zomba Boma and between us we designed a set of strong wooden boxes with hinged lids which neatly contained all our needs and were to serve us well. I also, reluctantly, invested in cheap china and glass – I refused to use dreary tin mugs and plates. Our only luxury when camping was our Mappin and Webb cutlery (a wedding present). I always counted out what we needed and replaced it myself in the big canteen, which contained twelve of everything.

Followed by a lorry carrying the tent, camp furniture, supplies, several Government messengers and Aflike, we would arrive at our destination. The village headman would have organised a camping site under trees, with a square bamboo stockade to enclose it. Some yards away from this compound, discreetly placed among the trees, a small roofless hut was erected, our *chimbuzi* (lavatory), which contained what was called a 'squat hole', a deep hole in the ground. Seasoned travellers took their portable lavatory seats with them. We had a strong torch, but I dreaded that journey last thing at night through the vibrant darkness, and always undertook it clutching my snake stick.

In the tent proper there was room for two camp beds with a narrow passage between; at the back, a semi-circular extension served as a bathroom containing a canvas bath and basin set on folding frames. The bath was low and square, about a foot high, and Ron's knees just about came up to his ears when he sat in it. The entrance to the tent had a roofed extension which gave us a tiny *khonde* where we sat out in the evening and for meals. The tent opening had strong fastenings which were done up at night. In the cold season the ground below our low beds rapidly cooled and by dawn we were chilled to the bone. I always slept badly under canvas, from sheer nerves and an over-active imagination. No matter how many experienced campers assured me kindly that the last thing a wild animal would do was to enter a tent, I never got over the feeling of vulnerability within the thin canvas walls. (These reassurances were simply not

true, as my extensive reading of books about Africa subsequently proved!)
Leaves and twigs fell onto the sloping roof and slid slowly off with a scratching
sound and mice or some other small animal rustled among our boxes. Hyenas
sometimes prowled and snuffled about the compound, occasionally brushing
against the guyropes, which made the canvas by our beds strain and creak
ominously. The bamboo canes supporting the mosquito nets touched the sides
of the tent and when there was a high wind the canvas pressed in on the canes,
which shook until the bed began to vibrate as if something were rubbing against
it. Aware of Ron's quiet, regular breathing in the bed opposite, I would lie with
my heart pounding, exhausted and feverish with unreasonable fears, cursing my
plight and vowing I would *never* go on *ulendo* again. Only when I heard the first
distant cockcrow did I relax and fall deeply, briefly asleep. It became one of the
most welcome sounds of Africa, and it still produces a sense of relief in me,
some thirty years later, when I hear it.

We got up very early in camp, and how marvellously restoring it was, in
the soft, mysterious lightening dark just before dawn, to drink the piping hot
tea Aflike brought and feel ready for another day. Ravenously hungry in the
clear cold air, we ate our eggs and tinned sausages in the rich, glowing light of
sun-rise. Pigeons began to coo in the trees, where every dew-washed leaf
glistened, and the pungent woodsmoke from newly-lit village fires stung our
nostrils.

The village headman always provided accommodation for Aflike, whose
cooking facilities appalled me – a hollow in the ground, flanked by two bricks
across which was laid a tin sheet; from this primitive arrangement he produced
incredibly good meals. He thoroughly enjoyed *ulendo* and having us to himself
to look after. At the end of a long day spent walking in the bush, the return to
camp made it all worth-while. There was a hot bath to soothe weary bones,
disinfectant for scratches, bites and blisters, and clean slacks and shirts, beautifully ironed, laid out on the beds for us. (Aflike used a big, heavy iron which
burned charcoal. Each side of the iron was perforated with holes, and by
swinging the iron from side to side, the charcoal was kept fanned into life.)
When we emerged, the drinks tray would be on the table on the little *khonde*
and we would sit quietly enjoying our well earned sundowners and watch the
stars come out. The African sky at night was always a marvel of beauty; in the
cold season in Nyasaland, it was a spectacle of transcendental splendour. The
sky stretched out all round us to the horizons, a vast, glittering dome like a lid
placed over the earth. The stars throng so thickly, large and small, all encrusted
and mixed together; it is not credible there can be space for one more. One is
aware that up in that teeming element they hang at different levels – a falling
star really does fall among and through its companions down the infinity of the
sky. In one evening we never failed to witness several of these brilliant de-
scents, like a drop of liquid diamond side-slipping into extinction. Like the sea,
the sky was always quick with life. The first impact of this experience haunted

my memory next day, only to be miraculously renewed that evening and for hundreds of evenings to come.

Extracts from my letters fill in the details of this period.

3rd April:

This morning we did the long drive to Balaka, where the DC is camping, as Ron had to attend a large council of the district chiefs with him. I watched the proceedings from the car, parked under a tree. The council was held in the village *bwalo*, a large square of ground shaded by big mango trees. There were seven chiefs, dressed either in long toga-like garments or in robes of shiny, striped material rather like Noel Coward dressing-gowns. They wore white caps, turbans or high red fezes. There are a lot of Muslims in the South and their dress always has an oriental touch about it. All the chiefs had presence and bore themselves with dignity, though the DC, when I remarked on this, said with feeling, 'That may be, but three of them are wily old rascals,' and I think he was watching his language! They sat in cane chairs in a semi-circle and about a hundred villagers squatted behind them. The DC and Ron sat at a table facing them and the DC addressed them through an interpreter. There were a great many flies and I lit a cigarette to discourage them. Ron caught the movement and his face became more and more strained as he realised where his cigarettes were! Afterwards we gave a lift to two large chiefs, who crushed into the back seat with Willis. I made polite conversation with them over my shoulder, as Ron had to concentrate on the dreadful road surface – like a turbulent river bed. They grumbled over the latest Government taxes the DC had been telling them about, and I said that the British grumbled too and in fact taxation was a sore subject the world over. Willis interpreted this, at some length, as usual. When we dropped them off, one of them nodded in my direction and said something quickly to Willis, who told me as we drove on that he had said, 'The young dona is a good wife for the ADC. She knows how to talk to chiefs!' Ron was *delighted*.

This is Easter weekend and everyone will be on holiday. We shall stay quietly here and get on with the garden. Ron starts distributing war medals next week, in the district.

One of the ADCs in Zomba is going on leave soon and Ron has an awful feeling he will be his replacement. The DC, who knows that we love Kasupi, told Ron in confidence this morning he has applied to the Provincial Commissioner's Office for a grant to enlarge our house, build a separate Post Office and a better Boma office, thus making a permanent sub-Boma with a proper residence for an ADC. He indicated that he hopes Ron will get the posting when the time comes. So we know, alas, that our days at Kasupi are numbered. It is no use moaning about it, as these sudden postings are to be expected in Colonial Service life, but I must confess my eyes fill with tears at the very thought of leaving. We are beginning to feel so at home. The villagers here are used to us, and in the district they recognise the car and wave and smile, and the women start up their ululating sound of welcome when we stop somewhere.

12th April:

I have little news for you because we spent Easter weekend quietly here. Yesterday Ron was in Zomba, working at the Boma, and I spent the whole day on my own, mainly in the garden.

Besides the two *machila* men who help with the garden, I have acquired a third helper – Akim, a sturdy fourteen-year-old boy. He was recently embroiled in a village fight and stabbed his best friend, who fortunately survived. He should have gone to a reform school but there is not room for him at present. Ron has decided to take him on as a garden boy for a few months, 'to keep an eye on him' as he put it. I know jolly well it will be *my* eye that will be kept on him most of the time, with Ron buried deep in paper work in the office or out in the district! So far Akim has been on his best behaviour and tries very hard to please. This afternoon I saw him, soaked to the skin in a sudden downpour, dashing backwards and forwards with his watering can, determined to finish his task, come rain or shine! I have bought myself a small red trowel which I keep strictly for my own use. The Africans tend to break 'gadgets' and are far better working in the garden with a flat stone or the all purpose *panga*, a primitive knife they use to cut the grass. Akim and the *machila* men are fascinated by my trowel, and stop working to stare at me whenever I use it. This gets on my nerves and I have to ask them politely to get on with their work, which they do, with much ingratiating rolling of eyes and flashing of teeth.

We now have two cane easy chairs which match the floor mats. A nice young South African couple who gave us lunch at Balaka when we sold maize there, commissioned them for us from a local craftsman and sent them via the car of two friends of theirs who were passing through on local leave. They called in with the chairs this morning, a lovely surprise, and stayed for coffee. He is with Barclays Bank in Blantyre. They were 'my kind', as far as interests go. As soon as they came in they made straight for our big bookcase, sat on the floor beside it and stayed there through the visit, letting their coffee get cold. We were soon deep in T.S. Eliot, Max Beerbohm and D.H. Lawrence. After they left, I found I was shaking! One gets so accustomed to keeping one's interests to oneself, the sudden relief of being able to air them was quite overwhelming.

We are definitely moving to Zomba soon – no date yet, which maddens me. Aflike has already arranged to have eggs and chickens from the village sent in by the bus – they are cheaper here, he says firmly. I think you will be glad to know we are going to Zomba, because it means I can have company some-times, also tennis, swimming, a library and cinema. We certainly mean to be happy wherever we are – and we shall have a diningroom *and a bathroom* – hurrah!

18th April:

We are so tired that although it is only 7.45 we are already in bed, ensconced under our mosquito nets with the lamps buzzing quietly beside us. We have had a long, hard day, a very 'African' day, which I shall tell you about presently.

At the weekend, a young woman with her little girl aged about three appeared on the doorstep. The child's foot had caught in the back wheel of her father's bicycle as she sat on the carrier, and a spoke had cut deeply into one side of her foot, laying it open. There is an African hospital about ten miles away, this side of Liwonde ferry, but they live in Kasupi, so they came straight up here. I got out Daddy's marvellous medicine chest, blessing him under my breath as I found everything I needed. [My father had stocked up from his surgery a sturdy wooden crate with an impressive supply of dressings, cotton wool, bandages, scissors, thermometers, sticking plasters, disinfectant, aspirin, iodine and ointments, including an ointment he made up himself. It saw us through many a cut and sore during childhood. We called it 'magic ointment'. Mother always said he would have made his fortune if he had patented it.] The child did not utter a sound, but her fathomless dark eyes were abrim with tears as I bathed it, put on a dressing of magic ointment and bound it up. Two days later they returned and I unwound the filthy bandage with shaking fingers, wondering what I was about to uncover. How thankful I was to find the wound clean and healing well, especially as a small group of spectators had accompanied them to the back *khonde*. Aflike hovered anxiously, concerned for me. He gave a little '*ai*' of satisfaction when I lifted off the dressing and there was a polite round of clapping! They are coming back in two days. I just pray my reputation does not spread. I do not want a clinic on my hands. Ron came back at lunchtime, having been out in the bush visiting a man who had been mauled by a lion. The man told him cheerfully that the thing to do was to give the lion a fist to chew on till help came! They are amazing people.

On Saturday morning we drove out to visit one of *the* big chiefs at his village, which is called by his name, Kawinga. He lives in some style and we had to watch our p's and q's. He is a splendid looking old man, tall, upright, with hooded, worldly eyes and magnificent teeth. He wore an ample orange turban – I longed to ask him to show me how he winds it – and round his neck a hefty necklace of lion's teeth (his own kill) over a robe of royal purple. He showed us his maize garden, climbed a steep hill to let us see the impressive view of his domain, and took us into his house, which is larger and more comfortable than ours. On one wall hung big framed photographs of the King, Churchill, the Governor of Nyasaland and himself! He then led us to his courthouse and we sat on chairs, made from local banana trees, on the wide *khonde*, in the shade, surrounded by the entire village population, who squatted sociably at a respectful distance, watching every move. We shared our thermos of tea with him, drinking from glass cups he ordered to be brought from the house. (I held the cup in my left hand, in a hopeful gesture towards hygiene!) It was really quite an occasion. He walked with us to the car and asked us to come again. I asked Willis to ask him if I might bring my camera, which brought a gleam of pleasure to his sombre eyes.

The rains have almost stopped and the weather should get cooler. At present it is the hottest since we came – fierce. All the blossom is coming out and Zomba is looking very beautiful. We have discovered we have a flame tree and a peach tree in our garden!

I am so tired I can hardly hold my pen but I must tell you briefly about today. Ron's latest task is to explain to the villagers a scheme to set up a grinding mill in the district, to be run on co-operative lines by the Africans themselves, who will use the profits to pay back the Government loan. It is quite a sophisticated idea to put across and has to be presented in simple, repetitive terms. At breakfast this morning Ron had the brainwave that I should talk to the women and he would talk to the men. The women do all the work of pounding the maize, using great heavy wooden pestles which they lift high and let fall on the grain – back breaking work. It makes me ache to watch them. So we took Willis and a second interpreter. We drove down the escarpment for a few miles towards Liwonde, left the car in the shade and set out across the plain in scorching heat, following paths among tall maize gardens. Between eight and one o'clock we walked five miles and stopped at four villages. As we approached each village we could tell by the smell the standard of cleanliness we would find. It depends on how good the village headman is. They were all small, typical villages, the huts built round orange and lemon trees, the surrounding earth beaten down hard and bare, where a few scraggy hens peered and poked. Half-starved pye dogs lay about, scratching and snapping at the clouds of flies, their coats mangy and spotted with clusters of bloated ticks. Sometimes they came tearing out of the village to meet us, barking and lunging at us, but always falling back. It makes the hairs on my arms and legs crawl with horror. At each village Ron explained to the headman what we wanted arranged. All the villagers were summoned – the children came too – and Willis and I sat under a tree with the women, Ron nearby with the men. We had discussed what we would say and as a first round, as it were, it seemed to go down well. The women certainly listened intently, laughing gently and uttering their 'ehs' and 'ahs' when I said, through the eloquent Willis, in his element, that I had seen the village women pounding maize and thought the new mill was a good idea, as it would save them this very heavy work, and they should urge their husbands to support the scheme.

At the furthest village we had a rest and ate some mangoes under a baobab tree, then set off back to the car. But I have recently done very little walking and my thigh muscles began to protest and I had to make a terrific effort to keep going. We still had about a mile to go when there was one of those sudden cloudbursts and we were absolutely drenched to the skin, but oh, the heavenly cool! It was great fun but the Africans hate rain and our two companions went into the sulks. When we got home Aflike fussed about, making lemon tea and pouring a hot bath. We plan to do the same tomorrow – if I can walk!

26th April:

The day after I wrote to you we had another day's driving, (a very long drive), walking and talking, covering a little more ground and visiting five villages. My legs were agonisingly stiff at first but gradually improved. At the fifth village, no child under nine had ever seen a white man or woman, so there was high excitement, lots of laughter and, from the babies, yells of fright and floods of tears. Some little boys trotted right back the six miles to the road with us, talking their heads off very quietly and daring each other to touch us! They had never seen a car and stood staring at it in disbelief. Ron opened a door for them to get inside but they would have none of it. Then he reached in and touched the horn, which has a very French sound! They screamed and took to their heels but were drawn irresistibly back. This performance was repeated several times. I think they thought it was alive! Next he took a penny out of his pocket and held it up, indicating that whoever dared to touch the horn got the penny. One of them, obviously the leader, stood quivering, torn between fear and fortune, finally forced himself to dart forward and hit the horn with his fist, grabbed the penny and was off like the wind, not even looking back once! The others tore after him, almost hysterical with laughter. I must start keeping a jar of boiled sweets in the car.

Next day we went to Balaka, where Ron had to inspect a road and organise transport to carry away the last of the maize stored there. We were to stay the night with the Hemmings, the young South African couple we know, but found they had moved to their new house thirty miles to the north, at a small station called Nsipe, just over the border, in the Central Province. They left a note begging us to go on and join them, so we did, stopping on the way while Ron visited an Indian who had a garage full of lorries for hire. He insisted on us taking our picnic basket into his house and lunching there. So we sat in a low, cool room with Indian rugs and a lot of brass bric-à-brac and ate our sandwiches while a Muslim service went on (it was Friday) in a 'mosque' across his courtyard, a little crude building of mud and thatch. We watched the people squat outside to remove their shoes before going in. Then on to Nsipe, where we found the Hemmings installed in a temporary house while their lovely new one awaits completion. They have an open outlook straight across to the bare mountains of the Central Province. We found ourselves hoping we would one day be posted to this Province. Ron was instinctively right in wanting to be posted there. It looks really African – wild and bare and spectacular, the mountains more like Scotland's because, unlike those in the South, they are not thickly afforested. It was bitterly cold at night and in the early morning, so that we could sleep without mosquito nets – lovely. We heard hyenas and jackals in the night, quite close, two distinguishable sounds, weird and a little scarey. But it was bliss to actually *snuggle down* under blankets.

Driving back next morning we found the cold season really upon us. At Liwonde the ferry heaved uncomfortably on noisy, ruffled water and a strong wind flayed the undergrowth and ripped to shreds the thin leaves of the banana trees. The Africans' dark faces turn livid and blotched, and they shiver and wrap themselves mournfully in a strange assortment of garments – cheap grey blankets, old KAR khaki jackets and discarded European coats of stylish vintage. When we got home Aflike had piled up logs in the big fireplace. The forgotten comfort of a fire made me hopelessly homesick!

We found a wire waiting for us, from Mathias Kantiki, our London Nyasalander friend. He is now an inspector of schools. It had come the day before, saying he was coming down from Dedza (Central Province) and would arrive on Saturday at Balaka at 1.30 p.m. and would have no transport. Well, this was Saturday and we had just come from there, over that bad road. We hoped he might get a lift, but by five o'clock he had not turned up, so we had to get into the car and go back. We crossed the ferry in a fiery sunset and it was pitch dark by the time we got to Balaka. Mathias was sitting in a little shack of a canteen by the bus stop and came rushing out into the car headlights. He looked exhausted and ill, quite unlike his dapper London self, his skin a blueish grey from malaria which he got the moment he arrived back a few weeks ago. He was very happy to see us and talked and talked on the drive back. We had a late dinner and crawled to bed, Mathias on a camp bed in the sittingroom. Aflike shook with excitement throughout the evening. A black man in a white household! All Sunday we sat out in the front garden, talking and resting – it was too cold in the house – while the village buzzed with the news, and people strolled near the house, trying to get a glimpse of us. Aflike guarded our privacy jealously. Next morning, very early, Mathias caught the bus for his long journey back to Dedza. Throughout his visit, he and Ron talked shop *non-stop*. I felt invisible!

3rd May:

Ron has been on *ulendo* for five days with the DC and I have been staying with Dorothy in Zomba. She was out all day working at the African hospital, but I managed to fill my time well enough. The garden is at its best and I spent at least an hour each morning gathering flowers and grasses and filling the house with great bowls and vases which the head boy produced from a store room. When the DC came back from *ulendo* and walked in, he stood transfixed and said, 'By Jove, there's been a woman in this house!' Ron likes him more and more as he works with him.

One morning early, on her way to the hospital, Dorothy dropped me off with her cook, Tobias, at the native market, which I had said I would like to see. What a fascinating place! Fruit and vegetables from local gardens and outlying villages are laid out for sale on dark green banana leaves in long colourful rows and tumbling heaps. Grapefruit, oranges, lemons, limes, strawberries, avocados, pineapples, tomatoes, bananas, carrots, egg plants and pimentos jostle each other in cornucopian profusion, smelling delicious in the fresh morning air, glowing and gleaming in the early, low-rayed sunlight. The whole scene looks like a vast Impressionist canvas of still life rather than the real thing. The cooks of the white households come here every morning to do the day's marketing. They look very clean and trim in their white or khaki shirts and shorts, or *kanzus*, longish tunics worn with a tight belt or cummerbund, and assume an air of superiority as they move with their baskets among the *hoi polloi*, gossiping about their employers among themselves, it is said, wickedly!

I walked slowly back to the DC's house, for the first time fully able to appreciate the wondrous beauty of Zomba in blossom time. The winding roads which climb from terrace to terrace are lined with tall jacaranda trees. In full bloom they have no leaves, just masses of blossom of an incomparable blue. The jacarandas on the first terrace spread out a sea of blossom level with the second terrace, and above that another vast canopy is spread, and so on all the way up for 4,000 feet. In the big gardens beyond the trees, there is the fine tracery of peach and apricot blossom, and the bolder, coarser African shrubs and creepers send a riot of colour blazing up against the dark-blue sky and cascading down over roofs and rocks: flame coloured flamboyantes, poinsettias with hot red petals and the brilliant foam of bouganvillaea and golden shower. Here and there, making a classical appearance amidst all this tropical extravagance, a slim, straight cypress stands dark and formal.

The men came back on Friday and Ron and I stayed overnight at the DC's house. We all went to the matinee at 4.30 of the film *Johnny Belinda*. We had seen it at Oxford but did not say so. At the interval the Club was full of children of all ages, back from school in England, South Africa and the Rhodesias, for the Easter 'hols'. There is something arrogant about colonial children which is not attractive. Perhaps it is simply a precocious sophistication lacking in their peers at home.

On Saturday morning there was a big official occasion. The King's African Rifles were being presented with new Colours and there was a great turn-out of spectators. I had not realised we would be officially involved, so had not brought a hat, or rather the only hat I have! So Dorothy lent me her gardening hat, a rather dashing Stetson-like brown felt. I was grateful for it as I was in the sun for well over an hour. The senior Government officers and their wives had seats in the Club overlooking the sports field, which is bordered by blue gums, bamboos and palms. The general public gathered in crowds right round the edge of the field. The Boma staff and their wives sat with all the chiefs of Zomba district on a row of chairs placed below the Club steps, so we had an excellent view. The Governor was there, handsome in uniform (though his face is plain), a great white plume in his tall helmet, medals and sword glittering. The African troops were most impressive, impeccably drilled. I felt an agonising pang of homesickness pierce my heart when the pipes and drums of the band played the 'Skye Boat Song', with a slightly alien tempo, a dying fall that was very moving. They also played, in slow marching time, 'Auld Lang Syne', as the old Colours were marched off the field. Every now and then the national anthem was played and everyone stood up, the officers in our group removing their hats, but, because of the sun, keeping their arms raised and their hats held just off their heads, in a kind of prolonged salute. For the first time, I felt *terribly* proud to be where I am! It was all very formal and colonial, but somehow fitting and natural. Everyone seemed specially friendly and relaxed in the Club afterwards, and we stayed for a drink and then, refusing several kind invitations to lunch, fled back to Kasupi. We are becoming real country cousins!

12th May:

The stars at night are beautiful beyond belief. The other evening for the first time we spotted the Plough – upside down!

We spent Saturday morning on business and shopping in Zomba, and found everyone in despair because there had been no flour in the shops for a fortnight. Every household makes its own bread, so this is tragic. We had just finished up our store, and we have been having biscuits with marmalade at breakfast, a most demoralising state of affairs!

Last week's *ulendo* was rather more interesting than usual. The headman told us there was an agricultural officer and his wife living not far from the camp, so in the evening, after a bath and change, we drove out to pay a courtesy call. We found the house in the middle of nowhere. Mrs Brown, the young wife, had not seen a white woman for over three months and almost fell into my arms with relief and pleasure. They have two small, pale children, so shy in the company of unaccustomed strangers they ran away, then hovered at the doorway, peeping at us. The house had no ceilings, simply a pointed roof with wooden beams stretching across and, while we sat talking in the lamplight, large domestic rats ran out along the beams and crouched there, cleaning their whiskers and baring their teeth soundlessly as they looked down on us with an air of sharing in this unusual social scene. I got the impression that the Browns hardly noticed them. I was glad to get back to our dinner under the stars!

It is windy in the cold season and, as the soil becomes more and more dry, sudden little gusts, like whirlwinds, produce what are known as 'dust devils' – spiralling columns of dusty red soil. We see miniature ones in our compound but out walking we see really big ones, rising eerily above the tall maize, whirling and twisting, then vanishing into thin air.

Later in the week we called at a Mission run by three Dutch Fathers, big cheerful men with shaggy hair and thick beards, whom we saw ricocheting hardily over their parish on motor bikes, their white robes fluttering round them and their beards flattened by the wind. They welcomed us so warmly and made a party of the occasion, plying us with red wine. To my dismay, one of them plumped down a bowl of sugar in front of me with the hearty remark, 'There! I know the ladies always like their wine very sweet!' I politely scattered in a few token grains, whereupon the hospitable Father seized the spoon from me and added a generous heap, exclaiming, 'No, no! Have more! Have more! There is plenty! There are no rations here!' Ugh! When I remarked on their gramophone, a lovely oldfashioned one with a horn amplifier shaped like a trumpet, he put on a record of a Dvořák piano quartet and we all sat listening spellbound. Of course it took me straight back to Dunalastair and Daddy's Flonzaley Quartet records, and I thought of listening on summer evenings and the six shimmering poplars in the garden, their leaves reflected on the drawingroom wall. When the music stopped there was a little silence while we all emerged from our private dream into reality again.

1st June:

Yesterday Ron went off on *ulendo* at 6.00 a.m. till Saturday. The weather is bitterly cold and it will be freezing in the tent, so he insisted I stay at home and keep warm. He is distributing war medals, a very boring job. He took Aflike and both interpreters with him, so I have only Hassani and Kidney for company, neither of whom speaks a word of English! A messenger comes up at sunset, with his wife and child, and they sleep in the office next door, so that I need not feel nervous. I was very touched to discover that it was *Willis* who suggested this arrangement!

There is great activity on the roads during the day. In the rains, people walked great distances at night to avoid the heat. Now, in the cold season, no travelling is done at night, because the lions come down from the hills and are a fearful menace, even on the main road, after dark. I have not yet heard one (and am not exactly longing to), but apparently they are very noisy at night in Zomba. The cold drives them down from the mountain. The Africans are terrified when they hear them. If they are man-eaters, they can easily tear down a native hut. A watchman sleeping on the *khonde* of an Indian store eight miles from here was seized the other night. Ron gets all the reports in his office. There is a Game Warden who lives in the district and he shoots the man-eaters.

We *still* have no date about our posting, so I have just gone ahead with my plans for the garden and have sent for 25*s.* worth of seeds from South Africa – lupins, phlox, sweet peas, carnations, begonias, foxgloves. I shall send you a plan of the garden once we have it planted. There are four smallish square beds and seven long narrow ones. I feel very ignorant about it all, but am game to try. I have some of our jasmine in a bowl beside me, and the heat from the log fire is bringing out the scent deliciously.

The cold weather has produced some unbelievable sunsets, turning the plain below completely golden and all the surrounding hills a deep rose. It is so alien I feel I am watching a coloured film on a screen!

On Saturday evening we went to a dance in Zomba, as the guests of Norman and Anne Hall. He is ex-army and is one of the ADCs in Zomba. They are kind, friendly people in their early forties. We dined at Kasupi by candlelight in evening dress, Aflike greatly approving, then Ron wrapped me in a sheet (I was wearing my wedding dress) and *carried* me to the car and packed me in like a parcel. It was exciting to emerge from the darkness into the lights of the Club, and hear the clink of ice in glasses, laughter and voices, and the band. We had a great evening and went back to the Halls for a very late nightcap. They love to talk! They came back with us for lunch at Kasupi and were, I think, rather shattered by the somewhat rustic arrangements. (*All* women loathe an outside loo.) This is their first tour and they have spent it in Zomba, where Anne has a job as a typist in one of the Departments. We found a wire from the Hemmings awaiting us, saying he had been transferred to the Northern Province, so they have had to leave Nsipe without ever living in their nice new house. I do not know when we shall see them again. I can see it is not going to be easy to make lasting friendships out here. [But I did.]

7th June:

Last week I wrote to you from my awful isolation! Nothing untoward happened while Ron was away, except that one night I was awakened by a loud thudding noise accompanied by thin shrieks. I was petrified for a moment and then not much relieved to realise that the noise came from the ceiling and there was obviously quite a large family of rats under the roof, scampering about, fighting and squealing. The noise went on for ages and I lay trying not to think of the sags and cracks in the rotting ceiling above my bed! It is high time this house was repaired – it will soon be beyond it.

Tomorrow, the King's Birthday holiday is going to be rather a bore. We are lunching at the DC's with a lot of other Government people, and helping to entertain about twenty chiefs and their headmen.

Ron came back on Saturday and how glad I was to see him – and Aflike! I am going with him on *ulendo* next week from Monday to Friday. There is a vacant house belonging to the Agricultural Department, so we shall stay there – it has a fireplace. It is about thirty miles from here, high up and very exposed, we are told.

16th June:

It is Friday afternoon and we have just come back from *ulendo*. The garden seeds arrived just before we went, and we spent a hectic day planting them, some in beds, most in boxes, which the garden boys look after, watering them every morning and evening.

Last Saturday we went to the King's Birthday celebrations. We were at the Watsons for cocktails and a stand-up curry lunch. It was all quite chaotic. There were twenty chiefs and their minions, all drinking at top speed. Dorothy told me later that my friend Kawinga drank half a bottle of whisky, neat, and walked perfectly steadily to the lorry waiting to take him home. They drank and had lunch sitting at tables at one end of the big *khonde*. The white guests drank their cocktails standing at the other end, and went into lunch after the Africans had departed, only to find that there was barely enough food left to go round! Some of us mingled for a while with the Africans, but it is not easy, and I think they just wanted to be left in peace to enjoy themselves. After lunch we went down to the sports field and watched the Africans running, bicycling and jumping – less impressive than I expected and the lack of a spirit of sportsmanship amusingly evident – sulks, tantrums and scuffles among the losers! There was a tug-of-war between twelve white and twelve African women, in which Anne Hall and I joined. To everyone's astonishment, the Africans, every single one, were on their knees within a minute. All the white women looked positively stunned with surprise!

Our *ulendo* was up into the wilds all right. We camped in a large, cold house which was overrun by hordes of weevils, seldom visible by day, but at night they mysteriously materialised, getting into the beds, and in the morning shoes and clothes were swarming with them, and all our boxes. The ceilings were made of bamboo matting, which housed hundreds of tiny insects called borers, and we could hear the faint pick-pick of their destructive activity while a constant fine shower of shavings fell down on hair, food, everything. There was a full moon and every night we lay scratching at the weevils and looking out of the uncurtained windows at the stars and white moonlight, which made the walls glimmer as if there were snow outside.

On our last evening we were returning to the house at dusk in the very last of the light, when it becomes difficult to focus on objects, and were just about to turn off on the short path to the house when a little way ahead of us a great shape lumbered out of the trees, crossed the road and vanished into the bush on the other side. It was a kind of iguana, a huge lizard creature which looked grotesque and prehistoric. It happened so quickly I feel now it only lumbered across my imagination, but Ron saw it too!

We learned on Saturday that we move to Zomba next weekend. Ron has some cases of tax defaulters to hear at Kasupi and means to visit it twice a week, so I shall be able to keep an eye on the garden. You see, I cannot let go of my beloved Kasupi.

Chapter 12

Extracts from my letters describe our first three months in Zomba.

23rd June:

On Saturday morning we went into Zomba, where at the Boma we heard definitely that we are to move into our house on Monday. After a morning of shopping and rushing about in the car on official errands, we presented ourselves at the Binghams at lunchtime. They are delightful people, in their fifties, very sophisticated and great fun. We have met them in the Club several times and Humphrey Bingham lunched with us once at Kasupi. He is Commissioner for Co-operative development and so Ron came into contact with him in connection with his organising and setting up of the maize mill in Kasupi district. Eve, his wife, was a member of the BBC's Children's Hour team as a young woman, and has written books for children and several books of African folk tales. We were given a great welcome and have not enjoyed any weekend since we came as much as this one. They have a charming bungalow, with a lot of their own beautiful furniture and precious *objets d'art*, books, fine prints, and artistic touches which most houses here tend to lack. (With the prospect of frequent postings, I can understand why.) They have been in Nyasaland for over twenty years. They have no family. We had a bathroom off our bedroom, bedside table lamps, rugs and all the civilised things one forgets exist.

After a long lunch we all retired for a rest, and after tea they drove us out to visit old friends of theirs who live on a beautiful estate, being retired from thirty years of tea planting in Nyasaland. I could hardly believe that such an enchanting place could be found, right in the middle of nowhere. The view was glorious, the garden huge and beautifully landscaped, and the house was like a perfect English country house. It had the same smell as West Coker – a mixture of lavender, wood fires and furniture polish. They had hundreds of old books, all in leatherbound sets, many of which I remembered from Grandfather's library, including *Mr Punch's History of the Great War* which I cannot have seen since I was about five! I used to sit on the rug in front of the fire by Grandfather's chair and turn the pages carefully. I loved the illustrations but of course the jokes were too grown up for me. Going back in the car I was speechless with homesickness. We had baths, changed into evening dress and joined in a dinner party for eight. The food was delicious, with several wines, and brandy afterwards. Then we all went down to the cinema to see *The Unfaithful*, an unpleasant film but well acted. We talked till late with masses of people in the Club and Eve introduced us to a quite different set from the one we know so far – KAR and heads of departments, not Administration, all older than we but very friendly, lively people. Dorothy has warned me that Zomba is a very cliquey place and I am beginning to see what she means!

During the somewhat short night I woke up suddenly and there was Ron's face pressed against my mosquito net and his voice whispering pathetically, 'Darling, can I come in? I am being eaten alive by ants.' I got up to investigate – marvellous just to switch on a light – and his bed was a black, moving mass of them! I had to dust him down a bit! When we reported this, somewhat diffidently, to Eve later, she said calmly, 'Ah yes, that bedroom has always had an ant problem!' We found a real English breakfast on the diningroom sideboard – grapefruit, cornflakes, kedgeree and scrambled eggs. We spent a lovely leisurely morning and afternoon at the Club, watching the Zomba cricket team play Mlanje. Humphrey is captain of the Zomba team and stayed at the Club for lunch, while Eve bore us off with a KAR officer and his wife to a splendid buffet lunch party in their tent – yes, I said tent! They have a dear little cottage which has been condemned – riddled with white ants – and while it is being repaired they have moved into two tents in their wonderful garden. There are a lot of keen gardeners in Zomba, always eager to talk gardeners' shop. We went back to see the end of the cricket, then up to the house to bath and change and back to the Club for the monthly Sunday recital of music on the radiogram. What a treat. We heard a Bach violin concerto, three lovely songs by Handel and Brahms's 4th symphony. I felt quite drunk with it all. We dined early with the Binghams and reluctantly hastened back to Kasupi to get to bed early in preparation for tomorrow.

Having met some of Eve's set, my first impressions of Zomba and colonials have expanded and perhaps been rounded off. The whole ambience is what I thought it would be like, at its best, only better, and I feel I can live with this atmosphere and make a good life within it.

Monday was a bit of a nightmare as Ron was away till teatime and I had all the packing to do. To complicate things, this month is Ramadan and I was worried about Aflike slaving away beside me, his empty stomach rumbling wildly all day. He sensed that I was bothered and said to me firmly, 'Madam must not be troubled. Fasting makes Aflike very strong.' So on we went! By yesterday morning at 8 o'clock, unbelievably, we were ready to go, and set off at about 15 m.p.h., as all the china was in boxes on the back seat. I held the glass in a case on my lap with my Laura Knight ballet picture beside me. A lorry with the boys and all our stuff followed us. On arrival, Ron left me, as he had to go off for the whole day again, and I unpacked. By the time he came back, having had no lunch, at three o'clock, everything but our clothes was in order, including curtains and pictures. I had even had time to do the flowers, and had arranged masses of roses and a lovely pink blossom rather like a giant hawthorn. We got our clothes unpacked by sunset and then had a bath in our gorgeous big bath. The DC had kindly offered us dinner, so we went thankfully there, about five minutes' run in the car.

The housing shortage is desperate, we are told, and we are temporarily occupying the Director of Agriculture's house – he is on leave – on the top level of the mountain road and quite out of keeping with our rank and salary, which will give Zomba something to hum about. (Housing is a very sensitive subject, I gather.) It has an enormous garden, with hundreds of roses in bloom, but all very neglected. The view is very like that from the DC's house, only wider. The house, after Kasupi, is a small palace and we have closed some of the rooms. We have electric light and hot water and a real lavatory which flushes – in fact we have two! There are a huge drawingroom and a delightful diningroom, both fully furnished, of course. Off our bedroom is a black and white tiled bathroom with a white dressingtable, and beyond that, Ron's dressingroom, which he keeps forgetting to use. Off the other side of the bathroom are a big linen cupboard and the loo. We also have a spare bedroom with its own dressingroom and bathroom, again all fully furnished. The kitchen and boys' quarters are legion and have electric light. Aflike is gratified but indicates subtly that things are merely as they should be!

27th June:

I am sitting in the sun in the garden, as brown as a berry, and thinking how Jess [my eldest sister] and Daddy would go wild over the birds, you over the flowers. There are exquisite little sun birds flitting about and hanging poised with their beaks in the blossom, and in the tree near me a lourie is awkwardly moving about the branches like a clumsy parrot. There are lots of birds in the morning; strange and exotic it is to hear them, not so much songs as noises; whoops, clucks, screeches, pops, bangs and an occasional piercing whistle. The only familiar sounds are from the wood pigeons, and even their notes are a little alien.

On Friday Ron rushed back from the office at 3.30 for an early tea, and then drove with me down to the Club. He had cricket practice till nearly five o'clock and I sat with Eve, who told me about a paper she is to read in Blantyre for the Nyasaland Women's Society. It is entitled 'The African idea of justice as seen in the folklore'. I would love to hear her, but *ulendo* plans make it unlikely I can accept her invitation to go as her guest – a great pity. On Saturday afternoon I played my first game of tennis from 2.30 - 4.45. I played with the Halls and a young man in need of a partner. Ron was in a doubles with the DC. We had a late tea at the Club and then a rushed bath as the Halls were coming to dinner and bridge. We spent the whole of Sunday at the Club watching Zomba play Blantyre at cricket. There was also a Zomba versus Blantyre tennis tournament being played, in blazing heat, all the players wearing hats, which looked odd.

Norman went off on *ulendo* yesterday, so Ron had a gruelling day on his own and came back looking exactly like a man who had been 'at the office' all day! I can always tell when it is noon and 3.30, because down in Zomba at the Boma, the Secretariat and other offices the cars begin to honk their horns and then comes the noise of engines climbing and gears being changed. At various glimpses I have of the red, winding road I catch a glint from a car roof crawling up the steep slopes of the mountain. Ron always honks his horn at the last hairpin bend, which involves a slight hiatus while he double declutches in order to manoeuvre it. Aflike leaps into life from nowhere, cook starts banging about in the kitchen and I dash out to meet the car.

5th July:

Our *ulendo* last week turned out to be pleasanter than I expected. We camped at Balaka, where the Hemmings used to be. One of their great friends, David Pike, a charming South African in Agriculture whom we had met at their house, called for tea the day we arrived and asked us to drive to his house, five miles away, for dinner that evening. We had a lovely dinner, played with his pet bush baby, a dear little creature which clung to him and gazed at us with its enormous dark eyes ringed with white, which makes it look terrified all the time, and listened to the nine o'clock news on his radio, a great treat! We got up at 4.30 on Saturday morning and drove back to Zomba, straight up to the house so that I could bath and change into decent clothes. I did some shopping, collected our mail at the Boma and stayed till noon helping Norman, who hates paper work!

In the evening we went to the cinema and saw a dreadful, sugary film, *Maytime in Mayfair*, with Anna Neagle and Michael Wilding! After *ulendo*, *any* film seems worth seeing. We had a quiet but busy Sunday, preparing for a marathon walking *ulendo* Ron and the DC are undertaking this week. It will take them to the Portugese border of Mozambique. After breakfast we drove into Zomba, or rather just beyond Zomba, to call on a Mr Kayes, who has a transport business and hires lorries to the Boma. He and his wife have been in Nyasaland for thirty years. He was one of the old pioneers and has done everything – tea, tobacco, dairy farming, and now maize milling and transport. He and his nice South African wife insisted we spend an hour with them over coffee. They have a lovely big bungalow with a swimming pool in the garden, down on the plain below Zomba. Their three children are all at school in Rhodesia. She took an honours degree in English literature and language at Cape Town and then did two years research in Middle English at Oxford, so for once *I* had somebody with whom to talk shop! They are very easy going, interesting people. When Dr Aitkens was out here studying Chinyanja he stayed with them. They have a beautiful big radiogram and a grand piano in the drawingroom which she plays. It is so exciting and unexpected to come upon these little havens of civilisation in the bush.

On Monday Ron and the DC set out for the Portugese border to deal with a border dispute. They had forty carriers! The lorry set off with their tents, luggage, messengers and boys, after breakfast, and after lunch Norman Hall, in his Daimler (yes, he is mad enough to bring a Daimler to Africa – he has a certain flamboyance) drove them about thirty-five miles to the point where the road stops and they start walking. Dorothy (who is now very pregnant) had said she would like to go for the drive, so I turned up too, but she wisely decided not to. What a road! We went over 'drifts', bridges thrown across defunct water-ways, built of several tree trunks laid out together and filled in with earth which the sun had dried and which crumbled away into dust when the car bumped over the trunks. We could feel the structure swaying and giving way as we drove over. There were also two deep drifts without a bridge which had to be ma-noeuvred – old, dried-up river beds with steeply sloping banks, at which Norman set the great car like a horse! He is a superb driver. While this was going on I sensed that we were all silently thinking of the return journey Norman and I were to make. The DC obviously thought we would be stranded for the night because he suggested we should take a messenger back with us in the car! Norman treated it all as a huge joke. However, on the journey back, he insisted that I get out and walk over all the drifts – not an easy exercise – in case the weight of the car collapsed them. He made it seem a light-hearted adventure and we always enjoy each other's company. All the same, when I got out of the car my knees were shaking so much I could hardly climb the *khonde* steps!

Since then I have been with Dorothy, who I think is glad of my company, as she misses her hospital work and finds the days long. She loves telling me about personalities in Nyasaland, so I give her a lead and away she goes. All the DCs give hospitality to Government people and visiting VIPs who are passing through their station, so Dorothy has met and entertained a great many people.

I keep thinking about Ron, walking eighteen miles a day – they start at six and stop at noon, to avoid the worst of the heat.

12th July:

Last week when your letter came I was staying with Dorothy and wrote to you from her house and here I am again!

We have discovered that Kidney is almost a half-wit, quite incapable of learning anything, so Aflike is looking for another boy, but it may take some time – so many of them seem to drink, steal or not work properly, in his opinion. I am thankful to have him. He is completely honest and trustworthy, which, to hear the women talk, are rare qualities.

We became country members of the Club (I automatically and free of charge, when Ron paid his subscription) about a month before we moved to Zomba, which is rather lucky, as the fee is halved for country members and yet here we are in Zomba. We only use it for films, dances and sport, and an occasional visit to read the latest magazines. I know that sounds a lot, but some people haunt the place day and night.

You ask about books. I read all I can beg and borrow, but at present have reached the point when I have read all the books which interest me in any of the bookcases I have access to in Zomba. People are very generous in lending books. I have a huge reading list which I add to each week from the *Observer* and *Spectator* reviews – very frustrating.

Ron and John came back on Saturday morning, both looking very lean and fit. We had had a quiet week and were delighted to see them back. They brought two large geese, two ducks, six chickens and masses of eggs, all presented to them. They walked seventy miles in five days, and Ron took it in his stride. He said it was a wonderful sight to see the forty porters balancing the luggage on their heads, winding through the bush paths, all singing cheerfully in improvised harmony. That is a thing the Africans do – burst into song when working. At the garage, often, when a man is pumping petrol, he suddenly starts singing in time to his movements and other Africans working nearby join in.

We had dinner on Saturday evening with the Watsons, eating one of the geese and hearing all about the *ulendo*. On Sunday the Halls came to us, to help eat the other goose! Yesterday Ron went off on another walking *ulendo* so that counted me out. (I am trying not to grumble about these wretched *ulendos*!) John has also gone, so Dorothy is glad to have me – her baby is due next week, when I believe Ron will be in the office and we shall have a brief few days of normal life together. Fourteen days' *ulendo* a month means Ron is away three weeks out of four, except at weekends – dreadful. Everyone is groaning and grumbling about it. One of the doctors at the hospital who dined with Dorothy and me last week told us he thought it will cause marital problems! It is the present Governor who has brought in the rule, which of course makes him unpopular with the Administration.

19th July:

Ron returned on Saturday leaner and browner than ever. In the evening we went on our own to a dance at the Club but Humphrey and Eve pounced on us at once and insisted we join their party, who were all Army. So I danced with the Commanding Officer of the KAR, with the major who lives in a tent and with a wonderful dancer, a young captain called Lorne Campbell, who had recently sailed round Mull and all along that coast (and been turned away from a jetty on Mull where he was seeking shelter from a sudden squall when it was discovered he was a Campbell) just before he came to Nyasaland! The Bingham party left around midnight but we danced on till 2 o'clock. We were down on the tennis court by 9.45 next morning and played all day with the Halls. In the evening we went to the monthly gramophone recital – lovely, all Bach.

Ramadan finished on Monday morning, thank goodness, and I gave Aflike the day off. All the Muslims in Zomba went mad! There were services and processions all day, which much chanting and laughter, flowers everywhere. I love to hear the Muezzin calling them to prayer – it always makes me feel I am in India. We have tennis planned for this week, and the film is a good one, *Kind Hearts and Coronets*. We are dining with the Halls and going with them. How I love Ron's week in the office.

25th July:

We are at Kasupi! We drove out yesterday after lunch and return to Zomba tomorrow. Ron discovered he still had two nights of *ulendo* to do. Apart from a little office work, he seems to me to have spent most of the time lying under the car! The whole thing is becoming a farce. Poor Norman has been out all week for a month and will continue that way for some time, because he had about eighty nights to make up, as his Daimler was out of order and he never left Zomba for six weeks.

You ask if Ron enjoys his work and if the life in Nyasaland suits him. The answer to both is 100% YES. He is perfectly happy and is living exactly as he would choose to live and doing the work he loves to do. I think this is true of most of the men out here. It is the wives who have to *create* a life for themselves. Most of Ron's work would bore me stiff, though of course I take a great interest in everything and help him when I can, and I love the beauty of the country and getting out into the bush and learning more about the African people. But I do have the occasional moment of crisis when I feel I am just wasting my substance.

On Saturday we drove out to Domasi, which lies between Zomba and Kasupi, to attend an agricultural show. It was not very interesting, and as it was terribly hot, the smell of hundreds of Africans and African cattle was really overpowering. But there were some lovely woven baskets and wood carvings, including a splendid chess set made of ivory and ebony. Eric Barnes, the Provincial Commissioner, opened the show. We had lunch in a marquee in the DC's garden (I mean the DC Domasi, who is a very pleasant Scot called Thomson. I discovered he is a great Kipling man, so we could talk.) Ron, the PC's charming wife Leslie and I had great fun together, while the PC sat on the opposite bench gazing across the table with envious eyes, absentmindedly eating his salad and not really listening to his neighbours! After lunch we slipped into the car park and escaped. It was *so* hot and the show went on till 5 o'clock. The Governor (known as HE) was to arrive at three, and we had to drive back at high speed in case we met him on his way out. There is an awful tendency here for people to talk in initials. E.g. 'Did you hear what the CO of the KAR said to HE at GH last night?' (GH = Government House.)

On Sunday we played tennis all day, as it was cloudy and quite cool. Yesterday morning a Mr Laycock arrived. We had agreed to put him up for a week, as he has come from another district and there is not a house for him till next weekend. He turned up with his own boy and masses of supplies, so we left him to it. (I had to borrow blankets from the hospital!) I walked up to Dorothy's for elevenses and found her most depressed as the doctor has just told her the baby will be late. Poor John had organised his *ulendo* so that he would not be away when the baby was expected, so of course he will be at home when it should arrive and away when it does! He is now trying to reorganise the whole thing. Organising a *ulendo* is far more complicated than people think.

When we came out here yesterday afternoon our first move was to dash out to the seed boxes (big petrol tins cut in half longways) and examine the little seedlings. No sign of lupin or phlox, but we have masses of candytuft, carnations and one precious begonia. Aflike's kitchen garden is magnificent – about twenty huge cauliflowers and lots of lettuce, tomatoes, carrots and beans. I am going to bring some cuttings from the Zomba garden and start a rose bed. The house has not been touched yet. Even if repairs started now it would not be ready before the rains. All they have done is clear the ground for the foundations of a new office at the foot of the drive. There was bright moonlight last night and Kasupi looked a dream. We are so happy to be here, however briefly.

2nd August:

We have been out at Kasupi again this week, a marvellous way of doing *ulendo*. I managed to get a lot of work done in the garden, planting out seedlings, a delicate job I like to do myself. We drove across the plain over very rough roads to Chagwa, where at last Ron saw the results of his hard work in the form of a maize mill, furiously grinding maize, setting up a fine white cloud of flour and a smell of oil, surrounded by a crowd of utterly spellbound – and petrified – villagers! Humphrey and the DC were also present, but it was really Ron's day. As the DC so kindly said, Ron's name will be remembered in Kasupi district for a long time.

Ron goes off on *ulendo* again with John, today, after lunch. They will take the rest of the day to cross Lake Chirwa in very primitive log canoes, with all their camping equipment. So I shall be up at Dorothy's till Saturday. She is very weary of waiting and terribly heavy.

There was a *chiperoni* at the weekend, which put a stop to tennis and lowered the temperature considerably. We had a roaring log fire. Chiperoni is a mountain in Mozambique, about eighty miles away. (On a clear day you can see it from Zomba mountain.) At this season, when the wind sometimes blows from that direction, it brings rain and a drifting cold mist, which usually lasts three days. It is our first experience of a *chiperoni* and I rather like it, as it reminds me of the West! I feel relaxed and at ease. Most people hate it.

As people become aware of us in Zomba, we are being asked out more and more, and on Sunday evening we went to a very pleasant Sundowner (drinks before dinner). We met a very nice couple from the Department of Agriculture, and I found a note from her this morning asking us to pre-lunch drinks next Sunday . . . and so it goes on. On 8th August we are going to our first Sundowner at Government House, along with about a hundred other guests. At the entrance to the driveway up to GH there is a small, manned sentry box on one side and a similar box opposite which contains on a shelf an enormous visitors' book. This is signed by all Government people on arrival in Zomba. It is also signed at New Year and before going on leave, when one puts the letters ppc after one's name. This stands for 'pour prendre congé' meaning 'permission to depart'. From this book the Aide-de-Camp (also confusingly called the ADC) makes up a list of guests for the cocktail parties which are held at regular intervals. I must say there is always something new to experience – at least it keeps me on my toes.

8th August:

I am writing one day early, as we are off on *ulendo* again tomorrow and will be many miles from a post office.

Great excitement! Aflike has just come back from the market. He met Tobias, the Watsons' cook, who told him Dorothy had a son yesterday! He came dashing in to tell me, so excited he poured out a flood of Chinyanja and when I looked blank, stemmed the flood, thought hard and burst out with 'Bwana DC has young'. They wanted a son so much. Dorothy said it would be just her fate to have a baby on August Bank holiday and she was right! The baby was twelve days late.

When I last wrote we had just come back from Kasupi and Ron was going off with the DC. Dorothy and I had a quiet but pleasant time. She was obviously finding the waiting rather a strain, but was quite lively and entertaining. She swears like a trooper when under stress! We expected the men back on Saturday morning. When we woke up, a *chiperoni* had set in and Lake Chirwa was hidden in a thick mist and the sky above it was a nasty stormy yellow. I walked down to the Boma to collect our mail and Norman asked me if I would like to go to Johannesburg with him and Anne for ten days. His Daimler has been giving trouble and the nearest agents, in J'burg, have got the necessary spare parts at last and according to the firm's guarantee, will do the job free of charge. As Ron will be on *ulendo* most of the time, it would have been a great break for me – an interesting journey, good company and a little bit of civilisation, such as getting my hair cut. Ron and the DC were expected back before lunch, so I thought I would just have time to get Ron's approval, some money and pack a bag. However, by 4 o'clock we were still waiting, and when the Halls called for me, I had to opt out – shame. Norman advised Dorothy to ring the Boma and ask them to arrange for a lorry to go out to the village where Ron had left his car, which she did. She is normally very level-headed but I could see she was getting panicky – as was I, inwardly. It got dark early, shortly after five, and the wind was rising. I made her sit down and we had an early drink. They finally arrived at nearly 6 o'clock, not foot sore but posterior sore! It had taken them seven hours to cross that wretched lake. Ron looks marvellously well and talked deliriously of the wonderful bird life he had seen. The DC looked as if he had had enough. They saw hundreds of pelicans and dozens of varieties of duck, two water bucks and eight hippos! (As Dorothy said later, 'Next day John had sunstroke and I had a son.')

Tomorrow we go off for *nine* days, returning on the 17th, so my next letter will be late. We drive about seventy miles north-east of Zomba and will have some walking to do. John should have been going, but for Dorothy's sake has decided against it. You say you are glad that when Ron is away I am in Zomba, not Kasupi, but it is actually the other way round! At Kasupi I did not mind being alone, though I was lonely, because at night – and that is what counts – I was not nervous, as the only things I might see or hear would be animals, *outside*. I had nothing to fear from the bush Africans. Here, in Zomba, there is a fearful spate of burglaries and the thought of finding a burglar in the house, a black one at that, is unnerving, to say the least. This big empty house is eerie at night and noisy – doors blow open and slam, the roof creaks, and things flop about on it; I think owls and monkeys. The town African is very different from his bush brother. Every house on our terrace has been burgled except the DC's and ours. Maybe it is because we are Boma people. Several of the chiefs have said, 'Next time you are in England and see the king, tell him . . . etc.' They think he is our personal friend!

16th August:

I am writing this on *ulendo* and will post it as soon as we get back. This is a very isolated spot and none of the villagers, children or grown ups, have ever seen a white woman, so I get stared at till I could scream. Aflike shoos away the children but they creep back and peep through the bamboo stockade. I can hear them now, whispering and giggling, as I sit at the table on the tent *khonde*. The women saunter past the entrance and linger to have a look – my face feels stiff with smiling. Their huts are all round us and on the first evening we could hear the buzz of excitement our presence was causing. Ron is still working on the settlement of the border dispute between Nyasaland and Mozambique.

On our first morning we visited the local chief, a very surly, suspicious man, and later Ron cycled round the area, planning what to undertake each day. I stayed in camp and had a slight contretemps with the women and children who, the moment Ron vanished, crowded into the compound and sat down all round the tent, prepared to stay and stare all morning. I let them have a good look for about five minutes and then called Aflike, who sent them flying, all laughing and screaming happily. At teatime a Father Delahaye, from the Dutch Mission twelve miles away, came to call: a huge man with a black beard and a tremendous voice, who shouted good-naturedly in fluent Chinyanja at the villagers.

On Friday we had a great day. We left at 8.00 a.m. and got back at 4.00 p.m. It was a blazing hot day with a slight breeze. We walked four miles to the 'lake' and found it covered in tall reeds, with no sign of water. Our guide was a wonderful looking boy, wearing a brilliant red loin cloth, only longer. He plunged into the reeds, which had terribly sharp edges, and Ron, Willis, our two messengers and I followed. I had bare legs, so I was in trouble. Every now and then we came to a thigh-deep black pool thronging with leeches, and Ron and I were carried over by the messengers. Ron went pick-a-back, and very funny he looked, but I insisted on sitting on their clasped wrists. I fail to see why the messengers are any less likely to get bilharzia than we are, but I did not argue. At last, when I was just beginning to flag, we came to a narrow stretch of water where two canoes – the usual hollowed-out tree trunks – were moored, and we set off on a wonderful little journey. We were poled slowly through a winding channel with high reeds on either side, which gradually widened as we glided over enormous water-lilies, lavender, blue and pink, till we came to the lake itself. There were birds everywhere: dainty white egrets fishing in the reeds so close we could almost touch them; large black eagles soaring above us; and a jacana, a long-legged wader with big webbed feet, which marched about from water-lily to water-lily as if it were on dry land. All round the horizon there were huge blue mountains, and the reed beds were brilliant green or gold – exactly like a gigantic version of Rannoch Moor, in scenery and colouring.

The crossing took half an hour and then we had a two mile walk to a village. My shoes had got soaked in the leaky canoe and my feet began to blister. In the village we found the boundary pillar Ron was looking for and he and the headman had a long talk and Ron made a lot of notes. Then we sat down under a tree, ate our picnic lunch and watched the birds. Afterwards we walked back to the canoes and crossed that lovely stretch of water again. By the time we had struggled back through the reeds to the road I was finished, not from exhaustion but from the pain of my lacerated legs and raw feet. (I am not complaining or making a fuss. I realised from the very first *ulendo* that I do not have suitable clothes for *ulendo*. I should be clothed like a man, in bush jacket, long trousers, thick socks and ankle boots, and where am I going to get these and who is going to pay for them?) Ron sent one of the messengers to find or borrow a bicycle and took me back to camp sitting on the handle-bars! Aflike took one look at my face and rushed off to heat up bath water. From then till now I have sat in the sunshine, reading, writing and playing Patience, and it is amazing how quickly all my cuts and blisters are healing. I can walk in socks and sandals.

On Saturday Ron went through *his* ordeal! He and Willis set off at 7.00 a.m. both with bicycles. On foot went a messenger carrying a thermos of tea and sandwiches. They cycled to the lake, hauling the bikes through the reeds (!) and taking them across in the canoes. One of the canoes went back for the messenger. They then cycled down the far side of the lake to inspect several more boundary pillars. They found, as usual, that distances were further than they were led to expect. (The Africans, when asked, always minimise distances, believing that this is what one wants to hear!) So they did not turn back till 1.30, having completed the task. By 4 o'clock Ron was so tired he gave up cycling and walked. He had eaten nothing all day except two mangoes, and had drunk nothing. He met the messenger at 4.30 and drank the tea. He still had two hours' journey ahead and it is dark by 5.30, so he just had to hurry on. They crossed the lake in the dark. Meanwhile I had had my bath and was practically chain smoking, pacing the compound in the lamplight. Every now and then Aflike peeped in with a grave face, shrugged eloquently and withdrew. About 6.30 I heard a distant shout from Ron, Aflike seized his hurricane lamp with an answering yell of 'Bwana' and fled along the path to meet him. I stepped into the dark tent – nowhere to sit, as the nets were tucked into the beds – stood shaking all over, held my head in my hands and wept briefly but bitterly from a mixture of relief and rage! I emerged to see Ron coming into the circle of lamplight, looking dead beat. We hugged, he sat down on a chair and lit a cigarette while I poured two stiff drinks, silently screaming, 'Where the *hell* have you been, and how *dare* you put me through this ordeal of waiting since you are obviously neither hurt nor dead?' And he knew this, because he loves me. Aflike carried in bath water while I calmed down and listened to his story. As a matter of fact it has taught him a lesson: there are only twenty-four hours in a day, and you cannot go on and on forever without food or water in this climate and with only so much daylight, and must therefore organise the working day accordingly. I may say I think it was a lesson he needed. He lay very low on Sunday and Monday, when the DC turned up with his tent and his nice cook, Tobias. Dorothy's baby weighed 9lb. 2oz. and was born in six hours. He obviously hated leaving her as she is far from well.

This morning Ron and John have gone out duck shooting. Tomorrow we go home. I must say I would not have missed this somewhat dramatic trip, although I only had one active day. I am very brown and bleached and am back to my old thinness, which I like.

23rd August:

We got back from *ulendo* on Thursday last week, very dirty and tired. We found the house sparking clean, flowers everywhere and piles of clean laundry. I forgot to tell you Aflike found another house boy, an old friend of his own age, with whom he had worked for fifteen years. His name is Willard and he is an excellent worker, so our house moves on well oiled wheels and I know I am very lucky. We have six fat young hens which Aflike bought on *ulendo* some weeks ago and he brought back a big cock from Kasupi, so our household expands!

On Saturday evening at the cinema we met Humphrey and Eve at the interval who invited us to dinner and a dance next Saturday. So there we are, involved in a party again. On Monday morning I got a lift up to the hospital to call on Dorothy. She really is a shadow of her former self, with a faint voice and a skin like fine porcelain. She has been very ill, but was to get up for the first time later today. The baby is a pet but frighteningly big! The Halls turned up at teatime, just back from Johannesburg, and told us all about their trip, which was very tiring and appallingly expensive, so it is as well I did not go. They found the whole experience rather unpleasant because of a strong anti-British atmosphere in South Africa. However, the Daimler is going like a bird!

Yesterday we drove out to Kasupi in the morning. 'Winter' is over and has left bare trees and all the high grass dead, so that we can see across country for miles. It is already warmer and there are signs of the African spring, which brings not a flush of green, but of *red*! As we drove through stretches of trees and savanna, we saw here and there, every few yards, young trees and bushes covered with tiny, flaming leaves. There is also a lot of gold colour, but I am told that also turns red. It is like a magnificent autumn scene at home. The sunlight is more golden, and with dead leaves drifting in the wind, I get all mixed up and do not quite know what I should be longing for – African spring, summer, or autumn in Scotland!

Next month the Director of Agriculture arrives, so we shall be moving again, but whither, no one yet knows, except that it will be Zomba. I shall not really mind leaving this house, but I have loved having the garden and the view.

30th August:

I am staying with Anne Hall, as Ron and Norman are both on *ulendo*. Ron has been sent on a three-day tobacco course from Tuesday to Friday (do not ask me why). Next week he is staying at a Mission where women are not welcome, and after that he has a walking *ulendo* which I have to admit is beyond me.

I have been working very hard! Eve put me in touch with the Director of Education, who interviewed me in the Secretariat. He gave me a MS of 100 pages in Chinyanja, written by an African, to edit. It is a history of the Alomwe tribe and contains some rather awful revelations and accusations against the Portuguese. He wants to publish the MS in the vernacular, but for diplomatic reasons must omit the offensive passages about Portuguese East Africa, which everyone calls Mozambique, by the way. It is a bit tricky, and anyone who has studied African history and anthropology will know perfectly well that the Alomwe fled to Nyasaland from Portuguese oppression. However, I am so fascinated I am going to read the whole thing before I take it back and probably advise him that it is impossible to do as he wishes. He has given me a very adequate Chinyanja dictionary compiled by one of the Missions. I am discovering that there are several books on Chinyanja, and dictionaries, and that Dr Aitken's was by no means the first in the field, but his approach and method are certainly the most scholarly.

Yesterday morning Ron left for Mlanje, which is a tea and tobacco growing district, and I came here, to the Halls' house on Naisi housing estate, three miles from Zomba. There are about twenty houses dotted over three terraces on a slope below the mountain. They look across to Lake Chirwa and, of course, Mlanje. Somehow it is there, wherever one looks, but I am beginning to fall in love with *Zomba* mountain!

5th September:

Here I am again at the Halls. These houses have rounded ends, which is attractive but makes it difficult to place the furniture, and thatched roofs. Today several Africans are squatting on the roof rethatching it. I can make out quite a lot of what they say, but not their fun, which is very fast. Sometimes they sing lazily, which is soothing.

I am looking forward to receiving the Vogue pattern and the Penguins. I am *so* glad you consulted Mr Jessiman. He would be more than ready to help and has such lovely manners.

I have been working all day on the Chinyanja MS, which I shall finish on Friday. I shall have to say I do not think it can be edited as he wants, so that will be the end of that, but I have learned some history.

Last Saturday Humphrey and Eve came to dinner, so we wore evening dress, as they always do. Afterwards, we had some very good bridge. I am progressing by leaps and bounds, Ron says.

13th September:

I am with the Halls again – they insisted, as the thought of me alone in the big house really worries them. I have borrowed Anne's sewing machine and am slowly but surely making such a pretty cotton dress, using the Vogue pattern. It is rather like working out a puzzle – things start to fall into place. I *never* thought I would become a dressmaker.

On Saturday evening we went to a dance with the Halls, just the four of us, and had a splendid time till 2.00 a.m. I was feeling particularly good as Anne had cut my hair very well and helped me home perm it very lightly – transformation scene. It took nearly four hours and I thought my arms would drop off, but it was worth it. We met Mike and Joan Saunders, the nice couple we knew at Oxford who were on the Second Devonshire Course and who gave us very sound advice about Nyasaland. He has been posted to the Secretariat and they have a house near the Halls. It was lovely to meet people we knew at home and we asked them to join us. Yesterday morning I walked up to their house and had coffee with Joan. Her Siamese cat has six tiny kittens, all tabbies, but they have their mother's blue eyes.

On Monday, alas, Ron once again went off for a week's walking *ulendo*. Norman drove him out sixty miles and I went for the run. You would not believe the dust just now, and it will go on till the rains in November. If you have ever seen a film photographed in sepia, strengthen that colour to a hot, hard tan and you will have the right impression. Most of the dirt roads are of red soil (in some areas black), and all the trees, bushes, plants and crops are covered with red dust for yards beyond the road. When a car passes, it sends up an immense double column of whirling dust, higher than the car, enveloping us in a blinding, thick, dust storm. So on the few occasions when Norman was challenged by an approaching car or lorry, he put his foot down and the Daimler fairly surged forward, an exciting sensation of sheer power. I found myself thinking of muscles and sinews!

Ron and I are very happy. The weekends are paradise after the lonely week and we try to be philosophical about it all, for if you give in to discontent or depression in this climate, you may as well go home.

18th September:

I am writing to you a day early, as tomorrow we go on *ulendo* until Saturday, far from a post office. You say in your last letter that you worry about me, because in some of the photos I have sent recently I have looked strained. It is simply that the blinding glare when I take off my sun glasses is very hard on my eyes. I assure you that if this wretched *ulendo* were less frequent, I would enjoy the life out here very much indeed. As it is, it is an unsettled way of living but I do not grumble about it to you – or anyone – because what is the use? I can honestly say it is not easy to find enough to keep me occupied but I manage fairly well. Besides, it is early days – there is so much to adjust to.

On Saturday evening the Saunders dined with us and then we went to see the Zomba Dramatic Society's production of *The Chiltern Hundreds*. We had very good seats and settled down to a wonderful evening's entertainment. All Zomba was there, including the Governor and his party. The play was beautifully presented and well acted.

On Sunday morning we had some excellent tennis with the Halls, one of the last games we shall have, I think, as the sun is directly overhead and astonishingly strong. The great thing is the heat slows everyone down together, so one is not really aware that the games are losing pace.

I am re-reading Sassoon's *Siegfried's Journey* and loving it. His writing gives me such a sense of his Englishness and of the English countryside.

27th September:

At last I am writing to you on the proper day and from the proper house! On Saturday morning when we came back, Ron practically went on strike and said he wanted a week in the office and John had the grace to grant it.

We had a very pleasant *ulendo* in spite of the heat. We were in a narrow valley surrounded by hills. Our tent was pitched near an old empty house, in which a famous Nyasaland character, known to everyone as Uncle Don, was camping. He has been out here for nearly thirty years and works in the Department of Agriculture. He is a bachelor and has the most wonderful old world manners towards women. I have been literally basking in this, I can tell you! He and Ron did a lot of walking together. Sharing the house with him was a very intelligent young agricultural officer. They both play bridge, so each evening we hung our lamps in a tree, placed the table under it and enjoyed some fine games. Uncle Don lent me Fitzroy Maclean's *Eastern Approaches*, which kept me happy all day, all week. The only flaw was the mosquitoes – huge brutes which bit me through my linen slacks. I nearly went mad and sat, smoking furiously, wrapped, sweating, in Ron's dressing gown over my clothes, to protect myself. The nights were gloriously moonlit, with a high, very warm wind.

We managed a whole day's tennis on Sunday, despite the heat. Zomba was playing Limbe in the last match of the season, so when we rested, we sat and watched some lovely tennis. We had just had a bath and were sitting on the *khonde* watching the last of the sunset when Nickie Hemmings turned up from Mponela, 240 miles further north. She had come down for dentistry and got a lift from friends. She stayed for dinner and we had a very nice evening, exchanging news.

Yesterday was full of interest. Ron had to drive out twenty miles to settle a land dispute at an agricultural prison farm. The countryside reminded me of Caithness – a huge flat plateau with the *tops* of mountains showing at the horizon. Then we got into tea-growing country, wonderful prosperous estates with (bliss) good roads, well laid out fields scattered with umbrella trees (to shade the tea) and a general sense of England in the landscaping. The roads were very straight, and lined with tall blue gums which in fact looked French. We found the house of the head of the prison farm and introduced ourselves. Well! His name is MacDougall and he comes from Lochgoilhead and knows that lovely little hotel at Loch Gair we all remember for the wonderful breakfast we once had there. In no time we were talking about Rest-and-be-thankful, Inveraray, Southend, the Mull, while Ron tried in vain to get a word in. He is a frightfully nice type of Scotsman, cultured, with good manners and wide interests. We had morning tea with him while Ron got down to business and then the Commissioner of the prison and another officer arrived and after more tea and discussion they showed us over everything. We saw the cells, cattle, poultry and food stores, and some prisoners working at carpentry and basket making. We got back to the Boma just before noon and Ron was given another job in the afternoon. So after lunch, out we went again, driving thirty-six miles over a vast plain of sparsely grassed land with *ten* great blue, pyramid shaped mountains on the horizon at one side of the car, Zomba mountain riding along the skyline behind, and Mlanje towering up in front – but all away at the edge of this wide, windy plain; the wind was *hot*. Driving back in the late afternoon sunshine was like an exhilarating dream – you have to pinch yourself to grasp that these splendid mountains are real! So we did 112 miles yesterday. I am not sure if I have ever mentioned it but we get a very reasonable petrol allowance which Ron claims at the end of each month.

In the evening we went to an enormous party given by Police acquaintances who are going home on leave next week. We had a mouthwatering, stand-up supper – a hot curry, and strawberries and icecream. Lots of people we know were there, all young, and we had a lovely evening.

I am rushing along with this, as Aflike is going to market and will post it for me. I was up early. I have asked him for another five minutes. He is impressed by the number and size of the letters I write, and has asked me to tell you this!

The four Penguins came yesterday, to our great delight, and I am trying to keep them for our next *ulendo*. Ron says to thank you for including one on Africa. The author was a lecturer at Oxford whom Ron always enjoyed listening to. The books took exactly a month and three days. It gave me such a thrill to see Henderson's green wrapping paper and white label, and Mr Jessiman's familiar, neat writing!

4th October:

The hot weather is upon us. By 9.30 the sun is so hot I cannot go out without a hat. Sitting reading the *Observer*, getting its pages entangled as I usually do, by the time I have straightened them I am bathed in sweat from the slight exertion. Flowers only last a day in the house, less in the garden. Mlanje lies invisible behind the heat haze, even at night. Zomba is a dream of scents and blossoms. Most people are lethargic and quiet, but I love the heat and feel alert and well.

On Thursday morning I walked very slowly up to see Dorothy, and found the garden absolutely radiant, all the flowers swaying and bobbing in the warm wind. Dorothy, looking positively svelte, was just putting George in his cot, which is covered with a pale blue mosquito net. He looks very well and very bright. She was glad to see me, as John was on *ulendo*, and settled down to a good gossip.

On Friday evening Mike and Joan Saunders called in for a drink. They are greatly taken with our big drawingroom and said how ideal it would be for a party and suggested that as we had not had a house-warming party we should have a house-leaving party! After they had gone we discussed it and decided it would be fun. I told Aflike, who was enthusiastic. Ron and I listed the guests, five couples, and Ron rang them all up from the Boma on Saturday morning. They all accepted, for Sunday evening, which is marvellous at such short notice – but Sunday evening can be very flat with that Monday morning feeling already raising its head, so it was a good idea. I shopped at alarming expense on Saturday morning, after a long consultation with Aflike, who behaves as if we throw parties every second day, which helps to calm my nerves. On Sunday morning I combed the garden early for flowers that would last, and nearly hanged myself on the jacaranda tree. Ron had to come and unhook me. (He chose to spend *his* morning in the garage pit under the car, covered in oil, perfectly happy and assuring me whenever I ran up to ask him something that the party would be a great success!) I filled the room with masses of jacaranda, bougainvillaea and honeysuckle, and organised chairs and little side tables, raiding the unused rooms. Then Nickie Hemmings appeared from Blantyre for lunch and announced she would be picked up by her friends at 5 o'clock. Help! I had to abandon everything and entertain her. Fortunately she left promptly and I rushed behind the scenes to find the kitchen a complete mess, but Aflike, Willard and Hassani working steadily among what was obviously organised chaos. At 6.30 the Halls arrived with cushions I had asked to borrow, then came the Saunders with extra glasses, then three young couples we have met several times at the Binghams, who love young people, and fill their house with them. We had drinks and small eats – home-made potato crisps, home-salted peanuts, and tiny hot Vienna sausages on sticks. About 8.30 we all went into the diningroom for a buffet supper –cold lamb, ham and chicken, mint sauce and home made salad dressings. All the butter dishes were lined with fresh lettuce leaves and the table was sprinkled with flower petals. There were also bowls of fresh vegetable salads, and for dessert, piles of strawberries and peaches. It was a great evening and next time I shall take far more part in preparation, as I saw ways of improving things. They all left about ten, as it was Sunday night, and I went through to thank the boys for their marvellous effort. They were just locking up and turned to me three black faces with long grins positively flashing in the moonlight! I have told you about this first party of ours in some detail, as I thought you would be interested.

13th October:

You ask if there is much more of the *ulendo* work to do. Of course, as it in-volves the basic field work of the job, and as long as we have the present HE, Ron will always have fourteen nights a month to do. Also, being in Zomba district and therefore under close scrutiny, these orders are carried out to the letter, whereas in the Central Province, I know, David Baxter (our nice friend from London days who learned Chinyanja with us) has hardly been on *ulendo* at all. However, the rains break in November and we think that will have some effect, as many of the bush roads we have travelled over will be impassable. David is taking a week's local leave starting this Friday, and we have invited him to spend as much of it as he likes with us.

Everyone here has been most intrigued over the phenomenon of the blue moon at home. It must have been very weird. I got into a discussion with Mike Saunders about the phrase 'once in a blue moon'. I firmly maintained that old sayings were always based on fact, and therefore this particular saying implied that it had happened before!

I was very glad to see Ron back last Friday. There had actually been some freak rainfall and when we got back to the big house, we found the garden bursting into life. All the rose bushes were pruned recently and every one is simply covered in new red shoots. There has been an army of penal labourers working on it in preparation for the Director of Agriculture's return on 18th October.

We had a splendid weekend, dancing on Saturday night into Sunday morning. The good news is that we have been allocated a house on Naisi estate! It means I shall have neighbours and therefore sleep soundly, as they are within scream-ing-for-help distance! There is a lovely view and we are high up, almost as high as the big Zomba houses. There are a sitting-room, a diningroom and a bed-room, a big store room, a bathroom and an attached outside thunder box. The kitchen is only a few yards away, which I do not like – such stupid design. The *khonde* is small, built into the front wall of the house, but adequate, and there is quite a big garden on three levels, laid out, but untouched, so I shall be kept busy. I can use Anne's machine to make new curtains, etc. We get £3 per month travelling allowance, as we are three miles from Zomba. I cannot tell you what a difference it will make to me. I need never be frightened at night again, and I can tell you now I have had several almost sleepless nights in that big, spooky house – so has Ron. In fact he sometimes took a golf club and prowled, with me behind him, similarly armed, right through every room, there were such odd noises.

17th October:

We have had a hectic time since I last wrote. David Baxter arrived for lunch on Saturday and we took him to the Club at noon to meet people. It was lovely to see him again – he is very thin and shows little fussy signs of bachelorhood, dear man. He went off after tea to Limbe to stay with friends, and is coming back to stay with us this week from Thursday till Sunday. On Sunday we packed, in awful heat, all day. The hot season is glorious in itself but it is not the time to move house. In the evening we went to the monthly gramophone concert and heard Haydn's London symphony and some Scottish songs, includ-ing a Hebridean one, 'Island Moon', which described the moon shining on white breakers, and the thought that in a far country it would shine on the wanderer but would not be the island moon. It was too much for me and I was glad of the low lights. I not only felt far from home, I also felt alien to everyone in that hall! Afterwards we got into a group and I felt quite apart from them all, with my secret.

On Monday afternoon we moved to Naisi. We were so tired with the heat we just left everything and gratefully accepted tea at the Halls. When we got back the beds were made up, the mosquito nets tucked in, and after a bath and some fresh fruit salad we went to bed, at 7.00 p.m. This morning Ron climbed over the trunks and went to the office, and when he came back at lunchtime the house was absolutely shining and completely ready, except for curtains and cushion covers. There are three terraces and we are on the middle one. The mountain soars up about 300 yards behind us. There are trees and gardens between the houses, so we are not conscious of other houses except at night when the lamps shine out and I do not mind that. We did not bring Hassani with us to Naisi. Two boys are enough in this small house and Aflike and Willard are happy with this arrangement, so boo to the DC, who said the minimum must be three! But they are exceptional workers.

Tomorrow we go to Blantyre and leave the car at the garage all day to have its first service. We have household shopping to do and I *must* get a hat. We stay the night at Ryall's and on Thursday morning we join up with David and all drive back together, which will be great fun. I am very tired now, with all the work today, which is why my writing is so shaky.

Chapter 13

24th October:

Our day's shopping in Blantyre was very successful. I found a hat, a Henry Heath, white felt with a Garbo-ish brim that can be worn up, down or sideways, so that is that. You know how I feel about hats! We went to a very well stocked Indian store to look for curtain and cushion material. I finally chose apple green linen for the curtains and a heavier, silvery grey with a small green motif on it for cushions. I want the room to look cool; it is too small for bright colours. The Indian who served us is my friend forever. [He was.] When he finished doing up our parcel he turned to Ron and said firmly, 'I would like to show Madam some silks,' and, flashing a quick sideways smile at me, he proceeded to ripple across the counter rolls of the most exquisite silk. I could not tear myself away and my eyes came to rest on a white, white silk with a scatter of tiny hand-painted red stars sprayed with gold dust. I just stood very still and looked at Ron in silence. Finally I brought myself to say in a hoarse voice – how I hate having no money of my own – 'It could be an anniversary, Christmas and birthday present,' and he gave in with good grace and bought me six yards, which cost £4 10*s*. I walked on air for the rest of the day, in spite of the terrible, debilitating heat. It is so much worse in Blantyre, with the pavements and concrete buildings reflecting it. We met up with David for a very lighthearted tea at Ryall's, and who should come in but Bill Wright, who took the Chinyanja course with us in London. He is ADC Blantyre and insisted we all go to his house for an early drink with him and his wife, Lois, whom we met once in London. She is ex-Wrens, sophisticated and funny. We had a very pleasant hour and then David had to dash off to get ready for a dinner party and we went back to dine at Ryall's, and so to bed, worn out with our 'day in town'! There was a host of fireflies in the bedroom, piercing the darkness with tiny intermittent points of light, enchanting.

On Thursday we collected the car at 8 o'clock from the garage and drove back to Zomba. David came later in time for lunch and the Halls came to tea to meet him. We had a lovely evening, talking and exchanging experiences. I think David is lonely and longs to have a wife. Next evening we broke a rule and walked up in bright moonlight to dine with the Saunders. It only took a few minutes but I was jumpy. We are too near the mountain to take risks at night. On Saturday after lunch we introduced David to the joys of Zomba mountain. It is such an exciting drive up – and such a relief to reach the plateau! Friends of his were on local leave and we found their rented cottage, perched literally two yards from the edge, bordered only by a low honeysuckle hedge. We had tea on the narrow *khonde*, looking out at that marvellous panoramic view culminating in Mlanje's great massif. What with the precipitous drop practically at our feet and the heady mountain air we all felt deliciously intoxicated. At dusk our hosts went inside to light a huge log fire and we drove down, as if wrapped in dark blue velvet, with the lights of Zomba gradually twinkling and spreading far below, as tiny as fireflies. The suddenness of the three thousand feet descent made us yawn but we were so happy we felt on top of the world for the rest of the evening. After quick baths and a change into evening dress we went to dine with the Halls, then on to the Club, where we watched a dreadful, rubbishy film. But David thoroughly enjoyed meeting our friends, including Humphrey and Eve, just back from their local leave in the North, full of beans. We had a lazy morning on Sunday and after lunch – he eats as much as we two together but is as thin as a bean pole – David piled up his car with big boxes of stores and set off on the long drive back to Ncheu, highly delighted with his leave and looking a different man. Ron and I felt exhausted!

Yesterday he went to Kasupi for five days and I stayed here to get sewing done. I have baulked at making the curtains and heavy cushion covers, and have arranged for an Indian to come from Zomba with his machine to do it for me – he will work out on the *khonde*. Norman is also away, so Anne at last has some return for all her hospitality and is here with me, but of course is out all day working.

1st November:

We have had a great upheaval in Zomba – The Rains Came, early! There has been a very hot spell, and last Wednesday it was suffocatingly close and lowering all day, with a sunless light that made the mountains, indeed the whole landscape, appear to have moved closer when one's back was turned, and an atmosphere of electric resonance as if the very earth were holding its breath in some cosmic expectation. Just before dark, as Anne and I were having a sundowner, a sudden strong gust of wind swept through the house and we became aware of a strange, steadily increasing sound. We jumped up and went out on the *khonde*. It was RAIN. A murky, solid wall of rain was advancing across the plain below us, with a mounting roar. The air was already astonishingly thinned and freshened with the smell of damp earth. We stood riveted as doors slammed, curtains (our precious new curtains) were sucked billowing out of windows and papers fluttered to the ground. Aflike came dashing through the house, closing windows and shouting reassurances above the din. I rushed in to help and then out again. A great fireball of lightning exploding in the garden almost at our feet with a simultaneous crash of thunder sent us leaping back. Never have I felt such a sense of exhilaration! The first big drops fell with a *slap* on the steps and then the rain was everywhere, like a brown snowstorm in the dusk, each drop visible as a separate streak as it fell faster and faster. The gutter round the house was soon a gurgling moat and the red soil on the terraces melted like lava. A fine mist drifted down from the bamboo ceiling as the thatch weakened under the onslaught and there was a horrible smell of rotting hay. It battered down for hours and we went through to bed early. We had to move the beds around to avoid two leaks, which kept us awake with a steady plonk, plonk, into pails Aflike set under them.

Next morning we woke to a weird, muffled atmosphere, and when we looked out we realised why – everything was enveloped in a thick grey mist. All the mountain streams and waterfalls were in full flood and in the distance made a deep pounding like the sea after a storm. The trees and undergrowth had been transformed during the night and were bursting with sap, swelling and smelling in the warm, damp air. Naisi road was unbelievable. It looked like a mess of red porridge stirred with a spoon. By lunchtime no cars had returned. They usually start to appear soon after noon. At last, at 1.15, Anne arrived – she gets a lift with a neighbour when Norman is away. Eight cars had got bogged down, one behind the other, in about two feet of almost liquid mud and all the occupants had been out struggling to pull and push each other free, drenched and plastered with mud. On Thursday it was just as bad and most of the men donned boots and walked the three miles into Zomba. We began to worry about Ron and Norman getting back, but on Friday the rain stopped, though the road remained a horror. Norman arrived at teatime and Ron about six, having got bogged down for an hour *one mile* from home! The trouble is you cannot just abandon your car and walk away, as the road is very narrow with a steep drop on one side, so there is very little room for other drivers to manoeuvre. Fortunately he had Willard with him and between them they managed, in the dark. Ron looked quite shaken, and it takes a lot to ruffle him in a car. The rains should not have started for another fortnight and everyone is talking about it, either grumbling or rejoicing. It is strange to hear the weather discussed at all! These are the 'small rains'. The rains proper come in mid-December. The sun blazed down again on Saturday and it has blazed ever since. The sudden changes in temperature are causing a lot of sickness. I have had a nasty few days of 'Zomba tummy'.

Joan Saunders has a wireless and we listen to it as we sit and sew companionably of a morning. I cannot tell you what a joy it is to hear good music, light music and the news – whatever is going pleases me. It is either the BBC World Service or from South Africa. The Saunders have some good books: I am reading an excellent one by Helen Waddell, *Peter Abelard*. I think it is better than George Moore's *Heloise and Abelard*. Joan is a marvellous dressmaker. I showed her my silk material and sketched the design I envisaged. In one morning she made up a perfect pattern in paper, fitting it on me with pins, and then cut out the material pinned to the pattern. It is going to be the loveliest evening dress I have ever had and there is enough for a long stole. Silk is difficult to handle, so I progress slowly. It must be ready for the Empire League Ball on 11th November.

On Sunday we started on the garden by planting dozens of geranium cuttings which Anne kindly sent up. Ron obtained, from the Department of Agriculture, Seychelles grass seedlings, a coarse grass which grows very fast and spreads out fanwise, ideal for our terraces, so we got them all safely planted – very finicky. Crouched down at our work we poured with sweat, which ran down our legs and made small pools. After a bath one feels purged, divinely clean!

Ron is on *ulendo* again next week. Then we have a week at home and after that a week's local leave. He is a bit run down and it is high time he had a break. We may go to the Lake for a few days, but that will depend on weather and our finances.

8th November:

I finished my dress before Ron came home on Friday, and I must say it does not look home-made at all.

This house is so small I have had to give a lot of thought to its arrangements and appearance, and I am gradually getting there. The houses on Naisi estate were built quickly and with cheap materials to cater for the sudden influx of personnel after the war, and are far less durable and attractive than the old bungalows in Zomba. The fireplace is hideous, the doors and windows ill-fitting, and cupboard doors and drawers warp and jam – there is a daily physical struggle with the maddening hostility of inanimate objects. The most adequate room in the house for its purpose is the storeroom, which is not all that roomy but has a big wire mesh food store on legs, which stand in tins of paraffin, to discourage the ever-active ants. Our water filter is of a more modern design than the truly ancient one at Kasupi. However, I would rather be here than on the other new estate down on the plain below Zomba, aptly named Misery Farm. The houses are bigger, but are boxlike, with tin roofs, so ugly, and they must be hot.

On Sunday afternoon the Halls took us in the Daimler on a very hot dusty drive some miles beyond Zomba to have tea with friends of theirs who have a tea estate. Whenever I go into a planter's house I realise where the money is in this little colony! They have a long, low, wooden house, absolutely lovely inside with cool rooms all leading into each other through arches – like a Dutch interior by an old master – and polished wood floors with a few pale rugs scattered. The drawingroom was all white and soft gold. We had tea from a cake-stand loaded with delicious home baking, and there was a silver kettle over a little flame, to replenish the silver tea pot. They are plain spoken north of

England folk but my word, they know how to live! They were proud to tell us they have three children at Cape Town University. I do not grudge them any of it, as all the planters and their wives work very hard, and in the early years must have had quite a struggle. In the car going back we laughed somewhat ruefully at the abyss which yawns between their life style and ours!

On Monday morning early we drove out to Kasupi, where we found the garden in full bloom. The crickets and cicadas flourish in the hot weather and produce a perpetual high-pitched sawing noise *all* day and well into the night. The heat here is absolutely shattering. At night we sleep with only a towel over our waists and wake up drenched in sweat – it is far hotter than Zomba. The wind is so hot it feels as if it were coming from an opened oven door. When one walks out of the house and into the sun one's body winces and droops. We get up early and do our walking and outside work before ten o'clock, when possible.

There is a Red Cross morning on Thursdays at Naisi, when nine of us gather at alternate houses from 9.00 a.m. till noon, to roll bandages, sew or knit for the African hospital. At first I was very unwilling, as I hate being organised and having to be with a lot of women, but I quite enjoy it and get some private amusement watching the women interact. There is such a mixture.

There is a perfect ferment of superiority and inferiority complexes just below the surface among British people from varying backgrounds artificially concertinaed into a small colonial community, in which the outward manifestations of this particular way of life are all very much the same, in that everyone is provided with a house, everyone has a car, everyone has servants, everyone is a member of the Club and everyone appears to live more or less the same kind of life despite differences in salary; whereas, in the larger horizons of home, we have all come from many different sections of society without having had much contact with those outside our own particular sphere. This kaleidoscopic society produces its own strains and tensions, one sign of which is the snobbery – and its equally vulgar counterpart, the readiness to attribute snobbery where none is intended – of those who feel uncertain of their position when forced into an unfamiliar environment. Of course the majority are well balanced people who behave in a perfectly civilised manner and would naturally do so anywhere. The fact remains there are definitely some large fish in this small pond, and some little fish who find the pond big, especially, I hate to have to say it, among the wives!

15th November:

Last Saturday morning I ironed my dress and stole and hung them in the bedroom. Every now and then I went in to peep at them, shimmering in the wardrobe, the bodice tiny and the skirt looking narrow but in fact swinging out in folds when I move. It is so wide I can hold it above my head when I pick it up by the hem. It will look great on a dance floor.

The Halls came to us for a drink before lunch. They had news for us which they did not want to be overheard in the Club. Norman has been made the new Aide-de-Camp to HE. Ron and others were also being considered and everyone has been on tenterhooks. All I can say is a selfish *thank God*. It is really a job for a bachelor, as there is not much scope for private life, to put it mildly. If you are young, it is a good start, provided you do it well, as it means HE's goodwill follows you around afterwards. Norman, at forty, is prepared to 'have a bash' at anything, he says, but Anne is not happy. They are leaving Naisi and moving to a small semi-detached bungalow on Blue Gum Avenue, in a rather dreary row of old bungalows on the road leading south out of Zomba. There are Indian stores, a Greek store and a mosque opposite, so it will be noisy. The one amenity is a telephone, to keep in touch with GH. Poor Anne.

On Saturday evening we dressed for the Ball. What excitement! Ron called in Aflike and Willard to let them see me in my dress, which shone and sparkled in the lamplight. I raised my arms above my head and spun round several times so that the dress swung out, then wrapped itself round me in clinging folds before unwinding and falling straight again. '*Ai, ai, ai,*' they murmured, clapping their hands softly and darting pleased glances at Ron. When they had bowed themselves out, teeth flashing and eyes agleam, Ron said it seemed such a shame we could not just ask them to have a drink with us! We went to a buffet supper at the Saunders, with two other young couples who live nearby, the Dales and the Jones-Walters. It was the greatest fun, because we women had bare shoulders and bare-ish backs, and the thousand, thousand night insects which one usually takes for granted, seemed to crawl all over us and fall down inside our dresses! The men had a high old time – 'just stand still and let me . . .' etc – hilarious! It was a very splendid evening, everyone dressed up to the nines, some of the older men in tails. The hall was most imaginatively decorated with poppies and carnations and there were fairy lights hung throughout the Club. Best of all, there were tables set out on the path by the playing fields and we sat in the soft warm air under that brilliant night sky, and *all* the men were good dancers – heaven!

We have been presented with a kitten from the Saunders' latest brood, mother Siamese, father a tabby. He has green eyes and his coat is a lovely grey with faint black stripes. We have named him Smoky.

The Saunders have acquired a canasta set and we have had several evenings learning to play. As you know, I am not really a 'games' person, but I can see it has possibilities. It has been too hot to eat a proper dinner, so we have sandwiches or salads, and fruit.

Each Saturday morning Joan and I walk down a path leading off Naisi Road, through a tung plantation laid out in terraces, until we reach the main road, where Ron meets us in the car, having slipped away from the Boma, and we get our shopping done before meeting the men at the Club before lunch. There are two big general stores where everyone buys most of their supplies, and an excellent little Greek store on Blue Gum Avenue which I try to avoid, as it sells luxuries like tinned caviar and black olives, at a price.

Our local leave began on Monday and we are enjoying it very much. We reluctantly decided we shall have to save up for a visit to the Lake later. On Monday it was so hot we pottered about at home till mid-afternoon, then went down to the Club and played four sets of tennis. As we were having a long drink afterwards, the Halls drifted in from choir practice and the men went off to the billiards room while Anne told me her troubles. She had been to see their bungalow on Blue Gum Avenue and was very depressed. The trees that give the avenue its name are lovely. They have long slender silver trunks and feathery foliage which begins high up. They mature into huge untidy trees with peeling bark hanging from their trunks. They are a type of eucalyptus and have a scent like fresh lemon, which always reminds me of our arrival in Nyasaland, when, dead tired, I smelt it in the taxi on the way to Ryall's. It was not at all how I expected Africa to smell, but now I think of it as its very essence.

We have been to the swimming pool three times before tennis. The water is cool and refreshing and we have the whole place to ourselves. The heat is so great one has to make an extraordinary effort simply to face that suffocating three miles drive into Zomba. We are going again today and to an informal Sundowner dance at the Club later. We both look and feel extremely fit. Ron is ready to go back to work with a will, and I think perhaps I have been the greater beneficiary of the break!

29th November:

We are back to normal and today Ron goes off on *ulendo* but only for two nights.

On Thursday morning we drove out to Kasupi, as someone from the Colonial Office was camping there with Humphrey Bingham. He wanted to see the maize mill at Chagwa, which is doing very well and is now a 'show piece' in the district. So we all went in Humphrey's car. The heat was tremendous down on the plain and I blistered my arm accidentally touching the hot metal of the car. On Friday it was too hot to do anything, and we sat reading and writing letters on the *khonde* all day. In the evening we had Pat Meek, Norman's replacement as co-ADC, to dinner, as he had just that day moved into his house on Naisi and had nothing organised. He is on his second tour, very charming, ex-Indian Army, and has shot big game with princes and nawabs in many parts of India. He is a keen birdwatcher and has a wide knowledge of African birds, so he and Ron have that great interest in common.

The weather is sultry and thundery, with spectacular sunrises and sunsets. We get the morning sun in the bedroom and later in the day in the sittingroom. The moon, which at present rises over Lake Chirwa, is almost blood red just now and seems far bigger than at home. This is the season for beer brewing and drinking, and every night, far into the night, we hear the drums answering each other from village to village across the plain.

6th December:

Ron came home on Friday, his birthday – twenty-seventh! He had got up that morning at 4.30, to go with Pat Meek on a day-long fruitless leopard hunt. I am glad I did not know about *that*! Mike Saunder's birthday was next day, so we gave a joint party at their house and I spent Saturday morning and afternoon helping Joan prepare for the evening party. She invited the Dales and the Jones-Walters and I invited the Halls, Pat Meek and the Watsons. I had not seen Dorothy for ages. We gave them a cold buffet supper which they all seemed to enjoy very much. Then we bundled into cars and went to the Club to see a dreadful film about American football called *Yes, Sir, That's My Baby*! At the interval I suggested we opt out of the second half and everyone chorused agreement! So we sat in the Club and talked over an early nightcap. On Sunday morning Ron was playing tennis at 9(!) with John and two others, so I took my book – Robert Graves's *King Jesus* – and read in the Club. Then Dorothy appeared and we watched the tennis, catching up on 'news' as Dorothy calls it – it is really gossip! We played canasta with the Saunders in the evening. On Monday it was so hot I just sat and read all day – an amazing book which Harold Nicholson reviewed somewhat sceptically in the *Observer* recently. Pat Meek lent it to me – *Operation Cicero*. It is very exciting but not quite convincing, perhaps because it is a translation. Today we mean to swim again. How monotonous it must all sound.

Please tell Daddy Aflike burnt his arm badly the other day and came to me in great pain with a raw wound the size of a small saucer. I opened up the tin of impregnated dressings for the first time and dressed it for two days, and today, the third day, it is completely dry, with a new skin. Aflike declares it is *ufiti* (magic), and really means it. I just hope I never fail him.

14th December:

The rains are expected any day and it is tremendously hot and sticky. One of the wives I meet at the Red Cross morning offered to cut my long hair, which I accepted gratefully, as it had become a positive burden. She came for tea on Monday and cut it shorter than I have worn it for years. Ron will be cross, but what a relief!

On Sunday morning we went to George Watson's christening. The church is small and rather crude but somehow appropriate. It was beautifully decorated with flowers. There were fifteen guests, including all the Boma people. George looked angelic and did not utter a sound. Afterwards we all went back and had a terrific party on the Watsons' *khonde*, with champagne flowing and a delicious curry lunch, a really hot curry which did what it is supposed to do – made us all stream with sweat! Dorothy, in great form – she can be very charming – gave the chaps permission to take off jackets and ties, which was so sensible. We all know each other well and it was a happy, relaxed occasion. In the evening we went to the record recital and heard Brahms, Mozart and the divine voice of Ernest Lough singing 'Hear ye, Israel'.

This week I sent off the few Christmas cards we can afford. In yours I enclosed a Christmas cheque. I suppose the mails may be a bit erratic with the Christmas rush, but I shall send off my weekly letter as usual.

21st December:

Our mail is most exciting just now. We already have twelve cards, all local so far, including a very posh one from GH. The Halls have asked us to join them on Christmas Day. They have a wireless so we may hear something from London.

Ron has been away for two days but comes back this evening and stays at home till the New Year. On Tuesday evening Pat Meek very kindly took me down in his car to the Club, where we heard a twenty-two voice choir made up of people from just about every Government department, singing Christmas carols. They waited till 6 o'clock, when darkness had just fallen, and suddenly there they were gathered on the back steps of the wide *khonde* singing 'Adeste Fideles'. Everyone stopped talking at once and there was no sound but the clink of ice in glasses as we all sank down wherever we happened to be, to listen. It was indescribably moving. As Dorothy said briskly afterwards, 'Hardly a dry eye in the house, my dear!' Everyone was in a friendly mood and wanting to talk, so Pat and I stayed on for a drink. It was a lovely experience and meant more to me than Christmas Day will, I think.

There have been some tremendous thunderstorms and heavy rains at night but nothing as dramatic as the advent of the 'small rains'.

To my great surprise I have received a cheque for 30s. for reading the Chinyanja MS. I had forgotten all about it! So I got a lift and went into one of the Indian stores on Blue Gum Avenue and found some fine cotton for a dress to wear at Christmas festivities, and I am sewing hard. As usual, Joan made up a pattern to my design.

We had a lovely anniversary weekend. Sunday 17th was a perfect day. We had breakfast about nine, and found the house full of gorgeous flowers. Aflike knew it was our anniversary, and got up in the small hours and 'procured' the flowers from Zomba – there are no flower shops, of course, so it was best to ask no questions at all! I spent a busy morning working with the boys, preparing small eats for our noonday party, while Ron marched to and from the Saunders, ostensibly borrowing things for me but I suspect spending most of the time under the car with Mike! Men go *mad* about cars here. However, they do have to keep them well maintained in this climate and the garages charge a lot. At five to twelve I changed into my white Irish linen dress and was nervously flitting about the sittingroom changing the position of things by half an inch when our guests started to arrive. We like parties that have a good mixture of senior and junior – at this party the most senior were Humphrey and Eve. They had been at the KAR Ball the night before and were feeling a little frail but they revived. The small room was packed with people, but in time they spilled out onto the *khonde* and even sat on the steps. It was that sort of party! I am beginning to get the feel of what makes a party go and I enjoy it.

My next letter will actually reach you in 1951, so now is the time to send our New Year greetings and good wishes, and oh, may it pass as quickly as this year has and bring us all together again in great joyfulness.

27th December:

We have had a much gayer Christmas than we planned, and I am very glad of a quiet day today.

On Friday evening we went to the Halls for a light supper and on to the cinema to see quite a good film called *East of Java*. At the Halls we met Harold and Margaret Jubb, who were the Halls' neighbours at Naisi. They had just been presented with a sucking pig and invited us four to help them eat it the next evening and go on to the first of the Christmas dances. On Saturday morning the Saunders went off to Cholo for Christmas and I shopped on my own. I met Dorothy by chance and we went to the Club, where we were joined by Ron and John for a Christmas drink before lunch. There is a great deal of drinking done at this season, I can see! In the evening we dressed up and went to the Jubbs, where we struggled somewhat through a magnificent dinner. Margaret Jubb is from Yorkshire and is a marvellous cook. Her husband Harold is in PWD and as he is the only trained plumber in Zomba he is a *very* important man, and knows it! The dance was very festive, with masses of streamers, balloons and paper bells. (The traditional Christmas decorations make one painfully homesick. Everyone feels it.)

On Christmas morning we had a very light breakfast at ten and opened our parcels – how marvellous of the entire family, including sisters and cousins and aunts, to concentrate on *books*! More of them later. We were so glad to receive the cable from you all yesterday.

We went to the Halls for a splendid Christmas lunch. They had decorated the house and there was a real Christmas atmosphere. Afterwards Anne and I sat talking, and Ron and Norman played golf! There was a fancy dress dance at the Club in the evening. We had decided we would just go in evening dress, but the Halls would not hear of it, saying that we would be most unpopular if we did that. So we all put our heads together and it was decided that Ron would go as Lawrence of Arabia (an absolute natural) and I as a Chinese coolie. We had a late tea with Christmas cake and did not get home till seven. We then had a bath and got ourselves dressed. Ron wore green pyjamas with a sash. I put a hand towel on his head and bound it twice with black cord, and then we draped him in a sheet. On his feet he wore flip-flops. He took his evening shoes with him. He looked uncannily like Lawrence. I wore Norman's white cotton pyjama trousers rolled up a bit, Aunt Isabel's flame-coloured Chinese jacket with the mandarin collar, and a large straw sun hat tied under the chin with the jacket belt. I made up my eyes and eyebrows, hid all my hair under the hat and wore a most convincing black pigtail down my back. The make-up and lack of hair changed my face so much hardly anyone recognised me. It was terrific fun to feel so anonymous among so many familiar faces! There were some wonderfully ingenious costumes and we were thankful we had joined in the spirit of it all. Everyone was in the highest of spirits and the KAR band was in great form. We finally got to bed at three and slept till noon. I felt very homesick all day, as I knew so well how Christmas would be going at home, but I think most people suffer, and we all help each other to put on a good front.

Yesterday we had a great day, reading and wandering round the garden, making plans and gloating over our achievements. The grass is flourishing and we now have two beds brilliant with three different shades of geraniums and a round bed full of carnations in bud. Outside the bedroom window there is a huge bed absolutely thick with zinnias in bud. My aim is massed colour and informality, nothing in regimented rows.

Our next big event is the New Year's Eve Ball. After that we shall be quiet, as Ron has his lower Chinyanja exam on the 9th. He will pass the written easily, but we worry about the wretched oral.

The heat is terrific at present. We wear as few clothes as possible, and still the perspiration trickles down our back and legs and papers stick to our arms.

Chapter 14

There was a small excitement on Boxing Day. We had a cyclone warning. It was moving up East Africa, causing considerable damage, and was expected to reach Nyasaland on Friday (29th). On that day the rain and wind never ceased for one moment and the trees tossed and bent until one felt they would collapse from exhaustion. In the afternoon the weather people sent out a warning that the cyclone was expected to hit Zomba at 7.00 p.m. We fought our way to the Saunders just before dark to play canasta and also to watch the storm; theirs is the highest house on Naisi. There were tremendous flashes of lightning all evening but no increase in wind or rain and next day we heard it had split in two over Mozambique and gone elsewhere. On Saturday evening we ventured the drive down that awful road to the Club. There was a most peculiar, eerie fog creeping swiftly at ground level round corners, like white steam blowing in the wind. The film was grim but excellent – *Give Us This Day*.

On Sunday the weather cleared and spirits rose as we dressed for the New Year's Eve Ball. We had a light supper and the Saunders joined us for coffee and liqueurs and we arrived at the Club at 9 o'clock. I have never seen so many people in the Club and there were lots of unfamiliar faces. There were obviously many house parties going on over the holiday and Mike pointed out people from the North and Central Province whom we had heard of but never met. He said just about all the Administration from these two Provinces were with us and the rest would be in Blantyre. On these occasions I am always struck by the number of good looking men and women there are in Nyasaland. John and Dorothy brought an enormous party, including the territory's most eligible bachelor, an Irishman called Cosmo Haskard, who is PC in the North. There was an exciting atmosphere of friendliness and flamboyant high spirits. We ate a superb buffet supper and people drifted about with their plates, coming up to talk to friends and be introduced to new young faces. At midnight balloons and streamers floated down and everyone embraced, shook hands and rushed in search of friends – and favourites! The Halls were in HE's party, of course, very much in attendance, but Norman managed to get away for his never-to-be-missed dance with me, an old-fashioned waltz. At 4 o'clock we went back to their house for a final coffee and brandy. It was light and the birds were in full voice as we drove into the sunrise, and the first long rays burnished the top of the mountain with gold. Aflike came grinning out of the kitchen to greet us. We went to bed till 1.30, then had a bath and a late, cold lunch by the fire.

10th January:

We have been having a quiet time, as Ron has been working hard in the evenings for his lower Chinyanja exam, and staying on at the Boma for an extra hour in the afternoon, to have oral coaching from Barnet, the head clerk. But we took time off at the weekend to watch a rugger match on Saturday afternoon and in the evening saw an excellent film, *Sorry, Wrong Number*. The suspense was excruciating and everyone gave a sigh when it ended. My knees were shaking so much I could hardly stand properly for 'God Save the King'. Sunday was a radiant day and we spent it on the *khonde*, working at Chinyanja. Ron sat the exam yesterday. He had the written in the morning and a very unpleasant oral in the afternoon. Both were fairly stiff, but I think he has a good chance of passing. He is such a bad examinee, one never knows. *If* he fails, I shall sit it with him next time, in July, so that we work together and I know how much he has done(!).

The kitten is a wonderful companion for me and follows me about like a dog. I am sure the boys think I am mad, for they must hear my voice in the house, talking to him. The Africans are not natural animal lovers. Cats and dogs in the villages are left to their own resources and kept strictly for the practical purpose of keeping down vermin. The men also take the dogs out hunting in the bush. We meet them on the paths sometimes, and how I hate to see a poor dog hirpling along, its lead a piece of string tied on one of its hind legs. However, African servants become fond of their employers' pets and treat them with indulgent kindness.

We had a lot of rain last week and I had a fire on all day. I found two good library books last weekend and read my way through them: Somerset Maugham's *The Razor's Edge* and Sinclair Lewis's *Ann Vickers*. On Saturday morning, walking through the tung plantation with Joan, we came upon two baby snakes, like long black worms, dead. I thought nervously it would be too bad if mama were still around, and sure enough, we saw her cross the road ahead of us and vanish into the bush. I described her to Aflike, who said she would be a cobra – four feet long and as thick as my wrist. I have seen/ encountered/confronted nine snakes now, but as I know your horror of them is as great as mine, I will not go into detail! On Sunday I got some plants from the Saunders' garden and filled another bed with chrysanthemums, delphiniums, foxgloves and portulaca, a lovely small plant in brilliant colours which spreads quickly over the ground.

Yesterday morning we came out here for the week, to the village of Lambilila, only twelve miles from home. The country is lovely, high up, with wide savanna between vast rocky stretches, and mountains blue in the distance. A strong wind was blowing after tea and we walked between rice fields, shimmering and wrinkling in the late afternoon sunshine. There are an agricultural officer, his wife, nine-year-old daughter and a dog, camping some yards from our compound. Ron goes off with him all this week to various villages. They have a wireless and I could hardly believe my ears this morning as I was brushing my teeth, when the strains of Rachmaninov's 2nd piano concerto came floating over to me! I was so enchanted I swallowed my toothpaste. I have nothing, but nothing, in common with the wife. I tried to hide quietly in the compound after breakfast but she barged in cheerfully, carrying her chair, so I share the mornings with her. She has interrupted this letter so often, I am afraid it must be disjointed. A messenger will take it to Zomba tomorrow, so it will not be late.

24th January:

Last Saturday afternoon we experienced our first earth tremor. We had had a rest and were lazily having tea in bed (our latest weekend vice) when there was a long, low rumble, the house shook for a few seconds, then the rumble subsided. I shot out of bed, whirled into my kimono exclaiming, 'Earthquake!' and Ron stayed where he was, saying, 'No, no, they are blasting somewhere.' In the kitchen the boys began to laugh wildly and I went out to investigate. They grinned and rolled their eyes at me and Aflike managed to convey to me that there had, indeed, been an earth tremor.

Our *ulendo* weather turned wet and windy for the last two days and what misery. The runaway dug round the tent flooded and we woke to find the beds standing in water! Clothes, bedding, everything was damp and the tent felt like a steamy bathroom. Walking in the slushy compound was very precarious. I got myself organised with a chair just inside the tent and settled down to read *The Kon-Tiki Expedition*, which is rather like a mixture of Conrad and Homer! Poor Ron got soaked to the skin, of course, but takes it all in his stride. We returned on Friday to find sweet peas and carnations in flower, the house shining clean and every vase we possess filled with zinnias by Willard. The Africans have a marvellously uninhibited touch with colours and mix them in a way that leaves me blinking.

Aflike and I have dreadful colds. His was developing on *ulendo* and I think I caught it from him. In the heat it is a real affliction. My head feels as big as a Chinese lantern. I gave him codeine, and such is his faith in my *mankwala* (medicine) chest, he swears he feels well again, which he patently is not.

Ron has passed his Chinyanja – what rejoicings and *what* a relief!

6th February:

The great excitement of the week was the dance at GH to celebrate the eighteenth birthday of Elizabeth, HE's daughter. Just as we were leaving the house, having timed ourselves to arrive at GH at exactly 9 o'clock, I heard faint, high-pitched shrieks and discovered to my horror I had caught a lizard in the hinge of the bedroom door, so I had to put it quickly out of its misery with the heel of my shoe, then rushed out to the car, where Ron was sitting with the engine running and an exaggerated expression of patience on his face. We soon caught up with other cars on Naisi road and in Zomba the terraces were momentarily floodlit as cars emerged from driveways and turned down the mountain roads. Everyone was so prompt there was a long queue of cars up the driveway and into the large car park. GH was ablaze with lights, its enormous wide *khonde* decorated with potted plants and tall vases of magnificent flowers set among tables and chairs informally scattered about. We were announced by Norman, on his best behaviour, and shook hands with HE, his wife and Elizabeth, at the entrance to the great reception room with its gleaming floor and high arches leading on to the *khonde* stretching down its length. On the opposite side of the room, quite high up, there is a long, graceful minstrels' gallery. Huge bowls of tropical and English garden flowers standing on pedestals filled the air with a heady mixture of scents, frangipani predominating. There were perhaps fifty couples, just enough to fill the floor without overcrowding, and we danced to a very good radiogram. We knew lots of people, including the Binghams and the Watsons. Elizabeth is keen on country dancing and Humphrey, who knows all the young people, cleared the floor and announced he was going to select dancers to perform in two sets of an eightsome reel. He very quickly picked sixteen dancers, including two kilted KAR officers (one of them my friend Lorne Campbell). 'Come on, young Ann,' he shouted, beckoning across the room, 'I want you in this,' so Ron and I took up our places. It is *so* wonderful when all the dancers know how to dance it properly. Everyone crowded round to watch and there was enthusiastic applause when we finished. As we bowed to each other, smiling and breathless, HE stepped forward, clapping and calling out, 'Bravo! Encore, encore,' and so we danced it all over again! I have never felt more fleet of foot than on that beautiful, wide, satin-smooth floor.

Shortly afterwards, when I was sitting alone smoking a cigarette on the *khonde*, cooling down with a glass of claret cup, HE came out and joined me. He is a shy man and, as you know, I am hopeless at small talk. Mercifully, I was inspired to admire the minstrels' gallery and went on to say that the only other one I had seen was in my uncle's house in West Coker. He brightened at once and said purposefully, taking my arm, 'Come with me and let me show you mine.' So up we went and stood looking down on the dancers. Ron was dancing with Dorothy and their faces were a picture when they looked up and saw us. I could read Dorothy's lips saying, 'However did she manage that?'! I was rather thrilled.

Joan Saunders has started to teach her son Peter, aged five, for an hour and a half in the morning, following a course of lessons sent from Rhodesia, which is used in conjunction with a half-hour broadcast. It is most interesting to watch and listen.

We are delighted to have the *Glasgow Herald* Christmas Quiz and are going to tackle it on *ulendo* this evening. We will remember other times when we all joined in at Dunalastair.

14th February:

The Byron biography has arrived at last. I am delighted with it and am trying to read it slowly! A thousand thanks.

We had a most enjoyable *ulendo* last week, although it rained heavily at night. The sun was hot and Aflike coped marvellously with getting everything out into the air to dry. I went out walking with Ron twice and we had one very interesting meeting which I followed throughout in Chinyanja. I am beginning to make out the quick asides and jokes. The weather was exactly right for walking – hot sun and a high, dry wind. The countryside looks so beautiful just now, lushly green, and the flanks of the mountains take on a purple, grape-like bloom. At moments I felt I was walking through paradise. We drove back on Friday evening through torrential rain. After dinner on Saturday we churned and slithered our way into Zomba to the Club to see *Rope*, a good Hitchcock thriller with James Stewart. Everyone was wrapped up in warm clothes and at the interval chilly gusts of rain came skittering across the *khonde* and we all crowded as far in as possible, round the bar. My tan was much admired.

Yesterday was a lovely day and I did some gardening. At the moment I have flowering carnations, sweet peas and geraniums. Aflike assured me that snakes do not like the smell of geraniums, so I have masses of them on either side of the front steps!

20th February:

Yes, I *am* becoming engrossed in gardening and spend about two hours every morning slowly pottering about. After that it is too hot.

How astonishing that Laga Dushmanitch [see Chapter 1] has married a Southern Rhodesian and is coming to live in Limbe. Poor girl: it looks like a small, defunct boom town. I do hope she gets in touch with me.

Last week was Ron's week in the Boma, and we had a quiet, pleasant time. Over the weekend Ron spent many hours working on the car, as the majority of men do. Every weekend at every house on Naisi you are likely to see a car in some state of déshabillé and a pair of feet emerging from under it – and occasionally a wife standing by patiently handing over cleaning cloths. Even Aflike raids my careful piles of dusters if Ron calls for one and I do not get there first, and later I find them in an indiscriminate heap of cotton, chamois, towelling and soft polishing cloths – maddening.

Yesterday Ron went on *ulendo* till Friday. I would have gone with him, but electric light (think of it) is being installed and the men are about the house all day, so I decided I must stay here.

Ron heard the other day that he is to be posted from the Boma to undertake resettlement work on part of a large area of land called Magomero Estate. Government is buying the land from planters who are selling up. His job will be to resettle Africans from overcrowded land in the area. It is not promotion, but it means 'they', the powers that be, think he can tackle it, and the DC says it is a good move, from the point of view of gaining experience. There is a lot of practical work to be done in preparation, including a census of the large population, choosing a site for a house and supervising its building. Magomero is about thirty miles from Zomba, and as far as we know there is no house available, so we just hope and pray we may be allowed to stay here at the weekends and camp during the week. It will be such a shame if we move when the house and garden are just right, but it often happens, so I must grin and bear it as best I can.

28th February:

Your letter last week came late. I discovered it had, mysteriously, gone up in the box to GH. Norman sent it down by messenger with a note, suggesting that it was perhaps a portent of things to come!

On Thursday after tea I went with Joan Saunders to a meeting at the Club to discuss the forming of a Film Society, which would endeavour to obtain continental, British and American films of good quality for a monthly showing. Dear Humphrey proposed me as a member of the committee (he is President) but I regretfully refused, for if we are to move to Magamero, I might find it difficult to attend regular committee meetings. However, I told Humphrey afterwards I would be happy to make suggestions informally and he was very pleased. We have heard that there has been a delay over the purchase of some of the land at Magomero. We have also heard that David Baxter has been given a resettlement job twelve miles from Zomba, starting in August, so we may see something of him again, which would be fun.

The weather is beautiful but terribly hot, with an occasional outbreak of thunder and rain. It is so hot by 7.30 a.m. that I pour with sweat as I go slowly about the garden cutting flowers for the house. Ron came home on Friday with a burnt nose, peeling lips and very long hair, so I had to set to and tidy him up a bit, as we are going to a dance at the Club next evening.

6th March:

There are now verbena and chrysanthemums blooming on one of the front terraces. I forgot to tell you Aflike has two terraces behind the house for his kitchen garden, which is flourishing. He obviously has green fingers.

The weather is treacherous just now – hot and thundery but with a sudden chilly wind that blows steadily at unexpected times. The mosquitos are at their height, in quantity and quality! However, the rains are lessening and we shall soon have the wonderfully cool, dry, brilliant weather of the cold season. I appreciate having been out here long enough to sense the subtle changes out of one season into the other. It makes me feel relaxed and at ease with my surroundings.

Tomorrow we go to Kasupi, which I always love to do, for three nights. Zomba Boma is in a turmoil again. There has been no progress with the land deal at Magomero. Pat Meek has been posted to the North and Mike Saunders goes home on leave in July. So John is going to be short of ADCs who know the district. . . . We shall see.

On Saturday morning John and Joyce Gourlay, who live near the Saunders and with whom we play bridge, kindly offered me a lift to Blantyre, where they were shopping for the morning. I had no money to spend, but as it was a lovely day for a drive I went with them. John vanished on business and Joyce and I window-shopped; a most boring and frustrating way of passing the time, I found. We discovered one of the stores served coffee, so we sat down, feeling very sophisticated and towny, and had elevenses. Such are our simple pleasures!

14th March:

The Saunders left on Saturday for a fortnight's *ulendo*, which is my idea of misery, especially as in a tent which Ron and I find just too small for comfort, they have to share with Peter, aged five, and a ridgeback puppy not yet house-trained! Ron and I have decided, since discussing the joys of *ulendo* with them, that we are just not the pioneer type at all.

Last week we had our three quiet days at Kasupi, which was looking like a dream. It is lovely to return there. The people in the district remember us well. Someone recognises the car, shouts to his neighbours, and everyone drops everything and comes running through the maize gardens to the roadside, to wave and smile. The old women arrive more slowly, giggling behind their hands and shaking their heads at life's surprises. The little girl whose foot I treated came up the hill to visit us, dressed in her Sunday best, a red cotton square, tiny bead bangles and a bead necklace; a little flower of a girl. She speaks only Yao, so it was all smiles and bows until Aflike came hurrying to the rescue. She brought us two eggs, cradled carefully in her cupped hands.

We returned to Zomba on Friday just in time to gloat over the garden before dark. The rains are on the wane, with a great flourish of thunderstorms. Saturday was one of those steamy tropical days when one feels that the bush is full of menace. Joan Saunders is on *ulendo* and the prospect of a lone walk down through the tung plantation was too much for me, so I stayed at home and Ron, none too pleased, took the shopping list! In the afternoon we were persuaded by the Gourlays, our bridge-playing friends, to go down to the Club with them to watch a soccer match between Zomba and an Indian team. Everyone was there and afterwards we four stayed on for a drink. It was dark and raining hard by the time we set out for home in the Gourlays' car. To avoid Naisi road, John drove along the main road and turned off at the short cut through the tung plantation. The car stuck in mud a mile from home but we managed to push it onto a terrace, where we abandoned it and walked in the dark up the road which I had not been able to face in broad daylight that morning! John and Joyce, who have not lived outside Zomba, seemed unaware of possible hazards. However, Ron started singing and we all joined in and made enough noise to scare off a herd of elephants!

On Sunday evening we donned evening dress for Pat Meek's very posh farewell party, held at the Watsons' house in their big drawingroom. He has been unexpectedly posted to the Northern Province. We arrived on the dot of seven and found just what we expected, that 'everyone' was there, that is, a lot of heads of departments, the upper echelons of the Police and KAR and all the Boma people. We decided to separate and cruise; a big party can be fun, occasionally, and I thoroughly enjoyed my evening except for an awkward few moments with the very shy Colonel of the KAR who obviously knew he had met me before but thought I was someone else. He suddenly loomed over me and asked benignly, 'And how is Maud?' Mercifully, I had no time to deal with this, as Humphrey, out of the blue, pounced on me and bore me off, 'like loot from a battlefield,' I said to him, breathless but grateful. We both found this remark terribly funny and clutched each other as we laughed affectionately. He is a pet.

Ron is away on three days *ulendo*. I just could not face another mosquito-haunted ordeal in a tent. Last week at Kasupi, even in the house, I was covered in bites. I attract them far more than Ron, and react more severely. By the end of the evening I begin to feel feverish. We take paludrine *every* morning at breakfast.

I am reading a fascinating book which you would all enjoy: *Naga Path*, by Ursula Graham Bowes, who as a young woman of twenty-three went to live in the Naga hills in India among the native people.

23rd March:

I am finding it difficult to concentrate this morning, as I am in some pain. Last night we had one of our odd whims which do not seem strange out here.

We were both tired and there was what seemed like an everlasting thunder-storm going on, which started at 5 o'clock. We decided we would spend the evening in bed. So we had a bath and got under our nets with cushions, pillows, ash trays, drinks and books. Aflike, getting into the spirit of things, opened a tin of soup as a surprise at supper. We do not have soup in the hot weather, but it was chilly last night. The tin was an unknown South African brand and, although I quite liked the soup, it has had a drastic effect on my usually iron digestion, and this morning I am spending my time sitting very still and grey in my armchair! I only keep tins of soup for *ulendo*, as Aflike makes delicious fresh ones.

I have started making notes for Ron, who has two law exams in the offing, and spend every morning ploughing through a huge tome called *Principles of Common Law* – heavy but interesting. Ron is very tired and very thin (so am I), and we have decided to go to the Lake for Whitsun to get a change of air and scene. The Gourlays are going, and Joyce spoke to me seriously about Ron and myself obviously needing a break, so that really made up our minds for us.

27th March:

Yesterday we were thinking of you all and hoping you had a lovely day for the wedding [my sister Elspeth's]. The weather was beautiful here, with a soft wind and lots of white clouds floating over their own shadows on the mountain and the plain. I made up a posy of verbena and small double zinnias and took it up to Joyce as an incoherent gesture to Elspeth, and she understood at once and took me round her garden, which is much more mature than ours, and cut a great mass of mixed blossoms, so that I was able to fill the house with flowers.

Today is so beautiful I just sit on the *khonde* and gaze and gaze, almost in disbelief, letting my whole being fill up to the brim with this vision of Africa. The air is definitely cooler and thinner. Our little puss senses the change and leaps madly about while I work in the garden, sometimes landing on my back. The garden is flourishing; the latest blooms are one chrysanthemum plant I got from Joan and a whole bed of lovely balsam, more colours in the verbena and some nasturtiums. Aflike's vegetable garden has produced a fine show of toma-toes, mint, parsley, onions and lettuce. There is also a row of ripening pineapples. I am filling the garden with everything I can get hold of, despite the question mark in my mind about how much longer we shall be here. The Magomero sale still hangs fire.

Did I tell you Joan [a cousin] sent me the wonderful *Boswell's London Jour-nal*, which must, I feel sure, be the most exciting literary discovery of the century? I was *speechless* when I opened the parcel and nearly burst into tears, I was so thrilled.

4th April:

Last week was quiet, as Ron was on *ulendo*. Joyce Gourlay has a typewriter, temporarily, and offered to set out the law notes I made for Ron at Oxford, so after tea each day I dictated them to her and she has typed them beautifully for him. He returned on Saturday morning, very brown. The Saunders go on home leave in July, and till then Mike has been posted to Kasupi, to supervise the building of a Boma there and get it working. We are so sorry it is not to be ours again. Ron especially is shattered. Listening to the men talk, I think their first district is probably rather special to them. I am beginning to feel that nothing is *lasting* in Africa, nothing is *mine,* so I am ready to move on as life moves on.

The weather is glorious, with a fresh wind and hot sun, and the garden is bright with colour. I have a front bed full of balsam in pretty shades of purple, red, orange, peach and pink.

Joyce is teaching me how to do smocking, and I have started, somewhat apprehensively, on a lawn nightie I made, at the waist and neckline. Can you believe it?!

9th April:

It is one of these divine golden African mornings, the time is 7.30 and Ron and I have just driven through clear, cool sunshine, to begin five days' *ulendo* about ten miles from Zomba, at a place I have visited once before. The tent is pitched right in the middle of the village, and at the moment there is a lot of screaming from small babies who do not like our pale faces, and a lot of laughter from the women. I admire them – they laugh easily at the slightest thing, and yet lead such hard lives.

It was such a beautiful day on Saturday I decided to spend it at the pool. I went down with Ron at 7.30 and after doing the shopping, settled down to relax, sunbathing, reading (a good book by Ernest Raymond called *The Witness of Canon Welcome*) and occasionally slipping into the pool to get cool. I had the whole place to myself and emerged at noon very bleached and dark brown. After lunch Ron joined me for the afternoon and we had tea in the Club. In the evening the Gourlays dined with us and we went to the Club to see Trevor Howard and a beautiful French girl, Anouk, in *The Golden Salamander*, most enjoyable. On Sunday there was cricket all day, which I love. Ron was playing, somewhat out of practice.

I am finding smocking quite fascinating!

18th April:

We had a pleasant five days' *ulendo* last week. Ron had to go back to Zomba twice and I went with him and sunbathed at the pool – the water is *cold* now. We did some walking, and drove into the bush on a road still under construction – a very hard drive – and came out onto a plateau looking down on a vast panoramic view of the plain, astonishingly far below. There were some red, rocky hills scattered about, and from our height they looked like sandcastles! We walked along a cliff path which dropped down into a gorge below, where we could hear water roaring under a thick canopy of steamy, bulbous vegetation and tangled creepers. It is absolutely virgin bush, yet only ten miles from Zomba. The nights were so cold we had to sleep in the same camp bed to keep warm, and woke up completely cramped and set in one position! Last time we camped here it was the hot season, and we did not realise how high the village is, which is *folly*. The Gourlays drove out one afternoon to have tea with us. They were appalled by the road out, which to us is an average bush road, but delighted with the tent and all our arrangements. They left saying they thought *ulendo* must be exciting. Huh! But it brought home to me how lucky we are to lead such a varied and interesting life, compared with people like them, who work in the Secretariat in jobs which have little contact with the African, and who never have the opportunity or the interest to seek out the non-Zomba scene, which is the real Africa. I am *not* criticising Zomba, may I hasten to add. I think I would die without it!

This week we are at home and enjoying it very much. On Monday I spent another day by the pool, but I think it may be my last for the present, as the water is so icy it is more of an ordeal than a pleasure, and I do not enjoy sunbathing without the cooling down of a swim afterwards – very frustrating.

25th April:

Our puss, Smoky, is lying on a small coffee table beside me, facing me, as he always does. He seems to know when Ron is away and never leaves me. He usually sleeps on his own cushion in the diningroom, but when I am alone he sleeps on Ron's bed, close up against my mosquito net!

The weather broke at the end of last week and Ron went off on *ulendo* on Monday shivering in the thin, chilly mist that hides everything beyond a few yards. It is most depressing. Last Friday evening we had a fire heaped with logs and ate a lazy supper on trays, silently consumed over books, except that we always keep remembering things we want to tell each other. Ron is away so much that we never get too settled and domesticated together, which is the one and only good aspect of *ulendo*, which otherwise I hate with a deep, black hatred! On Saturday we saw *The Inspector General*, good but not a patch on *Walter Mitty*. Today Ron is to be in Zomba, and is coming home for lunch, tea and dinner, and then, of all ridiculous things, must drive out six miles to the camp and sleep there, in order to make up his compulsory fourteen nights! We occasionally cheat and he has an extra night at home, leaves at the crack of dawn and is well away before Zomba is stirring. The DC knows, and turns a blind eye, but it is not wise to do it often – too many nosey people about!

I am trying to read Lin Yutang's *Moment in Peking*. I think my mind must be too modern to appreciate Chinese writing, as I never find it quite real.

2nd May:

My latest venture is a row of tiny grapefruit trees at the side of the house, which are growing amazingly quickly. The garden is a mass of colour and gives me great pleasure.

I had a quiet week, sewing and reading by the fire, and of course there are always letters to write, which I enjoy. Ron came back very tired, and full of aches and pains, poor man. The weather was so damp and sunless his clothes and bedding never had a chance to dry. So we lay low at the weekend and spoiled him.

11th May:

This is just a note scribbled on the day before our Whitsun weekend at the Lake. I cannot think how I forgot to mention the fact that next week, on Tuesday, Nyasaland celebrates its Jubilee – sixty years a Protectorate. There are all sorts of celebrations, and this First Day Cover has been issued, with special stamps. I thought you would all enjoy receiving one – they will become of value to stamp collectors. It is rather thrilling to think we have landed out here, on our first tour, at such a time. I am handing in the Cover to the Post Office, where it will be kept till Tuesday, when it will be franked and posted.

15th May:

I am writing this after breakfast, in the hope that I shall get it finished before Ron comes back from Zomba, where he is helping to organise preparations for a jubilee ceremony at the Boma, which we are to attend this morning. Messages of loyalty to the King are to be read out by the DC, a settler, a representative of the Indian community and the senior chief of Zomba District. It is expected to last about twenty minutes, and is the reason why we had to return from our holiday last night instead of today. There is a huge parade in Blantyre, which the Governor is attending.

We had a wonderful weekend at Lake Nyasa. The weather had been dull and chilly all week and I gloomily packed mainly warm clothes. However, on Saturday morning we woke at 5.30 to find the sun already warm, pouring into our bedroom. We leapt up and ate a big breakfast; the Gourlays arrived in their car at 7.30 and we climbed in to the back. It was so nice to have Ron beside me, able to look at the scenery with me instead of concentrating at the wheel, but like most men he would have preferred to be doing the driving! We called in at

Kasupi to show John and Joyce our little paradise. The Saunders were on *ulendo* so we just showed them the view. The house looked really dilapidated. At Liwonde, the ferrymen were delighted to see us again and sang strenuously to us during the crossing, greatly impressing our companions. They had not been north of Zomba. We stopped at 9.30 and had coffee and sandwiches and then went on, out of Zomba district and into Fort Johnston district, where Aflike comes from. It is very tropical-looking, with hundreds of palm trees. We hoped to glimpse some game but saw only birds and dozens of baboons. Fort Johnston is an attractive little place, with a wide sandy main street lined with trees and ending up at a jetty by the Lake, which was an incredibly deep blue. It was sheer heaven to see water again. I had not realised how much I miss it. Some of the houses on the street had low walls and garden gates – I had completely forgotten about gates and felt a surge of homesickness.

Our hotel, Palm Beach, is about ten miles beyond the Fort. We turned off the main road and bumped along a sandy track and there it was, in an enchanting setting on the edge of the Lake, which is enormous and looks like a sea. The hotel consists of a long, low building made up of a great open lounge and bar, with a diningroom beyond. On either side are small rondavels which are bed-rooms, all with running water and a shady *khonde* with deck chairs. There is another building at the back containing baths and lavatories. The hotel and bedrooms are built on the beach itself and the water lies about fifteen feet away. There are large leafy trees behind the rondavels and in front, growing just in the water, four tall palms. The hotel has its own generator and there are lights in all the trees. There is a small jetty with several rowing and motor boats. We spent the whole of Saturday and Sunday lazing on the beach and swimming in the cool, soft water of the Lake. There are high hills to the south, hills in the dim distance opposite, and to the north a scatter of small islands which, in the noonday heat, appear to float just above the water, like a mirage. It was *exactly* like the Highlands and seemed a world away from Africa. I felt completely at peace. The food was very good and the service perfect. We had morning tea in our dressing gowns on the *khonde* and watched a brilliantly hued kingfisher dive for his breakfast from one of the palms. In the early morning the water was so still one felt one could walk over it to the horizon.

16th May : [The same letter]

Ron came tearing back from the Boma yesterday morning, and surprised me writing this letter, so absorbed that I had not noticed the time! So I had to change in ten minutes. The ceremony was held outside the Boma and was more impressive than I had expected. There was a huge crowd of Africans gathered, smelling potently in the hot sun. (I wonder how we smell to them!) The four protagonists of the ceremony sat under an awning (the DC flanked by Mike Saunders and Ron). The official audience sat on chairs facing them – about forty Government and private sector men and their wives, and in another block of chairs, about the same number of Indians. The Boma court messengers in khaki and red fezes, came out and presented arms, and a bugler blew one long note. Then the DC stood up and opened the ceremony by reading his message of loyalty to the King. Each message was translated into Chinyanja by Barnet, the head clerk. The bugler then played reveille and we all stood up as the Union Jack was hoisted. It all looked like a picture from the past, John and Mike in their bemedalled white uniforms, swords and big white helmets. (Ron wore his demob suit! He is not required to wear uniform on his first tour.) Chief Chikowe and his councillors were in vivid robes and turbans of green, scarlet and purple. John then called for three cheers for the King and led a rather discreet hip-hip-hurrah. It was then Chikowe's turn and he leapt to his feet, flourished his stick with its long tassel of lion's hair and gave vent to a splendid, uninhibited sound which was joyfully taken up by the crowd, a kind of hoo-la-la-wumphhh! Everything then broke up, including Mike, who tripped over his sword and laid his elegant 6 feet 2 inches along several chairs. Invited guests went up to the DC's for drinks and Ron and I went happily home, John having forgotten to ask us. There was an African football match in the afternoon which we all had to attend, and we turned up to find John full of apologies and Dorothy fuming at him. He insisted on us staying on with him after the match to have a drink, while Dorothy rushed home to see George fed and put to bed.

To return to our holiday. The sunsets were spectacular and we sat out with our sundowners watching in awed silence – it is the water that provides the ultimate touch of magic. After dinner we played bridge and ended the evenings bathing at about 11.30, swimming among the reflected stars. On Monday we drove thirty miles to Monkey Bay, and on another ten to Cape Maclear, the main lake resort of Nyasaland, which has an airstrip. The road was very hard going and it took us nearly an hour. The surface was coarse gravel and the car hung on steep inclines with the tyres digging pits in the ground. The jagged edges of huge boulders which had been blasted, jutted out into the road and the driver had to dodge quickly round, only to meet another on the opposite side. Sometimes the road was so steep we passengers all stood up from our seats to look over the bonnet to discover which way the road turned next! (Shades of the road to the Isles.) It was so hot we were all drenched in sweat but it was worth it. The hotel, a large, two storied building with tall windows and deep *khondes*, stands in sloping grounds about fifty yards from a long, sandy beach lapped by dancing blue water, with small islands about half a mile out and the vast stretch of the lake into the distance. We went straight in to bathe for an hour, swimming out to a raft to sunbathe. We all agreed we felt *liberated*! We had a delicious lunch with a bottle of wine – sheerest luxury. There were lots of guests, most of them having flown up from Rhodesia, all very tanned and muscular – *so* colonial looking. We looked positively puny beside them! We got back to our small hotel for an early tea and regretfully turned our back on this newly discovered paradise. We crossed Liwonde ferry in a flaming sunset and climbing the escarpment saw a most spectacular falling star which seemed to take forever to slip down the sky. The Saunders had returned and their lamps twinkled through the trees on the hill at Kasupi and Ron and I uttered low sounds of envy and regret. We got back about eight, and walked in, so brown that Aflike hesitated in disbelief before coming forward to welcome us. We had a deep bath, a silent, dreamy supper and fell into bed. I feel better, just knowing the Lake is there, however unattainable it seems in everyday life!

29th May:

We have had a very sad thing happen. Our darling pussum has been missing since Sunday night. For two mornings Aflike and I searched the garden and this morning we found two enormous paw marks on the big flower bed below the bedroom window. So it now seems certain that the poor puss was taken by a leopard. Aflike says it happens all the time. It is quite unbearable to think about and I am missing him very much. He was such a companion and always made his special sound of greeting when he entered a room. It is so strange to look at the garden, all shining and blowy in the morning light, and think of it quiet and still in the night with a great cat moving soundlessly about. Not for the first time I am glad that the windows are barred.

On Saturday night at the cinema the British News was devoted entirely to the opening of the Festival. There was absolute silence throughout and I have never felt a Zomba audience so attentive. It all looked so British in the best sense, of pageantry, national pride, endeavour and achievement. The interval came immediately afterwards and everyone thronged round the bar, confessing to homesickness, enthusing and saying what a marvellous sight it made. Suddenly, right there in Zomba Club, I felt completely at home, exactly where I wanted to be.

The weather is *very* cold, with sunshine. I shiver all day unless in the sun. I think my blood must have thinned!

13th June:

I have forgotten what it feels like to be warm without a fire. Aflike lights a big log fire in the sittingroom before I get up and when Ron is on *ulendo* I have all my meals there. My flowers do not like the cold either and are wilting fast, except the antirrhinums, which I planted when we came to Naisi. They only began to bloom last week and are very fine.

I thought you would all appreciate the photo of the 'Beware of Elephants' sign on the way to Fort Johnston. The Saunders recently found themselves camping near a herd. Mike said he made Joan and his son, Peter, practise climbing an enormous baobab tree by the tent, just in case!

You ask about newspapers. The Club provides *The Times*, *Picture Post*, *Country Life*, *Tatler*, *Queen*, *Sphere*, *Vogue* and *Punch*. Occasionally one feels rather oppressed by the fact that all the news is late, but I am nonetheless grateful and pounce on them.

The great event last week was the KAR Ball. In the morning we had the King's Birthday Honours parade and presentation of medals, all very impressive but oh, so cold. There was a huge drinks party at the Watsons afterwards, with a big marquee in the garden for the chiefs and councillors, where they poured back whisky and brandy and ate piles of avocado sandwiches and iced fruit cake. Mike Saunders and I kept an eye on my old friend Kawinga, and between us reckoned he drank ten whiskies! My Chinyanja is much better than last year and I was able to do my bit among the chiefs. Ramadan had started that day and one of the chiefs, Msomala, whom I know quite well, is a Muslim, and could not eat or drink between sunrise and sunset, but made it clear he wanted his share of the food. So I found some paper napkins and each time he was offered a sandwich or piece of cake, he accepted it, handed it to me, and I made up two parcels for him to take home, amidst great hilarity! At last we got away and gave lunch to the Saunders, in from Kasupi for the occasion. They love being there, damn them!

In the evening we dressed for the KAR Ball and went off to the Stobbes cottage for a supper party. They are a couple who were living in tents in their garden when we met them. They are now back in their lovely renovated cottage. We found a tremendous party in progress, drink flowing and a fabulous cold buffet. About nine we all got into cars and drove off to the Officers' Mess, which was lit with hundreds of fairy lights. The dress uniform is extremely smart: tight black trousers with a red line down the side, and a fitted jacket with high collar and silver buttons. The entire evening was most impressive and stylish and we enjoyed it enormously. At 1.00 a.m. we had ham and eggs and coffee, most welcome, and left about 2, although the dance seemed still in full swing. Ron said at lunchtime on Saturday that he and the DC spent an unusually unproductive morning at the Boma, yawning and gossiping! In the evening we saw *Odette* – excellent.

I found Carla Oman's biography of Florence Nightingale in the library. It is heavy going but very interesting.

21st June:

The weather is simply appalling, with dark skies and a bitter wind which howls at night. It is unbelievably cold and I am thankful Ron is in this week. Yesterday there was rain all day – icy, drifting rain, and it is the same today: a really nasty *chiperoni*. It is so dark I am writing this by fire-light, at 8.00 a.m. Our electric light is only on from 5.30 p.m. – 10.30 p.m.

I have finished the Florence Nightingale. It is a magnificent book, and what a fascinating woman she was. I had no idea she was so beautiful, witty, cultured and clever. You would love the earliest part which tells of her childhood and youth. They had a glorious time as a family, travelling all over Europe and meeting the most famous people of the day.

I spent Friday afternoon at the Club, browsing through the papers, and had tea by the fire in the big lounge. It is always a nice time to be there, as people come in for the film matinee at 4.30 and stop to talk. Although we are such birds of passage in Zomba because of *ulendo*, it is surprising how many I know.

27th June:

Once again I am crouched over a large fire. I have just finished reading Duff Cooper's *Operation Heartbreak*, which I think quite perfect of its kind, written in a positively classical style – beautiful, controlled prose with a wealth of feeling below the surface.

Ron was in all last week and we had a lovely time together, eating meals in front of the fire, and long quiet evenings reading and talking. On two afternoons I went down to the Boma with him and helped him with routine paper work – how I hate it! His work really has a wide range and he copes with dozens of different problems.

The Watsons dined with us on Saturday evening. Dorothy had not been in a Naisi house before, and was interested to see everything, such as there is! Aflike and I had worked all day together and our little house was looking very pretty, filled with flowers. The dinner was a success. We had Aflike's home-made clear soup, chicken in a parsley sauce, with home-grown potatoes and vegetables, and a strawberry trifle, made by me from a recipe Joyce gave me. (She is going to teach me how to make pastry – hers is far better than mine.) At the Club later I heard Dorothy say to one of her Zomba friends, 'We've been dining at Naisi – quite a little bush village out there!' The film was good entertainment, *So Long at the Fair*, with Jean Simmons and Dirk Bogarde.

4th July:

The weather has been warmer and I have been able to work in the garden for hours – very therapeutic. The nights are very cold and in the evenings, Ron tells me, he has a big fire burning outside the tent by his chair. I love these warmer winter days. The little trees in the tung plantation have golden and red leaves which constantly float down the wind, and one or two have already put forth their snowy blossom. When the whole plantation is in flower, it looks like an apple orchard.

The Saunders go home on leave tomorrow and to my delight have offered to leave their wireless with us. What a difference it will make, especially to me.

The main event at the weekend was held on Sunday, a cricket match between 'the gentlemen of Zomba and Limbe', all players to be non-cricketers. In the end, a few very good cricketers were included, as they could not get enough volunteers. The whole thing was an elaborate joke, perfectly organised by a very popular senior officer in the Secretariat called Maurice Houle, a charming, witty man. He captained Zomba and Eric Barnes, our PC, captained Limbe. The teams turned up in their whites and wearing their school caps perched on their heads. The two captains withdrew from sight and then suddenly Maurice emerged onto the field, wearing a red striped blazer and an immaculate grey top hat, and riding his own beautiful horse, which he took right round the field. Accompanying him were two out-riders on bicycles – the PC, who is not tall, on a fairy cycle so small he had to push himself along with his feet, and a big man in the Police, on a very high bicycle. We were all helpless with laughter. The African spectators were silent for a few moments and then as they recognised the trio they let out yelps of joyous appreciation, set up a steady clapping and stamped their feet. The Acting Governor (HE is on leave) was batting first and as he walked onto the field, the African Police Band appeared from behind the Club and escorted him to the wicket, playing a rousing march. He acquitted himself quite well, but several players were out for a duck and were escorted off the field by the band, playing a funeral march. Maurice was waiting for them at the steps of the Club, where he solemnly presented them with a real duck on a silver tray. When it was Maurice's turn to bat, he raised a pair of binoculars and scanned the horizons. By this time some of his African fans – clerks in the Secretariat – were rolling on the ground, and their uninhibited mirth was most infectious. It may seem madly childish written down, but it really was hilarious – mad dogs and Englishmen, indeed!

Yesterday Mike Saunders was sitting his higher Chinyanja and brought Joan to Naisi at 8.00 a.m. to spend the day with me, which was very pleasant. He and John Watson were the only two examinees.

11th July:

We are very happy this week because we are on *ulendo* at Kasupi and Ron is in all next week. The weather has not been quite so cold, and here it is warm. The view is so comfortingly familiar and the atmosphere so peaceful. The Saunders left us an old bookcase and twenty Penguins, mostly thrillers. I am delighted to have another bookcase and, of course, their wireless. Ron does not have much office work to do, so we shall pay calls on the chiefs in the district, for old times' sake.

Ron has been told that when he goes to Magomero as Land Resettlement Officer, he can do the preparatory work as ordinary *ulendo*, from Zomba. This means we shall not have to leave our house and garden. Despite my new philosophical attitude, I am in fact ecstatic about this to the point of tears of thankfulness.

18th July:

This morning we left early for a two-day *ulendo* at Kasupi. There was rain in the night and we drove through a countryside sweetened and freshened. The rain has increased the cold and the Africans shiver, crouch and lament. Aflike has built up a crackling fire and I have just finished elevenses (at 9.30!) with Ron and a PWD man who came this morning to go over the house and determine what has to be done. Well, he saw for himself it is riddled with white ants, so they are going to pull it down and build a new one. What ages decisions take out here. By the time that is done we shall be home!

We had such a nice *ulendo* here last week. We did two hundred miles of travelling through magnificent scenery. Driving through the Chikala pass, notorious for its appalling surface, we had our first puncture ever, and while Ron changed the wheel I climbed a huge rock to get a better view. The Chikala hills are lovely: high, rugged and wooded, and as they drop down to the road there is tall, sandy-coloured grass growing among big boulders – typical lion country and I always hope to see one.

You may have heard on the news that two KAR battalions are being sent to Malaya, some of them Nyasaland troops. Our *ulendo* developed into a search for the DC, whose presence was required in Zomba to set matters in train. We missed him by a few hours in three different villages and finally found him walking in the bush with twenty carriers. He had left his car in a village and gone on foot. We walked with him back to our car, which was nearer, gave him lunch at Kasupi and took him back to Zomba on Thursday afternoon.

In the evenings we have been wallowing in the wireless programmes, delighted with everything we hear. What a joy to have good music again. It has quite transformed our life, especially mine. Aflike obviously enjoys our enjoyment. Last night we were to have a cosy dinner by the fire, and Aflike was setting the table. I was exploring the wavebands and stopped on the sound of a very unfamiliar language. Aflike caught my eye and said briefly, 'Portuguese. He is talking about money.' From what followed it was clear that the speaker had been announcing that the next record to be played was of Chaliapin singing an aria from *Le Coq d'Or*!

The first of the Film Society's monthly films was shown on Sunday evening to a full house – a marvellous start. It was *La Traviata*, the whole opera, sung by magnificent Italian singers in Italian, with a very brief commentary in English, in the form of a diary, between arias, very well done. The whole production was beautifully presented and the acting very good. Everyone emerged in a buzz of pleasure and we stayed on and spoke to a lot of people. Humphrey, who is President, was delighted with the general reaction and bought us a drink to celebrate.

On Monday evening we went to a Sundowner at GH, given by Mr Footman, the Acting Governor, and his wife. The atmosphere was friendly and informal and 'everyone' seemed to be there. We were offered good Virginian cigarettes stamped with the Nyasaland crest, specially made and sent from England for GH. We met the new Financial Secretary and his wife, Kenneth and Ruth Simmons, a very sophisticated, lively and amusing couple. They are new to Nyasaland, having been posted from Kenya.

25th July:

Yesterday Ron had to attend a meeting in Blantyre, and I went with him. We gave a lift to a Welsh girl, a friend of Joyce's, who works in the Secretariat. She is getting married next month and was desperate to get some shopping done. Her fiancé is one of the men who is going to Malaya with the KAR, and they are getting married now, so that she can go with him. She has only three weeks in which to gather together her trousseau. She asked me to go with her and help. It was heartbreaking. She is short and very overweight, and we saw several delightful dresses and suits, not one of which she could get into. (I suffered agonies – all these lovely clothes!) At last we found something she could wear, a cream shantung dress with a short jacket. She does not have much money and did not find a hat she could afford. I suggested the Greek tailor in Zomba might manage to concoct a tiny something from remnants. I felt so sorry for her I could have wept. She comes from a small village in a Welsh valley and wanted a very traditional, family wedding. Instead she is getting married in a short dress, to a man in sergeant's uniform, at the Boma by the DC – dreadful.

Today I have worked hard with the two garden boys, getting the garden re-dug and preparing a great number of boxes for my new seeds, newly arrived from South Africa. I am planting lupins, phlox, carnations, gypsophila, mignonette, lobelia, stocks, verbena, balsam, zinnias, antirrhinums and nasturtiums – some of these from garden seeds I already have.

30th July:

We are out on *ulendo* this week, but tomorrow we pass through Zomba on our way to another camp, so I shall post this and collect our mail at the Boma. We are camping in a very low-lying valley. There is an all-pervading smell of parched earth and a dry, warm wind at night. The stars hold us spellbound, and we sometimes spend the whole evening simply watching them and only occasionally talking.

On Friday the Gourlays went off to Salisbury on a week's local leave, to buy a new car, taking with them both our watches, which have been out of action for some months, and my wedding dress, which suddenly broke out in rust-coloured stains – the work of some wretched insect, I think. If it cannot be cleaned I shall have it dyed, which I meant to do in the end anyway.

On Sunday morning Ron and I worked at the Boma, in a desperate attempt to clear up his endless paper work, and returned for an hour after lunch. We made some headway but what a *bore* it is. We went on to the Club, where a tennis tournament was in progress, and after an early tea set off for this camp, about forty miles from Zomba.

It is now afternoon. I stopped this to go with Ron to a big meeting – about a hundred people. Ron spoke, and then answered questions, for over two hours. There was an amusing incident. The Africans speak Chinyanja and Ron works through an interpreter, although we both understand most of what is said. Some of the men in the villages have been African clerks and speak English very well. At one point, two young men, probably on leave, jumped up at the same time. One said to the other, 'Excuse me,' and the other said, 'Excuse me, *one* moment please,' and burst into a flood of Chinyanja. They both spoke with public school accents.

Yesterday we gave a lift to an old, old chief I had not met before, and Ron said to me when introducing us, 'The chief speaks English.' The chief said proudly, 'Yes, but as in Scotland.' It transpired that he had been to a Church of Scotland Mission school, years ago, and wanted his denomination understood.

The colours today are wonderful – purple mountains, red earth, scarlet and gold trees, and everything shimmering in the blessed heat.

13th August:

I have got hold of a library book which was well reviewed in the *Spectator* – *The Brave Bulls*, a very vivid, earthy book about the breeding of bulls for bullfighting, with the most beautiful woodcuts by the author, an American named Tom Lea.

The Saunders left their Siamese cat in our care, unaware perhaps that she is going to have kittens, so that will be my next responsibility!

The Gourlays arrived back three days late from their leave in Salisbury. My wedding dress, you will be glad to know, has been beautifully cleaned and is again flawless. I also have my watch back in working order, but Ron's was beyond repair, which is a disappointment. As a matter of fact, we both find now we are fairly accurate at telling the time by the sun. I had spoken to no one since Ron went off on Monday, so I was glad to see them. They had a great week in Salisbury, spent all their money and set off in good time to arrive back on Sunday afternoon. On Saturday morning, driving through a Native reserve (no fences) they saw ahead a *cow* on the road. John is a townsman and does not know much about cattle. He thought the cow would move to the side of the road when he honked his horn, but of course it did not and he drove smack into it at 40 m.p.h.! The miracle is that it got up and walked away and neither of them was hurt, though badly shaken. The car's engine was undamaged but the bonnet and front mudguards were badly buckled. Fortunately they were within fourteen miles of a small hotel which ran a garage – they might have been hundreds of miles from anywhere. A lorry came along quite soon and gave them a lift to the hotel, where a truck was organised to tow in the car. It took the garage staff three days to beat the bonnet into reasonable shape. The hotel was empty save for themselves, and had no fireplaces, so they froze. It was also dirty. They had very little money, no books and not enough warm clothes. They could not even go for a walk, as they were warned that the surrounding bush was 'stiff' with leopard. They are lucky to have got off so lightly. The hardest thing about the whole experience is to have to say they collided with a cow!

Ron has been told that our home leave has been provisionally approved by the PC for August 1952. It is wonderful to have a definite time to plan for and dream about. My mind reels in disbelief.

I have discovered that some people out here live in debt for a whole tour. We live very simply and therefore we have the money when a big bill turns up, e.g. the last car servicing bill. Recently, Ron has started to send a modest sum home to his bank.

We had a Sundowner party last Thursday, which was a great success. We owed quite a lot of hospitality, so we asked as many couples as the room would hold, a mixture of Boma, KAR and Police. With the boys there to do so much of the work, I have time to devote to detail, and did great things with flowers. Dorothy crowned the evening by asking me if I would like to have her sofa and two chairs when they go on leave in December! Everyone going on leave tries to 'farm out' as many of their perishable possessions as possible. Otherwise they are put into the PWD storerooms, susceptible to dampness and the depredations of white ants.   While I was shopping on Saturday I met Dorothy, wild with excitement, on her way to buy a bottle of champagne, as John had phoned from the Boma to say he had passed his higher Chinyanja, a real achievement. So I slipped into his office to congratulate him. He looked quite dazed, pulled at his moustache, a nervous habit he has, and said something rather incoherent about 'examiners . . . kind . . . act of charity'! He is a dear man. At the cinema that evening the British News showed quite a lot of Wimbledon, including Doris Hart winning the women's singles – exciting.

5th September:

I have been working in the garden this morning but had to give up, it was so hot, at 8.45! The sun is tremendously strong, although there is a high wind and lots of high clouds. We have had some rain, which is quite irregular. I suddenly decided to have a new, big bed full of a mixture from all the other beds, so the garden boys are preparing it now and I shall work on it tomorrow. The rain has brought on the seedlings wonderfully, and every morning early I rush out and transplant furiously.

Our local leave began on Monday, and so far we have done very well. Ron works from 7.30 till 2.30, with a short break for lunch. Then we go down to the Club for tennis and tea, then back for more work in the evening. It is not yet warm enough to swim, but the pool has been cleaned and filled.

There was no cinema last Saturday, as new sound apparatus, long overdue, is being installed. However, there was an informal dance, which was most enjoyable. The Watsons were there on their own and invited us to share their table. On Sunday Zomba's second eleven was playing the KAR and I spent all day at the Club, while Ron played in the match. We had lunch with the teams and had great fun. I was on my own, but not for long – kind chaps came and went, plying me with conversation, curry puffs and long drinks. Ron played well but has been like an old man ever since, he is so stiff!

I have got a very good book from the library, Stephen Spender's *World Within World*. It arrived among the latest batch from England and Joyce Gourlay, who is on the committee, very kindly laid it aside for me.

12th September:

Thank you for sending the Aflike article: 'Study in Black and White' to the *Glasgow Herald*. It might well be accepted for the Weekend Page – what fun!

Our leave has turned out rather different from what we planned. Until last Wednesday all went well, then the weather became cold and overcast and I got a severe chill, which laid me low with diarrhoea. Ron dashed up to the hospital and they gave him pills for me, which made me fearfully sick, and my temperature shot up to 102°F. However, I cooled down on Saturday and had no more symptoms, and got up on Monday. But I still feel rather shaky and am quite content to sit wrapped in a rug all day re-reading *Gone With The Wind*. It is much sadder than I remember. Ron has been working hard. I have been so thankful he is at home. David Baxter sent word to us that he suspects he has dysentery and is going into hospital today, so we are waiting for him to let us know whether he is fit enough to stay with us over the weekend and sit the exams or whether he has to go into hospital for treatment. *The Wooden Horse* is showing at the cinema this coming weekend and there is a Charities Ball on Saturday, so I am lying low and hope to be fit by then. Eve Bingham has asked me to help her with the flower arrangements and I do not want to let her down.

I loved Stephen Spender's *World Within World*. It is rather like a minor *Siegfried's Journey*, with vivid portraits of T.S. Eliot, Virginia Woolf, Harold Nicholson and other literary people – very much my kind of book.

The garden is looking lovely and I am so frustrated because I cannot go out and finish the transplanting. The garden boys, driven by Ron, are doing their best, but I do not trust them with the young plants. One thing they do beautifully, and that is cut grass. Our terraces are really lawn-like in appearance and people comment on the transformation made in the whole garden, which of course pleases me.

It was so dull to have to spend last weekend in bed. Ron could not bear the house without me, and had his meals on a tray sitting by my bed (although the smell of food did not give me much pleasure!), and kept wandering in to see me, till I suggested he bring his law books into the bedroom and get on with his work there.

20th September:

Since I last wrote to you I have been in bed and am still there, though I shall get up later today. The day I wrote to you I had an awful feeling I was in for one of my heavy colds and I was right. I think it is really a kind of 'flu which is going round Zomba. There is always a lot of illness at the change of seasons. Mercifully, Ron has somehow escaped it. So, I missed the film and the Ball. Aflike was terribly upset when I 'took to my bed', as it has not happened before. He tip-toed about with a grave face and brought in trays with dainty little meals for me. He was shocked when I refused baked custard (ugh), which he had obviously been taught was suitable food for an invalid. It was impossible to explain to him that it is an inherited aversion from both sides of my family!

David duly arrived on Saturday morning and sent up my temperature, we all got so excited. He and Ron retired to the sittingroom and worked hard, although every now and then I heard a burst of laughter. They talked to me through the open door at meals and I croaked back; and always came in for elevenses, tea, and coffee after lunch and dinner. It exhausted me but also cheered me up no end. The law exams were on Monday and Tuesday. Ron was sitting two, and David was boldly attempting all four. Being a bachelor, he has more time to work for them. It is hard to have exams looming, when the office work is completely overwhelming because of the time spent away on *ulendo*. All the Bomas are complaining bitterly.

David went into hospital on Wednesday for tests. He really is appallingly thin. Ron is going to ring the hospital for news of him this morning. He goes off on *ulendo* next week and life becomes 'normal', alas, once more. It has been a happy fortnight, despite my incapacities!

26th September:

I must set your mind at rest at once. I am very well again, rested and full of energy. I think I was very run down, in spirit as well as physically, after the wretched cold spell during which I spent so many, many hours alone, crouched over a fire.

Ron went off on Monday morning, very reluctantly, and I have been able to keep myself busy, as things had got slack in the house during my absence, as it were. It always surprises and pleases me when I realise how essential a woman's presence is in a house, however good the servants, and as time goes on I undertake more and more, and enjoy it. I 'spring cleaned' all my books yesterday, sitting on the floor in slacks, sloppy-joe and sandals, my hair falling round my face – a familiar sight to you, I thought. It took me a whole day, because of course I kept dipping into them – lovely!

The weather is simply glorious, with a hot sun and high, cool wind in the morning, which drops at noon and then it is warm and sticky for the rest of the day. I love it. Everyone is saying the hot season is going to be very hot indeed. The blossom came out while I was in bed, and when Ron drove me into Zomba on Saturday afternoon, I was enchanted to see the mountain terraces one mass of jacaranda blue and peach blossom. We wax nostalgic over memories of the big Mountain Road house, which provided such a magnificent setting and views at this time last year. There is no blossom at Naisi except the white tung trees, which we cannot see from the house, and I miss the peace and quiet of that big garden.

David came out of hospital on Saturday morning, earlier than we expected, and arrived in time for lunch. It was my first complete day up, so we made it a celebration. There was a great deal of talk and laughter, and Aflike went about beaming, shaking his head and saying '*ai, ai*' under his breath. David has had some kind of dysentery, but was cured in four days by the rather drastic methods they employ. He left on Sunday after tea, hoarse with talking, and is coming back next weekend for one night. He sleeps on a camp bed put up last thing at night in the sittingroom.

3rd October:

Aflike has just been telling me this is a bad year for illness in the villages and many people have died recently. Zomba is full of 'flu and fever. I hear that David has had a recurrence of dysentery and is very depressed. It must be awful for him, all alone. Everyone I meet exclaims in one breath how much weight I have lost and how very well I look! I go down to the pool every afternoon and already my swimming is much stronger and I am bleached and brown.

Zomba is breathtakingly beautiful, one great mass of blazing colours, and everywhere, everywhere, the divine blue of the jacarandas. It is all so lovely one feels it might suddenly vanish in the blinking of an eye. The weather is at its most magnificent, with flawless dark blue sky, heat haze hiding all the familiar landmarks, and in the morning a high wind. The garden is coming on very quickly and today I got six fat carnations for the house. Aflike takes a great interest too, and bosses the garden boys imperiously. He is very subdued just now because his wife, who went off some weeks ago to their village to hoe his 'garden' (plot of maize) is sick. I cheer him up by telling him the latest arrivals and departures and changes of houses. He loves this kind of 'gossip' with me.

Everyone has been anxiously following the news of the King's illness. When I told Aflike about it, he looked stricken and raised his arms about his head in an aimless gesture, a habit the Africans have when faced with something they do not know how to deal with, as if they are trying to cast off an unbearable burden.

Ron came back from *ulendo* on Saturday morning and was delighted to find me dashing about again. I went to the Boma with him to collect our mail and the DC took us into his office to give us the news that the arrangements for the Magomero Resettlement Scheme are now completed and Ron is to take up his work as Resettlement Officer shortly. We are to keep on the house at Naisi till we go on leave. Ron begins the work next week, and will be his own master, doing whatever *ulendo* is required but no longer under the fourteen days *ulendo* a month rule. Three pre-fabricated aluminium huts are to be erected on a site chosen by Ron and these will be our living quarters at Magomero and we shall come in to Naisi at weekends. This is at last definite. I am very pleased for Ron, as this new posting is a great opportunity for him. Since he heard seven months ago that he was to be the Land Resettlement Officer in due course, a lot of his *ulendo* has been out at Magomero and he has already completed a survey of the land and villages and has written two reports, both of which have been well received. He is tremendously interested in the work and is longing to get on with it, although very sad to be leaving Zomba Boma. All the African clerks are sorry he is leaving. Kayes, his personal clerk, a wonderful man, said 'Oh, Bwana, now I shall have no one to tell things to.' He has always been very helpful and gave Ron all sorts of insights into African affairs. The DC was hoping the posting would go to someone else and says he is 'shattered' to lose Ron.

This news, however expected, caused a general sense of upheaval, but we managed to give David another happy weekend. On Sunday morning we walked with him to visit Dave and Iris Davies, whom he knew in the Central Province, where Dave was DC, Ncheu. They have just returned from home leave and Dave is in the Secretariat – which, like all good DCs, he hates. They are living in one of the Naisi houses, quite near us. To my delight, Iris Davies is a kindred spirit – what a find! I have made many pleasant acquaintances out here, so far, but that is all, and suddenly, almost as our eyes met, one recognised the real thing. [I was right. We became lifelong friends.] She is ex-Wrens and worked in Intelligence in Vienna after the war. She is a great reader and has lent me Siegfried Sassoon's biography of Meredith. She is coming to the pool with me this afternoon.

On Monday evening we went to the KAR Mess to attend a farewell party for the officers who are going to Malaya. I had a great evening, meeting several young men I had not met before. It is not an easy life out here for young bachelors. I notice David just cannot stop talking when he is with us – he begins before he gets out of his car – and he is so grateful for what he calls 'the feminine touch', such as flowers in the house, a pretty table and nice bed-linen. He asked me to cut his hair on Sunday and sat on the *khonde* wrapped in a towel, placidly puffing at his pipe while I practically stood on my head trying to carry out his instructions. Joyce lent me scissors and clippers, and I took off masses. Aflike stood unobtrusively in the background, transfixed with interest in my latest undertaking!

10th October:

The weather is extraordinarily hot, much hotter than usual, Aflike says. I am loving every minute of it and spend my afternoons at the pool. Ron developed a very chesty cold and was persuaded, with great difficulty, to stay in bed for three days. He has been over-worked, over-tired and over-nervous for weeks, and I am thankful he is at least having the few days' rest.

Last Friday the Watsons gave a huge 'farewell' party, which was rather a fiasco, as the day before brought news that their leave had been postponed till March. Dorothy was still in a flaming temper and no wonder. When she heard the news at the Boma, Ron says her language made even his hair stand on end!

David turned up on Saturday morning to take me to shop, as Ron was too busy in the Boma to get away. After lunch we went to the pool, taking Iris Davies with us. She and I talked sixteen to the dozen all afternoon and would hardly take time off to swim! We feel exactly the same about a woman's life out here and had a great, rebellious grumble, besides talking of many other things. She is going into hospital today for tests, as she feels constantly ill, with dire, undiagnosed symptoms.

17th October:

Ron and I have been most enthralled by a new book which everyone is reading – we managed to borrow two copies – *The Cruel Sea* by Nicholas Monsarrat.

The weather continues to be incredibly hot and it is difficult to get to sleep. Very late last night we were at last dropping off when suddenly a bull frog started up a noise like a sea-lion just outside our windows. We both shot up in bed, sweating, cursing and wide awake. Ron gave his pillow a final pounding and murmured, 'Ah, those glamorous tropical nights!' The garden is doing its best to survive. I have one garden boy just going round and round watering all day.

Last week what I expected to happen did happen. Ron had to retire to bed for another three days. He was working far too hard in the Boma, trying to clear his desk before he goes off to Magomero, and his dreadful cough was wearing him out. He got up on Friday, having seen the doctor on Thursday afternoon, and went back to the Boma very cheerful, because the doctor advised against *ulendo* at Magomero this week. So here we are together for another week, very pleased with ourselves.

On Saturday afternoon we had just retired to rest when David, whom we were expecting for tea, roared up in his car and we tumbled out of bed and dressed while he stood just outside our door shouting all his news since he last saw us! He is *so* isolated at Chingali, the strain is beginning to show. In the evening we got dressed for the KAR Ball. David left on his own as he was in a different party. Our host was Lorne Campbell, whom I have mentioned before. We sat down ten to dinner in The Pig and Whistle, Zomba's first pub, opened recently. We enjoyed a very good dinner, with several wines, then went on to the Ball, rather late, so that as we drove up the hill we heard the sounds of revelry grow louder and louder. The Mess looked beautiful, with fairy lights everywhere within and all over the garden, where fountains with coloured lights were playing. One was aware of the misty African plain below and dim mountains beyond. It was actually cool, as the Mess is on the mountain side and the fountains also helped. We had a truly magnificent evening with the usual ham and eggs about 1.00 a.m. My last dance was with Lorne, a polka followed by a highland schottische, the first time I have found anyone out here who knows the proper steps. There were very few couples on the floor and a very appreciative audience on the sidelines, Ron among them. He said afterwards there was no doubt that two very wild Highlanders were leading the dance! I felt on wings and Lorne, equally airborne, found breath to utter high yippeees of elation. He is obviously a very popular officer. We left at 3 o'clock and heard next day that the party went on till daylight.

Ron goes out to Magomero next week. His work takes him out on marathon walks in the great heat, so I shall not accompany him yet. John Gourlay gives me a lift after lunch down to the pool, where my young KAR friends often come to swim and talk with me.

I am enjoying *The Loved and Envied*, by Enid Bagnold, a very sophisticated writer I have not come across before.

We now have a pink and red hollyhock looking in at our sittingroom window, with more to come, and about twenty-five lupins will be out in another week. There is a great show of zinnias, marigolds, phlox, gypsophila, linaria and petunias. I have about a dozen foxgloves getting bigger and bigger but with no sign of blooms. The earth is gasping for rain. In the heavy thundery heat the veins on my hands stand up blue, and I am constantly aware of the blood pulsing through my body.

On Friday I was most upset as the Saunders' cat had kittens in the night in her box in the sittingroom and I found her in a great state, with two out of five very messily dead. Aflike removed them and I cleaned up the box and calmed down the poor puss. The three kittens look quite Siamese though according to Aflike, who knows everything, the father is a grey tabby!

31st October:

The small rains have broken, which means deliciously cool, dampish weather, with snowy white mists floating along the mountain, suddenly thinning in places to reveal a sunlit crag. The heat mounts up again at night, then just before dawn a little breeze starts up and tingles one's nostrils with freshness.

Ron came home unexpectedly on Friday afternoon, and came down to find me at the Club, where I was changing library books: a lovely surprise for me. People stared at him, who is usually immaculate, striding into the Club in sweaty khaki shirt, shorts and stockings, absolutely black-limbed with the sun, his hair dusty and his nose peeling! He had had a very interesting week's *ulendo* at Magomero, and proceeded to tell me all about it, drawing maps on the back of his cigarette box, while I gazed at them and thought of other things – I am hopeless at map reading. There was no good cinema, so we spent a lazy weekend together, being very unsociable. There was marvellous music on the wireless on Sunday morning.

8th November:

The kittens are becoming adorable. Almost overnight grey stripes are showing through their white baby fur. They are so frail and dainty, with huge eyes and bones as light as a bird's.

This week Ron is at Magomero setting up our permanent camp of three aluminium huts. He has promised me to get the windows wired so that we can open them at night without fear of intruders! So I shall get some sleep on future *ulendo*. Our camp is about forty miles from Zomba, twenty along the Blantyre road and then we branch left onto a bush road.

The small rains are very much with us and the amount that has already fallen is beyond belief. Yesterday there was a freak storm and I watched the flowers being battered by hailstones the size of ice cubes. I have to send Willard through pelting rain into Zomba to post this – and he is happy to do so. Darkest Africa is a wonderful phenomenon.

14th November:

About Christmas: Ron and I would like the new Margot Fonteyn biography by William Cappell published by Cape. It is the sort of book one appreciates out here, to go back to again and again, whereas once a novel is read, it is put aside for a long time.

The rains have definitely come, and today is the first sunny day for almost a week. The flowers are all lifting up their heads again and the house is bright with vases of phlox, petunias, zinnias, salvias and marigolds. The nights are strident with frogs, crickets and cicadas. Walking along Naisi road the other day with Iris, we had to raise our voices above the piercing drilling of the cicadas. They are everywhere and I have yet to set eyes on one!

Ron is still organising things at Magomero. The huts are up – eighteen panels bolted together by one hundred and fifty nuts, with an aluminium panelled roof – and outbuildings built near them, including a kitchen and living quarters for Aflike. He has chosen a secluded spot on a hill, under trees, not within sight of a village, though there are several nearby. He has got basic furniture, mosquito nets and a portable typewriter. As far as I can gather, the work to be done will be interesting and I shall be glad to help Ron do the paper work.

I lunched with Iris on Thursday. The hospital think they know what is wrong, and she is getting penicillin and liver injections and is on a diet. People do get dreadful internal complaints here.

On Saturday morning Ron arrived, full of news, and then, five minutes later, in charged David, unexpectedly, asking if he could stay with us. I think he just suddenly felt overwhelmed with loneliness. I nearly burst into tears, I had planned such a nice weekend for Ron and myself. However, one must never grudge hospitality in Africa, and I soon recovered and we settled down to a delightful weekend. We spent two quiet evenings talking and listening to music. On Sunday Dave and Iris walked round for a drink at noon and the fun was fast and furious. The boys love to hear our laughter and Aflike flits about with shining eyes, obviously listening intently.

After tea David went back to Chingali, having thanked us devoutly for his weekend. He goes off this week on ten days' local leave with an Oxford friend who came out this year. They are going to climb Mlanje, and will either have magnificent weather, or, far more likely, be engulfed in freezing mist – not my idea of local leave at all!

Yesterday I did a tremendous amount of work in the garden and read right through a biography of Ivor Novello which I started rather scornfully, but it turned out to be fascinating.

21st November:

The last few days have been appallingly hot and sultry, with very little sun and great masses of thunderclouds. For the first time out here I feel that the climate is beginning to debilitate me. I do not mind the dry heat of hot sunshine, but in this overcast heat sweat does not dry, so one does not get cool. Even the kittens are flopping about in tiny heaps and I move them about the floor like chequers on a board to find them a fresh cool patch!

Ron is out on *ulendo* this week and next week the camp will be ready. He has taken endless trouble to make the camp comfortable, and I cannot wait to see everything and perhaps add some feminine touches. There is masses of work he wants me to do for him and he is bursting with enthusiasm about the whole thing. The responsibility and initiative this new post has given him have quite suddenly matured him, young as he looks.

The garden is one mass of flowers, with really green terraces, and there is a small bamboo fence all round, which gives it a finish.

We are not going to the Lake at Christmas, alas. After the £70 car bill was paid, some months ago, I wrote to cancel our booking!

I have been reading Peter Fleming's *The Sixth Column* and enjoyed it. I also struggled through Arthur Koestler's *The Age of Longing*, which I loathed.

Joyce has taught me how to make flaky pastry, and we had steak and kidney pie on Saturday, which delighted Ron, even in this heat!

Chapter 15

28th November:

I am at Magomero! We came out on Monday morning in blazing sunshine, and from then on there has been not a cloud in the sky during the day. The heat is unbelievable. Never, not even on the journey up from Cape Town, have I known anything like it. The huts are aluminium, which is supposed to reflect back the rays of the sun. This is just not so. In fact it retains the heat. At 7 o'clock this morning, after breakfast, the walls were so hot I could hardly touch them. It is now 9.30 and it is like sitting in an oven. My body feels as if I were badly sunburnt – ablaze all over, yet wet and quite cold to the touch. We work in Ron's office, and keep dipping our wrists in a basin of water, which of course is tepid, and are surrounded by sheets of blotting paper to mop up the sweat. Until this week, Ron has been out in the field all day, so he did not realise what it would be like to sit inside, doing paper work, which we have been deep in since I came. I feel sick and squeamish till about 4.30, when a heavenly, heavenly breeze comes stealing in, and by 6.30, after a bath, I am restored! The nights are magnificent, cool and clear, the stars like cut crystal in the heavens. It is too hot to have the lamp in the hut, as the walls take several hours after dark to cool down, and because of the insect night life we cannot sit out with the lamp, so we set it outside on a tall stand and sit, one on each side of the doorway in the darkness, with our books held out to the light, which attracts millions and millions of insects of every shape and size, which dance themselves to death round the fascinating brightness that blooms like a fatal flower for them in the African night. Their frenzied movements are so swift they seem to draw solid lines against the light, creating marvellous, ever changing geometrical designs. Thousands and thousands of charred wings and bodies lie on the path by the time we cross to our bedroom hut; our feet moving through them make a sound like walking through autumn leaves. We endlessly pick them out of our hair and shake them from our clothes.

The bedroom hut has our two beds, a small chest of drawers and a table which we use as a washstand. There is just enough room for a zinc bath which is carried in night and morning, all the water for it and other purposes being brought by lorry in tins from a muddy river a quarter of a mile away. The day hut contains a table, a cupboard and four upright chairs, to which we have added our two canvas camp chairs which are cooler and more comfortable. The floors are beaten down earth. The kitchen and store are small grass huts and it is a desperate problem to keep food fresh and free of dust. On my very first evening, a tremendous din suddenly arose from the direction of the kitchen, sounding as if Aflike were demolishing his entire quarters. Before we could make a move, he was at our doorway, his eyes staring and his face mottled with blue-grey patches, his black skin's reaction to shock. He explained breathlessly that as he was pulling out a wooden box from a dimly lit corner, a big puff adder reared up at him from the shadows. What we had heard was him battering it to death. To calm him we had to go out and look at it, lying like a piece of thick rope thrown down in the pool of lamplight. Though it was quite dead, the body was still uncoiling itself in sinister slow motion – not exactly an auspicious introduction to the camp!

I have been reading Irwin Shaw's *The Young Lions* in the evenings and think it one of the best war books I have read, though it is very terrible in places.

I spent last week doing a lot of odds and ends in the house. I found I have lost so much weight I had to remake my Indian silk evening dress, which was quite a task, but it is done. It poured every day, so it was cool and fresh, but of course I have only to come out to Magomero and the sky becomes *flawless*!

28th November:

The kittens are simply beautiful now, still very small, but plump and fluffy, with Siamese dark ears and tails and pale fur, through which the inevitable tabby stripes are gradually appearing. They have the Siamese call, which is a startling sound coming from such tiny creatures.

On Sunday evening we were at a Gilbert and Sullivan record rectial with Iris at the Club. Suddenly all the lights fused, the sound ground to a halt and we had to creep away by the light of matches and Ronsons, to find one candle lighting a very jolly, impromptu party at the bar.

A messenger is taking this by bicycle to the nearest Post Office, ten miles away. He is standing outside the hut, coughing politely, to let me know he is waiting.

5th December:

You will be glad to know that my torment ended a few hours after I had written what must have been a miserable, stupified letter to you. In other words, the rains came and at last we were cool. They broke with the greatest storm I have ever seen. There was only rain till dusk, which was impressive enough, as it made a frightful noise on the aluminium roofs. Then came deafening thunder and the most spectacular lightning. It began round the horizon and gradually spread all over the sky, long, lingering flares illuminating enormous thunder-clouds, and sudden vicious stabs of electricity knifing down to the ground. Finally, it all turned into a quivering, pale violet light, as if the entire earth were kindling towards complete conflagration. As the storm got under way, I was having a bath when an awful thought struck me and I yelled above the noise to Ron, 'Is zinc a conductor?' and he yelled back, 'Yes, of course it is.' I was out in one leap! I flung on my clothes and went out to look. The night was ink black and at every wavering flash the landscape appeared as if projected on a vast screen. I shall never forget it.

Until we left on Friday afternoon there was an occasional shower of rain, which kept the heat at bay, and I walked round several villages with Ron, helping him with the census work. We have no interpreter here and our Chinyanja improves by leaps and bounds. We have great fun with the villagers, who are the nicest type of African, little in contact with and therefore little influenced by white people. Some of the older women have so many children, relatives and hangers-on in their hut they cannot recall all their names and are prompted by their friends amid gales of laughter. I saved up two names for you: a boy called Friday Smoke and a girl called Ulalia Gusto! A study of the names in the census would be interesting, as they must reflect all sorts of influences – former employers whose names were adopted or whose sense of humour be-stowed many an odd appellation on an unsuspecting African; names brought back from journeys to the more sophisticated south and from far places visited by soldiers of the KAR, besides all the old traditional tribal choices.

I did not realise I had not told you much about Magomero. It was a huge estate of thousands of acres bought by a Scot, by the name of Bruce, in the nineteen twenties, for a bale of calico, so legend has it. Last year he sold some of it to other settlers in the area and what was left after these private sales, 18,000 acres, the Government bought. Not surprisingly, Mr Bruce has retired to his native land! Over the years the Africans have put up their huts and culti-vated the land in a haphazard and destructive fashion. Ron's job is to resettle the entire population in the most practical and economic way, grouping huts so as not to disturb village life or waste good agricultural land for the crops. He will then supervise their cultivation, ensuring that the 'gardens' are planted in the proper way for maximum production. He also deals with the *dandaulas* (complaints) from the villagers and is responsible for maintaining good rela-tions with the British, Dutch and Italian settlers whose estates are scattered over Magomero. Public relations between Government and the private Euro-pean sector have always been a matter of some delicacy, so it is a real challenge.

At present Ron and his rangers are covering the entire area, taking a census of the population, which will amount to about 10,000 names, all of which I enter, with other details, on specially printed cards which will be indexed for reference. Ron worked out the system himself and it will be more comprehensive than any census carried out so far. There are also two borers from the Water Development Department moving about the land, drilling boreholes where new villages will settle. They work in co-operation with two young surveyors who have a tent permanently pitched near our huts. The whole scheme is very interesting and Ron is blissfully happy. He is pushing himself very hard, but this is inevitable in the initial stages.

We drove back on Friday through blinding rain and came home to a lovely clean house full of flowers, the garden lush with green grass and bright blossoms, and the kittens fat and more heavily striped! I rushed into the bath and lay down, head and all. My hair was sticky with sweat and I was covered in a tiny heat rash which has not developed into prickly heat as I feared it would. I have stayed at Naisi this week. The heat at Magomero gave me awful diarrhoea, which is very weakening, and I want to recover quickly and go out again with Ron.

David spent the weekend with us, back from local leave camping on Mlanje plateau, in glorious weather – hot, sunny days and cold, clear nights with the stars, he said, 'crackling' in the sky! He is looking marvellously well and not quite so thin. We went to the Club on Sunday evening to see *Les Enfants du Paradis,*which we counted as a celebration for Ron's birthday. On a fourth viewing it still yielded new delights.

Ron came in on Wednesday, as we were invited to a cocktail party by the Simmonds', the new Financial Secretary and his wife, whom we met at GH and took to at once. It was a most enjoyable evening with a good mixture of people. Ron got up at 5.30 next morning to be off to Magomero, and I got up later and worked hard in the garden. It gets out of control so quickly in the rains.

We were thrilled to see my article on Aflike in print; and seven guineas is riches to me. God bless the *Glasgow Herald*!

13th December:

This has been a perfect week for me – and for Ron. On Monday morning he had a slight temperature and felt a weight on his chest, and while I completed the *ulendo* packing, he drove up to the hospital to see the doctor, who told him he must not go out to Magomero this week, as he has a bad chill on his chest. So he came home and with no fuss went to bed (which shows how unwell he felt), where he has stayed ever since, except to get up every morning (with a temperature and his chill) and drive up to the hospital in the treacherous early morning air to report to the doctor, who only visits patients who are 'really ill'! I wonder what Daddy thinks of *that*! I installed myself in the bedroom and produced all the letters which have accumulated unanswered, and we settled down to an orgy of Christmas mail, Ron writing to people who have not heard from him since he came out here! I also got some good library books so that we could have nice long evenings reading. Ron badly needed the rest – he *will* work himself to a standstill. He looks better today and is up, poking the typewriter with two fingers. We are so happy just being together and having time to enjoy relaxing in comfort. Iris called in yesterday and declared Ron a complete fraud, he looked so well. He will be ready to go to Magomero next week.

~~We have two little trees on one of the terraces which I have been cherishing~~ hopefully, and to my delight they are apple trees and are at present producing lovely delicate blossom. The scent comes into our bedroom at night. My carnations are magnificent – pink, yellow and crimson, and there are four shades of red on the hollyhocks. The lupins, very splendid, are all blue, which is not what the packet promised! There is also a thick border of gypsophila, which is most useful as a decoration with other flowers.

19th December:

I am full of plans for making things next tour, and mean to bring out rug-making kits and tapestry for a stool and a fire screen. How astonishing that I should ever think of such things!

We had such a happy time last week. I made Ron stay in bed till Sunday, as David was coming for the weekend and I knew Ron would overdo things. His blood test and X-ray are both negative, thank God. He got up on Sunday, full of beans, and we had a lovely day, with a morning visit to Dave and Iris, a quick dash up my magic mountain in the afternoon for a peaceful walk by the dam, and bridge in the evening with the Gourlays. Poor David is always reluctant to leave.

On Monday, out we came to Magomero and celebrated our anniversary all on our own. I had packed pretty candles and some exotic surprises for dinner, and Aflike produced a delicious meal. There has been a lot of rain and great masses of clouds, so we have been comfortably cool, though maddened by thousands of disgusting flies. The area is highly populated and it is impossible to get far enough away from the villages to escape them. However, I came armed with my Flitgun this week and have made headway. Aflike sweeps them up in heaps, as he does the millions of wings and bodies around the lampstand at the end of each evening.

Yesterday we had a most exciting event. John Grenfell-Williams paid us a flying visit. He is Overseas Director of the BBC and a good friend of Tom's [Ron's guardian]. In fact it was he who first gave Ron the idea of applying for the Colonial Service and later he was one of his sponsors. He is in Nyasaland for three days, arranging the setting up of a radio station in Zomba. On his way back to Blantyre yesterday, he called in for tea, having learned from the Public Relations Officer who was driving him around that Ron was camping only a short distance from the main road. He leaves today by plane and will be in London on Saturday. We were terribly pleased that with such a crowded schedule he found time to call on us. The PR man who brought him is a very pleasant

South African whom we know well and like very much, so we all had a happy teatime together in our wretched hut. Grenfell-Williams was obviously very interested to see Ron again and to meet me. He said Tom was doing exciting work in Nigeria, where he is responsible for setting up a network of radio stations.

27th December:

Next time I write to you it will be 1952, the year of our first home leave. Can you believe it?

We came to Magomero this morning, bringing a whole stack of mail which had accumulated at the Boma over Christmas. The weather has been dreadful and the roads today are appalling. We have hardly seen the sun since before Christmas and the days are damp, clammy and always wet by evening. All the bedding and our clothes smell musty and mould is appearing on shoes and books. However, we have had a very pleasant Christmas. We came into Zomba from a week of hard work and on Saturday morning completed our Christmas shopping. David arrived after lunch, having had a hair-raising drive from Chingali. If the car had stuck I think he would have walked! We were supposed to go to a concert at the Police Camp, taking Iris, but the rain was so torrential we stayed at home and listened to some great Christmas music on the wireless. On Sunday David spent the morning out visiting and I made sausage rolls and mince pies. I work on the diningroom table – the kitchen is still the sole domain of Aflike and Willard. They are responsible for the oven. My pastry is as light as air now.

There was a carol concert at the Club on Christmas Eve. The choir was formally dressed, the men in dinner jackets and the women in white blouses and long black skirts. The singing was beautiful. Eveyone stayed on for a drink afterwards and we met lots of people. It all felt much less strange than last year though homesickness was never far away! David was thrilled with his evening.

After a large breakfast on Christmas morning we had a happy session of present opening. We are delighted with the Penguins, which are our mainstay on *ulendo*. Aunt Kathie sent me Christopher Fry's *A Sleep of Prisoners* and Elspeth sent me Charles Morgan's *A Breeze at Morning*. We are also delighted with the big jigsaw and in the afternoon we three sat on the floor working at it. At noon we walked round to Dave and Iris and found a very lively drinks party in full swing. The heavens opened savagely just after we arrived and we had to shout above the noise of the thunder. We were given a lift home through crashing rain. We listened to a very atmospheric relay of the king's speech, but it was worth it just to hear his voice. When he gave the special message to those far from home I said in a shaky voice, 'That means *us*,' and we all had to blow our noses! Later we bathed and dressed and went up to dine with the Gourlays, who had also asked Dave and Iris. Joyce's table looked lovely, with red candles in tall ebony candlesticks, and red crackers. We took them a bottle of cognac and a box of petits fours, both of which were offered with the coffee. Joyce borrowed Aflike for the evening and it was he who carried in the blue-flaming plum pudding, his eyes, glistening with pleasure, turning to me, sharing the moment. A little before midnight Ron, David and I braved Naisi Road at its worst and slid, skidded and squelched our way down to the Club to join the dance for an hour. We spent Boxing Day quietly, all reading our new books. This morning David returned to Chingali and we came out here.

2nd January 1952:

We had a very damp, bleak, muggy five days at Magomero and were glad to get back to the comforts of the house on Saturday. We went to the Club in the evening, mainly to see and speak to people! The film was ridiculous – *Mark of the Gorilla*, which made everyone laugh as it was supposed to be set in Africa and the place was simply teeming with tigers! We sat next to John and Dorothy and we all got the giggles when the DC in the film solved everyone's problems in cavalier fashion. Sardonic laughter among the audience made people turn round and smile affectionately at dear John, who sat pulling at his moustache. The Film Society on Sunday evening showed the Marx Brothers in *A Night at the Opera* – sublime! Never have I heard such laughter in Zomba cinema. Everyone emerged in a good mood and we stayed on for a drink. Several people came up to ask us how we are getting on at Magomero, and not one failed to exclaim at how brown and thin we both are!

Next day David arrived in great form at teatime, thankful to be sharing New Year's Eve with us, We bathed, donned evening dress and had a very formal dinner, discreetly presided over by Aflike. He was trained to stand in the diningroom right through every meal, but Ron and I do not want that when we are alone. However, Aflike made it subtly plain to me that he should be present when we have guests, so I gave in! We went on to Iris and Dave for coffee and liqueurs and then we all went to the Ball, one of the most wonderful dances I have been to in Zomba, as all the men dance beautifully. We had two good eightsomes and a strip-the-willow. It ended at 3.30 and we were quite reluctant to go home. Today I have been sewing and yawning most of the time!

9th January:

I do not have your letter to answer this week, as we are at Magomero, in fearful weather. We came out here on Monday and it has poured, teemed, lashed and hammered with rain ever since, with colossal thunderstorms smashing overhead for hours on end, particularly at night, when we have to shout at each other – very headache making. Last night, for the first time, Ron was actually scared by the lightning, it was so near and so violent. I never am, because I accept Africa and all its phenomena as completely alien and leave it at that! We really are longing for the weather to improve. Everything is damp and mouldy and smells so. Neither our clothes nor bedding ever feel dry.

I am reading Churchill's *The Gathering Storm* and am utterly engrossed by it.

We did not come out here till after lunch on Monday, and I walked round to Iris in the morning, ostensibly to show her how to cut out a dress pattern, but as usual we had so much to talk about that very little was done, and when Ron called in for me at noon he found us sitting on the floor among pins, material and pattern, each flourishing a pair of scissors, in animated conversation!

16th January:

I have stayed at Naisi this week. Every now and then I come to the end of my tether over *ulendo*. We had dreadful days of cold and damp last week and the only thing which kept us going was that we had an immense amount of paper work to do and also, at night, with the lamp between us and the door closed, the hut felt quite cosy and warm.

I am reading Nevil Shute's *Round the Bend*. He is a very enjoyable story-teller. We came back from Magomero on Friday night to find the garden heavy with flowers and the house smelling of polish. There was the usual rush to bath and hair wash and the thankful sinking into early bed with our books, feeling deliciously clean. The weather cleared on Saturday morning and has been beautiful since, with sunshine, fleecy clouds and in the early evening a great storm of rain, which clears in an hour and leaves everything sweet, warm and steamy.

After lunch on Sunday Mike and Joan Saunders turned up, back from leave. It was delightful to see them again and I was thankful to hand over their cat, safe and sound but again heavily pregnant. We also, alas, had to part with the wireless, a dreadful blow.

23rd January:

We are at Magomero. You ask when the rains stop, and the answer is in late March, early April, and then, incredibly, we are into our third cold season, and I wonder how we shall fare, living in huts in the middle of nowhere on this vast, exposed plain.

We have Willard with us, as Aflike had to stay in Zomba to visit the dentist. On Sunday he came to me in desperation, asking for 'tooth *mankwala*' (medicine), which usually means toothpaste, as 'shoe *mankwala*' means shoe polish. As he does not use toothpaste, I was baffled, until he suddenly threw back his head and showed me a decayed molar in a mouth of otherwise perfect teeth. So I doped him with codeine for the day and sent him to the African hospital on Monday. It transpires that he has had toothache on and off for the past two years, which I now think explains his thinness and moods of deep melancholy. This has upset me very much – poor Aflike, such a stoic.

Here at Magomero the weather varies between intense heat and heavy rain, but I am getting used to it and I no longer feel ill – wonderful. I walked with Ron about eight miles yesterday and today, and at last have some colour again. My face had become quite pale, there has been so little sun; and one gets no exercise when the rain is so interminable. We are working on a plan for the house. Eventually there will also be a post office and a dispensary; quite a little settlement!

30th January:

I have never had – and I hope I never have again – such a strange birthday. Ron went off to Magomero on Monday morning and I have spoken to no one since and it is most unlikely that I shall until his return on Saturday. Iris is in hospital all week, having treatment for her wretched inside, and the Gourlays moved last weekend to a house in Zomba. There is no one now in Naisi whom I know or want to know. To make matters worse, there is something wrong with the mails just now and we have had no sea mail, i.e. newspapers, for a fortnight. I am spending the week reading and sewing – talk about make-do-and-mend – my undies are a work of art, positively filigree!

The rains continue unabated, with very little sunshine, but in the dry, bright moments the air is full of swallows gathering, soon to leave for Europe, lucky things. There is a rather unpleasant South African camping beside us at Magomero this week, helping Ron with some tobacco work. I am afraid I just could not face the prospect of having to be hospitable in the evenings. This is *very bad*, but Ron understands. They will pass the time talking endless shop, their only means of communication! The weather is strange and erratic. Last night it gave me the only fright I have had – having boasted to you quite recently that I am never scared of storms! There had been a thunderstorm clattering around for about two hours, which I had ceased to notice, and suddenly there was an increase of light in the curtained livingroom, brighter than the electric light, and I looked up from my book and realised it was lightning, quivering *in the room*. At the same moment the thunder gave an ear-splitting crack directly overhead and my heart seemed to stop for about five seconds as I awaited extinction. My head ached till bedtime. David had a strange experience with lightning at Lilongwe. He and the DC had desks on either side of the office, which had open French windows at each end. One afternoon, with no storm and no warning, a flash of lightning came in at one doorway, streaked horizontally through the office and went out at the other door, passing between the desks, not harming either of them. They sat glued to their chairs in a state of shock, unable to believe what had happened.

On Saturday morning we called in at the office of the Zomba architect and got his advice on our house plan. He said it was too complicated and modified it in helpful ways. I have an absolute obsession, from bitter experience, with providing adequate storage space and this was what had to be slightly curtailed. He is having a very detailed plan made for us. If we get our leave in August, as scheduled, we shall not see the completion of the house, but I do not care two hoots about that!

Ron got a letter from Tom in Nigeria, who had heard from Grenfell-Williams about his visit to Magomero. Tom quoted bits, which make good reading. 'He is highly thought of by the people at the top . . . that is why he was chosen for this ticklish job . . . Yes, Ron is making the grade all right, and with distinction.' We are thrilled. (From somewhere very deep inside me came the fleeting thought that it would have been nice if he had mentioned Ron's wife – but it was very fleeting and of course I said nothing.)

I have read, in one day, *The Dam Busters* – very exciting.

6th February:

Ron came bounding in on Saturday and I broke my week-long silence with some relief. We watched a good rugger match in the afternoon and at night went to the Club to see the film of Somerset Maugham's *Trio*, which was excellent. On Sunday we read and talked all day and in the early evening Dave and Iris called round unexpectedly for a drink. They had come to break the news that they have been posted to Fort Manning, about one hundred and fifty miles north, and they go off on 28th February. Iris and I can hardly bear to speak of it. We really have become close friends and I shall miss her terribly. On Sunday evening we went to the Film Society to see *Bicycle Thieves*, an outstanding Italian film. As we were coming out, I overheard one of the young Secretariat stenographers, a Scot, saying to her friends in her refined Kelvinside accent, 'Aye do dislayke foreign films – all those men in vests end the women in shebby bleck dresses'!

Ron stayed in overnight on Monday. He had a lot of business to do, and John and Dorothy were giving, for the second time, a farewell party that evening and were most insistent that we should be there. I cannot tell you how much that extra day, added to our usual brief two days in Zomba, meant to us. It was wonderful. This continual dashing to and fro from Magomero is so restless and uncomfortable, though thank God we are allowed to do it. We had tea at the Club, where I got four library books and talked to lots of people – in fact I spent the three days talking my head off! The Watsons' party was terrific because we were both in the mood to be sociable and people gave us a great welcome, as if they had not seen us for ages, as was so in several cases.

The rains are supposedly on their last lap, and it is a very long-drawn-out, violent one. Today was the first fine day for over a week and is a promise of things to come – warm sun, but positively cold indoors. Soon I shall be reorganising the garden.

15th February:

You would realise from my last letter that I had not yet heard of the King's death. Ron told me on Saturday morning. He got the news from a planter who called in at the Magomero office to say he had just heard it on his car radio. What a terrible thing for the royal family, especially Elizabeth. At the cinema, the national anthem was played at the end of the evening, as usual, and we stood looking at the blank screen instead of the customary coloured photo of the King. We all felt rather desolate.

We are having terrible weather. It began to rain yesterday about five in the afternoon, not lightly as often happens, but heavy, deafening rain, and now, at nine in the evening, it still comes down. Last night I could not sleep for the noise of water flowing down the *road*! All the garden terraces are under water with only the tall flowers' heads showing. The waterfalls down Zomba mountain are enormous and fill the air with a roaring sound. It is rather exhilarating, but in the black night not much fun, as the noise becomes alarming. On these occasions I always wish it were Aflike, and not Willard, who is sleeping in his hut nearby. The boys tell the time (to within a few minutes) by the sun, which has been invisible for three days, and this morning I found I was having my bath at 5.30. Willard simply had no idea, and just turned up when it got light, lit the fire and brought in my tea.

On Saturday afternoon we watched a rugger match between Zomba and Limbe, and at last met Laga Dushmanitch, now Carlyle. Her husband Clement was in the Limbe team and before the match asked someone in the Club if we were there, and so we were introduced. We sat all afternoon with Laga, who is delightful. She is tall, thin and dark and was wearing a scarlet linen dress and a white wool jacket which she had embroidered in brilliant colours in the Serbian style – exactly like Aunt Kathie's ancient brown one! It was uncanny – we just felt a mutual, deep affection at once! Con [her mother, a great friend of Aunt Kathie's: see Chapter 1] is up from Rhodesia visiting them, so we shall meet again after all those years. I asked Laga if Con still wore a monocle, and she said no, amazed that I should remember! Ron is going to ask for a day off next week and we shall go first to Blantyre, as the car needs attention, and go on to the Carlyles for lunch. I shall write and tell Aunt Kathie about it in due course. What a marvellous thing to happen! We could not wait on after the match, as we were dining with Kenneth and Ruth Simmonds. We saw a dreadful film called *Tokyo Joe*, during which my host slept soundly beside me, thereby cutting me off from cigarettes. We had a very good dinner, with wine flowing. They are the greatest fun.

I enjoyed, with reservations, Richard Aldington's biography of T.E. Lawrence, *Portrait of a Genius, But . . .* I do not approve of debunking when the man is not alive to defend himself, but I doubt if Lawrence would have cared. Now I am rereading *For Whom the Bell Tolls*: wonderful writing.

24th February:

I have a truly epic cold, and feel hot and vague, my head too big and heavy to concentrate properly. *Everyone* has a cold, because of the dampness and sudden drops in temperature. The rains continue furiously and everything looks over-grown and sodden.

Last Friday, the day of the King's funeral, Ron did not come in from Magomero, and David's car got bogged down on the way in from Chingali, so he was too late to attend the service. I was at Naisi, and he called in on the chance that I would be there. He arrived about eleven and stayed happily till teatime. He horrified me by saying quite casually that he had heard that Ron was to be asked to extend his tour. You can imagine what that did to the rest of my day – and night. Ron and I had already discussed this possibility and come to the decision that I should go on leave in August, as planned, whatever happened, but of course I now began to back-track at the thought of our separation and question if it was the right thing to do. Ron came in on Saturday morning and put me out of my misery. His leave has been postponed till November, which I think he was expecting. To cut a long story short, I shall go home in August. From September, Ron has to be out at Magomero all the time, supervising the building of the house, which will mean giving up this house and doing three months' camping, the very thought of which produced the most astonishing flood of tears from me, in an agony of indecision – 'If you can do it for three months, so can I . . . etc.' – but Ron was adamant and after some anguished argument I calmed down and agreed. It was such a relief to have it all cleared up so quickly. Ron is remarkably philosophical about it, but then he loves his work and wants to see the house finished. My reaction shook us both, as that is not at all how I usually deal with a crisis! Perhaps I am run down.

Our day off on Monday was wet and cold, except at dawn, when the sky was very beautiful. We set off early, left the car in the garage in Blantyre, and went to Ryall's for coffee, after which we did some dull but necessary shopping, and *then* I bought red wool for a twinset and wistfully tried on a very good, pencil-slim (like me!) skirt in a fine navy and grey check tweed. Ron said recklessly, 'We'll have that.' I think he wanted to cheer us both up! I persuaded him in turn to buy a very smart pair of much needed ankle boots for himself. So, broke but happy, we took a taxi about 11.30 to Limbe and found Laga's house. Con was sitting on the floor arranging flowers in a vase. The instant I saw and heard her I got a lump in my throat. She is so Scots, so genuine, so warm, reminding me of you, Aunt Kathie and all the friends of that marvellous generation. She looks frail and old, but her eyes are young and glowing. I just sank down on the floor beside her and we talked, oblivious of the others, till lunch. It was all most enjoyable, but Con carried the day. We stayed till five, when we had to tear ourselves away. I crept to bed when we got home, as my cold was just beginning and I felt dreadful – reaction to too much emotion one way and another, I reckon.

The *Glasgow Herald* Christmas Quiz, tucked into the *Observer*, arrived today and I am really taken aback at my ignorance. Were you?!

26th February:

I am at Magomero this week. My cold developed in its usual dreary fashion and was at its worst the day I wrote to you, but I did not go to bed, as I would have felt worse there, with Ron away. However, when he came in on Saturday morning he insisted that I go to bed, although the worst was over, so I did. He brought in a comfortable chair and books, and we stayed like that all weekend, quite happy and content. On Sunday morning Iris and Dave walked round for a last visit, and joined us in the bedroom for a farewell drink. After they had gone, we were rather depressed and the steady downpour of rain did not help. However, when we woke on Monday there was not a cloud in the sky – miraculous. So I leapt up, packed my case in a few minutes and we had a cheerful breakfast. We left Aflike in charge, to clean, polish and air the entire house and supervise the garden boys, and off we went with Willard, and are having a very pleasant time, with no rain for three days. The nights and mornings are really cold and there is an indefinable feel of the cold season in the air. At night the stars fairly snap in the sky. I think their light is more exciting than moonshine. We sit outside, well wrapped up, before dinner, as the insects have vanished with the cooler weather, praise be.

5th March:

I am at Magomero. It is deliciously fresh, almost cold, and the heat haze has completely gone. A wonderful landscape is revealed in bright sunshine today – cloud shadows racing over vivid green marshland, with blue pools and patches of golden maize rippling like giant corn in the steady wind. I have just counted twenty-eight mountains round the horizon. Yesterday we walked in a fine rain to look at a possible site for the house and it felt exactly like a wet day in the Highlands.

Ron is working on the plans for the house, sitting for hours beside me with his nose a few inches from the paper. His maths training is useful now and the plans are beautiful, drawn on graph paper with all the angles accurate and everything done to scale. I shall make a copy for you. I think it is extraordinary that Ron should be asked to build the house himself, but he is enthusiastic and has worked out all the costs of brick-making, timber, fencing and so on.

We had a very pleasant weekend last week. Alan and Joyce Dickinson, whom we met in London at the Chinyanja classes, have been posted to Zomba from the Central Province and are living in Dave and Iris's Naisi house. They asked us round for drinks on Saturday evening. It was fun to see them again. They are our age group and we miss young people. The Sunday Film Society was *The Search*, one of the best and most moving films I have seen – an American production filmed in Europe, telling the story of a mother's search for her lost son through the UNRRA children's camps in post-war Europe.

I have been writing in rather a rush, as one of the surveyors camping here is going to Blantyre and is waiting for me to give him this to post.

13th March:

I am at Magomero. The cold season has set in and the weather is at its best. I can walk for miles in this climate and have been out with Ron looking for a site for the house. We travel some distance on the back of an open lorry, enjoying a wonderful view and lots of sun and wind, and then we descend and plunge into the bush, which has an intricate network of paths worn by the Africans walking between villages. The grass is so tall at this time of year that it is well over my head and I get cross when Ron stops, stands on his toes, points with his stick and says, 'Over there would be great – just look at that view', when all I can see is brown stalks and the sky! The views are breathtakingly splendid. The best way to describe them to you is: take Glen Coe, pull all the mountains back so that there is an enormous expanse of flattish land, then raise the mountains by thousands of feet and throw in about twenty more!

On Sunday morning we walked round to the Dickinsons and were persuaded to join them on the golf course in the afternoon. It was a lovely day and I enjoyed walking along while the others played bad golf. It is an attractive course, with some lovely tall blue gums smelling of lemon and lots of smaller trees by a burn. We had a late tea in the Club and then home to bath and supper. Alan and Joyce have an excellent selection of books and have kindly offered us the freedom of their shelves. I have started with Karsavina's *Theatre Street* – lovely. The Dickinsons are quite stunned by Zomba's social life, having come from Kota Kota, a much smaller station by the Lake. Eve and Humphrey, always on the lookout for new young faces, grabbed them on their first week-end, gave a dinner party for them, with the Bingham abundance of good food and drink, and then swept them off to the cinema, where Alan, worn out, fell asleep! Joyce has made quite an impression on Zomba, with her white, translucent skin, short black hair and slanting green eyes in a pointed face.

19th March:

I am at Magomero. It is 9.20 a.m. and we have had a bath, breakfast, a four mile walk and rather early elevenses! It is a glorious day and my face is glowing with the wind and sun. This is the best kind of weather out here and of course similar to what we experienced when we arrived, which gives an extra touch of magic – nostalgia *already*! We are reminded of the marvellous shimmering mornings of Kasupi days. Every night now we get the classic African sunset. Down goes the sun in a blood-red sky which gradually turns to orange, to green, to lemon, with the mountains changing from purple to black silhouettes. This pale, luminous afterglow lasts for some minutes and then there is the sudden extinction of light, a leap into darkness which never fails to give me a frisson of excitement, a mixture of elation and fear. The nights are cold and the mornings shivery. We get very hungry!

Our weekend started badly as we had a puncture two miles from home on Saturday morning. However, Ron and Aflike between them changed the tyre in no time, while I sat by a cool, noisy waterfall and had a moment to see how beautiful Naisi is, apart from the awful road. David was in Zomba on business and called in for tea, much more like his old self, and we had our usual fun. In the evening Alan and Joyce came for supper and bridge. On Sunday we gave a drinks party at noon, I think perhaps our last. Kenneth and Ruth Simmonds, my favourite people, had to call off at the last moment, as they received a late invitation to lunch at GH with an unexpected VIP guest. Kenneth said in his note they would have loved to come and have a 'quickie' with us first, but he did not dare risk his big car getting bogged down on the notorious Naisi road. The party was such a success we had difficulty in bringing it to a close! Away from our somewhat stark life in the wilderness, we find we tire quite quickly in 'society'. Also, we both now find some difficulty with social conversation. This is bad and shows how isolated we have become at Magomero.

1st April:

I have just made an April fool of Ron! I ran into the office and told him there was a small black snake (i.e. a viper) in the bedroom hut. He took his walking stick and strode manfully away, calling for Aflike. I heard them banging about looking for it in vain and then they came out and saw the grin on my face! I had some difficulty in explaining the point to Aflike but he got there and shook with laughter, and is now going happily about his work, shaking his head and chuckling. He must think we are mad, to joke about snakes, which he hates and fears as much as I do, and is quite cunning at leaving their slaughter to someone else, usually me! Ron is now trying desperately to catch me out, but is being too obvious to succeed!

I shall soon be able to tell you my sailing date. I sail from Beira. This means only one night on the train and five weeks on the ship, which makes its leisurely way down the east coast, calling at Lorenço Marques, Durban, Port Elizabeth, East London and Cape Town. I must confess my thoughts occasionally stray in that direction and I begin to feel the first slight withdrawal from the African scene. This I do not speak of, as any mention of it brings a cloud to Ron's face and an answering tremor in my heart. Aflike has been very upset by the news of my departure. His eyes fill with tears every time our eyes meet. Oh damn, why is life so complicated?

We had a blissfully quiet weekend, as we were both very tired. On Sunday, Alan, Joyce and David, who was staying with them, walked round for tea. It felt strange to watch David walk away with them, but of course he knew them in London too.

9th April:

Ron is sitting beside me, his shirt dark with sweat. I have my hair piled up on the top of my head for coolness. The temptation is to cut it all off but I know I shall be glad of its warmth round my neck in the cold. Magomero this week has been exasperatingly hot for the last three days, as hot as at the height of the hot season, but I will not take up space and energy describing it – my first appalled reaction was enough, I am sure! We have been concentrating on paper work, which has been mounting, and doing no walking at all.

Another, very small, grass hut has been added to the camp. Aflike has built himself his own private mosque, into which he retreats at sunset, and we faintly hear the wailing chant of his prayers from our huts. He is enjoying considerable prestige among the local people, and as time goes on he is acquiring the status of a kind of unofficial liaison officer between Ron and the Africans, revealing a truly subtle sense of loyalty to both. He and Ron never gossip, nor does Ron question him, but occasionally he lingers over his work and makes a remark which indicates to Ron which way the wind is blowing in the villages.

We had a delightful weekend, driving back to Zomba in the cool of early morning, through a landscape as beautiful as paradise – blue mountains, dazzling white clouds like great ships at anchor in the sky, golden miles of swaying maize and green hillsides neatly terraced with tea and tobacco. We were so early the women were still walking to market, with their babies on their backs and tall baskets full of produce balanced on their heads. They carry everything that way, and I saw hoes, a plate with three maize cobs and a bunch of bananas. We had shopping and a lot of business to do in Zomba, and ended up at the Club for a drink and biscuits and cheese lunch. I browsed through the latest papers while Ron stayed in the bar, talking shop. Then I put the papers back on the table, went through with my drink and firmly joined in the conversation, leading it away to other subjects, which I am known for and teased about!

We had a very civilised Saturday evening. We went to dine with Bernard and Mary Kayes, settlers of long standing whom I have mentioned to you. They have a lovely bungalow on the plain below Zomba. I presented Mary with forty-three carnations from the garden, and she was so thrilled she rushed away and redid the flower arrangements for the table. Apparently carnations should not be in bloom just now! Alan and Joyce were the only other couple, so it was very relaxed. We sat on sofas on their wide *khonde*, looking between pillars onto the terraced garden, down to the swimming pool and out over the great plain, milky white in the moonlight. On the horizon, to the right, Mlanje loomed dimly, to the left our lovely Zomba mountain, with the lights from the high houses on Naisi twinkling faintly. We went in to an excellent dinner with delicious wines, and then coffee and liqueurs on the *khonde*, where we enjoyed music and conversation till 1.30, without noticing the time. We listened to Schumann's piano concerto, Mendelssohn's *A Midsummer Night's Dream* and some Bach. There was a party of a very different kind going on in a nearby village and between records we heard African laughter and chanting, and the beating of the drums – an extraordinary contrast. As we were leaving, the finishing touch to the evening was provided by a hyaena, invisible but very near in the garden, uttering its weird, choking bark. We all confessed the sound always made the hairs stand up on our bodies.

We had a wonderful lazy day on Sunday, too hot to do anything energetic. I went through weeks of home papers and added over a dozen books to my reading list. After a cold supper we went down to the Club to hear Zomba choir singing excerpts from *The Messiah*. It was quite an occasion, with the Governor and his party in evening dress, including the Bishop of Nyasaland in long purple robes and shorn hair. Mary Kayes had lent her beautiful grand piano for the evening, and the singing of the thirty-five members of the choir was excellent. The solos are really too taxing for amateurs, but were bravely tackled.

We return to Zomba on Thursday and do not come out here again till Tuesday morning – the longest time at home for months. David has invited us to spend Monday with him at Chingali. He wants me to see it before I go but it will depend on the weather. He has probably organised a picnic halfway up the mountain, if I know him! He does not realise – no one does – that we do so much travelling by car and on foot, and see so much of the country, that when we do get a chance to stay put we are not interested in picnics, walks, climbs or drives. These activities are part of our everyday lives and we sometimes *long* to escape them!

17th April:

The weather has settled down into 'winter', so our life at Magomero is an active one.

We had a very quiet Easter weekend. On Thursday evening we saw Gloria Swanson in *Sunset Boulevard*, a great performance. On Friday afternoon we were in the middle of a round of golf when we were caught in a sudden thunderstorm. Fortunately, we were just by the fourth green, which is across the road from The Pig and Whistle, so we dashed in there to shelter and have a cold drink. The place was rowdy with bachelors in from the bush for the holiday, and we did not linger. The atmosphere was positively Somerset Maugham-ish! Monday was dreary and cold and we stayed in all day: neither of us could face the prospect of Chingali. I read the whole of a marvellous book – *Venture into the Interior*, by Laurens Van Der Post. It is the story of his travels in Nyasaland when he undertook a survey of Mlanje and the Nyika plateau in the north, which was disrupted by tragedy. It has had a mixed reception here, and I can see why. He was given every possible assistance and hospitality, and some of his observations on people and colonial life are not exactly tactful. However, he is a bit of a mystic and I love his descriptive writing.

23rd April:

All is chaos around me! We are moving camp and pandemonium reigns. Our choice of site was finally decided for us when water was divined about two miles from this camp, on a site we were considering. It is higher up, with a glorious view, much superior to the one from here. We shall camp in a tent while cement is put down on the floors of the huts – Ron will be thankful to have his precious safe set into the bedroom hut floor! They are also putting grass on the roofs in a hopeful gesture towards keeping the huts cooler. I am in the only hut left standing! The bedroom and office ones are being dismantled at this moment and the noise is shattering. Ron is charging about, supervising the unscrewing of the bolts. In all, one hundred and eight sheets of aluminium will be undone and set up again on the new site today. Ron is determined the work will be completed by nightfall so that the cement laying can begin tomorrow. The place is swarming with Africans, all working very noisily but with a will. I can hear Ron's voice raised in mock anger and bursts of answering laughter. He is incredibly good tempered with them and of course it pays off.

We saw a good film at the weekend – *Chrome Yellow*, with Trevor Howard and Jean Simmons.

On Sunday Ron was playing cricket all day, and I was joined in the Club in the afternoon by David, who was staying with his former DC, who is now in the Secretariat. David has been in hospital with a frightfully poisoned foot which caused swelling right up to the top of his leg. He has had massive doses of penicillin and looks tired and run down – I suspect we do too.

Ron has just come in to take me to the new site.

1st May:

You will be glad to know our new camp was set up by sunset on the day I wrote to you. The men built a large stockade round the bedroom and day huts, so we have more privacy. There is a tremendous stretch of flat ground all round, which has been completely cleared of bush, and we are exposed to every wind that blows! At night we sit huddled by our 'brazier', which Aflike made by piercing holes in an old petrol tin and burning charcoal in it. In the small, coldest hours, the hut panels contract with loud, ringing bangs and we are jolted into wakefulness. Even during the day the air is cold indoors and I keep warm by leaning my back against the wall panels, which heat up in the sun.

Aflike has had a little grass summer house built for me at one corner of the stockade. Yesterday, just before tea, he came in and proudly announced it was finished. I went out to have a look, in a strong cold wind, and he immediately whipped out my chair, book and knitting and placed them firmly in the shelter. The men who had made it stood at a distance, laughing with pleasure that I should use it so soon, so for their sakes I sat there shivering for half an hour, gradually turning a darker brown as the fine dust blowing on the wind settled over me!

On Saturday morning we went back to Zomba and found everyone in woollies and tweed jackets. David arrived at teatime, obviously very happy to be with us again, and in the evening we went to see James Stewart in *Harvey*, a strange, funny-sad film about a man whose companion is an invisible white rabbit over six feet tall. On Sunday Ron was again playing cricket and I went down with him. David had to go back to Chingali, as he had work to do. We stayed for lunch at the Club – twenty-two men and me! We got home in time to bath, change, have dinner and get back to the Club to see the Film Society film, *The Yearling*, a very sentimental but pleasant film.

On Monday we came out to the camp and found the driller for the well had arrived, with a tall edifice about twenty feet high, which screeched deafeningly as it pounded and bored its way down through layers of rock and soil. His wife, ensconced in a caravan nearby, came out to introduce herself – a vision of young South African womanhood: neatly waved hair, heavy make-up, a tight, sleeveless dress and white high-heeled shoes with ankle straps. I doubtless presented to her eyes an equally representative vision of young British womanhood. I had on sandals, a sun-faded navy dirndl skirt and one of Elspeth's old Wren shirts, and my long straight hair was tied back with a blue scarf. We exchanged brief civilities, then politely went separate ways with mutual relief.

We left after lunch for a two day *ulendo*, thankful to escape from the noise. We drove about eight miles by car, then changed to our lorry for two miles over a dreadful road, and then walked three miles to our camp. The villagers had never seen a tent before and were wildly excited, so there was little privacy. Next day we did some walking, passing through sunflower gardens, great long fields of huge yellow flowers, taller than Ron, the blooms the size of a tea plate, with a marvellous heady scent. I felt like Alice in Wonderland among them. I got a nasty deep scratch on my foot from a thorn bush, fittingly called a 'wait-a-bit', which grows low on the ground and catches at one's feet. The scratch turned septic overnight, but I am dealing successfully with it, once again blessing Daddy for his 'magic ointment'! We packed up after lunch yesterday, walked in the hot afternoon to the lorry, drove to the car and on the way home stopped to have tea with a very nice Dutch planter (I cannot attempt to spell his name) who has called on us several times at Magomero. We met his wife and very old parents, who hardly spoke any English – it was a breath of Holland in the heart of Africa. The family has been in the seed trade for generations. We drove back in the dark and Aflike had the bath in the tent and hot water ready to pour. We actually had a 'glad to be home' feeling – everything is so relative!

8th May:

We came out here on Monday to find the well *in situ* and working – a turn of the big handle produces a most satisfactory gush of water. Ron had to put a guard there for the first few days, as the children from the surrounding villages came thronging round to see the new wonder, eager to swing on the handle and splash in the water so miraculously produced by the white man's magic. They uttered such piercing shrieks of excitement I kept rushing out, expecting to find some dreadful scene of disaster.

We had a very pleasant weekend, as usual. The News at the cinema included the Boat Race, which caused great excitement and partisan comments all round us. On Sunday we watched excellent cricket all day and in the evening attended a gramophone recital at the Club – a Mozart piano concerto, Beethoven's 7th Symphony and the Brahm's Variations on a Theme of Haydn – all lovely.

On Wednesday we had a visit from Ren Smith, who did the Oxford and Chinyanja courses with us. He is now in land resettlement too, and lives about fifteen miles from us. We are dining with him next Tuesday. He tells me he has a very good library!

We are surrounded by materials for the house, some of which are stored in the tent. Lorry-loads of stuff have been dumped in the compound! Doors, window frames, panes of glass, pipes and bathroom fittings, sacks of cement and long, sweet-smelling tree trunks for the ceiling beams. We now have a watchman, who has a small shelter at the entrance to the compound and keeps watch day and night. There is so much to organise and supervise that Ron wants to work straight through the weekend, so we shall dash into Zomba on Saturday morning to collect mail and stores. I have been in touch with Laga, and she and Clement are coming out to Magomero for tea this Sunday, as they are very interested to see our 'primitive life style', as Laga put it!

13th May:

We called in at the Boma on Saturday morning and there was a note to inform me that a passage has been booked for me on the *Durban Castle*, sailing from Beira in July, no date yet. I have a single first class cabin, No. 26. Poor Ron looked shattered by the news, as if he had been told for the first time that I was going, but he soon cheered up. I felt slightly sick for the rest of the day, a bit overwhelmed at the thought of all I have to do in preparation, but that will sort itself out. We were back at Magomero by noon, quite glad to have a quiet day in the office. We got through an enormous amount of paper work and by Sunday afternoon were very ready to welcome Laga and Clement for tea and a stroll over our little domain. They were interested in everything – the huts, the tent, the well, the stockade, the summer house, even the lavatory, and never ceased to marvel over the view. We persuaded them to stay on for a sundowner, to watch the splendours of the sunset, which was all we had promised, and they were thrilled. They wanted us to go back with them to Limbe for dinner and the cinema, but we did not have the proper clothes, and were both feeling so tired we did not really mind having to say no.

Last night we drove fifteen miles to dine with Ren Smith, whom I told you of last week. He has come down from the North to finish his first tour in Land Resettlement. Being a bachelor, he has been able to spend money on home comforts and we were impressed by his accumulation of local crafts. There were three good leopard-skin rugs; beautiful wooden carvings, spears and masks on the walls, a splendid bookcase, writing desk, drinks cabinet, arm-chair, dining table and four occasional tables. All this furniture is made of local wood, to his own design, costing in all about £14! He must have driven a very hard bargain. This is the African system in selling goods – there are no fixed prices, and they love the art of bargaining and are very skilled at it, I think. I am hopeless: I always feel I should pay more for their beautiful carvings than they seem to expect, especially when the seller is old and going blind, as is my favourite craftsman at Magomero. I have tried to enlist Aflike's help, but he will not be drawn in on either side. Only after the bargain has been struck will he indicate, in polite circumlocution, that – more often than not – he considers I have been robbed, and of course, when by chance I have made a good bargain, he is pleased and admiring and I retire from the fray feeling sorry and guilty!

I came away with a lovely supply of books from Ren's enviable library, so I feel very relaxed – my reading supply now completely controls my mood! I have started with Chester Wilmot's *The Struggle for Europe*, which is enthralling, and more objective and comprehensive than Churchill.

21st May:

First things first. My sailing date is 21st July!

The weather is glorious but very cold and I live in slacks and a sweater. Since our visit to Ren Smith, I have been eating my way through his books and am at present about halfway through *The Caine Mutiny* by an American, Herman Wouk. It makes a fascinating contrast with *The Cruel Sea*.

We went into Zomba at the weekend, feeling rather strange after our fortnight in the bush. I had so much shopping to do I borrowed a court messenger from the Boma to carry my two heavy baskets. In the evening we went to the Club to see Bing Crosby in *Mr Music* – good, light entertainment. We stayed on and talked to a lot of people who had noticed our absence from the social scene! I began to feel they are not quite real, I have so much on my mind – and in my heart. On Monday morning we had a lot to do in Zomba, ordering materials for the house, and we did not leave till about 9 o'clock. We are now known in the shops for arriving on Saturday looking wild and shabby, and calling in on Monday morning, very sleek and clean!

28th May:

It is cold, and I spend the days sewing and the evenings reading in the hut. I have managed to borrow a sewing machine for a fortnight, so I am fully occupied. I have made a dress out of old bedroom curtains, a blouse out of an old dress, and a dirndl out of another old dress, the bodice of which has given way after thousands of washings, and what washings the boys give things – wild slappings on stone unless I keep an eye on them and see that they use the bath.

Brick makers have been busy for some weeks, turning out slabs of mixed earth and water from crude wooden moulds and laying them out in rows, covered with straw, to dry in the sun. Then they were built up into big kilns with deep holes running through them along the base. Into these holes are thrust huge piles of firewood, and the other evening at sunset these furnaces were set alight, and the kilns are to burn for five days, beginning with a slow fire which is increasingly stoked up until their outlines undulate in the great heat. When the grass laid on the flat tops burst into flames, the fires will be allowed to die out. Before we go to bed, we walk over to the kilns to talk to the night watchmen and share our cigarettes with them. In the piercing chill of the night air, it is comforting to approach the black silhouettes of the kilns rising above the bamboo stockade surrounding them, and feel the warmth of their glowing infernos leap out to meet us. The men squat nearby, attending to the stoking of the fires, and the red light is reflected in their dark faces and shiny eyes with a striking effect of primitive beauty. Sometimes I am wakened in the night by the intense cold, and lying in my icy bed I listen to the murmur of their voices and long to join them.

Saturday morning was a holiday, so on Friday night we drove into Zomba through a splendid sunset. Willard had a huge fire burning and after a deep hot bath we had supper in our dressing-gowns beside it. Saturday was damp and bleak and we did not stir out at all. David arrived for tea and stayed the night. We talked, laughed and played some reckless rubbers of three-handed bridge. On Sunday morning we watched cricket, but it was too cold for comfort on the Club *khonde*. David left in a rush after lunch, as he suddenly remembered he was having guests for tea! In the evening we went to the Film Society cinema, an Italian comedy called *Four Steps in the Clouds*, pleasant but not up to the usual standard. We came back here on Monday and have been frozen all week.

Dust sweeps about in clouds, driven by strong wind, and immensely tall dust devils rise above the maize gardens in a whirling frenzy like mad snakes in a dance of death.

5th June:

We had a lovely Whitsun weekend. On Saturday evening we saw *Pandora and the Flying Dutchman*, a most lusciously photographed film, very good entertainment, though no one in the cast bothered to act. On Sunday and Monday there was a two day cricket match between officials and non-officials from all over Nyasaland. Last year it was held at Lilongwe, Central Province, and this year it was Zomba's turn. It is always a great occasion, with many visiting guests. We spent both days at the Club as spectators, and enjoyed it immensely, not only the cricket, but the relaxed, friendly, very English atmosphere – such a lot of nice looking, happy people gathering in talkative groups and calling out greetings to friends they had not seen for a long time. There was a Sundowner after the match, which we went to on impulse and enjoyed. We came back to Magomero on Tuesday morning, feeling very much the better of the little break in Zomba.

11th June:

It is very cold!

Things are really developing here. The fires in the kilns are out, the bricks are cooling and will be ready next week. The foundations of the house have been laid out and dug – it looks huge!

We had lovely weather here for the Queen's Birthday. I was quite sorry to miss the celebrations in Zomba, especially seeing all the chiefs again. We went to Ren Smith's for the day, and had such a pleasant time. He gave us a marvellous hot curry lunch and afterwards we walked down to a little pond near the house, a rather eerie place shut in by hills, with trees growing in the water. We spent a quiet afternoon in the sun and came back here after tea, laden with Penguins. On Saturday morning we rushed into Zomba early, as Ron had work to do and I wanted to do things in the house and garden before Ren arrived for tea, to stay overnight for the Red Cross Ball. There was the usual succession of baths, and we finally emerged and sat round a big log fire, as it was terribly cold, and had dinner on small tables beside it. The Ball was a great success. Halfway through there was a very clever cabaret show. I am always so impressed by our local talent. About 3 o'clock, Kenneth and Ruth Simmonds, who had been with a very dull party which had just broken up, made a bee-line for us and we had a delightful hour with them and were invited back to their house for coffee. By the time we got there dawn was breaking and Ruth decided on breakfast instead – bacon, eggs, sausage, toast and coffee, all of us wide awake and not yet feeling tired. In fact, Kenneth and I did *The Times* crossword between us! We drove back to Naisi in bright sunshine and went straight to bed till lunch time. We then ate a huge lunch and took Ren up the mountain for a short tour of its magic. The clarity of the views at this time of year is astounding and our heads were reeling in the thin, icy air – delicious, like chilled wine. Ren left after tea, very impressed with his first weekend in Zomba. Ron and I sat nodding over books, then gave up, had an early bath, went to bed and read, and had supper on trays handed in under the mosquito nets by Aflike, wearing an 'I told you so' expression on his face.

We had an early start next morning, as Vernon MacDonald, the man in charge of all the land resettlement schemes in the Southern Province, had asked Ron to go down to Cholo for the day to see some new villages which have been resettled there. He kindly suggested I go too and spend the day with his wife. (I would have liked to see the villages myself but of course could not say so.) We drove over the rough road to Blantyre and then had the pleasure of driving on twenty-five miles of tarmac, the longest stretch in Nyasaland, to Cholo. For almost the first time, Ron used the over-drive, which means a steady 50 m.p.h. with no gear changing – marvellous. Cholo is one of the main tea growing areas, and the landscape is most attractive. The tea terraces stretch for miles, immaculately tended, with many umbrella trees to provide the necessary shade. Great white estate houses stand among huge blue gums, and everywhere are planted avenues of trees and evergreen thickets, to give privacy. We arrived about 9.30 and after coffee the men went off and I knitted and talked to Mrs MacDonald, a delightful woman, who was doing an exquisite tapestry on a big frame – most impressive. They came here from Kenya years ago and have a beautiful bungalow in a mature garden, everything so perfectly looked after and in very good taste – the absolute height of luxury after our huts! We drove back through a blinding sunset. This is Ramadan and I was concerned for Aflike, who had come with us – he visited friends in a nearby village – and should have been on his prayer mat. However, he said he was all right and quietly spat out of the car window all the way back. As soon as we got to Magomero I sent him off to have some food.

18th June:

On Saturday morning at Naisi I was just going to wash my hair when suddenly I could not bear its mass any longer. To Ron's horror I seized the scissors and cut off two inches all round – it was so long it still looks exactly the same! That is the sort of mad impulse one would never have at home, but out here one has many! In the evening we went to the Club and saw *The Hasty Heart*, a good film we had seen at Oxford. I scarcely remembered it, which shows how full my head must have been of other things. We came out to Magomero after tea on Sunday, a frightfully bleak way to end the day, but Ron wanted an early start to the work on Monday morning, so it had to be. There is so much to be done, not only work on the house, which I do not mention much but it does go on, but also, Ron is responsible for road maintenance and we have being doing a lot of driving in the area. The road gangs are supervised by a *capitao* (overseer) but it sometimes requires a sterner approach to keep them at it, though we cannot help being amused by what we come across, time and time again. The labourers are warned by the tell-tale column of dust as the car approaches and by the time it comes into sight they have seized their hoes and flung themselves into action at a frenzied pace no man could keep up for five minutes. Sometimes they are all resting in the tall grass at the verges and when the car appears suddenly, there is a shout from the first man to catch sight of it and immediately a kind of fanning in movement occurs along the length of the road, as man after man springs to life and bends over his work, his whole body a study in self-righteous toil. Ron shouts words of encouragement out of the window and they laugh, lean on their hoes and spit. If he sees very little of the day's stint has been done, he gets out and calls for the *capitao* and has a talk with him. He keeps his temper so well, but not as well at this stage in the tour as he did at the start! Both David and Ren have said it is the same with them.

25th June:

I am having my second last week at Magomero, as after that I must plunge into packing. It is very odd, but as the time for leave draws nearer, everything seems to be simplified, and the thought of packing has ceased to worry me. For several weeks, also, I have felt some dread of the long, lone journey, and now that feeling too has gone. I suppose the longest journey I have done alone is on the train from Glasgow to London, and now I am about to cross half the world. However, Iris, who travelled out to Nyasaland alone to join Dave, assured me that I shall love it, that there is a feeling of great liberation in being a person in one's own right instead of being just Mr So-and-so's wife. I think I know exactly what she means!

Last weekend we found Zomba quite warm compared with here. We spent Saturday quietly, going over books and household things together, deciding what Ron wants left out. On Sunday there was a cricket match, and all our resolutions to go over Ron's clothes faded away and we spent a peaceful, restful day watching Zomba beat Blantyre. Word has got around that I am going soon, and people were constantly coming up to talk to me, which was nice, though it made me feel upset for Ron. However, there were many kind assurances that Ron would be most welcome to stay at weekends.

On Monday morning we went up to the hospital early, to be vaccinated, and then came out to Magomero. I have spent the time writing a lot of letters to precede my homecoming and doing endless paper work for Ron.

2nd July:

I am sitting here at Naisi in the most awful looking room, with no pictures, ornaments or books, and two open trunks and several tea chests on the floor! Ron went off on Monday morning and I plunged into packing, after shedding dismal tears into my coffee at the thought of how little time we have left together. It is proving a long week! Looking back, I cannot think how I endured those weeks alone here, and I find myself longing to be out at the Magomero camp. However, I have plenty to do and the packing is going very well. I pack away our pretty things with a feeling of love, they have meant so much to us out here, making what I call a 'haven' of each house we have lived in. Yesterday I packed my books in their big wooden chest, handling them very cautiously, as 'things', dead and alive, fall out of them — scorpions, cockroaches, beetles and spiders, despite the fact that I go over them every few months. Bernard and Mary Kayes, our nice settler friends, have very kindly offered us storage room in their big store attached to their bungalow, where they can keep an eye on our things so that is a great load off my mind.

FULL STOP! Willard has just brought in the mail, including a frenzied letter from the Passage Officer to say he has just had a telegram from Beira informing him that the *Durban Castle* is due in Beira on 14th July, so I must leave by train on 13th July! Poor Ron, he will get a shock when he comes back. Fortunately I shall easily have everything ready by then — it is almost a relief. Heavens, I *am* excited, and not a soul to tell about it. However, I am going to dinner with Alan and Joyce Dickinson this evening, so I can tell them, otherwise I feel I might burst.

I had my final week at Magomero last week, and left it without a pang, though it looked very beautiful in the early, golden mist, with Mlanje majestic among its lifting clouds. On Saturday night we saw *The Ghost Train* performed by the Blantyre dramatic club — not nearly as high a standard as our Zomba club — but amusing, and theatre night in Zomba always has a special atmosphere, with everyone in evening dress. I was able to provide Ron with a marvellous clovey carnation for his buttonhole. In the cold weather, flowers retain their scent deliciously. I have thirty-five carnations in Ron's rowing cup, beautiful among the ruins in the stark room and smelling divinely. On Sunday we were very busy with Ron's clothes and papers, and in the evening escaped from this depressing task to go to the Film Society film, Maurice Chevalier in *Le Roi S'Amuse*, a delightful film. I had never seen him and never particularly wanted to, but I was charmed. The Zomba audience came out looking very middle class and strait-laced!

This seems a scrappy letter but I am in rather a daze after the news. I am really very glad it cuts out a week of waiting. We both feel it a great strain. I know I am doing the right thing, but it is so hard to do, until it is done!

8th July:

Ron was rather devastated when he came in on Saturday morning and I broke the news to him. However, we decided to have a happy weekend. On Saturday night there was the monthly informal dance at the Club and we went on our own and had a lovely evening. On Sunday morning we had just decided recklessly to have breakfast in bed and work extra hard at the packing later, when a car drove up and David appeared. I had written to say good-bye. Ron was livid! Dear David. He had got my note on Saturday afternoon and roared up from Chingali to have a farewell breakfast with us! The walls of the house are very thin, and Ron could not let off steam loudly, so there he was in his dressingroom, his hair on end, his voice hoarse with indignation, standing gesticulating furiously in the direction of the sittingroom and mouthing a whisper to me, 'Our LAST weekend . . . silly idiot only wants to see YOU . . . that's all he's come for!' I shook with laughter, feeling slightly hysterical. We all ate a big breakfast, Ron fully recovered himself, and David made himself useful, helping to nail up crates, and in the end stayed for lunch, and went off about 3.30, his eyes full of tears, poor lonely man. Ron and I felt very depressed and sat on the floor talking among unpacked sherry glasses, straw and boxes till it was dark, not getting on with things at all. Ron went off on Monday and is coming in on Thursday evening. On Saturday we go to Limbe, staying the night in a big new hotel, The Shire Highlands, and my train leaves Limbe at 10.00 a.m. on Sunday.

The packing is going very well. The only awful bit is the china, which I shall tackle tomorrow. I keep finding things of awkward shape just when I have neatly filled up a crate. My worst moment was when I had completed the linen trunk, which has all our ornaments in it and I found I had overlooked our ebony procession of ten elephants, all knobbly and difficult! But in they went.

15th July:

I do not think the Gods love Ron and me. My date of departure has been altered *again*. The ship sails from Beira on Sunday 20th, and the last train from Limbe before that date is Thursday 17th. I hope I can go on board at once, otherwise I shall have to spend two nights at one of Beira's not too clean, wildly expensive hotels. It is all quite infuriating.

I came out to Magomero with Ron yesterday morning, leaving word at the Secretariat to send a message out here if the date is changed again! I got all the packing done last week by Thursday, the day Ron was coming in. I had everything planned so that I had left out just enough clothes to wear till my departure on the train on Sunday. At lunchtime I got notice of the changed date, too late to get word to Ron, so in he came to find me rather desperately unpacking clothes. He was glad to have me for the extra days and Aflike was radiant. Only I felt I could not stand this uncertainty much longer! However, we had a very nice long weekend. On Friday we went to the early cinema and saw an excellent comedy called *Born Yesterday*. So many people came up to say good-bye and promise me they would look after Ron, which touched me very much. On Saturday we did final shopping and packing and had a quiet evening reading by a big fire. On Sunday morning we visited the Kayes briefly, leaving our heavy luggage there to be stored. I had stripped the garden of flowers and presented Mary with an enormous bouquet, which astonished her. As usual, my garden has quite a lot of out-of-season flowers – I do not always follow the book of words, but most of them survive the wrong season very well!

On Monday morning we got up at five, to a marvellous red dawn, and finished our personal packing. At 8 o'clock someone from the housing department came and checked all the furniture, we locked up and handed over the keys. Then we drove off, too numb, we confessed to each other, to feel any pain at all. The lorry followed us out to Magomero and I spent the rest of the day making the huts look as nice as possible for Ron. The floors are covered with mats and there are two comfortable armchairs with big cushions, a small bookcase full of Ron's books and two small occasional tables – a very crowded hut but what a transformation! The bedroom hut is full of my luggage and we have been plunging about, knocking our shins and stubbing our toes. Ron and I are managing to be quite cheerful, but Aflike goes about looking like a tragic muse. The workers here thought I had gone on Sunday, and when I arrived yesterday they all gathered round in a great crowd, staring, laughing and clapping. Aflike gave them the latest news bulletin and sent them away with one of his imperious gestures of dismissal. I foresee quite a send off on Thursday, provided Aflike does not ruin everything by making an emotional scene. My next letter will be from the ship!

POSTSCRIPT

Iris was right, I did love the long voyage home alone, I did feel a sense of liberation and I did enjoy being a person in my own right, not just Mr So-and-so's wife. By the time I reached Tilbury I had come to the conclusion that my apprenticeship as a wife in Africa had been served in the last two and half years and was over. Henceforth I would try to create a more personal pattern of life for myself within the framework of marriage and the colonial way of life.

Ron's leave was further postponed till December, but he was home in time for Christmas. He had seen the completion of the house and handed it over, together with his duties as Land Resettlement Officer, to his successor. We never lived in the house, and as so often happened in Africa, we visited Magomero again only once, very briefly: a place which had become, for a time, part of the very fabric of our lives.

A month before the end of our leave, I received an air letter from Nyasaland. It was from Mary Kayes. It contained such devastating news she had felt she could not bring herself to inflict its brutal impact upon us by cable. She wrote, still in shock, to say that in a thunderstorm early one evening the previous week, their bungalow had been struck by lightning through the thatched roof and in a matter of minutes burnt to the ground. They had lost everything. 'Everything', of course, included their big store which housed all our possessions in the world.

When he heard this news, kind Uncle Teddie, my only wealthy relative, sat down at his desk and wrote me a cheque for £100 – in 1953 a large sum of money. Family and friends rallied to support us in this catastrophe. We were grateful for their generosity, but nothing in the world could give me back my books, my precious books, or those other treasures, mostly wedding presents and family gifts, which had breathed life into each 'haven' I had made for us. To this day I feel that old sense of loss when occasionally I seek out a book I have momentarily forgotten has not graced my bookshelves for more than thirty years. With this bitter blow, Africa had again demonstrated to me what I had only just begun to grasp – the inexorable inevitability of change, of having to let go, move on, re-design, take up again the challenge which was never going to go away.

Chapter 16

11th May, 1953: On board MV *Dunnottar Castle*

We arrive at Gibraltar tomorrow, and a Mrs Albas, a Gibraltese who sits at our table, has kindly offered to post this for me, so you should receive it quite soon.

Our last night in London could not have been more splendid – a magnificent evening at Covent Garden. We had a box opposite the Royal Box, which was occupied by Princess Margaret and her party. She looked lovely – huge bright eyes – but very selfconscious and desirous of attention. During the interval, in the bar, we stood next to Robert Helpman, Ninette de Valois and Arnold Haskell. I have yet to fail to see at least one famous face from the ballet world in the Covent Garden audience. Last time it was Moira Shearer. Margot Fonteyn was quite perfect in *Swan Lake*, partnered by Michael Soames. It was a highly emotional occasion for us, with the unspoken thought in our minds that tomorrow we would be setting sail for our second tour in Africa. The realisation kept coming between me and the performance and I had to concentrate very hard. London looked very clean, fresh and unfamiliar, with enormous spectator stands already in place for the Coronation. I was very glad when all the leave-taking was over and we left London. Joan [Joan Nathan, Uncle Teddie's elder daughter, one of the 'Chinese cousins', see Chapter 1] and I put on a marvellous show of self control by simply ignoring each other for the last half hour before our departure! She is an excellent hostess and we were very comfortable in her lovely flat.

The ship is a sister ship of the *Durban Castle*, so I quickly felt at home. We have an inside cabin, which is rather a bore as the weather warms up. We have made a threesome with Charles Gurd, a doctor whom we knew slightly in Zomba last tour. He is the only person from Nyasaland on board, so we are lucky. I always liked the look of him and he is great fun to be with. The weather is perfect and as the sun gets warmer we gradually turn brown. As I write, we are sailing down the Portuguese coast past Lisbon and this evening we will pass Cape St. Vincent. The sea is a deep, cobalt blue; just looking at it gives me a feeling of being healed. I have that awful sensation of raw, torn-up nerve ends but I shall soon settle down and 're-plant' myself, I know.

15th May: Genoa

Yesterday we had an interesting day at Marseille, going on a Cook's tour which culminated in a visit to Le Corbusier's astonishing new block of flats, high up above the town.

This morning we emerged on deck to behold Genoa, a beautiful city nestled among the lower slopes of the Apennines. We took a taxi to the Consulate and asked to see the British Consul, Aunt Kathie's friend, Count Stenboch, who welcomed us very warmly and was delighted to have news of Aunt Kathie, whom he had known for years in Belgrade. He had just returned from leave in Florence and was obviously overwhelmed with work, but he took time to plan our day, advising us to go to Portofino, about twenty-eight miles along the Riviera from Genoa, and writing down the name of the best restaurant to go to for lunch. He even wrote down what to eat (mouth-watering local fish) and drink (a delicious local wine). He then sent us off to the bus station in his own chauffeur-driven car with its CD number plate! The bus journey along the coast was absolutely breathtaking – so *exactly* like all the postcards, photographs and paintings of the Riviera that I can still hardly believe that there we were, really in the midst of it. Portofino is a very picturesque little port, besides showing all the signs of being the playground of millionaires. We lunched on the verandah of the restaurant, overlooking the harbour, which was packed with the most beautiful yachts imaginable. We got back in time to wander through Genoa's fascinating streets and had tea outside a café, under a striped umbrella, feeling very continental. I said to Ron when we got back to the ship I thought we were in the wrong Service!

20th May: Port Said

We have just reached Port Said, which looks so hot and dirty we have blasély decided not to go ashore. The weather is now HOT. Yesterday evening we sailed past the dark shape of Stromboli against the night sky, an ominous red glow at its peak and an occasional red hot rock tossing up through the smoke.

We have been swimming, playing deck tennis and lazing in the sun. In the evenings we play bridge with Charles and a retired Lieutenant Colonel who works in Locust Control and is bound for Aden, poor chap. They are both excellent players, so, in spite of nerves which make my fingers shake, I persist and already my game has improved. Charles assures me I could become a very good player. We lost more than half the passengers at Genoa, most of them holidaying in Europe, and now we only have people like ourselves, *en route* to work in Africa, so conversation tends to take on a deadly familiarity! I escape into my book or talk theatre with Charles.

I am feeling most excited about this part of the journey. We enter the Canal at midnight tonight, by arclight, and we are staying up to watch. We only do twenty-five miles in the night so we shall have plenty of time to enjoy it tomorrow. It was very misty this morning and I could not see much of the coast line. I feel very close to Elspeth, as I can imagine very well how much she would love all this – far more than I. It was the Mediterranean coast that thrilled me.

25th May:

We are approaching Port Sudan and I am writing this to post there. Since we left Port Said we have experienced terrific heat and completely new and exciting scenery. When I went up on deck on the morning after we entered the Canal, there was brilliant yellow desert on both sides and the ship was gliding quietly along in baking heat. It was a thrilling day and we left the deck only for meals. We saw Arabs, camels and isolated units of British army camps. The men raced down to the bank, howling like wolves when they saw the women on board and shouting lewd remarks about us to the men. Everyone laughed and waved. Now we are in the Red Sea, which really does have a reddish tinge due, I am told, to a certain kind of plankton. The heat is tremendous but I do not mind except at night in that wretched inside cabin. There is a strong wind this morning, so warm it makes one sweat. I have lost all sense of time and seem to have been at sea for aeons. I am reading a wonderful book called *The Sea Around Us* by Rachel Carson – most appropriate.

Coronation Day: Mombasa

The ship arrived here yesterday morning and I cannot tell you how awful it is! There are exactly nine first class passengers left, including Charles and ourselves. Today, of course, is a holiday, so the docks lie silent and lifeless around us and there is little to do or see in the town, likewise on holiday, so no market and shuttered shops. We do not sail till 7th June, and something tells me we will hate Mombasa by then – and I have always loved its pretty, exotic name, which seems to promise so much!

We had two days at Port Sudan and the ship fairly fried in the heat – the decks became so hot it was uncomfortable to walk on them. We did not go ashore but visited a beautiful underwater coral garden which we viewed through a glass-bottomed boat. There was a great pile of family mail for me at Aden – lovely. The ship arrived there late at night and sailed before we were up, so not a glimpse of the barren rocks did we get. To make matters worse, Charles is now without his bridge partner.

4th June:

The harbour has returned to normal and there is a constant movement of ships in and out which is always interesting to watch. Fortunately, it is the cold season and there is a breeze during the day. Last night after dinner we walked along the dock to visit an attractive-looking Lloyd Tristino ship, the *Africa*. We went on board and had a drink in its air-conditioned lounge. What a cosmopolitan atmosphere compared with our British ship! Everyone seemed to be speaking French or Italian. We had with us Charles, a Southern Rhodesian farmer, a German girl and an American girl (all from our tourist class) so our accents were fairly mixed but at least all in the same language!

Coronation Day dragged its weary length along! The Captain gave a huge cocktail party before lunch to which no passengers were invited, which seemed very odd. Then everyone went down to a very good lunch, at the end of which he proposed the toast to the Queen. At 4 o'clock we gathered to hear the broadcast of the procession returning from the Abbey but weather conditions were unfavourable and we heard nothing but loud atmospherics – terribly disappointing. Before going to bed we three walked along to the end of the docks to look at a destroyer flood-lit in the bay. She looked very British and very beautiful.

It is odd to think I am in Kenya at the moment!

8th June: Tanga

We sailed away from Mombasa this morning with lightened spirits. Eighty new passengers joined the ship yesterday, so life has acquired more normal proportions and we are rediscovering the art of conversation. We arrived here at sunset and leave the day after tomorrow. Our last port of call before Beira is Zanzibar, which should be fun, but the men, poor things, are now longing to get back to work. Ron is reading the Bible in Chinyanja and Charles is just going quietly mad. He has made this trip for us – a duller lot of passengers cannot be imagined! I am beginning to come to life again after this long, dreamlike spell of travelling through limbo, and I feel very ready to tackle whatever lies ahead.

We are anchored well out to sea, and it is wonderful to feel a fresh breeze again, and no longer smell that indescribable African port smell which we have been breathing in for a week. Sparkling in the dark, Tanga looks like a fairy town – they all do at night – and in the morning, I know, will look remarkably like all the other ports of darkest Africa!

15th June: Beira

We disembarked at 3 o'clock yesterday and made our way to the Savoy Hotel, which is our headquarters till 6.20 this evening when we board the train, which should arrive in Limbe tomorrow evening about 6. There is no news for us about our posting, so we must wait till Wednesday morning when Ron reports to the PC in Blantyre. The *Dunnottar Castle* is anchored opposite the hotel *khonde* where I am sitting. The train from Nyasaland got in early this morning and passengers from it will now be joyfully aboard, so the view has a certain poignancy for me! Ron and Charles have gone to clear the luggage through Customs and I am left in this ghastly Somerset Maughamish place, with its cane chairs, smelly potted plants, flies and trellised verandah. At present there is a cold mist over everything and I am waiting for the sun to break through and warm me.

Zanzibar was fascinating. We went ashore over huge green waves in a little launch, and it is true that you can smell the cloves as you approach land. The streets are narrow and Eastern in atmosphere and the entire population seems to communicate at the pitch of its lungs. The architecture is tall, with high walls enclosing inner courtyards, and the houses have magnificent heavy doors with beautiful brass hinges and handles. We saw the site of the old slave market, horrible to imagine, and then hired a car and were driven round the island, visiting a cloves factory *en route*.

I shall write from Blantyre to let you know our posting.

P.S. [Written on the back of the airletter] Posted to Mlanje – both pleased. A.

Chapter 17

22nd June:

Here I am at last, writing my first letter from Mlanje. I have not had a
moment to myself until now. We actually heard about our posting on the train
on the journey up. When we stopped at Port Herald, on the border, the DC
there, a Mr Talbot, boarded the train and travelled with us to Limbe. He gave us
the tentative news from his grapevine that we were posted to Mlanje, which
relieved us immensely, as it is a fairly civilised station, by all accounts. We
booked in at Ryall's with a strange feeling of déjà vu, as we occupied the same
bedroom as on our arrival last tour. However, this time I feel very much more in
control of myself and things to come.

Next morning Ron called on Eric Barnes, the PC, who confirmed the Mlanje
posting. While Ron was out, Aflike turned up, looking thinner than ever and so
thrilled to see me he could only laugh and throw his arms about wildly. When
he had calmed down we had a long talk, his English and my Chinyanja meeting
each other half way, as always – lovely. He had, of course, heard about the
Kayes' house burning down and was about to launch into a lament, but I hastily
changed the subject as I am not ready to speak of it yet. He said *I* was far too
thin and indicated his cooking would fatten me up! Ron arrived back with the
car and received an equally ardent welcome. In the evening we dined with Eric
Barnes and his sweet wife, Leslie. They were most sympathetic about the loss
of our things in the fire, but kept it brief, as they obviously realised I have not
yet come to terms with it – kind, tactful people.

On Thursday we drove to Zomba for the day, which was dull and cold. (I
have been frozen ever since I came but that may be self-generated – a state of
nervous anticipation of the unknown, despite my brave resolutions!) I must
confess the first sight of the outline of Zomba mountain on the skyline brought
a brimming of tears to my eyes. This mountain reaches a very deep place in me.
We went first to the Boma, where we collected mail and were warmly welcomed by Barnet, the head clerk who helped Ron so much last tour. We called
in on John Watson, who was looking very well and seemed delighted to see us
again. He promptly rang Dorothy and she came down at once in the car to bear
me off to the house for coffee. I thoroughly enjoyed my morning with her,

hearing all the news and gossip, delivered in her inimitable style! After a very happy, lively lunch with them, we went down to visit the Kayes' and found them flourishing. They have started a new garage and insurance business and are doing very well indeed. They showed us the foundations of the new house, which is rising on the site of the old one, and with many improvements. It is going to be magnificent. We felt glad for them but came away obscurely depressed about ourselves. However, they were able to hand over to us our canteen of cutlery, dinner service and some kitchen things, all of which Ron had packed at Magomero and delivered to Bernard at his Zomba office, where they remained – hence they escaped the fire. I felt as if they had given us riches. (I must write to Uncle Teddie and tell him his wedding present survives!) We had an early tea at the Club, as we were beginning to wilt, and were joined by Bill Melhuish (my travelling companion on the voyage home on the *Dunottar Castle*. He works in the Treasury), which was delightful. Our final call was on Mike and Geraldine Lamb, acquaintances from last tour, who are about to go on leave. Mike had left a message for Ron at the Boma, offering to lend us all their camping equipment, beds, bath, basin, table etc. We are enormously appreciative of this very kind and thoughtful gesture. All day people referred to the fire and were so nice about it I just had to pull myself together and speak lightly and normally about it, so that is a hurdle safely cleared, praise be.

On Friday morning we completed our shopping and set off for Mlanje after lunch, Aflike following in one of the Boma lorries with our luggage. It was very exciting to draw closer and closer to Mlanje mountain, which we have only known as a great massif on the horizon. The Boma and Government houses are clustered right at its base. There are nine houses on the station, most of which look out over big gardens to the plain just below. The DC's house, the second highest up, faces the mountain; a great stark peak soars up at the end of the garden. There is a swimming pool near the house which is available to everyone. Mlanje is officially a hot station and kerosene refrigerators are provided free; typically, there are not enough to go round, so couples with children have priority, which is perfectly fair. There is rainfall all the year round and the scenery is very tropical. Vegetables grow up from seed in six weeks. Local prices are incredibly low – seven bananas for 1*d*., four oranges, two grapefruit. TT milk from an estate is delivered daily to the whole station. We have two *machila* men and two penal labourers, free, who collect wood and work in the garden. (They are there now, 'working' in the shade of a big mango tree. I have been busy in the house and will not get going with them till tomorrow.) We are in an oval bush house again. It has just been done up and is fresh and clean. It is as well that we are not in a bigger house, as the sittingroom looks appallingly bare with only our diminished resources, as it were. (I shall not go on about this.) I hope to get floor mats, curtain and cushion material soon. I must say I am pleasantly surprised at the number of books we acquired, mostly presents, of course, before we left home. We have a big front lawn with surrounding flower beds and a huge (empty) vegetable garden, so I shall be busy. The view is green and restful and Mlanje towers up behind us. There are three other bush houses, not too near. The Boma is five minutes walk down the hill.

This is a tea-growing area and there are many prosperous estates for miles around, on the plain. There is a rickety old Club, with a tiny library and a cinema which shows a film, an old one, once a fortnight. Apart from the DC and ourselves there are another ADC (not yet arrived), a doctor, a policeman, an accountant and a PWD man, all married except for the PWD man. Everyone seems very welcoming and friendly. The DC has not been on *ulendo* since April (!) and said calmly that Ron would do what the job required and no more. (Ron and I avoided startled glances!) He also said there are a lot of rest houses in the district, so very little tent camping is done. I begin to count my blessings with a vengeance!

The DC, Peter Nicholson, and his wife Betty are very nice and very easy to get on with. They have four children aged between nineteen months and six years. They lived for many years in India and only came to Nyasaland in 1947. I think Betty suffers from the lack of good servants she has been accustomed to, but she manages to keep her sense of humour. We slept in their guest house and ate with them till today, and got most of our unpacking done over the weekend. It was *very* hot work.

Ron is having his first day in the Boma and will be home for tea at any moment, so I must be ready to welcome him.

29th June:

The Secretariat in Zomba sends my *Times* on to me. It is absolute heaven to be reading up-to-date news. I must write to the London office and give them the Mlanje address. [As a first move towards improving my own private life style, I used £19 of Uncle Teddie's £100 cheque to pay for a year's subscription to the airmail edition of the daily *London Times* – my one and only extravagance, admittedly an enormous one, in the otherwise careful expenditure of that money to build up our household goods again.]

We have had quite a week of settling in and now it is just a case of being patient while I gradually buy or make what I need to turn this house into a home for us. There is a carpenter on the station and I hope to contact him soon, as I want him to make a coffee table and four occasional tables I have designed. I have access to a sewing machine, kindly offered by Elsie Martin, the policeman's wife, who knew Iris at Ncheu.

Ron went off on *ulendo* today for the week, but I have plenty to keep me busy. He has left me Aflike [the second move for the enhancement of my life] and taken out a new boy who only appeared this morning. He was cook to a retired DC in Blantyre, so he is probably well trained. Aflike likes him, which is the main thing. I also have a night watchman, who sleeps on the front *khonde* when Ron is away [the third move]. This afternoon a neighbour is taking me to a Red Cross meeting at the Club, where I shall meet some of the planters' wives, which should be interesting.

The weather is simply lovely and I sit out in the garden every afternoon under a tree, which keeps me cool but still lets me get brown.

I have been using my new French cookery book – so far successfully. Ron is delighted.

David Baxter and his new wife arrived back yesterday. I am about to write a note of welcome to them.

6th July:

I have had a pleasant week here. After Ron went off on Monday I was engulfed for a few hours in desperate homesickness and self pity, out of which one just has to drag oneself or go under.

I was given a lift into Blantyre on Tuesday and at a sale at my nice Indian shop, where I was given a touching welcome, I bought dark rose material for the big chair cushions and kapok to stuff the linings (made of calico). So Ron will find the room transformed, though still somewhat spartan, when he comes back on Friday.

Today we had a letter from Tony Bridge, one of the ADCs in Zomba, telling us that when the workers at Magomero heard from Ren Smith (who took over from Ron at Magomero, prior to Tony Bridge) of our 'disaster', as he put it, they made us a bookcase designed like Ren's, which I had admired, and it is waiting in Zomba to be collected by lorry – such a pleasing thing to happen. Ron is thrilled and I can hardly wait to get rid of the very ugly PWD one. Ron only goes out on Tuesday and Wednesday this week, which is cheering. The *ulendo* is not strictly carried out here, but unfortunately we have arrived at a time when the approaching constitutional change, the Federation of Nyasaland with Northern and Southern Rhodesia, is causing a certain amount of unrest and trouble in the South, and the Boma staff have to appear in the district as much as possible to 'show the flag'. There is a certain tension in the air which all the DCs and their staff seem to be enjoying, as they feel they come into their own, doing a very necessary job. Ron says that was why John Watson was in such high spirits when we saw him in Zomba!

The second ADC and his wife have arrived – Ken and Monica Archer, ex-Army, ex-Control Commission, sophisticated and friendly.

Aflike looks after me very well and we have our little talks every day. I caught an awful cold in Blantyre – everyone had one – and almost lost my voice, which terrified him. I was nearly sick from drinking innumerable hot lemon (from the garden) drinks with which he kept plying me. However, after two miserable days I felt better, so I escaped my usual marathon. Exactly the same thing happened at the start of our last tour, as he reminded me. I had forgotten. The weather is dangerous – bitterly cold night and morning, always cold in the house and hot in the sun. I have given up cotton dresses and am in winter clothes (both of them – skirts, I mean – one day the navy, one day the check!)

We had a very quiet weekend, so different from the old days in Zomba, which we enjoyed so much.

15th July:

Betty Nicholson has asked me to look after her sewing machine while she is on leave and of course I have accepted with alacrity!

It is strange to hear of summer weather at home, for here it is damp and cold; I have a big log fire on all day.

The mountain fascinates me. It is not a warm, friendly mountain like Zomba. It is cold, threatening and sometimes the drifting mists that swirl so swiftly around its peaks give me a shivery feeling. It is too near! I much prefer to see it on the horizon.

Yesterday my Chinese rug kit arrived. It is going to be splendid, in beautiful colours. Ron was so excited he promptly sat down and completed four rows! Aflike nearly had hysterics at the sight of his bwana sitting on the floor working at a rug! I am making great headway with my Jacobean tapestry. I am not going to make it into a firescreen – too conventionally English for me. I shall enclose it under the glass top of the coffee table I have designed. Besides the four occasional tables, I have also designed a long, low table and a low seat to stand in front of the fireplace in the hot season. Ron will take the designs down to the Boma carpenter and ask him to call in to discuss them with me. So we shall soon have another 'haven' after all.

Now I must turn my attention to the flower garden. The vegetable garden is dug, ready for seeds, which we shall buy in Blantyre. (Talk about a game of patience!) Ron is in this week, which is lovely. He likes Pearson, the somewhat elderly cook, so that is satisfactory. Aflike is in great form, slinking about very smugly today in his new white uniform, his felt fez at a jaunty angle which only just avoids earning my corrective comment! He is very companionable when Ron is away, and fades so discreetly into the background when he is here.

On Monday evening we dined with Robin and Elsie Martin (Iris's friends, who were married from her house in Ncheu when Dave was DC there) and thoroughly enjoyed it. They have two sweet children, a boy and a girl. I also spent a pleasant morning with Betty Nicholson: I have far more in common with her than I thought, which became evident once I got her to myself.

21st July:

I had a friendly letter from Margaret Baxter a few days ago. They are living at Naisi Road, in one of the new houses, which have tin roofs and square ends, and a second bedroom. David is overwhelmed with work in the Secretariat and comes home late every night loaded with files. Ah well, at least she does not sleep alone. I am going to invite them here for a weekend and I will tell you why I can!

There has been something of a reshuffle here. The new DC, David Bolt, moves into the Nicholsons' house on 14th August with his wife and three young children. Ken and Monica Archer, after three weeks here, which gave them time to unpack everything, have now been posted to Zomba, if you please, to the Secretariat – they are delighted. Ron remains in Mlanje as ADC and is glad – he is beginning to get interested in the district. The Archers are living in a lovely house, the best on the station, and Peter Nicholson has given us permission to move in when they go next Monday – indeed he suggested it. It has a kitchen attached to the house, two big bedrooms, a diningroom, a huge airy drawingroom, a sun-room, a large, deep shady *khonde* and passages, instead of rooms opening out of each other, a lavatory which flushes, and hot and cold water in the bathroom. The rent is ten per cent of Ron's salary instead of the bush house five per cent, but it is well worth it and we shall actually, at last, live in a real old colonial bungalow with tall cool rooms, all well proportioned. The house, till last year, was allocated to the PWD, so it has all the extra finishing touches the others lack. It is higher up the hill, with a much wider view, a beautiful mature garden and a big, well planted vegetable garden. So we have taken the plunge and said we will move in. You have no idea what a difference it will make to live in a gracious house. I said nothing about my reaction to being reallocated a bush house, but it was one of near despair. Our neighbours will be the Martins (Police) and the Holmeses (doctor) so we should be well looked after! Now we shall have a spare room [my fourth condition for a better life] for our friends and for Joan [my cousin who was planning a visit to us] when the time comes. Ron is I think almost more pleased than I am, as he fully realises the difference it will make to my life.

I have been specially thrilled with *The Times*' reportage of Wimbledon and two accounts of Everest by Hillary – wonderful, modest, brave writing. You will be interested to know that Tensing's brother is the bandmaster of the Nyasaland Police band, and I have danced to his conducting on many occasions – a most surprising coincidence.

We had a pleasant week last week, with Ron out for only two nights. He is out all this week and for four nights next week, and then we have the excitement of moving and a week together – such are the simple pleasures to which we look forward! On Friday, a large contingent of the KAR set up camp by the Boma. They will be there for ten days, again to 'show the flag' to the anti-Federationists. The Archers gave a welcoming party for the officers last night, which was great fun and had quite a different flavour from Government parties, I suppose because there was hardly any shop talk. On Saturday night we called in at a dance at the Club but left quite soon – it really is a very bushy Club. On Sunday evening we had a drink with Peter and Betty and as always enjoyed them enormously. I am about to walk up to tea with Monica, who very kindly said she was sure I would enjoy a chance to re-cast my eyes over the house!

I feel on top of Africa now instead of being utterly smothered by it.

28th July:

I am busy with the rug and have done about eighteen inches, less than one eighth!

This week the weather is lovely and I feel a different person. It is still cold enough for a fire at night but during the day the doors and windows are all wide open and I keep wandering out to the garden to look up and see how the mountain is feeling!

The new DC, David Bolt, has arrived with his wife and three children, *all* in the throes of chickenpox, caught on the ship, so no one was willing to put them up for the next three weeks. They have moved for that time into 'our' house, which we hope to move into in about a month, after it has been fumigated. I do not mind the delay, as it means I have more time to save up to buy more curtain material, and some of my furniture should be made by then. I shall have to take up gardening seriously, as there is a flower garden and vegetables enough to run a market garden.

Ron played cricket on Sunday and had an accident which, though painful, has resulted blissfully for us, as he cannot go on *ulendo* for at least a month. We feel as if we are on holiday, having a whole month together. He and another fielder collided full tilt and Ron took the man's head right on his cracked rib, which promptly fractured. Poor Ron. He is all bound up in Elastoplast, so it is lucky it is not the hot season. He feels it very much when he moves about, but manages to go down to the Boma. Peter, overwhelmed with work and handing over to David Bolt, is delighted to have him in the office. Everyone is most amused at my apparently heartless reaction.

While Ron was on *ulendo* last week, Elsie Martin took me out to tea at the Roman Catholic Mission, which is run by American nuns – most unusual and somehow not at all convincingly nun-like! We arrived to find two of them lying flat under a beautiful black Bentley which rich parents had sent from America to one of them. They all have terrific Bronx accents (e.g. 'toin' for 'turn') and are much more outgoing and worldly than the one quiet English one. The Mother Superior is French. She is very shy and remained invisible. They asked me to bring Ron to tea when we have settled in. They are not supposed to read much but had somehow smuggled in and read some recent American novels of a fairly sophisticated nature, which they discussed with relish.

On Saturday Ron came in very early and surprised me drifting about in my kimono, sleepily drinking morning tea. We drove to Blantyre to attend a furniture sale we had seen advertised in the local paper, the *Central African Times*, known as the Cat. We shopped and after some searching found Charles's house

(Charles Gurd, the doctor who travelled out with us). He was very glad to see us, and, I think, lonely in his big house. He gave us an excellent curry lunch and played us Mendelssohn's Italian symphony on his very good radiogram. We went on to the sale, where wealthy Blantyre business people made it immediately apparent from their bidding that we would not be able to buy the sofa. It went, along with four chairs, for £70. However, during the morning we had come across an Indian shop which was offering a new one, a cancelled order, for £10, so we rushed back and bought it. Now I must save up for material to cover it. I went to my Indian friend and chose some corduroy which he has laid aside for me. (It would be all too easy to get into debt with the Indian shopkeepers, they are so obliging and persuasive!) That is one more domestic ambition satisfied – I HAVE A SOFA! We returned to Charles for a tea of bread and butter, home-made strawberry jam and clotted cream. Like Daddy, he visits several farms! He is moving to Zomba in August, which is sad. I like him enormously. We left after an early drink and drove the last ten miles in bright moonlight, the mountain ahead utterly unearthly against a sky thronged with stars so brilliant they looked almost blue.

On Sunday I watched cricket from the tumbledown *khonde* of the Club and in the afternoon witnessed Ron double up and collapse with a yelp of pain. I was sitting with Sandy Holmes, the doctor, who took over very efficiently at once, thank goodness.

We are hoping David and Margaret will come and stay as soon as we move into the bigger house. I also want to have Bill Melhuish, who is a great climber and could take the opportunity to go up Mlanje. I am hoping we will climb the mountain, but I would not want to go with Bill, who is six feet seven inches tall, with the longest legs I have ever seen on a man! I wrote to Joan about the house move and the spare bedroom, and yesterday came a letter from her, full of plans for her trip, which she thinks will be in next April/May, depending on a passage being available – most exciting!

5th August:

I knew how immensely relieved you would be that we have at last got the chance of a good house. The Bolts are still in it, and will remain there until the PWD does some cleaning and painting in the DC's house. David and Joan Bolt are very nice indeed, very *English*. They have been in England for over a year while he 'ate his dinners' and completed his law studies. Their children, in spite of chickenpox, look sturdy, round of limb and pink-complexioned, making one realise how pasty and skinny the children on the station are, poor wee things. Joan is highly strung and as terrified of snakes as I am, so I think we will be good for each other.

Our sofa arrived from Blantyre at the weekend and proved too big by *one inch* to get through the door of the bush house! So it sits temptingly on the *khonde* until Ron can get hold of a lorry to take it up to the house to await our arrival. The carpenter has done well, and produced four small tables and a long, low one. He is now working on the fireside seat and my coffee table, while I stitch furiously at my tapestry, which I should complete quite soon. It looks great. Aflike, the snob, is simply delighted about the coming move. He merely shrugged deprecatingly when I remarked that he will have more floors to polish and rooms to clean. He, Cook and I had a little misunderstanding in the kitchen early this morning, with the result that I had to throw out the sauce Cook had made for the curry – disgusting. I cannot think what was in it – certainly not the ingredients I asked for. I hastily made up a fresh one, while Cook and Aflike crept about looking scared stiff. Neither of them had ever seen me in one of my silent tempers, but I suppose my actions spoke for themselves. Aflike came in after lunch, stood to attention and apologised for them both, his eyes as liquid as a spaniel's. I felt mean and guilty and very nearly apologised too, but of course stopped short, said the heat caused everyone to make mistakes, gave them both the afternoon off and all is sweetness and light again.

I am reading a fascinating book which you would hate called *From Here to Eternity*, by an American, James Jones. It is crude and brutal in bits but is enthralling reading. It is making me neglect *The Times*, which is becoming a joke with Ron and me, as it tends to arrive in twos, or even threes, and keeping up to date becomes a bit of a nightmare, though we *love* it!

Ron and I are having a very happy time together. It makes me realise how wonderful life out here would be if only we were able to spend more of it together.

On Sunday two estate owners made a formal call on the new ADC and his wife at teatime, and we were delighted to welcome them – big, tough, friendly men. In the evening Betty Nicholson came for a lively supper and on Monday Peter came. They never go out together, as they do not like to leave the children alone in the house, even with servants.

I forgot to say that last Monday I went as guest to tea at the Club with the local branch of the Nyasaland Council of Women, known as The Naggers(!) and Betty proposed me as a member. It was a very pleasant sociable occasion. I gather they are quite a power in the land.

The Glorious Twelfth:

I can vividly remember the moors resounding with shots and the grouse as silent as the grave!

I was very glad to receive some *Observers* and *Spectators* last week, and Joan sent on the latest number of *Sight and Sound* [a high class film quarterly edited by Lindsay Anderson], so I am very well provided for.

Ron's rib, alas, seems to be mending well, and I think he will go on *ulendo* next week. He is longing to get back to district work. The Nicholsons left on

Sunday, almost missing their train, with the four children howling like ban-shees because they were being separated from their African nanny.

On Thursday last week we drove by moonlight along the base of the moun-tain and saw the opening into the Rhur valley and gorge, where Vance was lost in *Venture into the Interior*, on our way to dine with John Werner, a charming young tea planter who always seeks me out at the Club and sits beside me at cricket matches. A Mr and Mrs Sanderson, also in tea, were there. It was most interesting to talk to them and learn how different their attitude is from that of Government people. The planters in general here seem inclined to be hostile to the Boma, though prepared to accept individuals. It is quite a challenge to meet them and start from scratch, as it were, to win them over. (It was the same at Magomero, of course.)

On Sunday we sat out on the *khonde* all day, a beautiful, hot day. I had to give up working on the rug (now half done) as my hands were wet with sweat. Our little room looks rather overwhelmed with furniture, now that the carpenter is working so quickly. Our bookcase from Magomero arrives today, so I shall be glad when we can spread ourselves in the big house.

PWD workers moved into the DC's house on Monday and I am hoping the Bolts will move in fairly soon. Betty warned Joan Bolt that the house is occasionally plagued by *rats*. I have promised Joan I will accompany her as moral support when she goes over the house to measure for curtains, etc., though I imagine I will make a flying leap for the nearest raised surface if I glimpse so much as a whisker. Mice, yes, but rats – ugh!

Yesterday afternoon I went for the second time to the Naggers, and was made a member. Elsie Martin and I sat, our heads bowed over our embroidery, listening to them discuss gun licences, education and the Federal vote. I just have not got the sort of mind that allows me to join seriously in this kind of discussion with a lot of women. (I noticed no one knew the meaning of the word 'indigenous'!) They are nice women, very efficient in their voluntary work and rightly concerned with questions of education, but I am not sure about wider issues. I must get hold of their charter and see what their aims are. There was a tremendous tea and everyone was madly friendly. Help!

18th August:

Ron's rib is now healed and yesterday off he went, but only for two nights. Sandy Holmes took off the strapping on Monday and revealed what we had feared – an angry rash right round Ron's body. The days are gradually hotting up, and when he perspired he felt wildly itchy. However, he has a special powder to use, so we hope the rash soon goes.

Our bookcase arrived last week. It is a good, unusual design, with four rows of shelves divided in the middle, with a small cupboard for letters in the middle of the top shelf, and two larger ones for photograph albums (ours, of course, went in the fire) on either side of the bottom shelf. It is so broken up it is not really spacious and we actually have enough books to fill it. Ron can keep his files in one cupboard and the piles of *Times* which he accumulates 'to cut things out of'(!) in the other.

Our roof is being rethatched and the ceiling is dropping down thousands of dust motes all over me. There are two Africans on the roof, occasionally getting on with the work, while three others give them moral support from the ground, where they squat with straws in their mouths – a typical PWD tableau. The *capitao* (overseer) wanders about looking important, and raises his hat whenever he glances in at the window, which he frequently does. I could *scream* for lack of privacy.

The rug is well over the halfway mark and my tapestry is three-quarters done. Everyone on the station follows the progress of both with interest, especially the men, oddly enough. I suppose it soothes them to think that here is a real, old-fashioned little woman in the home. Every now and then in conversation with them I perceive that I have inadvertently dealt this image a shattering blow.

My neighbours have gone to Blantyre today, leaving me to feed two huge ridgebacks, a puppy and a cat. The station abounds with dogs and I am great friends with them all, though they lie panting on my flower beds and use our nice lawn rather too freely for decency.

There were great rejoicings and excitement last week when Aleni, Aflike's wife, arrived unexpectedly, two days early. At teatime he burst into the room, said, 'My wife comes,' and flew out to meet her – he had seen her walking up the road. We rushed through and there was a great reunion, Aflike tossing his arms and laughing, his wife – so beautiful – speechless with shyness, Ron talking to her in Chinyanja and taking forever to *say* anything, while I hovered, resisting the impulse to prompt. It was lovely to see that brilliant smile again.

There have been several morning coffee parties to welcome Joan Bolt and I get some amusement from watching the women metaphorically stalking round her with stiff legs and hackles raised until they decided she was nice and not at all DC's wife-ish.

We had a quiet weekend, spending Saturday at the Club watching cricket, Ron *hors de combat* beside me. He introduced me to Bill Rangeley, the second PC for the Southern Province. He is a bachelor, South African, and I like him very much. He fixed me with a sardonic eye and asked me if I had been up the mountain yet and written a book about it! Fortunately I picked up the reference. How they all dislike Mr Van Der Post.

26th August:

The weather is definitely hotting up and I am now longing to move to the other house. It has two bushes, one on either side of the front steps, with white, pale lavender and dark lavender flowers (each flower a separate colour, not mixed). They are called 'yesterday, today and tomorrow' and their exotic scent wafts into the house, especially at night. I have been offered cuttings of roses and other plants and am looking forward to a great gardening campaign. I mean to buy some tools *when* I get to Blantyre. The painters have almost finished in the DC's house, but there are still some alterations to be done. The thatching of our roof is completed, except for a long, untidy fringe all round which has yet to be trimmed. The new thatch has cooled down the rooms a little, but I shall be thankful to move out.

I wonder what you are all thinking about the gossip over Princess Margaret. Lady Colby came back from Rhodesia recently. Apparently the papers there were full of it, but I gather the British press has been remarkably discreet.

The carpenter has made all the furniture very well and I await the final detail – the glass top for my coffee table. Today, with much gesticulation and patience just under control I showed him once again exactly what I want and light seemed to dawn at last, but he went off shaking his head doubtfully over the dona's strange idea of what a table is. I saw him exchange a tolerant shrug with Aflike as they parted at the kitchen door. The tapestry is finished and looks splendid. I can hardly believe I did it!

On Saturday morning after shopping Elsie Martin drove me out to a tea planter's house for coffee. They have lived there for years and what a lovely place they have created. They have their own generator for power, running water, a roofed path between kitchen and house, and Venetian blinds all round the *khondes*, which have moonflowers trained up their columns. There is a beautiful garden full of English and tropical flowers. It looked like a film company's idea of a colonial house. A little orchard of grapefruit trees was in blossom and the scent filled the air. All round there were neat green terraces of tea stretching back towards Mlanje, which, inevitably, towers up just beyond the fields. Our hostess kindly cut my hair, taking off about three inches, which is a great relief – it was such a mane. Ron is not at all pleased!

3rd September:

I have little news for you this week, as life in a way has ground to a halt. I believe the BBC news has mentioned trouble in Nyasaland, so you may be wondering if there have been any incidents in Mlanje. Let me assure you at once all is quiet here, but because of a few disturbances in Cholo district, all *ulendo* has been cancelled for the present. The Government has been expecting a certain amount of trouble over Federation and has a most detailed and efficient security scheme to cover any emergency that might arise, and all administrative officers are cognisant of it.

Unfortunately, on this small station, a certain clash of personalities has emerged among the men, which has had repercussions among the more excitable planters who drink at the Club and pick up gossip and rumours.

Inevitably, some of the wives have allowed themselves to be drawn in and all this has created a highly uncomfortable atmosphere. My reaction has been to go to ground and keep myself to myself, as I cannot bear to get involved in unpleasantness or pettiness of any kind. It is not worth going into detail and I know it will blow over. The whole business is so unnecessary and so depressing. Ron, of course, presses on regardless! I tend to blame the mountain a bit – it is so oppressively on top of us all!

8th September:

I am very sorry that Nyasaland has hit the headlines at home. I now read of it in *The Times* and begin to comprehend the problems of reporting overseas events both realistically and in their true context for home readers. Even locally, rumours are rife. I was in Zomba yesterday and everyone I met asked me, to my astonishment, if I had 'cleared out' till the trouble was over! All has been, and is, quiet here, and trouble seems to have died down everywhere.

Our move has been further delayed by a typical mishap at the DC's house, where a wall had to be knocked down and promptly carried most of the ceiling with it. That house seems to have a hoodoo on it. The weather is getting steadily hotter (and my immediate neighbours steadily cooler!) so I *long* to move.

The rather awful atmosphere on the station has died down, thank goodness, but some community spring has been broken and there is very little socialising. The ban on *ulendo* continues and I am thankful to have Ron's company in the evenings. He of course, is getting bored in the office.

One morning last week the Bolts called unexpectedly in their car and offered me a drive. David had business with the richest estate manager in Mlanje district (Lyons Tea) and they thought I might welcome a change of scene. Would I just! It was only about fifteen miles away, but as soon as we turned off the main road we were in a different world, again among long slopes of tea terraces and, for the last five miles, on a road lined with huge jacarandas, just faintly budded with blue. It must be glorious in 'spring', in a few weeks' time. Yesterday David had to go to Limbe on business and again I went with them, after lunch. When we got there, he found the man he wanted to see had gone to Zomba, so off we went, to my delight. My mountain was looking enticing and peaceful. It is visible for miles before one reaches Zomba and I sat silently feasting my eyes on it. Outside the Secretariat I saw David's (Baxter) car and other familiar ones and nearly burst with frustration at not seeing the owners. However, I got out of the car to stretch my legs and glimpsed many familiar faces, some of whom came out to say hello – none, alas, my favourites. It felt odd to leave after only an hour, with no visits to anyone, but we had the children with us and a long drive back. We did one hundred and seventy-five miles altogether. I felt and looked so much better when I got back, Ron was quite envious but pleased for me.

15th September:

I was afraid you would worry about us as the papers make things read so much more alarming than the facts. Everyone's parents are writing anxious letters and we are all hastening to write back reassuringly. You may have read by now that everything has quietened down. There is still a contingent of Rhodesian police (very impressive), and the Bomas in the districts round Cholo remain watchful.

We were told today we will not move house until 3rd October, which is disappointing. I do not know the reason for this long delay – the workmen have been in the DC's house for five weeks – and I shall certainly not try to find out in case I exacerbate any bad feeling on the station – all such a *bore*. Today I had a very pleasant morning with Elsie Martin, who told me the great news that Iris and Dave arrive at her house for local leave on Monday. Seeing Iris here will be like meeting Aunt Kathie in the middle of a desert!

Aflike complained this morning of a 'hot feeling' inside his shoulder at the back. I suppose it could be rheumatism. I could only tell him I thought 'his bones had caught a cold', which he accepted. He has gone down to the hospital with a note from me. I do not like to give him codeine too often, it is so strong, and I know he was disappointed that I did not get out my *mankwala* chest.

On Sunday our salad at lunch was enhanced by a very good lettuce. Later I was half amused, half appalled when Aflike made a point of informing me with a contemptuous shrug that he had stolen it from my neighbour's garden! A severe talking to by me ensued, with Aflike refusing to meet my eye and indicating by shrugs and sighs that if I chose to starve myself of greens from now on he would not be held responsible. It is so unlike him. He knows, of course, all the boys do, that public relations on the station have been bad, but I cannot allow such behaviour.

24th September:

There is a warm wind today and already at 8.00 a.m. I feel sticky, having just come in from the garden. 'Spring' is here and all the trees on the mountain and in the gardens have turned bright red. The jacaranda is now fully out, so that there is a sudden gleam of that divine blue from unexpected places on the plain below us. I miss the sheer abundance of blossom in Zomba, with its terraced gardens on the mountain roads.

As you will have gathered, things have quietened down here and work goes on as usual except that there is so much paper work at present there is still no *ulendo*. However, that state of affairs cannot last longer than another week, I reckon.

We drove to Blantyre last Wednesday and had a weird experience on the journey. It was a frightful day here, pouring with rain, mist obscuring the mountain and so dark I could hardly see to sew or read. We left about nine and as we approached Cholo we found ourselves in thick white fog which reduced visibility to a few feet. It varied from mile to mile, so that sometimes it was down to the bonnet and we were absolutely road blind, then it would roll back a little. Miserable, shivering Africans kept looming up for a second and then fading out. An Indian driver ahead waved us on to pass him, and Ron had just accelerated and was level with him when a bus appeared, feet away, approaching us. Ron was helpless. The bus driver swerved almost into the deep ditch and we squeezed past by an inch, I swear. Ron was beside himself with rage and his language to the Indian cannot have done much for race relations. Within a few miles of Blantyre we emerged into daylight and in the town itself the sun was blazing in a brazen sky. It changed in exactly the same way on the journey back. We had a great day's shopping but sadly saw none of our friends. I collected the navy blue corduroy for the sofa, which I have decided must be upholstered – the material is too heavy for loose covers – so I bought masses of upholstery tacks. I do not know how on earth I am going to tackle it, but I shall work something out – I must!

We have had great excitement here, as Dave and Iris arrived on Monday on local leave, to stay with the Martins till Saturday. I went up there for coffee on Tuesday morning, returned with Ron for tea and we stayed till 8.00 p.m! It was such a joy to see Iris again, just the same, with her husky voice and laugh. For the first few minutes we sat and smiled delightedly at each other and then began to talk and talk, while Elsie looked at me in astonishment. She confessed she always found me so very quiet! Linden is now a dear wee girl of three. She insisted that she remembered me and appeared to be on very familiar terms with Ron! Dave is just the same too, with his sudden, devastatingly clever remarks. After tea Elsie brought out the gramophone and we had a wonderful nostalgic mixture of records – the Harry Lime Theme, Joan Hammond in an aria from *Tosca*, Elizabeth Schumann singing Lieder, and Richard Tauber. It got dark and a boy lit a lamp in the room behind while we stayed out on the *khonde* still talking. Elsie put the children to bed and let Iris stay out with us, which was very good of her – she is terribly kind. We laughed a great deal and Iris told us lots of news in her vivid, amusing way. Dave and Robin came back late from an unsuccessful fishing expedition and joined in the talk. Iris is going to slip down and see me by herself sometime during their stay.

When I finish this I am going down to the doctor's house for coffee. The Holmeses have gone to Salisbury for three weeks local leave and we have as locum a delightful Irishman, Dr Weir, and his nice wife. They are in Zomba on their first tour and simply hate it, poor things. They think Mlanje is marvellous – so friendly!

Ron is teaching me to play chess. I *love* it.

30th September:

It is 6.55 a.m. and I am on my first *ulendo* in Mlanje district, for four nights. We are in a three-roomed rest house with an indoor bathroom and basic furniture. The heat is shattering and I have to make a great effort to think straight on paper, even at this early hour.

Our frustration over the house situation continues, as our move has been put off for another six weeks at least. Everyone has known for months that the front wall of the DC's house bulges slightly. Somebody pointed this out to Joan Bolt, who thought of her children playing by it and decided it must come down, which means the inside wall will have to be redecorated after it goes up again. I am not going to go on about this – it will make me too hot!

Iris and Dave left on Saturday. She came down and spent the whole of Thursday morning with me. It was *wonderful* to be with someone with whom I have such an immense amount in common. I have not laughed so much since I left home, and she certainly helped me to get Mlanje station into perspective! On Thursday afternoon I went with her, Dave, Elsie and all the children to Likabula, a beautiful spot up a valley beyond the station. Mlanje seems to go on and on forever, peak after towering peak. There is a lovely pool, with huge boulders and overhanging trees, which with their red leaves could have been rowans and birches in autumn in the Highlands. There is a long stony stretch round the pool and there was not a sound except that of running water and the occasional bird call. Although it was a hot day, we could feel the breeze chill as it blew off the water, which was freezing – only the children bathed, screaming their heads off! In the evening Iris and Dave came down for a drink.

Ron and I have been playing chess every evening and I am improving slowly. It is rather like bridge in that one learns a lot very quickly at the beginning and then gets stuck at the same stage for some time. We have to stop quite early as otherwise I tend to dream about it – it is excellent for my concentration.

On Sunday I suddenly decided I could not face the four days alone this week. Iris's visit has unsettled me. So on Monday, loaded with books, several copies of *The Times* and sewing, I came out here with Ron (who is delighted, as is Aflike, who accompanies us) to Palombe, about thirty miles from Mlanje. The scenery on the way was superb – the mountain is quite inexhaustible in the changing aspects of its somewhat stark beauty. Yesterday we drove on another ten miles to have tea with a real 'bush' type, Fred Balestra, a Cockney who came out in 1927 to help his uncle run an estate, now his, which he can only keep up by working for Government in the Department of Agriculture. He has a comfortable wife and a comfortable colonial house, full of carved furniture, ivory tusks and leopard skins. He also has a marvellous collection of books and plied me with as many as I could carry, nice kind man.

6th October: [Air letter]

This is being written in a terrific hurry on Tuesday morning. We are going on *ulendo* today till Saturday, again to Palombe. The mail there is so uncertain my letter may be very late, so I thought I would warn you, in case you worried. I shall write later today from there and post it in faith and hope at the local shack if there is a collection before Saturday. Otherwise I shall post it when I come back here. *Ulendo* is in full swing again, curse it.

It is becoming very hot – there is not a breath of air in this bush house after 10.00 a.m. I am writing at 7.45 a.m, after an hour packing and organising. This morning is beautiful, very clear and fresh at present, with the birds calling in the garden (sounds like Tennyson's poem!) The air is filled with the scent of woodsmoke and the sound of the boys' voices, making me *homesick* for Kasupi. Am I going crazy?! I expect Ron in the car from the office, where he has been collecting files, in a few minutes, so I have just managed this in time. I hope my letter is not too late.

6th October:

We drove out here to Palombe in unbelievable heat and dust. The dryness is at its height and one feels the countryside would go up in an enormous blaze (it probably would) if one so much as touched a match to the grass. Mlanje looks literally fabulous, its lower slopes in the dim heat haze folding back and back on themselves, and the high bare rock faces gleaming austerely in the sun. The Africans get covered in red dust and have their faces perpetually screwed up in the strong, hot wind. I laughed with the car window open and immediately found my teeth grinding on a great shower of dust. Although the Peugeot is marvellous for keeping out dust, I could see a million fine red motes of it billowing in like smoke through the bodywork. Every now and then I think of Joan in such circumstances and I feel quite faint!

We had a very quiet weekend, as usual. In Zomba the weekend stood out as a real holiday each week, but here it tends to be exactly like any other day except, of course, that Ron is around, cleaning the car, preparing a case or just reading those endless files. However, on Sunday we had a lovely morning at the swimming pool, which is beautifully clean and full of icy water which pours into it down little concrete runways which are fed from a huge tank, which in turn is fed from the mountain streams. The setting is attractive but rather overwhelming, with Mlanje soaring above and its tropical forest overhanging the very pool. There were lots of strange birds chuckling and gurgling unseen, and every now and then a branch would shake and a monkey would peer down on us. My nerves were jumping by lunchtime and all morning I kept a sharp look out – my snake stick beside me – while Ron lay sunbathing, blissfully unaware of my irrational behaviour. I just cannot accept that 'the jungle is neutral!' We felt divinely refreshed when we left, after our dips in and out of the achingly cold water.

I am reading *Escape – or Die*, by Paul Brickhill, most exciting. So far I have managed very well with books, thanks to Elsie, but I do miss Zomba library, with its monthly stock of new books. I really did manage, as with films, to keep wonderfully up to date.

I began work on the sofa material yesterday, but only got as far as binding the corduroy edges and sewing three lengths together – a terribly hot task in this weather. I was at it from 7.30 till 12.30 and when Ron came in for lunch I was not fit to speak to, simmering in one of my private rages. Being Ron, he (quite rightly) took one look, assessed my mood, sat down and quietly opened *The Times*!

David wrote from Zomba the other day asking us to go and stay any weekend, and we hope to go soon. The trouble is with all this *ulendo*, Ron does not get in till about nine or later on Saturday morning, so there is not much weekend left. How I *hate* this restless, hot, smelly, futile, continual travelling.

14th October:

I am writing this week in the comparative cool and comfort of the house, instead of sweltering on a hard chair in a stuffy rest house. The heat last week at Palombe was almost unbearable and I have a dim recollection of writing a bad tempered letter as a result – sorry. However, I did manage to finish the rug, in a final desperate spurt. I was determined to get it done quickly, as it was becoming so hot to work at it that I nearly burst each time I tackled it. My arms ached and my fingers blistered and peeled, but on Friday morning it was finished. It now lies glowing on the floor and I sit and gaze at it with disbelief and love. I am hoping Ron will help me upholster the sofa at the weekend – it is a physical impossibility to do it on my own. So our household goods (and gods) assemble, just waiting to spread themselves in that lovely house.

Last week we dined with the Balestras. He has wonderful tales of the old days and of hunting expeditions. Only a few nights before as he was driving home late he saw four eyes shining in the headlights, which gradually revealed themselves as belonging to two huge male lions. He stopped the car and got out (!) with his gun, but he said they were so magnificent and dignified he just 'gave 'em good evening' and got back into his car! We hoped so much we might see them on our way back, but no such luck. We had a dreadful experience on the way back. We came upon a terrible forest fire, right down to the edge of the road. Ron drove past it at high speed. We could feel the heat – awful. There were reports like gun shots as trees exploded, blown apart by the fierce intensity of the heat at the heart of the fire. It looked as if they were being burnt alive – as indeed they were – with scarlet flames like blood licking and flickering along the trunks and branches. It was one of the most horrible sights I have ever seen and I cannot get it out of my mind.

There are a great many outbreaks of fire on the mountain. Sometimes at night I am wakened by the sound and smell of a forest fire burning and always feel compelled to get up and look out, to see if it is near. This fear of fire is an absolute curse on my life and there seems nothing I can do about it.

We came home on Saturday morning, the mountain looming gigantic through the heat haze. When we got out of the car at 8.30 the bodywork was too hot to touch. I went straight into a bath, dressed in clean everything and went off to coffee and shopping with Joan Bolt. She is always thankful to see me back.

On Sunday it got hotter and hotter as the morning wore on till we felt we could hardly breathe if we exerted ourselves at all. Ron was cleaning the car and I was crawling about the *khonde* cutting corduroy. We were both drenched in sweat – it was literally trickling off us. We kept an eye on the sky as we knew what was coming. Towards noon it was filled with storm clouds and dark orange right to the horizon. Just as we both decided to stop working, a *huge* jagged flash of lightning tore the sky apart with a loud 'zip-p-p' and thunder cracked a moment later. It seemed to roll along the mountain and come echoing back – the noise was awesome. After a few minutes of heavy rain it began to hail, pale hailstones the size of large pebbles, hitting the ground audibly and stotting off it. Our big lawn was one mass of queer, jerking movement as they bounced about and then lay still. We stood spellbound on the *khonde* while Aflike, laughing wildly, went rushing out with a bowl to collect 'ice cubes' for our drinks. The coolness afterwards was heavensent.

Yesterday I walked up early to Joan and watched her teaching the children. She is doing it by correspondence course and it takes from 7.45 till 10 every morning. Ricky is five and a half, Caroline six and a half, so Joan has one in the diningroom and one in the drawingroom and moves to and fro. I may help, but cannot undertake it regularly because of *ulendo*. The third child is Simon, eighteen months old, large and cheerful. They are all delightful.

This will be posted when Aflike takes Ron's teatray down to the Boma, five minutes away, carefully covered in embroidered mosquito netting. (I mean the tray.)

Ron is on *ulendo* this week, in a tent, on the hottest part of Palombe plain, and advised me that if I wanted to remain sane, I should give it a miss, so I took his word for it and stayed at home. The weather – I can only repeat – is indescribably hot and sticky. I suspect it is not hotter than Zomba, but the high humidity and the proximity of the mountain (all those rock faces reflecting) make it very trying. I never feel clean after a cold bath so I insist on a warm one, which means I go on and on drying myself and go on and on pouring with sweat. I really do not mind the heat but it is quite a battle to keep fresh.

David Bolt went off for two nights' *ulendo* on Tuesday, so I moved in with Joan, as she nearly goes frantic when left on her own. I had a pleasant time and was glad to be in 'our' house, so much cooler. Yesterday morning I helped her teach the children, which I found interesting and not a bit irritating as I thought it might be. They are bright little people.

I have just had a letter from Margaret Baxter saying they would love to have us for the weekend of 31st October, so if Eric Barnes (the PC) will give Ron permission to leave Mlanje district, we have that to look forward to.

I have very little news for you. On Sunday morning and afternoon Ron and I upholstered the sofa, a marathon effort in the heat. It took nearly five hours and looks very professional. Ron then took off our front door (!) and we moved the sofa in. It looks fine, but is too big for the room, of course.

On Saturday at lunchtime we got a *horrible* fright. Someone had started a small bush fire down on the plain to clear a space for a new 'garden', and the hot, high wind fanned the flames, which spread with appalling rapidity and noise from far below right up to the edge of the bush houses' vegetable gardens. If the fire had come a few yards nearer, the flying bits of burning wood, leaves and grass would have landed on the thatched roofs and away would have gone our houses. (Imagine my thoughts!) When I realised what might happen I took to my heels and started to tear headlong down the hill towards the Boma. Halfway I met Ron coming up. I fell into the car, too winded to speak and just pointed desperately. He took one look, leapt back into the car, raced up to our little prison further up the hill and in no time at all twenty-five prisoners were haring down the road armed with long leafy branches. They arrived only just in time to beat back the flames. Jeff Eyres, a forestry officer who happened to have called at the Boma, *heard* the flames and drove up to help. So he and Ron led the men and after about twenty-five minutes of hectic activity, the fire was put out. I admired so much Ron's prompt action and the way he took charge. If he had hesitated, four bush houses would no longer exist. He and Jeff returned black and soaked in sweat and immediately retired to the bathroom. What with running as fast as I could in the noonday sun, the heat from the fire and the heat generated in my body by acute apprehension, I was hotter than I have ever been in my life! The men cooled off over a beer while I crept away and had a cold bath, for once. Jeff stayed to lunch. I could not eat *one bite*, I was so utterly shaken.

I nearly forgot to tell you – last week Spencer Chapman (*The Jungle is Neutral*), who is touring Africa by caravan, gave a talk at the Club – 'Behind the Jap Lines in Malaya'. It was TERRIFIC. His appearance belies his undoubtedly sterling character. He looks a long-haired intellectual, rather affected in voice and manner, but with a heavenly gift for understatement and a delightful sense of humour. He held us all spellbound and was rewarded by some very good questions afterwards.

28th October:

It is just after 8.00 a.m., a beautiful day which will soon be scorching hot, but is perfect at the moment, with a cool breath of wind. I am writing at the desk and can see the mountain soaring up beyond the top of the window. It is already dimly blue in the heat haze although only a few hundred yards away.

Ron came charging in on Saturday morning with that wonderful 'end-of-*ulendo*' grin, and after coffee took me shopping. I was particularly glad to see him, as he had Aflike with him. I myself suggested this. Aflike was showing signs of feeling as I sometimes do, i.e. that he had been cooped up in Mlanje for months! So off he went and came back much more cheerful, thank goodness. I managed very well with Cook, who had an easy time of it, as I spent two days and nights with Joan, who was also alone. Last week another of my ambitions was fulfilled. Ken Archer has been transferred to Salisbury and kindly rang up from Zomba to offer us his excellent wireless for £25, bought two years ago for £45. So, it awaits us at the Baxters!

On Saturday evening we donned evening dress and after a good dinner went down to the Club about nine to the British Empire League Ball, which we found in full swing, with perhaps one hundred and fifty people. We danced all evening, only exchanging a few words with people we knew. Our nice tea planter friend, John Werner, asked us to join his table for supper, and we met several of his bachelor friends and spent a pleasant hour with them – all young, homesick, lonely Scotsmen (John himself is *very* English), stationed on tea estates in lonely places, lavishing affection on their dogs, drinking too much and going pale, fat and flabby, poor souls.

Last night, at last, the Coronation film was shown at the Club – *A Queen is Crowned*. We went down at seven to find the place rapidly filling up. Already arrived was the Administrator from Portuguese East with some of his staff, who pressed us to swim in their lovely pool over the border and drink Portuguese wine with them – charming men with lovely manners. I am told they live magnificently and wear their official white uniforms every day on duty! I thought the film was excellent. The moments that stand out in my mind are: 'Jerusalem' being sung as the camera moved over 'England's green and pleasant land'; the demeanour of the Queen in the Abbey; the one, lingering near close-up of the pale, fair maid-in-waiting, with a face like a flower; the amazing sequence of rank upon rank of marching men, each more exciting than the last; and finally, the look of breathless, moved surprise on the Queen's face as she came out on the balcony and saw that perfectly incredible, wonderful, teeming mass of humanity surging and swaying below. The chiefs and their minions are to see it tonight, with Ron in attendance, so I shall go too and take Aflike, who looks sick with excitement at the prospect.

We go off to Zomba on Saturday early – Ron has the morning off – and come back on Sunday night. I look forward to it immensely.

5th November:

The hot season is now in full swing and I cannot tell you just how hot it is. We have a big drum of extra water lying by the kitchen door – a huge thing about five feet long and bigger in circumference than a barrel. By *8.15* yesterday morning the water in it was beginning to come to the boil! I could hardly believe my ears when I heard it singing and bubbling to itself. I got the boys to roll it into the shade. It was the hottest day I have ever experienced. I could not settle to sew, read or write letters, and found myself aimlessly wandering about, *instantly* forgetting what I had decided to do – most disconcerting. The men came back from the office grey with exhaustion, poor chaps. Ron stands up to it well, however, and maintains that West Africa was worse, all the time – unthinkable! No wonder they do eighteen month tours.

Ron had a letter from Tom [his guardian] a few days ago, on leave in a monastery in Italy. He is obviously going to become a Roman Catholic as Ron prophesied years ago. His work in Nigeria finishes in April and he will be thankful, as the climate, he says, is rotting him physically and mentally. Help!

I feel we are having a real respite from the normal dreariness of this station. Ron was on *ulendo* only two days last week and is in for the next fortnight. Last week I went again to the Coronation film, the night the Africans and Indians went. We smuggled in Aflike, who was awed by the fact that he sat between two Boma clerks. The bush African thinks these 'white collar' young men are very superior beings. I would like to tell Aflike that in my opinion he is probably worth ten of any one of them, but of course I would only baffle and disturb him. The reactions to the film were interesting and not unexpected. They loved the colourful pageantry of the men marching in the streets and simply yelled with excitement at the crowds milling round the Palace at the end. But, inside the Abbey and with many outdoor shots (e.g. Nelson's Column) I doubt if they knew what they were looking at and why should they? Afterwards we found Aflike had taken refuge in the back of the car, his head in his hands, utterly worn out by the impact of it. He could only shrug, laugh and repeat in Chinyanja, 'I like it, I like it.'

On Saturday morning at 7.30 we set out for Zomba, taking Aflike with us – he has many friends there. It was a glorious day and as we drove into Zomba district and that delectable mountain appeared on the skyline, our hearts lifted and we felt we were back in all the freshness of last tour. This sense of the relativity of time and place happens to me only in Africa and I love it. It creates the slightly unearthly sensation of being in charge of both, for a sudden, revelationary moment when memory, visual and physical, takes over from the present, and *I go back in time*. When I spoke of this in the car to Ron, he said he had not experienced this but understood exactly what I meant. We passed the turn-off to Magomero and a few miles further on caught a glint from the aluminium (ugh) roof of 'the house that Ron built'. I remained unmoved – no time warp there!

We dropped Aflike near the market and at ten o'clock drew up at Zomba Boma, where John and Dorothy were just emerging from their car. They were delighted to see us and wanted us to spend some of our time with them over the weekend, but of course we had to decline. We then called at the Secretariat and found David in his office – looking taller than ever – and just as thin. He has the

Secretariat pallor and his eyes look tired, but he was in great form. We left him to it and drove along Naisi Road and found the house, where Margaret gave us coffee. She is a delight to look at – very pretty: tall, with soft dark brown hair, deep blue, wide-set eyes and a lovely smile. We took to her at once and found it easy to talk, which is a great relief. I must say I would not like to be in her position, coming out as a bride on her husband's second tour, not speaking a word of Chinyanja and having to take charge of servants who have only known David's bachelor ways. However, she seemed to be coping calmly with everything. I tried to keep a curb on reminiscences of last tour and shop talk, so that she would not feel excluded, but of course she will have to get used to the men talking shop, as I frankly told her, poor lass. At dinner we drank champagne provided by us. We went on to the cinema but it was an Abbot and Costello and no one interesting was there – a great disappointment. We walked out after twenty minutes and went back to their house to play records.

On Sunday morning at noon we drove down Naisi Road in raging heat, past our old house, its garden exactly as I had laid it out, with the row of grapefruit trees much taller. I found myself surveying the scene with complete dispassion – Naisi and nostalgia definitely do not go together! The Baxters had been invited to a curry lunch by Tony and Pam Bridge who, when they heard we would be with them, kindly asked them to bring us along. There were over thirty guests there, all on the big *khonde* in sun dresses and shorts in the great heat. It was the nicest party I have ever been to in Zomba, in part because we have few social occasions here, but mainly because we knew so many people and were pleased to see them, as indeed they were to see us. It felt like being in a very small, exclusive club! We talked to the Watsons, the Simmonds, the Dickinsons and many others. Just as we were finishing a delicious lunch, a tremendous thunderstorm broke over our heads, so deafening the only sensible thing to do was for us all to say goodbye and rush through the rain to our cars. After an early tea we left, both of us hoarse with talking! We hope to have a visit from the Baxters soon.

We thought we were moving house this week, but of course there has been another delay. However, I think we really will move next week, which will be quite an ordeal in this heat. How thankful we will be, all the same.

Walter and Barbara Sproule, the second ADC and his wife, have arrived and we had them round for a drink last night. They are very pleasant, middle-aged, ex-Army, back in Mlanje for the second time (poor souls) on their second tour, and very annoyed that they are not getting the good house, but too polite to blame us. How I long to leave this station.

11th November:

The heat is paralysing. It is only 7.45 now and I am bathed in sweat, having been doing flowers in a leisurely manner. It is quite a different heat from

Zomba because of the humidity, as I have said, and for the first time in Africa I wear a hat in the garden all the time, which I dislike, as I want the sun to bleach my hair, but it is too risky to go bareheaded here at this time of year. The other wives are simply invisible till the evening.

We are delighted with our wireless (an EKCO), which has a lovely tone and tunes in clearly to London in the evening – heaven to hear Big Ben and the news, and on Sunday evening 'Much Binding'. Also, there is always a wonderful programme of classical music from Salisbury on Sunday morning – such a treat. I have been feeling simply starved for music. I am sure it has been positively bad for us not to have it.

You will be happy to know we are in THE HOUSE! The Bolts moved up to the DC's house on Friday, we moved in here on Saturday morning and the Sproules moved from a disgusting old bush house where they have been camping out, into our bush house, which is in excellent condition, on Saturday afternoon. We only knew of this plan on Thursday evening, so I spent Friday packing in absolutely appalling heat which lessened in the afternoon after a monumental thunderstorm. I felt quite ill – any exertion in heat like this brings on diarrhoea – but I was so glad to be moving I just pressed on – how to lose weight quickly! We got up at 5.00 a.m. on Saturday to avoid the heat, and at 6 the lorry was being loaded with our stuff. By 9.30 we were installed and Aflike was all over the place, cleaning and polishing with a will. I cannot tell you what a difference it makes to be in a really attractive bungalow with large cool rooms. Everything looks better. We spent an ecstatic weekend arranging our possessions. The kitchen quarters are attached to the house and there are wonderful pantries and shelves. The sun room is Ron's study and my sewing room in the mornings. He has his Magomero bookcase there, full of papers, files and cuttings – thank goodness for the sake of tidiness in the rest of the house. There are big store cupboards everywhere, so all our trunks are out of sight and fully unpacked; at last my passion for storage space is fully satisfied. Our bedroom has one enormous mosquito net which fits over both beds and is much cooler to sleep under.

The garden is huge – far bigger than we realised. We have several very fruitful mango and peach trees, masses of flowering shrubs, a little cactus garden and all sorts of hedges and borders. The whole place is fragrant with masses of white jasmine, petunias, pride of India and the two marvellous bushes of 'yesterday, today and tomorrow'. There is even a bird bath on the big front lawn. There is a large vegetable garden about a quarter of a mile from the house by a stream, which I will have to maintain, but as I have no desire to go travelling in the bush when I want to visit my vegetables, I shall start a small kitchen garden behind the house. There must be a least twenty flower beds and no doubt more will materialise when the place is cleared. It has not been touched for over a year, which in the climate of Mlanje means a flourishing wilderness. Ron is going to organise a team of penal labourers to clear it for me. Our prison is only two hundred yards up the road and, as Ron is officer in charge, it is all very simple! The DC's house is further up the hill, about five minutes walk from here in the cold season, at least ten in the heat.

There was a murder in the district some weeks ago, and Ron held the preliminary enquiry – his first. Mr Justice Sinclair came over from Blantyre to hear the case, a big New Zealander with a shock of white hair and piercing blue eyes. He lunched with the Bolts, and we entertained the new, very young Crown Counsel and his charming stenographer. He lost his case to the extremely able Indian lawyer who was defending the African. As I walked down to the Boma to meet the judge afterwards, I passed the acquitted man, sitting surrounded by his friends, smoking a cigarette by the courtroom, which is just a little shack. He gave me a dazzling smile and a salute. I felt glad for him though he looked a bit of a villain! Sinclair was perched on the table in the DC's office, his wig askew, vigorously scratching his head! Ron said the heat and smell in court were beyond belief.

Yes, there is one particular book I would love for my birthday. I noted it down when I read the reviews. I suggest you order it in time to have a good look at it yourself, as I know you will appreciate it. It is called *Persona Grata* and has photographs by Cecil Beaton and letter press by Kenneth Tynan; it costs 21/– and is published by Wingate. I am sorry it is so expensive but good books are now.

The glass for the table has arrived and it looks stunning. I asked the carpenter to wait while I assembled the whole table with the tapestry stretched on a board and fitted under the glass. He was completely mollified by the result! Aflike thinks I am so clever.

19th November:

You ask about keeping food and drink fresh. Well, it is not easy! We have a surprisingly effective little charcoal cooler. It has a wooden cupboard framework, wire-netted, and all down both sides there is a layer of charcoal. Water is regularly poured along the top and it sinks into the charcoal and evaporates – et voilà! We keep drinking water and fats in it; no jelly will set in it but it is a help.

The rains came on Monday night so the days are much cooler and I have five times as much energy.

On Saturday we had the doctor and his wife to dine, Sandy and Mary Holmes. She is a nice Edinburgh girl and he is a Polish refugee who studied at Edinburgh University. They are both very intelligent and we had a pleasant, amusing evening.

We have had our penal labourers for several days moving, oh so slowly, over the garden, which is gradually emerging as the wonderful garden it is. I quail a little at the work ahead but I shall manage. The men feel the heat and tend to take long rests under the big mango tree, eating unripe mangos, so the best of luck to their insides! All Sunday morning a beautiful kingfisher with a bright red bill sat like a statue on the bird bath, so that Ron stood equally statuesque, with the shears poised over a bush for minutes on end watching it. There are lots of flowering shrubs and shrubs with coloured leaves which I have not yet identified. I think they are a species of croton. There are masses of bougainvillaea, oleander and frangipani and the air is full of scents, so heady one's head reels slightly. I have sixteen seed boxes on the *khonde*, filled with carnations, gypsophila, lobelia, phlox, dianthus, antirrhinums and verbena. I planted them on Sunday and today every single box shows little green shoots. Aflike bought me two big chunky native cooking pots which stand on either side of the *khonde* steps at the top. I am waiting for Mary Holmes to give me cuttings of moonflower and morning glory, which I shall train to climb up and hide two large drainpipes. By ten o'clock on Sunday it was too hot to go on working outside, so we both worked on the *khonde* and listened to the whole of *Figaro* from Salisbury.

On Monday we had one of those typically muddled days which sometimes occur out here. Ron had to go to Blantyre to deliver the Mlanje district enrolment forms for the Federal vote, calling on the way at Cholo to collect that district's supply. David Bolt wanted him back by lunchtime, so we left early, getting to Cholo by 8.30. There we were informed that Ron was required to wait till the DC Port Herald arrived with *his* supply, which he did, at *noon*! Poor Mrs Martin, the DC's wife, valiantly entertained us for hours! We went on to lunch with Vernon MacDonald (Ron's boss last tour at Magomero) and his nice wife – they heard we were around and sent a note to invite us. We got to Blantyre at 2 o'clock where Ron delivered his vast collection of forms at the PC's office and I did some hurried shopping. We were back here by 4 o'clock. Poor Ron reported to the DC, had supper and went off on *ulendo*, leaving me alone for the first time in this house, with the rain pounding around me. I am having quite a pleasant week as Joan and I go up to the pool with the children. We never see anyone else up there!

26th November:

You must not worry about the heat. It really does not affect Ron or myself, provided we are not rash in our activities in the garden, which we now limit to before 9.00 a.m. and after 5.00 p.m. There has been rain every day this week, accompanied by the usual ear-splitting thunderstorms that only Mlanje mountain knows how to create, so the air is less heavy – I can almost hear the garden growing.

I assure you this tour is not nearly as difficult to cope with as last tour, even though I have no one at all in Mlanje to share my particular interests. This house and garden make up for a lot and besides, my whole outlook is different –

I just have a more relaxed approach to life and go my own way much more. I am happy to say this attitude of mine has had a good effect on Ron, so that at last we are able to feel that Africa no longer comes between us but brings us closer. If he could just get his own district it would help very much. We both feel he is ready to take on a district.

The swimming pool is now abrim, cool and clean, with icy water pouring into it all day, and soon losing its iciness under the searing heat of the sun. I have been gradually browning and on Sunday morning, having played a game of chess by the pool in my bathing suit, I suddenly found I was deeply tanned, except for my face – the sun is so directly overhead it never shines on it and it is as white as when I left home. I have promised Ron to turn it up to the sun for ten minutes daily so that it is brown by the time he comes back on Saturday. On Monday before he went to *ulendo* he took me to the local Indian store and I bought masses of material for curtains. He is going to be so pleased when he returns to find them all made and hung.

3rd December:

Ron has been doing some hard thinking about the future. He says that at present the work of a district officer is rapidly deteriorating into that of a policeman and later may turn into something even worse. However, he must wait and see how the political scene develops. I only mention this as I know it will interest you.

The Baxters are coming to stay this weekend. They will be our first house guests. I have been very busy in the house and garden and (mentally) in the kitchen.

I am having to do a bit of bird watching, as the Bolts' daughter, Caroline, loves it and keeps describing birds which I have to look up in Ron's bird book, which we have replaced, having lost the first copy in the fire. Our latest find is an olive sunbird, very common, *but* we have also found its nest, a little long woven bag hanging from a banana tree out of reach on the steep slope by the DC's garden, but well within watching distance. I have told Joan she must encourage Caroline, as it is a marvellous training in using one's eyes – so it is – and will also give her a great hobby for a lifetime. (I can hear you all laughing at my hypocrisy.)

Christmas parcels are beginning to arrive and I put them away very firmly, as Ron starts pulling at string and paper, ready to say 'it just came away in my hand!' He is in this week, wonder of wonders. He had a lovely birthday on Tuesday. I gave him a diary and a chess set, which the Bolts managed to find for me in Blantyre. It is only plastic, but it looks all right, and he has already beaten me three times with it. Aflike knows the Baxters are coming and slaves away at our already highly polished floors, which have recently caused me one very dramatic downfall and several acrobatic near misses!

We are having a lot of rain and thunder, mainly at night or in the late evening. The days are hot and sunny. Every morning Joan, the children and I go up for a swim, and again, after tea, with husbands as well. The children are just beginning to learn to swim, except for the baby, Simon, who sits on the steps up to his neck in water, grinning at us all. So, what with the cooler weather, the swimming and Ron in for a week, I feel pretty good!

On Sunday evening we unexpectedly heard Bach's Air on the G String played very splendidly by a full orchestra and to my surprise and Ron's consternation I BURST into tears. Hi, ho, and who was boasting that she felt in command of life?! It was just Dunalastair and not to be borne. However, I was mopped up and smoothed down, and recovered in time to listen to 'Much Binding' – fun.

16th December:

The date seems utterly unreal, as at this moment, just after lunch, the air is thick and sticky, storm clouds are low over the house and thunder is rolling and echoing along the length of the mountain.

We had a wonderfully happy week last week, culminating in the Baxters' visit at the weekend. They came in time for tea on Saturday and left after tea on Sunday. They thought Mlanje as a station must be quite perfect and fell in love with our house and garden which in comparison with their pokey little house and garden seemed a dream of spaciousness. (How well I know the feeling.) I could have told them life on Mlanje station was far from perfect but did not bother. Margaret sensed I had reservations and would obviously have liked to have a good gossip about it, but I thought I would spare David's feelings, since he believes all his fellow men – and women – are as nice as he is, dear man. To my great delight they have asked us to stay with them at New Year, so for the third time we shall spend New Year's Eve in Zomba. It has given me something to look forward to, always a help.

24th December:

I gave myself a perfectly dreadful burn on my arm the other night. I got entangled in the curtains between Ron's study and the drawingroom, carrying a lamp, and in my efforts to clear the curtains my arm brushed against the top of the lamp and *stuck* to it, and the skin peeled off as I jerked my arm away. So, I have been treating a severe, raw burn with Daddy's marvellous dressings, but despite it drying up quickly and growing a new skin, I have a three inch long scarlet weal, like an ugly birthmark. It will go.

I have planted over 500 seedlings this week! I am training a fall of verbena over one terrace onto another. Yesterday the Bolts had to go to Blantyre and at 5.45 a.m. I received a note from Joan saying 'Wake up! We are going to

Blantyre. Be ready by seven'! I leapt up, to Aflike's flustered astonishment, and was ready by quarter to! We had a marvellous morning. David vanished into the PC's office to discuss the visit, in January, of Lord Llewellyn, the Governor General of the Federation, and Joan and I shopped and then had coffee (civilised bliss) in a new restaurant. I bought Ron a book on animals of Africa and some beautiful brown tie silk material to be made, by me, into a dressing-gown. He does not know I got this chance to visit Blantyre, so the presents will be a complete surprise.

Today Aflike and I are simply dashing about. Ron and I decided that as it is Christmas we would do the right thing, so we are giving a drinks party on Christmas morning at noon, having asked everyone on the station. To my amazement *everyone* has accepted, so there will be eighteen of us. I shall be busy making hundreds of small eats, called 'patsy-go-lows' out here, from the Chinyanja for 'before', *patsogolo*! Some of the guests will be visiting us in this house for the first time.

31st December:

I expect your letter will come by today's post, but as we go off to Zomba after lunch, I am writing this without waiting for it, so that you will get it at the usual time. David Bolt has very kindly given Ron this afternoon off, so we can stay in Zomba till Sunday.

Well, Christmas is over! I had a hectic time getting the house and garden ready, and making mince pies which I felt sure neither of us would want to eat in this hot, hot weather.

Caroline Bolt's seventh birthday was on Christmas Eve, so I walked up for tea (with the gift of a home-made frilly dress for her best doll) and for the first time in *years* saw a table spread for a children's party: plates of sandwiches with little labelled flags, home-made iced sponge cakes and, later, different coloured jellies wobbling on the sideboard. I felt positively drenched in nostalgia! In the morning I was at Mary Holmes's house for coffee. She, nice kind woman, had invited all the wives and their children, who were given presents from a lovely tree. It was the first time for weeks, indeed months, since we had all been together, but I found it quite easy, as I have grown beyond being unsettled by petty people. In the evening I washed my hair and was settling down with a book, determined not to give myself a minute to be homesick, when I heard the dearly loved sound of our car, and RON appeared! He was supposed to be out till Christmas morning, but said it suddenly came over him that it was criminal for us to be apart on Christmas Eve, for the sake of one more night's 'damned *ulendo* in the bloody bush' as he succinctly put it, so he just upped and came – wonderful!

Christmas Day was cloudy and very, very hot. I filled the house with flowers and we got quite light-headed on the scent of honeysuckle and jasmine. I had our cards displayed on every possible surface and the room looked lovely, Aflike having polished the floors and himself till he and they glistened, done all the silver (i.e. three pieces) [given to me by my father, after the fire], and the brass doorknobs and window handles. He, Cook and I quickly assembled a vast number of small eats. I got a wonderful surprise present from Ron, which David Bolt had bought in Blantyre and kindly sent out by special messenger to Ron's camp. It is a small travelling clock, to replace Aunt Kathie's present which I loved so much. I have not mentioned that it was stolen on *ulendo* – Aflike's fault, as he carried it in his back pocket and then went to a market. He hardly dared to tell me, poor man, and sweated pungently when he brought himself to do so. To his intense surprise, I took refuge in one of my deep silences. In the face of such grave domestic disasters I just retreat inside myself and *close the door*. We love all our presents from home, especially the T.S. Eliot book of poetry, Moray McLaren's *The Scots*, which Ron is now enjoying, and the book on chess – wonderful choices. Joan sent me two books she knew I wanted! A book on poetry by Herbert Read and the journals of Denton Welch. It is lovely to be able to enrich my depleted shelves.

To return to our party. The food was placed on two tables in the drawingroom and the bar was set up on the *khonde*. (Joan and Mary brought masses of ice.) People arrived promptly and by 12.15 they had all arrived. It went very well, everyone polite and friendly in the best Christmas spirit. No one coming in would have dreamed we were not all a collection of happy friends! A very good thing too. By 1.30 they had all gone. I cancelled our light lunch and we ate the remains of the titbits and had a post mortem drink – highly satisfactory. After tea we heard the Queen's speech, perfectly clearly. She is too young to make one feel as the King did, and I felt it was not the same kind of message at all. The only human note was the slight wistfulness in her voice when she mentioned her children. Then, to our delight, they broadcast the Nine Lessons and Carols from King's College, Cambridge, and that made Christmas for me. In the evening we went to the Holmeses for Christmas dinner. No one else from the station was there but they had two young Scottish couples staying with them and we had a great party. They sang, played games and told stories – not really 'me' but I joined in. Ron, to my astonishment, threw himself into it all and was marvellous! The rest of the weekend we spent quietly by ourselves, with the wireless and our new books.

Ron is in this week, so there is a feeling of well being in the house. Aflike is fussing over our evening clothes and there is much blowing on, and rattling of, charcoal as he presses them. It is wonderful to think of seeing Zomba mountain this afternoon and later meeting many friendly people.

Chapter 18

Yesterday I sent off a birthday card to you, which I bought on our last day in London! We were with Joan in Heals, choosing her present of eight beautiful plain glasses to replace her original ones lost in the fire. I saw the card and thought how much you would like it. I have kept it carefully put away in a drawer, but it still looked slightly soiled – sorry, it is the climate.

Last week I wrote on the day we went off to Zomba, a heavenly hot, shimmering day. We left after an early lunch and I felt absolutely happy. I enjoy the car very much now, I do so little travelling. As we approached that seductive blue mountain (it changes colour with the light) I felt like singing. We arrived in time for tea and were given a great welcome. Poor Margaret had a miscarriage some weeks ago and was not looking very well; David, understandably, was rather piano, so we set to and did our best to cheer them up. A young couple, Dick and Sheila Purdie, living in the new house at Kasupi on their first tour, arrived in the early evening. Sheila and I slept in the spare bedroom and Dick and Ron on camp beds in the sittingroom. Bryn and Chris Jones-Walters whom we knew and liked last tour in Zomba, came for dinner too, so it was a great party – all the men good dancers. (I wore my black taffeta halter-neck dress, which showed off my dark brown back and shoulders.) We had a lovely buffet supper and arrived at the Club to find it fuller than I have ever seen it and simply humming with festive spirit. The Governor and his party arrived soon after us, all looking well fed and perhaps faintly bored. Ruth Simmonds gave me a huge, friendly wink as she stalked past, with that slightly defiant, independent air she has. It strikes a chord in me – I would like to be like her! Eve and Humphrey Bingham, whom we had not yet seen this tour, rushed up and embraced me with real warmth, and wanted to hear all our news. My mind stumbled momentarily – there seemed so little to tell – but I managed. It was thrilling to be among so many friends and acquaintances, all so welcoming and pleased to see us. Charles (Gurd) was there and came over to talk. He has been posted to Fiji and departs in February. We hardly ever see him but it cast a shadow over the weekend to know he would soon be gone. [We were to come across each other years later, in the Pacific.] Bill Melhuish came up and, stooping solicitously from his great height, led me onto the dance floor. (I said to Ron later 'the only way I could see was to peep under his arm!') He insisted we lunch with him on Saturday, bringing the Baxters. This will be *marvellous* – he lives on Zomba mountain! Altogether it was a most exhilarating evening. I danced for hours and we did not leave till about 3.30.

On Saturday morning David went off to the office, Margaret had household affairs to attend to, and Ron and I went on our own in the car to Zomba, to consult Charles at the hospital about Ron's eyes. He has been having bad headaches and obviously needs a change of lenses. He is to see an eye specialist who comes up from Rhodesia to Blantyre once a month. We had a long talk with Charles and that was the last we saw of him. We did some business in Zomba and returned to Naisi. At lunchtime, we four drove in our car up the mountain to Bill's retreat – a dear little log cabin surrounded on three sides by pines, perched right on the edge of the mountain with a spectacular view. He is a wonderful host. During an excellent lunch the conversation touched on flying saucers, which are much in the news just now. Ron was at his usual trick of arguing on the side he does not agree with, and I made everyone laugh by saying, in quiet but furious exasperation, 'For someone with a science degree, Ron, you do say the most extraordinary things!' We had coffee in the sittingroom before a log fire. The climate up there is utterly different from Zomba and of course far more healthy, in that sublime mountain air. He has promised to come and stay with us at Mlanje. In the evening we dined with the Jones-Walters and saw an awful Errol Flynn film at the Club. Otherwise it was a delightful evening, as they are an attractive and interesting couple. It made me sorry we had not seen more of them last tour.

We reluctantly left for Mlanje next day after tea and got back about seven, to find the house apparently very spacious and very clean. Ron is in all this week so I still feel I am on holiday. The break livened us up immensely, despite the inevitable sense of returning to a vacuum. In Zomba Ron found in conversation with the men that there is considerable evidence of politics creeping into both Boma and Secretariat thinking. This worries and saddens him. He talks of 'the good old days' of last tour and reckons they have gone forever. Bryn agreed with him.

The weather is scorching hot and I live at the pool with Joan Bolt, Mary Holmes and a swarm of dark brown children. This morning, alone in the deep end, I suddenly found myself face to face with a snake – not a water snake, to judge by its behaviour. I think it must have been asleep on top of one of the concrete runaways, fallen into the water and been swept down into the pool. I called to Joan and Mary to get the children out and propelled myself backwards to the end of the pool. The snake was still floating towards me, half in and half out of the water, struggling to stay on the surface. I flung my body back and up out of the water onto the concrete edge of the pool, grazing myself spectacularly down one thigh and leg, rushed over for my snake stick, managed to sling the wretched creature (probably half drowned) over it and hurled it as hard as I could into the bush beyond the pool. We had another scare a few days ago when a long, thick black snake fell heavily out of a big tree and landed with a loud slap across Mary's shoulders where she stood in the shade. She whirled round, thinking someone had hit her with a towel! Fortunately, the snake, after writhing about on the ground, got its bearings and sped away into the bush. Mary was remarkably calm – fear of snakes does not happen to be one of her things. I do not believe it even occurred to her it might have bitten her. Witnessing the scene was enough to turn my knees to jelly and I just sank down on the ground without a sound. She never knew how I felt, but Joan did! These two episodes have made us very watchful.

14th January:

It is a perfect day at 8.00 a.m, already so hot I have given up the idea of either cutting flowers for the house or touring the garden to see what work has to be done. So three penal labourers have been left to their own devices, i.e. sitting in the shade. We have had a wonderful crop of peaches and have been living on fresh fruit salads of peaches, pineapples, paw-paw, mango and guava – all from the garden. I am now watching the avocado pear and passion fruit trees gradually ripening.

I have just made one more withdrawal from the Mlanje scene. I have felt such a misfit at the Naggers' meetings that I took my courage in both hands and sent in my letter of resignation. I wrote out about twelve versions and then decided in despair it did not really matter what I said, as I am bound to give offence anyway. The monthly meetings are considered by the women to be one of the highlights of Club life in the district. Well, I am sorry, but there it is.

The glorious weather has completely disorganised my days, as I go up to the pool morning, afternoon and early evening if I can. I think it worth seizing the chance, as the season for it is not long, and sometimes it rains for a week and I do not go at all. It helps me feel fit and well, which is essential here.

Ron went out on Thursday this week. He is only one and a half miles away and comes into the Boma every day as the paper work is piling up – so I have him for lunch, which brightens our day. It is all nonsense but has to be done to get in his fourteen nights.

On Tuesday Lord Llewellyn, the Governor General of the Federation, came on a half hour visit to Mlanje and met about two hundred people at the DC's house, which has an enormous lawn. It was a dull, damp, frightfully hot morning, with the mountain lurking almost invisible behind wet white mist which drifted down to the treetops of the garden. Robin Martin had his policemen out in the middle of the lawn as a guard of honour. The Africans and Indians lined the borders of the lawn and all the Government people stood on the big *khonde*. He inspected the police, accompanied by a charming young Aide-de-Camp, an Army major (who flashed a quick smile at Ron, no doubt glad to see a young, friendly face) and Bill Rangeley, co-PC of the Southern

Province. Lord Llewellyn was large, hot and crumpled in a white linen suit –
and very friendly. Joan Bolt, as his fleeting hostess, gave the first curtsey. She
looked terrible, as she has a badly poisoned foot and was grey with pain. I had
the Bolt children with me and had to unwind them from elaborate attempts at a
bow and curtsey respectively, in order to get them to produce a hand for Lord L.
to shake, while the DC, having introduced everyone with admirable clarity, said
vaguely, 'Oh, these are mine!' The old boy then went inside, had a cup of tea
and left. People faded away very quickly while the Bolts, the Holmeses, Ron
and I collapsed in the sittingroom and drank tea. The women kicked off their
shoes and rolled down their stockings. (I am so brown I got away with bare
legs.) Lord Llewellyn was to visit several tea estates and lunch at the biggest
one, Lujeri. Ron was furious and said it was a sign of the times that he had
lunch with a planter instead of with the DC of Mlanje district.

He went off after tea, leaving me alone for the first time since Christmas Eve.
I buried myself in *The Times*.

21st January:

We had a sudden change of weather on Friday. It rained all night, all next day
and all Sunday – glorious grey skies, a heavy, chilly downpour or else a lovely
fine drizzle, bringing a wonderful fresh smell and a flush of green over the
parched land. There has been very little rain this season and the maize crop is
poor; there is even talk of another famine.

On Sunday evening we had the biggest earth tremor for many years. Cook,
who must be approaching sixty, says he has never experienced one like it. We
have felt a few in Zomba, very fleeting ones, but this one lasted *thirty seconds*.
(Try counting slowly up to thirty.) It happened at 7.48 p.m. when we were
listening to 'Much Binding'. There was a noise like distant thunder which
gradually increased, the wireless made loud noises of protest, the doors and
windows shook and the entire house rocked slightly. The floor was undulating
and one felt vaguely off balance, a sensation which rapidly got worse. The
walls were vibrating visibly and there were loud bangs on the ceiling, while
plaster and dust came streaming down in sudden spurts, covering everything.
The tall wooden lampstand began to sway violently; I saw this just in time
to catch the lamp, which was moving in jerks towards the edge. Ron and I
sat looking at each other for a few seconds, then I said 'This is one of those
things . . . tremors.' Ron nodded and we got up. We seemed to move in slow
motion. He opened the door, felt the wall alongside and grinned in nervous
surprise when it moved against his hand. We stood together swaying, bewil-
dered by the noise and general upheaval round us. As the tremor reached its
height, Ron took the lamp from me and pulled me against him saying, 'Let's go
outside till this is over,' and we stepped onto the *khonde*. Almost immediately it
all began to subside and die very slowly away.

The odd thing is we came straight in, sat down and listened to 'Much Binding' till it finished at eight, before we said anything! My knees were shaking but I certainly was not aware of feeling frightened at the time, nor was Ron. I think my peculiar defence mechanism against Africa stood me in good stead. Aflike and Cook were really scared. They took quite a time to come through, giggling with nerves, to see how we were, survey the damage and begin to clear it up. The room was a sight and I told them to leave it till the morning. David Bolt, good man, made a round of the station with a hurricane lamp. He called in on us last, looking very white. He said most of the houses have cracked walls and ceilings, but nothing big fell down. Some of the wives had been almost hysterical with fear for the children. There was another, small, tremor on Tuesday evening and everyone was jumpy. This is not earthquake country. The tremors are caused by some geological disturbance in the Rift Valley.

On Thursday the Holmeses invited me to spend the day with them in Blantyre, which I was glad to do, as I needed odds and ends. We had a very pleasant day. I met several acquaintances from Zomba, and Mike and Joan Saunders, who were delighted to see me. They are at Chiradzulu, a one-man station between Limbe and Zomba, on the side of the mountain of that name, said to be the most beautiful station in Nyasaland. They love it, of course.

I am expecting Joan Bolt for coffee any minute. She has been completely immobilised for about ten days with a poisoned foot. A spider bit her at the pool and her foot swelled up and was most painful. Sandy Holmes had to lance an inch deep to find a great internal festering wound. She is very run-down, depressed and nervous. Sandy grimly gave the DC a certificate to say his wife is unfit for *ulendo* and unfit to be left alone, so that puts a stop to the DC's *ulendo*. Poor Ron will have a *fit* when I tell him! This afternoon I am off to Mary's to help her sew tapes on her son's school outfit.

28th January:

I had just settled to this at 8.30 this morning, when Joan Bolt arrived, looking very unwell, to tell me some woman on one of the estates had been rude to her on the phone, which had upset her and David was out for the day, so would I please go up and spend the morning and have lunch with her, to cheer her up. So I put this aside and went up. It was a most beautiful, brilliant morning with glorious cloudscapes and a high wind. We sat in their marvellously tropical garden all morning and had a hilarious lunch with the three sweet children. I came back shortly afterwards, as there are great storm clouds, thunder is rumbling and I wanted to get home before it breaks.

We have not been swimming for a few days, as there has been a panic over the water in the pool. Sandy Holmes discovered that the tank which provides the supply of water was not in good repair. He found mud, dead and alive frogs and other small creatures, including snails. As bilharzia is carried by a type of snail, there was an uproar! However, the snail was examined in the lab. and is not the bilharzia carrier. So, the tank has been cleaned and repaired and all is well. Sandy's report, incoherent with rage and Polish excitability, was very funny, and his African typist added mistakes to the fun.

Ron is on *ulendo* again, for the third week, so I shamelessly opened Joan's birthday parcel yesterday, to cheer myself up. It is five yards of lovely blue and white Horrocks cotton – a marvellous present. All I have to do now is wait till I next go to Blantyre, order a Vogue pattern book, wait for it, and when it comes, choose a pattern, send home for it and *wait for that!*

There has been a lot of rain, so the weather is cooler and I have been busy for hours in the garden, where the weeds grow as quickly as the flowers – my phloxes are already in bloom, though it seems no time since I put them in.

Ron has been investigating a case of corruption – fiddling Native Authority court books, and at the weekend distinguished himself by having a nightmare in Chinyanja, if you please, beating about with his hands and shouting, '*Ndani, ndani,*' (Who, who)! What it is to be a linguist!

Do you realise I shall be *thirty-two* on Saturday?

4th February:

Yes, Ron dislikes *ulendo* now, and does only what he has to do while he is out, whereas last tour he simply did everything he could possibly fit into a day. He often takes out files from the office and works on them, doing no walking at all – there is no need – very changed days and a very changed man. It is such a pity the Governor cannot be made to see the error of this particular rule, based entirely on *theory* – fatal.

My birthday book arrived on time and is *wonderful*. The photographs are magnificent and Tynan's letter press is a model of clever, witty writing. Ron is also enchanted with it. A thousand thanks.

Ron came in on Saturday morning and presented me with a large bottle of Eau de Cologne, which I have been without for months. Joan Bolt came with Caroline for coffee and gave me a beautiful, sweet-smelling bouquet of flowers. The Holmeses came for a drink at lunchtime and made a great fuss of me and I really felt I was having a birthday. We had a bottle of white wine at dinner to round off the day.

Sunday was boiling hot and we swam in the morning, returning in time to hear some of our lovely music from Salisbury. I am now nearly black with the sun.

11th February:

You may have heard by now that Joan sails on 20th April in the *City of Paris*, arriving about 26th May. I shall have to start getting the spare room organised for her – and thinking desperately of how to entertain her! I am going to ask her to bring out my corduroy suit, as I need more warm clothes.

The Holmeses are very kind to me when Ron is out, asking me down for an evening meal and canasta (which bores me). They took me to Blantyre with them on Tuesday, as Sandy had to attend a court case – an Indian had had his head chopped off with an axe! We went to visit St. Andrews, the primary co-educational boarding school which Robin, their son, aged seven, attends. What a pathetic sight the children were at playtime, some quite happy, others mooning about alone like little animals at bay. Robin walked over, said 'Hello,' to his mother, ignored his father and me, and silently spent his twenty minutes eating his way through a packet of ginger snaps Mary had given him. He left without a backward glance, and I saw Mary's eyes fill with tears. What a life it can be for a family out here.

There are five murder cases to be tried next week in Mlanje. The Chief Justice and Crown Counsel, plus stenographers, are descending on the station for a few days. I quickly offered to put up the CJ's stenographer, whom I know and like very much. I will not be asked to put up the young Crown Counsel, as Ron will be on *ulendo* – not the done thing at all!

18th February:

This is the season for tremendous swarms of bees, and there are ominous signs that they favour this house – there are at least a dozen humming maddeningly about the room at the moment.

I am very happy this week, as Ron has unexpectedly been 'in'. The Treasury Cashier was posted suddenly to Blantyre and the DC asked Ron to cancel his *ulendo* and stay in to help him cope with the money. Needless to say Ron was only too willing to oblige.

The Assizes opened on Tuesday, bringing an influx of visitors. The Assistant Judge, Mr Rigby (not the CJ) is staying with the Bolts. His stenographer has gastric trouble and has not come. Collet, the young Crown Counsel, unexpectedly brought his even younger wife with him and they are being put up at Elsie Martin's guest house. On Tuesday evening we went to the Club and saw Alec Guiness in *A Run for Your Money*. It was not a very good film, but his performance was flawless, as usual. We sat next to the Colletts, who told us the Baxters have been posted to Blantyre, where David takes on the job which threatened Ron – Personal Assistant to the PC, Eric Barnes. Margaret is very lucky – this is the second job David has had with no *ulendo* attached. They move on Saturday, so I must get in touch with them soon. They also told me Joyce Dickinson has had a daughter, Caroline Jane.

This is not a good letter – the bees are distracting me! I do not like to kill them, so I have been batting at them with a copy of the *Spectator* when they came too near for comfort.

26th February:

We have had a week of rain and I am thankful that this is Friday, as the long, damp days are very depressing, and poor Ron on *ulendo* must be feeling like a drowned rat.

On Monday we had a very pleasant day in Blantyre. Ron had to have his glasses changed and had an appointment with a specialist from Salisbury. His lenses are to remain the same but will be put in at a different angle. Sandy Holmes was also in town for the day, so we met him for lunch, which we had in a little new restaurant where they serve a mixed grill and cheese, as in an English pub. We sat there for ages. Sandy and Ron get on well together and hardly ever have the chance to talk. We were back by teatime and Ron went off after an early supper.

I discovered next day that while we were away in Blantyre a frightful row broke out on the station, starting between Joan Bolt and Elsie Martin over the sharing out of hospitality to official guests and as usual it has escalated via Club gossip to the estates. No one seems to have any sense of privacy here. Apparently our name was dragged in. I am horrified, as I have kept clear of everyone and gone on quietly in my own way. I refuse to have anything to do with it.

The High Court is still sitting, finishing today, and from Wednesday I have had Patsy Price, Mr Ridley's stenographer, staying with me. She was born in Nyasaland and educated at home; such a delightful, intelligent girl, so my evenings were very much brightened by her company. Ron comes in tomorrow morning and later in the day we are going out to Tuchila, the agricultural experimental station about ten miles from here, to stay with Bill and June Barber, a very nice young couple whom Ron sees on *ulendo* quite often. I travelled home on the *Dunottar Castle* with them but did not really know them. She is South African and Bill is a quiet, clever Englishman who has lived in Africa for most of his life, apart from the war, some of which he spent in a Japanese prison camp. I am so glad we are going to get away from the station for the weekend. We shall come back on Sunday night, and then Ron has a week in, so I shall have him for moral support, thank goodness. With this latest upheaval among the women I feel as if I had been struck in the face. Are they all *sick*, or something?

Aflike says it is going to rain all day, so I have decided to be a real martyr and have looked out a whole pile of mending!

4th March:

We heard some news in Blantyre yesterday which so far is an unofficial rumour, but having heard it from four different sources we think it must be true. The rumour is that Ron is to be posted to Zomba, to the Secretariat! I shall tell you about it when we know it is definite. All other news has been completely submerged by this latest bombshell.

By a miracle we have managed to steer clear of the row on the station, so that's that. David Bolt has had a complete nervous collapse and was taken yesterday to Zomba hospital with suspected ulcers. Fortunately, the Nicholsons arrive back next Saturday.

We enjoyed our weekend with the Barbers. I was desperately tired and was glad to sit quietly and talk with these nice people. On Sunday morning they took us for a walk over the whole station, which was interesting. We swam in their pool, a circular concrete tank, containing water which was positively warm compared with our Mlanje mountain water. We came back after an early supper, I laden with borrowed books, so I shall soon be falling terribly 'behind *The Times*', as we now call it.

11th March:

The news is the best possible: we *are* going to Zomba, Ron starting work in the Secretariat on 1st September, so we shall move house a few days before. It gives us time to think about it and plan, and it means we shall have Joan with us, to strengthen our plea for a decent house. It also means Joan will have three months on an out station before experiencing the bright lights of Zomba – interesting for her. Ron is very pleased, though he would like to get away from Mlanje *now*, as I would. I feel a different person – the prospect of this Mlanje limbo-like existence coming to an end is an immense relief. It has been crushing my spirit so much. I felt my letters never really said anything because I did not want to convey my unhappiness, so I was beginning to feel out of touch and therefore very homesick.

We are going through dismal days of mist and soaking, interminable heavy rain. It makes the house dark and damp and the garden is shooting ahead and my first carnation bloomed yesterday. The days have been passing quickly, partly because we have this good news to think about, and partly because Ron is in this week *again* and will be in next week. David Bolt came back on Saturday from hospital, looking simply ghastly, and asked Ron to stay in and help him at the Boma. The Bolts go off to Lilongwe, Central Province, tomorrow, when David becomes Resident Magistrate. The poor Nicholsons, who were supposed to arrive tomorrow, have been delayed, as their ship had to put in at Fremantle to land a passenger who was very ill. There is also an outbreak of measles on the ship, so any minute now, Peter wrote, the spots will appear, on all four children. Betty will be livid – with the ship, the disease, Peter and the children! They will arrive about the 20th, so for at least one week Ron is to be DC, Mlanje and has already been gazetted as such. He has not been looking at all well recently, but he is perking up already.

We have been doing a lot of reading, as the Barbers lent us ten Penguins – nothing very interesting except a re-reading of Harold Nicholson's superb *Public Faces*. Elspeth sent me a most marvellous collection of magazines,

French and English, which I was delighted to have. Sandy has asked me if he may borrow the French ones!

Ren Smith, one of our contemporaries at Oxford, who lived near Magomero at the end of last tour, has written to invite himself and his newly married wife to stay with us. She is a dentist, and was hoping to be able to practise out here. Instead she finds herself languishing in the bush at Chingali, where Ren carries on the resettlement work begun by David (Baxter) last tour.

We had an unexpected party at the Club on Tuesday evening. Two directors from Lyons were visiting the district for the first time, staying at Lujeri. They gave a champagne party at the Club, to which everyone on the station was invited. We went with the Holmeses and thoroughly enjoyed ourselves.

19th March:

We have had almost a fortnight's rain, but yesterday the blessed sun appeared and Mary and I rushed up to the pool for a delicious, icy swim. Today is perfect, a typical cold season day, the plain below hidden in beautiful white mist. All my carnations are fat-budded and badly need the sun to bring them out. I was afraid they were going to rot on their stems. The only flowers which flourish, come deluge or drought, are the tough little zinnias.

The Bolts left on Friday morning, thankful to be gone. Ron became DC at once and has been very busy and very happy ever since. He is definitely run down. He is just recovering from a bad cold and on Saturday developed a dreadful sore – I think the result of a poisonous bite on his bottom, which has been very painful and debilitating. However, Sandy gave him several penicillin injections, I have been dressing it with hot antifligistine, and it is slowly healing. It is the first time he has gone septic in this country.

We had a very quiet weekend indoors, with the rain ceaselessly battering outside. We shall soon be having a fire. All our shoes and clothes smell musty and yesterday Aflike and I put our entire wardrobe out in the sun to air. On Monday Ron had business in Blantyre and of course I leapt at the chance to go. I had a hair appointment (phoned from the Boma) at a new salon, but when I got there it turned out that the African assistant who made the appointment had not written it down in the book, and the hairdresser had gone to Zomba. Furious and desperate, I rushed into Michael's, the little Greek man's place, where Ron was having his hair cut. He really only cuts men's hair but I begged him to cut mine, which he did, with dedication. I hate it – I look like an effeminate boy. Ron, surprisingly, loves it – I expected him to have a fit. We had lunch with the Baxters and found them both looking well. Margaret thinks she is pregnant again and is over the moon with joy, as is David. They have told no one else yet. They are in a frightful slum of bush houses but are moving into a better house in a few weeks. They asked if they could come and stay again and we fixed it for the weekend of 3rd April. (I wish we were as popular in Mlanje as we are outside!) Apparently last time they came they thought our house and garden were a kind of Garden of Eden after Naisi, which I understand completely.

On Monday we went to the Club and saw an old but pleasant film, Bing Crosby in *Top of the Morning*. (You see how low I have to set my cultural sights!) We sat next to the Holmeses, and Sandy, turning to me with a wild Polish gesture to comment on something, struck his full pint glass of chilled beer off the arm of his chair and I found myself instantly and icily drenched! I was wearing a very full skirt, so in fact I just wrung out the wet section and spread it away from me to dry. I then took off my shoes, emptied them, curled up my legs under me and sat on my feet to warm them. All this was done very quickly and unobtrusively, and Sandy was so impressed he became almost hysterical with laughter at my calm, unfussed rearrangements of myself. People began to look round, while I sat very still and looked innocent. (Mary told me Sandy's reaction to my short hair was the plaintive remark 'Why does Ann have to make herself look like Joan of Arc – at the stake?'!)

Today Mary gets her first Chinyanja lesson from me. I do not know why we did not think of it before. My Chinyanja is simply dying away, as I never hear it except for Aflike and Cook. Last tour I heard it constantly on *ulendo* but now I never even think about it. It is a great pity to lose it so I jumped at the chance to revive it. My pronunciation is accurate, I know, so all I have to do is revise the grammar and get on with increasing my vocabulary.

The Nicholsons come back tomorrow, so I shall lose the sewing machine, which has been such a boon. I am looking forward very much to seeing them again and hoping their presence will have a good influence on the general atmosphere of Mlanje and its environs. Ron will drive to Luchenza, our nearest station, twelve miles away, to greet them.

24th March:

Ron went out on *ulendo* last night after supper and will sleep out for the rest of the week, but will be in for lunch every day, as he cannot leave the Boma for long – this *ulendo* is a complete fiasco. *Why* doesn't one of the PCs have the *guts* to spell it out to HE?

The inevitable has happened and Peter Nicholson is very sick indeed with what shows every sign of being measles, so Ron will carry on as DC for a little longer, which gives him great pleasure. The Nicholsons arrived on Saturday, absolutely worn out but thankful to be back. I waited till yesterday to call, as I know what it is like with two people settling in, and can therefore imagine the chaos of six! We drove up after tea, taking back Betty's sewing machine, which I have cleaned and oiled so well it is quite unrecognisable and goes like a bomb! Peter had retired to bed earlier in the day. Ron went in to have a talk with him and found him wearing dark glasses and generating enough feverish heat to make the room warm, poor chap. The four children were, as usual, romping about in high spirits. Betty looks very well and is as nice as ever. It is a great relief in a way to know that they are there. They are immensely popular and people were pouring in to see them, measles or no measles.

The cold weather has set in. After a fortnight's rain, which disguised the fact that the season was changing, the sun has returned in much diminished splendour, and I am now clad in slacks and sweater in the morning and skirt and sweater in the evening. It is cool enough to do things, so I have been dashing about the house and mean to do a great deal of gardening from now on. The first of the leaves are on the ground – mainly from our peach trees – and yesterday I got a sharp pang of homesickness as I watched the swallows gathering – they are at it again today, circling and swooping low over the house. (They have no telegraph wires to sit on, as they did at Dunalastair, twittering and glistening in the sun.) The weather is really beautiful, and warm if one stays in the sun. The bungalow itself, with its many windows, stone floors and carefully shaded rooms, is like a tomb in the cold season, but who cares.

Mary and I went blithely up to the pool yesterday morning – we want to go on as long as we can – and nearly screamed the place down when we felt the water temperature, but oh, what a marvellous feeling after the first shock. We sunbathed afterwards and it was delicious to pile on clothes and come away with a cold wind blowing, and sunburn glowing underneath.

I have started teaching Mary Chinyanja. We do an hour every day and then relax with *The Times* crossword – my favourite form of relaxation. Mary is an impressively quick learner, but is having difficulty with the pronunciation, she has such a strong Edinburgh accent. However, I insist that she persists – any pupil of mine must get it right!

We had a pleasant weekend with Ren Smith and his wife, Liz, but I was worn out by the end, with planning meals and keeping them entertained. I must get back into more sociable habits! I took to Liz. She is a mixture of Wales, Devon and France, the mixture taking place in her grandparents' time. The result is an attractive darkness of hair, eyes and skin, and she has a deep, soft voice. She obviously hates her present life but is too new and diffident to say so. She did say I was the first woman she had met in Nyasaland who had the honesty to say quite openly what I dislike about living in Africa – no other wife quite admits to this, she said – interesting! (I do not think Ren approved one little bit of this conversation!) Like the Baxters, they thought the house and garden absolutely lovely, and Ren began to wonder aloud what strings he can pull to get posted here when Ron goes in September. Ron told him it is definite that a new cadet is taking over.

On Monday we had a lovely surprise visit from Bryn Jones-Walters, over from Zomba. He works in the Secretariat and was able to tell Ron that his work will be in Security, co-ordinating intelligence from all over the territory, which should be very interesting, and Ron is now greatly looking forward to it.

31st March:

It has been raining since yesterday before lunch, without stopping, and the only sound is that of large drops plopping down with dreary monotony. We had a beautiful hot, sunny weekend, which brought out masses of my flowers, but now six carnations I have been cherishing are only half open and look as if they will rot before reaching full bloom – this never happened in Zomba. Ron went on *ulendo* on Monday evening and comes in first thing tomorrow morning, so I shall have had only three nights alone. He is looking very thin, pale and languid, and as soon as Peter has really taken up the reins again, he is going to ask for local leave – perhaps a week now and more later, to coincide with Joan's arrival. It is exactly noon now, and so dark and chilly I am cheering myself up with a glass of sherry before lunch. I drink half of it and put the rest in my soup.

The Baxters have invited themselves to stay this weekend, which is nice, but not terribly convenient, as they will coincide on Saturday evening with John Werner and John and Elizabeth Sanderson, whom we met at John's house. They are coming to dinner and I am not sure how good a mixture I shall have at my dinner table! I shall only enjoy the Baxters fully once Saturday night is over, as I always retire in to a shell of minute organisation and worry before any new venture in the way of guests.

On Friday we are going briefly to Blantyre for a visit to the dentist – I lost a filling the other day; such a nuisance. We are taking Aflike with us, as he has been having the most terrible toothache and not saying a word. A few days ago I was shocked to find him weeping helplessly with pain into the washing up. I was appalled and rushed to get him codeine. *Why* does he not come and tell me, foolish man.

Mary is learning Chinyanja very quickly and I find myself effortlessly producing whole sentences, now that it has come back into my mind.

We called on the Nicholsons on Monday after tea. Peter was up and about and looking splendid. What a great big charming man he is. He may not get back to work till next week. Misfortunes heap upon them. Their new car was involved in a goods train smash, between here and Beira!

7th April:

I forgot to say that Ron's sore has healed. It took three weeks of twice daily dressings to do it. I am worried about his thinness (I am like a pencil myself) and have persuaded him to ask for three weeks local leave from 20th May. He will then be free to take Joan about in the car. He may not get three weeks, but he will certainly get one or two, through a medical certificate from Sandy, if necessary.

The leaves are falling fast and already our view of the plain is greatly extended, through the bare branches of the trees. How I love this time of year.

The Baxters were not in good form at the weekend. I suspect Margaret was not well, though nothing was said, and David was subdued and restless, very unlike himself. On Saturday morning I got soaked to the skin in the garden (five days' solid rain till this morning!) cutting flowers for the house. I managed to dry out masses of phlox, honeysuckle and carnations, so the rooms looked and smelt lovely. The Sandersons and John Werner arrived promptly at seven and we had a delightful evening, except that I was worried about Margaret, she was so quiet, and dear old David took umbrage early on when Elizabeth Sanderson (who is charming) innocently criticised a remark on race relations made *months* ago by the Dean of St. Paul's, who is apparently greatly admired by David. However, Ron leapt to the rescue, conversationally, and the moment passed. I had decided on an informal meal rather than a sit-down dinner, and the buffet supper went without a hitch. Aflike's sweet tomato soup was praised, and with perfect timing, Mary Holmes arrived with two trifles I had made, which she had kept all day in her fridge, so that they were set and well chilled. She had had supper, but stayed to have a dish of trifle with us, lighting up the party with her robust Lowland Scot wit.

Peter has started going down to the Boma in the mornings, but he is clearly still far from well. I just hope he does not have a relapse. So Ron continues to enjoy his DC-ship, but is chafing at the kind of half-and-half authority Peter's presence inevitably imposes.

16th April:

This letter is going to be late. Yesterday at the last moment I decided to go with the Holmeses to Blantyre. Today I find the Post Office closed and there is a holiday on Monday. I do hope you will realise that Easter weekend will have upset the mails a bit.

We got back from Blantyre at dusk and I found a wonderful collection of mail (no male, alas – Ron is on *ulendo*) waiting for me. This has been a long week, mainly because it is the first of three during which Ron is to be out, and the first always seems appallingly long, as one knows there are two more to come. This is Good Friday and everyone is on holiday, but Ron has not come in. I only realised yesterday that this was Easter weekend – you see how vague I am becoming – and on our way back from Blantyre, we stopped near here at a village called Chonde, where I wrote a note to Ron telling him today is a holiday. Sandy has a dispensary in the village, and he gave my note to the dispenser, asking him to take it to Ron, who is camping about a mile off the main road. So I was hoping he would come in today, but no. He has probably calculated and discovered that he cannot fit in fourteen nights this month unless he can count tonight. There are times when I feel I would like to cast myself to the ground and scream myself senseless.

On Sunday morning our sacred routine was broken, as there was the first cricket practice of the season at ten o'clock. I went down with Ron, read out-of-date magazines and gingerly explored the filthy, dust-covered shelves of the library, to no avail. Various young bachelors from the estates wandered in and talked happily to me till the practice was over, and I quite enjoyed what I expected would be a pretty martyr-like morning. Ron and John Werner, more dead than alive after such unaccustomed exercise, joined me at noon and we stayed on for a drink.

On Wednesday Mary came up for her Chinyanja lesson and we had coffee. Aflike listens intently when he comes and goes with the tray, and can hear how quickly Mary is getting on (except for her accent – it makes him screw up his face at me!)

The weather has settled down in to the wonderful cold season pattern, with hot sun, cool or cold wind, crystal clear visibility and dazzling cloudscapes. Ron has asked for a week's local leave from 20th May and hopes to extend it. We thought we might go up Mlanje, but may wait for Joan, though I am not sure if she will be fit enough for such a climb. It is very steep and odd things happen to people who are out of condition, Sandy tells me. One woman found that her muscles, stiff from the climb up, simply refused to work and she appeared to be paralysed and had to be carried down. Another case was that of a young man who woke up next morning suffering from concussion and with two black eyes, caused by the jarring of his heels on the way down!

Isn't it *tragic* about the Comet? Everyone here is talking about it; people are cancelling their air passages home and going by sea, from sheer nerves.

21st April:

You ask about the Purdies, the young couple whom I mentioned as stationed at Kasupi on their first tour. They are the first couple from the next intake into the Service after us whom we have met, and it was most interesting to realise there is a definite gap between us and them – all of them. The great divide is, of course, the war. I may add that they do *not* make us feel old and settled! They are young and adaptable, yes, but so are we. But they *are* the next generation, and for that reason they expect – and get – more: better housing, better pay. Even the way they wear their *clothes* is different. The fact remains we liked Dick and Sheila very much.

I have discovered that Nyasaland has another link with Everest. There is an administrative officer in the Secretariat whom I have met once called Ronnie Noyce. His brother, Wilfred Noyce, was a member of the Everest expedition and kept a diary, some of which has been published. It includes poems which several keen climbers here have told me are marvellously vivid and evocative in their descriptions. Joan sent me a new magazine called *Encounter* a few months ago, and it contained a long excerpt from his diary which I found most interesting. I think it is extraordinary that Nyasaland should have two close associations with such a great enterprise.

We had a happy Easter, and I am thankful to say Ron looks much better, so he had a peaceful rest. He came in on Saturday morning and as usual, the tempo of existence suddenly quickened – even our penal labourers feel it and dash about the garden with watering cans slopping wildly. The rains have finished as much as they can ever be said to have finished in Mlanje, and the garden has to be watered twice a day. The weather was absolutely perfect all weekend – cool in the shade, very hot in the sun. I wore my new halter neck Horrocks and got darkened again, as I can never stay out of the sun for long in the cooler weather. We moved our chairs, wireless and little tables onto the *khonde* and lived there. On Saturday night we went down to the Holmeses for a drink – they see a lot of me, not nearly so much of Ron, whom they both enjoy. On Sunday we just sat about all day, simply filled to the brim with beautiful Easter music from all over the world. On Monday we had such a nice surprise. About eleven o'clock Pam and Tony Bridge (ADC Zomba and very kind to Ron last tour after I left) with their two delightful sons Mike and Chris, aged five and seven, unexpectedly arrived. We insisted they stay to lunch and loved their visit. Tony began his first tour here, and they were spending the weekend with Ramsden, manager of Lujeri, where John Werner works. They have asked us and John to stay with them in Zomba for the weekend of 8th May, for the Red Cross Ball and a cricket match next day, in which Ron, John and Tony are all playing. So that is something to look forward to.

Ron is out for four nights this week. He is actually staying with John Werner, who invited me too. At any other time I would have loved to accept, but I am very busy preparing for Joan's visit. I want the whole house and garden 'spring-cleaned' for her, and I have masses of sewing to do for her room.

28th April:

We had a lovely weekend, the weather behaving quite out of season, with blazing hot, still days. I had a heavenly surprise on Saturday morning. Ron had come in and gone down to the Boma, and I was tackling Joan's curtains when I looked up and saw *Iris* beaming at me from the doorway! They are now on their way home on leave, and were staying in the Martins' guest house for the weekend. She had had too much of a rush to write and let me know, and slipped away to see me and arrange further meetings over the weekend. She looked quite well, and wonderfully vivacious and happy at the prospect of leave. She and Dave called in after tea, to see Ron too, and on Sunday morning we went up to the pool with them and spent a blissfully happy morning. Iris and I kept standing in the shallow end talking instead of swimming. They came back with us for late elevenses and then we said goodbye. Iris is to be in Edinburgh with her parents and may visit you!

On Thursday evening I dined with Walter and Barbara Sproule and went on to the Club with them to see *The Chiltern Hundreds*, which I had seen on the ship coming out in 1950!

Ron has been given local leave from 4th May till 13th June – three whole weeks, just in time for Joan's arrival.

5th May:

I am feeling odd today. On Monday I woke up all shaky and fluey. I have dosed myself with various things and have almost kept it at bay.

On Sunday there was a cricket match against Limbe at the Club, and Ron went off looking beautifully turned out, in long white trousers, his St. Andrews sweater and blazer. I stayed on the *khonde*, listening to a perfectly wonderful Bach concert – a Prom recording, with Leon Goosens playing an Oboe d'Amore. The golden sound seemed to mingle with the gorgeous colours in the sun-drenched garden and I abandoned my sewing and allowed myself to be transported into that inner paradise I inhabit with great music. The spell was broken about eleven o'clock by John Werner driving up to persuade me to join everyone at the Club. Hi, ho. I arrived in time to see Ron out for a duck! However, he is one of their best bowlers and did well later. We came home for lunch and returned in the afternoon. They played till the light faded and I had to wait on while Ron helped entertain the Limbe team. It had been a boiling hot day, but as soon as the sun goes down, it gets cold, and I gradually froze, though I wrapped myself in Ron's blazer. Hence misery today.

I have had a letter from Joan Bolt, now settled at Lilongwe. She seems anxious to keep in touch and gave me their news. David loves his work as Resident Magistrate and is obviously much happier, so that is good news.

The garden is going to be wonderful for Joan's arrival. The poinsettias – we have nine bushes – will be absolutely blazing, and the 'yesterday, today and tomorrow' bushes are covered with buds. The carnations are splendid; my greatest success, always!

12th May:

I am interested to hear that you are reading *The Adventures of a Ballet Critic* by Richard Buckle. I wrote it down as soon as it came out – perhaps in some other life I shall *read* the books on my library list!

Yes, I certainly do the *Observer* and *Spectator* crosswords, on my own. (I *never* quite finish the *Spectator*!) I share *The Times* one with Mary very often, but I actually enjoy best doing it on my own.

The cold season is very much with us. I have an extra blanket at night, and for the first time had a fire on Monday evening. Ron is out on *ulendo* this week and next, and then his leave begins, thank goodness. My incipient cold never rose to the surface and after a few days faded away under the impact of hot toddies, aspirin and sheer willpower! Such a relief – Mlanje is enough to bear without being ill as well.

We left here on Saturday morning and stayed in Blantyre till after lunch. Ron spent a long time in the PC's office and I did some shopping and then sat in the car, knitting, and talking to various people I know who were calling in at the office. David (Baxter) came out to the car, looking simply terrible, to tell me that Margaret had another miscarriage a few days ago. I think she has been quite ill, but he was so withdrawn I felt I could not really ask questions. He obviously wanted to tell me but could not trust himself to say very much. Poor David, my heart aches for them both.

We had a late lunch at Ponsons, a mixed grill. Having breakfasted at 6.30 we were ravenous. I felt quite sleepy in the car but perked up when we got onto home ground. Mlanje gets so much rain it always looks green and fairly well covered on its lower slopes, but on the road to Zomba we saw the real signs of winter – the long grass withered and sere, leaves lying in great heaps, and the trees bare and gaunt against the sky. Even my mountain looked a little remote and chilly. It was a grey, overcast day and Zomba had its own peculiar quality of atmosphere – slightly cold yet muggy, a smell of wood smoke and sounds carrying far in the wintry air. We arrived at the Bridges in time for tea and then went down to the Club with Tony to watch a hockey match and see some familiar faces. John Werner joined us there, having stopped at the Club to drop off the cricket gear. Then we all went back to the house and sat talking till six o'clock. Pam had just begun to organise baths when who should call in but Ken and Cathie Robinson from Magomero (they kept the car for us during our leave) and Cleasby, a settler on one of the Magomero estates with whom Ron had many a clash. However, everyone was friendly and Ron heard all the news of the place, while I shuddered inwardly at every reminder and marvelled at how I endured it – the place, the climate, the life!

When they had gone a long relay of baths began and we emerged to find other guests had arrived and a great party had begun. (You do not know the guests so I will not go into detail.) After a wonderful buffet supper we went down to the Club, which was beautifully decorated and brimming with gaiety. I had scarcely sat down when Humphrey Bingham rushed across from his party and embraced me warmly. I was just smoothing myself down from that when Ruth Simmons came over from the same party to say how much they were looking forward to seeing us in September and invited us to stay with them while we settled in. I suddenly began to enjoy myself very much. We saw many familiar faces and exchanged many greetings. Tony is a beautiful dancer, John too, though so tall I have to hold him by the elbow! We left about four, the dance still in full swing, but as the cricket began at 9.15 that morning, we felt we must go. I discovered how out of practice with late nights I was and felt grateful to sit quietly watching the match till it finished at 3.30. During the morning I talked

her somewhat inefficient African nanny! Mary herse
younger. When she thanked us before getting out of th
ed being with us, because of our restful, serene relation
t.

tiful day and I spent it in the sun, as I was icy cold wit
to Luchenza in glorious early evening sunshine, stood or
other till 5.10, when black smoke told us the train was
ed on the platform when I saw Joan at a window looking
wearing a lovely yellow cotton dress. (ALL her cottons –
beautiful Horrocks, making me feel very plain Jane!) It
she could see the countryside. We got her luggage – an
into the car and all squashed into the front seat and drove
tly and smiling at each other. She looks so well, fresh and
ch less heavy. She has had a perfect trip, especially after
he officers mingled with the passengers (only twelve on the
ook her on trips ashore.

ge was so wonderful that Mlanje is quite a comedown in
she is interested in everything and thrilled with the house,
e – I am afraid he thinks she is Ron's second wife but, being
perfectly acceptable to him and a sign of increasing prosper-
oth look well but are very different from our 'home' selves –
how she put it! Ah well, that is Mlanje for you. Since she
ent the time talking while she was supposed to unpack. Ron
the day on Sunday, to play cricket, and came back to find us
o unpacking done. On Monday she unpacked a bit and I got all
ts and the clothes I had asked her to bring for me. She knows
ke and brought me *two* winter skirts, because they were so in-
a beautiful Horrocks dress which fits me perfectly – soft pastel
le grey background. *What* a joy really good clothes are! She
present a dream of a housecoat, also Horrocks, grey with tiny
ke a delicate Victorian wallpaper. She struck Ron speechless
echless!) by presenting him with a *fabulous* antique decanter.
evening the dear Holmeses came rushing in for a drink, eager to
treating her like an old friend. She was greatly taken with them
ee she charmed them – lovely for me – reflected glory! In the
n and Mike Saunders paid a delightful surprise visit, so she met
h' characters and enjoyed them immensely. I have warned her that
ople she meets will be as interesting and interested!
the forenoon we drove to Lujeri tea estate and John Sanderson
ver the factory. Joan asked all the right questions (while I stood
uely at the machinery and sneezing at the tea). We nearly had a bad
the way back along an estate road. A motorcyclist came round a
r quickly, panicked, and turned into the oncoming car instead of

with more people and had a drink with John Watson, glad to see me – so shy, nice man. Dorothy is expecting a baby in August and was lying low at home. We left about 4.30, taking with us a young policeman from Mlanje, about twenty, Ron Fitzhenry, a big handsome young man who treats Ron with defer- ence and tends to call him 'sir'. He has very good manners and makes me feel like Dresden china.

I must go on to another page because I have forgotten to tell you something interesting that happened at the Ball. Kenneth Simmonds came over to our table, asked my hostess if he could 'borrow Ann', took me to the bar, bought me a drink and led me to a secluded corner, where he talked seriously to me at some length. He said he had always remembered a conversation (so had I) with me when we first met, in which I made critical remarks about life in Africa. (How my innocent frankness of those days is catching up with me now!) He asked me if I still felt the same. I said yes, I thought I did, but in a more mature, controlled way – a kind of inner rebellion which I kept to myself. Well, he looked pleased with that, but proceeded to give me a long lecture on Empire, a sense of service, loyalty, etc – in short, all the things I feel very strongly about myself – and advised me on no account to think of giving up or encouraging Ron to give up. My reaction, apart from mortification, was a very deep, private anger. I said quietly that he had completely misread my character and that it would never enter my mind to 'give up' or encourage Ron to do so. He nodded, said 'Good,' and asked me to dance! Then he took me back to my table. Ron was bursting with curiosity – he said my eyes were 'glittering'!

Having thought about it and talked with Ron, I believe Kenneth was kindly and discreetly indicating to me that if I would just grin and bear it, life was full of promise for us both and could only improve. He is a very clever, charming man and I think it was frightfully good of him to take the trouble to try to help me. In the context of our miserable life right now, in Mlanje, it was no bad thing to be reminded by a man of his calibre of what the Colonial Service stands for.

19th May:

I have had a letter from Joan from Cape Town. She writes just as I feel on a voyage – in a complete daze and very inconsequential as to news and details. She spent her time most efficiently in Cape Town, 'doing' the National Gallery and Botanical Gardens. She also went up the mountain, sensible girl. All her comments on scenery and new things are excellent, while anything said on familiar things (e.g. shops, clothes, etc) are very blasé and critical – just wait till she is on her way home after some months here! The first shop she sees in South Africa will seem like a Paris haute couture salon!

I am rather bothered about food when Joan comes. I have not said much about it, but it is very difficult in such a hot station without a fridge, and when Ron is out I keep a very simple table. However, he pays off the car completely very soon, so perhaps we can buy a fridge after that. At least we eat plenty of fresh fruit and vegetables.

Ron came in on Saturday morning and blew away all my little nagging worries. At teatime Laga and Clement Carlyle arrived with the three children and a delicious Pekinese bitch called Kiko. It was a lovely surprise, and we were all delighted at the reunion and kept exchanging mutual apologies for not getting in touch till now. Laga and Clement look tired but well. The children are delightful, though David's petit mal is much in evidence and must worry them. Laga simply loathes Limbe now and they have hardly any friends. (I thought of the many nice people Ron and I know and silently and humbly counted my blessings.) She sat down and poured out her heart to me, while Ron and Clement talked and kept an eye on the children. They had tea and stayed on till it was dark, then accepted a drink and still Laga sat talking and laughing. She was enjoying herself so much that I suggested that the children (who were both wild and wilting) have supper and go to bed in our room, and they stay on to dinner and make a celebration of it. She jumped at the idea and the children enthusiastically ate a supper of boiled eggs, brown bread and marmite, apples and cocoa, and then meekly went to bed, dead tired. Aflike *loved* having them! We four had dinner later and they left about ten, asking when they could come back! I have promised to have them for a day as soon as Joan settles in. We both enjoyed them tremendously and they were obviously thankful to see and talk to us again.

We spent our usual peaceful Sunday in lovely sunshine and on Monday Ron triumphantly produced a poisoned finger which led to his *ulendo* being cancelled and brightened our lives very much, as it means he is in all this week and on leave for the next three. But it is worrying, as this is the second attack of poison this tour. I must try and feed him up.

26th May:

It is Ramadan and my nerves are suffering! Aflike has had an appalling cold which sounded as if it might develop into pneumonia. He refused codeine because of Ramadan and in the end I sent him away with strict instructions to go to bed for three days, which I am relieved to say he did. Thank goodness he comes back tomorrow! Meanwhile Cook has us in his tender care and the less said about that the better. Joan's room is ready; it looks a little bare, but will be pretty when she unpacks books and ornaments. She arrives on Saturday and we are going to Blantyre on Friday to do some last minute shopping – pillows, for one thing. Tonight we are dining in great state with Sandy and Mary, who are celebrating their ninth wedding anniversary.

Ron's leave began on Monday. He is enjoying every minute of it, and it is wonderful for me to have him about. The penal labourers have not quite known

what has hit them and
to look as trim and as
prefer a certain *embarr*
brand new. He has also
blow up and destroy eye

On Sunday morning we
family again descended o
enjoyable but tiring, as th
parents talk to us. They are
take us over the tobacco floc
exciting. Ron plans a visit to
take a small interest in the
arrival and the air hums wi
Sproule (who I like very muc
whole rows of ears flapped to

I am having to deal with a fe
our precious life together with
excited when I see that train stea
broken and is horrible! There is
dismal clouds drift along the mo
flowers are wet and wind tossed.
It is the sort of weather that can las
be exactly like this, but I doubt if sl

2nd June:

I feel I hardly know how to begin,
you, on Joan's arrival. I must first tell
was Sandy's and Mary's ninth wedding
no one else there – and had a great even
was the highlight. We took Mary to Blan
had a day off in Nyasaland without chi
having coffee, then shopping and a hairc
Humphrey Bingham joined us for coffee
his charm and conversation. He was at his
to her. We then went to Limbe and had an e
longing to meet. The house is pleasant but
hate. Laga does a lot of painting and has som
of Yugoslavia, the children and wild flower
Mary came away most enthusiastic about the
Blantyre and went to the cinema at 4.30 – a
Wife. We drove home in magnificent starlight a
Sandy subdued and exhausted after a day spen

218

month-old daughter and
looked about ten years
car she said she had lov
ship. Well, think of th
Saturday was a beau
excitement. We drove
one foot and then the
coming. I was transfi
marvellously tanned,
dozens of them – ar
was almost dark, bu
astonishing amount
back talking consta
most attractive, mu
Cape Town, when
City of Paris) and
I think the voya
many ways, thoug
the view, and Afli
a Muslim, that is
ity! Joan says we
'rather dead' wa
came we have sp
had to vanish fo
still talking and
the home presen
exactly what I l
expensive, and
flowers on a p
brought me as
roses, rather l
(yes, I said sp
On Tuesda
meet her and
and I could
morning, Joa
two real 'bus
not all the p
Today in
showed us
looking vag
accident or
blind corne

turning aside into the tea at the roadside. Fortunately Ron was going very slowly and swung the car sharply away from him, then stopped dead. The young man crashed into the right headlamp, and glass flew everywhere. He only has a badly cut leg, but his bike was damaged and our dearly cherished car has a nasty dent apart from the shattered lamp. It could have been much worse, so we can be thankful. Ron's reaction was absolutely split second. He reported it to Robin Martin as soon as we got back. Ron says there will be no unpleasantness and the insurance will cover the damage. The poor young man's wife, whose house is just by that corner, heard the crash and came running out. She nearly collapsed with relief when her husband got to his feet. I am thankful it happened at Lujeri, where all the people are so friendly.

After tea today we are going up to call on the Nicholsons, and on Friday we spend the day with Laga and go to a tobacco auction. It is very nice to have all these things to show Joan, for of course I have not seen any of them either. I am still finding it strange to combine Joan and Africa!

Joan is feverishly writing letters while I write this and so we are both quiet! Ron is pretending to read *The Times* but is asleep. He had a nightmare last night and when I woke him and asked what was wrong he said, 'Wolves, darling,' in a very affectionate voice and instantly fell asleep. I of course lay awake for ages. He is loving his leave and not really aware yet that Joan is here!

9th June:

We are in the middle of a bleak cold spell which keeps me pale and fireside-bound. We are gradually settling down and already Joan's arrival seems far away. It took me – not Ron or Joan – several days to get over the shock of the accident at Lujeri. I had a charming letter from Mrs Dacy, the injured man's wife, saying it was not our fault in the least and they realised that if Ron had not been so quick it would have been much worse. Her husband has had five stitches in his thigh (it looked so awful I expected there would be more) and has a sprained wrist, but feels well and cheerful. It was such a relief to get a friendly, sincere letter in Mlanje and I wrote back to tell her how much we appreciated their attitude. Joan feels she must have brought a 'hoodoo' with her on the car, and you may agree as I tell you our further adventures!

On Friday we went to Blantyre to take Joan to the dentist, and then on to Limbe to spend the day with the Carlyles. On the way, for the first time ever, we ran over a chicken, which survived but left practically all its feathers sticking to the bonnet of the car. (Worse is to come!) We spent a very pleasant day with Laga and the children, and Clement took us to the tobacco floors to watch an auction, which was interesting. One cannot, with an unpractised eye, see the men bidding at all. The auctioneer keeps up a continual singsong of mounting prices and his eyes flick from face to face while the bidders presumably wink, twitch or nod. Joan liked the Carlyle family very much. She tends to keep in the background and play with the children, which of course suits Laga, who loves talking with me. She has a lovely ranging mind and we never know what we shall end up talking about. After tea we visited friends of theirs, a Mr and Mrs Cook, to look at a litter of Pekinese puppies. Ron and I were sorely tempted, but they were all bitches and not very 'pure'. Mrs Cook is very Bohemian-looking, as was her home – Balkan embroidery *everywhere*. As we drove up we all distinctly saw a *cow* standing on the big *khonde*. Marvelling about this we got out of the car and discovered it was of painted cardboard, life size, to be used at the Agricultural Show! We entered the drawingroom to find a live baby waterbuck eyeing us from the sofa. Mrs Cook was quite put out that we had taken for a cow what was clearly a bull! We all got the giggles, including the children, who are as sharp as needles.

We returned to the Carlyles for dinner, and Laga found that the cook had had a mental block, and had only prepared soup and a pudding, leaving the pork joint untouched in the fridge, so we had an omelette instead. Laga laughed her head off at this minor disaster, which is one way of dealing with domestic crises! We left about 9.30 and *then*, between Limbe and Cholo, miles from anywhere, a terrific thumping developed in the car and it began to vibrate all over. We stopped in pitch darkness and Ron peered about with his torch but could find nothing wrong; he suspected that something awful had happened to the back axle. There was nothing for it, he announced, but to stay in the car all night, which we did, while it grew colder and colder and a thick fog gathered round us. A lorry stopped and we gave the African driver an SOS for Clement which he promised to deliver, but of course nothing came of it. Meantime we ate sweets, talked and dozed for odd moments, very fitfully. In the very middle of the fiendishly uncomfortable night we burst out laughing when I suddenly said in a dreamy voice, 'Wouldn't we have just LOVED the puppy if we had decided to have it and brought it with us in the car'? At first light, Ron, who was in fact very worried, got out and found that the trouble was only a loose tyre, which he put right in about four minutes, and we drove off thankfully if a bit sheepishly!

We passed a quiet Whitsun weekend. I am reading one of Laga's books, *Laughing Diplomat* by Daniele Vare, which I think you would love. Last night Barbara Sproule came for a drink and we went to the first cinema show held in the new Club, and Joan saw her first gathering of Mlanje Boma and district people. Her presence caused great interest. With my heart in my mouth I took her about and introduced her to everyone I knew. The film was *Oliver Twist*, very well done. We had the usual bacon and egg supper in a rather festive atmosphere. It is a lovely club and will look delightful when it is fully furnished and finished off. The acoustics are poor, but by hanging cloth from the ceiling they hope to improve them. I was shocked at the change in Barbara, so white and thin, though she is always beautifully turned out. (I was also shocked at Joan's reply when I said this to her – 'no more so than you'!) Walter, of course, is on the fourteen nights *ulendo* treadmill too. I know so well what she must endure.

Last week we took Joan up to call on Betty and Peter, who were, they announced at once, barely on speaking terms, so she saw that household in its usual state!

16th June:

This is being written in bed, whither I retired with one of my epic colds, acquired from Joan. As it is over a year since I had one I feel I cannot grumble. I think I have been run down in spirit, and the opting out is doing me good already – I just feel deadly tired. Joan wrote to you yesterday so by now you will know her first reactions, if she really tells you them. I think she is TERRIBLY bored! The weather has been bleak and miserable, which has rather restricted our plans for her entertainment. She is beginning to see what life has been like for us in Mlanje and wonders how we have endured it. We are all longing for Zomba. I feel I can only just bear Mlanje now that the end is in sight.

Last Thursday, on a wet, chilly afternoon, we drove to Limbe equipped with rugs, cushions and a thermos of tea against emergencies *en route*! Poor Joan has taken a lot of teasing. We arrived safely in time for tea, and till the time we left, after tea next day, Joan and I were absolutely frozen, and she developed the cold which I finally caught. In the evening we went to see *Moulin Rouge*, which I enjoyed very much. The costumes and settings were wonderful and Jose Ferrer outstanding. You would have loved the colours and the marvellous treatment of his paintings, posters and sketches. We spent next morning shopping in Blantyre and Joan got a haircut, visited the bank and shopped recklessly while I meekly piloted her about, spending very little myself. We came back to Mlanje with but a single thought – warmth – and sat for the rest of the day over a huge fire which Aflike had lighted early on, thoughtful Aflike. On Sunday we watched cricket and Joan has now met everyone on the station, besides John Werner and the nice Sandersons. Yesterday I crawled about feeling wretched and was persuaded by the other two to take to my bed, which I was thankful to do. I am sorry this is such a dull letter. My head feels like a balloon.

23rd June:

We have had a truly shattering piece of news this week. Eric Barnes, the PC, was here for the weekend, and on Saturday he saw Ron and told him he is *not* going to Zomba after all. It is very bad luck on Ron, as it has nothing to do with him. The Governor and Eric Barnes have apparently crossed swords in the past, and when HE went on leave about a month ago, he left strict orders that in spite of the shortage of administrative officers in the field, the Northern and Central

Provinces were to be fully staffed. He did not mention Barnes's Province, the South, so the result is that Barnes has been practically stripped of officers. He decided to hang on grimly to every man he could, and promptly informed the Secretariat that he could not spare Ron from field work, so they have had to dovetail two sections in the Secretariat and have one man doing Ron's work there as well as his own, while Ron continues in district work. So, we either stay here or go to Chiradzulu, a sub-Boma of Blantyre. I will not go into details until we know if we go there or stay in Mlanje. You can imagine our reactions, Joan included. It has been a bitter blow and I nearly went back to bed, having just got up! I am sorry to give such depressing news but you had to be told. We will soon adjust ourselves and get on with life.

I have not much other news. My cold ran its usual dismal course. Sandy came to see me and has put me on a very effective tonic. (He said my terrible colds may be psychosomatic, nothing to do with other people's germs – help!) I got up on Friday and on Saturday went shopping as usual. The weather has been frightful – bitterly cold and wet, with the roads in rainy season condition. I was glad to be in bed with a hot water bottle, and Ron and Joan had a huge fire going all day. Sunday was dreadful – dark and wet. The Carlyles came for the day, so we had the two children shut in with us all day – hectic. By the end of it I felt I was about to have a relapse. But we are all equally thankful to have found such kindred spirits.

Poor Ron went off on *ulendo* in pouring rain on Monday, looking much better in health, but as low in spirits as I think I have ever seen him – so unlike himself – absolutely silent with misery. This cancellation of his posting is a fearful disappointment, especially as he feels it for me as well, as of course I do for him, and we only had Saturday and Sunday in which to comfort each other.

I have been enjoying more of Laga's books: J.H. William's *Bandoola* (author of *Elephant Bill*) and a novel, *The Consul at Sunset* by Gerald Hanley which I think Daddy – and perhaps you – would enjoy. My *Times* and *Observers* suffered neglect, as it is impossible, I found, to read newspapers in bed! However, the weather keeps us crouched over a fire (poor Joan is FURIOUS about the weather) so there is lots of time for reading.

30th June:

I feel my last week's letter must have depressed you, with its sad news of no-Zomba. I did not realise perhaps just how much you also were counting on it for me, and yesterday when your letter came I knew from it that you were thankful to think we were leaving Mlanje. It made it all the worse for me to think I had to tell you. The worst of the disappointment is over and we are determined to make the best of things.

My cold has almost gone and I have that special feeling of well-being one has after a feeling of ill-being. On Friday Sandy is taking Joan and me to Blantyre.

I am going to buy shorts and take up tennis again with Mary. Charles Watt, a Church of Scotland minister who lives at a Mission near here, has lent us two racquets, so we can at last play again. [We lost our Slazengers in the fire.] Watt met Ron on *ulendo* not long ago, and offered to lend us them then. He brought them two Saturdays ago and stayed to lunch, which I forgot to mention.

The weather has improved, with sunshine and a high wind, all lovely to look at, but still far too cold for me. Joan loves it and has sunbathed several times in a sheltered spot in the garden. She has certainly settled down now, and it is so nice for me to have her, though I feel very sorry for anyone who has to live this sort of life at all!

Ron is out on *ulendo* again this week, but he will be in next week. Joan and I had a quiet time without him and were delighted when he charged in on us on Saturday morning. He had been out in the sun a lot and looks so much better. Unfortunately he was away in Limbe all day on Sunday, playing cricket, so I saw very little of him. I did not go with him as it is very chilly and dreary watching cricket in this weather, and I wanted to throw off my cold completely as soon as possible.

Last night Walter and Barbara Sproule met Joan and me having a walk just before it got dark, and came in to have a drink with us. They are nice, kind people and obviously like Joan.

Do not worry about us.

4th July: [Air letter]

This is just to let you know that on Saturday evening we heard that Ron has definitely been posted to Chiradzulu and we move on 19th July. You will be glad to know that we are absolutely *thankful* and looking forward to it! The station is a sub-Boma of Blantyre, as Kasupi was of Zomba, so Ron is responsible to the DC Blantyre, but is on his own at Chiradzulu, which means ten days *ulendo* a month, working out at two weeks in and two weeks out. Again like Kasupi, it is a one-man station. It is only forty miles from Zomba and twenty from Blantyre, and is about twelve miles off the main Zomba-Blantyre road, so we will be really far better off there than in Mlanje. It means we will shop in Blantyre, have the cinema and – heaven – library.

The Bolts spent a whole tour there and loved it. I believe the house is lovely. There is an enormous garden of about four acres, which includes an orchard planted years ago by Bill Rangeley. David Bolt installed a proper hot water and WC system and there are the remains of a large swimming pool. So all is well. I dread the packing a bit, as I cannot bear to think of any of our few bits and pieces being broken, but I expect it will be easier than I think. We are so glad to be leaving this dreadful place we all feel we are on holiday! Aflike goes around all smiles, wearing his fez at as cocky an angle as he dares. Ron is like a schoolboy – he has simply hated working in Mlanje.

I will write as usual on Wednesday. I just wanted to put you out of suspense and let you know that we are all cheerful!

8th July:

Yesterday Joan and I had tea with the Holmeses and then went down to the Club, where Mary and I played tennis. I was surprised how quickly it came back and thoroughly enjoyed myself. Today my shoulders and arms are aching. However, I got down to the books and packed them all, so now a different set of muscles ache! Ron left for Chiradzulu yesterday morning, to take over. I hear with some amusement that there is a battle royal raging on the station as to who gets this house!

On Friday Sandy took Joan and me to Blantyre, where we had a good day's shopping, with lunch at Ponson's where several Zomba people came over to say how sorry they were that we were not going to Zomba. I knew none of them well, and was terribly pleased that they should trouble to come and speak to me – very good for one's self-esteem, which has taken a beating after a year in Mlanje.

Ron came in on Saturday morning looking sunburned and well. We proceeded at once to enjoy the weekend. The Holmeses dined with us, bringing with them Roy Fitzhenry, the young policeman we met recently, and Joan was thrilled to meet him.

All the trunks and boxes are out, so by the time Ron returns from Chiradzulu most of the packing will be done. Sandy has just called in with two big tea chests he ordered for me from one of the estates. He is a great help when Ron is on *ulendo*, as with no phone and no car I feel I cannot get things done at all. Joan has cheered up immensely – she hates living so near the mountain and is longing to get away from 'this deadly place', to use her words.

14th July:

I am perfectly fit again, and standing up well to the exhausting packing.

I find it difficult to start on our news, as Ron being away at the weekend has completely confused my idea of time. He left last Wednesday and was to be back today, but phoned Sandy last night to say a spring in the car has broken and he will not be back till tomorrow. Ron told Sandy to tell me that Chiradzulu is lovely. Sandy said he sounded on top of the world. I have been packing gradually – how I hate it, as I expect to find things in pieces when next I see them. (This is a feeling I have developed since the fire. I think it is a kind of defence mechanism.) Joan is at her most melancholy and has taken four days to pack books and clothes in her own room while I have packed up the contents of an entire household!

On Sunday morning we were so desperate for company we walked down to the Club to watch cricket. I wore my new Horrocks cotton for the first time – it is lovely and raised my morale. I met people from Cholo whom I knew, and was then joined by a tea planter whom Ron and I met recently. His name is Peter Delapasteur and he is a friend of Roy Fitzhenry's. I introduced Joan and when Peter learned we were on our own, he insisted we have dinner with him that evening, transport being provided by Roy. I hesitated a little, but accepted. I could see Joan was dying for me to say yes. We had a great evening. He is a bachelor and a rolling stone, with a passion for racing cars and big game hunting. He looks like a very dare-devil version of the Indian cousins – dark, lean, with glowing eyes and hair touched with grey. He left Joan and Roy to talk together and concentrated entirely on me (!) all evening. I was prepared to listen, as I have not met his kind before. He struck tin in Uganda after a bad patch in Tasmania. Eventually he sold his mine to the CDC (Colonial Development Corporation). He now manages a tea estate called Mini-Mini in Mlanje district, about eight miles from us. It is bad luck that we should have discovered a possible friend so late in the day.

I feel I can just hang on here and no more. We hope to move to Chiradzulu by lunchtime on Monday. I am taking masses of cuttings from the garden – my lovely garden, my only regret! The weather has been much better and warm enough for cottons, but there is a cold wind today. I pray for a dry departure day.

Chapter 19

21st July: Chiradzulu

Ron came back from Chiradzulu on Thursday, full of enthusiasm and reassurance, but with the news that the *ulendo* is still fourteen days a month, an awful blow to us both. I know it is only four days' difference, but it means a lot in our life. He described everything and we bombarded him with questions. The great assets, he said, are a delightful house, a magnificent garden and a glorious outlook; he was quite right, as you will hear in a minute.

Our last weekend in Mlanje was very pleasant but I have already put all that firmly behind me. We left at 9.30 on Monday morning, closely followed by two lorries piled high with our household goods, our boys, their wives and children. We drove at 30 m.p.h., as we had to keep the lorries in sight, to prevent them stopping to chat with friends and take on illegal passengers. Chiradzulu is only seventeen miles from Blantyre, twelve from Limbe and thirty from Zomba, so we are even nearer to civilisation than we thought. We turned off the main road and drove eight miles along a very good bush road, passing hundreds of huts and swarms of Africans. This is the most densely populated area in the *whole* of Africa, with as many as four hundred people to the square mile. It serves as a 'dormitory' area for workers in Limbe and Blantyre. Ron says I need not even think of accompanying him on *ulendo* as there will be no privacy at all, and he will probably camp in the many court houses scattered throughout the district.

We are more than a thousand feet higher than at Mlanje and feel ten times more alive. At present it is coldish, but a dry pleasant cold, quite unlike the bone-aching damp of Mlanje. The house is about two-thirds of the way up Chiradzulu mountain, reached by a steep road lined with blue gums and jacarandas. There are six formidable hairpin bends, each more hair-raising than the last, but Ron deals with them effortlessly. The house has the most marvellous setting I have ever seen – breathtakingly lovely. It stands high on a narrow plateau, with a wide lawn and then a dramatically sheer drop down to the plain, and a view across low hills scattered over Palombe plain, straight out to the whole awesome length of Mlanje, which I now love deeply – from a distance of thirty-eight miles! The Boma is three minutes' walk from the house, along an avenue of tall blue gums. There is a drive of beautiful cypresses up to the house, which stands in grounds that look like English parkland. Behind are an enormous well-stocked vegetable garden and orchard, and beyond that a tennis court, in good condition. Behind it the mountain rises up – it is friendly, though covered in very primitive rain forest. On the other side the ground slopes steeply down to a colossal rockery and garden, culminating in a magnificent semi-natural swimming pool, twenty feet deep at its deepest. Two sides are made of shelving rock, the remainder of artificial walls. It is flanked on two sides by trees in which birds, squirrels and monkeys keep up a continuous cacophony of exotic noise. As I said, I have never seen a lovelier place. Unfortunately the pool was badly constructed and has never worked properly, but we shall see what can be done. There is an enormous bed of watercress growing on it, which Aflike already has his eye on for salads and soup!

The bungalow is old, spacious and has great character. The WC is outside Joan's bedroom, in a wired-in part of the side *khonde*, which has a door in it. So to reach it Ron and I can either go through Joan's room or out of the front door and round to the side. However, we have a thunderbox outside our bedroom which Ron means to convert into a proper water closet. [He never did.] We shall not use it; it can serve the small guest house nearby. There are an immense number of outhouses and boys' quarters, and a huge, dark kitchen with smoke-blackened walls and one tiny window in the roof. However, there is a big, airy pantry where food can be prepared for cooking. Aflike is perfectly happy with everything, which is all that matters. We have four *machila* men, free, to maintain the garden and grounds, which they do very well. They are all middle-aged and have been working here for years – such a marvellous help to me – I really quailed when I saw the extent of the grounds! All the cuttings from the Mlanje garden went in the day after we arrived and they flourish – the soil is dark and rich. I am full of plans.

We get very good African milk, and butter and meat (on Wednesday and Friday) from an estate on Magomero run by Cleasby, the Scotsman who gave Ron so much trouble last tour! The cattle are European stock. So, praise be, the food problem is much easier. (I *long* for a fridge, but Ron says I must wait till next tour.) We have a telephone in the house and at the Boma, so we feel in touch with the outside world, though our surroundings suggest the back of beyond. The bungalow has a drawingroom, a diningroom, two big bedrooms, one small (Ron's study), a bathroom, a wide front and side *khonde*. Joan's bedroom has French windows opening onto the wired section of the side *khonde*, where the WC is. There is a fireplace in her room, so it can become a real bed-sittingroom in the cold season. She is delighted with everything.

You need not worry about us *at all*.

P.S. I have discovered FOURTEEN DAFFODILS blooming in the rock garden! There are also thousands of big violets which fill the air with sweetness.

27th July:

We are settling down marvellously here. We sleep well and eat at least twice as much as we did at Mlanje. It is wonderful to have good meat. The nights and mornings are bitingly cold, and in the evening we have a wood fire which burns magnificently in the best fireplace we have yet had out here. The sun is hot, and shines on the side *khonde* in the morning, so Joan and I sit there, looking out onto the avenue of blue gums which leads to the Boma, and the avenue of cypresses which leads to the house. Yesterday morning we walked down to a solitary Indian store we had noted near the bottom of the drive, and bought material for the guest house – bright blue for bedspreads and for curtains a fresh leaf green with large white oval spots. It is going to be completely modern, and we are having a wonderful time planning it on about sixpence! I feel very lost without a sewing machine but with Joan's help, it is not so bad. (She *loves* doing monotonous work, and will happily sew hems for hours, while I feel I shall go mad and have to take a break and do something else.)

Ron goes out on *ulendo* next Monday, but till then is at the Boma, which he found in a chaotic state. We have been without Aflike since Saturday. His uncle (Hassani, our first cook) died, and he is now head of the family, so he had to go home to tidy up affairs and give a funeral feast. Cook has managed fairly well but I am thankful that Aflike returns today, bringing us, I hope, bamboo mats, ebony carvings for Joan, and some of Zomba's famous strawberries.

On Saturday morning Ron took us to Blantyre and we shopped while he attended to business at the PC's office. He saw David (Baxter), who said he hoped he and Margaret might come and see us soon. In the evening we dined with the Carlyles, whom I had *phoned* earlier in the week. They were very glad to see us and eager to visit us – everyone has heard of Chiradzulu, as it is famous for its beautiful situation. After dinner we went to see a most amusing film, *The Captain's Paradise*, with Alec Guiness and Celia Johnston. On Monday Tony Bridge called and had tea with us, giving us all the Zomba news. Joan was charmed by him. Dorothy Watson is expecting her baby in about three weeks' time, almost four years exactly since George was born. After next weekend we hope to start entertaining – I have the Holmeses down as our first weekend house guests. I promised to invite Peter Delapasteur and Roy Fitzhenry next. As you see, we have plenty of social activity ahead.

On Monday morning Ron had work to do at Magomero. Joan and I went with him and had a most interesting visit. Our house looks delightful, with a beautiful garden which Ren Smith laid out when he took over from Ron. The occupants of the house were out, so we did not go inside, but we walked all round and visited the office. The court messengers and other old retainers gave us a tremendous welcome. There is no doubt that Ron was very popular there. We also visited our camp site, almost completely reclaimed by the bush, and showed Joan where the tin huts had been. (Ugh!) Then we drove on to

Cleasby's estate and called on his wife, who showed us over the farm. It was lovely to see cattle and sheep grazing, and a host of ducks, turkeys and hens; also five young peacocks and two gorgeous bloodhound puppies in a white kennel, who bayed at us most convincingly! It was strange to stand in the Magomero garden and see Mlanje, Zomba and Chiradzulu round us – my three mountains and our three stations, all so near and yet, for me, so far. I am longing to show Joan Zomba, which has become a kind of Mecca in her mind!

The daffodils drive me nearly frantic with homesickness – those slim, cool leaves and the fresh yellow colour.

4th August:

Laga has offered to leave her sewing machine with me when she goes on leave in October, so that is a relief. At present I am just starting a cross-stitch theme which would interest you. There is a small open wardrobe in the guest house, and to hang across the front I have bought coarse white material and thick, bright blue *wool* to embroider a deep band on it. I found the design in a woman's magazine left in the house. It is Italian and has two highly stylised dragons rampant, facing each other across a stylised urn of flowers. I am doubling the size, which means quarter-inch stitches, all to be copied by eye onto the weave of the cloth, starting in the centre. It is the most ambitious embroidery I have ever attempted and will be simply gorgeous if it comes off. I can tell Ron and Joan are very sceptical, though too polite to say so! We shall see.

I have been busy with the little bit of garden which belongs to the guest house, and have planted verbena and geraniums. I got one of the *machila* men to make a high trellis between a tree and the wall, to hide the view of the back regions. Laga, a great gardener, is going to bring me a quick growing blue creeper to plant there.

The warmer weather is gradually making itself felt, to my delight – and Joan's – and already we are dark brown and my hair has returned to its bright yellow streakiness. Ron has had to cancel his *ulendo* this week, much to my pleasure, as the Boma is in a dreadful state and several financial crises have arisen. His predecessor obviously had an aversion to paper work! When Ron unlocked the confidential safe, masses of neglected letters, some dating back to 1952, fell out! He was livid, pushed them all back in, rang this man and told him he would like to take over from him properly so would he please return for a few days to enable him to do so. [This he did; all most embarrassing, as he had to stay with us.]

On Wednesday, Laga, Clement and the children came out for tea and simply fell in love with this place. No matter how often we tell them, they never realise that Ron works practically from dawn till dusk and is away more than half of each month, so they imagine we live a kind of country squire and wife existence and envy us accordingly. On Friday we went to Blantyre to shop, and I met the Baxters, who asked us to the Red Cross Ball in Blantyre this weekend, Joan included, of course, so she will at last attend a really big function. Ron and Joan were not with me when I saw them, so they have yet to meet Joan. David is thin and white, Margaret looks well.

On Sunday the Carlyles came for the day, bringing a friend who is an engineer. He told Ron he thought the pool could be 'patched up' for about £50, so that is one step forward. It was a perfect day and we played four sets of tennis. They came again on Monday afternoon for more tennis. We love having them.

11th August:

Chiradzulu is so healthy, bracing and lovely that we hardly feel we are in the same country as Mlanje. I have heard from Mary Holmes, who has fixed with me to come here for a weekend in September. She is missing me a lot and greatly envies us our more pleasant surroundings.

Joan and I spent a day last week preparing for our first weekend away since she came – a great orgy of hair washing (though we do that anyway), ironing, shoe and jewellery cleaning. I leave my earrings and rings in *gin* overnight – a tip I got from Joan Saunders last tour! The weather has been glorious and we embarked on a systematic sunbathing programme, with the result that we are wonderfully browned and bleached, and looked positively foreign among the pallid Blantyre faces. I have also been organising the garden, which takes up a lot of time: it is a great pleasure to me, with my four very helpful *machila* men. They speak not one word of English, so my Chinyanja, I am glad to say, is being stretched. I leave the vegetable garden and orchard to them. They tell me Bwana Rangeley (Bill Rangeley) comes once a year to prune the fruit trees which he himself planted some years ago, when he was stationed here. So that is all right.

We went to Blantyre on Friday to shop, and I met John Gourlay (from Naisi days), who said I looked better and 'livelier' than he had ever seen me. He added that he and Joyce (his wife) would like to come out and visit us. This giddy popularity is due entirely to Chiradzulu's reputation as a great beauty spot. Our weekly trip to Blantyre is always enjoyable, as there is the chance of meeting old friends and acquaintances, and it is interesting for Joan to meet people I have talked about.

We left for the Baxters on Saturday afternoon, arriving in time to find their house in daylight. They are on an estate of new houses, rather crowded together, but quite nice. Joan liked the Baxters at once, and everything went very well indeed. They had asked a very pleasant bachelor partner for Joan, a forestry officer called Brian Fuller. Joan wore a lovely Susan Small cotton dress and long jet earrings (Aunt Isabel's). She looked delightful, though she has put on some weight. I wore my Indian silk and prayed that no one from Zomba would be there to see such an old faithful, and no one was, except David, who loves it anyway. We had a wonderful evening. Ron was in great form and never missed a dance. Peter Delapasteur was there, and danced with Joan and me rather oftener than he should, not being in our party! He always attracts attention, with his grey flecked hair and young, dark face. We have nicknamed him 'the buccaneer'! He invited himself to Chiradzulu for the last weekend in August. Ron likes him, so we are all glad he is coming. (I wonder if he has his eye on Joan!) We left about three on Sunday, as everyone was feeling the effects of the late night. It was such a relief to come back willingly to Chiradzulu – it used to feel like returning to a prison when we went back to Mlanje.

Ron went off today on his first *ulendo* here – only a mile away – and comes back on Saturday morning. He is fearfully busy, but cheerful.

Aflike has accepted Joan and is her willing slave. She thinks him as much of a treasure as we do, and he goes up in her esteem more each time she visits another household and sees how much the servants vary in quality. We had a hilarious time last week. She decided to go on a diet for three days, a milk and banana diet which is very much in vogue at home. Of course there is no word for 'diet' in Chinyanja, and no African would understand such a concept anyway, so my orders for meals were a great trial to me and Aflike, and a source of amusement when I reported back to the other two. At first Aflike thought Joan was ill, and made her special clear soup to tempt her appetite, which of course she refused. He became steadily more baffled and sulky, I more distrait. Ron and Joan laughed and laughed while I got very cross! I really think he thought I was trying to starve her – the jealous older wife?! In the end the diet made her so liverish she gave it up and *then* I had to try to stem the constant supply of bananas which overloaded the table at every meal.

18th August:

I am reading a fascinating novel about India which Joan brought out with her. I think Daddy would like it – *The Near and the Far* by L.H. Myers.

I have been interrupted by a visitor, a Mr Hooper in PWD, who comes out daily from Limbe to supervise the building of a house for an agricultural officer, near the third hairpin bend. So in a few months' time we shall have a neighbour. Mr Hooper is from Somerset and knows West Coker. He took to Joan at once and they had a great talk – a real English countryman. He seems willing to spare a few boys to do some maintenance for us, so Joan and I are deep in discussions on coloured walls and a green bath. She is helping me with sewing for the guest house, which is looking pretty with its green spotted curtains, and royal blue bedspreads piped with white on the twin beds. I am enjoying my very difficult cross stitch creation – it is going to work, so there!

We had a *chiperoni* at the end of last week and to my delight Ron gave up *ulendo* and came in on Thursday, as everything was soaked. The whole place looked like the countryside on a November day at home, with trees looming out of the mist and everything dank and dripping. We had fires in the drawingroom, diningroom and Joan's bedroom – lovely. About 6.30 on Thursday, as I was roaming about the house sipping early morning tea – a favourite time of day with me – by chance I was standing in the bay window, looking out at the thick mist hanging low over everything, when suddenly a herd of wild pigs, big black creatures, materialised out of the mist and came hurtling down the slope below the path to the Boma, crossed the drive and disappeared into the trees on the other side. It was very eerie – a soundless, fleeting image of the Gadarene swine!

On Saturday morning we had a wet shopping trip to Blantyre and returned to Limbe in the evening to dine with the Carlyles and go to *Casablanca*, which we had all seen before but enjoyed very much. There was a very charming tobacco man there to partner Joan, which was nice for her. On Sunday Roy Fitzhenry (the young policeman from Mlanje) came for the day. We managed one set of tennis and a walk round the mountain side to our little dam, but the mist came down again and we stayed by a big fire for the rest of the day, sitting on the floor by my bookcase, talking books – lovely.

25th August:

I am feeling particularly isolated in spirit, despite Joan's presence, as this is Ron's third week of *ulendo* and our weekends have been so full that I have scarcely had a private word with him – ridiculous! He is very overworked and though he enjoys being on his own, he continues to feel the frustrations and setbacks which seem to be on the increase in district work nowadays. All his energies are taken up with getting through the work, and I just have to let it be that way until the burden lightens a bit. He looks very fit and is playing very good tennis. He came in early on Saturday while we were at breakfast, joined us and gave us some Zomba news. He had had to go there during the week – I nearly burst with envy. (*Why* did he not call in here and take us with him?) Later he took us to Blantyre and we spent the rest of the day quietly reading by the fire. On Sunday the Carlyles came and we played eight sets of tennis, while Joan coped angelically but exhaustingly with the children. They bring an African nanny always, but she is utterly useless, and has no control over the children. All this creates difficulties for me, but we like them so much and enjoy their company.

1st September:

I have finished my cross stitch! I did it in three eyesight-ruining weeks and the result is absolutely magnificent – Ron and Joan are full of admiration. I am rather pleased myself and keep stealing over to the guest house to look at it.

I do envy Daddy the Cézanne and Diaghilev exhibitions – the two events at the Edinburgh Festival I most want to see – he would be in heaven.

We had a quiet time last week, with Ron out. Clement and Laga came for tea on Friday; they like to have a run in the car after work each day and sometimes turn up here. It is only half an hour's drive. They usually stay on for a drink and watch the marvellous changing light on Mlanje at sunset, splendid mountain that it is. I *love* it.

On Saturday we shopped and came back in time for lunch. Afterwards I had just finished my preparations when our weekend guest, Peter Delapasteur, roared up in his nice maroon Citroen. He was a perfectly charming guest and we enjoyed every minute of his company. (Ron says it is *me* he has his eye on!) He drove us into Blantyre in the evening to see a wretched English film which he alone enjoyed. Sunday was a beautiful day and he and Ron played tennis all day. I let the men play, as they were evenly matched, while Joan and I sunned ourselves high up on the grass verge. He left about six, absolutely thrilled with Chiradzulu, and we sank back for a quiet Sunday evening and early bed.

On Monday night we went to dinner with 'Uncle Don' Bartlett, our nearest neighbour, about six miles away. You may remember we once shared a *ulendo* with him and played bridge under the trees by lamplight. He is a real old-timer and I was delighted that Joan had the chance to meet him – but it was a *disaster*, as they had nothing to say to each other! She now knows what it is like to sit silent throughout an entire evening listening to uninspiring shop talk, being utterly ignored and feeling that she is gradually becoming invisible. Nevertheless, he is a dear man and of course Ron enjoyed the evening. I was glad Joan had this experience, as it gave her some inkling of what a certain aspect of life in Africa does to my morale, socially. You will be interested to know she was appalled, so it is not just me being Ann!

Ron is in this week and I am beginning to feel like a human being again. The weather is hotting up beautifully and Joan and I are dark brown.

5th September:

You ask about the pool. There seems no doubt at all that it can be made usable. It just needs time, trouble and concentration to get it done, and Ron at present devotes all these to his work.

We had such a pleasant week with Ron in. He has been in this week too but goes out this afternoon for three nights. He and I have played tennis every day and my game is better than it has ever been. I invariably win the first set – I am quicker and have a better eye – and then his greater strength and stamina take over. I feel extremely fit. Joan and I do a *Times* crossword every day in the lovely civilised hour between bath and dinner, when we sink back with a drink and relax.

I have sent to Jo'burg for seeds and long to get them started. We have a large round rockery bed on the front lawn and I want more colour in it. There is a mass of orange blossom in the orchard. It makes the whole place incredibly sweet smelling; the scent sweeps in waves over the tennis court.

We had a lovely weekend being lazy – our first really lazy weekend here, with Sunday music from Salisbury and everything moved onto the front *khonde*, from which Mlanje was invisible in the heat haze. I do wish you could see this heavenly place. Joan remarked at breakfast this morning how much you would appreciate it.

15th September:

In desperation Joan and I have decided to go ahead ourselves about the pool. At this moment she is writing a letter to Shell in Southern Rhodesia, asking for advice on bituminous paints. (Laga's engineer friend told us how to go about it.) I have just come up from the pool, having supervised its cleaning since Monday. It is now scraped clean and when Ron gets cement for the cracks, all we have to do is paint the entire surface with this Shell product, Indasco. So our dream may yet come true. [It never did.]

The great heat is almost upon us and we are thinking of eating out on the *khonde* during the day. Tennis is still possible but by late afternoon the court feels airless and the smell of rotting vegetation, rather like wet nettles, only more primitive, comes drifting down from the mountain. My hair is the colour of corn, I wear no makeup except lipstick and look a picture of health, Ron says. Poor Joan steadily refuses to lose weight – I assure her she will when the heat sets in. Ron is on *ulendo*, was last week and will be all next week. He took us shopping on Saturday. We at last joined the library and I came back joyfully clutching *Old Men Forget* (Duff Cooper) and four others. Ron, of course, pounced on *Old Men Forget* and TOOK IT OUT ON *ULENDO*, so today I sent a small, furious note across country (not far) by a large, placid messenger, demanding its return – it is really too bad – he should jolly well choose his own books, not pinch mine.

On Saturday evening we went to a party at the Leaches, who live on an estate about twelve miles away and knew Ron at Magomero after I left. Joan wore a lovely brilliant green evening cotton and I my black-off-the-shoulder cotton, which Ron loves. He was thrilled with his two dark brown 'wives' and said we looked marvellous. We had been asked to wear the symbol of a book, so Ron put a slide rule in his breast pocket and went as Nevil Shute's autobiography of that name; Joan wore a drawing of a signpost which had a snake with its tail in its mouth – *From Here to Eternity*, and I (feebly) wore an ivory brooch of three monkeys to represent *Apes and Ivory*, a book by Joy Packer which is a best-seller just now. There were thirty-two people there, all wearing book symbols – I guessed seventeen and was the winner! I was given David (Baxter) as my partner in a dreadful improvised conversation game, which we won, and then played another game putting together cut pieces of a page of a newspaper and won *that*. (We are both old hands at jigsaws and assembled the pieces like lightning.) I loathe party games, as you know, and the only way to survive that kind of evening is to throw oneself into it, which Ron and I did. Joan withdrew into a shell of non-co-operation! Fortunately her partner was Arthur Monk, one of the ADCs in Blantyre, who is very relaxed and delightful. Most of the guests were in tobacco and seemed quite interesting. There was a buffet supper and later, about eleven, the floor was cleared for dancing and the party went on till one o'clock. I saw a lot of David during the evening, which was lovely, and Joan had a long talk with Margaret. It was all most enjoyable. Our social life is enough to make us feel sufficiently in touch with people again. P.S. Dorothy Watson has had another son.

22nd September:

I have been meaning to tell you this for ages: there is a large rookery below the Boma, about three hundred yards to the left of the house, and every evening after tea the noise is exactly like the rookery up the lane from Dunalastair! The crows fly home towards sunset, having a wonderful time on the air currents beyond our lawn. I thrilled Ron and Joan the other evening as we sat quietly watching them by suddenly speaking Macbeth's marvellous lines:

> Light thickens, and the crow
> Makes wing to the rooky wood.
> Good things of day begin to droop and drouse,
> While night's black agents to their preys do rouse.

The lower house is going up very slowly, at a typical PWD rate! We hear bangings and hammerings and can watch progress from high upon our platform of lawn.

Joan helps Ron with typing quite often. He is trying to get her a paid, part-time job, so that she can work perhaps all morning every day at the Boma. It would give her something definite to do each day. I have the house and garden to organise and usually am occupied with some ploy, but she has nothing at all to do. She knits unceasingly, but it will soon be too hot for that. Since she came she has knitted a beautiful cardigan for Ron, a sweater for Mary Holmes, a cardigan for Laga and three sweaters for herself, none of which she will ever wear, as she 'dislikes hand-knitted things'!

The weather gets warmer and more beautiful every day. Ron came in on Saturday and took us to Blantyre to shop. Gabe Pollard, the DC, Blantyre, has been posted to Fort Johnston. I have not mentioned him, as I only met him once, briefly. He has been replaced by the man he took over from, Ron Pincott, back from leave, whom Ron likes and considers a very able man who should go far. He is looking forward to working with him. In the evening we dined with the Carlyles and went to see Carol Reed's latest film, *The Man Between*. They are busy packing up but have not much to do, as they are letting the house. The film was disappointing; not up to his usual high standard. We spent a beautiful, lazy Sunday, and till now, Wednesday, Ron has been in, so life has been good.

We now have Kiko, the Carlyles's peke, with us till they return from leave. She is sweet, no trouble, and adores the whole place. At the moment she is chasing a pair of wagtails on the lawn, leaping in the air with stiff legs, like a little lamb. They are much too clever for her and tease her endlessly.

28th September:

We have more library books to keep us going, including the much publicised *Seven Years in Tibet*, which Joan is reading, and Marghanita Laski's *The Victorian Chaise Longue*, a rather grim, Henry Jamesian novel, very well written.

The weather is glorious and the days pass effortlessly when we can be out in the sun and play tennis. Joan has improved a lot and we both enjoy the exercise.

On Saturday, after shopping, we had lunch with John and Ray Grindall. John has taken over as agricultural officer in Chiradzulu for six months, and was out on *ulendo* with Ron last week, touring the district. They enjoyed it and will obviously work well together. His wife Ray studied ballet, which she teaches in Blantyre, Limbe and Zomba. They are charming, interesting and fun to be with. In the evening Ron and I went to the cinema in Limbe to see *Roman Holiday*, with Gregory Peck and Audrey Hepburn, the young girl discovered a few years ago by Colette, to play the lead in her play *Gigi*. She is quite enchanting. The film was shot in Rome, in strong sunlight and shadow – lovely. We saw lots of people we knew, as the place was packed for such a good film. Joan did not come: she has very definite likes and dislikes; so Ron and I were on our own and made it a special occasion.

Sunday was a sunny, breezy day. The Baxters arrived about ten, both obviously prepared to enjoy themselves. David is very white but was in his most delightful mood, reminding me of the old, light-hearted David, and Margaret was bright and relaxed. We played rather bad tennis and sat out on the *khonde* talking and laughing till dark. We were all so happy they were easily persuaded to stay on to supper. (I heard Ron say, 'It's all laid on, you know,' as I went out to the pantry, clutching my hair and wondering how I could possibly feed *five* people at such short notice!) However, Aflike and I put our heads together and I left him and Cook calmly preparing to cope. (This is one of the occasions which proves that I really do need a fridge.) Margaret told Joan I looked a different person since I left Mlanje. She said she had never seen anyone so small, thin and white as I was there. *Everyone* comments on the change, she said. Ah, well.

I have twelve seed boxes on the side *khonde* and will report progress.

7th October:

Yesterday Ron had to go to Limbe to attend a court case and took Joan and me to Blantyre for the morning. We explored the Indian stores and I found exactly what I wanted – a heavenly blue cotton – as always in my favourite store. We also went to the British Council building and joined the free library there. It is mainly non-fiction and has many books I have wanted to read for ages, including David Garnett's *The Golden Echo. Seven Years in Tibet*, which I finished the other day, was a great disappointment. It is, of course, a tremendously interesting and courageous adventure, but narrated in a flat, almost priggish style which I found irritating. I have also re-read *Operation Heartbreak* and found it as wonderful as ever.

I am feeling very cheerful as Ron is in this week. He came back last Friday, in time to see the Carlyles, who came for tea, to say goodbye – and deliver the sewing machine. They were both amazed at the difference in Kiko, who has put on weight and has a very healthy-looking coat. (I groom her every day.) She is a darling and gives us endless pleasure and amusement. She must find our big garden an absolute paradise after Limbe.

On Saturday we shopped and got back in time for me to do the hundred and one small things which make this house *my* house for my guests. Sandy and Mary (Holmes) arrived about three o'clock and we had a great reunion. Mary hates Mlanje and never sees anyone. (It really does seem to have a curse on it.) She was thankful to have a woman to talk to, in fact two. She likes Barbara Sproule, who has had a bad breakdown in health, mainly nervous, and is taking a long time to recover, keeping very much to herself. We played a great deal of tennis and they talked their heads off. When they left they said, with their dear, genuine affection, that they had loved every minute.

The weather is very hot and the jacaranda blossom is fully out. Chiradzulu really looks like paradise. We have ten jacaranda trees in the grounds, some of them growing on the steep slope below the lawn, so that we look out over a foaming sea of blossom. I occasionally get a dangerous urge to dive off the lawn into it! In every direction there is a great mass of blue – unbelievably beautiful. Our visitors just gasp when they step out of their car and see what lies before them.

11th October: [Air letter]

This is to let you know my letter will be late this week. On Friday we were thrown into some confusion by the arrival of a wire from Mzimba, capital of the Northern Province, from Joan's friends the Milners, who travelled out on the ship with her, to say that Bruce Wickham, an administrative officer living in Mzimba, is to be in Blantyre to collect a car and drive it up to Mzimba, setting out tomorrow, 12th October and stopping overnight at Lilongwe. He has gladly offered us a lift. It is four hundred and eighty miles north! It was such a bolt from the blue we took some time to decide. However, it is a wonderful chance which may not come again. Ron is out on *ulendo* for the next three weeks anyway, and urged me to go. It is very hot and the roads are rough, so it will be quite a journey for Joan. The Mlanje-Cholo-Blantyre-Limbe route has safeguarded her against any experience of roads elsewhere in the territory. We go through Zomba, Kasupi and cross Liwonde ferry – all so exciting to show her. Mzimba is only forty-five miles from the Lake, so we are hoping for a visit there too. I have made a lovely blue dress at high speed, done masses of washing, mending and tidying, besides organising supplies for Ron and Kiko, and making a plan for the distribution in the garden of masses of seedlings from my boxes, unfortunately at this moment ready for planting – all this in the tremendous heat. Joan, needless to say, has been in her room, fully occupied with 'packing', since Friday!

14th October: Mzimba

I must begin at the beginning and tell you about this very sudden trip. On Friday we received the Milners' wire telling us we could get a lift on Tuesday morning. It was so unexpected and left us so little time to organise ourselves that my immediate reaction was not to want to go, and Joan hesitated too. However, we discussed it, Ron saying I would always regret it if I did not take this chance opportunity and prevented Joan from taking it. I suddenly realised I had reached a stage, brought about by isolation, when I did not want to do anything unusual, out of routine, and was finding feeble excuses to get out of it, so I firmly made myself agree to go – and of course I am now thankful. I did an exhausting amount of planning, phoning and wiring and got it all straightened out. Ron went off on *ulendo* on Monday after lunch, very subdued but glad for my sake. At three, Mr Hooper, PWD, called for us and took us into Blantyre, where we stayed the night with the Baxters, who gave us a happy welcome. Bruce Wickham came to tea, having flown down that day. He has served in Nyasaland for thirteen years and is about to become DC, Rumpi, one of the districts in the North. At present he is PA (Personal Assistant) to the PC, Northern Province. He is terribly nice, easy either to talk to or be silent with. He was collecting a Morris Minor which has done six thousand miles in England and has just arrived by sea and rail. We were worried it would be a frightful squeeze but it was perfectly comfortable. Joan and I took turns at sitting in the front, as the back is hotter, dustier and bumpier.

On Tuesday David took us to the PC's office at 8.00 a.m. and there I ran into Eric Barnes (PC) and introduced Joan, looking somewhat larger than usual in corduroy slacks. I wore my old blue linen slacks and an ancient navy blue blouse, in the hope that it would not show up the dust. We drove to Zomba in great excitement and found it looking like the Garden of Eden, with every colour and shape of blossom pouring from every wall and hedge, the roads blue with fallen jacaranda blossom. Joan was enchanted. Bruce signed the book at the entrance of the drive at GH and then drove us all round Zomba, so I was able to point out to Joan the Boma, the Club and all the mountain road houses, including No 1, where we had lived. Then we went to the Secretariat, where Bruce had an hour's business, and Joan and I met Joyce Gourlay, Bryn (Jones-Walters) and Bill Melhuish, who was delighted to see me. He was looking very well indeed, and explained that he had just spent three weeks' 'local leave' in England with his wife and children. She had been left a legacy, and sent him a present of his fare, lucky man. Joan was most interested in everyone and everything, and adored the look and atmosphere of Zomba, including my mountain, its unforgettable profile peacefully dreaming in the hot sunshine.

We drove through a countryside so loved and familiar to my heart that for the first time ever in Africa I found myself looking at the scenery with eyes which recognised it as *my* landscape rather than an alien one. This discovery quite overwhelmed me. The country round Kasupi looked astonishingly beautiful, all the great hills covered in dove grey and scarlet trees, the colours of early spring. Between Zomba and Liwonde the road was worst of all, with potholes, corrugation and bright red dust, but Joan was too interested in everything to notice. We slowed down to look up the drive to the house at Kasupi, which is most attractive – white walls and a green roof. We drove down the escarpment to Liwonde, where it felt hotter than ever. There were some old women gathered there whom I remembered from the time of the famine. They did not seem to recognise me but when I spoke to them they touched me with frail, clawlike hands, giggling and cackling, and said, '*Inde, inde,*' (Yes, yes), they remembered the little Dona and the tall Bwana Hitchcock from Kasupi. I told them where we had been since Kasupi days, and they listened, exclaiming politely, '*Eh, eh, ai, ai,*' as I spoke. It was a lovely encounter. I expect they talked about it for the rest of the day, as indeed I thought about it. (Ron will be pleased.) The ferrymen were strangers but sang as they pulled us across, much to Joan's delight. It was the most special part of the whole journey for me, and I was moved by how vividly I remembered everything, with a deep sense of haunting homesickness – my eyes kept filling with tears.

We drove on till 1.30, stopping just over the Central Province border for a picnic lunch, then on till 4.00 p.m., when we reached Dedza, where we had tea with the DC, George Salter and his wife Kay, who once called in at Kasupi. The Central Province is much wilder than the South, the road passing over high, undulating tableland, with mountain tops showing on the horizon, very like the country in Caithness and Sutherland. We got to Lilongwe at 6.30. Bruce went to stay with friends, while we spent the night at the hotel, a most civilised place like an English pub, where we ate a huge dinner and I had one of the most welcome baths of my life! We felt tired, but not wearily so, and both slept wonderfully.

Bruce collected us at nine next morning. We had lunch at Kasungu, at the rest house, where we found Maurice Gandy (David's first DC), whom we had known in Zomba when he was in the Secretariat. He is now a lawyer but has been recalled to Administration, much to his displeasure. He had arrived only a few hours before us, to take over as DC, Kasungu. It is a very well laid-out station, most attractive and, as they all are, miles from anywhere. The distances between them are colossal. Zomba district is one hundred and eighty square miles and we considered that large – Mzimba is seven thousand square miles! We drove on without another break, except for a ten minutes' stop when we found a blue gum fallen across the road and Bruce organised a boy with an axe to clear enough branches for our neat little car to pass on. The country got wilder and wilder; I felt as if I were travelling along the top of the world – a glorious sensation, heady and almost supernatural.

We arrived here at 6.45, not even very tired, but absolutely filthy! The Milners are Scots and very nice. They have two small girls, aged seven and two. Tommy is Provincial Engineer, and is going to take us further north on *ulendo* to Livingstonia, and also to Nkata Bay, one of the most beautiful of the Lake stations. We have a little guest house with a bathroom to ourselves. This morning we woke up and looked out on a wide view from the top of a large, flat hill. There are twenty families in Mzimba, some of whom we are to meet. This morning we just sat talking and walked round the garden. It is very hot in the sun, but there is a cool, high wind, as the station stands at over four thousand feet. Joan is thrilled with everything and has come more alive than I have yet seen her out here. She was most excited at Kasungu yesterday when we met an old man with a long hunting spear and on impulse I said I would ask him if she could buy it. The Central Province Chinyanja is incredibly easy to understand (I think it is a matter of the accent we were taught being the same and I find my vocabulary flowing back). I had a long, friendly talk with him, and eventually told him Joan wanted to buy his spear and would pay whatever price he asked. He promptly sold it to her for 7/6. He had made it himself and used it for years, hunting in the bush. (Somehow I hated this transaction.)

I must stop before this gets too heavy. We think of staying for about ten days, but it really depends when we can get a lift back.

21st October:

We returned from a trip north last night (Wednesday) and I am writing this in time to catch the next plane, which goes out tomorrow. We have no definite date yet for returning, but we hear that Humphrey Bingham is at Karonga (right up at the tip of the North) and is driving back to Zomba about 26th-28th, so I have sent off a letter by someone who is arriving there today, asking him if he can give us a lift back. It seems an imposition to me, but apparently it is done all the time.

Joan and I continue to enjoy our holiday and have had a most marvellous trip, more than a hundred miles beyond Mzimba and only forty-five miles from Karonga, the furthest Boma in Nyasaland.

We spent the first few days in Mzimba. Margaret Milner gave a party for us, to meet all their friends. Two young ADCs are out on *ulendo* but we hope to meet them before we go. This is for Joan's benefit! They are all very pleasant, friendly people. Bruce Wickham's wife, Jean, is a darling and we find we have a lot in common. I would like to spend far more time with her. As with my first meeting with Iris, our eyes met and exchanged messages, though on a different wavelength. [We became lifelong friends.] I have just heard that Humphrey arrives here tomorrow and leaves for the South on Monday 25th, which is ideal for us and we are longing to hear if he will take us. Bruce says he is sure he will!

On Monday we left about 9.00 a.m. on *ulendo* – Tommy, Margaret, Joan, the two children and myself. They have a big roomy Vauxhall, and as I sat in the front all the way, except for a car-sick hour at first – there is quite a swing to the car at the back, which proved fatal for me – I had a most comfortable journey. I felt guilty not sharing it with Joan, but everyone saw that I could not cope: I was wilting, green and very apologetic! The scenery on the way to Mzimba was spectacular enough but NOTHING to what we saw beyond. It is almost indescribable – huge mountains, high rolling tableland, massive rocky outcrops and thick forests. We drove over the Vipya plateau and were spellbound by the magnificence of the scenery. We picnicked at Mzuzu, which at present is a collection of temporary buildings in the middle of nowhere but is to become the provincial capital instead of Mzimba. Tommy was on a working *ulendo* and stopped at several places to inspect roads and bridges.

After lunch we turned off the road north and dropped down thousands of feet to Nkata Bay, a beautiful Lakeshore station, which looks like a rather raw version of the Riviera in scenery and layout. The DC's house stands on a promontory and on a clear day the mountains in Tanganyika are visible. The rest house is on the edge of a cliff overlooking a little bay; the pleasure of watching sparkling blue water gradually becoming copper coloured in the sunset and then opalescent in the afterglow was tremendous, making me realise anew *how much* I miss living beside water. The sudden drop to Lake level played havoc with our eardrums, but after sleeping like tops we found they had recovered. We were shown over a fishery laboratory, where five young bachelors drooled over the sight of us. There is only one woman in Nkata Bay at present; even the DC is a bachelor.

We climbed back into the hot car and set off again. The heat and dust at this time of year make travelling an endurance test. We had lunch at Ekwendeni, with the PWD storekeeper, a slightly bush-happy South African, whose kitchen boy was holding a wedding feast in the garden. Joan took photos of the bride enveloped in yards of mosquito netting. We arrived at Rumpi, our destination, in time for tea in a large guest house set among massive hills, with the usual station buildings around – Boma, Post Office, Police, etc. – again, all in the middle of nowhere. I keep writing that phrase – I have to – it is a fact! There were five men staying there besides us. Joan and I had a little house to ourselves to sleep and wash in, but as there was NO water, we just slept – awful. I used up almost a whole bottle of eau de cologne to feel clean – the only liquid I had! Joan saw her first snake on the steps as we went across from the main building to our bedroom. I, of course, with my sixth sense, saw it beyond the light of my torch as a vague but sinister shape and pulled her back. She shone her torch on it and it slithered slowly down a drain. It looked to me like a black mamba (which is not actually black; I know, because I killed one in the kitchen garden at Mlanje). She was thrilled – only my nerves thrilled, as I lay sleepless in bed, recovering. I do not know if it is because she is just a visitor out here, but it seems to me Joan has left her sense of fear at home.

We left at nine next morning for the most wonderful scenery of all, along the foothills of the great Nyika plateau. Huge mountains pile up one behind the other, and the road climbs up and down over hill and valley, suddenly appearing ahead from nowhere. We climbed thousands of feet in a matter of minutes and could hardly believe our eyes – and ears, which behaved in an extraordinary way as the pressure kept changing. We reached Livingstonia about eleven, and had tea with a Scottish mission family. (There is no Boma at Livingstonia, only Mission people.) Their name is Gemmel and both came from Glasgow – with accents to match! They were delightful. From their garden we looked out over the Lake but could not see far, because of the heat haze. Tommy then drove a few miles further to let us see the famous escarpment with twenty-three hairpin bends which leads to Karonga. The Lake lay far below us, brilliant blue in long curving bays with a thin edge of pale sand. Tropical forest-clad mountains rear straight up from its shores. The escarpment road winds down the edge of a mountain with a sheer drop on the side, and we saw sixteen of the bends, like an enormous snake flung down, as we stood at the top. I just gasped with excitement. In the car I felt very odd indeed – as if the back of my head was going to float off – the road is so narrow I could only see the drop, not the edge. Tommy drove down round one bend, to let us get the sensation. I bet some people walk it! We had a picnic lunch on a ledge, looking across to the beautiful Manchewe Falls, which drop down three hundred feet. We watched a terrible forest fire raging up a mountain before the wind. We then turned back, stopping for tea at an isolated house with a PWD man and his wife, who get eighteen bottles of milk a day and make cream, butter, cheese and cooking fat with it (!) and arrived back at Mzimba, at seven, in the dark. Unfortunately we saw not one scrap of game throughout our journeyings, which is a great disappointment. We were very tired, slept deeply and feel fit and well today.

The Club committee has organised a treasure hunt and dance for us on Saturday and on Monday we hope to leave with Humphrey. By the time we get back we shall have done well over a thousand miles. I am now longing to get back to Ron and my own house and garden: so is Joan, but it has been a marvellous experience and has done us both a lot of good. The Milners make a great fuss of Joan, who blossoms and I am glad for her, while I stay quietly in my shell. However, Humphrey will change all that!

[My next letter went missing and never reached my mother. The main item of interest in it was our meeting with the two young ADCs, back from *ulendo* in time for the treasure hunt and dance. One of them, John Carver, became a dear friend and still writes to me from South Africa. Everybody at Mzimba waited with bated breath for John to 'fall' for Joan. Amusingly, he 'fell', with a crash which reverberated throughout the station, for the wrong cousin – me! We have laughed about this together ever since.]

3rd November: Chiradzulu

We are gradually settling down. I still feel slightly detached and have to make an effort to remember to run the house!

I wrote to you last Tuesday, two days before we left Mzimba. By then I was thoroughly enjoying myself and Joan was beginning to feel miserable. John Carver gave us a wonderful farewell party and we danced on the *khonde* to his gramophone. (I shall always think of him when I hear 'Smoke gets in your eyes'!) On Wednesday afternoon at teatime Humphrey called in, early in schedule and eager to be off on Thursday at 8.00 a.m. instead of after lunch. He swears that he said, 'Oh hell,' when he was handed my letter and told it was from someone wanting a lift, and then said, 'Ah, heaven,' when he opened it and saw my signature! We spent a quiet last evening with the Milners.

Next morning we were having breakfast when dear John turned up with a packet of peppermints for the journey. As we bade each other a fond farewell he said, 'Thank God for the tourist trade!' Joan and I sat in the front of Humphrey's big Ford, I in the middle – because there is nothing of me at all, according to his inaccurate powers of measurement by eye! He was an entrancing travelling companion, vividly recounting interesting stories about the country, which he obviously adores. He has become one of my most favourite people in Nyasaland. I had to sit very still so as not to disturb his driving and got very hot and stiff, but one adapts very quickly to hours of heat and dust.

We got to Kasungu about ten, and had a cold drink with Maurice and Bunty Gandy, which was wonderfully reviving. We arrived at Lilongwe hotel in time for a late, very good lunch. On again, and we reached Dedza at teatime. We stayed the night there at its very pleasant hotel *The Angoni Highlands*. Joan found some lovely ebony eggcups to take back and I bought four ebony ashtrays for Ron, which he is delighted with. Next morning we had a very light-hearted breakfast and were off at 8 o'clock. Humphrey was very impressed throughout the journey by our punctuality (managed by sheer will power and insistence on my part). The drive south was the hottest of all. The countryside is utterly dry and parched, as inflammable as tinder. We got to Zomba at noon exactly and drove up to their lovely bungalow. Eve greeted me most affectionately and was greatly taken with Joan. She gave us one of her marvellous curry lunches, which we shared with David Longden (Resident Magistrate) and Dougie Lomax (Police and a near neighbour at Naisi). It was lovely for me to sit back and absorb the old familiar Zomba ambience and I enjoyed it immensely, as did Joan, who found it all very much as I had described.

Ron arrived for an early tea, looking brown but tired. He then thankfully bore us back to Chiradzulu, where I found a frivolous selection of food and drink in the store, and a most dismaying mixture of seedlings growing in all the wrong places in the garden, which is going to look very odd indeed – after all my cherished plans! Aflike's cousin Allan, whom I have been waiting for since we came back from leave, has at last turned up and our old cook has retired. They work marvellously together, so I can now relax and leave it to them, which is a relief in the great heat. Aflike was quite upset that I had been away 'too far, too long'. However, I had a long talk with him, describing my journeys, and he could not conceal his delight that I had seen so much of his homeland – more than he ever has. Kiko has been overfed but is simply gorgeous, with a thick, clean coat. She looks a real pukka peke now, except for her lamentable tail which continues to droop slightly instead of curling up over her back. She follows Joan and me about and lies affectionately on our feet at every opportunity, to make sure we really are going to stay with her.

Ron worked very hard while we were away and now has a week in with me. I think he found the house at the weekends rather dismal on his own and says he missed me terribly. (Huh, what about *week* after *week*?) We found the weather very much hotter when we came back, but on Sunday the small rains broke and there have been showers since, which have cooled the air wonderfully. We spent a lazy weekend. Joan had eleven letters waiting for her, I three! Iris has at last written, an air letter, full of life and interest – she loved her day in St. Andrews and her visit – 'especially Mother' she says! I have a vast pile of *Times* and *Observers* to catch up on.

In a way you are right in thinking Ron and I are lucky to be in the South – on the journey up and back I had cause to count my blessings. All those Central and Northern Province stations are out in the blue, and once one is up there, there is no escape and no amount of magnificent scenery is going to compensate for that. On the other hand, the Northern Province in particular struck me as being the *real* Africa and I got a very strong feeling I would like the chance to meet the challenge of that way of life. I just have a feeling in my bones for it. Ron, of course, would love it and listened avidly to all I could tell him. (I did not say so, but if we were posted there, I would insist on several concessions – the car, a fridge, and various other amenities that occurred to me.)

10th November:

I am feeling very homesick today, as the weather is quite lovely and very like home – a soft, damp wind moaning in the chimneys; in the garden everything fresh, sweet smelling and slightly bedraggled after a night's rain.

I am glad you found my two letters from the North interesting. It is always difficult to settle down to write a proper letter in a strange place, without privacy, especially when all I have seen is so utterly alien to home, I despair before I begin of being able to convey the very special atmosphere and appearance of things. Being on the move all the time, the images were fleeting, which made it difficult for me to capture their essence and distil it onto the page.

I have been replanting all the seedlings planted in the wrong places during my absence, a marathon task, but it had to be done and I have not lost any of them in the process. Ron noticed at once when he came back from *ulendo* and was very impressed.

We had a most marvellous storm last night which gave Joan her first view of what lightning can be like in the tropics. Outlined against flickering violet light, the black bulk of Mlanje seemed to loom closer to us across the plain, which was under assault from great forks of lightning, audible between the onslaught of the thunder. The rain poured down all night and this morning the lawn and the foothills beyond are perceptibly greener. My carnations, all slips which I brought from Mlanje, are simply bursting into bloom – I picked fourteen yesterday and twelve this morning.

On Saturday we lunched with the DC, Blantyre, Ron Pincott and his wife Coralie. They are warm, friendly people and I can see that my Ron will work well with him. I should hate to see those two up against each other – they are very alike in that one senses the inner drive with which they approach their work.

I found David Garnett's *The Golden Echo* deteriorated as it went on. There is something unpleasant and furtive in him which I cannot quite put my finger on.

On Monday a young policeman called on business and stayed for tea – Ron was out. He had been in the thick of the emergency in Malaya. Months after Michael Codner ('John' in *The Wooden Horse*) was killed at Tanjon Malim, this young man arrested a group of ambushed terrorists, among whom was a woman carrying Michael Codner's revolver, so she was among those who ambushed his men and murdered him. He was fascinated to learn that I had met Michael at Oxford.

On Saturday Ron came in early and we had a long morning in Blantyre, during which I went to have my hair thinned and shaped. The South African girl who did it was new to the salon and did not know my hair. When she had apparently finished, she hesitated and then said, 'I am sorry, this marvellous head of hair is so thick I do not seem to have made the slightest impression on it, so may I start all over again?' My head feels so much cooler and lighter. I bought some lovely black and white cotton for an evening dress Vogue pattern I have had for some time. It is more complicated than anything I have ever attempted, so I decided to make a short dress from some old curtain material as a trial. It has turned out delightful, so I shall dye it black and wear it as a cocktail dress. The curtain material is the lavender from Joan's bedroom at Mlanje. It turned out that the one colour she loathes is lavender, so you can imagine how I felt in Mlanje, after all the loving care taken to decorate her room entirely in lavender!

We had a wet, quiet weekend, listening to the wireless and reading. I read, for the first time, one of Iris Compton-Burnett's novels. I happen not to have come across her before, though I know her by reputation. Well, I find her completely unreadable – just too artificial for my taste. Joan and I have been doing a *Times* crossword every evening and now find we finish it in half an hour, so we do two between bath and dinner! She is frightfully good at anagrams and does them in her head, sometimes so quickly that I have not even had time to write down the letters in order to work them out. However, I come into my own with quotations and a much wider vocabulary.

All the beds in the garden are sprinkled with spring green, lovely to see against the black earth. The vegetable garden is bursting with produce and we are going to have literally thousands of peaches, apricots, plums, paw-paws and mangoes. The *machila* men have indicated politely to me that there is an established tradition that whoever is stationed at Chiradzulu is expected to supply the PC's office staff with boxes of fruit throughout the season. This I shall be happy to do.

The rain has brought out the usual hosts of insects of every shape and size. Kiko pounces on them, sits chewing them with loud relish and then brings them up, equally loudly, revolting little beast.

I must tell you about 'our' leopard. When Ron is in, Joan and I often walk to the office after tea to meet him, taking Kiko with us. The Boma is built near the edge of a very deep, wide gully, and on more than one occasion we have heard the hoarse, coughing bark of a leopard coming from somewhere on the opposite side. Ron's clerk tells us it lives among a group of huge boulders halfway up the steep slope of the gully. Leopards are known to have a penchant for dogs, so I always turn back with Kiko when I hear it – a very feral sound which makes the hairs stand up on my arms. Kiko, little 'lion dog' that she is, barks back defiantly, all the hairs on her coat fluffing out, and snuffles furiously in protest when I pick her up and hurry home.

One evening last week when Ron was on *ulendo*, I walked round, as I always do, to the side *khonde* and went into the wired-in part on my way to the loo. Darkness had just fallen, and Joan's lamp shone out of her open French windows. She was sitting at her dressing table, brushing her hair. When I came out of the loo I became aware of rustling and breathy sounds coming from beyond and below the *khonde*, where there is a narrow flowerbed. I thought it was Kiko, who is not allowed out after dark. I walked over, leaned down with my face close to the netting and said in the special voice I have for her, 'What are you doing out there in the dark, you naughty little thing? Come in at once, come on, round to the front.' Four things then happened simultaneously. I heard Joan's voice from the bedroom saying, 'I do not know who you think you are talking to. Kiko is in here with me'; I made out a long solid shape in the dark flowerbed; I heard a deep, rumbling growl come from below and my nostrils were assailed by an awful, foetid stench. (All this happened in a matter of seconds.) As I realised the presence of the leopard, I leapt backwards the entire breadth of the *khonde* – something I would find physically impossible in normal circumstances – landing in Joan's doorway, with my back to her room. I grabbed the doors and shut them with a crash, turned round, ignored Joan, jumped over Kiko and flew through the house, yelling repeatedly at the pitch of my lungs, 'Aflike, *nyalugwe, nyalugwe*' (Leopard, leopard). He was in the pantry and came running in. I said 'Help me. Close the doors,' and rushed past him into the drawingroom, across to the big bay window which looks out on the side *khonde*. Its windows were wide open, as it was a hot night. (Only the bedroom windows are wired over.) As I shut them I heard Aflike slam shut the diningroom doors and a moment later he was behind me shutting the front ones. We then faced each other, he perfectly calm but with eyes anxious for me, I gasping for breath. I made an enormous effort and managed to tell him what happened. With one of his eloquent, fatalistic shrugs, he said, 'The leopard smells the little dog.' (In other words, 'what do you expect?') As he left the room, Joan came in smiling, carrying Kiko, who was all fluffed up and snuffling horribly. I sank down on a chair and Joan poured me a brandy, which I could barely hold with both hands. I reckon she has *no* sense of danger out here. Later, of course, I saw the funny side and was able to make an amusing story of it when I told Ron. But for the rest of that evening we sat and sweated, as I could not bring myself to open up the house. I wish I had a gun and knew how to use it if necessary. I just cannot *stand* feeling helpless.

24th November:

I am happy this week as Ron is in. About ten days ago he got a *njiga* (tick) known as a 'jigger' embedded in his foot, which gradually went septic, swelling his foot and groin. He went into Blantyre to see a doctor, and was given an injection and told not to go out on *ulendo* this week. Typically, the doctor did not tell him to stay in bed or that he would probably run a temperature, so we were rather worried when he started to burn merrily on Monday afternoon. Since then he has remained in bed, getting a very much needed rest, and the Hospital Assistant from our local African hospital comes up each day to give him an injection, which we hope will disperse the poison. He is perfectly happy and thoroughly spoiled.

Joan has at last managed to get her trip to Salisbury to visit the
Dushmanitches organised, and flies there from Chileka, our local airport (outside Blantyre) on Sunday. She plans to stay for a fortnight and then go to
Bechuanaland, where friends she met on the ship live at a place called
Gaberones. They are going to the Natal coast for sixteen days over Christmas
and have asked her to join them. There will be surfing, picnics, and lots of
festivities. It means she will be away over Christmas, but I had no hesitation in
telling her to go, as Christmas means so little here and will be terribly quiet for
her. She has also been told she cannot get a passage home on a City ship till
May, so this will make a good break in the middle of her visit. It will be a
wonderful trip: I feel quite refreshed by all the planning and enthusing.

There are two very good films in Limbe and Blantyre this week – an
embarras de richesse after many weeks of nothing but rubbish. We are being
extravagant tomorrow, going to the matinee of *Shane*, the Western which became an instant classic. We get a lift in the afternoon in Mr Hooper's car, and
come back by TAXI! We hope Ron will be mobile again by Saturday and have
booked again for *Julius Caesar*. After that I have my visit to Mlanje in early
December to look forward to.

We went into Blantyre on Saturday and stayed to lunch with the Baxters.
Margaret had another miscarriage six weeks ago and was in bed, again hoping
that she is pregnant. She has lost faith in the doctors out here and has sought no
advice, just doing as she thinks best – worrying. David looks white and unhappy. I have given them an open invitation to Chiradzulu whenever they want
to come. The change of scene might do Margaret good and she could stay for as
long as she likes in our dear little guest house.

1st December:

As you see, it is Ron's birthday, and I have just watched him stride along
the blue gum avenue to the Boma, with sweet Kiko leaping and scampering
behind him. It is one of those golden African days which fills my being with
light, and I feel I want to gather it into myself as a memory forever. Ron is
absolutely thrilled this morning as Joan and I combined and gave him a Parker
51 pen and pencil in a case. I have a bottle of very good French wine to produce
as a surprise this evening. He is feeling much better and is back at work,
fortunately at the Boma this week. He and I are blissfully happy. Joan went
off to Salisbury on Saturday, and it is absolutely wonderful to be on our own
again for a bit. He has been working in his little study, while I have been
making my cotton evening dress. It is lovely and looks exactly like a pukka
Horrocks.

Last week Joan and I went to the matinee of *Shane* and came back by taxi,
rather nerve-wracked, as the African driver was put in a panic by a thick white
fog which engulfed us on our bush road, and then got into a worse panic when

he had to deal with the hairpin bends. However, it was worth it, as the film was wonderful. On Friday it was quite evident that Ron would not be up by Saturday, so I gave my shopping list to a messenger and off he went on his bicycle. However, Joan had to get in to see about money, passport, passage, etc., so in we went after lunch, again with the obliging Mr Hooper. We went to the 4.30 showing of *Julius Caesar* and came back by taxi – an Indian driver this time, who coped very well. The two films and the journey cost 36/–, but it was worth it. The film was magnificent, with everyone except the two women – who gave dreadful performances – on top of their form. The scenery was overwhelmingly Roman – great white colonnaded buildings casting huge black shadows. The crowd scenes were most marvellously managed, with the rise and fall of sound heightening the drama. I came away physically and mentally exhausted and, very unlike me, fell asleep in the taxi!

On Saturday Joan got a lift into Blantyre, stayed the night in Ryall's and flew to Salisbury on Sunday, just missing a tremendous thunderstorm. She plans to come back early in January. Next week I go to Mlanje to stay with the Holmeses, and Ron joins me for the weekend. There is a dance to celebrate the official opening of the Club on Saturday.

The weather continues to provide plenty of rain, but the sun is scorchingly hot when it does get through, with the result that our fruit trees are laden with *hundreds* of big ripe peaches glowing among their leaves. I have only to run my hand along a branch and they fall off, sun-warmed and simply spurting juice. The loveliest sight is the plum trees, with their dark purple, bloomy fruit. I have a constant pain from overeating, but Ron seems able to eat his fill without paying any penalty! Our wooden fruit bowl is a sight to see, piled with cornucopian plenty on the breakfast table.

It is strange to think of all the dark, dead gardens at home while mine is leaping into life. I keep up a constant supply of twenty carnations in the house, in eight marvellous shades. I had two long borders made in front of the house, when I came back from Mzimba, and filled them with portulaca. That was a month ago and yesterday seven plants were in bloom. I have a whole bed full of pansies which are growing visibly every day. It would give you such pleasure to see this big garden coming alive. From our rain gauge, I can tell we have had between six and seven inches of rain since 31st October, without being very conscious of it.

8th December: Mlanje

This will probably be rather a rushed letter, as the Holmes household is not exactly peaceful! We are going into Blantyre in forty minutes, so I shall post this there.

On Sunday afternoon Ron took me to Blantyre and we had tea at The Tavern with Sandy and Mary, and then I went off with them. They pounced on me like a long-lost friend. Ron went back to comfort Kiko and have the unusual experience of a lone Sunday evening. He is out on *ulendo* this week and comes here on Saturday in time for lunch.

Mlanje is tremendously hot and humid – far more so than I remember and everyone says it is a particularly hot wet season here. I cannot imagine how Ron and I lived in this climate. I do not mind it but I am sure it is terribly unhealthy. This house is an absolute sun trap and does not have enough windows – even the cat gasps for air!

On Monday afternoon Mary and I went up to the DC's house, where the Boma Red Cross meetings are now held. There was no one there (I breathed a sigh of relief) except Betty, a Mrs Cox whom I knew from Zomba days, and Peter's mother, who has come out from England to visit them. She is seventy-five and was feeling the heat terribly, though she lived in India for thirty-five years. We went back there in the evening for drinks, apparently offered in my honour, as Mary said she and Sandy never see the Nicholsons – so *plus ça change, plus c'est la même chose*, on Mlanje station! It was a very pleasant evening, Betty and Peter very relaxed and friendly. Yesterday was a lovely day and we made a beeline for the pool, where we spent a wonderful morning swimming and sunning ourselves. The water was absolutely *freezing*. After lunch it poured with rain, as only Mlanje can rain, and so cooled the air that we decided on tennis after tea. We had to get boys to brush the water off the court before we could go on. We played two hard sets, winning one each, which was satisfactory. You should have seen us afterwards, with sweat-soaked hair and streaming faces. After a bath we had an early supper and went back to the Club to see an old, very dreary film. At the interval I saw all the old familiar faces and felt I now lived in another world from them. Dear Peter Delapasteur, looking more Edwardian than ever in narrow trousers, a silk shirt and a spotted necktie, came bounding up to me and in two minutes Mary, mesmerised, had asked him to dinner on Thursday. He is a most charming and unusual person, and looks very out of place among the tough Mlanje planters, though I suspect he may be tougher than any of them!

Today we go to Blantyre for Christmas shopping – a dreadful ordeal in this heat, especially as I have none to do, and will simply trail around. At 4.30 we go to St. Andrews school to pick up Robin and attend a carol service, then back to Mlanje. For the rest of the week we intend to live at the pool.

I read a lovely book last week which you would enjoy – Cynthia Asquith's *Haply I may remember*.

15th December: Chiradzulu

I thoroughly enjoyed my week at Mlanje. The shopping trip to Blantyre was, as predicted, absolutely exhausting! We spent a great deal of time at the pool and I gradually darkened and bleached. Robin and Elsie Martin asked us for a drink one evening, which went very well. Again, Mary was surprised, as she never sees them. Late on Friday night one of Mlanje's great thunderstorms burst upon us and lasted till dawn, with lightning apparently hopping about my bedroom. It eventually broke my nerve and I ended up with the sheet over my head. It went on raining till we left on Sunday afternoon; steady tropical rain that is terrible to watch, it is so destructive, flooding the gardens and melting the roads.

Ron arrived at lunchtime on Saturday, looking very well and fully recovered from his bad foot. We donned evening dress and were down at the Club by seven to hear Peter Nicholson open the Club, making a good, short speech. Barbara and Walter Sproule came for about two hours and joined us. Barbara looks well but somehow frail. We spent a long time with Ian Strachan, the very new ADC, a young, shy, clever Aberdonian. I told him he was the first atomic scientist I had met, which seemed to please him very much! We talked to many people and the atmosphere was very friendly. Everyone said how well I looked and I attributed it to our enjoyment of Chiradzulu, which is true, though I actually acquired my tan at Mlanje pool. Ron and I were glad we went, as we were able to leave Mlanje with a better taste in our mouths.

We found Chiradzulu wet, chilly and lushly green. Things have grown incredibly quickly in a week – including Kiko, who is disgustingly fat. I think Aflike and Allan spoil her terribly when I am not there. The four moonflower twigs I brought from Mlanje are now about two feet high, all bearing flowers, and my twig of 'yesterday, today and tomorrow' is covered in leaves and has nine buds, though less than a foot tall. The vegetable garden is almost obscenely fecund and has sixty huge lettuces, all ready for eating. There are more plums, but all the peaches have gone. They have a very short life, shortened in our absence, I suspect, by PWD workers from the building site. However, there are several late-bearing trees which I hope will contain themselves till Joan comes back.

Ron went off on *ulendo* on Monday after tea and I was well and truly on my own, the most isolated I have ever been. It took me a little time to settle down but I am now quite all right, keeping myself fully occupied. He is coming in on Friday for our anniversary.

I had a nightmarish experience last night after I went to bed – my own fault. It was so terribly hot I threw off the mosquito net. I was reading, with the lamp beside me and all the windows (wired) wide open for air. I suddenly heard a swish of sound and looking up, saw *thousands* of flying ants floating into the room in a thick cloud. In no time they had darkened the walls and were all over and in the bed, in my hair, my eyes, everywhere. I put out the lamp and just had to lie waiting for them to settle, and for half an hour nearly went mad as they crawled and fluttered all over me and the room in the darkness – awful! Meanwhile, Kiko, under the bed, was also being maddened by them. The floor this morning was half an inch thick with their wings. I found dozens squashed in the bed, and picked out corpses from my hair, feeling quite sick. Kiko has had hiccups all morning, looking at me reproachfully. So, my word, mosquito net from now on.

The mail has just come in, bringing a long letter from Joan, in a hectic household in Gaberones, about to leave for the Natal coast in an impressive Chevrolet. She sounds most cheerful and happy, and I expect the break is as much appreciated by her as by us! Life has been positively winged with lightness and love in this house with just Ron and me.

22nd December:

We hear the news from London every night at eight and then 'Home news from Britain', also from London, and at 8.20 we get the Federal news from Salisbury. Our wireless is such a boon to me and the reception is wonderful except when thunderstorms make it impossible to have it on at all. The lightning sometimes makes our telephone ring, which always reminds me of Dunalastair, where the same thing happened. Do you remember?

My morale is low today, in the middle of the second week alone, so I have been cheering myself up by browsing through poetry books – lovely.

I survived last week very well. Ron came in on Friday at 6.30 p.m. I had given him up and was in a state verging on melancholia when I heard the impertinent little 'toot' that he always gives the horn, when he turns into the first hairpin. He found me smiling and waving a lamp at him, the house full of flowers, Kiko sleek with grooming, and dinner on the trolley by the fire – roast duck, garden peas, garden plum tart, his favourite blue cheese and a bottle of red wine. He is combining an anniversary and Christmas present for me, so I am waiting till Christmas for it. It is going to be a really good one – I think earrings, which will be thrilling. I have always LONGED for presents of jewellery from my husband!

We had a wet weekend and spent it quietly reading and listening to music. This is being a very wet rainy season and I am getting pale again.

Ron went off on Monday night after dinner and called in to see me yesterday. Tomorrow we are going to see the Everest film with David, who suggested it himself, to my delight. Margaret is still in bed. I shall spend tomorrow night on *ulendo* with Ron in a house, and then we come in on Christmas Eve, and will celebrate next day alone. Ron is in for the next two weeks, so I feel my ordeal is almost over.

30th December:

Ron and I had a lovely holiday together and look forward to another this weekend. We began to enjoy ourselves on Thursday, when he came in for an early tea before we drove to Limbe to meet David at the cinema. He was looking, as always now, white and strained, but cheered up very much as time went on, and it felt just like the old days in Zomba, sitting between the two of them in the cinema. To my great pleasure, the short film before *Everest* was *Crin Blanc*, which no doubt you have read about – it won prizes at the Cannes and Edinburgh Festivals. It is about a boy and his wild white horse in the Camargue. I felt sorry I had to see it and then *Everest*, as the tremendous impact of the latter drove everything else from my mind. What a triumphant film! I think it impressed me more, seeing it so long after the event. At the time there were so many reports, articles and photographs that it all became rather familiar, but to be suddenly reminded again made me think about it anew. I got a most moving impression of the courage, endurance, friendships and simple decency of the men, and Tensing shone radiantly throughout, with his beautiful face like a laughing saint. Hillary (*so* like David!) has tremendous charm and bravery, and Hunt himself stood out as a magnificent leader, his face getting more and more strained as time went on, and showing the most emotion of them all when the two men returned, speechless from their achievement. We went back with David for dinner, and I had a long talk with Margaret, while the men stayed in the sittingroom. She is still in bed and intends to remain there. She is often in pain, but is quite cheerful though not very hopeful. I feel the situation has somehow got out of control – dreadful.

We spent the night in an empty house where Ron had been on *ulendo*, at Mombezi – dirty, just disgusting, and came back here after breakfast, I simmering silently about how Ron lives on *ulendo* without me – what a *bore* it all is. I suddenly felt I could not bear to go through with Christmas at all. When one of those awful bouts of homesickness and rebellion takes me by the throat there is only one thing to do – shut myself away and weep it out of my system.

We opened all our presents as we drank early morning tea. We are delighted with everything and I shall be writing special thank you letters to all the family. Ron had a letter from Tom [his guardian], who has returned to Nigeria for one more tour. He seems more settled, having become a Catholic during his leave. Ron presented me with the most beautiful earrings, which I wore all weekend to get used to them. They are marcasite, drop earrings, pear shaped, an inch long and so delicately hung they quiver and shoot out brilliance all the time. I am so delighted I keep taking them off to look at them. We listened to lots of Christmas music; carols and oratorios. We heard the Queen at five, our time. I felt several times she must be addressing me personally! We spent a peaceful day, talking, reading and enjoying the wireless. The weather is dreary – cloudy sun, very hot and sticky, with a lot of rain and thunder – *what* thunder. On Sunday we had over two and a half inches of rain! I was glad to have Ron with me as the lightning was having great fun in the garden. It is thundering merrily now, and I can see Aflike setting off for the Boma with an umbrella and RAF raincoat for Ron, who has phoned me three times from his office just to chat! We have the New Year's Ball in Zomba tomorrow evening if we feel like it.

Everyone books a table and goes in large parties. It will take some courage just to walk in on our own, but why not? We shall see.

Chapter 20

15th January 1955:

I am feeling guilty about last week's letter, as I am sure it must have depressed you to hear how homesick I had been. That fortnight on my own really brought me very low, but I am better now. We went to Zomba for New Year and I am *amazed* at the difference. I am eating more and feel twice as alive. It really is the loneliness that reduces one to mere breathing, not living at all.

Last week the weather was very wet and stormy, and we had ominous news of flooding and bridges down in the district. On Thursday night we had a storm which lasted two hours and produced over two inches of rain, and Friday, New Year's eve, was wet and sultry, a sure sign of things to come. However, I washed my hair and Aflike pressed our evening clothes. Ron came in at teatime, slightly pessimistic, and by five the clouds were piling up round the horizon. At six the lightning became continuous all round us and the thunder came half an hour later, with the rain. The lightning was so severe it was not safe to have a bath till about eight, and by the time we had bathed and dressed it was 8.45 and we sat down to dinner, still wondering if we were mad to drive all the way to Zomba in such awful weather. (Aflike looked grave, but said nothing.) Well, at 9.30 we decided to go, and at the very last minute I threw some clothes, undies, shoes and toilet things into a case – I thought we might get stuck or perhaps spend the night in Zomba. We drove through heavy rain but there was no thunder. By the time we got to Zomba (10.40) we were in high spirits. We walked into the Club, took a deep breath and as we stood on the threshold of the big lounge getting our bearings, a familiar clear voice said, 'Well, now, isn't this fun, here are the Hitchcocks,' and Ruth Simmonds promptly swept us into her party and in two minutes had settled the fact that we would stay with them and stay till Sunday! (She thought Joan would be with us and was *horrified* to learn we had spent Christmas on our own, and nearly New Year as well. I began to feel very much better!) Her party consisted of the Binghams, in great form, the Watsons ('how *clever* of you to think of coming to Zomba' – Dorothy!), the Norman-Walkers, Jane and Hugh, back from a year in Salisbury, which they hated, Anthony Mott, one of our KAR friends, a lawyer just arrived from home called Deny Roberts (who has written a bestseller, *Smugglers Circuit*) and at last, Dr Murcott [a friend of Aunt Kathie's from Glasgow University days who worked in Nyasaland]. He is a little, ordinary-looking man with a red, wrinkled face and bluff manner, who does not seem very popular, but I found him delightful and we plunged into family reminiscences. (He followed me with his eyes, like a dog, for the rest of the evening.) We were given a great welcome by everyone. Humphrey soon whisked me off to dance. It was lovely to walk with him among the tables and see many familiar, smiling faces and more when we stepped onto the dance floor; people waving and calling out greetings. It was a dream of an evening, and went so quickly, though it was after four when we left. I had a long talk with Dorothy, at her nicest, which is very nice. I saw a lot of the Binghams and Bill Melhuish, and had great fun with Ron and John Watson, who at last has lost his shyness with us. Most of the time I was dancing, but I managed to talk with everyone in the party, particularly Kenneth, who took me deep into Macphail genealogy. (He is definitely related to the Macphails of Mull through his mother's side of the family.) About 4.30 we went up to the Norman-Walkers for bacon and eggs and ate them as the milky dawn light began to steal over the garden.

Everyone agreed it was a pity to go to bed, so we all quickly changed into day clothes and in two cars went up the mountain to watch the sunrise. Kenneth drove us, Ruth and their six-year-old son Oliver (known as Oli) in his big, comfortable Plymouth. I will try to tell you what it was like. The narrow road, as you know, winds steeply up, and one looks out of the car window into space. The entire, vast plain below was cloud covered to a great depth, but here and there was a break, a roundish hole, which revealed a vista of more cloud, another hole, and so through to a furthest gap, which showed Mlanje's rugged flanks gleaming wetly beyond. All the time, more and more colour, from palest pastels, was deepening into strong, golden sunlight. I shall never forget it. (What a sight for little Oli to remember.) We all sat in silence watching this marvellous transformation scene. Then Kenneth got briskly out of the car (he is always on the move, a great 'doer') and went off for half an hour's fishing with Ron and Oli, while Ruth and I talked quietly in the car, our eyes fixed on the perpetually changing majesty of Mlanje. Underneath that sophisticated shell there is a warm, kind woman, vulnerable and brave. Suddenly the others were back and we all went down and, by now ravenous, had a second breakfast at the Simmonds' which went on and on into elevenses. Ruth then ordered us all down to the Club for a pre-lunch drink. After an early lunch we went off to their little guest house and slept till six, had a cup of tea, donned evening dress and off we all went to dine at the Norman-Walkers and on to the cinema. I had not brought my glasses with me and the ever resourceful Kenneth produced a spare pair of his, enormous black-rimmed ones which he said made me look 'like a bashful owl', but they enabled me to see perfectly a very bad film called *Springfield Rifle* with an aging Gary Cooper. Hugh Norman-Walker was up the mountain playing bridge with Bill Melhuish, so Jane had found herself a partner, Colin Baker, a young ADC who came out in September and is at Chingali, where David was last tour. He loves it and does not mind being on his own, which is not surprising, as he spends every weekend in Zomba. We left on Sunday morning, having had a splendid time and feeling our friendship with the Simmonds' is firmly established. They live at a fast pace, *never* (ah bliss) talk shop, are highly intelligent and cultured, and can be amusing or serious at will. Ruth is almost a beauty and has a marvellous dress sense. Kenneth is plain but attractive, with a cool, light voice and the inner poise of a man who knows he is heading for the top of his profession. He has a passion for painting and photography – an interesting mixture. I do not know how popular they are in Zomba but we have always been drawn to them.

We both came back bursting with energy. I seized the advantage of sunny weather on Monday and Tuesday and 'spring-cleaned' three rooms, washing all the curtains myself and, I fear, wearying even Aflike with extra work. The damp stormy weather is back, so I am now cleaning the books and pictures. Next week I shall do Joan's room, dyeing the loathed lavender bedspread and cushions as a surprise for her. There is a wonderful array of parcels and cards waiting for her. I am giving her two beautifully carved ebony spear heads which happen to be the only native things I have ever wanted to have in a room with me, but I know she adores them, so at least I know my gift is the right one.

12th January:

A million thanks for the shortbread, which brightens up teatime when I do not usually eat anything. I showed Aflike the picture on the lid, saying it was the golf course in my 'home town', and he immediately pointed to the Royal and Ancient and said firmly 'And this is the Club'! Out here the Club is the tribal meeting place of the white man, in the eyes of the Africans, and as Zomba Club is next to the golf course, it was natural that the R and A should be identified!

I had a postcard from Joan from *City of Paris*, saying she would be back on 17th January, i.e. this Saturday, so I am now waiting for a wire to hear when her plane arrives. We have our shopping morning on Saturday, and will either stay in Blantyre and meet her after lunch, or make a second journey later in the day. Her room is like a new pin – indeed the whole house looks delightful. My carnations fill the rooms; I have an average of forty always in the house. Some surprises from my predecessor's wonderful gift for gardening have come up in the rain, and I make myself homesick by bringing in huge bunches of sharp scented chrysanthemums and dahlias – a wonderful autumn mixture.

We went to Blantyre on Friday afternoon last week to shop, as Ron had business to do there. The result was that Friday felt like Saturday, so our 'last' weekend alone together seemed delightfully long. Sunday was a beautiful day and we sat on the front *khonde*, I nipping out into the fierce sun for twenty minutes and nipping in again, tan and bleach swiftly acquired. It is damp and rainy again this week. The wet season this year is phenomenally wet, and just as the BBC home news is full of bad weather reports, so is our Federal news full of reports of bridges down, roads impassable and storm damage, mostly in the Rhodesias. After lunch today cloud came right down to ground level, and the mist was drifting round like smoke – lovely, rather like being at sea in a fog. My Celtic taste for mournful weather astonishes people, as I rapturously tell them of dripping trees and ghostly outlines. David's eyes once filled with tears when I told him I always thought the mists swirling round Mlanje's great peaks were singing, but we had lost the primitive sensitivity to hear them.

Jane Norman-Walker and our KAR friend, Anthony Mott, have invited themselves for the day on Sunday, as they want a base from which to climb Chiradzulu. It will take them some time, so we shall not see much of them. I have asked Ruth and Kenneth to come for lunch too. I am wondering what Joan will think of them all. If it is a very wet day, the Simmonds will not come, as they are dining at GH in the evening and do not want to risk being stuck in the mud on their way home – no excuse except illness is allowed for non-attendance at GH. Jane actually invited herself for the weekend, but owing to Joan's arrival I really had to say no.

I have just had a phone call from Mathias Kantiki, our London/Nyasalander friend, who is out visiting a patient at the African hospital. He diffidently asked if he might call in for a short time. You should have heard the change in his nervous voice when I exclaimed with pleasure at his name and told him to come, at once. Pause as he approaches.

He has just gone. He is very thin, and very African. His sophistication has vanished. I think he has found it terribly difficult to settle down to being a 'black' man again, after the experience of living in London and having white friends. Aflike was thrilled to be remembered but devastated that he would not stay to tea. Kiko loved him and lay on his feet, which obviously pleased him.

19th January:

Ron is out this week, only four miles away. He has so much paper work to do, he is going to come in once or twice during the day to get on with it. He was out last week too, so he has only one more to do this month. I was so busy last week that the time went very quickly. I was determined to have everything perfect for Joan's return.

On Friday afternoon I had a phone call from Chileka airport to say a Miss Nathan had arrived and had got a lift to Limbe, after trying fruitlessly to get through to me. I just had time to lay out all her parcels and letters, which now cover her bed, when the phone rang again (how I love it!) and there was Joan, having tea in a hotel in Limbe, and about to come out here by taxi. She sounded odd, and of course it turns out that she became ill with jaundice on the *City of Paris*. She managed to get up and leave the ship at Beira, where she was told she could not travel by train, so she flew on a dreadful Portuguese plane to Salisbury, intending to spend a night with the Dushmanitch family. However, it turned out that Dana was suffering from a mild attack of polio, so that was that. Joan thought for three days on the ship that she might be sickening for polio herself, as there is the worst epidemic of it ever known in Africa at the moment – only one case in Nyasaland, but hundreds in the Rhodesias and Natal. So you can imagine how she must have felt. She spent one night in Salisbury in a hotel, then flew here next day, arriving on Friday instead of Saturday. The Binghams were in Beira, Humphrey being there to welcome the KAR back from Malaya. Typically, they enquired if there was anyone from Nyasaland on the ship, and so visited Joan on her sick bed! She should really have still been in bed and was very yellow, but *thankful* to be back. She said the house looked marvellously clean and tidy, so I got my reward. The stay in Natal with her friends was not a success and the only bit of the whole trip that she enjoyed was her stay with the Dushmanitch family at the beginning. She is charmed with them all. I gave her a great welcome and had a fire lit in her room to cheer her up and a bottle in her bed. She just sank into a chair and poured out the whole story. She said she had never in her life been so pleased to hear a voice as she was when she heard mine on the phone to Limbe! We seem to have been talking ever since, as there was lots of news on both sides to exchange. She thought I was much brighter in spirits than when she left, Ron too. He arrived on Saturday morning in time for breakfast and we all sat talking for ages, and then Joan spent the morning by the fire and we drove to Blantyre in pouring rain and did our shopping. Joan was looking much better by lunchtime and has begun to eat again, though only certain things. She is so glad to be back it is a pleasure to see.

On Sunday it was a lovely day, our first for ages, and I dashed about putting finishing touches everywhere. I had lots of carnations, a lovely autumn bowl of chrysanthemums and dahlias, and a huge arrangement in Daddy's blue vase of beautiful long grasses, salvia and some spikey lilies I have never seen before. Jane and Anthony turned up at 9.45 (far too late for their climbing expedition) and settled down to coffee. Then off they went and I continued to dash about, this time organising lunch, with Joan helping. We were just standing back admiring our handiwork when the Simmonds' arrived, with Oli, and they proceeded to explore our 'estate', absolutely delighted with everything, including the house. The grounds were looking glorious, especially down by the swimming pool, where Oli, with the eye of a true connoisseur, nearly went mad over the easily-climbed trees – I longed to join him – and had his day crowned by the presentation to him of a pomegranate straight off the tree! He, Ron and Ruth went further afield to see the view from the Boma and Kenneth stayed on the *khonde* with Joan and me, setting up his camera on a table, ready to get a photo of Mlanje whenever the cloud on it lifted. He caught sight of Joan's music stand, so she had to produce her flute, which he promptly learned to play. He plays the bagpipes and recorder and was soon 'fluting' happily. Joan, of course, was at her most charming and was a great help throughout the day. At noon we all sat on cushions on the *khonde*, looking out into blazing sunshine and the heavenly view and had drinks till lunchtime. The mountaineers arrived back about 12.30, worn out and not having got very far, so they both had hot baths and joined us. After a marvellously lively lunch, Ruth took Oli down to the pool and slept while he pottered about, Jane and Anthony sunbathed on the lawn, Joan retired to her room to rest, Ron pretended to read on the sofa, and Kenneth, always on the go, got out his paints and proceeded to create a very reasonable picture of our view, in about an hour and a half, while I curled up at his feet and entertained him. He asked for a glass of water, and thinking he wanted to drink it, I brought him one of my beautiful Heals glasses, and of course he promptly dipped his *paint brush* in it! I managed not to react at all!

Finally, I collected everyone and we had tea inside, in the middle of which my ballet picture suddenly broke through its cord and fell with a crash into the fireplace, missing Ruth by about a quarter of an inch and sending glass splinters all over the room. She took it very calmly and said that was another of her lives gone! Kenneth presented me with his painting, signed and dated. I shall certainly keep that. [I have it still.] They all left about five, the Simmonds' genuinely enchanted with their day in the bush – Kenneth said it was the most civilised day he had spent in Nyasaland, which of course pleased me very much. I found I was exhausted but happy about the day and we three held a very satisfactory post mortem.

Next day Ron went off on *ulendo*, most unwillingly, and Joan and I took up our old routine. She is nearly better and has lost her very yellow look. She is now busy answering her dozens of Christmas letters. She was quite overwhelmed by my present of the spear heads, knowing how I love them, but was persuaded to accept when I promised to try to replace them.

26th January:

Last night (Burns Night) we heard records of the Glasgow Orpheus Choir and a tenor sang 'Land o' Heart's Desire' which I can only just bear to listen to out here – an exquisite song.

Ron is out this week, but in next, so I have that to look forward to. On Saturday I bought some royal blue corduroy to make winter slacks. I had difficulty in convincing the Indian girl that two yards were sufficient, and she only believed me after she had measured me! At noon we went to have a farewell drink with Arthur Monk (ADC Blantyre) and his wife, who go on leave very shortly. We were joined by Colin Baker, the young ADC we met in Zomba, who is taking over from Arthur. We shall no doubt see him at Chiradzulu, as he is delightful. David came in from the office, with Ron. He stayed for fifteen minutes, talking only to me in a distraught manner about Margaret, still in bed. I wish he would come out on his own to Chiradzulu for the day at a weekend, just to *get away*.

We had a very quiet weekend. We brought back eleven library books, so we were all happily occupied. I plodded through the pedestrian but oddly attractive *As It Happened*, Clement Atlee's understatement of his life, lit up by uncanny flashes of astonishingly robust humour! In bed at night I am reading *England Have My Bones* by T.H. White, the man who wrote *The Goshawk* and who has just published a 'book of beasts', a mediaeval bestiary which I would love to have, but it is in the luxury class in production and price.

Eric Barnes, the PC, Southern Province, is retiring at the end of February, having been out here since 1922! He is a much loved administrator. In Blantyre district alone the Africans have contributed over £200 for a present. On Sunday he is to be in Chiradzulu to receive tributes at a school prize giving, and he and his wife Leslie are coming to lunch first. I am so glad we are seeing them privately before they go, and that Joan will meet two of the nicest people we know in Nyasaland.

3rd February:

We are having the wettest wet season for years. Up here the rain is often accompanied by a wonderful, wild, howling wind. The house is going to be incredibly cold in the cold season, as even now there are whistling draughts everywhere. I am wearing my new royal blue slacks, which look most decorative. Kiko loves the wind and gallops round and round the lawn with her ears flying. Her favourite indoor game is to be pushed backwards across the slippery floor at high speed, regain her grip after a stationary struggle and then come tearing and skidding back for more.

I had a very pleasant birthday. Ron give me a tiny bottle of scent as a token, and I am to choose material for another evening dress with him, which will be lovely. Joan gave me a perfectly beautiful pale blue glass bowl which she bought in a Swedish shop in Durban and carried carefully home – she has impeccable taste. Eric and Leslie Barnes and our neighbour 'Uncle Don' Barnett came to lunch, which was a great success. (I was determined it would be, and not a repetition of the disastrous evening with Uncle Don.) The Barnes' are thankful to be leaving. He has seen such a lot of changes in his time, and is not happy with what he sees happening now, as the nationalist movement (the African National Congress) gathers momentum and undermines the authority of the DCs.

After lunch we all, except Joan, went off in our cars to a village five miles away, to a Muslim school where Barnes was given farewell presents. There were hundreds of African spectators, all in vivid clothes, lining three sides of the *bwalo* (village square), the fourth being occupied by a grass shelter in which sat the PC and his wife, the DC and wife, Ron and myself and various missionaries and educational people. There was a gymnastic display done to the 'music' of drums, whistles and bits of iron knocked together. The noise and the smell was indescribable! The sad thing is *nothing* is done well on these occasions, as it is a mixture of black and white culture at their worst: what they think we want to see of ours and what they are prepared to show us of theirs – pathetic. During the performance rain crashed down and black umbrellas went up in hundreds, while drops fell down our necks as the grass roof became saturated. We drank tea and tried not to have to eat some highly coloured cakes, no doubt prepared with loving care. I slipped mine into my raincoat pocket and was appalled to discover when I got home my 'pocket' was one huge hole and there was no cake! The afternoon ended with us all standing while the entire school sang the whole of 'The Queen' in Chinyanja.

Today I got a letter from Ruth Simmonds asking us three to Zomba for the monthly dance on 19th February, so we have that to look forward to. At last Joan will attend a function in Zomba and see all the people.

16th February:

I made my evening dress in four days, except for the hem (six yards of skirt)! It cost £3 16s. and you would never know it was home made. Ron is delighted with it. Joan has decided not to come to the dance in Zomba, as she says she still gets easily tired. Her awful post-jaundice depression has lifted at last, praise be, as life has been pretty gloomy. We shall only be away for one night, and Aflike will sleep in the house.

On Friday a Mrs Vickers and her husband called, as he was recruiting labour in the district. (He is in charge of organising what is called 'migrant labour', Nyasaland Africans who go down to the Rhodesias and South Africa to work mainly in the South African mines.) She knows the Carlyles, and had heard from them that we did not get about much. She has just settled into a house in Blantyre and called in to introduce herself and ask us to stay with her any time when Ron was on *ulendo*. Her daughter has recently gone to boarding school and she is very lonely, as her husband travels a lot. I thought it was sweet of her. So we will arrange something.

Ron came in on Saturday, gloriously brown after a walking *ulendo*, looking just as he used to in Zomba days, peeling nose and all. (Why does he always get a peeling nose just before a dance when I want him to look at his best?)

Joan has started to learn chess. With the help of my book I am forging ahead, much to Ron's perturbation!

There is to be a dinner party for all members of the Administration in Nyasaland who can turn up, in Blantyre on Friday, as a farewell to Eric Barnes. David, who is helping to organise it, has asked if he may borrow Aflike for the evening. He is thrilled, of course, and is wearing his cap at a very pert angle today. Ron will stay the night with the Baxters and come back on Saturday morning and we leave for Zomba after lunch. When Ron told me about the dinner I threw down my book and said indignantly I thought that it was *typical* of this territory that these occasions are always for men only, and why did not men face facts and realise that the *wives* deserved just as much to be fêted, after all the help and support they had given their husbands, and all the energy and courage they had expended on mere survival! Ron was momentarily stunned by my outburst, then laughed and said he quite agreed! Sometimes I could scream.

23rd February:

The farewell dinner was a tremendous success. Ron came in next morning about nine, looking tired and unshaven, but absolutely thrilled with the evening. He stayed the night with the Baxters and walked out early in the morning, to find several uninvited guests asleep in the sitting room! There were about forty-five officers there, which was less than expected, but bad roads put a stop to the attendance of men from the North and Central provinces. Ron said all the speeches were first class, and Barnes delighted him and others by firmly pointing out that nowadays people tended to lose sight of the fact that the district man was still the core of the government and without him it would collapse. Ron talked to masses of people, including John Watson, Pat O'Riordan and Peter Nicholson. He said everyone was at his very best and it was a moving experience to see all 'the chaps' who keep this country going, sitting there in immaculate evening dress, at ease with themselves and their surroundings. Joan and I sat enthralled. Afterwards I hugged Ron and apologised for my ill tempered criticism. Aflike told me his side of the evening while he and I co-operated in ironing my dress, a marathon task. He simply loved seeing all the 'big Bwanas' as he calls important people (i.e. the Administration, in his eyes), and was specially thrilled because John Watson and Pat O'Riordan recognised him and spoke to him.

We left for Zomba at three, leaving Joan and Kiko to hold the fort. It was a lovely afternoon, with the tall maize golden in the sun, a thousand snow-white clouds suspended in the sky and my mountain purple-patched with shadows. We got to the Simmonds' at four and settled down for a long talk. There was a farewell dinner for the Barnes' at GH which they had to attend, so their party was organised to meet and dine at the Pig and Whistle, Zomba's one pub. My dress looked lovely and was much admired. There were fourteen people in the party, those you know being the Norman-Walkers, Anthony Mott and Bill Melhuish. We had an excellent dinner which I hardly noticed as my neighbours were Bill and Hugh, both in tremendous form and I was really kept on my toes. We then went on to the Club and were joined later by Ruth, Kenneth and the Binghams. It was a great evening for me, as there were lots of good dancers in our party. Ron and Hugh had a long talk, which they always enjoy. We went on till four, hardly noticing the time, and slept till about 10.30. We spent the rest of the morning talking and looking at some of Kenneth's impressive collection of photographs. After lunch he and Ron played a game of chess while I watched and decided I am now fit to play with people outside the family. We had an early tea and got back to Chiradzulu at dusk and promptly sat down to tell Joan all about it.

The Carlyles are coming out on Friday afternoon. It will be so nice to see them again. So we hand over Kiko and the sewing machine, both devastating losses!

2nd March:

We are at last having better weather, which is such a relief and greatly helps one's spirits. Ron is in this week and next so I feel very cheerful.

Laga phoned last week and postponed their visit till today. Kiko has had a bath and looks like a very large powder puff. The poor wee thingie senses that something unpleasant is going to happen, and has been lying either on my feet or Joan's all morning, gazing with trusting eyes into our faces till we nearly weep! Aflike is going around with his mourning look and his cap dead straight on his head, a very bad sign!

We had another visit from Mrs Vickers and have arranged to go and stay with her for the week beginning 14th March. We met David on Saturday while shopping. He was looking far from well and I nearly walked past him. It is so sad to see, and I keep thinking of Margaret all day by herself, for weeks on end now, just lying in bed. Joan and I will go and visit her when we are staying in Blantyre.

We spent a very peaceful weekend, sitting out on the *khonde* again at long last and enjoying the warmth and blessed dryness. I have been reading *The Hill of Devi* by E.M. Foster and loving it. This week we have had several callers in for coffee or lunch, all official and not interesting enough to write about. Ron thinks the Rhodesias, in a few years, with Nyasaland not far behind, will get rid of British rule and perhaps two more tours might see the end of our life out here. He talks about it more frequently as time goes on, and always when he has been in Zomba, with a chance to discuss it with colleagues. I do not write of it to you, as I do not want to worry you with uncertainties.

We are having the most glorious sunsets, the best we have ever seen at Chiradzulu, and after tea our games of chess suffer, as we keep going out to gaze in wonder at Mlanje, pink and gold, floating on a deep purple plain, and revealing gullies, flanks and plateaux that one is hardly aware of during the day. In the morning the whole plain is a vast sea of thick white cloud and I feel I could swim to Mlanje, which floats on the horizon like a great Pacific island.

11th March:

Ron is in for the second week running, so there is a feeling of well being to the days, and we heard some news about *ulendo* on Monday which cheered us even more. He has been finding it impossible to be out of the office for three weeks each month and get through the ever-increasing amount of paper work he has to do. The DC, who knows how hard he works, finally sat down and put forward a case for the reduction of *ulendo* at Chiradzulu, a one-man station. We waited cynically for the result, but to our joy and amazement, the Governor immediately informed the DC that *ulendo* at Chiradzulu was to be reduced from fourteen to ten nights out each month. It will make all the difference in the world here and Ron will do alternate weeks in and out. He is transformed by the news and has already regained some of his old enthusiasm for the work.

By chance one evening last week we heard it announced that Dylan Thomas's *Under Milk Wood* would be broadcast after dinner, a repeat of the original production – wonderfully exciting and stimulating radio. Reception was good and the beautiful Welsh voices seemed to be in the room with us.

The cold season definitely approaches: the mornings and nights are cold, clear and lovely. We still get heat during the day, as the storm clouds build up. Today the mist is down to the doorstep and we have the three fires burning, to warm up the house and get rid of the smell of damp which hangs everywhere.

Last Friday the Carlyles arrived for tea and stayed till seven, as usual! It was lovely to see them again, all looking very fit and relaxed. There is an outbreak of rabies in Limbe, so they asked us to keep Kiko safely up here till it is over – *what* a reprieve!

Now that I have no sewing machine, I have taken on a marathon knitting task which I want to complete while Joan, the expert knitter, is still here to give advice and moral support. It is a very elegant jacket, a Vogue pattern, royal blue with a fleck of white in the wool. The stitching is so clever that from a distance it looks like tweed. Fortunately I have now got into the way of it and can read as I work, to Ron's astonishment.

17th March: Blantyre

I do not have your letter yet this week, as we are in Blantyre and all our mail languishes at Chiradzulu. We came in here on Monday afternoon and Ron collects us on Saturday morning. It is being a perfectly delightful week. The Vickers live in a huge house in the wealthy residential part of Blantyre; one forgets that the Blantyre of stores, shacks and 'shanty town' appearance, exists. There are lovely colonial houses in their own grounds all round, and a marvellous cacophony of sounds goes on in the early morning – trains hoot and shunt in the distance, cars sound expensive horns and the boys hoover all the *carpets*.

We have a huge bedroom with its own bathroom; electric lights are in every conceivable position. The food is delicious and it is such bliss not to know anything about it beforehand. The drawing-room looks Spanish, with decorative wrought iron over all the windows, huge Persian carpets and a lot of low tables with exotic, gleaming ornaments on them. Mr Vickers is up north on *ulendo*, and Mrs V. works in his office all day in his absence. They have lived abroad for many years and acquired a sophistication which makes it difficult to 'place' them and their background. She comes from Kilmarnock and has not lost her accent. She is charming, has done a lot of interesting things and is an excellent talker. They have lots of money and life out here seems incredibly improved by such a state of affairs! I realise with a shock how near the edge of security Ron and I live, and how far from anything but the essentials, materially: all very interesting.

We go out in the morning and walk the half mile into town to do our leisurely shopping. I had my hair done yesterday and it is wonderful to have a light, neat head. I found exactly the material I wanted for a winter dress – red corduroy velvet. The Vogue pattern is so simple I can make it in a day. Today we are lunching with the Baxters and spending the afternoon with Margaret, who is apparently longing for visitors. She has offered me her sewing machine for a few days when I go back to Chiradzulu – good.

Last week I sent Aflike off on Tuesday for three days holiday in Zomba, during which time he was to find ebony carvings and bamboo mats for Joan. He arrived back on *Monday* morning, if you please, worn out, having gone up to Fort Johnston to get what Joan wanted. I was going to be very cross with him, but of course realised he had done it all out of loyalty, and found myself instead telling him to have a rest this week! Allan managed quite well on his own, as I did a considerable amount myself.

On Sunday John Grindall, who has been acting Agricultural Officer for five months in Chiradzulu during the closed season in tobacco, and who has just gone back to his tobacco job, came out for the day with Ray, his wife and their two delightful children. He and Ron have worked wonders together in the district and are good friends. Joan enjoyed their company very much and of course loved the children, who were as good as gold.

24th March:

Joan sails from Beira on 5th May, on her beloved *City of Paris*, and will leave here by train on Sunday 1st May.

I am feeling much refreshed by our luxurious stay in Blantyre. We lunched with the Baxters last Thursday. Margaret is pregnant again and spends all her time in bed. She was quite cheerful, though finding life very dull.

Two nights ago I heard Max Bruch's violin concerto, which I love. It was not played as well as Heifitz plays it on our old recording!

Ron is out this week, and then, ah bliss, has a fortnight in. On Sunday Colin Baker came for the day. He brought with him the whole album of records of *La Traviata*, his favourite opera, which he had just bought second-hand and played them through *twice*! (We all got splitting headaches and Kiko was sick!) He left at 10.00 p.m. delighted with his day.

On Monday a young agricultural engineer arrived and moved into the new house below us, which he will share with the Agricultural Officer, who comes in May. We gave him lunch, sent down three boys to clean the house before he arrived, and also provided stacks of dry wood and had huge fires going to dry out the house for him; and he lapped it all up with never a word of thanks, so from now on he can jolly well get on with things alone! On Tuesday dear Humphrey Bingham was in the district, and Joan and I entertained him to lunch. What a pet he is. We felt so light-hearted and civilised – so different from yesterday!

Tomorrow Ray Grindall is giving us a lift to Zomba, where we are lunching with the Watsons. Ray holds her ballet class there on Fridays and Dorothy plays the piano for her. Ray will drive us back to Limbe, to her house, where Ron will join us for dinner and the cinema. We will then come home, about midnight. What a long day it will be but of course I am looking forward to it immensely.

We have plans for local leave on Zomba mountain and await developments. I shall tell you more details next week.

When Aflike was away he ordered some ebony for Joan and it had arrived when we got back on Saturday. I let Joan do her own bargaining, I dislike so much doing it, as you know – and she got nineteen pieces for £3 15*s*. Then, another, older man arrived this week with mats, lovely things made in Fort Johnston, which were quite irresistible. I bought a large one for 6*s*. 8*d*. for the dining room and as a farewell present Joan gave me a big round one which tones beautifully with the colours in the drawing room. She also bought three for herself. The man was a real bush African, for whom I have real respect and affection. We had a great exchange of greetings, courtesies and jokes. The boys' wives came round from the back and squatted on the steps by the *khonde* to enjoy the proceedings, and of course Aflike hovered in silence in the background. When the transactions were completed I presented the man with six copies of the *Observer*, which I knew he could barter for food in Zomba. He pointedly said, 'Paper will not fill my stomach on the journey home,' and everyone roared with laughter. So of course I gave him money for *posho* (rations).

30th March:

I am feeling very cheerful today, as Ron is in and the sun is out, at last. We have had such cold and damp that all the fires have been on and Joan and I wear slacks and sweaters. The cold season is very much with us, but is usually sunny, and probably is, elsewhere; Chiradzulu draws down the clouds. However, we woke this morning to a brilliant clear sky and cool breeze. Joan and I sat sun-worshipping on the steps from eight till nearly ten, letting the warmth soak into us, and now I have a wonderful glow on my face and arms and renewed energy. Kiko sunbathes with us; her coat gets quite bleached and her skin goes black! At first we thought it was a skin disease, but someone who knows about dogs said it was pure sunburn and would fade.

Our day in Zomba was a great success. Ron took us to Limbe and left us at the Grindalls, while he attended meetings in Blantyre which lasted all day. It was the first sunny day for weeks, and the only one until today, so we were lucky. We arrived at 11.30 and went to the Post Office, where we coincided with Dorothy. It was an awkward meeting, as she and Joan were wearing the same Horrocks dress!!! However, it was exclaimed over, laughed off and all was well. We transferred to Dorothy's car and went to the Boma to pick up John. They are both looking blooming, though their three years are up in July, when they go on leave. Charles, the six-month-old baby, is absolutely gorgeous, exactly like George at the same age – large, serene and terribly friendly! Both the Watsons were at their very best and the time passed quickly. Joan was greatly taken with them. After lunch Dorothy took us down to the Club and went off to play the piano at Ray's ballet class. I showed Joan all over the Club and grounds, which she thought lovely, and then we sat reading magazines, as I used to do in the old days, little thinking I would one day have Joan beside me in those familiar surroundings! Dorothy collected us at tea-time and we went back there and stayed till Ray fetched us about 5.30. It was a most enjoyable day and I felt the Watsons were genuinely glad to see me. They want us to go over for a Sunday soon, so that they see Ron too. I came away thinking how much nicer it would be to live in Zomba now than when we lived there last tour when we were new, green and inexperienced. I could certainly cope with it all now! We drove back through a flaming sunset with a tiny new moon getting brighter and brighter as the colour faded from the sky. We got back to Limbe feeling surprisingly untired. Ron was already there. We dined and went on to the cinema to see *Front Page Story*, which was disappointing. By the time we got back to Chiradzulu it was midnight and I fell into bed, but was persuaded by Ron to give him an account of my day. So I did, fighting off sleep till I suddenly noticed the breathing of my supposed listener – he was asleep!

On Sunday morning we had a most marvellous day's music on the wireless, and a surprise visit from John Grindall and Ronnie Noyce. They had coffee and then climbed the mountain, returning about noon, when they had a drink and then went home – two charming men. We enjoyed their visit so much, especially as neither of them uttered a word of shop, a great recommendation to me!

Our local leave is granted for a fortnight, starting on 16th May. Humphrey Bingham is trying to get hold of a cottage on Zomba mountain which we can rent for about ten days. We shall be near Bill Melhuish and we have our Zomba friends to visit. I think it will be great fun, though it means I still have to cope with boys and running the house, which is what one longs to get away from. It will be cold and healthy up there, with a wonderful view, lovely walks and Zomba down below when we want company. It will tide me over the days after Joan's departure, though I do not contemplate having any trouble about that.

7th April:

The weather is perfect, hot, hot sun and a cool breeze. The view is at its most splendid, with seas of white cloud over the plain in the early morning and in bright moonlight. Joan is certainly seeing her last of Nyasaland just at the most beautiful point of the two seasons. I am dark brown and very blonde. In the evenings it is cold enough to have a fire, despite glowing sunburn. The house has at last got a chance to dry out and the garden is lifting its head again. It is quite amazing what a difference a change of weather makes to one's mood – no doubt you know that very well at home, though I do not really know what your weather is – this newspaper strike is maddening and frustrating, especially at the time of Churchill's defeat. We listen to the news twice a day, but it is not the same as settling down with *The Times*.

We have put our local leave back, to begin on 7th May, so that we shall be in Zomba to see the Dramatic Society's latest production, *Clutterbuck*, in which Ruth and Jane have the leading roles. We have been invited to dine with Kenneth and attend the play. All this still depends on Humphrey finding a cottage for us.

Today we are going into Limbe after lunch to shop, have tea with the Grindalls and meet David at the Club at 4.30, to take him to the film *The Moon is Blue,* a sophisticated comedy which had good reviews.

I am reading Cynthia Asquith's *Portrait of Barrie* – most interesting.

13th April:

I am feeling and looking a different person since the sun came 'on' again, and I have my ration of an hour's sunbathing every morning. By teatime the house is cold and by bath time we have the fire lit. I have been revising the garden, a huge task, and the *machila* men are flat out cutting the grass, a marathon at this time of year. They could really do with scythes. The time goes so quickly in good weather and Joan's visit is rapidly nearing its end.

The Carlyles have asked if they can come to the station to see her off, and the Holmeses are going from Mlanje to Luchenza to see her there. That is where we met her when she arrived – which seems a hundred years ago.

We have had quite a pleasant Easter holiday, the best thing about it being the glorious weather, which makes this place look astonishingly beautiful. We had a good afternoon in Limbe on Thursday and then dashed off to meet David at the cinema. He looked a little better and was obviously thankful for some light entertainment. This was his first film since *Everest* with us at Christmas. *The Moon is Blue* was slightly 'blue' and most amusing. We parted from David and went to the Carlyles, both in excellent form and delighted to see us. We had a quiet day on Friday and Saturday, going to dinner on Saturday evening with a bachelor neighbour, eight miles away, Dick Buckingham, in tobacco. He is delightful and a very good conversationalist, rare out here. On Monday Ren and Liz Smith, whom we have not seen for a year, when they spent a weekend at Mlanje, came, self-invited, for the day, with their five-month-old son, Gavin, a nice wee baby and as good as gold. They also brought their huge ridgeback, who gave Kiko a somewhat overwhelming day's companionship! It was a pleasant day, with lots of news to exchange and I always enjoy being with people of our own age.

20th April:

It is the most lovely day. Joan and I are sitting out in the garden with our backs to the sun (bare backs, of course) and a cool breeze continually blows our hats off. The *khonde* looks like a dress shop, with all Joan's cottons hanging out to air. She has been packing for some days now and we take her heavy luggage to Limbe station on Saturday. Ron is out all this week and next, then he has a week in, a fortnight's local leave and another week in, so a kind of heaven stretches ahead. Our leave is from 7th – 22nd May, and we have been offered two cottages on the mountain, thanks to the efforts of Humphrey and Bill Melhuish. I am now in the final stages of negotiation, all most satisfactory.

I am feeling quite useless and idle today, as I have finished my Vogue knitted jacket almost before I realised it. It is *stunning*. It makes me want to scrap my entire wardrobe and start again!

We are thankful to hear the English newspaper strike is over. I shall be most grateful for the *Scotsman* to fill in the gap – for once Scotland was the better-off part of Britain. I must say I think there is something wrong with the spirit of the age, that there should exist such a crippling device as strike action, which has increased so much in recent years.

Do tell me what reaction there is to Billy Graham. Uncle Teddie and Ann [his younger daughter] saw him on television and he 'left them cold', and struck Uncle Teddie as 'vulgar, selfish, insincere and in a huge money-making racket' – strong words from him.

We are becoming great chess addicts, and although Ron is still better than I, I have advanced enough to give him a good game, beat him enough to encourage me, and even tackle (unsuccessfully) the problems in the *Observer*.

In Blantyre on Saturday we stayed on to lunch with Sandy and Mary Holmes at the Tavern, as a farewell for Joan. They go on leave in July and have the new found energy and high spirits which go with such a pleasant prospect.

On Friday Ron was out in the district with several agricultural men and took sandwiches, expecting to be out all day. At noon he brought them all back to the house for a drink, as they had finished early. I delayed lunch to entertain them while they ate their sandwiches and Joan and I sat with our stomachs rumbling and our mouths watering at the interesting selections of fillings we saw on their plates!

28th April:

The weather this week has changed completely – bleak and dull, so Joan and I are confined to the house, have a fire on and are going gradually pale brown. Ron is on *ulendo* but comes back tomorrow, thank goodness. Joan is in one of her melancholy moods. I think she reacts to bad weather even more than I do.

We have got our cottage on Zomba mountain – three guineas a week rent, with everything provided except food and lamp fuel. It is next to Bill Melhuish, who will 'keep an eye' on us, as he puts it!

The Times began to arrive again on Thursday, and I felt quite exhausted after reading it. There was a very good supplement with a summary of news for each day missed, so I picked up the essentials. I am reading Compton MacKenzie's *Sinister Street*, a marvellous record of a boy's childhood and early manhood, very sensitive and vivid. We heard from Sandy Holmes that Peter Nicholson's mother, who is still with the Nicholsons at Mlanje, had a slight stroke, from which she fully recovered, but she is longing to go home earlier than had been planned. Joan pleased me very much by immediately offering to share her double cabin with the old lady and give her the moral support of her company. The Nicholsons have gladly accepted, so she will get home comfortably.

This week I tried to dye my rose cushions navy blue and they emerged a deep, rich violet, frightfully depressing, so now I must un-dye them and try again. Aflike will think me mad, as he greatly admires their new colour. Ramadan has just begun, so all is very slightly fey and will continue so for the next month, which unfortunately includes our local leave. His strict regime carried out on the chilly heights of the mountain will be quite weakening, I feel sure, and he is very susceptible to heavy colds.

On our way to Blantyre on Saturday we delivered Joan's heavy luggage at Limbe station. In the evening I laid on a special dinner party for her, with lots of flowers, and candles at dinner. The Grindalls came, also Dick Buckingham, our nice bachelor neighbour. It was a great success and Joan was in good form. On Sunday the Carlyles came for a birthday tea. Joan forbade me to tell them it was her birthday and then told them herself and Laga immediately wondered why I had not said so – ah me. They took Kiko back with them, alas. The house feels like an abandoned ship. I phoned on Monday and was told she had settled down very well, having first routed their huge cat, which is longer and taller than she is!

5th May:

Joan left yesterday. This last week has been grey and chill with clouds covering Mlanje, but yesterday morning was superb, with a deep bank of cloud on the plain and on the horizon Mlanje's peaks soaring above it, against a piercingly blue sky, so Joan saw the last of Chiradzulu and its view at its most beautiful. The boys were very sorry to see her go, especially Aflike, whose poor face was all screwed up with emotion. But, as Joan said as we drove off, 'They laugh easily so perhaps they cry easily too!' At Limbe station we found Laga, Kiko and the children. I had felt perfectly all right till then, but the psychological effect of seeing that train thronged with people going *home* was absolutely devastating! I felt a real pang at saying goodbye to Joan, but it was the general effect of the place that did the damage, and I had a splitting headache for the rest of the day. Ron cheerfully whisked me into Blantyre and bought me a brandy!

Last Saturday Joan had her last morning's shop in Blantyre and we all went on to the Baxters for a farewell lunch. David was in great form, livelier than I have seen him this tour. Margaret was in bed, but got up for tea, looking well and relaxed. She is now in the hands of a very good GP, as a private patient.

I have plenty to do, getting ready for local leave. Today we are moving into Joan's bedroom, which is the nicer of the two bedrooms, though smaller. It leads off the drawing room, has the bathroom off one side and the lavatory off the other, on the closed-in *khonde*. So there will be no more wandering along *khondes* to get to it. In the really cold weather I shall have a fire on at night and build it up before I put out my lamp – lovely.

This letter is very disjointed, as the boys are moving furniture about and I am only half concentrated on this anyway, as I have not quite 'come to' from yesterday.

10th May: Zomba mountain

It is nine o'clock, we have just eaten a big breakfast and are now sitting in front of a blazing fire which has logs the size of young trees on it. The weather is as we expected, a hot sun and simply freezing indoors, so that in the cottage we wear slacks and sweaters, which we have to change out of whenever we go out! The cottage is old, dark and primitive, but comfortable and of course the view is glorious. We are right on the edge, with just a few yards of rocky garden and then a great drop to Zomba. We both felt the cold very much at first and the high altitude gave me a cracking head, but we are getting acclimatised and I am sure we could not have chose a better place, for already we are full of energy and my appetite has doubled!

We spent the few days after Joan left in getting ready. Now, of course, it feels as if she had never been here. We left Chiradzulu on Saturday after an early lunch, with Aflike and all our luggage simply bulging from every seam, as it were. It was a glorious day and driving into that familiar landscape felt like re-entering paradise. Our landlord, a settler called Thorneycroft, was waiting to hand over our keys. He had organised water and wood, and had had the whole place aired, so we settled in at once and everything was in its place by teatime. Bill Melhuish is 'next door', invisible among trees. There is a well worn path between the cottages, as a great friend of his lived here not long ago, who died in very tragic circumstances. [On a very wet night his car skidded off the road and plunged him to his death below.] We drove down in unearthly moonlight, with the lights of Zomba twinkling in a most civilised way below us, and arrived at the Simmonds' before seven, to find Ruth perfectly calm and as usual the centre of the party. Kenneth is acting Chief Secretary at present, as HE is on leave and Footman, the Chief Secretary, is acting Governor. He and his charming wife were there, and a Mr and Mrs Ingham, who have come back to Nyasaland after eight years in Kenya. He is now Secretary for African Affairs. They were all very friendly and easy and I quickly began to enjoy myself.

(Ruth found an excuse to get me to herself in her bedroom, sat me down on the bed and said firmly, 'Ann, why do you allow that man of yours to drag you from the top of one bloody mountain to the top of another bloody mountain for local leave when he should damn well take you to the Lake?' I was so taken aback I just gave a little shrug and shook my head! Fortunately, she had to dash away to the Club to dress and put on her make-up.)

We had a very happy party and an excellent dinner. We had marvellous seats right at the front and it was thrilling to look round and recognise so many faces. The play, *Clutterbuck*, was a piece of nonsense, but the two sets, as always, were beautifully done and the cast was excellent, especially Ruth, just being a little more outrageous than usual! We were invited to the party on stage afterwards where a splendid cold buffet was spread out and drink was flowing. We stayed for an hour and took our leave, with the greatest difficulty as the Simmonds' wanted us to press on and then breakfast with them, but we were actually very tired. I had a long talk with the Binghams, and then with Alan Dickinson, who told me the dreadful news that the Baxters have lost their baby. That was really why I could not bear to stay on at the party. I know no details, simply that Margaret gave birth to the baby on Wednesday, four days after we saw her, and it died on Friday. It was premature, being only six and a half months, and probably had little chance, less still out here. It is so difficult to write to them, for there is nothing to say.

19th May: Zomba Mountain

I had my first letter from Joan yesterday, posted in Durban. She was having a lovely time, with lots of attention and admiration. Old Mrs Nicholson seems well and is enjoying the voyage. Joan's letter was really a sort of 'thank you' letter. What she picked out most of all to thank me for will interest you – 'the chance to see how a marriage could endure in adverse circumstances'! Well, well.

I have not heard from David, but am hoping for a note this week. I have said that if Margaret wants to get away for a little, she can come to Chiradzulu and David can join her at the weekend. We have Bill Melhuish coming for the first weekend in June, a mixture of business and pleasure, as he has to audit the Boma accounts. Then Iris comes, on her way back to Lilongwe – she has had a whole year at home. So I shall be kept busy, which is a very good thing.

We are still enjoying life up here, but the weather has broken, which limits our activities. We are seeing a lot of Bill, lonely man, who is obviously delighted to have neighbours, and calls in every day with our mail or without it. We meant to do a lot of walking this week, but on Sunday down came the mist and it was as dark and chill as a foggy November day. We have huge fires and spend all day inside with books, chess and the wireless – Ron loves it and I enjoy it with him but feel I might as well be at Chiradzulu! (Ruth had a point.) On Tuesday we had to go down to shop, and lunch with the Watsons. We found the road a quagmire – not comfortable driving and my heart was in my mouth. We enjoyed seeing John and Dorothy again. After our shopping we called in on Ruth for an early tea before we braved the road. She was thrilled to have us to herself, and sat on the floor talking hard and chain smoking, like a very young Aunt Kathie. Both she and the Watsons invited us to stay the night if we could not face the road but we felt we should try and off we went – a marvellous feat of good driving on Ron's part and co-operative silence from me! The trouble was the road had just been 'repaired' with heaps of red earth, then came this unexpected heavy rain, and then several Forestry lorries churned up ruts about nine inches deep of squelching mud. However, road gangs with stones and shovels have been at it since and the weather is clear again, otherwise we would have sat here for as long as the wet weather continued. Bill reports that it is all right again; otherwise, of course, I would not have told you all this!

On Saturday we had a drink with him before lunch, sitting on his *khonde* gazing out at the unbelievable view we have from here. We calculated that simply by sweeping our eyes round in a semi-circle we could see in that one glance between five and six hundred hills. In the evening we went down to the cinema to see *West of Zanzibar*, absolute tripe, but lovely photography and some lovely familiar shots of Zanzibar itself. Ruth saw us at the interval and gathered us into her party, consisting of the people I like least in Zomba. However, Kenneth drew me behind a pillar and we hid there and talked! As acting Chief Secretary he flies to and from Salisbury very often and is working about fourteen hours a day and thriving on it.

This Saturday we have been asked to dine and go to the cinema with Liz and Ren Smith, so we shall see everyone again before we leave on Sunday after lunch, to be back in Chiradzulu before dark. My knitted Vogue jacket has been much admired and no one believes I made it myself. As I got out of the car at the Simmonds', Ruth said, 'My God, Ann, you look as if you've stepped straight out of Vogue.' I struck a pose and said 'My dear, I have!' I have just started on another Vogue knit, a very chic Italian pattern in black and white. It is two-ply wool on No.13 needles, so you can expect to hear of its progress for a long time to come!

Election Day!: [26th May] Chiradzulu

I have been sitting in the sun, getting my quota of inner warmth for the day! It is absolutely perfect cold season weather, with brilliant sunshine and visibility like a knife edge on Mlanje. Our own mountain, with its craggy face, is looking very Scottish today. We came back to find the garden and grounds beautifully groomed and neat, and the tennis court ready for marking, so now there is only the tall bamboo fence to be put up round it. Ron went off on *ulendo* rather reluctantly yesterday, but comes back on Saturday. He thinks he may do a few days out each week, so that I shall not be alone for a whole week. After the somewhat dark pokiness of the cottage, the house seems very high, wide and handsome, and *so* clean! I have just made and dyed some cushion covers from old calico curtains, and they have turned out a perfect navy blue, so when Aflike has finished ironing them I shall put them on the chairs and the drawingroom will be much improved. The calico cost only 1/6 a yard, but looks much nicer than it sounds, and will do until I can get advice on my poor purple failures!

When I last wrote from Zomba we were hopeful about the weather and looking forward to our night out. Well, there seemed to be an improvement, but Bill came in on Saturday at lunchtime, looking white and weary, and said he had stuck twice on the way up, and passed, with difficulty, another car, completely stuck. He said we would get down well enough, but he would be prepared to bet that we would not get up again, especially at night in thick mist. So we phoned the Smiths and cancelled our cinema evening. Bill, of course, was delighted, and promptly asked us to dinner (which was as well, as our stores were right down to basics), and afterwards we played three-handed bridge, in which I got some very useful coaching – he is an excellent player. We woke into bright sunshine on Sunday, to our enormous relief, and spent the morning packing, listening to the concert and sitting gratefully in the sun. After lunch we closed up everything and left the cottage as we found it, only cleaner, then made our way perfectly well down the mountain, where dried mud tyre marks showed just how awful Bill's daily journeys must have been. We called in at the Simmonds' to say goodbye and were given an early tea. They had not realised our difficulties with the road and had been wondering why they had not seen more of us. We then went on to the Smiths to explain in detail why we had put off our evening with them. It was quite difficult to convince them of our plight. The whole of Zomba is tarmaced and they just did not grasp our problem.

We drove through a glorious sunset and arrived home about six. We immediately lit a roaring fire, had supper in front of it and fell into bed. I spent Thursday getting things straight and was thrilled when Ron came in at lunchtime to tell me the next day was Empire Day and therefore a holiday, a fact only discovered to us by David ringing up to ask if he and Margaret could come out and spend the day with us. We were delighted. It was a beautiful day for them, praise be – I could not have borne a day huddled indoors over the fire in their circumstances – and we sat outside looking at the incomparable view, walked peacefully in the garden and talked companionably. David was cheerful and Margaret looked well, but they were both a little withdrawn, dear people. Margaret asked me to take her down to the pool, and there we sat on a rock and she told me all about the baby and we wept together in the bright sunlight. I will not harrow you with the details – so cruel. I felt sick for them both. They are going to Salisbury on local leave soon, and Margaret will see a specialist there.

2nd June:

It is 7.25 a.m. and a heavenly day. I am writing at this early hour as I want this to go off with today's mail.

Bill Melhuish comes tomorrow and we are both looking forward to his visit. On Saturday, Jim Reeve, one of the senior DCs whom Ron likes immensely, and who is working in Blantyre in Land Settlement (and hating it) is coming for one night, so I shall have three men to feed. I have quite a lunch party on Sunday as the Simmonds' are coming for the day – a great collection of interesting people, which I love.

Ron came in from *ulendo* on Saturday with a frightful throat which has developed into a tremendous cold. Fortunately, he gets these appalling colds without feeling ill, so it is not so bad. Of course, I have been dreading the inevitable, but have so far escaped.

We brought back some good library books on Saturday, which have kept me engrossed this week, except Joyce Carey's much lauded latest *Not Honour More*. I cannot read him. I tried *The Horse's Mouth* and had to leave it too, from sheer boredom – strange. We had a quiet Whitsun, with a visit from Dick Buckingham, who brought me a tremendous bunch of sweetpeas which are still filling the room with scent and making me homesick.

Bill is determined that I climb Chiradzulu with him. I am very unwilling, as he is so tall and so fit, but pride will probably drive me to do it!

8th June:

The weather continues to be absolutely flawless, and the place looks so beautiful I could sit out in the sun all day just absorbing the African essence of it. There is also a full moon at night and the landscape glimmers a dim honey colour. The moon is huge, soars up behind the black profile of Mlanje and shines straight onto the front *khonde* and into the drawingroom. I am sure all this beauty is good for the soul and helps to sustain me.

'Big Bill' arrived on Friday morning, delighted to be here and full of enthusiasm for everything in the house and garden. After lunch Ron and I dashed into Blantyre and shopped colossally for the weekend. He got caught up in the Boma for over an hour, so we had to tear back to get home before dark – I was afraid Bill might blow up the lamps, lighting them, as they are very temperamental. However, we got back at 5.25, just in time, as Bill was returning from the lower garden which he had been exploring. We had a very nice evening and managed a fairly early night, to be ready for the rest of the weekend which, as I anticipated, was hectic! On Saturday the men departed for the Boma (funny to see the two of them striding along the path together, Ron looking quite *small* beside Bill) for the morning and Aflike and I went into action, on food and the many odds and ends only I think of, which everyone attributes to 'good servants'! The men came back for pre-lunch drinks on the *khonde* and we sat down to a cold lunch. We then retired till teatime and I was just up in time to welcome Jim Reeve. He is one of the nicest men I have ever met – quiet, cultured and clever, with a delicious sense of humour. After dinner we settled down to bridge: Bill playing an excellent conventional game as my partner, carefully curbing any flights of fancy on my part; Jim playing beautiful, daring, unexpected bridge, with Ron supporting him admirably. There is no doubt that I *thrive* on the company of men!

We had breakfast at seven on Sunday, in preparation for our climb up Chiradzulu. I was rather apprehensive, as I have had no regular exercise since tennis last year and was also wondering if I had the stamina. It is a fairly sharp climb of two thousand feet. We set off at 8.15, Bill in front, then me, then Jim, then Ron. The path, such as it was, had been cleared by penal labourers right up to the top, so it was made as easy as possible. At first it was a long, steepish climb in the sun, and I began to feel slightly sick with the continuous, steady effort. However, that must have been nerves, for I got my second wind after twenty minutes. Then we moved into thick rain forest, very steamy and tropical, with great festoons of creeper hanging from the trees – actually the kind of scenery I find exciting. Sometimes the path was over boulders, and the going almost as steep as on a ladder, but we were in thick shade and Bill occasionally reached down a hand (which I was *not* too proud to grasp). Finally, about two-thirds of the way up, we suddenly emerged into sunlight and found we had to go along a very narrow, winding path absolutely on the rim of the mountain. To our horror, it turned out that Jim suffers from vertigo and he was quite overcome by the sudden exposure to this naked edge. He backed off into the trees and said he would wait for us there. We left him eating an apple and pressed on. He had fully recovered when we got down to him again. It must be a most dreadful affliction and was painful to see in a big, strong man. I kept my eyes on the path till we finally reached the top, which is not any wider than our front lawn. It took us one hour and fifteen minutes, going slowly. (John Grindall, who is very fit, did it on his own in three quarters of an hour.) We three sat down to eat our apples and marvel at what lay before us.

The view was the best I have seen in Nyasaland, better than Zomba, because we could see right round the horizon. We reckoned we must be able to see about a hundred miles! I would not have missed the experience for anything. Bill was absolutely thrilled with it all and I have no doubt is still boring Zomba dinner tables with his enthusiasm! We stayed for half an hour and then came down – in thirty-five minutes – great fun, simply hurtling down the slopes, catching on to trees on the way to steady up. I did a magnificent Tarzan act, when at full speed I grabbed what I thought was a branch, which turned out to be an endless, soft but tough creeper, and I fairly sailed forward over steep rocks, fortunately landing upright in a bed of leaves. Ron said it looked simply marvellous – as if I had meant it! When we came to the long gradual slope at the end of which involved controlled walking, my knees at last protested and went all spongy. I had to concentrate hard to walk back to the house without showing what an effort it was, of course! Ron and Jim had also found it quite tough going (to my surprise) but dear Bill, with his long legs and long walks on Zomba plateau every weekend, was in perfect training and chatted amicably *all* the way up, while we took it in turns to puff a reply. I immediately had a hot bath and was only just ready when I heard the Simmonds' car. Ruth had brought Oli and his friend, Ian Corrie. They retired to the lower garden with a picnic basket and behaved like angels for the rest of the day – so sensible of Ruth to provide a companion for Oli. Kenneth had come straight from a Secretariat meeting and was looking frightfully Whitehall-ish in a dark suit, silk shirt and tie, but soon managed to look rumpled when I relieved him of his jacket and tie and lent him one of Ron's pullovers. He arrived looking cross, tired and jaded, and still furious with Ruth, who had given up waiting for him and was actually moving off when he came running down the Secretariat steps to the car. However, we sensed trouble, Ron coped with Ruth and the children while I got the others talking and in half an hour Kenneth was the life of the party, relaxed and very amusing. (He caused consternation among the *men* by telling me my 'flies' were undone. He was referring to the slit at the back of my very narrow tweed skirt, which has three buttons and button holes, all of which I wear undone, otherwise I cannot walk!) We had the happiest party we have ever had at Chiradzulu, with everyone joining in. There was one dire moment, when I was kneeling in front of the fire putting on logs and I made to get up in one supple movement, as it were, and my stiffened muscles took their revenge. I muttered 'ouch' under my breath and looked round to see if anyone had noticed. I caught Bill's eye and he winked – he knew! After coffee people wandered round the garden or sat in the sun talking. We had an early tea and they all gradually went off. Ron and I sank into chairs, delighted with our weekend.

15th June:

It is a flawless morning, after several dull days, so I shall go out and sit in the sun for a bit after I have finished this. When we were in Blantyre last Friday we called in on David to hear his news and invited ourselves to tea. Margaret has had an operation and is still in Salisbury. We asked him to spend Sunday with us. On Saturday evening we dined with the Carlyles and went on to see Danny Kaye in a hilarious film – *Knock on Wood*. We went back for coffee and stayed talking till two! We slept late on Sunday and had just finished breakfast when David arrived. There was a *chiperoni* blowing and the mist was drifting past the windows. We had a lovely day sitting round a big fire. David looked relaxed and happy and it was just like the old days. Aflike was delighted to see him and fussed round us whenever he had the chance.

Yesterday we had a visit from Ron Pincott, the DC, and discussed the future with him. He said Ron would undoubtedly get his own district next tour, and that being such a good field man he would be kept in the district if the PC could possibly manage it. However, he agreed with us that it was time Ron got experience in the Secretariat, and said he thought the best thing to do was to apply to be posted there next tour. I have not yet seen Ron alone to discuss what he thinks, but I feel sure he will take his advice.

I am reading *South Col*, by Wilfred Noyce, and enjoying it immensely.

28th June:

I am feeling rather empty and sad this morning, as Iris and Dave (Davies) have just left for Lilongwe. It has been quite wonderful to see her again, but it is upsetting, as it emphasises the dearth of such people around us. On Saturday evening I had just had a bath when I heard Ron talking in the drawingroom. I slipped on my kimono and peeped in, and there was Dave, just arrived from Lilongwe! He swears he gave his date of arrival as Saturday, but I know it was Sunday! However, we were ready for him and glad to see him. It was a heavenly morning on Sunday and he simply could not get over the beauty of the place. He left for the airport after an early lunch, obviously bursting with excitement, and they were back by teatime. Iris looks wonderful, with a dark brown face and all her vivacity to the fore. She thought Chiradzulu lovely, and greatly admired the house. Linden is a perfect little darling, loving and very responsive to affection. She followed me everywhere, like a wee dog. She was, of course, wildly excited, and sick and fretful so that Iris got no sleep the first night. She and I talked and talked, guiltily breaking off when one of the men came in. We all walked in the garden after tea. Iris and I kept sitting down on logs and rocks, the better to concentrate on our conversation! Dave took Linden off for a bath and supper, while we settled down to our threesome and she told us all about her ten days in Bonn, giving us a detailed picture of the political set-up in Germany, which was fascinating. She has had a wonderful fourteen months, in spite of illness. On Monday they went to Blantyre for the morning to shop, and in the afternoon Iris had a sleep and recovered from her journey at last. Ron and I kept firmly off shop and personalities out here, and she said gratefully she felt she had not yet left home. She was thrilled that I knew so much about what was happening at home – that is thanks to *The Times*! Their visit was an extraordinary strain in a way, because we each know so well how the other feels, and maintain two emotional levels at once – the unspoken one and the one made by whatever we happen to be talking about. We are both intensely aware of the weight of our shared area of non-acceptance of life in Africa, about which there is nothing more to be said. They left this morning about eight, Iris repeating firmly that I must go up there and stay with them. PS: Iris spoke of her visit to you. She thinks I am extraordinarily like you in looks and character!

6th July:

Ron and I are in a state of elation today. He got a letter from Bill Rangeley, the PC, *directing* him to take his leave after the middle of March, an unheard-of occurrence till now. We even know who is taking over from him. It also suggests very strongly that his next posting is settled. The letter followed hard upon Ron's talk with the DC, so Rangeley may now know of Ron's intention to apply for the Secretariat.

Margaret Baxter arrived home last Thursday and is taking things very easily, but hopes to spend a few days with me soon.

I have had a letter from Iris, so grateful to us for introducing her gently to her return. She says all her cheerful resolutions have deserted her already. They have a little box of a house with an uncultivated garden and dust everywhere.

I have just finished a wonderful book called *The Bronte Story* by Margaret Lane – a reassessment of Mrs Gaskell's *Life*, in the light of later documents. What an extraordinary, fascinating, tragic family they were.

Ron was out for three nights last week, but is in all this week, which is delightful. On Saturday after shopping we called in on Ray and John Grindall and were invited to stay on for lunch. Sunday was a glorious day, clear and crisp, and we spent it on the side *khonde*, with wonderful morning music from Salisbury. I nearly overdid my sun worship but had the sense to come into the shade just in time. Ron started sketching the view and did so well he means to go on with it. He says he finds it very restful.

After tea yesterday we wandered round the garden. There was a faint blue mist everywhere and the damp brought out a most nostalgic autumn smell; golden leaves were slowly falling from the trees. The sounds are lovely at that time of the day – crows cawing, dogs occasionally barking, wood pigeons murmuring to each other and cows lowing at milking time in the village below.

The daffodils are a foot high, all fourteen of them, and I have had a sudden success with my pansy plants. I must go and change out of my slacks, as the Carlyles are coming to tea. The room is full of carnations and some very floppy roses.

25th July:

I should be working in the garden, but Ron has just sent over your wonderful long letter and I know that it is no use trying to do anything else but write to you. I am thrilled with the photos, especially the one of you in the garden. I went through and showed it to Aflike, and he beamed, pointed at your face, then at mine, and said 'same like'! Joan must have lost *pounds* on her way home. I know she was determined she would. I have had a long letter from her, written in St. Andrews, telling me all about her visit to you, most enthusiastically. I am happy that you all liked your presents.

Ron is definitely tiring, and showing the usual signs of strain that all the men begin to show out here after about two years. It is amazing how definite is the line drawn at two years as a maximum period of efficiency – and the settlers are urging that the tour for Government people should be extended to four years – rubbish.

On Saturday we called in at the Baxters. Margaret looks very well indeed. She now wants me to stay with them for a few days rather than come out here. The Grindalls and the Carlyles have also invited me, which gives me a good feeling – somebody cares! In the evening we dined with Laga and Clement and went to the cinema to see *From Here to Eternity*, wonderful! Our wireless battery is away being charged, so our Sunday morning was silent, and I got on with my knitting and reading – a book of memoirs you would enjoy called *Bricks and Flowers* by Kathleen Everett, an Irish woman of seventy-six who writes of the old days in Ireland.

Tonight we are going to a party at the Grindalls. Ray has just had an enormous success with her ballet pupils, who have done very well in exams judged by someone from England, so this is a celebration in honour of the examiner, whom I shall be interested to meet.

26th July:

The party was a great success. The examiner was a Miss Oliver, of the Royal Academy of Dancing, who does an eight months tour all over the world. She was charming, in her mid-fifties and very English. The evening was refreshing for me, as I knew not a single person in the room and it was a relief to meet new people and find one or two interesting ones among them. Just outside Limbe, we saw three huge hyaenas in the car lights, the biggest we have ever seen, so the excitement of that swept us happily into a roomful of strangers. As we were leaving Ray asked us to lunch next day, as the Watsons were to be there, about to go on leave. (They sailed on Sunday.) So we went back on Thursday. John and Dorothy were delighted to see us to say goodbye, and we had a very long, pleasant lunch with them. Miss Oliver was still there and was obviously intrigued to meet people from 'the bush'. Ron then went off on one night's *ulendo* and I stayed with the Grindalls. Next morning Ray gave a coffee party for all the mothers of the Limbe pupils and again I knew none of the sixteen women who came. Miss Oliver rose to the occasion and talked in a fascinating way about the ballet world and held her audience spellbound. Ron arrived for lunch and we left just as Miss Oliver was leaving for the airport to start all over again in Bulawayo.

On Saturday Laga phoned early to ask us to call in before lunch, as they had to put off their Sunday visit, David having had a nasty fall from his bicycle, damaging his face, which had gone septic inside his mouth. While shopping in Blantyre we met Tony Hardwick, a great friend of the Carlyles, who Ron knows slightly. He had obviously heard a great deal about us and seemed eager to know us. So we asked him, his wife and three children to come to lunch on Sunday instead of the Carlyles! We found David barely conscious in bed and Laga dead tired, having been up for most of the night, but glad to see us and have a talk.

On Sunday, a lovely day, Dick Buckingham called in with flowers for me, had coffee and stayed on to meet the Hardwicks, who were enchanted with Chiradzulu. Tony is a delightful man, interested in films and music. His wife Sybil is a large, motherly Rhodesian. The three children, aged six, nine and ten were thrilled that I had arranged for them to lunch together at a table on the front *khonde* before the grown-ups sat down in the diningroom. (I did not know what ages they were, so thought this the safest plan.) They left about five, inviting us to a musical evening in a fortnight's time. Today is cold and wet. Yesterday was sunny but the coldest day we have had this year, with a wind that made my teeth chatter and Aflike's colour turn a greyish-blue!

10th August:

We are having the coldest cold season this country has had for years. We had a blessedly warm weekend but are plunged back into cold again. We have a fire every night in the bedroom, a lovely idea for both comfort and the pleasure of lying in the dark with it flickering on the walls – it takes me back to Dunalastair!

Ron was in last week, so life was very pleasant. On Friday we shopped in Blantyre and had a quick tea in the Tavern, where we were joined by Bill Melhuish, delighted to see us. We then met up with the Carlyles and the Hardwicks and saw *Beau Brummel*, an awful film, as I expected. We were glad to go on to the Hardwicks and hear some lovely records – several Kathleen

Ferrier, Bruch's violin concerto and some Chopin. We had a good dinner and enjoyed it all very much. We had a quiet day on Saturday and on Sunday the Carlyles came for the day, a perfect blue, warm day, and we sat outside soaking up the sun when we were not playing tennis – our first game of the season, which has resulted in me behaving like a cripple ever since. Every muscle from neck to ankle is aching – disgraceful.

I am reading Noel Coward's *Future Indefinite* and finding it cheap stuff. I have just finished David Cecil's *The Young Melbourne*, a beautifully-written book, and have my name down for the sequel, *Lord M*. I have to comb the shelves of the public library now to find something to read, but the British Council is still a good supplier.

Ron finds *ulendo* very unpleasant in this cold weather, and positively luxuriates in whatever comforts I can arrange for him at home, poor man.

18th August:

We had a quiet weekend, mainly so that we would have each other to ourselves, as Ron was out last week and is out this week, coming in tomorrow, Friday. I find I can fill the days, but the evenings alone are deadly, deadly. We played several sets of tennis on Sunday, a lovely day, and got very brown. This time I was not stiff at all afterwards. We are hoping very much that the worst of the cold is over – this week has been warm enough not to have a fire till teatime and I have snatched a half hour's sunbathing each morning.

All our thoughts and energies are turned to Saturday, and I shall be thankful when it is over. About a year ago, the Imperial Tobacco Company, known as ITC, gave some land to Chiradzulu district, as hundreds of Africans working in their factories come from this district. The Boma head clerk, a very able man called Sasuze (of mixed Portuguese and African blood) thought it would be a good idea to build a hall on this land and form a Welfare Society. The district is one of the most troubled in the territory, as the people are so much influenced by life in the towns. The young men loiter about looking for trouble, with nowhere to go and nothing to occupy them, as they have become spoiled by town life and can no longer fit into village life – there are hundreds of them – spivish smart alecs, potential hooligans. By a tremendous amount of hard work, Sasuze and Ron formed the Society, collected money and organised the building of the hall, which is designed by Ron. On Saturday the hall is being opened by the manager of ITC, and at the same time there is a huge agricultural show being held in the 'grounds' which will be opened by Bill Rangeley, the PC. They expect about ten thousand Africans will attend! You just cannot imagine the organisation needed to get everything ready and Ron has put his heart and soul, as well as all his energy, into it. The show begins at ten and we have no idea when we will get away. I have to attend it, so lunch for ten people I shall have to leave in the hands of Aflike and Allan, which should be all right, but I shall get up at dawn on the day and do the ground work. On Sunday the Baxters are coming, which will help me wind down!

25th August:

I am thankful to say that on Friday the first sign of the hot season's approach appeared – Mlanje was completely hidden behind a haze of dust and heat, and we have only seen a ghostly outline of it since. The sun is beginning to prick my skin with its heat and my hands sweat all day. We have had no fire for five nights and the bed covers have been thinned out – bliss!

We had a lovely day for the show on Saturday: brilliant sunshine and a soft breeze. I had everything ready by nine o'clock when Ron came charging in – he had a quick shave, bath, and breakfast on the *khonde* and off we went. The hall looked spick and span, there were lines of flags flapping everywhere and a huge bamboo compound in which all the agricultural exhibits were laid out. There were hundreds and hundreds of Africans all dressed up in their best clothes, absolutely dazzling in their bright colours. (One can see how joining the Federation has boosted the economy in Nyasaland. In our first tour, gatherings of Africans were drab affairs, with only the chiefs and their wives brightly clad.) There was quite a number of Europeans from the district and of course our guests. Nearly all of us were judging something, so we went into the compound, and I dealt swiftly with prizes for sewing, ironing (!), knitting and beadwork. A small boy had a fit beside me but nothing else went wrong. There were speeches, the hall was opened and a plaque unveiled by Mr Loney (head of ITC). Then the day really began for the Africans. We left about noon, amazed to get away so soon. Ray Grindall drove me back about five minutes before the others, just giving us time to slip into the bedroom and thankfully rip off stockings and belts! We all had drinks on the front *khonde* and then a cold buffet lunch which everyone enjoyed – some had three helpings! Bill Rangeley was in excellent spirits and the Grindalls were a great help in keeping things going. Mr Loney was pleasant enough. He could not get over the fact that we had no private power plant to provide us with electricity. I smiled sweetly and said, 'Well, we're Government, you know,' and looked at the PC, and everyone laughed. Commercial salaries are known to be higher than those of Government servants. After lunch everyone melted away. John Grindall and Ron went back to the show to give out prizes, and Ray and I enjoyed a quiet afternoon on the *khonde*. Everyone was most impressed with the whole day and Ron – and Sasuze – received many kind words and praise, as was right.

Next day the Baxters came. The weather was lovely and we sat out on the *khonde* till teatime, very lazy and relaxed. Listening to the men talk, it was evident to me that Ron, out in the district, is more aware of the changing atmosphere in the territory – the weight of commercial and political interests influencing not only government thinking but also the role of the district officer, no longer a paternalistic figure. Ron first spoke of this to me in Mlanje, when bitterly unhappy in his work after the 'troubles'. David seemed reluctant to agree with him.

1st September:

I am writing this early. It is a glorious morning, hot already (7.20) with a high wind. Ron has gone off for the day to a distant court case, and I nearly went with him, just for once, but remembering the heat, the smells and the hours of waiting, I decided to go on keeping away from all that! He is in this week and we are having a happy time, with tennis every day after an early tea.

I have been reading *Georgiana*, the letters of the Duchess of Devonshire, and will shortly go on to those of 'Dearest Bess', her boon companion. They are both mentioned in *The Young Lord Melbourne* and Ron and I have been reading as much as we can find of that fascinating period.

On Saturday afternoon, that sacred time, Bill Rangeley drove up in his car. He had, dear man, come to prune the fruit trees, which were planted by him years ago, and which he comes to prune every year, wherever he may be stationed. Ron woke up, said some awful things (!) and went up to the orchard to help him. He stayed for tea; such a nice, shy man.

The garden is full of birds just now, and as there are damp mists at night and before dawn, the flowerbeds are green with young plants shooting up, especially pansies, carnations, poppies, verbena and portulaca. I am going out into the sun to wander round now.

8th September: Blantyre

I came here to the Baxters yesterday and Ron will fetch me on Saturday when he comes back from *ulendo*. Jim Reeve came for dinner last night and we played some rather bad bridge. I have been sewing furiously and have almost finished two seersucker skirts. Margaret and I are enjoying long talks together and David comes back from the office very ready to talk. Tomorrow evening they are giving a party for fourteen people to pay back all the accumulated hospitality David received while Margaret was in hospital, so we shall have a busy day preparing *patsi-go-lows*.

I am so thankful for our lovely house and garden, compared with this little box in suburbia.

15th September: [Air letter, in answer to a letter from my mother telling me of the sudden death of my father.]

Your air letter has just come. It was wonderful of you not to cable, for I could not have borne not to have more words from you. Ron is on *ulendo*, not far away, and I have sent a messenger on a bicycle with a note, for I must have him with me. It is a great shock and I should perhaps not write at once, but I want so much to feel near you. I am trying hard to think of the comforting things – that it was not a long suffering, that he had had a happy retirement and been reconciled with his family in Glasgow. There will be many people who will grieve for him in gratitude and affection, remembering all the years of his magnificent service to others. I just wish with all my heart that I could be with you. You will be constantly in my thoughts. I cannot write any more.

22nd September:

Your long letter came today, one day late, so I am afraid this one of mine may be late too. I wanted to have yours before I wrote. I also got your air letter telling me about the funeral. It has been such a comfort to feel really in touch again and I am so grateful for all the details you give me. I have been very worried about you, as the shock must have been so great and it is such a relief to hear that you are feeling better. I know Jess must have been a tremendous strength and comfort. [My sister Elspeth was on board ship, on her way to Barbados with her husband.]

The letters and the kindness of friends must have been very wonderful, and everyone – family, friends and acquaintances – seems to have done everything possible to help. It is so nice that the people in the shops have shown such sympathy and interest, but then, I am sure Daddy had established himself as one of the most endearing characters about the town.

Your air letter telling me the news came on 7th September, about 11.15 a.m. Ron was on *ulendo* and came back about three hours later. I managed to hold on quite calmly till he came, so he was with me when I finally gave in. Being so far away was almost the worst of all to bear, as I was longing to share everything and help and be helped. I have felt very tired since and terribly restless. I roam about and find it difficult to concentrate. Ron had to go out again the next afternoon, but came in after only one night, and has arranged things so that he has been in all this week. He has been wonderful, a great help.

That same evening, we decided that I would go home in time for Christmas. As I want to be with Ron as long as possible, and even more as I cannot face the prospect of a prolonged journey, I shall fly. David Baxter very kindly offered to arrange it all. I have no details but I leave on 17th December and arrive in London on the 19th. I have written to Joan to suggest that if she wants to see me, could she meet the plane. We could stay a night in a hotel, and I would take the train north on the 20th. She can book my ticket well in advance, as no doubt the trains will be crowded. Clothes and luggage are a huge problem, but nothing really matters except that I am coming home – dear Ron at once suggested it. The irony is we heard yesterday that we have passages on the *Dunottar Castle*, sailing on 16th March from Beira, the earliest possible date for Ron, so very lucky. Now everything is settled we both feel less hanging in the air. When I get over the effects of shock, I know I shall be thankful that my time here is nearly over. Ron leaves almost exactly three months after me and will have five weeks' good sea air – he is so tired and thin.

Laga phoned yesterday, having just got back from two weeks in Salisbury with Con. When she heard my news she immediately said she would like to come out and see me. So they came for tea, and Laga just could not have been nicer or proved herself more of a friend. She brought me a glorious mass of flowers from her garden, and said everything that could most help and comfort me, for which I shall always be grateful. Her behaviour was perfect.

We were to have had the Grindalls and their friends the Grahams on Sunday, but the Graham children have got chickenpox and their visit was cancelled. We though we might as well let the Grindalls come. I was so dazed and restless, Ron suggested it might help me through the day to have people about and he was right. He told them what had happened, and we had a quiet, friendly day, but I was thankful when they went, I was so tired.

29th September:

I am glad you had a nice letter from Joan. I do not know whether you realise that she always thought 'Uncle James' wonderful, and used to talk to me about him out here so very understandingly – she really did appreciate him and I am glad she managed to convey so much of her impression of him to you when she wrote.

Ron is being quite perfect and has not uttered a word of his disappointment at losing me before March. He is thin, tired, easily depressed and needs all the looking after he can have. Fortunately, I can rely on Aflike to do his best.

I expect you heard on the news of the hurricane in Barbados – Elspeth and Harry will be arriving in the middle of the emergency, which will be hard on them. I wonder if you have noticed that when HE retires in March, Sir Robert Armitage, ex-Governor of Cyprus, takes over. That should help – I hope the new broom sweeps Ron into the Secretariat!

The weather is lovely and I sunbathe for a short time every morning – I was just beginning to go grey! Ruth and Kenneth are coming to have a farewell lunch with us on 16th October, provided Kenneth has recovered from a fearful attack of gout which has landed him in hospital. We dine with Laga tomorrow after shopping in the afternoon.

7th October:

You ask about the Welfare Hall. It has a library and is a meeting place for sports teams and the committee, at the moment, but Ron is trying to encourage Scouts, Guides, sewing bees and other activities. They tend to sit back and wait for him to think of things for them to do, but it is really nothing to do with him, so he keeps firmly in the background. But as Sasuze, his head clerk, is president, they discuss it a lot and Ron knows how things are going. On the night of the opening day, some Congress youths broke a window and slashed two curtains, but Ron has his own spy system (he prefers to call it his 'grape vine'!) and knew who were responsible and dealt with them forthwith. The most promising material for the ANC to work on is the young and discontented and this Welfare Society, with its obvious Government support in the form of Ron, is just what it does not want in the district.

There is not much news for you this week. We shopped in Blantyre on Friday afternoon and went to the Carlyles for an early dinner and on to Tony and Sybil Hardwick to hear some lovely operatic records. I was not very happy, as I find music upsetting – it is *so* full of memories of Daddy and Dunalastair. The rest of the weekend we spent very quietly here – shut into the house with a fire and a stock of good books, and, at last, my knitting again! We were shrouded in mist for two days, a *chiperoni* in fact, and it actually rained quite hard, with the result that the garden is flourishing and my carnations are thick in every vase I possess. The weather cleared on Monday and I have been out in the sun every morning getting it back into my bones and am now very brown (and look about five years younger!). Ron has been in all this week, so we have had a happy time. He is very tired just now, and we are perfectly happy to live quietly and get lots of sleep. I have been reading another book on the Devonshires – *The Face Without a Frown*, and am enjoying it very much.

12th October:

The time is passing very quickly and I am glad, for I feel I have had enough. Ron and I are continually very tired – we can only think the height at which we are living is beginning to tell. I am getting plenty of sunshine and feel far more able to cope with people – for a time I wanted to see no one and it was an effort to concentrate on simply getting through the day.

A parcel from Joan arrived today – a great excitement. There is a watch for Aflike, who is in *heaven* about it, a box of soap for Ron, a white blouse and a delightful cotton dress for me. I had an air letter from her yesterday, incoherent over my return, and saying she would book us a room in the *Ritz* if necessary.

We have been very quiet here. Ron was in all last week and goes out this afternoon till Saturday morning; only three nights so I cannot grumble. The weather is perfect and I have to be careful not to stay in the sun too long at a time. The jacarandas are in full bloom and I spend (I refuse to say 'waste') an awful lot of time sitting on the front *khonde* gazing at them. There are several pink oleander bushes, white moonflowers, deep blue periwinkles all over the wired side *khonde*, and orange Japanese honeysuckle and ivy geraniums cascading down from big tubs and at night the scent of the honeysuckle is lovely. Mlanje is never more than a dim shadow, if there at all, the haze is so dense.

The Simmonds come for lunch on Sunday by themselves, and we are looking forward to that. I think we have more in common with them than with anyone else out here except Iris. Kenneth may already know Ron's posting for next tour but of course we would not dream of asking him. Ron will certainly try to find out before he leaves.

19th October:

I am in bed with 'flu! It could not be more inconvenient. All is chaos and panic around me, caused by the news that Ron has been posted to the Secretariat *now*! We move on Friday 28th, so when you answer this our address will be c/o The Secretariat, Zomba. It was confirmed on Monday, when Bill Wright, who takes over from Ron here, arrived without warning to stay till tomorrow, so I have been playing hostess from my bed, my mind in a whirl, my temperature rocketing as I think of packing, moving, unpacking and repacking for myself, all in tremendous heat. The irony of it is shattering. Having prayed for a Secretariat posting for many moons, we get it at a time when I shall share exactly six weeks, then leave Ron to it. The car is on its last legs, the boys' uniforms were being made to last till March, out here where no one sees them, and Ron's clothes are barely decent; he is dead tired and will be without my private and public support. The blessings are as follows: I am going home, so am willing in the short interval to move to Timbuctoo, if asked, so little does it mean any more. If Ron does well in this short lap, there is no doubt he will go straight back into the Secretariat next tour. We have a reasonable house to go to, at the edge of a suburban estate called Misery Farm, within a quarter of a mile from Zomba. Most important of all, we have six weeks together in which to get Ron nicely organised. He is at the end of his tether over *ulendo*, and the isolation here is beginning to tell on us both. I think the move to Zomba, the change of work, the stimulation of people and the knowledge that he *must* make a success of his new post will pep him up no end. I hope you will gather from that long rigmarole that underneath the superficial panic we are both taking the news calmly and are not sorry to leave Chiradzulu, though I feel in my bones I shall never, never have such a lovely house and garden again. Really, *nothing* happens for months on end and then *bang*, off we go.

Ron was out for three nights last week, and that's the end of that, as he certainly will do no more *ulendo* between now and next Friday. He does not know it yet, but he will do very little office work either, for with the aftermath of 'flu and in this scorching pre-rains weather, I must have assistance, for once, with packing up. I have never asked for it before but the situation is fairly desperate.

On Sunday Kenneth and Ruth came for the day, and we had such a happy, relaxed time sitting on the *khonde* talking. Kenneth is acting Chief Secretary at present; he told us he had just approved Ron's move to Zomba, and that he would get official notice on Monday, which he did. They are delighted that we are to be in Zomba, but very sorry I shall be off so soon, though they approved wholeheartedly with my decision to go home. Ruth, so like her, got me in the bedroom, took me by the shoulders and said firmly, '*Stop* feeling guilty and apologetic about going home. Your mother needs you now. You and Ron have *years* together, she doesn't.' I promptly sat down and shed tears of gratitude. After they left I suddenly realised with horror that I was not feeling at all well and crawled into bed, cursing my fate. However, my temperature is coming down and I shall get up tomorrow.

On Saturday we shall have a final shop in Blantyre and I shall close accounts, close our two library lists, do all the normal food buying, plus some extra things for myself, and be with Ron when he chooses some new shirts, socks and material for two pairs of trousers – all this in about two hours, with, no doubt, people stopping to talk. Help!

My dear Humphrey Bingham went home on retirement leave two weeks ago, and there is the oddest feeling that things are not quite the same with them gone – Eve was quite a character too.

That is all my news, I think. Do not worry about a thing. It will all work out smoothly, I do believe. After all, it is up to Ron, with or without me, to do his work well, and why should I doubt him?

P.S. As I finish this, there has been a huge flash of lightning with a clap of thunder right on top of the house – first of the season, with no warning and nothing yet to follow!

27th October:

This will be rather a hurried letter, as it is our last day here and we are surrounded by open packing cases, trunks and tea chests. We got through our mammoth morning's shopping very well, getting everything I had written down in a formidable list, the most interesting item being some very good brown gabardine for trousers for Ron in the hot season. The local tailor is bringing up the finished article today – two pairs made in four days, copied from an old pair of very well tailored flannels. We went to the Baxters for lunch and found them in fairly good form. We went on to the Carlyles for tea, and as it would be our last visit for some time, we stayed on for dinner and had a lovely evening. I was still feeling rather shaky, but began to improve yesterday. Ron, of course, has now got a heavy cold and is feeling frightful, but at least he does not get 'flu, ever. We had a last, beautiful Sunday, very hot and sunny, and shamelessly lazed away the whole day. This week we have got up every day at five to get the heavy packing done before the heat of the day. Ron has helped almost all the time, which has transformed packing for me, as he does all the things I hate doing, e.g. small tables and lamps.

On Tuesday Ron phoned Zomba to find out about housing and was told the house on Misery Farm was not available and we were being given one of the old, oval-shaped bungalows at Naisi. He was furious and argued for hours on a bad line, to no avail. So we decided the only thing to do was to pack up everything – we could not get all our belongings into a bush house now – and leave the absolute minimum to camp out with at Naisi. So, we had to unpack everything, as we had just thrown it all together temporarily, to be taken to Zomba in the lorry, and repack it properly for storing. I was exhausted and wept into the tea chests, but I told Ron not to be upset for me – I was weeping with *rage!* We hope to get Ron a room in the Government Hostel, which is inexpensive and just across the road from the Secretariat. He would keep Aflike on. To crown everything, Zomba phoned this morning to say there was just the possibility of a better house, in Zomba itself, but it is too late now, as all our stuff is crated and ready for storing. So much for our wonderful new start in Zomba!

2nd November:

I hasten to apologise for my dismal letter last week. We were both suffering from deep depression, which has lifted now. We left Chiradzulu on a beautiful morning but were too tired to suffer any reaction. We got to Zomba about ten and called in at the PWD to collect the keys of the house, which is number twenty-two, the last one and in the best position. It stands very high, has neighbours on one side only and a lovely view, with bush houses only in the middle distance, out over the plain. We can even see a shoulder of Mlanje. The house has not been occupied for five months and I cannot describe to you the filth – bats', rats' and birds' droppings literally thick on the floors, and ants everywhere – there still are. There is no garden at all, just a small flat terrace of hot red earth which reflects the heat frightfully; I have never known such heat in Zomba. Everyone is complaining about it. I simply have not got light enough clothes and am desperately sewing sun tops by hand! We took all our heavy stuff to the PWD store and there it stays till next tour. Our silver, good china and small furniture will be looked after by the Carlyles and the Grindalls – *all* of it insured, as you can imagine! I have put up curtains in the bedroom and bathroom only, and for the rest we just camp – under bare electric bulbs at night, but oh, the bliss of electricity! All the wives at Naisi seem to work in offices, so I am left, thankfully, alone – so far! We had settled in by teatime on Friday, and after tea Gordon and Rosemary Landreth walked round from their house to offer meals, which was very kind but we are self-sufficent. He came out as a bachelor about a year after us, also in Administration, and is a great friend of David's.

Ron did not have to report to the office till Monday so on Saturday morning we shopped and drove round signing the various books – at GH and at the Simmonds', where the book was, as usual, on the *khonde*, and we slipped quietly up to sign, but of course Ruth spied us from a window and came rushing out in a great state to say we were supposed to be staying with them while we settled in, and that she at home and Kenneth at the office had been trying for several days to get through to us at Chiradzulu. We explained that we were not 'settling' at all, just camping out, but it was nice to know somebody cared! Before lunch we had a drink in the Club with Bill Melhuish, who is leaving for good in three weeks time. I shall miss him, nice man that he is. The film that evening was rubbish (as it is this week too), so we spent our weekend quietly, very much as at Chiradzulu, except that on Sunday we could hear at least four wirelesses besides our own, and saw a constant stream of cars going off to the Club. The boys' quarters are all over the place and they make such a lot of noise, especially when the wives go down to work and leave them to run the house, which they do not do, but stand shouting to each other across the gardens. We have got rid of Allan, thank goodness. He had been behaving strangely for some time and we suspect he may have some debilitating disease. I made him promise to go to the African hospital for a check up when he left. We now have Aflike and Lajeb, his very intelligent son, aged fifteen, whom we shall keep on as a second boy next tour. The house is so small and bare that there is little to do. Aflike manages very well and of course his cooking is excellent. Food is so easy here, it is such a relief after Chiradzulu. We have both developed enormous appetites, probably because we are coming alive again, and in Ron's case because he is finding the work very interesting and stimulating. He shows me files and I help him to draft reports and discuss things with him. I can be very useful to him: he says I see things with a fresh eye where he is bogged down in official jargon!

Ron went off to the office on Monday looking so nice in brown gabardine trousers and a new long-sleeved white shirt, having spent ages wondering which *tie* to wear! He said no one was in the least interested in his arrival at the Secretariat except Kenneth, who gave him a warm welcome and grinned from ear to ear when Ron called him 'sir'. When Ron said he felt very confused about everything, Kenneth said, 'That's nothing. I have been in the Secretariat for fifteen years and I am still confused about everything!' He thinks the work will not be very difficult, though it will involve a lot of hard work, especially at first. (His 'title' is Assistant Secretary, Finance.) He is finding it fascinating to see everything from a wider point of view. He comes home promptly for lunch, and about 4.30 in the afternoon (5.15 at Chiradzulu, usually) loaded with files which he reads all evening at present, occasionally reading out tit-bits or asking my advice.

9th November:

There has been tremendous heat here, which broke yesterday, with a thunder-storm and Zomba's first rain this season, which of course made Naisi road a sea of red mud. Although I love the heat, I really was glad of a little respite – I am missing my lovely garden, where I could stroll under the trees and feel cool.

We are trying hard to keep out of things socially, as we cannot return hospitality, but it is difficult. Ron took me down to Zomba on Friday afternoon, my first visit that week, and after shopping, I walked up to the Club and spent a happy afternoon reading the papers and magazines. I was about to order tea when I looked up and found Kenneth beaming down on me. He had discovered from Ron that I was in Zomba for the afternoon and invited himself to tea with us, the first time he had ever had tea at the Club. He and I had a delightful half hour together. This bond between Scots people is strong, and no matter how little one thinks about it, consciously, it is there. Ron arrived and then Ruth, bringing Oli to the film matinee. We stayed in till it was dark and met quite a number of old acquaintances and it began to feel like a party for us, though it happens in the Club every day! We were easily persuaded to go back to the house for a drink and dinner. Ruth put on some of her lovely records and Kenneth produced more of his old photograph albums, and so the evening passed very pleasantly. We are taking them to dinner next Saturday at the Pig and Whistle and on to a film, *The Malta Story*.

We had a quiet day on Saturday and on Sunday went into Zomba for a Remembrance Day ceremony which took place at the KAR monument on the outskirts of the town. The monument is hideous, but surrounded by absolutely blazing flamboyant trees in full bloom, and it was a dazzling scene, with the chiefs (some old friends among them) in their vivid robes and a lot of the Secretariat men in their immaculate white uniforms. There was a roofed stand for the women, some of whom had on very smart frocks and hats. I felt definitely end-of-tourishly dressed! It was an ordeal for everyone, in stunning heat, and the girl next to me fainted. Afterwards we got into the car and dashed joyfully up the mountain to Bill's, where the men changed into shorts and I into sandals. We had a very happy hour with him, alone, and then the Nances, Ian and Joan, who are great friends of his, arrived. Ian is DC Zomba at present, but has spent most of his fifteen years' service in the north. Bill had told us a lot about them, and them about us, I think, and we all settled down in a very relaxed way round the lunch table.

Ron has been allocated a room in the hostel, which is a great relief. Everything included costs him only £11 per month!

On Monday Ron had to attend a court case in Limbe, so I went with him and spent an hour with Ray Grindall, who was just recovering from one of the many strange infections people are prey to at this time of year when the dust is at its worst. All her glands swelled up like golf balls and she felt very ill. She was secretly convinced she had polio – people always think of that first out here.

I am beginning to feel better about leaving Ron, because he is so absorbed in his work. He goes at it from the time he comes back from the office till eleven every night. It is heavenly just to have him come in every evening.

We have heard on the grape vine that David Baxter has amoebic dysentery. I think he has had it since last tour, when he got so thin. I hope he has not neglected it for so long that it cannot be cured. I am going to write to Margaret now and ask how he is.

17th November:

It is so hot in the afternoons that I have had to give up reading *The Times* then – too strenuous, turning the pages!

Last Wednesday we went to John Firth's farewell party. (We knew him in London on the Chinyanja course.) It was a typical, packed Zomba gathering, but I was happy to roam about. I talked a lot to Rosemary Landreth. I discovered she read history at Oxford and is as bright as a button – nice. Ren Smith's wife Liz was there, staying with friends in Zomba while Ren was on *ulendo* – they do not like Kasupi! I think I managed to hide my astonishment. Liz came up next day and spent the morning with me. I enjoyed her liveliness and intelligence.

We were settling down to a hot, quiet day on Sunday, Ron reading files, I was just reading, when the Grindalls arrived, to our surprise and pleasure. They were going up Zomba mountain for the day, and thought we might like to join them. Ron had to work, but I went with them, glad to get up to cooler air. We had a lovely picnic by the river, under the trees, with the children in navy blue knickers (like us three at that age!) ploutering about in the water and sitting on stones, while we lay back and talked. Then we drove all over the plateau, which I had never done –gorgeous scenery like the border country, with thick clumps of trees in the gullies of rolling hills, and white, chalky stones scattered on the hillside so that one felt the sea must be just over the hill on the other side. We got back about 4.30 and found Ron in *bathing* trunks up to his chin in files and sweating profusely. The heat is phenomenal this year and almost monopolises all conversation!

30th November:

This is my second last letter to you written from Naisi! I feel I should have a bottle of champagne by my side! We are having the odd shower of rain, which has cooled everything down, and my sun tan is not as striking as it was, though very marked beside poor Ron's office pallor.

The Times book man wrote a lovely article a few weeks ago on books he remembered which made him laugh out loud, and gave a list compiled by himself and his friends, which set me thinking, and now today he has an article on those which made him cry – animals apparently win with everyone, Dickens does well but not as well as Hardy's Tess (no wonder) and someone, I am gratified to see, includes Galsworthy – I always cry over the death of Soames.

But as Kenneth pointed out, actual laughing and crying over books lessens as one gets older!

Up here during the week Zomba seems as far away as it did at Chiradzulu, and it is always pleasant to be in it on Friday afternoon when I shop and go to the Club, but we are both feeling too end-of-tourish to want any more than that.

On Saturday afternoon we went to Chiradzulu and had a very ceremonious tea at the Welfare Hall, with speeches and a great fuss made over Ron. We then went on and stayed the night with the Grindalls, going to a lovely film, *The Glass Slipper* with Lesley Caron. I have bought *Baron at the Ballet* for Ron's birthday, a magnificent book, the forerunner of *Baron Encore* which I bought on leave with money from David Baxter who wanted me to buy a book for my 'new' collection after the fire, dear man. The Grindalls have invited us to stay the last night with them, which means a reasonable start in the morning – the plane leaves at 10.50, and leaves Nairobi next day at 2.30 p.m. Ron is getting very subdued, but is cheerful about his work, which I knew he would be, given time.

7th December:

This is my last letter! I now feel very odd and restless, with most of the packing done. The rains are slow in setting in and I am going to miss the most wretched weeks. We have had some tremendous thunderstorms with lightning zipping and crackling within feet of the house, or so it seems. I sit with my back to the curtainless windows, but the great violet bars are actually reflected on the wall opposite! Ron and I indulge in a kind of nerve test to see who succumbs to alarm first!

On Friday Rosemary Landreth came for coffee and took me down to shop, in pouring rain, over that fearful road. She is an excellent driver, else I would have stayed at home. She sees only me during the week and is grateful for the least gesture, like handing on the *Spectator* to her and telling her the BBC news. The atmospherics are so bad at this season that only a powerful radio can pick up London, and hers does not utter a sound. I see myself last tour in her and it makes me heartsick – the loneliness and the brave façade which occasionally cracks a bit.

The Secretariat is buzzing with industry, as HE has just returned from Northern Rhodesia and Legislative Council meetings are in full swing. Ron has been working till about midnight and going to the office at 6.00 a.m. and seems to thrive on it. I, on the other hand, find I can sleep twelve hours a night – really good, sound sleep, which makes me feel wonderful – such a relief after countless months of bad nights when Ron was on *ulendo* – I never overcame my nervousness.

I have been tidying things up and looking out clothes, and I think I have so few decent things left that I shall manage to pack them all without being overweight. As usual, everything is much simpler when I get down to it, and after a frenzy of worrying, I have reached the calm stage when not even the discovery (yesterday!) that my passport is out of date moved me beyond reasonable reaction. Ron gets quieter and quieter, and smiles a lot, always a sign of inner disquiet! Alfike is subdued but not tearful. I think he feels end-of-tourish too.

Joan says she is going to phone you soon, so you can exchange excitements! I shall phone you from London – *halleluiah*!

Chapter 21

4th November 1956: SS *Braemar Castle*, approaching Las Palmas

Here is a nice surprise for you. At Las Palmas we are handing over a bag of mail to a home-bound sister ship, and I am told you should have this about the 10th or 11th, long before you will be looking for a letter. The usual raw ache has set in and I feel I shall not 'come to' till we are settled in Zomba. However, knowing our posting makes me feel much more ready to enjoy the voyage.

It seems ages since I left Scotland. I resisted the temptation to phone with great difficulty, while in London, and sent you the flowers instead, which are much better than three or six minutes of agonised conversation. We had a most enjoyable lunch with Uncle Teddie, Joan and Ann on Sunday at his Club. He was looking very well indeed, and was at his best. We spent the evening quietly with Joan, none of us capable of eating dinner after our splendid lunch, combined with that awful 'last evening' feeling, which even Ron felt.

The ship is pleasant and we have an outside cabin with its own bathroom – wonderful. There are several Nyasalanders on board, none of them very interesting. Anne Daly, a contemporary of my latter student days at St. Andrews, is on board, going to Cape Town. I never knew her, but we recognised each other at once and we have had several good talks about people in the old days. The weather has been cold and stormy, but today is humid and sunny and I am beginning to feel physically alive. We made a surprise call at Rotterdam, where the wind was like a knife and it rained constantly. We did not even venture out on deck, let alone go ashore.

The news about Suez is dreadful, and it is most frustrating not to have good newspapers, but we do get radio news twice a day. Ron thinks Anthony Eden has done the right thing and that it may all lead to prestige for Britain. [How wrong he was.] I feel wonderfully armed against the world by all the memories of my perfect leave. We hope to be in Cape Town on 17th November.

14th November: [Air Letter]

We arrive in Cape Town early on Saturday morning, where I shall post this and I hope find some very welcome mail awaiting me. There is not much to tell

297

you about this trip, as it has somehow lacked the magic of our first two. It is
perhaps lack of congenial company. The weather cleared up into glorious
sunshine from the morning I wrote to you, but we only had a week of that, and
for the last few days we have been going through rain and tremendous winds, so
that the noise is deafening – this morning the ship is bucking like a horse; but
we both enjoy this kind of weather, so all is well. We are deeply tanned, having
taken every chance to swim and play deck games. When it rains we play bridge
with a very charming older couple, a Brigadier Drew and his wife. I have been
seeing a lot of Anne Daly, who turns out to be a most delightful person. She is
now married and her name is Bennett. I have been truly thankful for her
company. We hear from a Nyasaland couple who have already done the journey
by car from Cape Town that it is a perfectly straightforward trip, with good
roads right through to Portuguese territory, and plenty of hotels and garages *en
route*, so we are not worried about that journey at all.

We went ashore the day before yesterday at St. Helena (my third visit) and,
just our two selves, drove in a small closed car up the escarpment to Longwood.
It was a soft day of mist and rain and the island smelt exactly like the Highlands
in similar weather, so I felt relaxed as a cat with cream. The house has been
restored and we were allowed inside to wander through the rather desolate
rooms – the walls of one bedroom are still covered in the original linen. I was
again impressed by the marvellous historical atmosphere the whole place has
retained since Napoleon's time.

I am beginning to think about packing, and I must say our one thought is to
get to Zomba and settle down. I feel very far away from everything and
everyone I love except Ron. I shall try to send you news on our way up.

18th November: Cape Town [Air Letter]

We arrived here yesterday and I was very glad to find your letter waiting for
me. We have had to stay over the weekend, as the car [a Vauxhall Velox, pur-
chased on leave] has to be unloaded from the ship and serviced. We plan to leave
some time tomorrow and Ron thinks we shall arrive in Zomba on the 26th. Also
waiting for us was a letter from Jean and Philip Richardson, ex-Solomons, whom
we came to know quite well towards the end of last tour, saying they would be unable to put us up as planned, because they had been landed with long-term guests,
and Jane and Hugh Norman-Walker would be glad to have us. It will only be for a
few nights. We shall want to move into our own house as soon as possible.

We are thankful to be off the ship and are now champing at the delay. It is
cloudy but bright and I am writing this sitting on the verandah. The weather has
been erratic and there has been no great heat but I have no doubt we shall drive
into it as we go north. We have bought an excellent road guide of South Africa
– the equivalent of our AA Book – which gives all the routes, distances and
hotels, so we undertake the journey without any qualms.

19th November: Swellendam (134 miles from Cape Town) [Air Letter]

As you see, we have not gone very far on our first day! The car was not ready till after lunch, and we decided to make a short day of it. Yesterday we did very little but sit in the sun. I did some washing and repacking. I spent this morning in Cape Town, buying stores for the journey, and met Ron for elevenses. The drive here was through wonderful country, rather like Austria, if one did not look too closely and see how sparse the vegetation is on the hot, dusty red soil. There are vast tracts of country visible for miles, with white, colonial style farm houses scattered on the hills. The roads are excellent, with long straight stretches for miles on end and hardly a passing car in either direction. When they do pass, the driver usually is a farmer and never fails to salute us. We are feeling very cheerful, simply because we are on the move, on the last lap. The weather is ideal for travelling, cool and sunny, without much dust, but of course we are travelling into the heat.

There has been absolute chaos over shipping, as you can imagine, with the Canal closed, and we are told that Durban has a queue of forty ships waiting to enter her docks. Our ship was turning there, and all remaining passengers were transshipping to the *Dunottar*, to get to Mombasa, the final port of call now for Union Castle Ships.

This is an absolute shanty town, the hotel full of Afrikaners, all speaking their hideous language!

P.S. Tell Aunt Kathie that the mountains today looked as dramatic and jagged as the Dolomites and I felt quite indignant that Europe and Africa could look so alike! But it makes the world seem smaller – comforting thought.

22nd November: Heidelberg, Transvaal [Air Letter]

Although it is only three days since I wrote, it seems more like three weeks, we have literally covered so much ground. We left Swellendam so early in the morning I had no opportunity to find the local Post Office, which is usually buried in a general store somewhere. We travelled 433 miles that day, to Grahamstown, through magnificent country, which seemed to be on the top of the world, with tremendous ranges of mountains all round, into which we plunged, then up again on splendid escarpment roads. By the time we stop in the late afternoon about 5.30, we only want a bath, a drink, dinner and bed. Elevenses and lunch we take with us in the car – sandwiches from the hotel, fruit, cheese, a flask of tea and a bottle of water – a sad come-down from our delicious continental lunches of last summer! Yesterday we travelled through the Transvei, a wonderful native reserve with deep, rolling hills. All the travelling by the Africans in this region is done on horseback – small horses more like ponies. [They are in fact Basuto ponies.] Everything seemed to be the colour of burnt sienna – the soil, the horses, the short cloaks the men wear, and even the African faces – most attractive.

One gets the impression of the *size* of Africa when driving through it. Sometimes the road stretches straight and empty for thirty miles ahead, like a ribbon, and the car cruises at 70 without us even noticing. The windscreen gets covered with the corpses of squashed insects and we have to stop regularly to clean them off. All the 'towns' are small shanty communities, with really tough-looking people populating them. The garage men are always friendly though – they never say 'Are you English?' but 'Are you Overseas?', they can tell that by the number plate, and like all people whose lives depend on transport, they are passionately interested in everything about the car.

Last night we spent at Ixopo, 480 miles from Grahamstown, a tiny place high up in the mountains, which we approached, very tired, as it was getting dark, through rain and ground level cloud – the hotel was called 'Off Saddle Inn' and was very comfortable. The sheer comfort of good lodgings when travelling these enormous distances is a kind of primitive pleasure. Today we did some 350 miles and are at Heidelberg, right in the middle of the gold-mining area – a horrible place and a truly horrible hotel! We expect to arrive in Nyasaland on Sunday and plan to stay the night in Limbe with John and Ray Grindall, going on to Zomba next day. We have wired the Norman-Walkers to expect us on Monday 26th. I may not write again till we arrive, as this is my last air letter and our one thought during the day is to get on. We are thoroughly enjoying this journey!

27th November: Zomba

It is Tuesday afternoon and at last I have a chance to escape and write to you.

Last time I wrote was from Heidelberg, in a dreadful hotel, the only bad one we stayed at during the entire journey. Next day we did another mammoth stretch from there to Beit Bridge, the border post between South Africa and Southern Rhodesia, where we stayed at a lovely little inn. The scenery that day was again splendid, and we had the excitement of seeing Johannesburg, which I approached without much interest, but when I caught sight of bright 'bings' of golden slag like great triangular nuggets of gold, I sat up and stared. The town itself is the usual mixture of beautiful colonial buildings, skyscrapers and awful slums, but I shall never forget the sunlight on all that yellow rubbish which symbolised the enormous wealth of the area. The next day we covered almost the whole of Southern Rhodesia, through featureless bush country, utterly wild, with hundreds of miles of seemingly uninhabited land. We reached Mtoko, the Portuguese border post about five o'clock, and there met up with Alan and Pat Monk, PWD, who were on the ship. We had a drink and dinner with them at a delightful hotel run by an old Lithuanian who came to Rhodesia forty-five years ago and could tell fascinating stories of the early days when he built a small shack as a bar and the men paid for their drinks in *gold*!

At Alan's suggestion we left next morning at 4.30, just before dawn, to do the last 300 miles of frightful roads through Mozambique and into Nyasaland. After the wonderful surfaces in South Africa, the river bed texture of these awful roads was a bit of a nightmare. Fortunately, it was a cloudy day, so we were very lucky, as we only had a few hours in the Zambesi valley, of suffocating heat. We crossed the river in blazing sunshine at about 11 o'clock. Even on the water there was not a breath of air and the sweat was dripping off our legs and forming pools at our feet. It was reassuring to have the Monks with us, in case there was a hiccup during that difficult stretch. We got to Blantyre about five and went straight to Limbe to the Grindalls, who gave us a great welcome. They both feel and look very end-of-tourish. We were dead tired and had an early night.

Next morning we called in to present ourselves to Bill Rangeley, the PC, and Peter Nicholson, both glad to see us, and in Limbe called in on the Carlyles, only to find that Laga is in Salisbury and Clement was out, so we left a chit. Then we drove to Zomba. For the first time since 1950 the rains have come at the right time – they have always been late – so we drove through thick mist and rain without a glimpse of my mountain. I was stricken by a feeling that this was a bad omen. We passed the back of Chiradzulu and I felt a pang, thinking of some ADC's poor young wife keeping lonely vigil up on that lovely station; though it would be far from lovely that day.

Hugh and Jane gave us a warm welcome and put us in a huge bed-sittingroom with its own bathroom. Aflike was there waiting for us, just the same, tossing his arms aimlessly with excitement, his eyes liquid with tears at the sight of us. To see him has lightened my heart a little. Already our clothes are washed and pressed; he brings in morning tea and murmurs, '*Moni*, m'am' as he lifts up the mosquito net. We have unpacked only a few clothes and can hardly wait to get into our house. After tea yesterday we went down and had a look at it. It is a semi-detached bungalow, with big rooms, high ceilings, a precipitous garden and a glorious view straight out over Zomba and Palombe plain to Mlanje. *Of course* it is not ready for occupation, though we have arrived here ten days late (because of the ship being so slow) and only with luck will we move in by the end of the week – typical. I shall describe it in detail later. It has character and charm, and I am bursting to get busy on it. We had another early night and spent this morning in dismal rain getting our things out of store and going over the house with the PWD supervisor, a Scot from Brechin who wasted an hour telling us how difficult it was to get labour and materials, while he dispiritedly knocked holes in the wall plaster to show us how much needed to be done. What a place! I then came back here while Ron called in at the Boma to see John Watson and reported to the Secretariat. There have been a lot of moves there. Everyone seems pleased to see us and already the invitations for the near future are pouring in.

Tomorrow we go to Limbe to get our things through Customs – we sent up the long player, the carpet and one trunk by train. [During our leave, Aunt

Isobel died, and with the small legacy she left me I bought the marvellous Pye 'Black Box' record player and twelve long-playing records.] It will be a rushed day, as we have shopping to do as well. I really do feel perfectly cheerful, despite the inevitable bleakness which always settles on my spirit at the start of a tour.

You mention the anti-British feeling in Cape Town. The odd thing is that this time the atmosphere was quite changed – friendly and co-operative. In the cinema the audience actually clapped when on the News we saw British troops in Egypt.

5th December:

Since I last wrote we have been having rather a dreadful time! We spent the day in Blantyre on Wednesday, working our way through an enormous shopping list without the car, which was being serviced. Our three items of luggage, which we expected to pick up, had not arrived, and we are still waiting – maddening, as the carpet is one, also the household trunk, which contains my precious curtain material, lamp shades and many other things for the house. Ron went to the office on Thursday and I somehow managed to fill in the time. I have played several games of Scrabble with Jane, and can see its possibilities. The weather is humid and wet, and I am longing for the sun! Work on the house began on Thursday and we looked at it each day in horror and despair, feeling we would *never* get in! On Saturday at noon we went to a drinks party with the Norman-Walkers and met a lot of people we knew – all of them complaining bitterly about the very wet weather. All *I* wanted to talk about was my wonderful trip to Europe in the summer, but I am learning – *not a word!*

On Sunday we jolly well moved into the house, in spite of the mess, and have been picnicking ever since, with a dozen or so Africans wandering about doing nothing. The diningroom walls are rotten, so everything in it was moved into the drawingroom, which is full of cases, boxes and trunks. I managed to get the bedroom and bathroom in working order. Aflike is as marvellous as ever, and his son Lajeb is going to make a very good second house boy. We have taken on the Bingham's old cook, theoretically. He vanished on Saturday to collect wives and belongings from his village, and has not been seen since, which is no surprise to me and I do not doubt he will turn up. Meanwhile Aflike cooks very well.

Everything has gone wrong since we moved in. We bought a fridge in Blantyre which has simply not been delivered. The wiring has to be redone and has not been touched. The new pelmets in the bedroom were put up too low, so that the mosquito frames, which open inwards, would not open, so I could not get my hand through to open the windows! And so it goes on. The electric light failed on our first evening and we had not so much as a candle in the place! Occasionally I feel quite sick, but fortunately I have plenty to do, unpacking everything – when I can find a surface on which to pile things up. We can get nothing aired, there is so much rain, and laundry mounts ominously.

In spite of all this, I am fairly cheerful, as I can see in the far future that our house will be charming. Aflike's devotion is reassuring, and when things get on top of me I go out and have a talk with him. He has a nice kitchen, a sink on the back *khonde* and two big store rooms, one with moveable shelves which can be taken out and scrubbed. Our drawingroom is big, with a wide bow window, and French doors. Off a very spacious *khonde* is a little room the size of our tiny guest house at Chiradzulu, so all my pretty things for it made by hand by Joan and me go in there and give us a spare bedroom. Off it and behind the drawingroom is a rather dark diningroom. Off the other side of the drawingroom is the bedroom, with three steps up into a small alcove where I have the dressingtable, and through an open archway is a large airy bedroom, with a big bathroom (lavatory in it – heaven!) off it. I shall draw a plan of it later when I feel able! Basic furniture is the usual stuff, in reasonable condition and now shining mirror bright, thanks to Lajeb and Mansion Polish. The house has been unoccupied for some time, and was therefore full of enormous cockroaches, but I have a very good insecticide spray (called Killem!) and my aim has been satisfactorily deadly. When I feel one of my silent rages surging up I go cockroach hunting and vent my spleen on the poor creatures.

I have had one very nice visitor, Coralie Pincott (her husband was DC Blantyre when we were at Chiradzulu and is now rapidly making his way up the Secretariat ladder). Yesterday afternoon we went to have tea with Gordon and Rosemary Landreth, who go on leave in about ten days time. Jennifer, their small daughter, has been constantly ill and they are both worn out. They said David (Baxter) had reached Cape Town and is now driving up in his new Vanguard, with Margaret and their baby daughter. I do not envy him the latter part of that journey, in all this rain. It is only 2.45 now, and almost dark, with the rain thudding down – I never remember just how heavy tropical rain is. The garden is very precipitous, with a lot of grass, rocks and trees, but in time it will look all right. The sunsets are glorious – Mlanje *and* Chiradzulu – wonderful. We also have an attractive glimpse of Government House, flag flying through the trees.

13th December:

I have lost all sense of time and am thrilled when I receive another letter from you, which means a week has gone by.

Ron's uniform has arrived – very splendid. Aflike is delighted with it. An amusing mistake has been made. Instead of a large, flat button-like tip in the top of the helmet, a more senior tip has been sent in the form of a colossal brass spike like a spear head which screws into the top and looks tremendously impressive. Needless to say it will be returned forthwith.

The Times has started to arrive – we have had four now – and already I feel very much more in touch with events. I am also thankful to have your *Spectator* and *Observer* by sea mail.

Here things happen with maddening slowness. On Thursday Ron suddenly rushed back up here at 8.00 a.m. to say we must dash to Limbe in five minutes (!) to collect our heavy stuff from Customs. So I leapt into fresh clothes and made up a hasty shopping list over which I needed to take careful time. Ron cleared the luggage while I rushed out and got lamp fittings and other vital things, including two lovely ebony lamp stands for my beautiful shades. We met up in the Tavern (the small restaurant where Joan and I used to wait for Ron after shopping). Ron brought the Black Box back in the car and made the great mistake of leaving the carpet and trunk (which contains my curtain material) at the station to be brought over by lorry that afternoon. Well, that was a week ago and they *still* have not come, and so we cannot invite anyone here to this bare, echoing room and I am going quietly mad. The final blow was when we fitted up the Black Box, only to find that a small, vital part, two inches long, which works the arm, had been broken in transit and the machine hummed pleasantly but refused to lower the arm onto the record – a bitter blow. Ron has sent home for a new part, which is in an almost impossible place to get at without proper tools. None of my lovely lamps is working, as the shops await the arrival of a supply of the correct plugs! The fridge came at last, ten days late. It is sheer heaven to have, about the only nice thing that has happened since we moved in!

My faithful Indian tailor came up and re-covered the sofa with a strong, grey material like fine hessian, with two bright red linen cushions. The room is going to look lovely, so I must possess my soul in patience. Yesterday I re-upholstered our window seat (made at Mlanje) in red linen and finished the fabulous cross-stitch tapestry I bought in St. Andrews and worked at steadily on the voyage. It looks splendid under the glass of the coffee table and will contribute to the colour scheme of the room. The bedroom, bathroom, diningroom and guest room are all completely ready and look very nice. After the slow torture of assembling the drawingroom is over, I must attend to the garden.

On Monday after tea we called on Barbara Firth. She is John Firth's wife, a contemporary of ours. Last tour in Zomba she got polio when she was expecting her third child, and was flown home, critically ill. Well, she has come back here with him and the three children, ranging in age from nineteen months to seven years. She lives in a very well designed wheelchair which responds to the slightest touch of her one mobile hand. She has a good head boy, an excellent coloured nannie and a boy who pushes her chair about Zomba. The children are lovely. They pay attention to everything she says to them. It was terrible to see the concentration on her face and the little boy's when he was in difficulties with his dressing gown and she could not help him but told him to stand still and then do certain things – he refuses help from anyone and gets almost hysterical if one persists. I do not think we have much in common except a love of music.

Not a hope of a driving lesson so far. Ron works in the office till six, except for two nights a week when he plays bridge at the Club till 8.30. It's a man's world! I hope to have more sociable and good tempered news for you next week! P.S. We have bought Scrabble and find it quite an absorbing time consumer. I am, at present, streets ahead of Ron at it, but no doubt the scientific approach will tell, in time!

20th December:

I am sorry my last letter was so depressed. Things all came together the very next day with the result that the house is at last in order and I am in a reasonable frame of mind. Poor Ron has been walking like Agag ever since we came back, I have been so temperamental! The weather is very dreary – thunder, mist, rain, wind, with only the most occasional glimpse of the sun. My odd rheumatic wrist aches all the time and positively squeaks when I move it.

Our delayed luggage arrived and Ron came home triumphantly with my two ebony lamp stands fitted ready to switch on. It was lovely to unpack everything and put things in their places. The tailor made up the curtains in no time and hung them for me – they make the room, as I knew they would. The white carpet looks wonderful. The Binghams' cook has sent a message to say he will arrive on 1st January, but by that time I hope Aflike will have found a less expensive one. We have spent a lot of money settling into the house and I shall have to start entertaining soon. The cost of living in Zomba has more than doubled, I would say, since our first tour.

On Sunday morning we went to a drinks party at the Watsons which was pleasant. I found myself in a sudden silence describing to a large group of people an extraordinary sight we saw in South Africa on the journey up. We were driving along a road with dense rain forest on either side when we passed a sign: 'You are now entering the Tropic of Capricorn'. Instantly the rain forest vanished and we were driving past huge cacti as tall as trees, growing on a sandy plain. There were some sounds of dubiety. Fortunately for me the Chief Conservator of Forests was there and he came to my rescue, saying firmly, 'Ann is perfectly right,' and proceed to explain this extraordinary phenomenon.

On Tuesday morning I walked down to visit Barbara Firth, following a path Aflike told me about, which takes me there, very steeply, in three and a half minutes instead of half an hour by the main road. She was very glad to see me and did most of the talking, which is all right with me. Yesterday we went to the cinema to see, for the second time, that marvellous film *Mandy*. We saw only two faces we knew! We are giving a drinks party (house warming really) on Saturday at noon, asking all the people we like (i.e. about twelve)! I miss the Simmonds'. We have had a Christmas card from each of them!

28th December:

The weather continues to be simply appalling – one prolonged *chiperoni* in fact. Last Friday Ron managed to get the morning off (everyone was taking time off to do Christmas shopping) and we went to Blantyre, mainly to see if the shop which sells LPs could provide us with the spare part needed for mine and put it in. They can fit it, but had no spare part. Hi, ho. We bought some interesting food and drink for Christmas, plus all the other things one cannot get in Zomba. In the last shop we visited, who should walk in but Laga. We fell into each other's arms, very near to tears. [Her mother, the marvellous Con Dushmanitch, had died recently in Salisbury.] She looks quite worn out and has obviously been through a bad time. We said we had only just got the house in order and were having a quiet Christmas. She promptly begged us to spend Christmas Day with them, saying we were the only people they wanted to have, so soon after losing Con and of course we agreed. (Frankly, I have felt *so un-settled* since we came back that I did not have the heart to give any thought to Christmas, I am ashamed to say.) Ivan [Laga's brother] is with them for a few months. So, we went back to Zomba much cheered at the thought of a 'family' Christmas.

On Saturday morning, the first sunny day for days, I rushed about preparing for a drinks party we were giving at noon – twelve people and ourselves. The house looked lovely and as fresh as paint. We had quite a mixture of people, some of whom you would not know, whom I did not know either; people who had been good to Ron when he was in the Hostel. The Pincotts were there, and Jean and Philip Richardson – who asked us to go to the New Year's Eve Ball in their party, which pleased me. Jean adored the house and called Philip in from the *khonde* to see everything and that brought everybody else in and they all had a good look – nice.

On Sunday we had a great day to ourselves, hearing lovely Christmas music from Salisbury and the César Franck Symphonic Variations, also lovely. In the evening Ron put on his new suit, I my best yellow Horrocks, and off we went to the Kayes' annual carols party – 160 people all milling about, so noisy the singers were scarcely noticed, which was a shame. Christmas Eve was a horrible dark day of continuous rain, and by evening I was in a state of acute misery – how I *loathe* Christmas out here. We drove through a *chiperoni* on Christmas morning and got to the Carlyles about 10.30. The children look marvellous and were so affectionate. Ivan, very white, thin and *very* Slav looking, accepted us at once but kept very quiet for most of the time. He seems devoted to Laga, who is so kind and gentle with him. Poor Laga wore dark glasses all day, and I think she cried a good deal, for she was constantly blowing her nose. However, she talked about her mother a lot, as she always has done, and was obviously very glad to have us there. She had decorated the house beautifully and made a most exquisite manger scene in the fireplace, which was lit up at night – very

Serbian. She had no cook, so she and I worked companionably in the kitchen till lunch time and we had a cold buffet lunch of turkey, with marvellous salads and plum pudding. Then we played Scrabble till it was time to go to tea with Tony and Sybil Hardwick, the people who used to ask us to musical evenings in Limbe when we were at Chiradzulu. We had an enormous Christmas tea, again in a lovely family atmosphere. In fact we could not have been with nicer people and Laga felt the same, I know. She is very tired and listless and sees nobody, but she now drives her own Morris Minor and is most eager to come over and spend the day with me once the children go back to school, which will be delightful for me, for one can never be bored in her company, though sometimes tired! We left about 10.30 and drove back through thick white mist and heavy rain. We had a quiet, very pleasant Boxing Day, reading and listening to the wireless, after a late, huge breakfast. Ron was duty officer and had to go down to the Secretariat about 10.00 to see that the mail was sorted and to take up the Chief Secretary's mail to his house, if you please. There was none, but Ron politely went up to the house to say so.

Yesterday I had quite a day, as we were having the Watsons for dinner and I was determined everything would be perfect. Well, it all went very smoothly. Of course, John talked shop to Ron all evening, except at dinner, when I always firmly take charge of the conversation and keep everyone on one subject. Dorothy seemed perfectly content to fill me in on all the gossip I had missed by being on leave. What a lot of ears must have been burning during the evening. New Year's Eve is coming up next, and then back to normal, whatever *that* means.

3rd January 1957:

The weather continues to be dreadful, which accounts I think for most of the acute depression I have been feeling since I returned. I have never seen such rain since Mlanje, and the thunder is tremendous, really awesome. Life goes on, with just enough happening to make one realise that one still exists, however faintly! I think that in time I shall be able to make a pleasant enough existence in Zomba. I am trying to be patient and give things time. After all, we have only been back five weeks.

I have discovered that the huge tree which shades the end of the house and hangs over the roof is a jacaranda, so in blossom time that wonderful blue will be just outside the windows. There is also a large avocado pear tree, so we will be popular! I am becoming very fond of the house and the view, and I have no doubt that when the better weather comes I shall feel very much more pleased about everything. All the wives are saying they feel depressed.

On Monday evening I wore my sea green chiffon (my back is *cream* coloured, not brown!) and we drove to the Richardsons through pelting rain, where we found the Pincotts, the Youens', the Roberts' and the Davidsons, Bunny and

Alex, friends of the Richardsons from the Solomons. They seem rather nice. They are the long-term guests who prevented the Richardsons from putting us up when we arrived. They are waiting for a house on a new housing estate just south of Zomba, called Kalimbuka. The party was made up entirely of pleasant people and all the men were good dancers so I was happy to dance away the evening. There were a lot of new faces, and the Club was simply teeming with people. Quite a number of women came up to say 'hello' and invite me to coffee one morning, including Jean Wickham (Mzimba, wife of Bruce, who drove Joan and me to the North). She seemed thankful to see someone she knew from the past and greeted me with great warmth. People who have served in the North are known to dislike Zomba at first, it is so different, and having had a glimpse of the North, I can understand this. We left at 3.30 and came home simply starving, to eat cheese and biscuits and talk till the cocks were crowing. Next day we spent very peacefully, reading, listening to the wireless and playing Scrabble. I used to beat Ron every time till we both got bored, but recently he has improved and often beats me. He has the scientific approach, of course, but *I* have the vocabulary! He is working very hard indeed, but enjoys it, though he will be glad when Kenneth comes back from long leave.

We still await the spare part for the LP. We are in touch with a Rhodesian firm which someone recommended. The wireless is my constant companion and I now know where to find the best programmes. I have even heard Amalia Rodrigues, the husky voiced Portuguese singer who specialises in *fada* – Lorenço Marques broadcasts her records. I used to listen to her at Chiradzulu, late at night.

9th January:

We have had three perfect days of sunshine, so I am blooming and my spirits have shot up – about time, too.

After tea on Friday, *at last* we joined the library and I came back feeling immune to everything, with six books, including Guy Chapman's wonderful book on the Dreyfus case, which, needless to say, *Ron* is reading! On Saturday we gave a big drinks party at lunchtime, to catch up on hospitality and introduce some new faces. Jean and Bruce Wickham came, and are obviously very anxious to be friends. It was a glorious day and everyone stayed out on the *khonde*, which I always like, as people are more relaxed in the open air. We had a very hot, quiet Sunday with a great concert in the morning which included the New World and Brahms' 2nd piano concerto. On Monday evening Hugh and Jane came to dine. To my relief, it all went very well and *not* a word of shop all evening. They stayed on late, as Hugh was obviously enjoying himself immensely. Poor Jane was yawning openly. Yesterday morning I walked down my useful shortcut to have coffee with Jean Wickham, who welcomed me thankfully. They are finding Zomba unbelievably unfriendly and cliquish after their with more people and had a drink with John Watson, glad to see me – so shy, nice man. Dorothy is expecting a baby in August and was lying low at home. We left about 4.30, taking with us a young policeman from Mlanje, about twenty, Ron Fitzhenry, a big handsome young man who treats Ron with deference and tends to call him 'sir'. He has very good manners and makes me feel like Dresden china.

I must go on to another page because I have forgotten to tell you something interesting that happened at the Ball. Kenneth Simmonds came over to our table, asked my hostess if he could 'borrow Ann', took me to the bar, bought me a drink and led me to a secluded corner, where he talked seriously to me at some length. He said he had always remembered a conversation (so had I) with me when we first met, in which I made critical remarks about life in Africa. (How my innocent frankness of those days is catching up with me now!) He asked me if I still felt the same. I said yes, I thought I did, but in a more mature, controlled way – a kind of inner rebellion which I kept to myself. Well, he looked pleased with that, but proceeded to give me a long lecture on Empire, a sense of service, loyalty, etc – in short, all the things I feel very strongly about myself – and advised me on no account to think of giving up or encouraging Ron to give up. My reaction, apart from mortification, was a very deep, private anger. I said quietly that he had completely misread my character and that it would never enter my mind to 'give up' or encourage Ron to do so. He nodded, said 'Good,' and asked me to dance! Then he took me back to my table. Ron was bursting with curiosity – he said my eyes were 'glittering'!

Having thought about it and talked with Ron, I believe Kenneth was kindly and discreetly indicating to me that if I would just grin and bear it, life was full of promise for us both and could only improve. He is a very clever, charming man and I think it was frightfully good of him to take the trouble to try to help me. In the context of our miserable life right now, in Mlanje, it was no bad thing to be reminded by a man of his calibre of what the Colonial Service stands for.

19th May:

I have had a letter from Joan from Cape Town. She writes just as I feel on a voyage – in a complete daze and very inconsequential as to news and details. She spent her time most efficiently in Cape Town, 'doing' the National Gallery and Botanical Gardens. She also went up the mountain, sensible girl. All her comments on scenery and new things are excellent, while anything said on familiar things (e.g. shops, clothes, etc) are very blasé and critical – just wait till she is on her way home after some months here! The first shop she sees in South Africa will seem like a Paris haute couture salon!

I am rather bothered about food when Joan comes. I have not said much about it, but it is very difficult in such a hot station without a fridge, and when Ron is out I keep a very simple table. However, he pays off the car completely very soon, so perhaps we can buy a fridge after that. At least we eat plenty of fresh fruit and vegetables.

Ron came in on Saturday morning and blew away all my little nagging worries. At teatime Laga and Clement Carlyle arrived with the three children and a delicious Pekinese bitch called Kiko. It was a lovely surprise, and we were all delighted at the reunion and kept exchanging mutual apologies for not getting in touch till now. Laga and Clement look tired but well. The children are delightful, though David's petit mal is much in evidence and must worry them. Laga simply loathes Limbe now and they have hardly any friends. (I thought of the many nice people Ron and I know and silently and humbly counted my blessings.) She sat down and poured out her heart to me, while Ron and Clement talked and kept an eye on the children. They had tea and stayed on till it was dark, then accepted a drink and still Laga sat talking and laughing. She was enjoying herself so much that I suggested that the children (who were both wild and wilting) have supper and go to bed in our room, and they stay on to dinner and make a celebration of it. She jumped at the idea and the children enthusiastically ate a supper of boiled eggs, brown bread and marmite, apples and cocoa, and then meekly went to bed, dead tired. Aflike *loved* having them! We four had dinner later and they left about ten, asking when they could come back! I have promised to have them for a day as soon as Joan settles in. We both enjoyed them tremendously and they were obviously thankful to see and talk to us again.

We spent our usual peaceful Sunday in lovely sunshine and on Monday Ron triumphantly produced a poisoned finger which led to his *ulendo* being cancelled and brightened our lives very much, as it means he is in all this week and on leave for the next three. But it is worrying, as this is the second attack of poison this tour. I must try and feed him up.

26th May:

It is Ramadan and my nerves are suffering! Aflike has had an appalling cold which sounded as if it might develop into pneumonia. He refused codeine because of Ramadan and in the end I sent him away with strict instructions to go to bed for three days, which I am relieved to say he did. Thank goodness he comes back tomorrow! Meanwhile Cook has us in his tender care and the less said about that the better. Joan's room is ready; it looks a little bare, but will be pretty when she unpacks books and ornaments. She arrives on Saturday and we are going to Blantyre on Friday to do some last minute shopping – pillows, for one thing. Tonight we are dining in great state with Sandy and Mary, who are celebrating their ninth wedding anniversary.

Ron's leave began on Monday. He is enjoying every minute of it, and it is wonderful for me to have him about. The penal labourers have not quite known what has hit them and are working furiously for him – the garden is beginning to look as trim and as neat as an English one (which I do not really like – I prefer a certain *embarras de richesse*!) Ron polishes the car daily and it looks brand new. He has also cleaned the lamps, which recently have threatened to blow up and destroy eyebrows and stray locks of hair, which I hate.

On Sunday morning we were on the *khonde* listening to music when Laga and family again descended on us and stayed till five o'clock. We find them most enjoyable but tiring, as the children are more or less turned loose while the parents talk to us. They are going to have us for the day when Joan arrives and take us over the tobacco floors and to attend an auction, which I believe is quite exciting. Ron plans a visit to Lujeri tea estate and factory, so I shall be able to take a small interest in the district. People have got wind of Joan's imminent arrival and the air hums with curiosity. Last night at the cinema Barbara Sproule (who I like very much) asked me when Joan was expected, and two whole rows of ears flapped to try and catch my low-voiced reply!

I am having to deal with a feeling of regret that Ron and I are about to share our precious life together with another person, but I know that I shall be very excited when I see that train steam in to Luchenza. The weather, of course, has broken and is horrible! There is a damp, howling wind, scurries of rain, and dismal clouds drift along the mountain and hang low over the plain. All the flowers are wet and wind tossed. Today could be a dreary autumn day at home. It is the sort of weather that can last for days in Mlanje. I warned Joan it might be exactly like this, but I doubt if she really believed me.

2nd June:

I feel I hardly know how to begin, with this sudden spate of news I have for you, on Joan's arrival. I must first tell you our news prior to Joan. Wednesday was Sandy's and Mary's ninth wedding anniversary and we dined with them – no one else there – and had a great evening, with lots of champagne. But Friday was the highlight. We took Mary to Blantyre for the day – the first time she had had a day off in Nyasaland without children or husband. We did it in style, having coffee, then shopping and a haircut each, and lunch in Ponson's where Humphrey Bingham joined us for coffee and completely enchanted Mary with his charm and conversation. He was at his best and I enjoyed showing him off to her. We then went to Limbe and had an early tea with Laga, whom Mary was longing to meet. The house is pleasant but has no view at all, which I would hate. Laga does a lot of painting and has some delightful pictures on the walls, of Yugoslavia, the children and wild flowers. She is obviously very talented. Mary came away most enthusiastic about the whole family. We then returned to Blantyre and went to the cinema at 4.30 – a very light comedy called *Dream Wife*. We drove home in magnificent starlight and arrived at nine o'clock to find Sandy subdued and exhausted after a day spent with his very active eighteen-

month-old daughter and her somewhat inefficient African nanny! Mary herself
looked about ten years younger. When she thanked us before getting out of the
car she said she had loved being with us, because of our restful, serene relationship. Well, think of that.

Saturday was a beautiful day and I spent it in the sun, as I was icy cold with
excitement. We drove to Luchenza in glorious early evening sunshine, stood on
one foot and then the other till 5.10, when black smoke told us the train was
coming. I was transfixed on the platform when I saw Joan at a window looking
marvellously tanned, wearing a lovely yellow cotton dress. (ALL her cottons –
dozens of them – are beautiful Horrocks, making me feel very plain Jane!) It
was almost dark, but she could see the countryside. We got her luggage – an
astonishing amount – into the car and all squashed into the front seat and drove
back talking constantly and smiling at each other. She looks so well, fresh and
most attractive, much less heavy. She has had a perfect trip, especially after
Cape Town, when the officers mingled with the passengers (only twelve on the
City of Paris) and took her on trips ashore.

I think the voyage was so wonderful that Mlanje is quite a comedown in
many ways, though she is interested in everything and thrilled with the house,
the view, and Aflike – I am afraid he thinks she is Ron's second wife but, being
a Muslim, that is perfectly acceptable to him and a sign of increasing prosper-
ity! Joan says we both look well but are very different from our 'home' selves –
'rather dead' was how she put it! Ah well, that is Mlanje for you. Since she
came we have spent the time talking while she was supposed to unpack. Ron
had to vanish for the day on Sunday, to play cricket, and came back to find us
still talking and no unpacking done. On Monday she unpacked a bit and I got all
the home presents and the clothes I had asked her to bring for me. She knows
exactly what I like and brought me *two* winter skirts, because they were so inexpensive, and a beautiful Horrocks dress which fits me perfectly – soft pastel
flowers on a pale grey background. *What* a joy really good clothes are! She
brought me as a present a dream of a housecoat, also Horrocks, grey with tiny
roses, rather like a delicate Victorian wallpaper. She struck Ron speechless
(yes, I said speechless!) by presenting him with a *fabulous* antique decanter.

On Tuesday evening the dear Holmeses came rushing in for a drink, eager to
meet her and treating her like an old friend. She was greatly taken with them
and I could see she charmed them – lovely for me – reflected glory! In the
morning, Joan and Mike Saunders paid a delightful surprise visit, so she met
two real 'bush' characters and enjoyed them immensely. I have warned her that
not all the people she meets will be as interesting and interested!

Today in the forenoon we drove to Lujeri tea estate and John Sanderson
showed us over the factory. Joan asked all the right questions (while I stood
looking vaguely at the machinery and sneezing at the tea). We nearly had a bad
accident on the way back along an estate road. A motorcyclist came round a
blind corner quickly, panicked, and turned into the oncoming car instead of

years in the casual, friendly and interdependent bush life of the North. Having circled round the subject discreetly, we found that we liked and disliked the same people or kinds of people, and then talked of other things for the rest of the morning.

I must tell you that I am not now in the awful state I was in when I came back. I felt I was threshing about in a cage of utter futility and frustration – it is all still there – the cage, futility, frustration – but now I sit quietly and pick out which corner is most comfortable! So, a lone private battle has been won. It is a strange thing to say but I think the only person aware of it has been Aflike.

16th January:

The latest in the saga of the LP is that the firm in Bulawayo to whom we wrote quickly sent us back the *wrong* spare part, though we had described it minutely and given the reference number. Ron nearly blew up, and wrote them a scathing letter. We wait on.

Ron was sure the new Prime Minister would be Mr Butler and I said I would bet him anything he liked it would most certainly not be Mr Butler but Mr Macmillan. I was right, only, of course, because I read so many home papers that I get the feel of things, but it shook Ron!

On Saturday Laga and Clement came over for the evening. We had a very good dinner and they loved the house, Laga raving about the colour schemes. She was looking very elegant in a tailored bottle-green dress. They loved *To Catch a Thief* and Laga's horse laugh rang out. I felt proud to have them as our guests in the Club, and people noticed them – they stand out, with that attractive Bohemian air they have, which I love. They came back to the house for a nightcap and stayed till 1 o'clock! We all enjoyed the evening equally, and I felt that wonderful satisfied feeling of having spent time with real people, real friends. Laga lent me Nicholas Monsarrat's *The Tribe that Lost its Head*, a huge bestseller which I devoured on Sunday and finished on Monday. I cannot recommend it to you as you would hate it, but it is brilliantly clever and most ingeniously worked out. It is also gratifyingly pro-Colonial Service! There is something slightly second-rate about him which I cannot put my finger on. I got this same impression when I saw him on TV.

There is a Ball in aid of Hungarian Relief on Saturday. We have been asked to join Mr and Mrs Ingham's party – he is Secretary for African Affairs – we met them at Ruth's last tour. They are both charming. This morning I am going to coffee with Coralie Pincott, who lives quite near.

23rd January:

I am thinking of getting a phone installed. Already several people have said they had looked me up in the book and, not finding me there, left it at that, as they could not spare a boy to bring me a chit. I have not quite decided whether I might be better to remain slightly unget-at-able! I have just written a long letter to Joan, full of the Nyasaland gossip she dearly loves. If my letters to her ever burst open in the Post Office, I shall end up in court!

Almost imperceptibly we are getting more involved in Zomba life as the weeks go by. Last week after I wrote to you I walked along to have coffee with Coralie Pincott. It was a lovely morning and I enjoyed the touch of the blazing sun on my skin and the sudden coolness in the shade. Coralie was delighted to see me and we found lots to talk about, so much so that she walked me back.

On Friday we went down to the Club after tea, as usual, and visited the library. I got *The Petrov Story* which is badly written but interesting enough; and a book you would enjoy, *The Glitter and the Gold*, by Consuelo Vanderbilt, who was married off to the Duke of Marlborough when she was eighteen. I found it fascinating. At the Club we came across Barbara Firth, ensconced in a corner on her own, so we joined her for a drink and had a pleasant hour.

On Saturday morning Joyce Dickinson called in for a few minutes, looking enchantingly feline, as usual. I was glad to see her, though we have very little in common. In the evening we dressed up and went to the Inghams' party for the Hungarian Relief Ball. They live in the big house which we inhabited when we first came to Zomba, and it was strange to see it again – it seemed to have shrunk! I went along feeling rather half-hearted about the whole thing but it turned out to be a delightful evening, and all the men were good dancers. Sitting out a dance with John Ingham, I innocently asked him who the handsome man was, sitting across the room from us and he replied, 'My dear Ann, that is Sir Robert Armitage, you new Governor.' Thank goodness I found him handsome, otherwise I might have used a more pithy adjective! Lennox-Boyd, who is in Nyasaland on a visit, was not there, but his dashing wife Patricia was. She was a Guinness, married at nineteen and at the age of thirty-eight has a son of seventeen at Eton. The son, Simon, has been charming everyone, apparently, but has flown home, back to school! She looked startlingly like Ruth Simmonds, though less thin and highly strung, and she even spoke like her. She was wearing a rather odd blue ballet-length dress and had two red hibiscus flowers – real ones – fixed in her hair with a glittering diamond pin. To complete the outfit she wore *chunky* sapphires round her neck and wrists. Anyone else with this mixture would have looked a tramp, but she carried it off and looked splendid. The Ball collected over £200, which is very good, considering it was so soon after Christmas and New Year festivities.

We had Bruce and Jean Wickham for a drink on Monday evening. They are very nice and easy, and it was a relief to ask them at the last moment, without any fuss about dressing up.

I am gradually extending my menus. Yesterday I made delicious brandy snaps, only a quarter of an inch thick and adamant in their adherence to the baking tin, so Aflike and I scraped them off with knives and instead of brandy snaps with cream in them we had cream with brandy snaps in it and Ron said it was the best pudding he had tasted since we came back!

The weather is beautiful – hence my lifted spirits.

30th January:

Tonight we dine with the Wickhams and go to see Alec Guinness in *The Man in the White Suit*. I know it will be first class. I also know I shall not find it as funny as the English find it – I never do, though I know exactly when they are going to laugh!

The weather is suddenly horrible – damp and dark. I have just ordered a fish soufflé for lunch and will try once more to make these wretched brandy snaps. We get wonderful cream from one of the settlers' farms, but it arrives at unexpected times and I have to rush into the kitchen and make something to eat with it!

I wonder if you read of Kenneth Simmonds' appointment as Chief Secretary, Aden. Opinion here is it may be a way of marking time till our own CS retires in two years time and Kenneth makes a triumphant return.

At the library I pounced on Angus Wilson's *Anglo-Saxon Attitudes* and Rene Clair's *Reflections on the Cinema* and some others, so I came away with a light heart. In the evening we went to a big Sundowner at the CS's. I wore my off-the-shoulder black cotton and was shattered to find nearly all the women covered up. Dorothy kept me company with her usual plunging neckline! She is always very décolletée, even in the daytime. On Saturday evening Derek and Micky Barson came to dinner. They came out in 1949 and did one tour in the North and then he went into the Secretariat. They were kind to Ron when he was in the Hostel and it was high time I entertained them. We had a lovely evening and they did not leave till nearly midnight.

Eight people from Salisbury, members of a Fiscal Review, are coming to Zomba at the weekend and we are putting up one of them. Poor Ron will be on the go *all* weekend. On Sunday we have to attend a cocktail party which the Norman-Walkers are giving for them. Worse is to come! On Tuesday there is the ceremonial opening of the new Legislative Council (known as Leg Co, pronounced ledge-co) building by HE. Ron is a *train bearer* and I have received an official invitation to attend. As if that were not enough, we have been asked to proceed from there to GH for a sherry party from 11–12 noon. I shall be interested to meet the Armitages. It is just the bore of having to dress up and *wear a hat*. After all these trials are over I shall ask the Carlyles to come over and celebrate.

We have had one of the most tremendous nights of rain and thunder I can remember in Nyasaland. The storm seemed to sit over us all night and I am sure no one in Zomba got more than two hours sleep, if that. The morning now is simply wonderful, with mist and cloud gradually clearing to reveal more and more of that Godsent view. I have just heard the 8 o'clock news very clearly as the atmosphere has been well washed and the thunder gone.

We have a pair of squirrels who live in the jacaranda tree. They come onto the roof and in at the top ventilator window; they gaze down at me with bright, inquisitive eyes. I sit very still and they forget about me and talk to each other.

We have got through our dreaded programme and, as nearly always happens, it turned out to be an enjoyable experience. On Saturday early Ron went off to Chileka airport to meet the eight members of the Fiscal Commission and accompany them to Cholo and other places, while I spent a quiet day alone, grudging every moment of our weekend apart. He came back at six with our guest, a Mr Cawood, Southern Rhodesian, junior secretary to the Commission, with a thick accent we had difficulty with at first – as he definitely had with Ron's! All these chaps regard Nyasaland as a dear little anachronism – one of the last parochial outposts, where people still work for the Empire, not for the 'whites'. Ron was out with him all Sunday, except for lunch, having attended a meeting at GH in the morning (and met the Governor for the first time). After lunch here he drove some of the party up Zomba mountain. Two men were accompanied by their wives – Sir Jeremy Raicman, chairman (thirty years in IN-diah) and Professor Britnell, a charming Canadian – who gamely went everywhere with them. (*Why* could *I* not have gone up the mountain too?) In all, Ron drove over 300 miles. He and Mr Cawood came back with two forestry officers at six. I had not even had my bath, so vanished at high speed while Ron gave them a drink. At seven we all went to the Sundowner at the Norman-Walkers, where I met the other members of the Commission – all shrewd business men – and the two wives. It was *heavenly* to meet nice friendly people from the outside world and I enjoyed that party more than any other since we came back. The wives pounced on me and said they were thrilled with Ron as guide. The CS later thanked him for giving the guests such a pleasant tour. He also told him they had all said how well everything had been organised, which pleased him very much.

On Monday, a glorious morning, we went off to Chileka. I stayed discreetly in the background till Ron had got them all on board, then I went up into the lounge and onto the verandah to watch the aircraft take off. An airport is such a thrilling place, especially in the middle of Africa. My heart went up into the sky with that plane and then came down with a bump. We sat and blandly drank a tall glass of chilled beer at 9.30 in the morning, feeling very sophisticated and miles away from our usual world. On our way through Blantyre we collected the LP, *mended* at last, and tore back to Zomba. I sat glued to the player for the rest of the day – the records are simply splendid, especially the Vivaldi. It is wonderful to have music whenever I want it. Yesterday morning as I did the flowers, I put on a record of Chopin played by Cortot and really with the golden sunshine pouring in and the music pouring out, I felt quite lightheaded. With music, I can survive *anything*!

On Tuesday, another lovely morning, we dressed for the opening ceremony of the Legislative Council building (quite hideous, outside and in). Ron looked handsome and poised in his uniform, and the boys and their wives crooned when he walked out, dazzling, to the car, I following in my dear old green linen suit and my Italian straw hat. We got there at nine, I was taken to my place and Ron went off to some inner sanctum where his berobed Speaker awaited him. There were about seventy guests, the majority being the wives of officials, some settlers, missionaries and so on. It was all most impressive in timing, ceremony and atmosphere: HE sitting in a black uniform on a scarlet throne flanked by his two ADCs, and the four Speakers in wigs and gowns. Ron looked very tall and serious when he came in. He had to stand all through the ceremony with his helmet under one arm, and as soon as he took it off he looked about five years younger! There were some very good looking men on the Leg Co benches and of course the uniform is very flattering, so altogether it was a splendid sight. Afterwards we just had time to come home for Ron to change and drive us up to GH with a mass of other cars. The sherry party ended *exactly* at noon! We went into the big reception room with the minstrels' gallery. HE and his wife seem charming, very relaxed and friendly, with a kind of glamour about them. I drank tonic water with a dash of gin in it, as I could not face sherry in that heat. Some of the dresses and hats were so dull I felt quite bucked!

Yesterday morning I walked down to have coffee with Barbara Firth, who wanted to hear all about the Leg Co ceremony, and this morning I am going to Jean Wickham's, which I always enjoy very much. Next Tuesday Anne Bennett is coming to stay for a fortnight! You know I urged her that having come this far (Cape Town) she should take the opportunity to see as much of Africa as possible. Well, last week, having received a long, persuasive letter from me, she wired to say she would arrive at Chileka on Tuesday! I am delighted and so is Ron. I am now busy planning who she must meet and what we can manage to show her. She is full of life, interested in everything *and* an extrovert, thank goodness: just what I need just now!

13th February:

This letter will be a little disjointed, as Anne is sitting opposite me, also writing home, and we tend to stop and talk!

On Friday afternoon we collected more books at the Library, including Father Huddleston's desperately depressing *Naught for Your Comfort*. We stayed on to look at magazines and then joined Barbara Firth, who was alone, for a drink. I told her about Anne coming and she suggested we all went out to Chiradzulu one Sunday, a marvellous idea. She knows Charlie and Lorna Young, who are stationed there and will phone them to arrange it. On Saturday evening we went by ourselves to see *The Desperate Hours*, which was excellent. We had a quiet Sunday with lots of music. On Monday Diana Youens asked me to play bridge with her and two friends, so I walked round to her house, which looks right out over the plain to Mlanje and Lake Chirwa, rather like our view from Naisi, only from higher up. The friend who made up the four has gone on home leave, and Diana would like me to take her place, on Monday mornings. I think I will.

Yesterday Ron got most of the day off and we set out at 11.30 on a sizzling hot morning, and reached Chileka just as Anne stepped off the plane. It was wonderful to see her and we drove off talking hard, to Blantyre, where we had lunch at the Tavern. We then shopped and came back here, thankful to get away from the heat of the town. Anne is thrilled with everything – except the insects and creepy-crawlies. It is delightful for me to have such an enthusiastic companion. It puts me – and Aflike – on our mettle. We are giving our biggest party yet, twenty-one people, for her on Friday evening and I have filled both weekends. During the week I shall take her to pay several morning calls. The weather is glorious at present but of course one never knows how long it will last; and there is a rumour that the pool is to be re-opened, so I may at last get some colour again. It has been closed for some weeks, as there have been several cases of polio in Zomba.

19th February:

We are thoroughly enjoying Anne's visit. She likes everything – the climate, the view, the house, the boys, the food and all the entertainment we provide for her. It has done my morale as a hostess a world of good. Ron likes her enormously – she quickly learned that he can argue for three hours that black is white, and she gives as good as she gets, which amuses me! We have more in common than I thought on the ship; the same sense of humour and the same reactions to and views on Africa! She told me she only came up to see us because she was fascinated by what I had said and obviously *not* said about our life, when I spoke about it on the ship. So I opened up and told her a great deal more. It is *marvellous* for me to have someone of her mental calibre around, and it has been good for Ron too. She married four years ago. Her husband is a St. Andrews man, whose parents still live there. His name is Ian Bennett, he is thirty-six and first officer on the *Perthshire*, a Clan Line ship. His trips round Africa take three months, so she sees him three times a year for six weeks. Both her parents are dead and she lives in the old family house at Kilcreggan, and teaches French and German at schools within reach of home. It seems a strange life, but at least while her husband is 'on *ulendo*' she lives in her own home in her own country and has a satisfying job. She knows all the wealthy Clyde families and is mad keen on sailing.

We have been doing quite a lot! The day Anne arrived the weather cleared and it has been lovely until today, when it has rained on and off. We have been spending a lot of time at the newly opened and very clean pool. The result is we are both very blonde and brown and I feel magnificently recovered from those dreary weeks of dull weather, full of energy, which I need. We have had two library evenings at the Club. Anne saw HE come off the golf course and was most impressed by the look of him. I introduced her to Hugh Norman-Walker and they got on like a house on fire. She said something very sharp about the Stock Exchange and Hugh turned to me and said, 'Ann, bring your friend up to my house for a drink *now*. I want to hear more!' So we went up with Ron and had a drink. Ron and I sat back and watched Anne entertain Hugh. She is really making her mark on Zomba and of course I am so pleased, because she is a *Scot*!

We have had coffee twice with Barbara Firth, whose house is *en route* to the pool, and Jean Richardson, who is a sweet woman, is laying on a large morning party, so Anne will see a group of wives together, something I did not want to do myself! She is very much struck by the pallor of the women, their narrowness of outlook, their brusqueness with their servants – I am honourably exempted – and their conversation, which takes no account of a stranger and concentrates on local affairs. (You see how good she is for me – she reassures me that in my initial reactions I was *not* mad, as indeed Joan did too.)

On Friday I had a hectic day getting ready for our guests, of whom you will know by name the Inghams, the Kayes, the Watsons, the Richardsons, the Davidsons, the Dickinsons, the Pincotts, the Youens and the Wickhams. (I also had Ray Grindall for lunch. She teaches dancing over here every Friday and from now on will come to us for lunch. I am glad to be able to repay her kindness and hospitality.) Anne was a great help and together we prepared a thousand and one small eats. As she and I were standing in the doorway waiting for the guests to arrive, she suddenly said, 'Don't move,' seized a copy of the *Spectator*, folded it and took a great swipe at the skirt of my dress, where an enormous locust was clinging on a fold. It went hurtling out onto the *khonde* and flew away. It was so good of her to do it as she really loathes any insect of any size. The drawingroom was looking lovely and I was quite overwhelmed at the very appreciative comments. People now say to me, 'I hear you have a lovely house.' So it was worth all the effort and expense, and I feel they now see some expression of the real me when they come. Ron is very gratified that all his doubts were unfounded. The party was a tremendous success and Anne, as guest of honour, was simply wonderful, talking to everyone and obviously having a whale of a time. When it was over we settled amidst the debris and over sandwiches and coffee held a hilarious post mortem. All great fun. I always feel sick before my parties and wonderful afterwards!

On Saturday night we dressed up and went to see Alec Guinness in *The Lady Killers*. I knew I would not like it much, but I always enjoy watching him. Anne saw Zomba society in full regalia. HE and his party were there and the place was packed. On Sunday morning we drove up the mountain and all over it, in brilliant sunshine, except once when a cloud *below* suddenly sailed up over the edge and poured inland. making everything momentarily darken eerily. Anne treated us to lunch at the new Kuchawe Inn, built by Homer Cox, who retired two years ago from the Treasury. He and his South African wife have made a delightful little haven, right on the edge of the plateau, with a breathtaking view. After lunch the mist closed in on us and we went down on the 3.30 'clock' in pouring rain. In the evening we had a quiet time playing records. On Monday afternoon we went to the pool and had a drink with Ron when he came in late from the office. Now that his satisfying fiscal job is over, he is having an unpleasant time as a 'rover', that is, the odd jobs man. However, it widens his Secretariat experience.

I have had a very nice letter from Kenneth, who arrived in Aden on the 10th, having had to curtail his leave by three months. He is sad to leave Nyasaland but as usual full of interest in the next thing to be done. He had a sad leave, too, as his mother died just before Christmas and he left his father ill.

Next Sunday we are taking Barbara Firth and her children, with Anne, to Chiradzulu for lunch. I am praying for a good day, as I shall want to show Anne over that beautiful place. The old Boma is now a house for a PWD man. Ron designed the new one just before we left, so it will be interesting to see it. I am hoping to bring back some moonflower and honeysuckle cuttings.

21st February:

We have had a wonderful spell of sunny weather again after some rain last week. Anne has certainly seen and done a lot in her time here. On Thursday morning we went to coffee with Jean Richardson, who had invited some friends to meet Anne. It was very pleasant but the noise was terrific and we both left with splitting headaches. On Friday we went to the matinee of *On the Water-front*, with Marlon Brando. It was very good indeed, but too violent for my taste. On Saturday we pottered about in the house, as it rained all day, and in the evening went to the Wickhams' pre-dance party. I wore my old white Indian silk, which looks as good as ever. Anne, at least, had not seen it before! We found a nice collection of guests, as always, at the Wickhams, all the men good dancers. Jean had asked Bryn Jones-Walters, whose wife Chris is in England, as a partner for Anne, but he did not turn up. When we got to the Club, there he was in another party – he had completely forgotten and had accepted a later invitation! He was absolutely devastated, made profuse apologies to Jean and was charming to Anne. Of course Jean forgave him. We had a magnificent evening's dancing, with a perfectly danced eightsome made up from our party. The band left at two, and with our Chiradzulu outing in mind I tried to get us home, but someone put on the radiogram and before I knew where I was we were all back on the floor and it was 4.30 when I finally got us away! Anne had a lovely time and was never allowed to feel she was without a partner – Bruce saw to that.

We left for Chiradzulu, by an enormous effort of will, at 8.45, collected Barbara and one child (the other two were ill) and went off in high spirits. It was a heavenly day, with great clouds floating high over their shadows, hot sun and a cool breeze. Chiradzulu was wearing its look of paradise and I felt a *piercing* desire to be back there, which confused me, because I have learned to let go. The Youngs, who are two years junior to us, made us very welcome and simply told us to go ahead and show Anne everything, while they talked with Barbara, so we did. The house was unrecognisable, as Lorna Young has completely different taste from mine, and the garden looked a bit wild. We walked Anne all over the grounds and she was most impressed and interested. There are now three other houses built and occupied, so the character of the place has changed, but no one and nothing could change that divine view and Ron and I kept stealing out onto the *khonde* to feast our eyes. It was a tremendous pleasure to see everything again, but inevitably we came away with mixed feelings. I brought back moonflower, geranium and honeysuckle cuttings, which I put in at once. They all originated in my garden at Mlanje! My lovingly tended 'yesterday, today and tomorrow' bush had vanished, to my distress, but the moonflowers are now thriving bushes, so I have left something of myself there, which is lovely. By the end of our day Barbara looked a different person, the change had done her so much good.

On Monday Anne and I spent the morning in glorious sunshine at the pool and came back dark brown and nearly burnt! In the evening we went to drinks at the Inghams with whom Anne has friends in common in South Africa. So she saw the big house we lived in when we first came to Zomba. There were a lot of people and we all enjoyed it. Yesterday Anne and I were taken by Jean Richardson to have coffee at Joyce Dickinson's. She now lives in a modern bungalow on a new estate built at the opposite end of the mountain from Naisi. She has an electric kitchen and a very clean house, but I still prefer the old, cool, rambling bungalows, in spite of their disadvantages. In the afternoon we went to the pool, had tea at the Club and later changed to go and dine with the Norman-Walkers, who had a charming young American staying with them. It was a very enjoyable evening. Today Ron got the morning off and we took Anne to Chileka. She has loved being here and was very unwilling to go, and we felt really sorry to lose her, though it is nice to be on our own again. So I now withdraw into my rather isolated life, but I prefer it to uncongenial company, and I see enough of the nice people in Zomba. I am now going to start work in the garden. We took Aflike with us to the airport, his first visit, so he was very excited. Anne thinks he is a wonderful man. She left expressing a great respect for the people who run what is left of the Empire in this part of the world and we have at least achieved something in sending home an ardent ambassadress!

I am writing this after breakfast and will not finish before I go off to Blantyre for the day with Jean Wickham. I have not much money to spend, but am always glad to get away and she will be a good companion for the day. I went to my first Red Cross meeting last Thursday morning and was surprised to find that I quite enjoyed it. I feel now that I have been in Nyasaland long enough for my reputation, good or bad, to have been established in this gossipy place, so I just relax and get on with being myself. Friday was a lovely day and I put on records and did masses of things I had let slide while Anne was here. After having Ray Grindall for lunch I went down to the pool and swam steadily all afternoon, to get exercise. I am now so brown there is no fear of burning. I had tea in the Club, visited the library and watched the Zomba world go by till Ron came in, very tired but feeling sociable, so we stayed on for a drink and talked to a Mr and Mrs Carmichael, who play bridge with Ron. He is one of the four top players, they told me. They are ex-India tea planters and he has an obscure job in Medical Stores. She comes from Edinburgh and is very well read, as indeed is he. On Saturday evening we went to a buffet supper at the Pincotts – delicious food and good conversation. People came up to me and said what a marvellous girl my friend is. I must tell her when I write. We all left in pouring rain about 11.00 and Jean Wickham asked us back for coffee, so we were not in bed till after one. We had a lovely quiet Sunday and that evening went to see a devastating French film called *Les Jeux Interdits*, so harrowing it took me all Monday to recover from it.

On Monday morning I had my second bridge session, with the same people at Diana Youens' house. They are all nice, quiet women, older than I, and they do not gossip or make a noise, two things I cannot cope with just now!

I have had a happy day in Blantyre. Jean and I were both quite hoarse with talking when we got back. It was a hot day of radiant sunshine and the drive over and back was beautiful. I think I know that road by heart now. I love it. I hope when I am old I travel it in my dreams. We had a rather hasty lunch with the Baxters and at last saw the baby, a sweet wee thing, pretty and dainty. The Baxters were in good form.

I am off to the garden as it is a cool enough day to work outside. There are signs of the cold season – the mornings deliciously fresh and nose tingling.

13th March:

We have had tremendous rain every day in the afternoon recently, which has not done my moonflower cuttings any good. I am struggling with a lazy and inexperienced garden boy, who causes me much stress and strain. I find I just cannot bear any more with the African unreliability and fits of stupidity, and I get silent rages when things go wrong, especially in the house. The trouble is, they all show up so badly in comparison with Aflike. Enough of that.

The cold season is definitely on the way, and I am actually wearing a cardigan. I have always meant to say that the little long white cotton one from Paris that Jess gave me has been perfect and worn constantly – and always admired. I had it on over a white blouse and my black skirt one bleak day at the Club recently, and a woman I hardly know came up to me in the library and said, 'I love your outfit. You always look straight out of Vogue.' (Shades of Ruth!) I am hoping for a few more days at the pool, but the weather is rather uncertain. There is a lot of illness about, especially among the children – there always is at this time of year.

On Saturday morning I had a visit from Joan Weir, the wife of Norton Weir, a very nice doctor whom we met in Mlanje when he did locum for Sandy Holmes. He is a charming man and a first class doctor, so everyone is thankful to see him back. I have asked them to come to the Golf Ball, which takes place in about a month's time. I have also asked Alex and Bunny Davidson (new people from the Solomons whom we met at the Richardsons) and Bryn and Chris Jones-Walters whom we have known since we come out here and like very much. In the evening we asked Jean and Bruce for an informal supper and music. They brought up some lovely LPs, mainly tangos, so we spent the evening dancing on our *khonde*, which is ideal, as it is smooth and polished. They are as mad about dancing as we are. They left about two and we staggered to bed.

On Sunday two stenographers who live in the Hostel came to lunch. They are both very musical and used to play their records to Ron and were generally very good to him when he lived there. One of them was rather nice, with good manners and she left at three. The other, though intelligent and interesting enough, had bad manners and stayed till 6.30, having come at 10.30. (I was *wilting*.) She was very taken up with her host but showed no interest *at all* in her hostess, who decided fairly early on she would not be invited to this house again! On Monday morning I had our bridge four here, which we all enjoyed.

20th March:

Today I am in slacks for warmth for the first time. It is a dull, chilly morning – as it happens, the morning I decided to try a new recipe for icecream! I have the cream, so we shall just have to freeze over it at lunch.

I had my usual Red Cross morning last week; not many there, so rather nice. Friday was a lovely day and I had a peaceful afternoon by myself at the pool, water pretty cold. On Saturday morning I went to coffee with a charming woman called Stella Bowden, wife of a Major in the KAR. We met them at the Inghams and she and I instantly liked each other. It was interesting to see the Army set-up. She had three KAR wives to meet me, all very well turned out but oh, so bored and discontented with their life in Zomba. I came home, sat down and very firmly counted my blessings! Sunday was another lovely day and I actually got Ron down to the pool in the morning before hordes of people arrived. In the early evening I was in the bath when to my astonishment I heard the unmistakable voice of *Iris* in the drawingroom. Ron had had tea in bed and was still lazing about in his dressing-gown. He sounded rather put out, so I whizzed into my kimono and went through, to find her with two friends who had brought her from Blantyre. She had flown down from Lilongwe to have some dentistry done. She was looking wonderfully vivid and well; her hair in front has gone almost white and looks most attractive against her brown face. She and I just sat and talked without a single pause for breath, for almost an hour. She was so thrilled to see us and left very wistfully, dear Iris. We had a terrific rush to get dressed and go to the Wickhams for supper and the Sunday French film. We had a wonderful evening. It was Jean Cocteau's *Les Enfants Terribles*, an extremely odd, avant-garde and rather horrible story about a brother and sister, but I adored it. The music, extraordinarily unexpected, but perfect for it, was my favourite Bach, the concerto for four pianos. I came out absolutely quivering with enjoyment and was glad to find the others had also been enthralled.

On Monday, a beautiful day, I walked, quickly, to get warm, to Diana's for bridge. I like going there. Her drawingroom is restful and the view glorious. Today I have the whole morning to myself and I am glad. I am getting the garden into order gradually and also, I want to try out a new dish – Viennese stuffed potatoes, my French book calls it! So.

27th March:

We have had quite a sociable week. On Thursday we went to dine with Gwenda and Peter Long. (She is a West Indian from Jamaica and he is a nice big Englishman in the Police.) They played us a lot of *The Messiah*, which was lovely. We now wonder how we ever survived without our music and we play something every day. I am sure it is the main reason why I am settling down. I just wish Aunt Isabel could have known what a blessing it is.

On Friday afternoon I went down to the Club at 1.30 to be sure of getting tickets for this Saturday's film, *Richard III*. The booking did not open till 4 o'clock, but having asked four people, I wanted to ensure I would get good seats. There were about fifteen wives with the same idea, but fortunately I was second in the 'queue', which was in fact a piece of paper on which we wrote our names as we arrived. I passed the time by playing bridge with two of the best players in Zomba and another woman not as good as I. After a few minutes of nerves I settled down and thoroughly enjoyed myself. (I was lucky, I had very good cards.) I then had tea with Barbara Firth, who came in just after I had booked the seats. Then Ron came in with the Wickhams and after a drink they came back with us for some music, bringing their fish soufflé in a pyrex dish while we ate our own fish and chips supper! It was the kind of informal evening we all enjoy. They are delightful people and are becoming real friends. They do something for us which Kenneth and Ruth did – make us feel we can relax and be absolutely ourselves, which of course is one of the conditions of friendship. They both have degrees. I read a marvellous remark the other day, in the *Observer*, which fitted in precisely with my own feeling about having a degree *out here.* 'Degrees are like false teeth. You do not like to admit that you have them, but would hate to be without them!' On Saturday night we dined with Bryn and Chris Jones-Walters, and found Norton and Joan Weir there. We had a very friendly, relaxed evening and saw a slight but pleasant American film called *All That Heaven Allows*, which everyone had mixed up with *All This and Heaven Too*, a very different matter! We went back for coffee afterwards and listened to *Swan Lake* on Bryn's beautiful LP.

On Sunday we had a late breakfast and a lazy day, recovering from three late nights last week. On Monday I had my usual escapist morning, deep in bridge. It is so nice, and gets more so as we get to know each other better, both socially and as bridge players. Last night we had to go to a Sundowner at GH. It was quite an experience, as we knew hardly anyone. The new Governor and his lady are very multiracially-minded and mix us all up together – Africans, Indians and British – which was barely attempted in the previous regime.

This morning Barbara Firth at last made the journey up to see me. She blossoms when away from her own household and I enjoyed having her. We sat out on the *khonde* – she has no view – and I put on my Chopin record. She was in raptures.

3rd April:

Ron listened to the Boat Race at the Wickhams and said it was a most exciting race. Our wireless battery was finished – and *my* battery so low that I chose to go to bed and have a good sleep!

On Thursday evening the Wickhams gave a huge cocktail party for thirty-two people. We went down early and while Ron played with Jonathan, aged four, in a dressing-gown, I helped Jean arrange hundreds of patsy-go-lows on plates. It takes ages to do it artistically, but is worth the trouble. It was a very good party, despite the fact that the guests were not chosen as a congenial mixture, but were mostly people whom they had to have and would not have again. (This is when entertaining becomes nonsense and a waste of time.) We had been invited to stay on for a scrambled eggs supper and we had to wait till 9.30 to get it, as there was the inevitable hard core who would not leave. When they did, we sat down and ravenously ate plates of scrambled eggs on our knees and supper was over in about five minutes! Then Bruce got out his collection of dance music and we danced till midnight.

On Saturday I had a busy day preparing for a dinner party. I made a magnificent chocolate mousse from a recipe Laga gave me – my first attempt, which was risky but all was well. Our guests were the Wickhams and the Carmichaels, Ron's bridge partners. The film was *Richard III* and the Club was festive with excitement. It was fun to be the hostess and see one's guests replete with pleasure. We stayed on for a drink afterwards, just to watch the big parties and hear the comments. Next day I was exhausted after the strain of entertaining during Ramadan, when it is a struggle to get any sense out of the boys. Aflike copes, but in an average-witted boy like Lajeb, disasters lurk. This morning at breakfast Ron asked Lajeb for his table napkin and Lajeb carefully brought in a slice of lemon on a plate – tableau! Poor Jean is giving a dinner party tonight for their tenth wedding anniversary. This morning we sent down a bottle of champagne and I wrote a poem, a parody of 'Drink to me only'. Ron thinks it is very clever. (So do I!)

10th April:

The Wickhams' party was terrific, though it got off to a shaky start, as the lights failed throughout Zomba just as we were all getting bathed and dressed. We had an excellent dinner and then danced to their jazz records. The other guests were Bryn and Chris, and a Mr and Mrs King (Legal Department) who have come from Hong Kong. We were persuaded to stay on after the others left and danced till three! Next morning I staggered up to get things ready for the Red Cross people, who were coming to my house of course, just when I would have given anything for a quiet morning. However, I survived. On Friday afternoon I went down to the pool with Joan Weir and her two nice children. I swam a lot and completely restored my sun tan and energy – good. The water will soon be very cold indeed. In the evening we went down to the Club after supper to see *The Trouble with Harry*. On Saturday I never came to rest till 6.00 p.m., as I had my Golf Ball party to prepare for. As the month of Ramadan progresses, domestic arrangements falter and I just never stopped. I can see why some hostesses refuse to entertain. I wore my sea-green chiffon which looked good against my dark brown skin. We had the Jones-Walters, the Weirs and the Davidsons, a highly successful mixture, as it turned out. We had a buffet supper with a hot middle course, because most men, I find, dislike cold meals, and went on to the Club where I had booked a table. All the men dance well and all are good talkers, so I was in heaven! The evening went so quickly it was 3 o'clock before we knew where we were. It was the first time this tour we had made up our own party for dinner and a dance, and I think everyone enjoyed themselves.

On Sunday evening, after a day of torrential rain, we went to dine with the Weirs, where we met the new surgeon and his wife – very charming, intelligent South African Jews, and very pro-British, which was a relief. We went to the Club to see Jacque Tati in *Monsieur Hulot's Holiday*. It was simply delectable, and achingly funny. There was no dialogue except in the background among groups, and no close-ups. What a clever man.

17th April:

I had a letter from Rosemary Landreth the other day. They are on leave and simply loving it. She is thrilled with the early spring. She does not know how she will face coming back. They have been posted to Mlanje, poor things. She does not know what is in store and I certainly shall not tell her.

I am writing this at high speed, as I suddenly realised it should go off this morning, as the long holiday, Friday to Monday, will bring everything to a standstill. I am going shopping shortly with Jean Wickham. It is a fearful morning of pelting rain with thick white cloud sitting on the mountain – visibility about ten yards! I have on my grey skirt and a blouse and am thinking of adding a cardigan. It is not really cold yet, but the mornings and evenings definitely feel, and smell, different.

On Saturday evening we were invited to the Wickhams for a haggis dinner and a quiet evening. Ron borrowed a kilt and I wore my long red tartan scarf as a stole. Down we went, to find both of them in kilts – Bruce looking too Scottish for words! Jean's maiden name is Sharrer, and her grandparents were Orcadians. We duly ate the haggis, to the accompaniment of Jimmy Shand's band on an LP, so nostalgic I could hardly eat. Then we got on to other music and in no time the furniture was pushed back, our shoes were off, and we settled down to dance. I have never before met a couple who equally share my passion, and of course it infects Ron. We are having a quiet week. Ron is working terribly hard at the moment and is rather piano, but seems to find his second wind at the weekend!

24th April:

Here excitement mounts as the Queen Mother's visit approaches. As you can imagine, the preparations for such an event are on a colossal scale. I hate all the scheming and clothes talk that is going on, but I shall certainly be thrilled to see her.

We had a very pleasant Easter. The weather was poor, as it often is, and we were happy to laze about and read, though Ron went to the office on Friday morning. The Wickhams came up after dinner and we played some of my records and we introduced them to Scrabble, which they enjoyed. On Saturday evening they came for dinner – I gave them duck, the only thing left on my menus they had not eaten! I had a bottle of very good French wine to go with it and we were bubbling with high spirits by the time we arrived at the Club for an informal dance which turned out to be a great success, though a lot of people were away on holiday. In the bar I met Peter Delapasteur, the charming planter from Mlanje. He had just crashed his nice Citroen, travelling at 80 m.p.h. when a tyre burst and the car dived over three times 'like a dolphin' he said. He survived *and* climbed out of the car, though when he got to hospital they found that his back was broken. He looked a trifle fine-drawn but was as quick and courtly as ever. On Sunday we slept late and were only just up when Bruce called in to say we must go down to them at once as Jean had decided to open the champagne we gave them, so down we eventually went and had a splendid treat of champagne and caviare! They have a gift for turning any occasion into a celebration. We had had breakfast at 11.30, so we skipped lunch and had tea with them.

On Monday we went off to the Baxters in time for elevenses. They are both looking better than they did last tour, though neither looks really healthy. It was lovely to see them again and we had a very light-hearted day. Margaret is very much absorbed with the child; David, to my surprise, not so, though clearly he adores her. He kept harping back to 'the good old days'. It is plain to me that he and Ron are now poles apart, in many ways, though still the best of friends. They both thought I was looking *so* much better than last tour and kept saying how well and bright I was: that should cheer you.

2nd May:

I must remember to tell you, Ron came back from the office the other day, very fed up, and said, 'God, I wish I could go off to the estuary with Jess and birdwatch.' It is unusual for him to be nostalgic for home, but in fact I notice he does it more and more – rather nice!

The cold season will soon be upon us, though the sun is still hot, and for the last two mornings I have gone down to the pool with Joan Weir and her two children, who are on holiday. The water is freezing, but I feel wonderful afterwards, and of course I am blooming and full of energy. Joan is learning to drive and Norton has offered to teach me as well; I said I would think about it but *of course* I shall accept. Ron says it is an excellent idea. I cannot imagine Norton as a very patient man, but we get on very well indeed and pride concentrates the mind wonderfully!

Yesterday Jim Reeve, one of the senior DCs and a friend from Chiradzulu days, came to dine, with the Wickhams, whom he has known for years. After dinner the three men and I played bridge, while Jean watched. It was first class bridge, and Ron was absolutely thrilled at my play, and slightly taken aback, as I was his opponent. At 12.30 they all left and there was I, bright as a button, and Ron dead tired. In the end he put a pillow over my face to stop me talking!

8th May:

The cold season is suddenly very much with us and I am sitting by our first fire in this house, clad in my Gor-ray skirt, navy blue twinset, stockings and the big tartan scarf wound round me. Needless to say, I am still cold! Our view gets better and better as the atmosphere clears, and Mlanje seems to have moved inches nearer during the night. The garden is depressing me, as the soil is really finished and things just will not grow except for my indomitable moonflowers and geraniums. I am now cherishing a gardenia slip which Jean Wickham gave me. She is incredibly kind and thoughtful. She calls in for me by car when there are apples or melons to be had in the shops, which I never know about, and yesterday, in pouring rain, she came up just before 10.00 to drive me down to Barbara Firth, as she knew I would get soaked, walking down.

Last Thursday, after tea, Joan Weir arrived to say Norton was taking her out to the airfield for a driving lesson and would I like to come? Out I went, horribly nervous, but all went well and he was an angel of patience. Joan went for a walk while I had my lesson, then I did the same while she had hers. I had another lesson on Monday, which went well. My difficulty is that I have *no* confidence at all. Norton's car is a Ford Consul, smaller than our great hulking brute, but with the same gears. It is amazing how much more alive I feel because I have the prospect of learning one more skill, and doing it well, or rather being determined to do it well.

Friday was a glorious day, the last we have had, and in the morning I walked down to have coffee with Chris Jones-Walters, whom I like very much indeed, though we are apt to upset each other as we both long for home and worry about our mothers. In the afternoon I went down to the pool with Joan Weir and had a marvellous roast in the sun – water simply freezing. We had a quiet evening's music on Saturday as the film was rubbish, and on Sunday evening went with the Wickhams to an excellent French film called *Marchandes d'illusions*. It was based on fact, and was about the work of a welfare worker among the prostitutes of Paris – very strong meat, which left us all a little exhausted. On Monday I had my happy three hours' bridge. Though I say it myself, I am now streets ahead of the other three. They are such nice women and I get interesting little glimpses into their lives as we talk at our coffee break. (I have the Vivaldi playing joyously on this grey morning.)

Ramadan is over, so I can breathe more freely, though I have decided Lajeb must go, as he is bone lazy and makes no effort to improve. It is so stupid of him, as he could have learned so much from Aflike and me, and fitted in to this peaceful household. I seem doomed never to find anyone one hundreth part as good as his father. He and I dislike the cold and both shrink visibly!

15th May:

On Friday afternoon Norton appeared, without his wife, and after paying a professional call at one of the estates, took me out to the airfield where I did so well he told me to drive back to Zomba, which I did. He is delighted with my progress. I gave a dinner party in the evening for the Richardsons and a very nice, quiet South African couple, John and Jean Kenan. She was brought up on an isolated farm and did not travel on a train till she was seventeen when she left home to go to university. The Richardsons are English and very sophisticated. It gave me great pleasure to bring these two couples together at my dinner table, so far apart they could have lived on different planets! We went on to see *The End of the Affair*, which was excellent. On Saturday evening we dressed up and went to dine with the Wickhams, where we were joined by the Weirs and a young couple in PWD. We had a marvellous dinner, as always, and a terrific evening's dancing at the Club, with *three* eightsomes made up by our party. We left about three and went back to the Wickhams, where I saw the astonishing spectacle of Ron producing the most delicious scrambled eggs for eight people! You would have thought he had prepared a twelve course dinner, he was so pleased with himself.

The weather is really cold now, but as long as the sun shines it is bearable. The bad days are the *chiperoni* days when the mist is down and the damp seems to enter one's bones – actually in my case it attacks the small of my back, my weak spot. Last week *both* my wrists were creaking with rheumatism. In spite of these signs of age, Ron tells me that I have never looked better. (But he never saw me when I was three, did he?)

22nd May:

Today is another in a succession of frightfully depressing days – mist, rain, chill, and the constant sound of water from the trees dripping on the roof.

I got my provisional licence yesterday and am to drive on the main road, whenever Norton can get away. He is very strict with me now and on the odd occasion we both get red in the face, but no temper has been lost yet. (Ron takes no interest, or pretends to take no interest. I think he is secretly unwilling to share the car with me, which is just *too bad*. Ron has never realised how much effort and planning – all without a car or telephone – go into our life.)

On Friday evening we went to dine with a Mr and Mrs Hugh Watson (ex-India) who play bridge with Ron. Also there was another ex-India couple, quite elderly. Ron and I had an amusing evening playing the roles of ingénues, as our ages were obviously wildly underestimated. As a matter of fact we enjoyed it very much and so did the dear old boy I entertained, while Ron sent his wife into fits of girlish laughter. The film was *The Man Who Knew Too Much*, not one of Hitchcock's best. On Sunday we watched cricket in the morning and in the evening went to see *Il Travatore*, done by the Rome Opera Company – heavenly singing but a very bad film.

30th May:

I am thrilled to hear that Anne and Ian Bennett paid you a visit. She is one of the nicest people I have ever met. It was quite a test to have her, whom we hardly knew, for a fortnight, and she stood up to it nobly.

Last week we had a lovely long weekend, with the Empire Day holiday on Friday. I was feeling very tired – I think it is the cold weather – but was persuaded by the Wickhams to join them on Friday for a picnic on the mountain. It was a lovely day and I was thankful that I went. The sun was hot and a wild wind was rippling the long golden grasses. We sheltered by some flat, warm rocks and Jean and I spread out a magnificent feast while the men took the two children bird watching. (Jonathan is four, David sixteen months!) I just lay down and let the warmth soak into me. By the time we left my face and limbs were glowing nicely. In the evening we went to a rather highly coloured but fascinating film called *The Naked Jungle*, about the ants which march across certain parts of Africa (not here!) and South America, literally eating everything in their path – human, animal and vegetation. On Saturday night we went to see *The Inspector Calls* done by the Zomba Dramatic Society, a rather dreary play very well performed, its last two minutes enlivened by the fact that the leading man, a young KAR officer who had been thrown from his horse the day before, fainted right in the middle of the stage, whole six feet three of him, gradually subsiding along the length of a sideboard he was leaning on because he felt ill. With him were swept some glasses and silver candlesticks belonging to the Norman-Walkers. The curtain came down, he was removed and they finished the play!

On Sunday we went to a curry lunch at the Wickhams to meet a friend of theirs from the North, a charming Highlander called Lorrie Bain. We had a marvellous curry with ten side dishes of garnish, including pickled limes and prunes in gin. (Jean was born in Kenya.) We stayed on for tea, as the Baxters were coming, and they turned up an hour late, with cot, carry-cot, pots and pans, blankets, toys – what paraphernalia. David is in Zomba for a week doing a course of some kind. Last night I had them, the Wickhams and Lorrie Bain for dinner and the cinema – *The Grace Moore Story*. I had been feeling awful all day, shaky and sick, and I received them in my dressing gown, as I intended going to bed as soon as I had given them dinner. Bruce, however, would not hear of this, saying firmly I only needed some sympathetic company and I would be all right. He is so sweet and kind. He just took over, sent Ron for brandy, insisted I eat dinner, then wrapped me in a rug (after I had got dressed) and bore me down to the Club! Well, it worked, though I sat in an aisle seat in case I had to dash.

I shall be better next week and able to write a less distrait letter! I am really hating the cold.

5th June:

I had a driving lesson today and Norton said I was coming on very well, though he wondered aloud when I was having difficulty with double-declutching if perhaps my co-ordination was not very good. (I pride myself on my co-ordination and was seething inwardly.) So, we stopped the car and he put me through two tests – patting my head with one hand and rubbing my chest with the other; then patting one knee with one hand and rubbing the other in a circular movement. I simply did both exercises as if I were doing something

I did a hundred times a day, and he was stunned. After that there was no more talk of unco-ordinated movements! (Ron could not get either of them right!)

On Friday morning Margaret Baxter came for a coffee and was thrilled to have a talk with me alone. She seems to look on me as a great friend, which is nice. In the afternoon I *drove* to the Club with Norton to change library books, then drove us back to the house. After supper the Wickhams came up for an hour, mainly to see if I was really better.

On Sunday I was fairly busy preparing for a small dinner party I was giving for Barbara Firth, having persuaded her that between them Ron and Bruce could cope with her chair. At about 5.30 she sent up a chit to say she had a bad cold and could not decide whether to come or not and would I go down and have a drink with her while she decided what to do. Of course I could not go at that hour – I had not even bathed and dressed – so I had to send a chit back saying I would expect her. However, she did not come.

The weather has settled for the moment to heavenly days of hot sun and cold wind. I feel a different person without the damp gnawing into me. Tonight the Weirs are coming to supper and Norton has his first bridge lesson. I have asked Joan to send out an LP of Chopin's 2nd piano concerto as a present to Norton for the driving lessons.

13th June:

I am sorry I am a day late with my letter. I had a last-minute invitation from Jean to go to Blantyre yesterday and of course today is a holiday. It is a bleak day, and Ron has just left, at 9.00 a.m., dressed in uniform, to act as an usher at the Club where there is the Trooping the Colours. Ironically, the first time I want to go, and have the right clothes (my spring suit), I am not to be there. The ceremony begins at 10.00 a.m., and Ron has to be there at 9.00 a.m. I flatly refuse to go down with him and freeze for an hour – gone are the days when I meekly accept my fate as a junior wife, hanging about while her husband fulfils some menial task. Tonight there is a huge cocktail party at the KAR Mess, so my holiday will not be too flat.

Yes, I am feeling the cold here more than at Chiradzulu, for a very simple reason – firewood in Zomba is expensive and I try to be economical with it. At Chiradzulu it cost us nothing and I could have fires all day and night. Also, this is a very cold house, as it has so many windows and communicating doors.

Ron is terribly overworked and tired, but I am hoping that after the Queen Mother's visit he will be less hard-pressed. For the first time ever he has not been easy to live with – sheer exhaustion, both physical and mental. However, he realised he was being difficult and is better now, poor man. The work demanded of the Assistant Secretaries is quite unbelievable.

My driving lessons will soon be over. I could easily pass the test in Norton's Ford Consul, but I have had to face our big Velox. I went out for an hour with

Norton yesterday and came back soaked in sweat and absolutely drained. No one can know the agonies of the unmechanically-minded, especially if there is an utter lack of a sense of direction and of visual memory thrown in for good measure.

On Saturday evening we went to the Red Cross Ball in the Jones-Walters' party. The Weirs were there and two couples we hardly know. Chris had a huge fire going in the drawingroom and we ate our delicious buffet dinner gathered round it. We had a great evening, very lively and happy, but the beastly cold got at me and we were actually the first to leave – an unheard of occurrence with the Hitchcocks. I wonder if I am run down.

On Sunday there was a cricket match and we watched all day, well wrapped up, with Bruce and Jonathan. Jean was packing. They go on leave next month. On Thursday evening we went to dine and play bridge with the new surgeon and his wife, Bertie and Berry Hammar; both simply charming, bursting with brains and intelligence. I was not nervous at all and loved the whole evening.

Yesterday Jean and I had a lovely day in Blantyre, I spending very little, by sheer will power – the shops are bulging with pretty things for the Queen Mother's visit. We lunched at the Baxters. David had a bad cold and was very piano, Margaret cheerful, the baby delicious.

I have a dinner party for seven coming up on Saturday, but as none of them has dined with us before, I can give them my standard dinner menu which goes like clockwork – famous last words.

19th June:

I am feeling far more cheerful, mainly because of the weather, which thank goodness is glorious – flawless blue sky, hot sun, though cold indoors.

We had a lovely party at the KAR Mess on Empire Day. They always do things in great style. I roamed about and talked to all sorts of people, including John and Dorothy, both flourishing. They are enjoying living in Blantyre. We went back to the Wickhams for a scrambled egg supper. Jean has an electric stove in her kitchen, which is within the house, so she can cook the odd meal herself and send the boys away, a thing I long to be able to do. I would willingly cook supper every night and have some privacy.

I have at last got the feel of the Velox and must arrange to go to Blantyre soon to take my test. We went out yesterday after tea and I drove Norton to an estate he had to visit. It was a golden day and we had a happy time. I love getting away from Zomba and Norton and I enjoy each other. I intend to use the car as much as I can instead of sitting incarcerated here sending out chits and waiting for people to come and give me a lift. I hate being obliged and besides, it sometimes means I have to get more involved with people's lives than I care to be. My next achievement must be to have the telephone installed. I did not mind at the beginning but now feel it would be an advantage. Ron is not keen, as he does not want to be made too available!

We spent Sunday with the Wickhams, eating a magnificent curry lunch to mark the last Sunday they would be able to entertain, as they are now in the midst of packing. In the evening we all went to a French film, *Souvenirs Perdus*, scrappy but beautifully done, with the exquisite Edwige Feuillère – my first sight of her. On Monday I had my blessed morning bridge and in the afternoon played tennis with Joan Weir and two others. We are thinking of making it a regular arrangement. It was a lovely day and I got some sun into me.

26th June:

I am sure you will be delighted to hear that my ability to cope absolutely with the car just came, completely suddenly, yesterday. Norton made me do everything possible in the most difficult circumstances, even in the dark, and I did them all, calmly and competently. We were so elated we nearly ditched the car on the way back, we were talking and laughing so much. The examiner does not come to Zomba again till November, so that means Blantyre. I met Joyce Gourlay the other day, who told me she had just passed her test and that the examiner is a dear old boy, whom I have discovered I once lunched with at the Baxters.

Ron should be less overworked after the Queen Mother's visit – now referred to by everyone as simply the Visit – as he will be dealing with one section instead of two, but it will be new to him and is a hard worked section, African Affairs. He is actually taking over from Bruce now. He will work under John Ingham, one of the best liked men in the Secretariat.

I have something exciting to tell you so will not bother with our social activities, which were very much the same as usual, except that we went up the mountain for an all day picnic with the Wickhams on Sunday and had a glorious relaxing day in hot sunshine. We all looked and felt marvellous when we came down.

A few days ago Ron came back from the office about six, looking slightly secretive and nervous. He sat us both down with a drink, told me to keep calm and listen carefully. He had just been approached by Jock Corrie, ADC to the Governor, who asked him if I would be willing to act as hostess to two members of the Queen Mother's entourage: her private secretary (a woman) and the Clerk Comptroller of the Household (a man). Well, I nearly choked on my drink and started making squeaks of protest, but Ron pressed on. Jock would arrange that we would move from this small house into a much bigger one (always allocated to the Attorney General, who has just retired and not yet been replaced) and stay there for the duration of the Visit. The house is furnished, of course, with PWD furniture and I would take my own linen, china, glass, cutlery and kitchen equipment. Jock said I could spend as much as I wanted on food, drink and cigarettes, and simply present him with the bills. It is quite a challenge and I knew I was going to agree even before Ron stopped speaking. Besides, it would be positively shaming to refuse. Ron was jubilant and delighted with me. So, another new experience to be dealt with, and fun, I hope!

2nd July:

The weather continues to be glorious and my spirits therefore continue high. I am playing a lot of tennis and that helps too.

I am spending the whole day in Blantyre tomorrow. I have been provided with a Government car (a *Humber*) and a driver, to do shopping for my English guests. I have an enormous list, which continues to grow as I think of another item. It will take hours to get through it. I have offered Joan Weir a seat in the car. She is very practical and will be a help. We are to lunch with the Baxters.

We have seen over the big house, which is a bit grim, though it could be lovely. There are hundreds of roses in the garden, so I shall be able to brighten it up a bit. We will sleep in a little guest house which is attached to the house, and our two guests will have a big bedroom and bathroom each, at opposite ends of the house *upstairs*! (Apart from Government House, there is only one other house in Zomba that has two storeys.) I have decided to take pictures, ornaments, lamps, books and the Black Box, to humanise the drawingroom. At the moment I want it to be over, but it may be fun.

Tomorrow I am going to buy some plain linen and make up my Vogue dress pattern. Barbara Firth has offered me her machine.

10th July: At the big house

The weather is perfect and everyone is praying it will hold. It is cold in the house but the sun blazes outside and the sky is a blinding blue. I can just stand the glare on this paper with my dark glasses on. I have bought a vast pile of firewood, so our guests will be warm. I am sitting out on the side *khonde* drying my hair and looking out on a most lovely garden, now overgrown but still sweet with roses, carnations and peach blossom. A garden boy is burning leaves and I am suffering waves of homesickness! I have *so much* on my mind I could scream, and like everyone else in Zomba will be glad when it is Monday morning.

Here we have been having quite a time. My shopping in Blantyre was a great success and I even managed to have my hair trimmed and thinned. We had lunch with the Baxters, who were in good form. I bought some beautiful material for a wedding coming up in August – powder blue, dull grosgrain, a very sophisticated texture. I bought it in utter defiance of Ron's taste, but to my surprise and pleasure he said it was lovely!

On Friday morning Jean and Bruce called in, took me shopping and came in at lunch time for a farewell drink. They are staying for their last two nights with the Kings (Legal Department). There is a very big blank left by their departure, but at the moment I am too busy to notice it. I have 'borrowed' Jean's old cook and two house boys to help Aflike over the weekend. He, of course, is very excited and very much on his mettle. On Monday by a marathon effort we moved in here and I had everything unpacked by evening. I was nearly dead with exhaustion and so depressed at the rather bitty appearance of what could be a lovely house. However, it is wonderful what one can do with flowers, ornaments and a change around of furniture. The bathrooms are *heavenly* and now smell of expensive soap! When I finish this I am going to settle down and write out every menu in minute detail, and also make out a last shopping list to be done in Zomba. Our guests arrive at teatime on Friday.

17th July:

What a relief it will be for me to put down in this letter the details of what has been a most glorious experience for us, and for everyone else, including, by all accounts, the royal household.

When I wrote to you last week I was feeling rather down about our house, but by the time I had everything ready it really looked very nice indeed. I had four tall black candles in silver candlesticks (some borrowing had to be done!) and four jade ones in my own ebony candlesticks on the oval diningroom table, which transformed the room, especially at night. Aflike and I had several conferences over the last few days and we both had everything at our fingertips – not a single moment of panic. The weather remained perfect throughout the Visit – hot, with a slight breeze and not a cloud in the brilliant cobalt blue sky. Zomba looked like paradise, with all the blossom out, everything spotless, white paint everywhere, banners and flags flying gaily. Our guests arrived about 4.30 on Friday: the Clerk Comptroller, a Mr Wickers, about forty, a most charming man who spoke *exactly* like Ralph Richardson, and the Queen Mother's private secretary, Miss Dunlop, about thirty-six, born in London but a Scot. She was plain and yet attractive – what the French call a *jolie laide*, and had great charm and warmth of personality. In voice and manner she reminded me poignantly of Aunt Isabel. They were thrilled with everything from beginning to end, as apparently were the Queen Mother and all the staff. The equerries and ladies-in-waiting stayed at GH, and the valet and hairdresser were put up by our local dentist and his wife. The Rhodesias had not had the same atmosphere and the arrangements for the staff had not been so good. Mary Dunlop just relaxed at once and we became friends very quickly. Mr Wickers, though very easy, was less intimate with us because he was in charge of the Household and had constant telephone calls and queries to attend to, so that he felt himself on duty all the time. They went down to work at GH after tea and again after dinner that night, coming back about midnight. I left out a tray of drinks, a thermos of coffee and sandwiches. They were unfailingly appreciative of small details like that.

On Saturday Mr Wickers worked all day, but Mary, to her delight, was free to come with me to the huge *baraza* (the African equivalent of an Indian *durbar*) held in the grounds of the Club. She has worked in the Household only two years, (formerly with the Duchess of Kent) and has not been on an overseas tour before. Mr Wickers has been on every tour for the last twelve years. Ron was ushering, so he left early; Mary and I were later swept down in one of the royal cars with its standard fluttering on the bonnet. We had excellent seats in the second front row. The entire population of Zomba, black and white, seemed to have turned out. The playing fields in front of the Club were lined with hundreds and hundreds of Africans, all dressed in their bright cottons and wild with anticipation. A dais with a canopy had been placed by the Club steps and facing this were rows and rows of chairs, occupied by all the DCs (wearing their immaculate white uniforms) in the territory, along with all the chiefs of every district. (Imagine the organisation required to achieve this!) The Queen Mother and the Governor sat on the dais, flanked by the three PCs. I saw people I had not seen for years, and picked out some of the wives from upcountry whom I have not yet met – pretty women in stunning hats. In fact all the women were very smart – Mary was tremendously impressed by this, which pleased me. The atmosphere throbbed with happy excitement and there was an overwhelming sense of a great occasion shared.

At 11 o'clock exactly the big black car came gliding in and drew up, the band played the national anthem and the Queen Mother, accompanied by HE, stepped out and proceeded to inspect the Guard of Honour. She has a great sense of theatre, and stood for a moment before moving forward, waiting for her presence to make its full impact on her audience. Standing beside HE, who was taller than ever in his plumed helmet, she looked tiny and regal in a full-length, fitted silver gown, with a blue chiffon stole which moved gracefully in the breeze. She wore a magnificent tiara which reflected the high, blazing African sun, and with every movement of her head the colours of the jewels flashed and changed, creating an extraordinary illusion that she was wearing a band of living fire round her head. The effect on the Africans was electric. From hundreds of black throats there came a deep, spontaneous gasping roar of wonder, awe and admiration. I shall never forget that sound.

After the inspection she sat down on the dais, about ten yards away, in profile, for the next hour and a half and I looked my fill. The PCs introduced each DC of their province, who in turn introduced the chiefs of their district. The chiefs looked tremendously impressive, so dignified and courteous. Presents were exchanged and little speeches made, and she gave her radiant smile to each and every one. When these ceremonies were over, she left in the car, which drove slowly right round the field, allowing everyone to have a good view of her. We went back to the house for lunch, reluctantly leaving everyone making a bee line for the Club! By the time I had supervised everything the day was over. I was ironing my green chiffon dress when the Queen Mother in her car passed on the road beyond our garden. (We live next to GH, at right angles, and from the top verandah we could see all the activity in the lit-up corridors – such fun.) I caught a glimpse of her and the boys could have touched her car – they were all lined up on the verge of the road, falling about with excitement. The Wickhams' old cook drinks, so I had to be on the watch in case celebrations got out of hand!

After dinner our two guests accompanied us to a huge party given by Barbara and Jock Corrie (ADC to HE) – a very glamorous occasion with everyone looking marvellous. There were candles in jam jars hanging on all the trees and charcoal braziers (made out of petrol tins) glowing warmly beside little tables: all this in white moonlight – the moon was full, so lucky. There must have been about seventy guests and Ron and I met many old acquaintances and were kept busy introducing our guests, who loved every minute. About 11.00, the high-ups from the State Banquet arrived, and Nancy Ingham, starry-eyed, told me all about it and how wonderfully informal the Queen Mother made it. She is apparently as thrilled with Zomba as Zomba is with her, and appeared completely relaxed and enjoying herself. At midnight Barbara served piping-hot kedgeree, just right. We left about 1 o'clock, quite deliberately, as there were signs that a really high-spirited party was beginning to develop and we wanted our guests to see Zomba society only at its best!

On Sunday they worked and we lazed in the garden, or rather Ron did and I got in about ten minutes before they came back for a curry lunch. We then took them up the mountain (closely followed by the Queen Mother and six cars!) Ron knew where the royal cars were going and managed not to coincide as he drove our people about. Eventually we waited by the clock, at the top, and saw them all drive past: the two ladies-in-waiting, Mrs Mullholland and Viscountess Hambledon looked very elegant and attractive women. Then we nipped back into the car and followed the procession down, as Mr Wickers had to get back to GH at once. At the bottom there were groups of people at the edge of the road all the way back, waving and smiling to all the cars. Mary and Mr Wickers waved back, while Ron and I went slightly pink with suppressed mirth as we sat beside them and looked out at heads of departments waving to us! It was interesting to get such an impression of happy faces and realise what the Queen Mother's presence meant to everyone. We had a long. relaxed evening, after a very good dinner, talking with them till after midnight. I forgot to say that on Sunday a secretary rang from GH to say the Queen Mother wished to thank those people who had given hospitality to her staff, so would we present ourselves at GH on Monday at 8.30 in the morning? By that time I was enjoying myself so much that I simply put down the phone, marched out to Ron and said calmly we were to meet the Queen Mother next morning, I had nothing to wear and did not know how to curtsey. Mary showed me how to curtsey and said to wear a simple cotton frock, as it was so early.

I took leave of our guests in my housecoat (I did not want to crush my dress) at 8.15 and at 8.25 I was in the car with Ron on our way to GH. We waited in the front hall and saw all the staff leave the building – equerries, ladies-in-waiting, everyone, and then the Queen Mother came out of a door opposite with HE, who presented us, Ron and me first. She is hardly taller than I, with a warm voice, deeper than it sounds through a microphone. She was dressed entirely in blue and looked completely rested and at ease, and one immediately relaxed with her. In the end we were in a group round her instead of in a row, as we began. She then drove off, smiling and waving to us. It was a perfect finish to a perfect weekend and I felt I had been far away on a long holiday. I went back and started the beastly task of packing up. We left the house yesterday after lunch, came back here and I unpacked everything, having first had to clean the house, which in a week of being empty was filthy, full of ant excavations and cockroaches. By evening it was all done – quite a task. When I put on my black slacks this morning – the weather broke yesterday – they *fell* onto my hips. I must have lost at least an inch in the last fortnight! However, I feel terrific. Tomorrow the Davies' come for two days and on Sunday I am having the Weirs and the Hammars for a curry lunch. Then I shall come down to earth with a bump. It has been a marvellous experience and very good for my morale. I would not have missed it for the world.

25th July:

I have been more in touch with Zomba this week and have been hearing how smoothly the whole visit went and how much everyone loved seeing the Queen Mother. I duly handed over all the bills, including firewood, telephone and electricity, and the boys' wages, to Jock Corrie, who accepted them without even casting a glance and thanked me very charmingly.

We quickly settled down here again and were ready to welcome Iris, Dave and Linden on Thursday at lunch time. They are all looking well and not a bit end-of-tourish. Iris has been playing tennis and hockey, and working hard as provincial president of the Red Cross; she has survived this last tour very well. She looked wonderful – brown face, shining eyes and her attractively greying hair. Linden, sweet as ever, could not get over how much Iris talked when she was with me – we were doing the kind of thing our family does: following each other from room to room and stopping what we were doing to lean on something and talk. In the end Linden said, 'Mummy, I know why you and Ann have so much to say to one another. You both have the same kind of eyes!' These were the three happiest days I have had since we came back. She truly is the only *close* friend I have out here (apart from Laga, who is close on another wavelength) and we are in perfect accord. Her visit did Ron a lot of good too and he cheered up noticeably. I worry about him just now; he is tired, not himself. They left on Saturday morning. In the evening we went to dine with Bernard and Mary Kayes, a delightful evening, with a little music – Brahm's violin concerto. The curry lunch on Sunday went very well. They were all bursting to hear about our time in the big house.

Next Thursday I go over to Blantyre in our car with Norton to take my driving test. So, fingers crossed, legs crossed, everything crossed!

8th August:

Well, to put everyone out of their agony, I passed the test! Norton took the day off, and we left about nine, in holiday mood, in spite of my inner nerves. I drove, and drove in Blantyre to get used to the traffic. We went to Ryall's for lunch. It is transformed, with a new diningroom and lounge. I ate hardly a bite and talked non-stop, to give us both something to think about. At two o'clock we presented ourselves at the office of Mr Oliver, the examiner. Norton practically *ran* away to do some shopping. His nerves were as bad as mine. I am the first person he has taught and his pride was at stake too. Mr Oliver took me all over Blantyre and I was concentrating so hard I forgot about nerves. Twenty minutes later we were back at his office and he told me I was a safe driver and had plenty of confidence (huh!) and only needed practice. Then he went off and in a daze I waited for Norton, who came towards the car with his face one huge question mark. I said, 'All is well,' and he promptly dropped his parcels and kissed me. He got lipstick on his chin, which I removed with my hanky, saying in the stress of the moment, 'We mustn't cop our blotty books now!' We did some more shopping and had a long, relaxed tea at Ryall's. We drove back in the late sunshine, I very tired and smoking madly. When we got back Norton came in for a drink (and to see Ron's face!) Ron was really delighted, though of course he had to be heavy-handed about it. I am now waiting for the office to send me my licence.

On Saturday we went to the Haskard wedding reception at GH: a huge affair with champagne flowing and lovely food. He was PC of the North and is now in the Secretariat. She is a stenographer and is the daughter of an ex-Governor of Northern Rhodesia and the Solomons. There were lots of people we knew, so we enjoyed it. In the evening we dined with the best man and his wife, a delightful South African couple, Julien and Sue Theunnisen, and the two bridesmaids, whom Ron knew in the hostel, and we held a great post mortem on the day. On Sunday evening we had supper with the Weirs and found Bertie and Berry Hammar there. They were eager to hear about the wedding, so we held forth.

Ron has taken up squash again and plays regularly with Bertie Hammar. I am delighted, as he badly needs the exercise. I am playing a lot of tennis. I have felt once or twice lately that I would just like to go to bed and be ill – not like me.

However, passing my driving test has been some sort of watershed and I feel much better.

15th August:

Our cold season seems to be over, thank heavens. It was so hot yesterday afternoon on the tennis court we began to think we would have to stop playing.

My morale, spirits and general well being have been mercifully up-lifted by a most wonderful offer of a job, quite unthought of and unsought by me. The day I wrote to you last week Ron came back at lunch time with the first piece of good news. John Kennan, at present Clerk of Leg Co, asked him if I would take on the job of indexing the local *Hansard*, a job I could do at home. It would take about a fortnight, at 27*s*. 6*d*. per day. I said instantly that I would do it and that afternoon John came up to the house with a frightful pile of Leg Co sittings reports – about 600 pages, to be indexed with references and cross-references – complicated work, mostly sheer slog but far from being without interest.

But, that was not all. The same evening Ron came back grinning with delight. Bryn Jones-Walters had asked him if I would be interested in a full-time job in *his* (Information) Department – the only work in the entire colonial spectrum that really interests me. (Why the hell don't these chaps ask *me*?) The work is usually done by an Administrative Officer, but they are short-staffed and Bryn said I was the only person he could think of – blow me down! I would have the official status of a Departmental Assistant. [In fact my official title was 'temporary female departmental assistant'!] I start at £41 per month. The work involves supplying HE and the Secretariat with press cuttings from home and colonial newspapers, writing the weekly Bulletin for African consumption, supervising the two African assistants (both very intelligent), collecting information on the work of Government Departments and editing that. Again I jumped at it before Ron stopped speaking! I went down (*in the car!*) to see Bryn about it yesterday. We had a long talk and it is all settled. I start whenever this enormous index is completed. By reading these *Hansard* reports, I am amassing a good background of information with which to begin the other work. At present I am toiling through Kenneth's Budget speech and the 122 pages of debate which followed; fascinating, oddly enough.

The African members' speeches make very trying reading. They are politically semi-educated pedants, interested only in the sound of their own voices. They speak English as they would Chinyanja, i.e. say the same thing in ten different ways at great length and full speed, raking their way through their English vocabulary with relish. They pay scant attention to procedure and hold up the business of the meeting exhaustingly. If I had to sit and listen to them I think I would have apoplexy.

Another nice thing about the job with Bryn is that I shall meet a lot of people who come to his office from both within and outside Nyasaland, especially the press. In time I think I shall have a fascinating job and Bryn assured me I would never be bored. I am to share his present office with him till his new one, in process of being built, is completed. So there we are. I shall have money to save for my own affairs, and a fully occupied day, doing something, at last, in my own line. Ron is absolutely thrilled (and talking about new slacks and a spare tyre for the car)! I begin on Monday, 26th August, provided the index is finished by then.

Norton's Chopin record arrived and he and Joan came down one evening for a drink and I gave it to him. He was very, very pleased, and loved the long piece of doggeral verse I had written, in the form of a thank-you letter, for putting up with my efforts for so long.

Next month, in spite of my working days, we shall have to start entertaining again – I hope it is a case of the more you have to do, the more you can do, in a day!

22nd August:

Yes, I most certainly want the *Spectator*. I shall send a cheque next week, as our finances will be shared by then and I would like to pay for it myself.

I am reading, with a mixture of interest and depression, Sinclair Lewis's *Main Street*, which Berry Hammar lent me. She had a son on Saturday.

I had a long letter from Jean Wickham a few days ago, now in England. Africa is, of course, her home, and she senses she is not quite 'at home' in England, though she went to school and university there.

Now that I am to be working all day, I feel wonderfully freed from the bonds of Zomba and will doubtless soon be out of touch with its gossip and atmosphere – and a very good thing too. People's reactions to the news of my job have been interesting. The men, who know what it involves, are full of interest and enthusiasm. The women are slightly put out and say, 'But I thought you could not do typing and shorthand.' When I point out that I shall not have anything to do with that, they are even more put out – and one said, 'Oh, so it's a *man's* job really.'(!) With the greatest of pleasure I said, 'Yes'!

I shall have the index ready to hand in on Saturday morning. It has been good experience but hard on my eyes and patience. It is looking very neat and legible. I saw Bryn again to finalise the details of the job. He is delighted to have more help in the office and obviously believes I will become very useful.

We had a quiet weekend, as I had to press on with *Hansard* and Ron was content to do very little. On Sunday he played squash and I joined him to watch some very good cricket for an hour before lunch. In the evening we dined with Alex and Bunny Davidson, charming people whom we both like very much. They took us to a good but very depressing French film called *Nous Sommes Tous Les Assassins*, about capital punishment – horrible! We went back with them for a nightcap and sat talking till one. Bunny was born and brought up in

Tenerife. Alex is a Scot brought up in England. They have two small daughters, aged two and four. They have served in the Solomons and we were introduced to them by Jean Richardson. I have mentioned them before but you may not place them.

I have had a letter from Kenneth, acting Governor of Aden just now. He has Ruth and the boys with him on holiday. He loves my letters, and says I keep Zomba vividly alive for him!

27th August:

Your letter arrived yesterday afternoon and I read it as I walked home at 3.30 from my first day in the office, getting the only exercise possible till I can reorganise my tennis.

The weather is very warm, and looks and smells like autumn, with the scent of bonfires, and the golden leaves drifting down into heaps on the roads and in the garden. The jacaranda is early this year and our own tree is in bud, while others surprised me a few mornings ago by creating misty blue patches among Zomba's many trees. September is going to be a most beautiful month of blossom. I am into cotton now, with a cardigan indoors in the morning.

Here life has suddenly become very full indeed. By driving myself, I finished the *Hansard* index, as planned, on Saturday at noon exactly and handed it in on Monday morning. I hear, through Ron, who is on the grapevine of Secretariat news, that 'They' are delighted with it. They have never had it done so thoroughly before, and, alas, they want me to do it in the future. I shall be interested to read the comments on it at the next Leg Co meeting, as the members are very touchy about being fully reported and will no doubt look themselves up to see if I have dealt with them properly – and I certainly have!

I watched cricket on Sunday morning while Ron played squash. By the evening I had a knot in my stomach, exactly like that awful 'Sunday night' feeling I used to get before exams as a school girl! However, it is all most interesting and Bryn is very kind and easy to work with. It is quite overwhelmingly detailed at present and I feel in a whirl, but I know that in time I shall be very happy. It is far more interesting than I expected, with all sorts of work which Bryn had not mentioned, knowing it would crop up as we go along. I am up to my chin in press cuttings, world news sheets and fat files to read through to get the background. I have met all the African staff, who seem bright, pleasant and keen on their jobs. The Government Print is our lifeline and I have met the staff there and been shown through the printing works. I have to visit people in the Secretariat to get facts and figures. At present I am a novelty there, and some of the men I meet stop and say, 'Good heavens, what are *you* doing in this place?' Their offices have doors and windows opening into the main corridor and I cannot avoid catching their eyes as heads turn at the sound of high heels approaching. Bryn rates my intelligence at an alarming height and casually gives me the most (at present) hair-raising instructions, all of which I accept with inner panic but, I hope, outer calm. I feel in my bones that I shall shortly be settled down and working at high speed. It all seems a kind of miracle.

There is a Parliamentary delegation of eight British MPs coming on Monday for a week and I have just got hold of the local paper and have been feverishly memorising their names and politics. Today a man from Lusaka came in to see Bryn and said, 'Hmmm! You have a neat little office here. I see you pick your assistant to match it.' (I sit in a corner behind a rather small table.) Some of the Assistant Secretaries have been in on business, and as they went out, directed an enormous wink at Bryn, who just stared back at them, bold and cool!

3rd September:

I am writing this while I have tea, on a glorious hot afternoon. As Ron does not leave his office till much later, I walk home, and it is the nicest time of day – the great relief that another day has proved that nothing drastic has happened because of my attention to Nyasaland affairs, and the lovely sight of all the trees and gardens in blossom. My beloved jacaranda is really flourishing now, along with 'yesterday, today and tomorrow' and simply oceans of bougainvillaea and poinsettia. You will be interested to know I do not smoke while working, so now I have my first cigarette at teatime, instead of after lunch. A slightly hectic feeling is beginning to come over me by that time, but I manage!

I stopped this briefly, as Joan Weir called in with a huge bunch of heavenly sweet peas, smelling of honey. I walked up with her to her house for exercise – it is at the top of a very steep hill and has one of the best views in Zomba. Norton suddenly remembered he had a visit to make (!) and so took me back in his car and we sat for a bit and had a talk. I think he misses our time together.

I was paid £25 for the *Hansard* index. I have to check the beastly thing in proof.

Mary Dunlop has sent us an LP, to thank us for making her visit such a happy one. It is Brahms's 2nd piano concerto played by Backhaus and the Vienna Philharmonic – a lovely recording. I am playing it now, turned up loud!

Last week was quite an experience and I am glad it is over; but my work can only get better now. Bryn is a great standby and is not rushing me. On Monday he was away all day and in the ensuing chaos I just had to cope and got through all right. Once I know where to find information and how to assemble it in the most effective way I shall get on very well. Ron is a great help, as he is interested and makes excellent suggestions. To my astonishment, when I told Aflike I was going to work all day in an office, he was devastated. He tossed his arms in lament and said, 'I shall never see you now. You might as well be in England!' I held his hands and managed to calm him down. What a thing! I get back about quarter to four on most days. Tea is on the trolley when I enter the house – he must keep a look out for me and make it when he sees me coming up the hill. As I drink tea, he stands beside me. We plan meals and shopping for the next day, and exchange little bits of news and he goes away happy – dear man. *What* would I do without him?

On Friday evening we dined at the Hammars with the Weirs, in great style – champagne to celebrate the birth of the baby, a dear wee mite. On Saturday we dined with the Weirs and Chris and Bryn. It felt a little strange to be with Bryn socially – our relationship in the office is so special; private but *professional*. We went on to the Club and saw the Bader film *Reach for the Sky*, the best film I have seen for a long time. We went back for coffee and stayed late talking, everyone stimulated by the film. On Sunday, bliss, I breakfasted at 10.00, and then did a huge laundry (I wash all my precious cottons myself) and did some much needed mending. We had a quiet day, with records and reading, and I felt very much restored.

There is a wonderful woman who works in the Department in her own small office next door. Her name is Kathie Smith and she is one of three remarkable sisters, the daughters of Scots missionaries who came out to Nyasaland many years ago. They were born and brought up here, and speak Chinyanja as well as they do English. Though all attractive, none has married. Kathie is in her forties, with a strong, tired Scottish face, and a quiet flat voice. She knows the African inside out and is invaluable to Bryn. She writes a Chinyanja newspaper called *Msimbi*, which means 'one who talks' and does countless other things in her office beside innumerable 'good works' outside. We get on very well indeed, as she also does with Ron, who used to work with her through Zomba Boma. Her sister Etta used to call on us at Chiradzulu, where she ran a women's guild.

Looking back, I truly think I was on the brink of melancholia when Bryn offered me this job. It has just about saved my sanity. Timing *is* all, as you have always said.

11th September:

It is another glorious afternoon. The hot season is here, and I am thriving on it. I am having tea out in the garden, to get some sun – gone are the days of morning sunbathing! I actually found myself singing to myself in the house the other day, which has not happened for many a moon. Bryn, nice man, told Ron that I was going to be 'invaluable', and today when my first unaided Bulletin came over from the Print for a final check, he was delighted with it and said the standard was higher already. We enjoy working in the same office, cramped as we are, and I shall be sorry when he moves into his new one. He finds me useful as a sounding board while he thinks aloud over a new idea. He is one of the nicest men I have ever met. He is forty-one but looks younger – tallish, broad-shouldered, black-haired as Daddy must have been, with fine dark eyes, a brown complexion and a beautiful speaking voice, with a slight Welsh accent which increases most attractively when he gets excited, which is often. He started this Department in 1953 and is now Chief Information Officer in Nyasaland. He has been a DC in the Central and Northern Provinces and done a stint in the Secretariat. He respects my brain – I say this in all humility. I am just glad that I have the chance to prove to *someone* out here that I have one!

Last week on Thursday I was asked to make up a tennis doubles after the office, and I am playing again tomorrow and on Sunday morning when Ron plays squash. On Saturday I rushed home at lunch time, did the flowers, made a pudding, put new candles in the candlesticks – things I used to fill my mornings with. In the evening we had the Longs (Police) and the Theunnisens (Administration) to dinner. The film was not much good, but we had a good dinner and brought them back for coffee and dancing to the Wickhams' records. They seemed to enjoy it, as they stayed on till 2.30! We had a lovely lazy Sunday. I started to read the Alanbrook diaries, *The Turn of the Tide*, which Norton lent me – most interesting.

Mabuka, the old paralysed chief from Mlanje district, whose photo was in the last *London News* we received, died a few days ago, much mourned, as he was one of the best and most loyal. I am glad he met the Queen Mother at the *baraza*.

18th September:

Here I am writing on Tuesday evening at 6.30, as I stayed late in the office to get something urgent done. My work goes well and it is just a case of concentrating harder and harder to improve the quality. Bryn seems pleased with my progress. He now lets me have access to the confidential files – most interesting. Ron is simply delighted that I am 'in the picture', as it were, and can now discuss things as I could never find the interest to do before. I have made firm friends in our office and in the Print, and there is a very easy and pleasant atmosphere in our Department, initiated, of course, by Bryn's personality. Our accountant is a Scot from Edinburgh (very broad), Alice Rutherford, and George, her husband, sees to the production of my Bulletin.

On Friday Bryn and Chris came for supper and we went to see *The Rose Tattoo*. They loved it and were happy to come back for coffee. Ron and Chris, who get on very well, sat in one corner and talked, and Bryn and I in another. He and I covered a lot of ground – Dylan Thomas, Orson Welles, Robert Flaherty, Edward Murrows and much more. We got to bed about one, I so pleased with my evening I was as bright as a button and could not get to sleep. Saturday morning in the office was a very piano affair! At lunch time we had the great thrill of seeing twelve Vampire jets fly over Zomba to celebrate Battle of Britain Day. The sound and sight were so nostalgic I felt sick, but I love it and the boys were almost delirious, having never seen or heard jets before. In the evening we went to the Davidsons and on to the RAF Ball, a lovely evening shared with the Theunnisens and Cosmo and Phylida Haskard, the newly-weds.

On Tuesday John Carver, the charming young ADC who pursued me so ardently at Mzimba, arrived to work in the Secretariat, and Ron brought him back to the house for a drink. He is as nice as ever, and, thank goodness, is going to get on well with Ron. They circled around each other like wary dogs but in the end were perfectly at ease. Today I had a very hard day in the office, with Bryn away in Blantyre, but it is good for me and I enjoy it.

I am very much behind with my home newspapers, as I now have to read the local and Rhodesian papers very thoroughly and listen to local and Federal news on the wireless. The time is flying and the weekends follow hard upon each other – incredible! Aflike is managing nobly and things in the house go on very much as they did before, except that entertaining has to be very well planned, as I do a lot before a dinner party.

25th September:

I am having tea, feeling very hot and sweaty. The walk home is a dream. The jacaranda is in full blossom. The colour does not dazzle but rather dazes the eye, I have decided. Our *khonde*, paths and flowerbeds are pure blue from the fallen petals.

Here things go at a great pace, as Bryn is away on *ulendo*, covering Roy Welensky's visit and I am on my own. I was given a terrific boost to my morale last week. The titular head of our Department is Vernon McDonald, who in fact has one of those hush-hush jobs which are covered by a nominal label from another Department. As the figurehead of ours, he takes an interest in all our doings, and has been reading the Bulletin since its inception. He told Bryn last week's was the *best ever*! And it was full of news items I had thought up myself. Bryn always looks it over and has more than once found a political indiscretion which I at once removed, so it will be just too bad if there are any this week, because it goes to press before he returns. He left in a whirlwind on Monday morning, leaving me with a long list of horrid tasks to do while he is away!

On Friday evening after tennis we had a drink with John Carver and he came back here for an informal supper and records, which was nice. I think he is a bit lonely but he will soon make friends in Zomba, he is so likeable; a very eligible bachelor, in fact. On Saturday evening the Davidsons came to dine. I was terribly tired and they willingly skipped the film and spent a quiet evening with us, talking and playing records. On Sunday morning I played tennis (and fell, economically but crashingly, on one knee, now rather spongy) while Ron had his squash. After lunch I went shamelessly to bed till six o'clock and had a quiet evening reading. On Monday evening we drove up Naisi road to have supper with John Carver, just the two of us. How did we ever live in one of those oval houses? John is a delight to be with, and I laugh with him as I used to laugh with David (Baxter). His cook produced a marvellous dinner.

Yesterday Roy Welensky was making a speech in Blantyre, and Ron, as Assistant Secretary, African Affairs, went off with his chief, John Ingham, to hear him. He came back at 8 o'clock and we sat up late, talking. Welensky is not unimpressive, Ron said, and his obvious determination to get African-based rather than British-based rule for the Federation suggests strongly that the days of the British are numbered. It is a fearful worry in the minds of all the men serving here: men with young families, men with no qualifications or other training, and men who may find themselves at the age of forty or forty-five looking for a new career.

I must stop now and do my laundry, write to the Chief Secretary to accept my job, write out a shopping list for tomorrow, go through the accounts, and then read carefully through the local papers *and* think up something for supper. We are having a drinks party on Saturday for John Carver, to meet people. He will also lunch with us, as it is his birthday. How I am going to tackle the arrangements for that is something I must think about in the bath tonight, otherwise I shall wake at 3.00 a.m. and do so then!

1st October:

The weather is fantastically hot and I find the afternoons in the office very hard going as far as concentration is concerned. We have a small fan, but even so, one's wrists and arms smudge everything and tempers rise and fall amusingly. Fortunately it is a happy office and nobody minds.

There have been some terrible bush fires on the mountain – there always are at this time of year. Yesterday I saw the worst one I have ever known in Zomba, about a mile away. Black ash drifted over and landed on my moist arms as I watched it from the office doorway. Its smoke rolled over the sun and produced a most splendid sunset like a winter one at home. After dark the spine of the mountain was outlined in flames and occasionally an extra gust of wind sent the tongues of fire licking further. We heard and smelt it during the night, a most ominous and disturbing presence, and I thanked God I was not at Mlanje. Today from the office I can see the enormous swathe of damage done. In fact the slopes of Zomba mountain have very effective fire-breaks.

Our drinks party on Saturday went off very well. We had fourteen people. As I had no time to prepare small eats, I ordered a vast quantity of curry puffs from an Indian store. They were delicious and so spicy everyone burst out in beads of sweat – and went on eating them. I asked Chris to stay on for lunch with John, as Bryn was not arriving back from his Welensky trip till later in the day. Chris is English and a delightful person. I would say she is at least two inches smaller than I am, with a face and voice very like Glynis Johns, which makes one assume automatically that she is Welsh. I have always liked her and we have an oddly close friendship without seeing very much of each other. Ron enjoys her company too, so we always have a happy time together. In the evening we dressed up to go and dine with the Davidsons and see the Zomba Dramatic Society perform in *Love is a Luxury*, a very bad play well done, as usual. We went back to the Davidsons, and as we all confessed to being hungry we had coffee and scrambled eggs. We discovered they had never been up the mountain to see the sunrise and they jumped at the idea of going, so we went home, bathed and changed, and they came to pick us up in their car. So they shared with us that marvellous experience; a cool, birdsong-filled dawn and then the huge red sun surging up over the horizon and that low, golden light bringing the plateau suddenly to life, all the lovely leaves and grasses shimmering and gleaming. Alex's car stuck on a stony track leading down to the water, and as we were pushing it a large pebble shot out from under the churning back wheels and cracked me on my shin, which promptly split open about three inches down the front of my leg! It was horribly, breathtakingly painful and for a moment I thought I was going to pass out. I was wearing close-fitting toreador trousers which would not roll up, so I did not see the damage till I got home – blood everywhere. It was not all that deep – a kind of raw abrasion. Later at the Club I met Norton, who nearly had a fit when he saw it. I was wearing a skirt and had left it uncovered. He said I must go up to the hospital and have a proper dressing put on, otherwise it would go septic, with so much dust about and in this heat. So it is to be covered up for three days. It will be perfectly healed over by then, he says, but my poor shin bone is aching and I cannot play tennis. Alex was appalled when he got out of the car and saw my white face.

I was glad to see Bryn on Monday morning, but that week on my own came just at the right time. I discovered I keep calm when there is a 'flap' on. I now go on with my own work without having to consult Bryn, who quite wistfully asks if I need any help! However, only the routine work is like that, and we have long talks over new ideas for articles. I am preparing a story on poultry today, which will be illustrated by captioned photographs. I had to go and see the Director of Veterinary Services to get all the details – seven frantic pages of them – he never knew I was not using shorthand. So my practice at writing quickly as a student comes in useful now!

9th October:

My abrasion healed beautifully and Norton is astonished that the scar is quite faint already. [I still have it!] He says I must be very healthy!

Here I am kept busy and feel wonderfully the better for it. People tell me how well and happy I look, which pleases me. The weather is phenomenally hot, day after blazing day. I love it, but the afternoons in the office are quite an ordeal,

and I plan all my 'thinking' work for the mornings and do reading and copying during those two gruelling hours. One's nerves and temper are definitely
affected, and one gets all het up over very little. Bryn is usually meticulous in
his use of language in front of women, but in this heat he sits quietly swearing
under his breath. I sigh, scrape my feet and occasionally utter a mild curse
which always gets an answering chuckle from him. *What* a nice man he is. Today I signed the Official Secrets Act, which means I have access to top secret
files. I read a wonderfully high-powered one this afternoon – most exciting.

Friday was Alex Davidson's thirty-eighth birthday, and Bunny asked us for
supper, which we ate sitting out on their *khonde*, the only cool spot. We drank
ice-cold Pimms, the brandy-based one, a delicious, heady brew! He is ex-Navy,
and was torpedoed three times during the war. He swallowed oil, which damaged the lining of his stomach, and has had major surgery to deal with duodenal
ulcers which unfortunately have recurred. He makes light of this affliction, but
obviously suffers a lot of pain. Bunny was born and brought up in Tenerife and
speaks fluent Spanish. She is English, but has an attractive exoticism about her,
in manner and gesture. I think she feels rather out of her element here.

At lunch time on Saturday I dashed home from the office to prepare for a
dinner party, and found the diningroom fragrant with roses and carnations
produced by Aflike. As my garden sadly lacks such bounty, I accepted them
gratefully and asked no questions! The Hammars and the Youens' dined with us
– a marvellous mixture – I mean the people, not the dinner! We went on to see
Bing Crosby and Jeanmaire in *Anything Goes*. It was a most enjoyable evening,
despite the tremendous heat. On Sunday we went off with the Davidsons to
spend the day at Chiradzulu, which we wanted them to see in jacaranda time. It
was, of course, looking like paradise. After calling on the ADC, we went down
to the pool and picnicked under an enormous jacaranda which kept dropping
blossom on us. The Davidsons have hardly moved from Zomba since they came
a year ago, and were in raptures over everything. We went back to them for
supper, silent and drugged by the long hours in the sun.

Last night while Ron was at bridge, Norton called in to say he had to go to
Blantyre on Thursday and would I like a day's shopping if I could get permission? Would I just. Bryn kindly said yes, so I have a huge list of things I cannot
get here, and a huge list for my friends in the office.

I had to phone David (Baxter) from the office the other morning on business.
He did not realise this and we had a baffled, hilarious conversation, as he
thought I was in Blantyre and asked me to lunch! He was very cheerful and said
he was delighted about my job, dear man.

15th October:

The terrific heat continues unabated and relentlessly.

I had a lovely day on Thursday with Norton. It is always fun to get away to different places and faces. We had a leisurely day's shopping. I bought a very becoming yellow bathing suit and a really good pair of dainty gold kid evening shoes, the first since my wedding ones in 1948, so I felt I could afford to splash. We drove out to Chileka airport and had a very good Italian lunch. The planes kept coming and going; it was interesting to watch the passengers. We had an early tea and drove back in the late golden sunlight. Norton was delighted with his day too. It was the first of ten days' local leave, which they are spending on Zomba mountain, in the KAR cottage, which has electric light and a civilised bathroom.

On Saturday evening we dined with John and Jean Kennan. I thought it was going to be a disaster, as Ron and I both intensely dislike the other couple who were there. My heart sank into my boots when they came in and I did not dare look at Ron. The man especially is an absolute *bête noir* of Ron's. However, we like the Kennans very much and somehow rallied. I managed to do quite a lot of talking – my office experience with meeting and talking to people is a great help socially, both for subject matter and the confidence to use it.

On Sunday we cast aside all the cares and went off at 8 o'clock with the Davidsons for a picnic at Mlanje. The tea country in Cholo district was looking lovely and they were interested in everything. Mlanje was unbearably hot – the pool has had no water for two months and the station is rationed. We paid a five-minute courtesy call on the DC and fled along the valley to the Tuchila pool, where we found enough water to immerse ourselves – lovely soft brown water, in the middle of rocks too hot to walk bare-foot on. We had lunch under the trees: a Spanish omelette provided by Bunny, fruit and a bottle of wine contributed by us which we cooled in the burn. We had a divinely relaxing few hours and left about four to drive the ninety miles back, all on tarmac. They came here for supper. We were all gloriously tired, glowing with sunburn, and sat about sleepily listening to music. I managed to bring the evening to an end early. I cannot stand late Sunday nights now.

Yesterday after tea the Hammars came in for a talk. Bertie has been offered a magnificent post in Salisbury as the surgeon of a brand new hospital, and they leave Nyasaland on the 24th. We shall miss them, as we have lots in common. They have loved Zomba and are sorry to go. They are giving a farewell party for forty people on Wednesday and on Friday John Carver is doing the same for them. I dread these mid-week parties, because I have to get up at 6.20 next morning, though of course I enjoy them.

The work goes on very well. I have just written a short history of the Secretariat for some curious ass who wants the information – hard ploughing through archives, but as usual I found lots of interesting reading, not altogether relevant to the subject! My knowledge of Nyasaland is certainly building up and when the Davidsons ask questions I find I have nipped in with the answer while Ron utters his preliminary 'aaaaahh'!

23rd October:

We too have Asian 'flu here. There has been quite a lot of it, though not very serious. There has also been a case of polio – Gerald Collett, one of the Crown Counsels, aged twenty-six, collapsed in court when he was on circuit in the North. However, that was six weeks ago and I saw him walking with a stick in the Club on Saturday – one of the lucky ones. It cast a feeling of horror over Zomba, especially for people with young children.

The weather is blazing hot and I continue to thrive on it but people are beginning to wish it was over. I feel happier than I have ever felt out here. This job has given me something that was entirely lacking – a sense of confidence in life in general, and now confidence in the job itself, so that whatever I have to do I just sit down and calmly do it. Today Bryn said the Bulletin was absolutely first class, and he felt I could now help him more with his work and would put me on to some next week. My memory is very good and in spite of the enormous amount of reading I do I can usually pinpoint sources of news later, when HE or someone in the Secretariat wants the original context. Of course they always want it *at once*. The visit of Lord Hume has produced most interesting behind-the-scenes files and I have been combing through all his speeches to pick out what should be printed for the African, and what is their significance for Nyasaland. He seems a most statesmanlike man.

The Hammars gave their big party on Wednesday, and a few of us stayed on to supper. It is so hot at present that food is almost incidental, except at lunch time when I am always hungry. We had supper on Thursday with Kathie Smith. The only other guest was a very dour Scottish doctor with whom I coped, as I could sense that Ron, who was very tired, was almost dying of boredom! All the way home in the car he kept saying 'God' and I got the giggles. We went up to Naisi to John's party for the Hammars. It was fun but I was wilting and we left fairly early. On Saturday at lunch time we went to the Inghams for drinks, to meet someone from the Colonial Office. There were so many people there he never got round to me, but I had a pleasant hour cruising about. In the evening we dined with the Davidsons and went to see *The Battle of the River Plate* – bad acting, but oh, those lovely ships, and the memories roused by that gallant string of names: Ajax, Achilles and Exeter. We had a desperately needed quiet Sunday, when I was able to catch up on myself and my domestic affairs.

Joan has sent me two very nice tailored blouses and skirts for wear in the office. I asked for stripes because they make one look cooler than in fact one is! The heat is colossal.

30th October:

It is after tea and *so hot* that my hands are trembling and wet. The weather is absolutely phenomenal and people literally groan and gasp at their desks. This afternoon I had a difficult piece of work to do, and Bryn gave me the key to his small recording room behind the Leg Co chamber. The whole building is air-conditioned, so I sat in clammy coolness with a clear head and did an enormous amount of work for two hours. Meanwhile Alice, in the office, drank my whole thermos of iced tea!

Everyone is cutting down on social occasions because of the heat. We had a quiet week and saved our energies for the Police Ball on Saturday, held at the Mess, a most pukka affair with all the Police in very smart Mess kit and a lot of the guests in tails. We sat outside under fairy lights and watched the 300 guests milling about. The Police band is always splendid and Ron and I enjoyed some good dancing. We were with a very mixed group, none of whom we knew except our host and hostess. It was delightful till about one o'clock, and then we began to tire. We could not leave the Mess till our host did, so we had to survive till four! We had a quiet day on Sunday, i.e. Ron slept late and I got up and did all the tasks that accumulate during the week. The Davidsons were at the Lake for the weekend and were grateful to come back for a late supper with us – glowing with sunburn and thrilled with their visit, particularly the Lake itself. They served in the Pacific for ten years and miss the sea.

We had our tennis and squash yesterday and had a drink afterwards. Tennis was poor in the great heat, but I like the exercise and the setting is so lovely. The jacaranda is nearly over, but the flamboyant and bougainvillaea are burning bright all over the place. Mlanje has been hidden in haze for days. The nights are incredibly beautiful, though very still and hot.

Work goes on as usual, but no one is really doing it as well or as quickly as they should, and some of the women are miserable and have to take days off. Bryn is not at all happy in this extreme heat but retains his equanimity wonderfully.

This is not a good letter, but my head is fuzzy with heat and that hard work this afternoon.

P.S. An enormous flash of lightning just now! I nearly hit the roof!

5th November:

I am having tea, with my harpsichord record on and have just changed into shorts and a loose shirt. I am sure you must be bored by mention of it again, but the heat is greater than ever and even I feel regularly sick by about three o'clock, which is zero hour for everyone, and we begin to feel weak and shaky. My best African assistant has just gone on long leave and I am having difficulties with his stand-in, Aubrey (!) Kachingwe, a clever, over-polite young man who has been to England. I have no doubt who will win the subtle battle we are conducting, but I wish I could have fought it in the cold season!

The Davidsons have acquired a wee plump poodle puppy. He looks like a lamb and is called Pablo. We all take it in turns to pick him up and cuddle him; he loves it and gets very limp and sleepy.

We have just had a short visit from our new Governor General, Lord Dalhousie, a big shy Scotsman with a square but chiselled face. Bryn was among those who met him at the airport and said he was terribly nervous, but charming.

After a quiet week we had a splendid evening on Saturday, when the Davidsons joined us on an expedition to Blantyre. Bunny and I wore short dresses (I my cotton with the long velvet bow at the back) and Ron and Alex did us proud in Red Sea rig – black evening trousers, black cummerbund, and white open-necked, short sleeved shirts. We took both cars and swopped spouses for the hour's drive, in bright moonlight, to a new restaurant outside Blantyre called *The Flamingo* – check table cloths, red candles in wine bottles, fairy lights inside and masses of people; Greeks, Italians, Portuguese and British. We all had piri-piri chicken, red wine, cheese and coffee – lovely. It felt utterly unlike Africa and we had a very civilised evening. On the way home I suddenly began to sing, something I had forgotten I used to do. Alex was enchanted.

Work gets more and more interesting. Bryn thrilled me today by asking me to try my hand at a draft for HE's Christmas broadcast. The theme is 'good manners' (multi-racial, of course). Bryn writes one too, also the Federal Information Officer, and then the Chief Secretary 'bashes them about', as Bryn puts it, and finally HE finishes them off! I shall brood over it for a few days and then put pen to paper.

I have discarded my cushion when I drive, even though it means my eyes are practically on a level with the bonnet of the car!

13th November:

Here there is little news and only one subject – the *heat*. By 8.30 this morning it was 94°F in our office! There was lightning over Mlanje last night but that was all. It really is appalling. From three in the afternoon till seven the whole place is like a furnace, and one simply concentrates on breathing. The only thing to do is to sit up late and get cool; lying in bed is wretchedly uncomfortable. I go through one set of clothes a day, and another in the evening. I breakfast in my kimono, pouring with sweat, and then bath and dress for the office. Everyone walks slowly and I find myself doing the stupidest things with great deliberation. I work hard in the mornings and have some satisfaction in getting a lot done. The Bulletin somehow gets filled up. The articles are getting more interesting to write as I discover how to put things over to the Africans. Bryn, who is feeling the heat terribly, has given me some of his work to do and is realising that he need not do everything himself, but he is a very skilful delegator and never overloads me. No one remembers weather like this and Bryn says it is as trying as the climate in parts of India. There is little entertaining going on, as people just crawl home and sit out on their *khonde*. We have the occasional evening's Scrabble with the Davidsons. Last Wednesday

Ron hurt another rib at squash, and took Thursday afternoon off to rest it, as he was determined not to go to the hospital and have it strapped up in this unbearable heat. On Saturday we drove up the mountain in milk white moonlight, with Bunny and Alex, and had dinner in the cool diningroom – heaven. We went on to the British Ex-Servicemen's Ball, which was most enjoyable, in spite of the heat. Sorry, I always come back to that!

19th November:

John Carver has just left. He gave me a lift home this afternoon and I asked him in for tea and a little music. He has settled down very well and loves being in Zomba.

I have had a horrible day today, struggling with Kachingwe, who inserts articles he has written into the Bulletin, wherever he can find the space, without telling me. They are politically slanted and would lose me my precious job. Bryn is away on *ulendo* in the North all week, so I feel particularly vulnerable. Apart from that I am enjoying everything and have plenty to keep me busy. The heat continues mercilessly and we almost literally pray for rain.

There is very little social news as we are all lying low, lacking in energy. We did go down to the Davidsons last Wednesday after dinner, to meet a friend of theirs from the Solomons who has just arrived in Nyasaland and is to be in the Secretariat. His name is Dick Fairlie, and as he is handsome, rich and a bachelor, he is causing quite a stir. He is very sophisticated and great fun. On Saturday evening Jean and Philip Richardson (also ex-Solomons) gave a dinner for him and later we all went to the Club to see Alastair Sims in *The Green Man*, not a good film. The heat in the cinema was truly awful and the men were so hot their shirts were completely dark with sweat. We bath twice and sometimes three times a day and have so far avoided prickly heat, which is rampant.

On Sunday, Dick, the Davidsons and ourselves met at 11.30 and drove up the mountain to show Dick the marvellous view, not at its best, as Mlanje is invisible. We had lunch at Kuchawe and sat out on the *khonde*, and had a blessedly cool few hours of pleasure. Dick is enchanted by the beauty of Zomba. In the evening he came to us for supper, with the Davidsons, as he has not yet bought any stores. Bunny helped him move into his quarters and he has had a very easy, welcoming introduction to Zomba, which he appreciates. I met him yesterday in the corridor, on his first day at the office, looking like a boy on his first day at school, and he gave me a rather tremulous wink!

27th November:

There is still no let up in the heat, so this letter will be as limp as all my recent ones. I have never done less with my leisure hours. We eat supper on the *khonde*, as the fridge in the diningroom makes the temperature unbearable. We live on omelettes, salads and cold food, so it is easy for Aflike. My long thick hair finally defeated me a few days ago and with great difficulty I pulled it back and pinned it up. It will take time to learn how to do it properly. It feels blissfully cool. Ron likes it and everyone says how nice it is (except Bryn, who politely says nothing but I *know* he likes it down, and Norton, who says I look like a school marm!) Ron eventually gave in and consulted Norton about his rib, and he is now strapped up in a thick, woolly bandage, so he is pretty miserable by the end of the afternoon, when it is soaked in sweat and smelling of damp wool. You can imagine how Ron loathes that!

Byrn came back from *ulendo* on Monday, noticeably thinner. The North was like an inferno – there was a constant, scorching wind and one of his African clerks fainted with the heat in the Landrover. (An African policeman died of heat stroke at Port Herald, which is very low lying, the other day.) I cope with it very well, on the whole, but I have no energy or will to do anything but the minimum. Bryn found things (outwardly!) very much in control on his return and consequently *piled* work on to me, which is really very welcome.

On Saturday evening, with the Davidsons, we had another lovely evening at The Flamingo, which is quite high up on a hill, so we were comfortable. On Sunday Dick Fairlie joined us and we went off to Mlanje, starting out at eight. We went to a pool in an enormous gorge far along the mountain, where we had a magnificent day of swimming, sunbathing and picnicking – absolute bliss. It is wonderful what a day away does for one.

Norton phoned me this morning to apologise for giving me a fright (!) in the car yesterday when we met somewhat suddenly on a blind corner. He thought I coped very well! He said the hospital is absolutely full.

We are giving a drinks party for twenty-four people on Friday. I have ordered small eats from a new inn in Zomba, as it takes a whole day to do them myself. What it is to have a job, no time and a little money to pay for the fact!

4th December:

Let me say at once that we had some rain at the weekend and on Monday night, so I am a little more capable of a coherent letter, though there is once more not a cloud in the brazen sky. Towards sunset the sky has a coppery look. Ron and I are both quite thin after all the heat. I wear my hair down at the week-end, for social occasions, but otherwise it is up. I am getting better at doing it. It is now very long.

Ron had a splendid birthday, and celebrated it for three days! On Friday we gave our big drinks party, which went with a great swing, to my relief, as I had to do things in bits and pieces when I had time, and so felt unco-ordinated. However, all was well, and our last guests departed at 9.30. It was a hot night and people were drinking a lot. Bunny has a huge fridge and kept the beer in it overnight, so it was beautifully chilled. She also brought an enormous thermos of ice. The small eats were excellent and beautifully laid out. Alice Rutherford, the Scots girl in the office, came with George, her husband, both nervous to be among the Toffs, as they said, but I saw to it that they enjoyed themselves. I had asked Kathie Smith, but she could not come. Next morning Alice had a long coffee session in Kathie's office, telling her in a low voice all about it. Kathie came out later and said, 'It was, I hear, a lovely party for Alice!'

On Saturday night Bunny gave Ron a splendid birthday dinner, for which I provided the wine. It rained hard all night so Zomba slept well for the first time in months. On Sunday as Dick's guests we four went up the mountain for lunch, seeing Mlanje magnificent in the clean air for the first time since Dick arrived. He was ecstatic and full of plans to climb it!

We have been having a very busy time in the office, with several 'flaps' which arise every now and then. Yesterday Bryn completed his Christmas draft for HE, but is not at all happy with it. He is very hard pressed just now. I sat down and wrote out mine, which had been taking shape in my mind, and in an hour it was done and typed. Bryn is in Blantyre today and will see it tomorrow. I showed Ron the draft last night and he said it was excellent. It will be interesting to see how much of it is left after 'They' have dealt with it – if anything.

Our new offices are complete. Bryn moved in yesterday and I organised mine today. His is beyond mine, with a communicating door which stands open. I am in the front one, with a phone connected with his, so that I act as a buffer between him and the public, physically and telephonically! He is extremely busy and gives me lots to do. The offices are pleasant – dark green floors, pale green walls and grey doors. My office is tiny, but I only need my nice small desk with its two trays attached and the label 'Information Assistant' on my door, which is always open! I now feel as if I had been in the office a long time, able to answer queries or know where to find the answers.

We have decided to go away for Christmas, as Ron is due for local leave. We have booked at the Lake at Palm Beach, and the Davidsons with their two children are joining us. It will be heaven to get away by the *water*, and we shall have sun, swimming and sailing. Tomorrow Bunny and I are going to Blantyre for a day's shopping, which will be fun. I may buy an evening or cocktail dress. It is lovely to have my own money to splurge if I want to.

I hope this letter has seemed more alive!

11th December:

We have had rain daily for almost a week and the air feels thundery, stuffy and damp. Ron's rib seems to be healing well. He took off the bandage at lunch time yesterday because he could not stand the constriction, and by going carefully has managed to do without it since.

Bunny and I had a lovely day in Blantyre last week. We went in their car and had the whole day, getting back to our slightly miffed husbands about 5.30! I found my evening dress in the first shop we visited, a new shop with lovely dresses which made us feel absolute frumps, run by two very smart South African women. I just walked into the dress as if it had been made to measure. It is ballet length and the most sophisticated dress I have ever possessed. It is flame coloured, made of stiffened layers of nylon which looks like chiffon. It has a full skirt, a tight waist and a strapless boned bodice made of soft folds, and a line of small red sequins along the top, which gleam in the light. There is a very delicate stole to go with it. I hardly dared ask the price and was thrilled to discover it was only 10 guineas – I was prepared to pay far more. I walked on air for the rest of the day. We bought Christmas presents and some good red Spanish wine which Bunny chose. We discovered a new café run by a Coloured woman and had the sort of lunch we both enjoy – rolls and butter, an omelette and coffee. On Friday we all met in the Club for a drink with Dick Fairlie and they came up to our house for supper and records. Dick is a dark horse. I have discovered he reads poetry and knows all my favourite moderns very well – C. Day Lewis was his house master at school.

I am enjoying my new office and am amazed at the difference that light and cleanness make to one's working morale. I also have far fewer interruptions, with the result that I do far more work in a day (and feel far more tired)! Bryn is next door, with the door open, and we talk quite a bit, mainly shop. I am at present writing a pamphlet on Federation.

18th December:

Christmas cards are pouring in. John Carver and I have a game (very childish, I admit, but he makes me childish) we play about them. Each morning as I pass his office after collecting my mail from Ron, I pop my head in at his window and announce my score and he announces his. The Chief Secretary was coming along unnoticed behind me when I said, '14' this morning, and John said rather loudly in his beautiful, carrying voice, 'Ha, *16!*' I caught the CS's raised eyebrows out of the tail of my eye as I turned away and hurried on!

The weather has been damp, grey and cool until today when I welcomed the sight and feel of the sun again, but it will not be as hot now as before the rains. Everyone is very tired. I am absolutely up to my eyes in sewing, mending, washing, letter writing, Christmas presents and parcels – chaos!

My Christmas draft for HE was the one chosen to go up to him, with one new paragraph added, and, unheard of thing, it came back without a single alteration and the famous red ink at the end in comment, 'Thank you. A very good draft.' Wonderful boost to my morale. Bryn was delighted – almost speechless with pleasure!

We had a good weekend. At noon on Saturday we went for drinks with Cosmo and Phylida Haskard, who have a lovely house on what is called Naisi Spur, high up, with a magnificent view of the whole of Mlanje. A small Siamese kitten attached itself round my neck for the social hour the party lasted. On Sunday evening the Davidsons came for supper and we went, in pelting rain, to a lovely French film called *The Moment of Truth*, with Michele Morgan and Jean Gabin – perfectly done. It has not left me since.

24th December:

This is going to be written in rather a rush, as I have a lot to do. We leave for the Lake at 3.30 this afternoon, picking up the men at the office on our way!

Disaster hit me on Friday morning, the day of the KAR Ball, when I woke up with a sore throat and that awful 'fluey' feeling. You can imagine the scene at breakfast, me trying to make little of it, Ron looking at me in horror! I am so tired and run down I knew I had not much resistance, and I also knew that if I gave in and went to bed I would not surface until after the New Year. So I took the risk and kept on my feet, going down to the office *full* of brandy and Disprin! Bryn, of course, saw at once that I was not well, and wanted to pack me off to bed, but I begged him to let me just get on with it, which he did, very reluctantly, which made me feel worse. I even went to the Ball at night – the usual magnificent occasion. Dancing with Bryn, he said I felt hot, and told me to take Saturday morning off, which was sweet of him. Sunday and yesterday were miserable and I felt I did not care if I never saw the Lake or anyone ever again! However, this morning I definitely am better and have been dashing about getting things ready. Everyone is feeling very festive. Ron went to a big party last night (I went to bed!) It has been a horrible few days and I have not got over the depression yet, but I think I shall feel different when we are on our way. I am so tired of *doing* things. The weather is dark and wet, but we are hoping that it is local, as it often is at this time of year. I have not had a single cold this tour, so I suppose I am lucky, but what *frightful* ill-timing this has been! Apart from feeling ill, I got a terrific depression as well – all too beastly.

I am sorry this letter is so dull. There is no news except my cold!

I must help Ron finish his packing – you can imagine – where's this, where's that!

Chapter 22

2nd January 1958:

I last wrote to you while in the throes of my terrible cold, which is still with me a little. It did not in the least spoil a truly lovely holiday at the Lake. We set off at 3.30 on Christmas Eve in pouring rain, I shaking like a leaf with the effort to give the impression I was all right. By the time we passed Kasupi the sun was out and from then on we had perfect weather except for rain at night which cooled the air nicely. Palm Beach was full, and there were only two people from Zomba whom we hardly know. It was good to be anonymous among strangers, who were in fact very friendly. We did nothing but lie in the sun, swim, eat, drink, dance and go sailing. We all got gloriously brown and bleached and the others ate mightily, I hardly at all, as of course I lost my sense of taste. We had a table to ourselves but occasionally joined our host and hostess for a drink before lunch or dinner. He is an ex-DC. We came back on Sunday, leaving after lunch, and found Zomba plunged in gloomy storm clouds. My sunburn glowed among the pallid faces next day in the office. It had rained right through Christmas, as it often does in Zomba. Everyone said how well I looked and were startled when I produced my deep cough, which is just on its way out now. The sun and the swimming really helped me, as it is the kind of cold that can go on seemingly forever.

We had two full office days in which we all tended to sit on each other's desks talking, and then came the New Year's Eve Ball. I wore my new flame-coloured dress and felt marvellous, with my dark brown shoulders and back. Peter Youens said, 'I would like to pick you up and put you on the top of the Christmas tree.' We dined at the Davidsons'. Bunny had decorated the whole house most beautifully before she went to the Lake. It was a small party – ourselves, Dick Fairlie, the Richardsons and the Youens – but delightful, all the men very good dancers. I think it was the best New Year's Eve Ball ever. We left at 4.45, and everything was still in full swing. We all met again at noon, to house-warm Dick's lovely modern flat, and another marvellous party developed and lasted into the late afternoon. Ron and I ended up in bed at 7.15! I felt more homesick at New Year than at Christmas, which was such a happy, sunny time.

8th January:

For once I am *not* enjoying my work! I am struggling with the Constitution Amendment Bill, a very complicated piece of legislation. I must get it absolutely at my finger tips, as I have to explain it in very simple terms to the Africans – fearful. However, it is interesting, and good discipline for my vague approach to detail!

John Carver's father is here on a visit from Southern Rhodesia: an ex-missionary and a real charmer. They dined with us on Saturday, along with the Milners (PWD, Joan's and my host and hostess at Mzimba). I knew jolly well that Ron and Tommy Milner would dislike each other on sight, but I had to have them, because of all their kindness to Joan and me. We went on to the Club to see a highly inappropriate American film called *The Proud and the Profane*. It was just *not* my evening, though they all laughed very nicely when I apologised to Mr Carver for the film.

On Sunday morning Ron played squash with Dick Fairlie and we went back to his flat for lunch, joined by the Davidsons. We went up the mountain for tea and they came back to us for supper, all wonderfully friendly and relaxing. Dick's flat is beautiful, with his own very modern furniture from Harrods and beautiful Persian rugs. (His father was a diplomat.) I was wearing yellow toreador pants and a jade blouse. Dick made me sit in one of the chairs in a relaxed pose and took photographs. He said I looked like something out of the *New Yorker* – a marvellous magazine he takes and now hands on to me. I also read Alex's *Weekly Times*, so I feel very up to date with world events – a relief after the sometimes dreary African affairs I have to know about.

On Twelfth Night we went to the Youens' and drank mulled claret: nice. Last night John Carver brought his father in for a drink and to say goodbye, as he goes home tomorrow. He said to me he thought John had made 'lovely friends' in Zomba. My word, I can see where John gets his charm!

5th February:

I had a lovely birthday. Ron gave me a bottle of Chanel No. 22 – I just adore it. It was clever of him to think it would suit me. Bunny gave me a gorgeous royal blue tailored poplin blouse for the office and Alex gave me a kind of wire-aertex portable cushion for the car which is very popular here, as it is cool. I am delighted; the leather seat can get terribly hot, and the one inch or so difference in height helps me to see over the bonnet more comfortably. Apparently my head hardly shows and it looks as if the car is driving itself when I am at the wheel. Bunny had prepared a delicious light supper, which we ate in the garden, in moonlight, while Pablo, their little poodle, flitted about like a ghost. On Friday we went to a drinks party at Dick's. He asked us to stay on to supper and then introduced us to his very fine collection of LPs. We sat and listened spellbound to Elgar's *Dream of Gerontius* – a lovely unexpected evening of pleasure.

We have been invited to a dinner and dance at GH on 22nd February, which may be rather fun. The guest of honour is Margery Perham, an Oxford don who lectured to us on Colonial History at Oxford.

I have been asked to take part in a broadcast inter-territorial quiz! We record it here and it is broadcast in Salisbury a few days later. It takes place on 24th February at 5.30 p.m. Hugh Norman-Walker and someone from the private sector in Blantyre not yet chosen, are the other members of the team. The question-master is Cooper, the editor of the *Central African Times*, a man I do not much care for, as he takes facts from my Bulletin and twists them into criticism of the Government, whose policy I am supposed to be 'putting across' to the Africans. There are seven teams, and we start against Livingstone. I am filled with misgivings, but am thrilled to have been asked. The questions are set by two professors of the University of Rhodesia and Nyasaland and the Clerk of the Federal Assembly. Ron, of course, is delighted. I feel I must take all these challenges as they come my way. We get paid one guinea for the ordeal!

12th February:

I have at last caught up with *War and Peace*. We had Dick and the Davidsons for dinner and then went on to the Club. It was just *not* the book. The retreat from Moscow was unforgettable and Audrey Hepburn did very well. Both André and Pierre were hopelessly miscast, especially poor Henry Fonda and of course the American accents were deplorably out of place. At the Club we met Walter and Barbara Sproule, whom we knew in Mlanje. By an incredible coincidence Joan has taken over their rented cottage at home. They were so pleased to see us and to give me news of Coker, which they loved. They had met Uncle Teddie and liked him immensely, as I knew they would. On Sunday evening we drove up the mountain to watch the sunset with the Davidsons. Alex's ulcer is having one of its periodic flare-ups and he is in constant pain. It is dreadful to see a big man literally sweating it out, without a word. Like all the men, he is overworked, and worry aggravates the ulcer, which apparently also produces a tendency to worry, so it becomes a vicious circle.

Life is hectic in the office, as Leg Co is sitting this week. All hands are on deck in our Department. We make a verbatim recording which is checked with the notes of teams of two stenographers who change, without a break in the taking down of notes, every twenty minutes. They work late, typing out their shorthand and checking it against the recording. The scripts are passed on to the Print, where the men work till two or three, and next morning at 9.00 a.m. *Hansard* is out, and sold out by lunch time! I go in and sit in the Press Gallery each day for a time, and find it all most interesting, though the thought of the index is not amusing, especially as the African members find more and more to say. Tempers were frayed this morning, and the Speaker had to intervene. He is an innovation. Up till now the Governor has been in the chair, which is awkward, as his impartiality can be questioned. So we have imported a Mr Henry Wilcox Wilson, QC, a tall, elderly man with a juicy voice and considerable presence, especially in his black robe and long white wig. It is all very formal, but as we are 'on the inside', we can flit quietly in and out.

19th February:

We are having tremendous sporadic rain. I had my first experience of driving through it the other day, and was not very happy. I was shaking when I got into the office and of course drenched in the few seconds it took to dash from the car. But I shall learn to cope with that.

We are all very busy with the aftermath of Leg Co to deal with. I paid a long overdue visit to the library on Friday and found a wonderful novel called *Justine*, by Lawrence Durrell, whose *Bitter Lemons*, about his experiences as an information officer in Cyprus, has been one of the books of the year.

On Saturday we were asked to noon drinks at Jock and Barbara Corrie's. It was pleasant, as Dick was there to talk to, and I also had a long conversation with Hugh Norman-Walker, whom I always enjoy. Diana and Peter Youens were also there. Diana rides every day past my office, and I now slip out and have a few minutes with her, weather permitting. She is so nice, I wish I saw more of her. She rides a white horse and is always accompanied by her white bull terrier. They make a striking trio! In the evening we went on our own to a very bad film, but saw some good News from home and a film of Welensky's Nyasaland tour in which Bryn figured prominently and unselfconsciously. In it we also saw David (Baxter) and John Watson, their faces exaggerated on film – David's longer than ever, John's rounder. On Sunday we took the Davidson children up the mountain after tea to collect fir cones for cold season fires.

Today the film of the Queen Mother's visit, in colour, arrived at last, and at 3.30 the Information Department staff, plus husbands and wives, all went down to our workshop, where we saw it run through, with sound – quite lovely, with excellent colour. It was fun to see all the familiar faces, a bit tense and unlike their relaxed Zomba selves.

25th February:

Life goes on pleasantly here. On Saturday evening we dressed up (I in my flame coloured dress) and presented ourselves at GH, where the ADC met us and showed us the seating arrangements for dinner – forty guests, with Margery Perham the guest of honour. Ron had been with her all morning, taking her

round the Secretariat, where she spent exactly half an hour with various heads
of departments, including Bryn, so I met her: a formidable personality, but so
tired and full of what she had done and must do that she did not make much of
an impression. She is sixty-two, but looks younger, is very decisive and not
very receptive to what she does not want to hear! We then went into a
drawingroom and had a drink with the other guests. At 8.15 exactly we went
into dinner, I, to our delight, on John Carver's arm. HE and Lady Armitage sat
in the middle of the long table, on either side, with John Carver at one end and
the ADC at the other, beside whom I sat. His name is Russell Rowan, and I
discovered his family owns Rowan's of Glasgow. I said, 'Oh, my father always
bought his hats there.' He was not amused, silly little man! We had a simple
dinner, served by boys in white (-ish!) gloves and we each had a crested card
with our name. We had tinned mushroom soup, tinned salmon soufflé, casserole
chicken with new potatoes, local beans and marrow (ugh), and a fluffy pine-
apple pudding. The drinks were sherry, white and red wine, liqueurs and port. I
avoided the port (too heavy) and toasted 'The Queen' in water. We had coffee
and GH cigarettes at the table, and then Lady A. gathered the ladies' eyes and
we went off to freshen up, then were joined by the men in the drawingroom,
where I talked with Miss Perham, who looked exhausted. She had already
excused herself from the dance. The ADC then came up and asked Ron and me
to leave for the dance, with others following and the top guests came ten
minutes later with HE and his wife. We had a lovely evening, dancing all the
time, as the men had to go the rounds. I met a Mr Leonard Born from Blantyre,
whom I discovered was to be chairman of the quiz on Monday, and we thoroughly enjoyed each other. Lady Armitage kept entirely to her senior guests,
but HE danced with everyone. He is a quiet, charming man, shy but with an
easy manner. We got on to the Information Department at once and I did most
of the talking and managed to keep him amused. The party broke up about 1.30,
and we were promptly invited to join Diana Youens's party, to which we had
originally been invited, and stayed on, to have a lovely time, till 4.30. Dick,
Ron and I went back to the Davidsons' for coffee and then had a swim in the
pool. At seven we drove up the mountain to Kuchawe, where we had a splendid
breakfast – grapefruit, kippers, bacon, sausages, eggs, toast and coffee! We all
felt marvellous – the swim was a terrific idea.

   On Monday morning I realised the full force of what lay before me at 5.30,
and fought with my nerves all day. I went home alone (a mistake!) for tea, had a
bath and at five drove shakily down to the studio in pouring rain. There I joined
Hugh, Mr Born and the Rev. Neil Barnard, the third member of the team. We
sat at a table with a small mike in the middle, and put on earphones, through
which we heard Salisbury, which was recording the programme, and
Livingstone, our rival team. Opposite us was a glass partition, behind which sat
the engineer (from Salisbury) and Dave Williams, the Federal Information
Officer, Zomba, who organised the programme. We were to start at 5.30, but

there were fearful atmospherics and technical complications which were amusing to hear, until 6.35, by which time we were all tired and in a state of frightful nervousness; the room was blue with cigarette smoke and we all confessed to be simply longing for a drink! Then we began, and as soon as we had to concentrate, we enjoyed it. There were seven questions each, in three parts, quite difficult, and finally a 'quickie' which had to be answered in five seconds, 'true' or 'false'. The score was Zomba 11, Livingstone 10½, and the tension was awful. The question was: 'Rachmaninoff did *not* write a violin concerto – true or false'? The other two looked horrified and waved me on, so I took the plunge (I was pretty sure) and said 'true' and we had won! If I have time I shall write out the questions for you. We scored 60%, which was not bad, considering the strain of that wretched delay. So now we have to do it *again*! I drove through a cloudburst in thick darkness, shaking all over, to Bunny's, where they were waiting anxiously for me, and I must confess I drank a very cold whisky and soda with the greatest of ease without realising it! It really was fun, but that hour of waiting, with comparative strangers, all of us keyed up, was a real ordeal. The news has spread today and everyone is going to listen on Friday at nine, to the broadcast. Jean Richardson has asked us, with the Davidsons and Dick, to supper. I rather dread what the mike will do to my voice. However, I would not miss it for anything. Ron, of course, is as pleased as Punch. I have not quite recovered apparently, as Bryn says I am 'as jumpy as a cat' today. Huh!

5th March:

You ask about the garden. It is utterly hopeless – even my sturdy moonflower cuttings failed. I have had one solitary success. Jean Wickham gave me a slip from her gardenia bush, which I put in, without much hope, when the rains began. Well, it is now about two feet high and has produced two beautiful flowers and I think I can safely say it is well established.

On Friday we went, with the Davidsons and Dick, to dine with the Richardsons, and during a late dinner we listened to a rather atmospheric broadcast of the quiz, which went more swiftly and vivaciously than I could have thought possible at the time. It turned out that I answered quite a lot and I was much congratulated, though I myself know I could have done better. The amusing thing was that everyone was expecting a marked Scots voice and accent, as I sound on the telephone. Well, though I say it myself, my voice sounded wonderful (I know it was not a true impression, but still!) It sounded low, slightly husky, very feminine, with a tentative note of enquiry in it – great fun to watch people's faces when I began! Our next recording is on Monday 10th, and our rivals are Salisbury, which has a strong team, I am told. We should be less nervous and so able to think more quickly and clearly.

We went to the Youens's for drinks on Saturday at lunch time. Ron had a short ride in their huge garden on Diana's horse, Goldflake, and Peter and I did a very good quiz he had found in Punch. In the evening we went to The Flamingo with the Davidsons and had a great dinner. On Sunday we lunched with them at Dick's. Typical of him, he insisted that we all go as his guests to introduce *him* to The Flamingo – not a Sunday evening thing to do at all, but we were persuaded. Dick likes to get his own way. So we had another enjoyable outing and a late night, which I paid for next day.

Work goes on as usual, and there is never a day without interest. My latest task is to explain in the Bulletin that although the Queen gives Royal Assent to our Federal Bills, the Africans must not blame her for the unpopular ones. (I ask you!) I have been putting it off for ages, but pressure was brought to bear today (!) so do it I must.

19th March:

The mornings and evenings are now cold, and there is a chill feeling all day indoors and wonderfully clear, tempting sunshine outside. I spend odd moments just standing in the sun outside the office, to get warm, while I occupy myself by plucking off the dead heads from the red roses which grow in a long flowerbed by the office. There are a great many blooms and I put a single bud daily in a vase on Bryn's desk, which I know he loves. There is a big Airedale called Murphy who *will* wander about Zomba. (He belongs to the Director of Public Works.) Murphy knows me now and hangs about outside my office, waiting for me to go out to the roses. He also follows me about faithfully, much to the amusement of the chaps in the Secretariat, who hear me telling him to 'sit', while I go into their offices. He is very obedient, though he sometimes gives a tiny little whine to remind me he is there. I do a great deal of walking about and Murphy thinks I am exercising him! A nice doggum, though not really my type. I greatly impressed Diana and Peter when we had drinks with them last week, by sending their bull terrier, Flash, into a 'dwaum' in one minute, so that he went limp and collapsed on my feet, to remain there for the rest of the visit.

The Monday quiz recording session was again late in beginning, and alas, we *just* lost to Salisbury. Dave Williams, the Federal Information Officer, was desperately disappointed, as he was convinced the Nyasaland team was unbeatable. He even expressed the opinion that Salisbury got an easier set of questions. However, here are some of ours:

How did Ghana get its name?

What would you do with potassium nitrate – stain floors, blow up Parliament, develop films?

What form of low marine life was described by a scientist as 'sitting on its head and waving its legs to get food'?

What famous Rhodesian also became Prime Minister of the Cape Province?

What do these mean – Eureka, Amen, Kismet?

Who composed 'The Consul'?

Name an International Trust Territory in Africa.

Answers next week please! We all went down to Bryn's office on Friday evening and listened on his marvellous big office radio. The reception was perfect and my voice sounded better than ever, so there!

Another Leg Co sitting began on Monday and I attended for some hours. The Federal Electoral Bill was stormily passed, after the African members had walked out in protest – How they *hate* Federation. Leg Co finished yesterday and I have had an exhausting struggle to condense the Financial Secretary's speech, full of technicalities and high finance – dreadful to my layman's mind. However, I broke its back this afternoon, much to Bryn's relief, as he was beginning to think he would have to offer to take over! I am so tired I can hardly hold my pen, but it is a satisfying tiredness.

1st April:

Last week we were all shocked to hear of the death of our very popular PC, Bill Rangeley, at the age of forty-eight, on a fishing trip during his long leave in South Africa. It was very sudden and totally unexpected. Ron attended a memorial service held in Blantyre. It is really a tragedy for Nyasaland.

The weather has become blissfully unseasonable and I am in cottons again and of course blooming gently in the warmth and getting honey coloured in snatched moments in the sun and at weekends.

The Wickhams are back from leave and are staying in Zomba over Easter with friends. I saw them on Friday morning, both looking very well. They came for dinner that evening. We had such a happy time, but they stayed till one and I felt very exhausted after a hard week in the office. They have been posted to the North again, and Jean is not happy about it, but as wives do, is putting on a very cheerful front in public. On Saturday evening we had Walter and Barbara Sproule to dine and saw *Ill Met by Moonlight*, quite a good war film. They live very quietly and are always very appreciative guests. Everyone is longing for the nice long break at Easter.

I am plunged into writing electoral propaganda, interesting but difficult.

8th April:

We have had a most glorious Easter, my only regret being that we saw no more than glimpses of the Wickhams. I asked them twice again, but they were busy with other friends, which made me feel better, as it means they were not counting too much on seeing us often, which was impossible, with all our Easter plans made. We began to enjoy ourselves on Thursday when we went with Bunny and Alex to The Flamingo. Ramadan is in full swing – that is *not* the correct phrase for it, by any means. Aflike and I are avoiding each other as much as *I* possibly can!

On Saturday Jean and Philip Richardson, Alex and I in their car, Ron, Bunny, the children and their nannie in Ron's, all left at 8.00 a.m. and drove 110 miles to Portuguese East Africa – beyond Mlanje, which they call Milange. It was fun to be actually out of Nyasaland and in a territory so differently administered. The churches are white, with orange tiled roofs, and there is a splendid avenue with a double carriageway up to the Boma, modelled on the famous avenue in Lisbon. Bunny has picked up Portuguese, so she called on the Administrator (equivalent to our Provincial Commissioners) and he charmingly gave us permission to use his magnificent pool, high up with a view for miles around, backed by a splendid villa, all quite out of Africa in atmosphere, and continental in an exotic way – most stimulating. It was a beautiful day and we all got sun-burned in the two hours we spent there. We then went down into the small settlement and had lunch in a café: white and red tiled walls, iron-legged, marble-topped tables, too much furniture in the lounge and a real bidet in the bathroom. Each of us came out saying 'I say, *did* you see . . .?'! We had a gorgeous lunch – wine, huge steaks, figs in ginger, and cheese. We got back about six to find Zomba awash with rain which had been falling all day. We had a quick bath, supper and the cinema, *A Place in the Sun*, grim but excellent. On Sunday we went up the mountain to lunch at Kuchawe with Dick who was at his most charming, teasing and funny. In the evening Ron and Bunny played Scrabble and Alex and I went down to the Club to buy cigarettes. There was an informal dance going on, and we joined the Wickhams and John Carver for half an hour. We had a quiet day on Monday as I simply had to catch up with household chores.

I feel a new woman today. Everyone is grumbling about the rain over the weekend and my holiday seems to have been far better than anyone else's! This morning, with Bryn's permission, I came up here and had elevenses with Bruce while I handed over all the things we had looked after for them. We shall miss their jazz records very much. They go north tomorrow and are calling at the office to say goodbye.

23rd April: [Air Letter]

I meant to write a long letter but there is not a great deal of news and as usual I am pressed for time. I have to go down to the Club to pay for some cinema tickets I had forgotten about which will be cancelled if I do not pay by this evening. I am frantically busy in the office and enjoying every minute of it, though by four o'clock I can hardly move, physically or mentally, and Scrabble, the game of the moment, is an agony of effort, especially now that the standard is most competitively high!

Fiona Davidson, aged five, is in hospital with jaundice and seems to be enjoying herself there, which is a great surprise to Bunny. She was left in Tenerife with Bunny's sister, while Bunny went to England to have Lope, and she has never felt secure since, Bunny thinks.

We had a good film on Saturday – *Giant*, with James Dean, whom I had not seen.

Dick Fairlie has moved into the Chief Secretary's house for six months to 'keep it warm' while the CS acts as Governor. We went up for a drink at lunch time on Sunday and I enjoyed the glorious view from the big *khonde*.

30th April:

Bryn stopped suddenly the other day as he was passing through my office and said out of the blue, 'You're a happy girl, aren't you?' So there we are!

The cold season is coming more slowly than usual – flawless skies and blazing sun, but cool indoors and cold, cold in the mornings and evenings. Everyone loves it except puddocks like me. The sun comes directly in at my office window till 8.30, so till then I sit blooming, then it rises above the roof and that is me withered for the day! The hot season whites I like so much are vanishing from the Secretariat, but I also enjoy the homely sight of the chaps in flannels and tweeds. Summer clothes are classless, as regards women, but in the cold season I can tell a lot about background by looking carefully at how they dress – fascinating!

On Saturday, the Zomba Dramatic Society was putting on the play *Rope*. We were invited to dine with Mike and Geraldine Lamb, who are about eight years senior to us. He is Senior Assistant Secretary in the Secretariat, and I have quite a lot to do with him, as he has to pass some of my work before it can be published. Their other guests were John and Dorothy (Watson), over from Blantyre for the weekend. It was pleasant to see them again and of course John and Ron had to be prized apart, they had so much to say to each other. The play was very well done, especially the dénouement, when the lame poet whips a sword out of his harmless-looking walking stick. I wondered who had been able to provide such an authentic looking 'prop', and was told it had been specially made by a KAR officer, clever man. The set was just right and the acting above average. We went back for a nightcap, and crawled home about one, bone weary with the cold.

We had a happy Sunday with the Davidsons, very peaceful, as Fiona is still in hospital and Lope was out most of the day with the nannie. Alex and I bathed

Pablo, their poodle, who had rolled on something unmentionable and was creeping about hating himself and hating us for hating him! It was a damp and strenuous business but worth it. He went mad with joy and leapt high in the air down the terraces of the garden, his legs stiff like a spring lamb.

The office continues to be very busy. Tomorrow I have my first 'outside' assignment. I have to take a Mr Spoodley, United Kingdom Trade Commissioner for the Federation, up Zomba mountain (in a Government Humber), show him the sights and give him tea at Kuchawe. He will probably ask me all about altitude, temperature (about which I am vague – I must swot them up) and *timber*, but I must start sometime, according to Bryn, so I said, 'Yes sir.' Ron is overworked and occasionally has a quiet mood, when he is 'just quiet' (!), but he is usually cheerful and enjoying life too.

7th May: [Air Letter]

I am sorry about this blue flimsy again. I have had another of my terrible colds and am not yet feeling very bright, nor do I have much to tell. However, it has been a short, sharp bout and in the colder weather will not linger on as the last one did. There is nothing worse than being stuffy nosed and trying to breathe in an atmosphere like an oven. The cold season is definitely 'on' now.

On Thursday afternoon, a golden day, I went up the mountain with our VIP, Mr Spoodley, plus his wife and two children (a boy of four and a girl of seven), all delightful and most refreshing to meet. They loved the plateau, especially the 'Queen Mother's View', so called because she was enchanted by this particular spot. They all ate a huge tea at the Inn and were enthusiastic about everything, including whatever I chose to introduce about Nyasaland into the conversation, which I tried to do. The sun vanished about 3.30 behind a peak, and a cold wind froze me, so that by the time we came down at 5.30 my throat was sore and I knew I was in for it. I went to the office and with Veganin felt reasonably well at the weekend, managing a visit to The Flamingo and a quiet day with the Davidsons on Sunday, but on Monday morning I could barely breathe, hear or speak, so I stayed in bed and got up on Tuesday afternoon, and today went to the office. The worst is over, but deep melancholia has set in, and I was glad to have a busy day, though I did some stupid things which fortunately dawned on me after a time lag, so that they were put right. Bryn came as near as he dared to telling me to wear warm undies! He had a violent headache and some form of hay fever, so we spent quite a lot of time sitting back and talking to each other through the open door, with pauses for furious nose blowing. The road in front of the Secretariat is up and Zomba's traffic is in a fine mess, so Ron and I nip down on foot – a lovely walk in the fresh, glittering mornings. I got some reading done in bed and am up to date with my home newspapers. What a huge paper the *Observer* now is. I find I always turn to the *Spectator* first. I do think it is more balanced than the *Observer*.

14th May: [Air Letter]

Another of these horrid things, but I am still a little bit low and feel I would not write a long letter anyway. My cold is dying down. It has left me feeling limp and dull, and I have been working rather badly, though glad to be back to the companionship and something to do with my mind.

On Saturday we had to go to a curry lunch with a senior couple. There I found Diana Youens, also full of cold, so we exchanged germs very happily together – an excuse for not being as sociable as we should! There also were John and Nancy Ingham, back from leave. He is Secretary for African Affairs and Ron's chief, a nice shy man to whom I always enjoy talking. Last night Bryn and Chris gave a buffet supper, with a *fire* in the drawingroom, especially for me, kind people. The Weirs and the Theunnisens were there and we had a very relaxed, happy evening. On Monday, I forgot to say, Bunny and I went to Blantyre in my car, and had a mammoth shopping expedition. I bought two pairs of shoes for the office and a lovely cocktail dress – a model Susan Small, costing 12 guineas; navy blue jersey, very close fitting, no belt, and a big collar tied with a silk navy and white sailor's tie. It is perfect for the cold weather, and we go to a Sundowner at GH tomorrow.

I shall be better next week.

27th May:

You must all be thinking a lot about Joan and her plans. [She had become engaged to a Church of England parson.] I wracked my brains over a wedding present – a cheque is so dull – and decided I would send her some really good local carvings. She took a lot home with her, but like me, she may have given them all away. I have two beautiful candlesticks which could be converted to bed lamps, and six wooden napkin rings which she would love, as they are chunky and modern looking. I shall gradually collect items as I come across them. I feel she has so much, and these are the kind of things she cannot buy at home.

My cold has gone except for an occasional spectacular bark which makes people jump. I am feeling cheerful and not so tired. We have Saturday morning off for Empire Day, so the slightly longer weekend will set me up again. I think that terrible hot season has had a lasting effect on everyone, for there is a great deal of illness about.

We had a quiet weekend last week, as the film was not worth seeing and the weather was damp and chilly. On Thursday we went to a Sundowner at GH, and I wore my Susan Small model, which was much admired, though Norton told me I am far too thin. However, it is truly elegant and I felt wonderful in it and enjoyed the evening. Kathie Smith was there and, typical of her, introduced me to an African woman, the wife of one of the Leg Co members. I could have throttled Kathie, because from experience, I knew how the conversation would go, and it did. Faced by a white woman across a vast cultural gap, the African woman invariably asks, 'How many children have you?' My reply of 'None' simply throws her, and I have to rush in and ask the names of hers and we take it from there. It is surprising how many Europeans just cannot stand the new policy of GH Sundowners being multi-racial. I do not mind in the least, but it is uncomfortable to talk to an African and become aware of people's stares of disapproval, and the Africans themselves are very stiff and ready to take offence. Most unfortunate of all, in most cases they are not accustomed to the strong drinks on offer, with embarrassing consequences. However, in time we shall be a multi-racial society and the old (and young) diehards will just have to face it.

Tomorrow I am having a morning in Blantyre with Bunny, as I did not get all my shopping done last time. Bryn is very generous with time off for his girls, as he calls Kathie, Alice and me. He knows we work hard.

28th May:

Things are just at present a little under the weather. *Everybody* has colds, very virulent ones and it is a vicious circle, at home and in the office, with people passing the infection round and round. Ron has a dreadful chest cold and today I seem to be in for something, as I confessed to Bryn, who promptly said he was feeling the same. So, time will tell.

We had a lovely evening at The Flamingo on Friday, temporarily marred by Ron, who ate a very hot piri-piri chicken for the first time. (It is served mild, medium and hot.) Five minutes after we set out for home he suddenly asked Alex to stop the car and proceeded to be violently sick in the dark outside! He got in again perfectly cheerful and was simply starving when we got home! He was Duty Officer on Saturday, and while he dealt with that I dashed about the house and got masses of odds and ends done, which was most satisfying. The Davidsons came to lunch and went off to a wedding. We had a long rest and dined with them at night. On Sunday I went resolutely into purdah and had a very quiet day in the house, in the hope that I could shake off my 'below par' feeling. I returned to work on Monday very much rested.

I am working very hard to make up for a few stupid days last week when I felt too limp to concentrate. The work pours in, but never to the point of being too much, though I sit on difficult problems till I absolutely have to tackle them and then do them quickly, which seems to be the right technique for dealing with them.

4th June:

The time is flying so fast I get a shock at the beginning of each new month.

You ask about Federation. I will send you a copy of the pamphlet I wrote about it. Federation has done far more for Nyasaland than is ever admitted by the political Africans. It is very difficult for visiting journalists and British MPs to get the correct picture, so Bryn has arranged for our local *Hansard* to be sent home to newspapers and MPs and already has received reports that it is proving an eye-opener, which is great!

My cold developed into a chesty one, which is easier to deal with than a nose one, though I have to rush away sometimes and cough things over. Bunny gave me some very good medicine she had had for hers, and I am much better and not so tired, as I have shamelessly been taking tea in bed and resting till bath time, surrounded by newspapers.

9th June:

I am feeling much better, in spite of the fact that the weather has suddenly got cold, very cold indeed, with heavy rain and a bleak wind. We now have a fire in the evening. I am into thick tweeds and twinsets.

Bunny and Alex came for drinks at lunch time on Saturday and we toasted Joan. [It was her wedding day.] I found myself having to hold back a sudden surge of homesickness – the tears were stinging behind my eyes and my hands shook. Hi, ho. In the evening, as a celebration, we drove up the mountain with the Davidsons, for dinner at Kuchawe. It was a beautiful clear, moonlit night, very cold, and we sat by the enormous log fire before dinner and saw familiar faces from Mlanje, who had come over for a cricket match next day. It was strange to see them again – all tea planters, nice ones, who hailed us cheerily and raised their glasses. I suddenly had a vision of myself at Mlanje, then thought of myself now, and silently thanked God, or rather Bryn, for the transformation! We had a nice quiet Sunday, with crosswords, Scrabble, bath for Pablo and a visit to the Club to see how the cricket was getting on – Zomba lost.

Work in the office piles up, as this is nearly the end of the financial year and backlogs are being cleared up, fresh plans made.

Dear Dick Fairlie has just bought one of the new Citroens. We went up to his house for half an hour yesterday to see it – a beautiful, complicated car, with techniques involved in its construction far beyond my comprehension – and Dick's! Something to do with hydraulics!

18th June:

There is a lot of illness about still. Bryn has had a very bad throat which I immediately caught, though not as badly as he. We croak at each other in the office. However, I have reached the wonderful stage when I am beginning to feel bouncy again. Ron has been tired and quite extraordinarily listless for three weeks, and has been complaining of a queasy inside. Today I persuaded him to go and see Norton, who says the symptoms suggest dysentery. We will know tomorrow when the tests are analysed. These days it is quickly cured, but the very name makes me shudder. Ron is so relieved to know why he has been feeling so low that he is quite cheerful about the diagnosis. After all our years in the bush it seems ironic that it should happen here. There has been a particularly bad plague of flies this season, but I thought I had kept them at bay with drastic spraying. There has been a disaster in the Davidson family. Lope (pronounced Lopay) aged nearly three, tripped over her feet in the garden on Monday morning, and fell awkwardly. She was in fearful pain, and it turned out that she had *broken* her leg, right up at the top. The surgeon set it today and she is bandaged and hung up on a pulley off the bed from below the waist, to be there for six weeks. Poor Bunny has been wildly upset.

I forgot to tell you in last week's letter that we had the excitement of the Southern Rhodesian election. Bryn had to be in Blantyre on the day the results came through, so I sat all day in his office, with light music on the wireless continuously, which was interrupted as the latest results were read out, which I had to phone to several of the chaps upstairs, as the names came in: all great fun. People kept phoning and coming in for the latest figures, so I had to keep my wits about me, what with all the odd names and even odder spellings.

We had a very pleasant Queen's Birthday last week. I stayed at home and did all sorts of chores that were screaming for attention, and Ron went to the parade. Then we, Dick and the Davidsons went to the Richardsons for a mar-vellous curry lunch – the fun was fast and furious. On Saturday evening we had a lovely hour at Kuchawe by the fire, where we heard the News and talked to some very pleasant strangers from Lusaka, and then came down here for sup-per.

The weather is very cold and sunny. Yesterday morning I picked a flawless red rose for Bryn's desk. It felt crisp and frosty, and smelt of a rose in autumn, a very special scent to me. All the leaves are scarlet and gold, and drift down all day – too nostalgic to think about overmuch!

28th June: [Air Letter]

Another small letter this week, because I was delayed at the office this afternoon and am home late, with a bacon and egg pie to make and my nails to do!

The weather is so cold that by 3.30 I am almost as helpless and useless as I was in the heat. I think Bryn will eventually get me a radiator. I am gradually wearing him down to a state of manly pity for the dear little soul shivering next door to him. He does not seem to feel the cold at all. He has started negotiations for a rise in my pay, as he thinks I deserve more and also he wants to give me more work to complete my training as a full Information Officer. He said the other day I have a definite aptitude for it. There is a great deal going on in the office in preparation for the Budget session of Leg Co next week, which I shall attend when I can get away.

Ron has had tests taken at the hospital and Norton says he had not got dysentery, but *might* have amoebic dysentery, which is difficult to detect. The cure is eight days of miracle pills, and he is to take them, as they will cure him if need be, and do no harm if not. From the way Ron feels Norton is pretty sure he has it, I think. We are thankful the cure is so simple nowadays. It used to be frightful, with enemas and all sorts of indignities!

Zomba is *thick* with 'flu. The Secretariat corridors echo with coughs, sneezes and nose blowings. I am much better and working well again, thank goodness. One of my Bulletin articles was quoted on the Federal News the other night – it gave me a funny feeling! They have very few sources of news out here, so it is nothing to get proud about. (Ron is, of course!)

1st July:

Ron finished his course of pills today and is looking and feeling very much better already. I have had another brief, bad cold and on Norton's suggestion have started taking vitamins, which are obviously doing me a lot of good, after only six days – such a relief to have energy again!

Life is hectic, as Leg Co began on Monday, and I have to take the place of Arthur Mell, who is the Southern Province Information Officer, stationed in Blantyre. He was to come over and take notes on all the African members' speeches, assemble them from *Hansard* next day, get them typed, do the same thing with the Government replies and have the whole collection printed and sent out to all DCs, to counteract the one-sided version the Congress people will present. Arthur's sailing date for home leave was suddenly put forward by a week, so he is out of it. I am, of course, delighted and have been sitting in the Press gallery scribbling hard since Monday at 9.30. It is an excellent chance to show 'them' I can do it *just as well as a man*! (It might influence that rise in pay Bryn is having such a battle over.)

I have just been down again, and have come home, as the debate has been adjourned till tomorrow and they are now on to Bills, which do not concern me. Ron is working late collecting material for the Government replies tomorrow. It is a time of great pressure on everyone.

My party for the Red Cross has dwindled to ourselves and the Davidsons. Dick was invited to GH, and of course had to accept. Diana and Peter Youens also excused themselves. Peter is acting CS and felt he should not leave Zomba – we are dining at The Flamingo. (Diana said to me in private that in fact he felt it was infra dig for an acting CS to go to The Flamingo!) So, off we dashed to Blantyre and had a mixed grill and red wine. We dashed back, changed and went to the Ball, which was fun, but almost spoiled for everyone because of the intense cold. We danced every dance, to keep warm. Sunday was very leisurely and piano after the late night.

Monday began with a bang and I feel I have not stopped since, but it is all most interesting, though the African members are as long-winded and unco-operative as ever. I am sorry this is written hurriedly, but I still have things to do.

9th July:

You will be glad to hear Ron has finished his course of pills and is absolutely himself again. I, after nine weeks, am almost entirely free at last from cold, though I still produce the occasional tremendous bark out of the blue which sends Bryn, working next door, practically through the roof. The Establishments people are being difficult about my rise in pay, entirely on technical, red tape grounds, and Bryn is now going to suggest they make me a full Information Officer right now, with salary to match. He says I am really as fully trained as is possible, have actually covered all types of work required and he considers I am absolutely qualified and fit to be one. We can now only wait and see. I think my Leg Co work finally made up his mind for him – a lucky chance, which I thoroughly enjoyed and which did not worry me in the least. I have been fully occupied since, compiling and editing all the material straight out of *Hansard*. I cut it out, paste it on foolscap, and it is whisked off to the Print. The next Bulletin is a Leg Co number – my idea – and I shall send a copy to you. None of it is actually written by me, of course, except the headings and 'leads in', but it will be interesting for you to see how it is made up and the cumulative effect of the articles. It will also give you an impression of the African members, though I have had to edit out nearly all the rudeness.

The best performance of the session was Peter Youens's speech for the Government, as acting CS. It was simply splendid, and one of the reporters from Northern Rhodesia, Jim Biddulph, a very experienced man, said to me it was the best political speech he had ever heard. Taking my courage in both hands, I rang the CS's office and asked if I could speak to the CS for a moment. Peter came to the phone and I told him I was ringing from my office to tell him Jim Biddulph's comment, which I though he would like to know. He was absolutely delighted and gratified.

We have a number of visiting journalists about just now, on the spot for the arrival of Dr Hastings Banda, which happened without incident on Sunday. He has returned to Nyasaland after forty-three years, with the stated intention of leading his people to Independence. Colin Legum, the journalist who is on the *Observer* staff, appears to be very close to Banda, as guide and mentor. He is on a five months' roving commission in Africa. He is a South African Jew, very smooth and agreeable to talk to. He takes no notes, as he has obviously decided already exactly what he is going to write(!). He nevertheless asks for interviews with all our top chaps. I give him as little help as I dare with all the charm I can muster!

16th July:

The Leg Co number of the Bulletin came out today and I shall send it off to you tomorrow, by air mail.

Ron and I spend a great deal of time talking shop, which as you know I used to deplore, but now that I am in the picture, with everything at such an interesting stage, and he is in African Affairs instead of in field work, we can discuss things and help each other by thinking aloud – all most stimulating and unbelievably different from the bad old days.

It is still very cold, but there is no doubt the sun is warmer, and a few more weeks will bring blessed relief. Some of the stenographers are back to cotton dresses. I am now a standing joke with several chaps I meet in the course of my duties. Whether Mrs Hitchcock has her tweed coat on, just round her shoulders or not at all, is regarded as a barometer of the weather outside, however they may feel!

Ron and I are both feeling absolutely fit again, though I am very thin. The vitamins increased my appetite and one day at lunch when I demolished a large bowl of strawberries, Ron looked positively alarmed and said, 'For God's sake get me some vitamins too, or I shall never keep up with you!'

The work in the office is interesting. I am now writing a pamphlet for newcomers to Nyasaland, and had great satisfaction today writing a very carefully worded chapter on servants. I have also started the marathon exercise of indexing the latest *Hansard*, which I know practically by heart, as I produced a big digest of it for the DCs which has proved so useful that it is in great demand on the top corridor, where they can read their contribution to the debate in convenient form. Bryn and I work so well together now that we talk in half sentences and he sometimes looks a little taken aback, then laughs, shrugs and leaves me to it.

On Saturday evening the Davidsons dined with us here, and then for a change, we drove over to Limbe to attend a Horse Show dance, which was most enjoyable but horribly cold, as Limbe always is. There was a strong damp wind blowing, and in the short dash from the car to the Club my hair fell disastrously and bothered me all evening, as I was wearing it down and it is very heavy and long. It was fun to see some unfamiliar faces and dresses. There was an hour's dress show, with some lovely summer models, all from a little shop called 'Boutique Meganne' where I always go, as it stocks small sizes.

Ron had to umpire a cricket match on Sunday between the Administration and Agriculture, and we spent the day watching, I wrapped up to the eyes. It was a bleak, grey day but everyone enjoyed it, as it was a Protectorate match, and there were people from all over the territory. The wrong side won and Ron had sore feet, but it was a happy day and I talked to many people. It is the kind of occasion I love.

Yesterday the Baxters, on local leave, called in. They were both astonished and delighted at the change in me – 'Out of the chrysalis at last,' said David, with great affection. Margaret is well, and expecting another child in December. Katherine is a dear wee girl, with David's long face – not pretty, but attractive.

30th July:

Ron and I are fit and well, but there is no doubt that we both need local leave. I am rather down today as Ron has been chosen to go to Salisbury to attend a course on African affairs from 24th August–5th September, almost exactly the dates I had fixed for my local leave too. It is typical Secretariat that they ask a man on local leave to go off and work for them, so that they do not need to replace anyone more than once, as it were. I have thought about going with him, but the air fare is £18 (Government will pay Ron's fare, of course, and an allowance, so he will not lose any money on it, though no doubt as a result he will spend more money in Salisbury!) and I would have to stay in a hotel. Ron is to stay in a hostel at the University, where the course is being held, which is some way out. He will have a few days off when he comes back and we shall have a long weekend at the Lake. I shall take some more days off after that – a good idea, really, as by then I may be able to go to the pool.

The cold season is still very much with us, but it is now hot in the sun and the end is in sight, and as always one's cottons look awful: limp, crumpled and out of date! However, I shall not so much as hang mine up for another month! The sun is moving round again and in the morning I get about twenty minutes of it in my office – lovely. Bryn has to listen to the 8 o'clock news, so we have light music softly from 7.30, and with the sun and the music the place seems very gay and bright and we start off the day very relaxed and pleased with each other! He went off to the North today, and Kathie is on local leave, so I am in charge. Fortunately everyone knows he is away and the telephone is fairly quiet. John Carver (of Mzimba days) has been transferred to our Department and has been learning the ropes for a few days. As far as I was concerned it was a waste of time, as he was far too busy teasing me and making me laugh, to take in all that I was trying to tell him. He has now gone to Blantyre to take over our office there. I shall miss him very much.

We had a very pleasant evening with Kathie Smith and some of her friends last week. People shirk entertaining in the cold season, as it is so difficult to have a warm room – screens, blankets along the doorways, shawls, *everything* is laid on and still we all shiver. It was so nice to meet different people and talk about all sorts of things. On Saturday the Davidsons dined with us and we went to see *The Yangtse Incident*, which, after a run of poor films seemed almost perfect. The *Amethyst* was the same type of ship as *Kite*, one of Alex's ships which was torpedoed, so he was filled with memories. (He had a very bad war.)

Ron had a letter from Tom [his guardian, Tom Chalmers], happily working in Dar-es-Salaam and longing for us to go and see him. (Huh! *He* is the one with the big salary.)

6th August:

If I had an air letter I would be sending it, as I have planned things badly this week and left myself with little time today. However, I am starting this before going to the office after lunch and will finish it at teatime.

Everyone is feeling rather dull after the holiday, an ungrateful feeling but it almost always happens! On Thursday Ron and I were invited to a party at the Collards (Commissioner of Labour). They had the seven Labour Officers from the whole territory there, gathered for a conference, with one rather lost wife. Dick was there, and the rest were eight African Labour Assistants with two wives – not two each, just two. I found it all very trying as Claud Collard insisted on saying I worked in the Information Department when he introduced me, and it is a well known fact that the Department is by no means universally popular among the better educated Africans, and the idea of a white woman working in it even less so! Of course they all shut up like clams, and they are dabs at that. The two wives were too petrified to be audible – a most exhausting and unrewarding evening for us both. We asked Dick back for a grumble and a nightcap. I tossed off my shoes and lay on the sofa, groaning.

On Saturday evening I took Ron and the Davidsons to The Flamingo as a holiday treat. About half of Zomba seemed to be there, all in the same holiday mood. As a change we had huge mushroom omelettes. Sunday was really warm and we had a lovely day at the Davidsons, on the *khonde* and out in the sun, being very lazy. The weather has stayed warm and I actually have on a blouse and cardigan – marvellous uplift to my spirits. On Monday we made an expedition to Chileka airport and had a delicious lunch. I had piri-piri chicken, Ron had pasta, Bunny and Alex had Portuguese steak, and we all had red Chianti, bottled in Florence – a lovely continental meal, with salad and cheese. It has made me brood about good food ever since, which is usually a sign that one needs leave! We had a quiet evening with a strong Sunday night feeling and went back to the office on Tuesday with a strong Monday morning feeling! Bryn was back from the north, full of interesting stories, so I had an easy morning listening to him. He has been asked by someone Upstairs (as we call the top corridor) to try to find Moscow at 9.30 a.m. on the wireless, and listen to certain news items. We have not found the station yet, but fiddle about for ten minutes every morning, Bryn working the wave band and I the needle. Cosmo Haskard came in this morning and discovered us both standing leaning our

foreheads on the set, engrossed in a magnificent performance of Rachmaninoff's 2nd piano concerto which we had just picked up. Tableau!

Wild excitement! Iris has just come in, back with Linden after eleven months
leave, to rejóin Dave. They are on their way north, and are staying up the
mountain, so we are going to see them tonight – heavenly! I must walk dowñ
and tell Ron, in case he decides to work late.

12th August:

The grouse will be lying doggo on the moors, bless them!

Your nice fat letter arrived yesterday morning. Alex called in at my office for
something and said there was a letter for me which he had just seen on Ron's
desk, written in 'a large bold hand', and I said it would be yours, whereupon he
said he rather thought it might be, as it was the handwriting of his mother's
generation!

The weather has dealt everyone a cruel blow. It was really warm till Saturday, and then in the evening it rained and since then it has been damp with a
bitter wind – temperatures in Salisbury *below zero* – it is much higher. Everyone is complaining – even Bryn's nose was red today. The electricity supply
was so over-loaded with radiator burning that a special notice was sent round
asking people to be more spartan! Alice went home at lunch time and found her
boy ironing in the kitchen with the electric oven fully on and the oven door
open!

Lope's leg has set perfectly and every afternoon Bunny takes her home for a
few hours. She walked, with help, at once, and will soon manage alone. She
looks rather dazed and is entirely dependent on attention, having been as good
as gold in hospital and entertained herself for hours. Fiona is finding the
competition for attention very hard, and is very difficult, poor wee girl, but they
will settle down.

The brief visit with the Davies' was wonderful. We went up to Kuchawe on
Wednesday evening and stayed till the 9.30 clock, and on Thursday went up
again for dinner, coming down at 10.30. We saw Linden for a few minutes in
bed, very delightful and precocious, and more amenable after school in England. Iris was looking splendid; brown face, flashing eyes and teeth, and her
hair going very becomingly white all round her face, though dark at the back.
She loathed coming back, of course, but was still buoyed up by eleven months
at home. She said how lovely it was to start off again by being with friends who
eased her down to earth gently. She said Ron and I seem to be as fresh and alive
as people at home, which was good to hear, and Dave said my having interesting work had changed me *completely*. I told Iris she must come here whenever
she likes, once Linden goes back to school, and stay for as long as she likes.
Their visit was like a breath of fresh air. Our weekend was quiet, very much an
indoors affair, because of the sudden beastly change in weather.

Things seem in a state of suspension at present, as everyone is waiting for the warm weather. The Governor arrived back from leave two days ago and already one senses the stiffening of the Secretariat spine, as the files come down with peremptory minutes in red ink. The political situation is getting more complicated, with Dr Banda behind the scenes – all very interesting.

20th August:

The weather improved over this last weekend and is now behaving as it should, getting warmer almost daily. There was a Civil Service dance on Saturday and we and the Davidsons had a lovely evening, dining up the mountain, warmed by log fires, and then getting a table by the fire in the lounge of the Club, so we were most comfortable. There were not many people there, which meant there was plenty of room to dance. We had a beautiful warm day on Sunday and I kept out in the sun as much as I could. We watched cricket at the Club for an hour in the morning, and I had a pleasant talk with some of my favourite people. Ron is preparing for his Salisbury trip. He is looking forward more to being away from the office than to the actual experience, I think. I shall try to get some household chores and sewing done while he is away, and be ready to go to the Lake with a clear conscience. I am feeling very well, but quite definitely need to get away from Zomba for a few days. I love the office and am perfectly happy there, but I get very tired by the end of the day and small things upset me – some of our African staff I could gladly fell to the ground! However, a few days in the sun will fix that. I am also, of course, dreading sleeping alone in the house. Bunny has invited me to stay with them, but quite frankly I do not think in my present state I could stand the noise and chaos created by the children. It will be the longest *ulendo* Ron has done!

26th August:

I am realising how much better it is to be working when one's husband is on *ulendo*. The days flash by as usual, and I get a lot done in the evenings. I have been well visited by Bunny and Alex, and yesterday I went to tea with Barbara and Walter Sproule. I had a delightful time with them. Barbara is a different person now that she is away from Mlanje, and it is quite obvious that to them I am too. They confessed they hated the climate there, and the people. They were eager for news of Joan, and Barbara got out a magnifying glass quite shamelessly in order to have a really good look at a small photo of Cecil. Her comment, in relieved tones, was that he looked far too nice to be a parson! They are charming people.

On Sunday morning we went through the usual chaos of Ron packing – the key of his suitcase just not to be found, what was Laga's address, where was his briefcase key, why were there not more clean hankies and his *tennis shoes* had a broken lace, etc. etc. etc. to the last moment, when all was put right and the Davidsons bore us off in their car, Ron perfectly relaxed, I quivering all over! We had an hour at the airport watching masses of people arrive and depart, and at 12.50 Ron departed with a roar in a Viscount. We drove back rather subdued and after tea with them, Alex took me home and I had an early night. Contrary to expectation I have slept well.

Tonight I am going to supper with Bunny and Alex and we shall have a threesome at Scrabble. Lope is walking well now, though still a little stiff, with a wobble before she tackles steps.

I still have not begun writing the many letters I owe, but will make a start tomorrow. I saw the Secretariat Christmas card today, a very lovely photo of Mlanje, and wrote the caption for it, so you must have one, when the time comes. Our departmental one has not yet been produced – awful to think of Christmas things already!

2nd September:

Let me start off by telling you at once that the *hot* season is here! On Sunday I woke up pouring with sweat and tossed the blanket off with joy. Today I am in a cotton skirt and blouse, without a cardigan – wonderful. The change is so sudden it is quite startling. I have not yet heard from Ron, which hurts my pride, because people kindly enquire for news of him. The mails are ridiculously slow, but I feel he cannot have written on Wednesday, as arranged. However, I must just wait. The time has gone remarkably quickly and I can hardly believe I shall be meeting him on Saturday. He brings me (on my cheque) a mended watch, if worth mending, my pearls restrung, some glamourous undies and, I hope, a present from him.

Life here goes on pleasantly though I am hanging on for next week when we are off to the Lake. I can believe we are going, now that the weather is warm, and have been getting out holiday garb, very crushed and musty. The Davidsons have been looking after me very well. On Saturday evening we went up the mountain for a pre-dinner drink, and there found Hugh and Jane Norman-Walker entertaining a very lively naval Commander. He and Alex reminisced hugely. I thought him great fun but Alex's verdict was he 'knew the type – one of those shore men'. Baffling! On Sunday morning I turned the wireless up loud and dashed about, happy to be domesticated for a short time. I had lunch and tea with the Davidsons and then came back for an early night. I have had one bad night, when there was a high wind and all sorts of noises, but otherwise I have slept remarkably well.

I had tea again with the Sproules, who were very glad to see me. I think they feel lonely and out of date here now, though they enjoy the general amenities. Barbara lent me three Vogues, and I am depressed by the ugliness of much of the fashions and glad we do not have to be too up to date here – what a thing for *me* to say! I am buying some more office clothes on Saturday. Last hot season just wore everything out and they are all going at the same time, as they always do.

There is rather a lull in work, which I do not like; just enough to keep me occupied. The next Leg Co session is in October, which will liven things up.

11th September: Palm Beach

I was very glad when Saturday came last week, though the time had not dragged. I was just beginning to sleep badly, which was a bore, and made me very tired and nervy during the day. On Saturday morning I left at 7.30 and had a lovely lone drive to Blantyre, singing to myself. I did a lot of shopping, very quickly, with great success, including a stone-coloured, straight linen skirt, extremely smart. I even had time for a coffee and was at Chileka at 11, where I ran into John and Nancy Ingham. They were about to fly to Salisbury and had just taken travel pills which made them feel odd, so we had a funny and light-headed conversation till Ron's plane came in and he joined us three for half an hour till they left, rather comatose. Ron was worked off his feet and had done wonders in getting my shopping list completed – my watch, new camera, undies, pearls and a bottle of heavenly French scent plus a lovely cotton skirt which tones with both the blouses I bought for the office. I am delighted. He enjoyed the course very much and says it was all very worthwhile. He took a three-page letter written in pencil out of his pocket and gave it to me – no envelope, no stamp! He had seen the Hammars and had dinner with Clement and Dana [Laga's sister]. Laga and the children are in Serbia. He says Dana is very Slav, like Ivan. We had a very good lunch at the airport, talking hard, and then drove home, Ron sweating in the heat, having left Zomba before it began. There was a lot of talk and untidy unpacking, then we bathed and dressed for the Golf Ball and went to dine with the Davidsons, who gave him a great welcome. We had a lovely evening, leaving about one, as Ron was very tired by then. We watched cricket all day on Sunday and in the evening went to see *Monsieur Hulot's Holiday*, which Bunny and Alex had not seen. They absolutely loved it.

Work suddenly piled up on Monday and Tuesday at the office, and yesterday I finished by 2.30, shaking with effort, and tore up to the house to load the car, and was outside Ron's office at exactly three. I drove to Liwonde Ferry, past my beautiful Kasupi, everything bathed in the thick gold sunshine of mid-afternoon, and then Ron took over. We arrived here at 5.50, just after sunset – the air warm and sticky, and the unforgettable smell of the Lake strong in my nostrils.

We have a lovely big room with bathroom and lavatory attached, and a roofed *khonde* with deck chairs, and the water only five yards away. The weather is perfect; hot, with a breeze, and we have been swimming, sunbathing and doing absolutely nothing all day. Ron is rather red now (4.15) but I have gone instantly brown. Neither of us feels quite unwound yet, but that will come.

There are masses of Rhodesians here, and no one from Zomba – bliss. All my summer clothes are too big for me, but as I am eating like a horse, this may change soon! I have never been so thin, but I feel absolutely fit.

17th September:

I had my first nightmare for years at the Lake. Something or somebody was climbing in at the window and I was unable to make out what it was without my specs – horrible!

We are back in Zomba, both simply bursting with energy and high spirits, and as brown as is possible. It was a marvellous break, exactly when we needed it. The Davidsons arrived with the children and their nannie on Thursday before lunch and in ten minutes had joined us for a swim. Bunny and Ron went out sailing every morning – not very interesting, as the water was very still, especially in the mornings. The nannie bore Lope away, and Alex, Fiona and I spent peaceful mornings together, with the result that she could swim by the time we left, as I spent hours with her in the water. She relaxes with me and behaves very well. We came back on Sunday, to find a queue of twenty-three cars at the ferry! We had to wait for two and a half hours. However, we had tea, crosswords and Scrabble with us, so it was not too wearying, except for the children after dark. We crossed at seven and were home by eight.

The men started in next morning as usual. I dashed about at home, as I have done ever since and got masses of things off my conscience, including some letter-writing, which is a wonderful feeling. I went to Blantyre yesterday, and had my hair thinned and tapered; so it remains as long as ever and I can wear it up or down. At night I twist it into a short rope, for coolness in bed. This morning we woke up to pouring rain and it has not stopped. I have cleaned all my books, washed my two big lampshades, made a pie, a pudding and mayonnaise, and done some shopping – I have the car.

I feel wonderfully well and rested, and enjoy being at home, as I know it is not for long! I called in at the office yesterday and it was nice to see Bryn's face light up. He said, 'Gosh, you look marvellous!' He had saved up a list of interesting items to tell me about the work going on, and I stayed for quite a while. He takes a week off next week, so I shall be plunged *in medias res* all right.

24th September: [Air Letter]

I sent the garden boy to the Post Office for this, which is why it is so dilapidated. I am sorry it is a short one this week, but I am back in the office and also, I wrote the news of local leave last week and do not have much more yet! I got off seven huge, overdue letters last week and feel very much the better for it. I can now sit back for a while and await replies.

I had a really lovely week off in Zomba, spending hours at the pool and doing lots of things in the house with the LP keeping me company. I feel very well indeed and everyone has commented on the difference. On Sunday night we saw an Italian film, *La Strada* – marvellous, but unmitigated gloom throughout, with agony piled on agony. Ron and I have begun to play tennis again. I am just going to collect him at the office.

1st October:

The weather has settled down to being hot and I am blissfully enjoying it. As soon as it settled, the jacaranda performed their yearly miracle of being colourless one day and almost overnight bursting forth into full, glorious bloom. The whole place is simply overwhelmed with them – masses and masses of blue trees already covering the roads with petals. The startling thing is that they have no leaves at all when in bloom, so the entire tree is blue.

Ron and I have been playing tennis every weekday. We go down at four and play till the light begins to fail at 5.30, have a drink at the Club, then home for a bath and sometimes Scrabble with the Davidsons. I do not really enjoy Scrabble during the week, as my mind is too tired to concentrate.

We gave a noon party for sixteen people, which was a great success, on Saturday. Bryn allowed me to go off at 11.30 to see to 'things', and I found everything ready but not all *quite* right, so I was glad of that half-hour's grace. We had the Sproules and several new people from the Secretariat, including a very nice couple from Bermuda, Bobby and Hazel Lowe, whom I think we shall see more of. It was a glorious day and everyone stayed out on the *khonde*. I sat out in the sun almost the whole weekend!

Bryn came back on Monday, looking very well and very brown. There is the usual lull in work that comes at this time of year, but later this month we shall be extremely busy, with Leg Co. Our African artist has produced a perfect Christmas card which I saw in draft, and I am looking forward to having a really satisfactory one to send from our department.

I am getting more reading done and am at present greatly enjoying Ian Fleming's *The Diamond Smugglers*; a true account of the tremendous trade in Africa in illicit diamonds. I have used the Zomba library for so long it takes me ages to dig out something interesting, unless I am lucky enough to find a new book.

Ron has just come in, at 4.30, not wanting tennis, so we shall probably have a game of Scrabble before a bath and supper with the Davidsons. He has had another letter from Tom, who would, brave man, like to drive down from Tanganyika to see us. It would be interesting to have him here for a time. His main reason for writing was to ask us to listen to the wireless on Sunday evening at 8.30, which we did, and heard him introducing excerpts from the B Minor Mass, which is a favourite of his and Ron's. It was most nostalgic to hear his soft, deep voice again, with all the little affectations on top of that very perfect BBC English.

8th October: [Air Letter]

A short letter this week, as various things have cropped up and we have car trouble today, so that I am home late and am going out soon. It was Alex's birthday on Saturday and he took us to Kuchawe for a very good dinner – the main course was veal, and we drank beautifully chilled hock with it. It was a lovely evening, the restaurant full and humming with enjoyment. We had a lazy, sunny Sunday and in the evening went to see *Miss Julie*, a very good, but strange Swedish film. There was some ham acting, but Miss Julie herself was perfect. It was all utterly miserable and reminded me of Russian short stories – mood, seduction, madness and suicide – the lot!

Work in the office is on the increase again, so I am happy and busy. Bryn is still trying to cut through red tape and get me more pay and the title of Information Officer.

22nd October:

The weather is beautifully hot and I am blossoming. The Met. people predict another exceptionally hot season, so we are certainly having a hard tour as far as the seasons are concerned. I still think people are suffering from last year's heat, followed by a very cold season and a sudden change to heat again.

I have become editor of a new venture, a monthly Students' Newspaper, which had its first issue last month – a dull beginning but it will soon improve. The tentative 1,000 copies printed vanished like snow. I shall be writing the editorials but the object is to get the African staff to write for it. I also have two 'photo features' in production – big posters with a series of captioned pictures which tell the story of one of the Government schemes to improve the lot of the African villagers.

We had a good weekend and on Sunday evening went to see Sucksdorff's *The Great Adventure*, a glorious nature film which entranced Ron and me. The most exhilarating shot in it was of an owl sitting rigid with tension on a bare tree branch gazing straight up into the sky where four jet planes screamed over the sky with feathery patterns streaming behind them. Ron was in transports over the birds. It has not yet left my mind. I asked for it specially and now have *carte blanche* to ask for more, the committee was so delighted with my find. *Sight and Sound* keeps me very well informed, and I can supply its good reviews which are put up with the advertisement.

We have been playing lots of tennis, but today it is actually too hot, so Ron has arranged to have a hair cut instead.

6th November:

The heat is tremendous, but my office is not nearly as stuffy as the one I occupied last year, and when people come in, they remark on its comparative coolness. I am not feeling the heat hard on me as I did last year, though our tennis is not as frequent as it was. We played yesterday, a very spongy game, and came off drenched in perspiration to the roots of our hair. Thank goodness I can put mine up. It soaks and dries about three times a day.

I now cope with the *Spectator* crossword very well, and feel inferior if I do not almost finish it. The *Observer* one I do in about 20 minutes, and Alex and I tackle the *Weekly Times* one every Sunday, usually leaving one maddening clue unresolved!

I am completely exhausted after a very hot, busy day, and am getting my second wind over tea. A high powered representative of *Time Magazine* descended upon the office this morning, unannounced, and as Bryn and Kathie are both on *ulendo*, I had to (almost literally) leap into the breach and arrange his 'program' on the spot – interviews with the Chief Secretary and a number of Heads of Departments, lunch, pamphlets, *Hansard*, everything I could throw at him! 'They' each gave him half an hour, so we await his articles in *Time* with interest. His name is Prendergast! He left in a yards long green car with huge fins on it, apparently extremely satisfied with his day.

Ron and I were gloriously happy to have your cable [Elspeth had given birth to a daughter], and I feel too utterly relieved that it is safely over. I am simply delighted that it is a daughter, in spite of the inevitable, conventional expectation of a son. I love the names, especially Alison (reminding me of the lovely early English poem with the line 'my heart to Alison is lent'). I am sorry there is no family name included, but perhaps Elspeth had no say in that.

I have recently been given a great deal of work. To my relief, Bryn realises that I work at my best when I know I have a great deal to get through, and he has been piling it on. I now prepare the Government press Communiqués, and so have completely covered all the work of an Information Officer. (Bryn is still battling over my status and salary.) The Students' Newspaper improves, but slowly. I still have to think up ideas for our African Assistants to tackle – quizzes, crosswords, articles on sport and interesting 'Do You Know' items taken from the Encyclopedia Britannica!

Ron and I dragged ourselves to a drinks party given by one of the settlers, on Friday evening, and it was as dreary as I had anticipated, except that the patsy-go-lows, which I seldom touch, were delicious. I stood gloomily involved with a bishop and ate steadily through caviare, smoked salmon and shrimps. We had a restful weekend, with the Sunday night film a delight – Jack Buchanan, slim and debonair, in *The Notebooks of Major Thomson*. We continue to play tennis, though not every day, as the heat is sometimes too oppressive when there is thunder about.

I must now make an enormous effort, go over the bills and write cheques –
hateful task when I am tired.

19th November:

I am drinking hot tea. It is far better than a cold drink in the hot weather, as it
makes one burst out into sweat from every pore and therefore feel cooler! The
weather is blazing hot and life for me is rather trying at the moment, as Aflike
went off last Friday to Fort Johnston to see to his 'garden', and did not return,
as arranged, on Sunday. Today, Wednesday, we had word that he is in Lilongwe
hospital, ill with some kind of fever. I have only a very young garden boy and
Stephen, our house boy, aged about eighteen. We are managing, but only just,
and any extra duties at home in this heat are almost the last straw. We are
nevertheless having pleasant meals of cheese, fruit, salads, fish and cold meat,
in somewhat monotonous rotation!

My title of Temporary Female Departmental Assistant may be changed to
that of Information Officer by a recent development. The Annual Report of the
territory is usually done by an Assistant Secretary (same as Ron) and was done
last year by John Carver, who is now in our office in Blantyre. There was a
terrific flap when it dawned on the chaps upstairs that he was no longer available, and Bryn was summoned to discuss the problem. When he came back he
said, in effect, that he really did not know what to do about it, as *he* certainly
did not have the time. Something made me say, on impulse, 'Is there any reason
why *I* should not do it?' and he stopped in his tracks, snapped his fingers at me
and said 'Right! You're on!' And that was that! It is quite a task, involving
meticulous attention to detail, and the chivvying of heads of Departments to
send in the relevant material, with statistics (which everyone seems to hate
producing). It is published for the Colonial Office by Her Majesty's Stationery
Office. The Government Printer tells me there is tremendous rivalry among the
African colonies to be the first to send their Report home, so the Print is always
desperately anxious to have the proofs flowing in. I have read four thick
background files on it and feel a certain alarm about the whole undertaking, but
it will be excellent experience and a tremendous chance to prove I can do it – of
course I can, but it will be an enormous grind. Everyone at work teases me
about it and commiserates with me. You will no doubt be sick of the subject
before it is finished – sometime in January/February!

I have sent off all our Christmas cards except yours, which I shall send by
airmail later. I had such a lovely selection that I sent off a Red Cross one to
Jess, a Secretariat one to Elspeth, and you will receive the Information Department card, which I love. It was done by Cawinga, our cartoonist, the utter
and complete bane of the entire office – hopeless at anything he touches except
his artistic work, which is good. He is a type I never want to meet again – an
African who believes having a talent (in his case drawing) entitles him to live

by that alone and he has assiduously cultivated an artistic temperament to get out of doing any work at all except drawing. As we are short-staffed, this attitude does not contribute to the smooth running of the office routine! He drives Bryn wild with exasperation and reduces me to terrible silent rages. Everyone's temper is precarious at this time of year anyway.

27th November: [Air Letter]

The weather is very tiring, with terrific heat piling up and then great storms of rain and thunder. There is the continual risk of getting chilled from the sudden fall in temperature. I have a shaky, 'fluey feeling today, but lots of people have had it without anything more happening, so it is probably that and I shall ignore it. I am also having anti-rabies injections – no cause for alarm, so do not panic. There is not the remotest chance of infection, but it is an absolute medical rule that anyone who has had contact, however slight, must be treated. A bull terrier puppy who plays with the Davidsons' Pablo, was found to have rabies, and as it had played round Alex and me in the garden for about a minute, we had to present ourselves. Ron and Bunny had no contact at all, so they are excused, but Fiona and Lope may have had contact, so they are being done. The full dose is fourteen injections, but Norton said a shorter course of seven would suffice. The nurse said my stomach area would just about take seven – there is tremendous swelling and the second seven have to be given on top of the swelling, which I am told is agony. I had my first today – not painful, but a long, slow, nauseating process, and I shall be glad when they are over. It itches madly, like a bad mosquito bite. Poor Pablo, of course, was immediately put to sleep, which has upset everyone, especially the children. He was such a pet, with a sweet, trusting nature and the most endearing ways.

My workload is now massive and I am thriving on it. The days simply melt away. I have Leg Co next week, so I shall be really on the go – lovely.

We had a relaxed weekend, with a delicious dinner at Kuchawe on Saturday – a premature birthday treat for Ron, as Aflike was still off and it was definitely my turn to feed the Davidsons! Aflike came back on Monday, looking well and rested. He says he had a fever, but it was not malaria.

Ron is also very much burdened with work – less pleasant than mine, alas, but he bears up well.

2nd December: [Air Letter]

I am sorry I only have time for one of these blue flimsies, but there is not much news and I am a bit under the weather. My incipient cold did not, thank heavens, materialise and I finished my course of injections yesterday – a most exhausting business, which has left me with a persistent temperature. The reaction only set in this morning, when my tummy suddenly broke into scarlet weals which have run into each other and it is blazing hot, itching desperately and looks as if it has been scalded. It is uncomfortable rather than sore, and produces a feeling of constant nausea. There, enough of that! I must be thankful I only needed seven – fourteen must be a nightmare. The scare continues, several people having been bitten and a number of dogs destroyed – all very unpleasant and made worse by the heat. I have been in Leg Co yesterday and today and it has been very difficult to sit still for hours. The air conditioning has broken down, as often happens, so the chamber is stifling.

The Annual Report progresses. I have stopped dreaming about it (!) and have just settled down to cope. Last night we had a rather dull Sundowner at GH, with everyone limp and moist. I had a long talk with Lady Armitage, who is very nice indeed. Today the Wickhams arrived from the North, posted to Zomba again – all simply bursting with health, due to the excellent climate at Mzuzu (to the north of Mzimba).

Ron's birthday was a lovely day. I got someone to make him a magnificent cake with marzipan and icing, and we 'hanselled' it on Sunday, so that the Davidson family could share it. I gave him two beautiful wooden carvings of a male and female koodoo, done by a Masai, now working in Tanganyika. He comes down every year; Joan bought a magnificent ebony head from him. I have always wanted to have something of his and it felt wonderful to have the money to do so, for Ron.

10th December:

I knew you would hate the thought of the anti-rabies injections, but I hope you realised I would never have told you if there had been any cause for worry. It is all well over now, and apart from fading bruises, I might never have had them. My worst day was in Leg Co last week, sitting there all day in stifling heat on a hard chair and leaning forward to write. I tried every position, endlessly. A very amusing incident happened which has gone the rounds of Zomba, and I am mercilessly teased about it. The Press Gallery is directly opposite and to the left of the Speaker, a doddery old retired judge with a ginny voice, short-sighted and slightly deaf. He can see only my head and shoulders, visible over the long bench top where we sit. It was a very hot afternoon. I had Don Penny, our new Press Officer, on my left, and on my right Bill Ferris, the Federal Information Officer. Bill had fallen asleep, woke up with a start and, at the same time as I, saw the Speaker suddenly stiffen, casting a baleful eye in the direction of our gallery. Bill thought he was going to be put out for nodding off, I thought I was going to be asked to leave because of my constant fidgeting. As we sat petrified, the Speaker leaned forward to his Clerk, who sits in front of him (John Kennan, an Assistant Secretary), and said, 'Where are the orders about dress?' John said, 'On your desk, sir.' The Speaker fumbled irritably with bits of paper and then said angrily to John, 'There's a chap in the Press Gallery without a tie. I think we must ask him to leave. He is improperly dressed.' John gazed across and saw two perfectly be-tied men, and me, wearing a tailored yellow blouse with an open neck and short sleeves. I had my hair up. He shook with laughter and said, 'That's no chap, sir. It's a *lady*'. The Speaker collapsed into rheumy mirth, which came over the mikes distinctly, and everyone stared at us, wondering what was going on. The Speaker waved the proceedings on, and we sat baffled, crimson and perspiring. John told Ron the story afterwards, also all the members of Leg Co, and next morning as I drifted innocently in before the day began, the men smiled and said, 'You are improperly dressed,' or 'Where's your tie?' In the afternoon I slipped in, wearing a black velvet ribbon as a bow tie, and all the Government benchers grinned happily. The Speaker, I knew, would be too short-sighted and somnolent to notice, so I risked the joke, which was much appreciated, as I learned later. I shall not live it down for a long time.

There was a tremendous amount of work to do on the *Hansard Digest*, but I cleared it in a day, leaving the office at six, triumphant and exhausted. Bryn was furious when he found out, and insisted I have a day off next week. So I shall have a last pre-Christmas shopping day in Blantyre and have my hair done – lovely. The great heat continues and I am happily adjusted to it. We get sudden coolness after the thunderstorms, which are terrific this year. I no longer meet them with quite the aplomb of former years! The lightning is savage, and one is amazed that all Zomba does not explode like a bombed city under the barrage.

The Wickhams are settling in and Bruce has taken over Ron's job in African Affairs. Ron has acquired a completely new post, Assistant to the Information Adviser, Vernon McDonald, who was his chief in Land Resettlement at Magomero. They never seemed to me to quite hit it off then, but they have both mellowed, and Vernon asked particularly for Ron. The job is actually intelligence and security, and Vernon's title is merely a cover up for his work, though he does advise our department quite naturally as part of his job. Ron was getting bored where he was and is enjoying the new experience. It is not promotion in salary, but just to be appointed to a newly created post is a boost in itself. He has moved into a cooler (and less open to the public) office, which the chaps upstairs have already christened the Orangery, because every file that goes in is orange, which means secret; green ones are confidential and buff ones are open, i.e. harmless. The only difficulty is that he now knows so much that he hardly dares talk shop at all, and you will understand what a blow *that* is to Ron!

I press on with the Annual Report. There is a lull just now, as all the departments are busy preparing their material, but I have plenty to do, choosing photos, arranging for maps, ordering covers and writing up my own bits – very disjointed – I have seventeen files on the go at present. We have acquired a stenographer, a Mrs Payne, now Jean to all of us, from near Glasgow. I am learning the art of dictation, which made me tongue-tied at first, but is now a most helpful process, I find, and the words fairly flow from me, much to Bryn's amusement, as he had difficulty in persuading me to make use of her at all. He has only a few more months to go and is feeling the effects of his fourth hot season this tour, but he is invariably good tempered and friendly, and the office is a happy place, much envied, I believe.

PS. I am giving Ron ten guineas as a 10th anniversary present, to start a fund for a pair of *field glasses*!

16th December:

Because of the heat and general pre-Christmas tiredness, I find I am doing stupid things. I was giggling feebly to myself the other day over this when my 'messenger' came in to clear my *out* tray. As I was alone in the office, he must have thought I was mad! All I can think of now is lying in the sun at the Lake. Christmas cards and letters are pouring in, which I love. Joan's Christmas present to me is a renewed subscription to *Sight and Sound*, which delights me.

On Wednesday evening we went to a most enjoyable drinks party at Naisi, given by Bobby and Hazel Lowe, contemporaries who arrived from Bermuda (his native country) whom we find very friendly and attractive. They came to our last noon drinks party, among other newcomers and, it turns out, were thrilled to be asked, as they found Zomba very clique-ridden, with very little effort made to welcome newcomers – in this case I mean newcomers from other territories. We had a cooling hour at Kuchawe on Saturday evening, where we are now very much of the family – cats and dogs pour out to greet us. (I am now a little chary of *all* pets!)

Bryn is on *ulendo* in the North and I am snowed under, but the Report material is being passed on to the Print in a steady flow and everyone (so far) is most helpful. The panic comes in January, but by then I hope to be a new woman, full of energy. Ron is enjoying his work, though finding it hard going. He has an enormous amount of background reading to do.

23rd December: [Air Letter]

It is a blazing hot day and I find it difficult to think that tomorrow is Christmas Eve. However, cards and parcels continue to arrive, and through my tiredness I have a little glimmer of the festive spirit stirring. I have been hectically busy but just the thought of the holiday has given me a bit of second wind to see me through. I had a lovely day in Blantyre all by myself on Friday, shopped very successfully and had my hair washed and set in a long, thick pageboy, which I had to put up today, because of the heat. I called in and saw David (Baxter) for ten minutes, to his great surprise and pleasure. Margaret went down to Salisbury to have her baby, and they now have another daughter, Rosemary. On Saturday the Sproules and the Wickhams came to dine and go on with us to see quite a good play, *Plaintiff with a Pretty Hat.* Barbara simply loved it as she adores live theatre and had never been in Zomba. Today our office had a Christmas lunch party at Kathie's, to which we all contributed. (I staggered up at 5.30 to make the blessed pudding, which was a great success!) Tonight we have a party at the Wickhams and some time between now and 3.30 tomorrow we shall pack! I shall get off at 3 and come up to load the car and shut the house – wonderful to think we shall have sun and swimming – and there will be a full moon!

31st December:

I am writing this after tea. I was given permission to take 22 perfect red roses from the office garden and they are now arranged to my satisfaction, and filling the room with their divine scent. Bunny and Alex are coming for a drink at seven, and then we are going up the mountain for dinner. The restaurant is fully booked – forty people – so it should be fun. We shall go down to the Ball in time for midnight.

Our four days at the Lake were wonderful – perfect weather, with hot, hot sun and a light breeze. Bunny and Ron sailed every day, and Alex and I lazed on the beach with the children from dawn to dusk – heavenly. The food and service have vastly improved and we had a very grand Christmas dinner. I ate enormously, to my surprise – two fried eggs and masses of ham for breakfast every morning. The place was full, with lots of children, who had a magnificent party on Christmas afternoon, with a lovely tree covered in presents for everyone. We are beautifully tanned and bleached and stand out startlingly among the white Zomba faces. I would have dearly liked another week off, but the four days have set us both on our feet again, and I am ready for anything! No one has felt like working between Christmas and New Year, everyone feeling sociable and still festive!

6th January 1959:

Ron is working very hard and I am feeling the strain as I get material piled upon me. The end of the year brought it flooding in and there is more to come. I live in fear of being held up by lack of statistics, the compiling of which, I am learning, is loathed by most heads of departments. But go in they must. Geoffrey Fricker, acting Deputy Chief Secretary, is a great help. I have to pass everything to him for approval – drafts, galleys and page proofs are the three stages, and the amount of paper involved is mountainous. I should be well informed by the time I finish!

We had the Wickhams for dinner on Friday evening, as we missed them in the crowds at the Ball, to wish them a happy new year. They are as energetic as ever, and I now wonder how we ever kept up with them – and how Jean does it, as she has no nannie and is on the go all the time. She never goes to bed before midnight! On Sunday we dined with the Davidsons and went to see a marvellous Film Society film: *Secrets of the Reef*, photographed in colour in Florida, all under water and absolutely enthralling, especially a marvellous sequence with a sea horse. Do you remember how we loved watching them at Edinburgh Zoo? They are only six inches long but this one was magnified many times and looked like a huge, elaborately carved chess piece.

The New Year's Ball was a splendid evening, as always. We had a magnificent dinner at Kuchawe, everyone in tearing spirits – we were the quietest table there and we were festive enough. We went down on the 11.30 clock and got to the Club just before midnight. It was very hot and noisy, but everyone was madly friendly – the men were hunting for their favourite women almost in packs, quite shamelessly – great fun!

13th January:

The rains are well and truly here, so it is cooler and we all have more energy.

There is not much news, as far as I can remember. The time goes so quickly I get mixed up about what happened when. In spite of the stress and strain, I shall miss my Report, but no doubt something else will land with a bang on my desk. I am hoping to take over entirely the editing of *Hansard*, as well as the index, but cannot be too sure of what will come my way after Bryn goes on leave, two months today – horror! Arthur Mell, who is on leave and was the Provincial Information Officer, Blantyre, is to 'sit in' for Bryn. He is thirty-eight, I think, half French, a live wire and very amusing. I dread the change over, as Bryn has been so wonderful to me and Arthur is quite a different type. However, we shall see. Alice goes on leave soon too, which is sad, as I am very fond of her and have become her guide, philosopher and friend. Her husband George, who is Reader in the Print, will be a great loss to me, but at least he will be here to see me through the final pangs of getting out the Annual Report. I am also on excellent terms with the Government Printer, a tough Cockney who spent some years in West Africa.

I am reading Montgomery's Memoirs, and to my surprise immensely enjoying the book – hard, plain, lucid thought and prose, which I gather is making him even more enemies since its publication than before, though doubtless also making him vast sums of money. Ron is ploughing through Pasternak, but is so tired he only reads a little in bed. He comes in about seven these days, absolutely whacked. He has to attend masses of highly secret meetings and write the minutes later, so that his normal work piles up terribly. I read over his drafts – a fearful grind (after dinner) which on the last occasion took me till after 11 – awful after a hard day myself, but he likes me to do the polishing, as it does make for a better presentation. (This procedure, of course, is not known in the Secretariat.)

We had a quiet weekend, as Ron was very tired. On Sunday we gave lunch to a Mr Cameron, Director of Federal Prisons, and Julien Theunnisen, a charming ex-DC whom we know well. He has a new post in collaboration with Ron, all very hush-hush. I shall have to get used to them stopping their shop talk when I enter the room! Mr Cameron was very smooth and *very* lively, and we felt quite refreshed by his visit.

21st January:

After days of dismal weather, the sun is out again and the air is baking hot and very sultry. I am glad, of course, but these sudden changes in temperature leave one absolutely limp. We have also had an unusually active social life and being out of practice, have found the pace rather much. On Friday the Davidsons gave a big party, and we were asked to stay on for supper, which is fatal, as people linger on and on, and we ended up eating very late, almost speechless with exhaustion. However, there were lots of nice people there and I had a great evening. I had a long talk with Norton, whom I had not seen for weeks. On Saturday we had a lovely dinner at Kuchawe, driving up and down in bright moonlight, and had an early night. Ron worked in the office all day on Sunday, and I was busy in the house – what a lot I can get through now, because I have to! We had a supper party and film. Diana and Peter Youens, whom we always enjoy, came, with Bobby and Hazel Lowe (the newcomers from Bermuda). Supper went with a great swing and we were all reluctant to go and sit quietly in the cinema. However, the film was simply beautiful – *Madam Butterfly*, filmed in Japan with a Japanese cast and dubbed with splendid Italian singers' voices. The scenery was exquisite, the acting excellent and the music very lovely – sentimental and restful in its familiarity. Hazel, who has never been to an opera, was in raptures and emerged at the end in a complete daze. In the love duet at the end of Act I, the camera roamed over a starry sky while the voices soared up with it. Butterfly was tiny and dainty as a flower, and the Consul and Pinkerton were both convincing types, definitely American, but I did not know their names. The cinema was packed and absolutely still and attentive, which is rare in Zomba. We were all emotionally exhausted at the end and stayed on for a nightcap to unwind.

Yesterday Ron woke up with a fearful cold and is feeling miserable in the stuffy heat. He drank a *huge* hot toddy in bed last night and got quite hilarious, but he is very subdued this morning, and, I noticed, took two Alka-Seltzers when he got up!

The pressure is on in the office, and I sit down at 7.30 and raise my head at noon, with fifteen minutes break for the ritual of swallowing two cups of coffee rather quickly. Now that I know exactly what I am doing, I am enjoying the work, but it is tiring, because I have to rely on other people to provide the material and have to discover polite ways of persuasion!

I shall be thirty-seven next week – think of it! There are no new lines on my face but those I have are deeper!

27th January:

I realised you would read about the 'riots' in Zomba. As usual, the Press reports make everything sound so much worse than what actually happened. We heard the crowd and the smoke bombs going off, from the office *khonde*. The crowd sounded quite good natured at first, but there were rabble rousers among them who know how to incite them into a state of unpredictable excitement. The police never really lost control and the pattern of events automatically evolved, with the DC reading the Riot Act when the crowd refused to disperse. The DC, Mike Leonard, has a stutter which he usually manages with considerable aplomb, but in the stress of the moment it got the better of him and he had to hand over the paper to the policeman in the van with him and allow him to read for him. I now know a lot of what goes on behind the scenes and it is becoming apparent that troubled times lie ahead. Ron is appallingly overworked and comes in about seven, usually very depressed about the mess that we are in – such a tragedy for Nyasaland, which has been a stable, happy territory; and of course what is happening in other parts of Africa has its effect here and the black politicians are precipitated into making demands the Government is not yet prepared to grant.

On Saturday evening Jean Wickham gave a magnificent Burns Supper – home-made broth, herring with oat cakes, and haggis with 'neeps'. The table was lighted with ten candles stuck into ten different brands of whisky bottles, and there was a sprig of white heather at each place, and name cards, each with a different tartan background. She really does things beautifully. They played Scottish music on their LP all evening, and everyone enjoyed themselves.

We are in the middle of a mild cyclone, which began last night – a tearing wind, torrential rain, and mist seething round the mountain – rather exhilarating but *very* damp!

I am now doing the *Hansard* index and the Report, so the days fly and I am stammering with weariness by evening, but I enjoy it very much.

4th February:

I had a lovely birthday weekend. Ron gave me a beautiful silk square and money to get myself a new evening bag. (Your old black bead one has at last disintegrated)! Alex gave me a Mantovani record of lots of nostalgic film themes and a bottle of Chanel No. 22, now my favourite scent. Bunny and the children each gave me a tailored blouse for the office, all beautifully made by Bunny. My birthday dinner was a great success. I tried a new recipe for ham cooked in brandy and spices; it was delicious. On Saturday evening the

Davidsons took us up to Kuchawe for dinner. Homer Cox, the owner of Kuchawe, is in England for a month, so Theo, his wife, is on her own. Ron volunteered to be barman for the evening and enjoyed himself hugely. The dinner was marvellous, with magnificent steaks grilled for three minutes in brandy. We ate in dedicated silence! We finished up with ginger icecream.

The last of the material for the Annual Report comes in tomorrow, and already the Print is grinding away at the opening chapters – Alice's George is working overtime and making *pounds* of extra pay. The Print is the only department which pays overtime, unfortunately! So, all the worry is over and now it is a case of checking the proofs, which is a very exacting job, but worth the effort. It is amazing how many mistakes can be missed. I read each line along the edge of my ruler while Jean (Payne) reads out from the original text – hundreds of foolscap pages. The Government Printer has given me a little book to read up on the correct marginal signs indicating errors and corrections required. So I shall soon be twiddling my thumbs unless Bryn has something up his sleeve for me. Ron is working terribly hard but seems to have got into his stride again and is less strained and keyed-up – what a pair we have been recently! It is not that the work is too difficult, but simply that there is so much, all the time, day after day. His cold is almost better and I have escaped it by a miracle.

18th February:

Ron's leave is fixed for November and we are actually booked on a City ship for the 11th. I want to work on till August, at least, which gives me a two years' contract and means half pay during leave, which would be most welcome. The political situation is so uncertain that Ron's leave just *might* be put off, but I can always come home anyway, and I will certainly not delay any longer than November, if even till then. Of course I have my loyalty to the office to consider now. Ron's future *appears* to be back in a district as DC next tour and I am wondering very much about myself. I really and truly feel I could never do it again – or be expected to, and am wondering about trying to keep on my job in Zomba. I do not want to be selfish, but there comes a time, I think, when one simply must consider one's survival in terms of oneself as well as others. I have known about the posting for some time and could not decide whether to tell you or not. However, I want you to know what I am having to think about. Should I just go meekly back to the old, bush life and fade away, or should I try to find a compromise for my own sake, having at last become a useful – and happy – member of society? It is all terribly difficult, especially as I have kept it entirely to myself, but every time I think of being on a bush station I know in my heart I must fight against it. I dare not talk to Bryn about it, as I would like to do, because I am not calm enough within myself to discuss it without perhaps getting wildly upset. Hi, ho, indeed. We have made no plans for leave, as it seems so far away. My main thought is simply being home again with you and the family. I cannot possibly ask Ron to interfere in any way with Government's plans for him. He has his own career to think about and of course good field men are needed in the districts at this stage of political development, and Ron is – no doubt about it – a 'natural' field man. I know Bryn wants to keep me. We are short-staffed in this office and again, Information is now so important there is a very strong case for my continued work there. Anyway, these are the problems I am having to think about, and round and round they go unceasingly in my poor head.

The weather is dreadful – rain, heat and appalling thunderstorms, the worst I can remember. (I say this every year!) The Report is in its last stages and I am in a spin all day and dead beat at the end of it. But I have loved doing it and when it is over I shall feel as if my little world were suddenly standing still!

We went swimming on Sunday afternoon, as it was so sticky and sultry. It was lovely, though only just refreshing, as the water was warm. I am stiff from the unaccustomed exercise. I am now going to hunt down two blasted mosquitoes which have been feasting on me since I began this letter – maddening!

24th February:

I have had a letter from Laga. Clement has got a permanent job in Salisbury, so they are all together at Con's house in Borrowdale (a suburb of Salisbury) – the Carlyles and the children, Dana and Ivan. They are building another house in the grounds of their present one, so they will end up living a communal life together – very Serbian! Dana still runs the market garden. Our friendship never flagged. It was simply overwhelmed by the pressure of events, on both sides, and I know we will keep in touch forever. [We do.]

Things are a bit rushed here. I am writing this at lunch time and will finish it at tea. I have a dinner party on Friday and am cleaning the carpet when I come home, so will not have time to write a full letter then.

The weather is still depressing: damp, thundery and wet, and I feel a chill in the air in the mornings and evenings, although no one else seems to. I have a nose for seasonal changes and so, I think, does Bryn! I am extremely busy in the office and Ron is hard pressed, but cheerful and well, as I am. The odd spot of trouble has been breaking out in different parts of the territory, but all is calm here. The radio and newspapers make the most of their information, which infuriates us, as we all have family at home and know how they will worry, as they did in 1953, when we were at Mlanje. You may be sure that I shall tell you how things are with us, so please do not worry.

We had a very quiet weekend. Ron had to work all day on Sunday, as there was a lot of decoding of Intelligence cables to be done in the Secretariat. So, Aflike and I had a very domestic day together!

I have cleaned half the carpet – I did the other half yesterday. It has given me great pleasure, but I shall have it dyed grey at the end of this tour. On Friday I am giving a dinner for the Davidsons, Kathie Smith – as guest of honour, long overdue – and Geoffrey Fricker, with whom I have worked in perfect harmony producing the Report. It should have been published in record time but has been held up by two departments not submitting statistics on time – terribly disappointing, as it would have been a triumph. However, there is no time to brood over that. The *Press* has moved in on us, like vultures, for news, but have had to make the best (or should I say the worst) of not very much, which of course the wretches do.

It is odd to hear of the days getting longer at home, because here it actually gets dark a little earlier as the cold season approaches.

4th March: [Air Letter]

This is just a quickie to reassure you. I shall write more fully next week. A huge packet of Press cuttings from home has arrived by air mail today, and we are all shattered at the frightfully dramatic way our affairs are being reported, except by *The Times* and the *Manchester Guardian*. Kathie had a letter from someone on leave who said even the BBC made it all sound very serious, which of course it is. The declaration of a State of Emergency, made yesterday, was inevitable, in the end, and hastened by Southern Rhodesia declaring one there. Everyone is relieved in a way that the situation has been brought out into the open and Government taken steps to pull the territory together. Things have been quiet in Zomba itself, apart from the fact that it is bristling with Federal troops and police.

Since yesterday, the African civil servants have not come to work here, though they have in Blantyre and Limbe. It has done everyone's morale a power of good to knuckle down and show we can run the place on our own! The Secretariat is very empty as a result, and there is a tremendous amount for us all to do, especially in our Department, with all the Press Releases and enquiries and importuning journalists. All the men are frantically busy. Ron spent last night in his office, as did Julien, and I slept at the Davidsons. Banda and a great many Congress people were arrested during the night and spirited away to prison in Southern Rhodesia. It was meticulously planned and was quickly over. There is a lull at present, and either things will die down or, more likely, flare up and have to be dealt with. Everyone goes about as usual and *no one* carries firearms, contrary to what the papers have said. I would really like to write about it all much more fully, but until we can be sure that letters get away safely and quickly, it is probably better not to. The point is none of us is in a state of alarm and despondency and the whole situation has been anticipated and prepared for, for months. Of course now rumours are being buzzed about by people who know nothing more than what they can dream up. We are all tired, as office hours are very elastic. I spent the afternoon today in the Print, folding and wrapping a special Gazette to be out tomorrow. (The Report, of course, is at a standstill, as the Print is simply churning out Government stuff.) Our household is at peace and perfectly calm, I am glad to say. Aflike shows agitation only over the fact that we both work longer hours and he never knows when one of us is going to rush in and ask for a flask of coffee and vanish! I shall write more fully next week. I hope this reassures you that the Flag flies high!

11th March:

The Press cuttings from home flood in daily, and the popular press is really sickening in its presentation of news. About forty journalists have descended on us and base themselves in Blantyre, where public relations are being absolutely nobly maintained by Arthur Mell, just back from leave – and only just in time, as John Carver seems rather overwhelmed. Bryn's leave, inevitably, was put off for a month, so he is still in the chair, except that he never is. He is here, there and everywhere, marvellous man. The better papers seem fairly level headed, but *no one* who has not lived out here can really accurately grasp the situation, least of all journalists who come from other trouble spots and think that every territory in Africa is the same, i.e. has the same problems. We have come off very lightly in the Southern Province, and Zomba has been undisturbed. I am glad for Ron's sake we were not in a district where things might have been difficult for him. There has been nothing to worry about here at all, but of course it was upsetting to learn of the disturbances elsewhere, and more so to know that people at home would have cause to think the worst. All our African civil servants are back at work and our Department is normal, except that the African staff are all a bit subdued – and having to work very hard – there is at least twice as much work to do, as all sorts of leaflets, pamphlets and other paper work have to be produced for dropping by air over the countryside. I am worked off my feet and so is Kathie, with the constant demand for her Chinyanja translations.

Ron, having worked behind the scenes for weeks beforehand, felt the anticlimax when others went into action in the field, but all sorts of new problems will continue to arise, so he will be kept busy, therefore happy, too. As you can imagine, he would have given just about *anything* to have his own district at this time. I know more than a little of how he felt. The night of the arrests Ron insisted that I stay at the Davidsons, as he was in the Secretariat all night. I could not sleep, and lay wide awake, thinking of all the chaps we know having to go against the grain and get on with the night's work. Finally, in desperation, I got up, dressed, and went through to the kitchen, where I found Alex fully dressed, sitting at the table with an ash tray full of butt ends. I just sank onto a chair, tears spurting from my eyes. He gave me a brandy and we sat talking through the night till just before dawn, when we went to bath and put on fresh clothes. What an *awful* night for Nyasaland.

The North, as was expected, is the main trouble spot, and of course up there Europeans can be very isolated – there are practically none except Government and Missions. I have the task of keeping a huge chart, pinned on the wall of my office, with date, place, event, damage, casualties, arrests, detentions – everything – which I fill in every day. It has proved extremely useful – and impressive – as all sorts of people have been ringing up or calling in to enquire about details they are too busy to collect themselves and I can instantly provide them. We have a local 'Blue Band' radio station which broadcasts news compiled in our Department at 6.30 a.m. and 6.00 p.m. Kathie Smith then reads out exactly the same news in Chinyanja. We always have our household in to listen – in fact we have borrowed Aflike's radio! Things are now very much quieter, even in the North, though by no means settled there. There is so much that one could quickly say about the whole business but it takes longer on paper, and as we are both very much in the middle of the 'back room' side, it is wiser not to write too much. Ron is marvellously discreet but I can put two and two together and Bryn tells me what he can.

Life goes on as usual. The children have gone back to school, and people are going to Blantyre again, to shop. We had dinner with Bunny and Alex last Wednesday, Bunny's birthday – nothing to buy her in Zomba except toiletries – and she was showered, poor girl, with bath salts, talc, soap, scent and powder! On Saturday we gave her a birthday dinner on the mountain, a lovely clear, starry night.

The Governor was filmed for TV in the garden of GH on Saturday, so you may see him on the news this week or early next. I met his interviewer and cameraman beforehand – they had just been in Uganda with the Queen Mother; a wonderful tour, apparently. Today a BBC man called in to see me. He had just spent a week with Tom! He had been an ADC in Nigeria, and through Tom had transferred to broadcasting there.

All is well with us, I promise you.

17th March:

The mails are perfectly normal again and life goes on absolutely as usual, except that being in our Department I hear all the news from elsewhere, and there are still disturbances. After having about forty journalists in Blantyre coming to and fro, plus BBC men, the place suddenly seems deserted, as a few have gone north and the rest almost in a body to Northern Rhodesia to cover the elections on 20th March. I have finished all the details, to the very last, of the Report, which is now being printed, but I have lots of other work to do. There are hundreds and hundreds of Press cuttings to sort and arrange before they are filed and sent up to HE. What a difficult thing to grasp 'truth' is! I have never read so much rubbish in my life. My blood pressure must be high by the end of each session with these cuttings. I never want to *see* an *Observer* again at the moment and now the *Guardian* appears to have gone mad. Some of the best, most balanced comments, apart from *The Times*, which has not let itself down yet, are from provincial papers like the *Yorkshire Post*, *Western Gazette*, *Cardiff News* and some more obscure. I just hope our Government feels the time is ripe to charge in with answers to all the calumnies and nonsense spoken and written about it at home. I read a profile of Dr Banda in the *Observer* and with a quick count I found 14 points which were either untrue or contradictory!

The weather is lovely again, but there is a nip in the air in the mornings and at night, and I am into thick skirts and blouses, though no one else is. I am reading Duff Cooper's *Old Men Forget* and loving it. It links up with his wife's autobiography, which I read some months ago. Tonight we are going to have a drink with the Sproules, whom we have not seen for some time. I sat out in the sun all day on Sunday and as a result am transformed into a tanned blonde!

I now bring work home with me and go on till about six – Bryn does not know, but I have to, as he forbids me to stay on in the office after 3.30. He is desperately tired, but has the prospect of leave very soon. Ron is not overworked now, and gets home at the reasonable hour of 5.00 or 5.30 – and then settles down to swear over the Press cuttings, which I smuggle home for him to see!

24th March:

This is a memorable day, as the Nyasaland Protectorate Annual Report was published, a month behind schedule, because of the Emergency, but still ahead of Uganda, which is apparently all that matters! John Morris, head of Colonial Office information, who has been here for a few days, was flying to Uganda today and at 8.30 this morning was given practically the first copy to hand to Uganda's Government Printer with the compliments of our Government Printer (known as GP), who was beaming all over his nice Cockney face. I gathered it would be a bitter moment in Uganda! There is tremendous protocol over its public appearance, and I, poor thing, who produced it, will not have my copy for a few days! Bryn's leave has been put off *again*, for another three weeks, and Arthur Mell has practically taken over, as far as the office is concerned, so Bryn is free for all the hush-hush work being done upstairs. I am now smothered in Press cutting files and today took on the job of organising the distribution of reading matter to detention camps. I shall bombard them with Government publications (produced in my office). Kathie, bless her, when consulted, grimly added three religious magazines to my list! The Bulletin, which had a circulation of 17,000 when I took it over, rose to 25,000 after a year, and now, believe it or not, has suddenly shot up to 70,000! So there are lots of Africans anxious to read reliable material.

Last week I got Thursday off and had a marvellous day in Blantyre. The roads were quiet and Blantyre itself slightly less full of traffic, which was most welcome. It was a beautiful day, with high clouds, blazing sun and a breeze rippling the maize gardens by the roadside. Chiradzulu looked a dream and there was wonderful clear visibility. I had my hair done and bought some much needed make-up and undies. I also bought a lovely cocktail dress, perfectly plain and straight, in a beautiful shade of misty coral – for under £5! I got back at 3.45, tired but feeling a new woman, having had a change of scene.

On Saturday Bunny and Alex dined here and we went to *Carve her Name with Pride*, a wonderful film based on the true story of one of the 'Odettes' of the war, with Virginia MacKenna and Paul Schofield. Sunday was warm and cloudless and we had a lazy day at the Davidsons. Life is absolutely normal here and things are quietening down in the Central and Northern Provinces. It seems now to be a case of 'mopping up' and repairing damaged roads and bridges. Ramadan, alas, has begun, and Aflike goes about with glittering eyes, spitting endlessly and doing his domestic chores in the wrong order, but I have learned to grin and bear it. Ron and I are very well and cheerful. The strain of all the disturbances was greater than one realised, and the easing up has been positively exhilarating to experience, in contrast.

1st April:

1st April and I forgot about it until too late to 'fool' Ron. I wonder if anyone got you! I am writing this after tea, having had a hectic day and with the prospect of more to come, as I have been asked to undertake the United Nations Organisation Report. What next! Bryn tells me my edition of the Annual Report has been declared the best yet, by the chaps upstairs, which is nice. I asked Bryn about the TV film you saw, and he says it was definitely Mike Leonard in Zomba district, so you without a doubt saw villages Ron and I had passed through and possibly camped in. Would you ever have believed it? Chris Chataway was here for a day at Easter, interviewing HE for ITV, but I did not meet him. The general impression he gave was not very favourable, but possibly we are all hypersensitive to Press and Broadcasting people from home just now.

I had a letter from Mary Dunlop this week (the Queen Mother's secretary). She was anxious to hear how things were with us, which was nice to know. She had been on the Kenya and Uganda visits and had had a wonderful time, but apparently the Zomba visit remains the highlight of her African experience.

We had a lovely Easter, with glorious weather, and I feel rested and unwound. Ron and Alex worked every day, as did most of the men in the Secretariat. On Friday we went up the mountain for a pre-lunch drink – our first visit in daylight for a long time and well worth it. The view was magnificent and there were lots of strangers who were all willing to talk. Kuchawe has a most companionable little bar and there is always someone new to meet. On

Saturday we went to a delightful buffet lunch at the house of Mr and Mrs Robbins (Local Government). They live in one of the big new houses on Naisi Spur, with a splendid view. Peter Youens was there. Diana flew home last week to be with the children, as Peter's leave has been put off till June. Bryn and Chris were also there and I greeted him like a long lost friend; I see so little of him at present – and will soon have to get used to not seeing him at all. I met Mr and Mrs Aitkins, from Glasgow. He is the new Director of Geological Surveys. He and I had a hilarious conversation about geology, with me hanging on, politely, by the skin of my teeth, to the subject, which he soon realised! We had a quiet Sunday, with another short visit in moonlight to Kuchawe. On Monday Ron was Duty Officer and Bunny and the children were out all day on a picnic with two of Fiona's school friends. Geoffrey Fricker asked Ron, Alex and me for a drink at the Club before lunch and we had a very gay and entertaining hour with him. Then Ron and Alex went back to the office and I came home and read my book in the garden. Yesterday morning was awful, everyone disgruntled to be back in the office, but we soon cheered up.

7th April:

Office life is hectic beyond words, as everyone, but everyone is preparing for the Commission of Inquiry (into the State of Emergency) whose members arrive on Saturday. [It became known as the Devlin Commission.] HE keeps sending down long red minutes on his latest ideas for their reception in the form of *masses* of reading matter. I shall have to put aside my other work and concentrate on preparing all the Press cuttings under different headings – a nightmare task, as there are over 2,000 and they are still pouring in. I have eighteen files of them already. HE keeps changing his mind about their presentation and I have to reorganise them. The sheer physical boredom of opening them out, arranging them in order, trimming them, pasting them in and labelling them is simply killing, and the pressure of other work I should be doing and people asking for research to be done on what *they* have to prepare is unbelievable. By 3.30 I am shaking all over and my temper is fraying. I nearly snapped at Peter Youens this morning, which just will not do! Everyone is similarly hard pressed and the atmosphere fairly sizzles! The problem of finding offices for the Commission members and their staff is acute, but is being worked out. I dash into an office to find it empty, immaculate and well stocked with typewriter and office equipment. I then have to tear around in search of the usual occupant and of course phoning is complete chaos, as the wrong man answers from the office *he* is now in!

We may go and see the Dramatic Society do *I am a Camera* tomorrow night. It is only a dress rehearsal, as one of the principals has had to give up, from pressure of work (Commission again!) and the full scale production has been cancelled.

Things are quiet, with only a few arrests occasionally reported in the North. Most people here think back on it as a bad dream now, but being in the office keeps me aware that it will be a long time before things settle down.

15th April:

You ask about the United Nations Organisation Report. It is brought up to date every year, working from the latest Annual Report, so I am on familiar ground – or rather I shall be. It has been completely shelved for the present, as I am engulfed in work for the Commission. They arrived on Saturday and are staying at Kuchawe. We looked them over (discreetly, of course) when we went up the mountain for a drink before dinner. Devlin is small and frail, with a slightly hunched back, a massive head and a real 'judge's' face, clever and aloof, but not cruel, as the photos suggested. Without his wig he looks human and a bit grotesque. Primrose is a big hearty Scot, Wyn-Harris a Governor of the old type – square, bluff, with lots of common sense but I should think not very sensitive, utterly unlike Evelyn Baring, for example, or our own Sir Robert. Williams looked supremely intelligent and as sharp as a needle. There are four high powered stenographers (200 words a minute in three languages, for Elspeth's benefit!) and lots of underlings with whom I come in contact. None of the Big Four is security minded and they drift out of their offices blithely leaving the door open with dozens of hair-raisingly Secret files lying about on their desks. So now there is a policeman on duty so that they can go in and out as they are apparently accustomed to do. All our men lock their offices even if they are only going to the loo, and I *sit* on Secret files I am working on – hidden under my cushion! I am able to observe their activities, as their offices are opposite mine, in the Leg Co building and I have to be over there a lot, delivering my files to the Secretary, a small, pompous, slightly common little man who was very superior at first, but now knows where he stands with our department. (!) His stenographer is very pleasant, a Colonial Office employee of about thirty-five. I enjoy talking to her when we have time. In order to keep things impartial, none of them is accepting social invitations. It is amusing how often we change our remarks in mid-stream in case we are being indiscreet – all very inhibiting.

I never have a moment to spare and everyone is the same. I worked till 5.45 yesterday, standing at my table all day, bending over files of newspapers – they want absolutely *everything*, from the local press as well as the home papers, and as our African clerk is hopeless, none of the local files have been kept up to date and I have worked my way through ten grubby Rhodesian and local papers, most of them daily, from July 1958, cutting out six different subjects. Then I have to paste them into files and all the time HE is thinking up more special subjects to be selected, so that I have to go and ask for the completed files, again go through them, cut out the references, only just pasted in, tidy up the gaps and repaste in *another* file! No wonder I do it in my sleep: I am the authority on everything that has ever happened now! It is interesting in a way, but monotonous and tiring, and the time limit factor is just exhausting. Bryn goes off on leave tomorrow and Arthur is in a fine state of nerves and needs constant reassurance. We had the Wickhams in for a drink last night, Bruce tired and very cross because he has nothing to do with the Commission and feels out of things, Jean exhausted because she is organising the Red Cross Ball. Ron is slaving away. He has ninety detainees' appeals to cope with, which is an enormous and depressing undertaking. It is all very stimulating and interesting, and I am not grumbling. We are having Scrabble and supper with Bunny and Alex tonight, which will be a pleasant relaxation, provided we can resist the temptation to talk shop! Sorry this is such a dull letter – you will be glad when the Commission goes to Blantyre at the weekend!

21st April:

We have given very little thought to leave – life is so urgent it is difficult to stop and go off on another tack. We are both very tired, and there is no doubt that as the months after two years mount up, one feels oneself not exactly slowing down but having to push oneself a bit to keep up the pace. I sometimes feel temperamental in the office, which is most unusual, I think mainly due to Arthur, who demands as much support from me as I would like to have myself, whereas Bryn was as steady as a rock and could always be turned to. However, it all means more responsibility and experience, so I do not really mind. Arthur is trying to get himself onto TV, interviewing the Governor, so you may see my temporary chief within the next few weeks, which will be interesting for you. He has jet black, very sleek hair, a tiny neat moustache and beard, a pleasant voice and smooth manner and will probably photograph beautifully. He is able at his work, in a flamboyant way which goes down well with the Africans and, more important at present, with the Press.

The Commission went to Blantyre on Sunday, but their presence still makes itself felt in the Secretariat – on Sunday Ron worked from 7.00 a.m. till 7.00 p.m. for them, and till after seven last night. I am almost finished my immediate tasks for them and hope to get on to the wretched UNO report tomorrow. Everyone is lying low socially. I had a very scrappy Sunday, with Ron making irregular appearances for meals, poor man.

This Saturday is the Red Cross Ball and I am going to Blantyre in the morning to have my hair done. Our party of ten meets at Kuchawe at seven for dinner. I have saved up for that treat. There will be ourselves, the Sproules, the Davidsons, Philip Richardson (just back from leave without Jean, who is at home till after the school holidays) and Mr and Mrs Freeman and their seventeen-year-old daughter. (I have not been able to find a young man for her.) He is the new Director of Education and seems delightful. It should be a very enjoyable gathering, and it is such a relief not to have to worry about dinner. I have seen the menu: grapefruit served in ice cubes tinted and flavoured with crème de menthe, marinated mussels, steak grilled in brandy and chocolate mousse!

It will amuse you to hear that in the latest press cuttings from home *I* am mentioned as 'Officials of the Secretariat have prepared thousands of Press cuttings as material for the Commission'! Also, HE wrote in one of his red minutes that the work on the Press cuttings had been 'quite admirable'. Fame at last! (I wish Bryn were here – he would be so delighted for me.)

29th April: [Air Letter]

Your welcome air letter came yesterday, with, as usual, a surprising amount of news fitted into it! I am replying in kind, as there does not seem to be much news this week, or I am too tired to contemplate a large sheet of paper!

The weather is lovely, but cold indoors, and I am in sweaters and my warmest skirt already. Work goes at a great pace. Arthur, quite rightly, 'had a word' with me about the neglected state of the Bulletin – HE's fault, not mine, but I was too proud to say so! Well, I pounced on it fiercely and there is an enormous improvement, to *his* great satisfaction. He is only interested in work that brings 'kudos' to his department – no back room stuff for Arthur! He was, however, horrified to find how poorly I am paid, and asked me to write out all I had done – quite a list – and has followed up Bryn's efforts, asking for the official title of Temporary Information Officer, back-dated to last July, which would mean a salary of over £700 instead of £490. So now we must hope for the best. It would be *so nice!*

I had a terrific day on Saturday. I left for Blantyre at seven and got there just after eight, did some shopping, had my hair done, picked up several parcels for the Red Cross Ball organisers, including a 10lb. ham, collected a new ball gown for Joyce Dickinson and got back at 12.30, very tired, to find several people in for a drink before lunch! They seemed to stay for ever, but I had quite a long rest in the afternoon. At seven we went up the mountain and met our guests. We had a very happy hour and then a magnificent dinner, much appreciated by everyone, and went down to the Ball at 9.30. I had managed to book a very good table in the lounge, away from draughts. It was a lovely evening. The Freemans' daughter, aged 17, seemed to enjoy it, as she kept her parents there till three! The Sproules, who are not members of the Club and can only go there by members' invitation, were simply delighted with their evening. We got home about four, and got up around 9.30 to have a very piano but pleasant day with the Davidsons, ending with Scrabble and supper here.

6th May:

Yes, I have met George Clay – one of the more civilised and reasonable of the British journalists. He wanted me to let him see his contributions to the *Scotsman*, as he has a feeling they were being edited. I told him they, and all his

Observer articles, were filed and with the Commission, which seemed to disconcert him more than please him! He has nice manners and is clean, though bearded. The Commission has left Blantyre and is now in the North, fairly bursting the rest houses at the seams, as of course they cannot stay with Government people. It is a pity that, because of the general climate of opinion, they have met with official defensiveness, as far as I can judge, though heaven knows the material given to them must speak for itself. Life seems normal again, but there are lots of problems. My Bulletin is now filled with Government propaganda, written by me on strict instructions from Arthur, who of course gets his orders from upstairs. It is certainly a much more interesting document than before the Emergency. We now get lots of letters from official and unofficial white sources, most in praise, though a few are devastating!

I feel this has been a long tour – as indeed it will be by the time we come home, but it really has not felt as long as either of the others – the first tour seemed as if it lasted years and years. Ron and I are working hard but have apparently found our second or third wind, or else the colder weather has sharpened our wits and energies. I am toiling stoically through the UNO report, with no supervision at all from Geoffrey Fricker, who is buried in some madly important salaries revision scheme which Alex is also heavily involved in. No news yet about how my financial position is being reviewed.

Arthur is great fun in the office but I miss Bryn more than I would have thought possible. He was always there to help me – now I am always there to help Arthur! Kathie deals with him in a most marvellous dead-pan, Scottish way, but I never have the heart to squash him. He puts me on my mettle and I work extremely hard for him in a defensive sort of way which is unrelaxing, whereas with Bryn I worked just as hard, but never felt I was having to prove anything. Ah well, *men*!

12th May: [Air Letter]

I am only just home (5.30) and can scarcely think straight. I shall write a long letter next week, as I have a very nice photo of me to enclose, taken by Percy Litete, our staff photographer, a nice, normal straightforward man who is far and away the best of our African staff. He insisted on taking me working at my desk, so apparently that is how he thinks of me. (He took Alice against a background of flowers in the garden of Leg Co!)

My rise in status and salary is completely stymied by red tape, lack of precedent and, I suspect, male prejudice, but I am to receive a charge allowance, which means a rise in salary and back pay. The file is still moving among the chaps, but I know that much from my private spies. Ron has been given a 'female clerk', the wife of a senior police officer, but that is what she is called, so he now has his head above water, as she is madly efficient. I worked till six last night and got through an enormous amount. It is wonderfully quiet and peaceful after 3.30, when the lower ranks leap into their cars and head for the Club, but after dark, (5.30-ish) just now, one begins to wilt, I think because of the ghastly strip-lighting we have in the offices. I dash up and have a cup of tea from Ron's tray and then come back. Arthur keeps his small dachshund with him in his office – Fifi, corrupted, alas, to Filthy. You can imagine the doggie talk from him, me and the dog! She sings and talks in a most companionable way to me and is as good as gold, except at coffee time when she comes and sits up swaying in front of me, her eyes fixed pleadingly on mine. However, I never eat anything, so she is disappointed. Arthur drinks tea *all* day and nibbles biscuits. He then starts worrying about his waistline and embarks on a two-day diet which seems to consist of raw steak and prunes. It makes him nervy and irritable, but I remain unmoved. Today he suddenly stopped on his way through my office and said in peeved tones, '*Why*, Mrs Hitchcock, do you have to sit there looking so *slim* and cool?' We understand each other!

The Baxters have had a short tour and gone on short leave, as David is needed later to take over some job in Blantyre. I was sorry not to hear from them before they left. Alice and George also went, two weeks ago. I miss Alice very much – I got to know a great deal about Zomba from her! The weather is lovely and not yet too cold.

20th May:

After months and months I have another of my crashing colds – full head, sore throat, earache, cough. However, I think today will have been the worst one, and with the help of gargle, Veganin and hot toddy I shall doubtless survive. I was so dazed and shaky this morning that I fell *flat* out on my way up the steps to the car while Ron sat with his back to my plight, with *patience* written all over the attitude of his body. He nearly had a fit when I crawled in, speechless, and began to pick small stones out of the palms of my hands! Fortunately I did not hurt myself in the least.

Last week there was a tremendous panic over the UNO report, as Peter Youens suddenly decided that in spite of the Emergency, the Commission and other pressing work, it must be ready by its deadline, Monday. So, I was provided with three extra stenographers, to whom I handed out the material as I finished each page. They then typed it on tin foil, and handed me back a page at a time for checking before they took it across to the Print, where it was dipped in something and immediately processed to produce the 25 copies required by London. It was rather a nightmare, especially as some of these girls take no interest or pride in their work. We finished ahead of time (as I was determined to do) and 25 bound copies went off by air mail on Saturday at 9.00 a.m. and I then took a copy up to Peter Youens, who was immensely surprised and gratified. Jean Payne, our own stenographer, who had worked like a beaver, said when she and I were sitting back afterwards, 'All right, Ann, you can put

away your whip now!' Arthur, as head of Department, was of course beaming
with pride and talking to people of how '*we* had beaten the clock'. All he had
done throughout the entire exercise was give me his devastating smile, say, 'I
rely *entirely* on you, Ann darling', and proceed to carry out these words *to the
letter*! It has been amusing to see his reaction to my cold – sympathy up to a
point but keep the girl on her feet at all costs!

On Saturday evening we dined at the Davidsons with Geoffrey Fricker and
Philip Richardson, both good company socially, and went on to see the film of
The Pajama Game – disappointing for an American musical, but with several
wonderful numbers scattered through it. We all stayed on afterwards for a
nightcap and ended up having a very late night, thoroughly enjoying ourselves.
We are having a quiet week, as I feel pretty done by the evening. I am hoping to
feel better for our long weekend holiday – the cricket season has begun and
there will be a match to watch.

26th May:

My cold has been dreadful, but the worst is over. I had a bit of excitement
when feeling least like it, last Thursday. Kathie was suddenly summoned after
lunch to appear before the Commission, in Blantyre, and would not be back in
time for her Chinyanja broadcast at 6 o'clock. Arthur was furious and I hastily
offered to do it. Kathie was so thankful and in such a hurry she just said 'Yes'
very firmly to Arthur and fled. We decided I had better record it there and then,
as I tend to be very hoarse by evening. So I read the script out loud to myself
twice and then went over to the recording room. The engineer played it back to
me – a rather husky flow of clear, quick Chinyanja. I called in at Ron's office on
my way back and told him to be home at six for a surprise broadcast. Aflike
came in to listen and was greatly taken with my performance. I think I would
enjoy broadcasting work. Obviously, with training, I have the right kind of
voice for it. There will be a working studio here in Zomba within the next few
years, I feel sure.

The weather was glorious throughout the weekend and we were lazy, pottering
and reading; Ron actually managed to stay away from the office. We watched a
great cricket match all Sunday and I enjoyed talking to lots of people at the Club.

3rd June:

I am beginning to feel better, though I am very tired. I got the day off on
Friday and went to Blantyre, where I bought a very smart warm skirt for the
office, some vitamin pills, and had my hair done. Alex was also there at a Wages
Advisory Board meeting, and we had lunch together at Ryall's, my first meal
'out', as it were, since my lunch with Norton the day I passed my driving test,
all of which seems in another world now. I bought three new tyres for the car

and fairly raced back to Zomba. There are three stretches of the road on which it is easy to cruise along at 70 without even noticing. That evening Bunny and Alex dined with us and we went to see *The Silent Service*, a film about Commander Crabbe's exploits during the war, very well done. On Saturday we and the Davidsons dined with Walter and Barbara, to celebrate her birthday, and had a most civilised and delightful evening, Walter being a marvellously entertaining host. We had a quiet day on Sunday and I went to bed at six (as I also did on Monday), just to rest my cold. Yesterday I began to feel human again and in the evening we went to a party given by Tony and Pam Bridge, whom we knew here in 1951. It was a terrific party, but we firmly left about 10.

I have been given a charge allowance of £12 10s. a month back-dated to October last year, which gives me £100 back pay and a salary of £53 10s. a month from now on, so that is better than nothing. Bryn will be pleased for me. The £100 goes straight into Premium Bonds!

10th June: [Air Letter]

Ron was actually *offered* two days off next week, Monday and Tuesday, and by almost going down on my knees I got Arthur's consent for the same, so we are off very early on Monday and intend to be at Palm Beach at 8 for breakfast, leaving next day in the late afternoon! Leave is now almost a reality and one grudges spending any extra money, so we are not going for the weekend as well. I would do it, just for the rest, but Ron feels very strongly it is not worth the expense.

We had such a nice, quiet weekend. We watched cricket on Sunday morning, and the Davidsons dined with us on Saturday.

The weather is getting much colder, very suddenly, and I am into my tweed skirt and last season's coral twinset.

Wonderful news reached the office on Monday of the birth of a *son* to Bryn and Chris after twelve years of marriage. Only a few days ago he was gazetted as Chief Information Officer, Nyasaland. (He has till now only been acting.) So Bryn's cup is certainly overflowing. The air must have hummed with cables, as they are very much liked and have served in all three provinces. *Everyone* was waiting with bated breath for that baby! Dear Bryn.

17th June: [Air Letter]

I promised a long letter this week but I am home late from the office and am going out later, so I must use one of these again. I am sure I can get in all the news.

We have had a marvellous two days at the Lake, the laziest we have ever spent. We were so tired we could hardly face the prospect of making the effort to go away at all – a very bad sign. I am thankful I persuaded Ron and he now agrees it would have paid us, despite the expense, to have gone on Saturday. However, we had a very quiet weekend and at 4.30 on Monday drank early tea in what seemed the middle of the night, ate a brief breakfast at 5, feeling cold and cross (!), left at 5.30 under a starry but lightening sky and drove furiously (tarmac all the way now) watching the glorious sunrise, to the ferry, which looked Japanese – wrapped in opal mist with ducks hurtling out of the obscurity of two yards' visibility over our heads. The ferry works by diesel now and we were over at 6.10 and at the Lake by 7.45, to find sparkling blue water and all the little boats heaving in the breeze. It is such a magical scene to come upon that I always have the strangest feeling that it only exists when I actually see it! We breakfasted, got into bathing suits and out in the sun. I slept for nearly two hours – astonishing for me. The water was cold enough to be bracing and by the end of the day we were brown, bleached and glowing. It was cool in the evening. We played Scrabble and read. Ron had *four* lamb chops for dinner. We both slept well and had exactly the same shamelessly lazy day on Tuesday. It was agony to come away at 4.30 in the afternoon but we both feel unbelievably revived. I was able to wear a blouse and cardigan today, as my glowing skin kept me warm all day! I get through an enormous amount of work and am able to stop thinking 'shop' when I am away from the office, which I was incapable of doing before the break.

There is now a suggestion afoot that I undertake the entire production of the five-day *Hansard* of Leg Co, which opens its session on 6th July. Last week I would have been appalled, as it would mean working till about 11 every night, but I did not turn a hair at the idea today! It would pay Government to be more generous with local leave.

24th June: [Air Letter]

Another of these things, I am afraid. Now that I have my better pay, I hardly ever leave the office at 3.30, as Arthur, quite rightly, loads my *in* tray with work.

It is odd to hear of high summer at home, as the weather here is cold, though bright, and the landscape definitely wintry, with thinning trees and an increase in the leaves to rustle through as I walk home. We have not had a fire yet, and it is not nearly as cold as last year – July is the coldest month, but it has definitely been a short season, I am glad to say. I am suddenly feeling very fit again and have been dashing about the house doing some unseasonal 'spring cleaning' with Aflike. Ron has been feeling off-colour this week with a vague queasy inside. He has promised to go and see Norton if it does not clear up soon. He really has been desperately overworked recently, but says it is easing off now. I am up to my eyes, but have it under control.

Last week Arthur lent me a record called 'At the drop of a hat': a piano and two singers, Michael Flanders and Donald Swann; very sophisticated 'patter' between very witty, clever songs. The best one (inspired by a car number) is called 'I'm a Gnu'. Flanders has had polio and sits in a wheelchair. We had the Davidsons for dinner on Saturday and played it to them before dinner – too English for Bunny, I think, but Alex loved it. We went on to see *Wild is the Wind*, very wild indeed, with a splendid performance from Anna Magnani, all hair and teeth. Last night Ron had an urge to play bridge and spent a good evening's relaxation at the Club, coming back 7s. richer. I firmly refuse to have people here to play or go to them, as I am far too tired after the office to cope, and it is more an ordeal than a pleasure. I have never played enough at a stretch to take it up again without being nervous and unsure, and I do not want to have these feelings about anything, *ever again.* Tomorrow night we are dining with Jean Payne and her husband, Rex, whom I hardly know. It will be interesting to see their house, which I am told is perfect – he is as domesticated as she, and even does the shopping. Can you imagine Ron . . .?!

1st July: [Air Letter]

I am sorry to write a short letter again. The pre-Leg Co 'flap' is on and I left the office at five, had tea, made a ham and egg pie, washed stockings and am now sitting down to this at last!

Here everything is geared to Leg Co next week, the Budget session and HE's Speech from the Throne, which this year is even more hush-hush than the Budget, as it will comment on the Emergency and the coming constitutional changes. I have been spared the production of *Hansard*, but will undertake the final editing and the index, as usual. Arthur has not had any experience of Leg Co and is in a state of tremendous nerves, eating biscuits all day ('My dear, I'm simply *burning* up energy') and of course drinking gallons of tea. He drives us all to near-hysterics, but I have got the hang of him and manage better than some. Ron is working hard, feels better and so is more cheerful. His queasy inside has died down again and he eats very well, so let us hope that is the end of that.

We had a very enjoyable evening with Jean and Rex Payne last week. The Government Printer, Dick Martin and his wife were there, and it was a gay and quite stimulating evening – a nice house with some beautiful old furniture. They are going to settle in Africa, which makes an enormous difference to one's attitude to what one buys and collects. As a result, I had a long, hard look at our house and it is now being ruthlessly spring-cleaned – the weather is perfect for it, as things are washed, ironed and up or on again in a day. The drawingroom is positively sparkling. The weather is coldish, but we still have no fire in the evenings, without any hardship.

7th July:

My Press cuttings files have become a small, fascinating library, unbelievably useful. I now supply the Police with special files. I have to read them *all* myself, so you can imagine how much I should know, if my memory could retain everything. However, I usually know where to find what is wanted, which is the main thing; for example, when someone comes in with a garbled request for 'a cutting from the *Scotsman*, sometime in May, I think, which mentioned something HE said in an after dinner speech when he was home in April '58'!

We are in the middle of Leg Co, so the office hums like a beehive. I did not get in at all on Monday for the opening and Budget, as I was holding Arthur's hand all day – floods of swearing in French, leanings of head on arm on wall, and pacings to and fro, but of course he copes perfectly well. All the cables went off at the right time (three journeys by me to the Post Office by car, one on foot when I found our car immovable behind two others!) HE's speech was all right, but fell flat as permission to speak on constitutional reform was withheld by the Colonial Office. The final cable confirming this arrived only five minutes before HE went in to the opening ceremony. The new mace was presented and is in use – very yellow-looking, but beautifully carved. The Speaker is in his usual form, ginny-voiced, deaf and sleepy. He is fairly shaky with rheumatism and the effects of polio, bless him, and his progress towards the throne is agonisingly precarious, with the whole Government front bench of lovely strong men poised ready to leap to prevent his downfall. Bruce Wickham is Clerk of the Council this session, and looks more than ever like a small grey lion in his wig, which he absent-mindedly tilts to scratch his head every now and then. I was in all yesterday and today, taking notes, as the three African members are speaking. The two firebrands are missing – Chiume is 'abroad' and Chipembere is Inside. Nothing spectacular has happened, but it is interesting to hear the reactions to the Emergency and how they are dealt with. *Hansard* is being edited by a different assistant secretary each day, and it was Ron's turn today, so he will be home late. He came in for a quick lunch and seemed quite happy. I visited him this afternoon and found him looking rather sheepish, surrounded by four stenographers with ear-phones on, typing furiously. The final editing lands on my desk next week, with the index.

On Saturday I was so exhausted I went to bed after lunch and stayed there till supper time. On Sunday evening Ron and I went to see *The Red Balloon*, a perfect French film, and a Russian opera-ballet film: some heavy but beautiful singing, and extracts from *Romeo and Juliet* and *Swan Lake*, with Ulanova, and the *Prince Igor* dances – gorgeous stuff.

It has been much colder in the last few days, but lovely clear weather.

15th July: [Air Letter]

Another of these! We are working late in the office every night just now, and I am so tired my hands have not yet stopped shaking!

The weather has been slightly warmer for the last two days and the African staff told me in the office today that they consider the cold season is on the wane, marvellous thought, though I have not actually suffered from it at all.

We had a quiet weekend, with a Saturday evening visit to Kuchawe before dinner. I am too tired to be sociable just now, though I shall have to make an effort to catch up on entertaining soon.

Leg Co went on for an extra day last week, so we were flat out. Ron was interested in his experience as editor and said it was just the job for me.

The Devlin Commission Report arrived last night from London. This was meant to be very hush-hush, but I had heard mutterings on the top corridor and guessed when Alex was suddenly detailed to go to Chileka to meet a plane yesterday afternoon. One can positively *hear* the Secretariat machine quickening up to meet the coming spate of extra work which is no doubt in store for us all, heaven help us! As Aunt Isabel used to say, 'If it's not one damned thing, it's another!'

23rd July:

There has been a contretemps over our leave arrangements, which is not quite settled yet but I may as well tell you now, as I have the time and energy. We are booked on the *City of Perth* on 11th November. It is a cargo ship with only twelve passenger berths and I have always been doubtful about it, as just one uncongenial passenger could ruin the trip. Well, my doubts were confirmed the other day when I heard that a couple from Nyasaland would be on board. It just so happens that they are *bêtes noirs* of both Ron and me. Ron was equally horrified and has set about seeking alternative passages. I have been so upset by this episode, I realise I am really very weary and end of tour-ish, though I love my work. I just seem to flare up at the slightest setback.

The Devlin Report comes out tomorrow, with various timed statements from various Government officials, and Arthur spends hours upstairs getting hush-hush instructions as to how to handle the Press. At first the rumours flying around were fairly reassuring but a bitter note has crept in and Arthur said grimly today that several heads would roll shortly. I think everyone will feel sick at heart if we are not backed up. The Press is trickling in from home, and there is a TV team – long hair and suede shoes – drifting about looking significant. All the top corridor chaps are difficult to deal with, which is unusual, and the best thing to do when one meets them is to say good morning, duck, and hurry past. Ron went to Chileka this morning and came in staggering under a load of mail bags bristling with emblazoned seals. There is an atmosphere of imminent disaster, but perhaps we are all being unduly pessimistic. Time will tell – I never thought I would feel so strongly about it, but I do.

We had a very successful dinner party on Saturday, with the Paynes, the Wickhams and an ADC (now a DC) who was staying with them, whom I had met at Mzimba, Squiffy Jones, a very Welsh Welshman, much mellowed since 1954. The film was fun, a comedy with Clark Gable and Doris Day. Ron and Alex had to work *all* day on Sunday, so we met at Bunny's for supper. I got lots done in the house, which is always a relief. I am reading *Anastasia*, the novel about the woman who claimed she was the daughter of the Czar – fascinating, but these Russian stories are so depressing, and I could do without that just now. I had a pleasant day all by myself in Blantyre on Friday, spending little but doing a lot of shopping for other people. I had coffee in a new café run by a Yugoslav woman – a lovely clean little place, serving delicious espresso coffee, quite out of this world. I had no opportunity to talk to her but I would like to, another time.

28th July:

I weighed myself in Blantyre last week – 6 stones 12 pounds, which seems ridiculous, as I am not all that thin. We had rain yesterday which suddenly froze everyone, with the damp seeping into one's bones. Today is chill and cloudy.

All our thoughts and energies have been concentrated on the Devlin Report. Copies for the general public are still in transit, having been twice mislaid at airports *en route*, which seems disgraceful. There was a leak here, of course, and I learned of its outlines from Ron. It is perfectly obvious that there was also one at home – to the Labour party. This is clear from the home Press, which I have been devouring. Today the comments on its publication have come, but I only rushed through them this afternoon. It could be worse. The Governor is vindicated in declaring a State of Emergency and public opinion at home seems to accept this, which saves Lennox-Boyd's bacon. The crashing blow would have been if HE had been condemned. What effect it will have on public opinion out here is a very different matter, because the Commission has reacted extraordinarily to Dr Banda – evidence of violence intended by Congress and so on, but no definite criticism of him – a kind of whitewashing which is highly dangerous here. The Africans will understand only that Banda has not been criticised. The sophisticated approach to there being evidence of intent to murder but not massacre makes no sense in a country of primitive people who can be easily incited to violence. As HE said, massacre may be a matter of quantity, but murder is murder. My word, if *one* white man or woman had been killed, British public opinion would have been up in arms and HE a disgraced man. Ron managed to get a copy from upstairs and he read it till one this morning. I went to bed at 10.30, slept a little, but was awake when he came in, and we lay and talked for ages, unable to relax and sleep, so we had a very short night.

I am longing to brood over the Report myself now and dissect it with Ron. He is fascinated by Devlin, and the possibilities of how his character and background may have influenced him and his approach to the personality of Banda.

Arthur had to put out a Press Release, which he did very skilfully, using direct quotations to ram home his points. We had dozens of cables giving long paragraphs from the leading papers, and to save time I had to read them out, in decent English, with punctuation, while Jean typed them straight on to paper. We produced seven Releases on Friday and were both utterly exhausted to the point of helpless laughter towards the end. The cables are all in journalese – cablese, not easy to convert instantly into good, readable prose, which was what was asked of me, and I got tied up in knots. It required complete concentration, not helped by Arthur rushing in every few minutes to grab another page. It was great team work and we ignored telephones, enquiries and people coming in. I think Arthur was really pleased with us. It will be even worse tomorrow!

On Sunday Alex put Bunny and the children on the train at Limbe, on their way to Tenerife. Bunny decided quite suddenly, in view of her father's death, to go and visit her mother, who is very old, and failing.

I am afraid the Report has loomed very large in this letter, but I thought you would be interested in a glimpse behind the scenes!

5th August: [Air Letter]

A dreadfully sad thing has happened. Bunny left for Beira on Sunday, and yesterday Alex got a cable from Tenerife to say her mother died on Monday. It is so frightful for her I have been upset all day thinking of her. The ship does not sail till tomorrow, so she may decide to come back.

August bank holiday has been one of disasters here, with two Europeans killed in road accidents, another from a fall from his horse just before the Turf Club races were to begin, and our Information Assistant, Max Osman, who helps me with the Bulletin, in his brand new little car for which not a penny has yet been paid back to Government, killed a cyclist and injured another, whose leg has since been amputated. He is in hospital himself and faces a charge of manslaughter, which means a prison sentence, and that is the end of him as far as Government service is concerned. It is tragic for him. He has changed since he returned from attending a course in England, and has been difficult, lazy and hostile, but he has talent and it is such an appalling waste of his education. So we are all feeling very subdued.

The Devlin Report is still very much with us, and I am ploughing through it. HE has returned from London, 'mentally and physically exhausted', according to Arthur's Release, and went off on local leave yesterday for an unspecified time to an unspecified place, so we have a breathing space before things quicken up again. The weather, to my delight, is definitely getting warmer.

This Saturday we are going in a party to the latest play: *Affairs of State* in which Bruce Wickham has the leading part, so it is of special interest. The Freemans (Director of Education) are taking us. It will be the last Club function, as they are pulling down the hall and re-building it for cinemascope at last! There is a new cinema in Limbe, which gets very good up-to-date films, so we may make a few expeditions there, if we have the energy.

My hair is getting so long it is exhausting to wash and dry and feels hot and heavy, so I am going to have it cut. The good hairdresser in Blantyre who advised me about it is now, to everyone's delight, married to a police officer in Zomba, so at last Zomba has a hairdresser. We are both feeling the better of our long, restful weekend and Ron is playing squash regularly again and feels less tired.

12th August: [Air Letter]

Good luck to the grouse!

There is not much news, so I am writing this before I go to the library. The Sproules have invited themselves for an early drink, which I like, so I have to be ready for them at six – hectic as usual!

Last Friday I went with Kathie to the African hospital to visit Max Osman, who looked terrible, all the sophisticated façade knocked out of him. He was discharged yesterday and we are wondering how his case will go. He was in a big ward, and the smell and squalor which a group of sick Africans generated were unbelievable. I had completely forgotten that particular smell, which took me straight back to the memory of some of the filthier villages during the famine.

We had a lovely evening on Saturday. The Freemans had invited two other couples, also in education, so the shop talk was new and most refreshing. It did not feel like Zomba at all! We had a quiet Sunday, and have Alex here for supper at least once a week. He is so overworked I think he is glad of the quiet at home and is certainly getting more sleep! I had Norton for tea the other day. He goes off on leave in September and is very ready for it.

19th August:

Bryn has been asked to shorten his leave, so we expect him about the middle of November. It seems hard, but I expect he will want to be back, in the thick of things. There is some talk of Ron's leave being put off till February again – nothing definite, but it seems likely. Having fiddled about with passages already it is all rather difficult, but I think I shall go on the December ship, our latest booking, still not confirmed. Ron thinks he will be useless as a worker by February, but realises it will give him leave at the best time of year, so he is fairly philosophical about it.

The event of the week for me was my visit to the hairdresser on Friday afternoon. Well, off it all came and I felt quite shaken to see about eight inches drop away. She cut it beautifully, very short, in layers, and gently curled all over. Everyone has admired it, and Ron says it takes years off me. I felt rather odd for a few days and slightly panicky whenever I caught sight of myself, but I am happy about it now. Arthur *loves* it and calls me his *petite gamine!* (Alex said I looked like a very pukka terrier!) It has sent everyone in the office rushing to the phone to make an appointment.

On Saturday Ron, Alex and I went to the 4.30 matinee of the new cinema in Limbe – multi-racial (not a single African in sight but quite a few Indians), air-conditioned, with a bar and coffee room – great fun. We saw four trailers, American News, a cartoon and a glossy American film called *Ten North Frederick*, with Gary Cooper and the very beautiful model, Suzy Parker. It was excellent entertainment and we all enjoyed it. We then went on for dinner at our old haunt, The Flamingo, and had piri-piri chicken, salad, cheese and a bottle of Chianti. It was a very relaxing outing and lifted us right out of the Zomba rut. There was the yearly cricket match between Agriculture and Administration on Sunday, and we spent a lovely day at the Club, meeting old familiar faces – Peter Nicholson, Pat O'Riordan, Jim Reeve and others.

Ron has had a streaming cold for some days and it went down to his chest on Monday and developed into 'flu, which is very prevalent just now (touch wood for me). On Tuesday morning he actually said he would stay in bed, which terrified me, as you know what he is like. So I phoned Norton, who came to see him, said it was 'flu, and gave him some pills and medicine which have miraculously made him feel much better already. He is having tomorrow off and thinks he will go back the next day. He has had a good rest, plenty of sleep and is eating like a horse. Alex came for a drink last night and we played Scrabble on the bed.

Iris and Dave are coming south next week from Kota Kota, and will be with us on Wednesday night, which will be wonderful. Iris is flying home with Linden to settle her at school and will stay till January, to miss the hot season. I can hardly wait to see her.

We have been slightly less pushed in the office, but there is something big about to break, I can tell, all very hush-hush at present. There has been a *chiperoni* since yesterday, and the mist is right down, with cold, steady rain falling – miserable, just when we were all relaxing in the sun. I am enjoying dashing off on my own in the car, always far more punctual without Ron! He seems to be greatly missed in the office – all the stenographers ask tenderly about him. I have just brought him four thrillers from the library, so I should have a quiet evening!

25th August:

Ron's leave is definitely in early February, and he is arranging for me to sail on the *City of Port Elizabeth*, which has now been put back to 25th November, so I shall with luck be home for Christmas, provided I get a berth. She carries 100 passengers and sails at such an unpopular time of year that there is every chance.

I have been preparing for the Davies' visit tomorrow – what a demand on linen and blankets. Some of our sheets and pillow cases are in a disgracefully threadbare state. The weather is warm during the day but the nights are cold, and coming from the Lake shore, they will need plenty of covering on their beds. It is wonderful how we have managed to have so many brief but happy visits from them over the years.

We had a quiet weekend. Alex came up the mountain with us on Saturday before dinner here. He is glad of some good meals, as the boys produce very monotonous fare and he has no time or energy to plan for himself. On Sunday we visited the Sproules in the morning and found them both very shaky from the aftermath of 'flu. Ron recovered remarkably quickly, and was back in the office on Friday, to find Julien about to go down with it. I still go unscathed, so let us hope I shall be lucky. Tomorrow I shall have been working for exactly two years, and I intend to celebrate in the office by sharing a packet of chocolate biscuits at elevenses. Arthur is on a new diet and there will be screams of pain as he resists the temptation to join in!

3rd September:

We had a great disappointment last week, when Dave arrived alone, having seen off Iris and Linden that morning. They had just had three weeks local leave in Southern Rhodesia and Dave could not linger away from his station any longer. It was a bitter blow, and we could hardly give him the warm welcome we should have. However, we asked Alex to join us for the special dinner I had planned for Iris – her favourite wine and light food – and we all enjoyed the evening. Dave is utterly absorbed in his work and he and Ron had a great talk about the districts in the Emergency and we all talked shop about the state of Nyasaland in general. We parted rather quickly in the morning and Dave set off for Kota Kota.

On Saturday at lunch time we went to Alex's, to have a drink with Jean and Philip Richardson and their children – Mike, aged fourteen, and Jo, aged nine, both tiny, like their parents. Mike is a perfect public school boy (Rugby) with a delightful poise and a breaking voice, Jo *very* English spoken, having left here a year ago with a very Southern Rhodesian accent. Jean had to stay behind at the end of their leave to have an unexpected operation, and then flew to Salisbury to have a second one, nearer to Philip, who was able to visit her. She seems to have made a good recovery and looks bright and well. We had a very happy hour with them. Jean was not interested in telling us about their leave, but wanted to hear all about the Emergency at its height, which she missed. In the evening we went up to Kuchawe with Alex and sat by the fire, talking companionably with people.

Today we are plunged into another *chiperoni*. Ron is having a day in Blantyre, attending to his detainees' affairs and visiting Kanjedza, the holding centre. I am glad he is getting away for a day, though it will be horribly cold in Blantyre. He has fully recovered from his 'flu. Alex's ulcer has flared up again and he is living on milk and omelettes. Bunny was to arrive in Tenerife on Sunday, so she will be settling in. Her sister is married to a Spaniard and has four children, so they will make a nice big family together. We play far less Scrabble now that Bunny has gone, though three make the best game, I find. We talk a lot of shop, which never interested her.

Today, on instructions, I wrote a long piece on David Livingstone, for his centenary, which I shall send you in the Bulletin next week. It was not at all easy, considering recent events – what do the Africans care about Livingstone now? – and it took me *all day*.

9th September:

The weather has settled down to lovely warmth, and I am full of bounce and high spirits. Arthur has suddenly broken out in a rash on his arm, which looks like, and may well be, ringworm. I had to rally round to deal with the panic, nausea, disgust, near-hysterics, etc. He has been given an ointment to be applied four times a day, and contrives to do it three times in my office! (I refuse to touch him. It is very contagious, I believe.) This morning he appeared with a small bell, if you please, which he pretends to ring as he walks upstairs to call on the chaps. He really is very funny, which is also contagious in my present mood. The roses by the office are in full bloom again, and the other morning I put a big, long-stemmed one between my teeth and danced into his office, flamenco style, clicking imaginary castanets, to find Kathie there too, at her most Scots and dour, not willing to be amused so early in the morning! Arthur, of course, loved it, gave me his most flashing smile and preened himself, which he always does when I set out to amuse him!

Last weekend Alex had to put up a guest from Salisbury, a man called Hingley, who has been on secondment to Salisbury. We all went up the mountain on Saturday and had a very good dinner and marvellous conversation. It was stimulating to see a new face and hear about Federation from the point of view of the south, even though it makes one's blood run cold to hear just how 'pro' Federation they all are. There were lots of people there, and as our conversation was by far the most lively, we had an interested audience, some of whom joined in eventually. Sunday was a dull, sultry day and I got dug into a book and hardly noticed it pass, till Scrabble and supper here with Alex. Tonight we are dining with Bobby and Hazel Lowe (Bermuda). This weekend a Rhodesian pilot is staying with Alex, flying some VIPs in on Saturday and returning on Sunday, so we are having them both to dinner, which should be interesting. Ron and he can talk a different kind of shop.

There is still this merciful lull in the office, and I am quietly clearing up all the skeletons which have lurked in my 'pending' tray over the months, so that I can leave with a good conscience. My word, Arthur is going to miss his little maid-of-all-work!

The time is flying and I am beginning to think of all the clearing out of wardrobes and cupboards. However, the weather has given me what I think must be my third wind, so all is well.

16th September:

We have had another *chiperoni* and felt chilled and depressed by it, but it lasted only two days, and the hot season is definitely here, though I shall want it far hotter than this. The jacaranda blossom is suddenly bursting into bloom and Zomba is beginning to look its most beautiful. It will be even better in a week's time, when the blossom is really thick. I never tire of looking at it with love and gratitude. We seem to have far more birds in the garden this year, and at the moment (4.30) they are all noisy in the long low golden light of the sun, which will soon disappear behind my mountain.

Our Rhodesian pilot did not come to Zomba after all, so my nice dinner on Saturday was eaten by Ron, Alex and myself, after a visit to Kuchawe, where we had a pleasant time with quite an interesting company. There was cricket to watch on Sunday, always a soothing and restful way to pass the day. We had a marvellous evening last Wednesday with Hazel and Bobby Lowe. Arthur and Bill Ferris (Federal Information Officer) and his wife Pat were there. Arthur was absolutely on top of his form and kept us all in fits. After dinner we played quite an amusing game called Americano, which I unexpectedly enjoyed – a mixture of poker and rummy – *not* my cup of tea at all, usually!

I have just read Graham Green's *Our Man in Havana*, very clever and funny, but the Catholic sense of humour is not for me, though I see the joke. I prefer him serious, I must confess.

23rd September: [Air Letter]

Another of these, as this is one of these weeks when I am snowed under. Arthur has gone off to a conference in Salisbury, and I am so determined that the office will prove itself capable of doing well without him that I am going over everything twice just to make sure all is well. He comes back tomorrow afternoon and we shall all have to brace ourselves for the whirlwind!

Norton called in to say goodbye today. He goes home to do a fourteen-month course on anaesthetics, which will get him the post of the only anaesthetist in the Federation. He is dreading going back to studying again, after being away so long. He is also terrified of flying, so he was not very happy about the coming journey. It is surprising how many people hate it, even in these days when it is such an ordinary mode of travel. All the school children here treat them as we did buses – what a hideous sentence, sorry!

The PCs' conference which decides postings begins at the end of next week, and there is every hope that Ron returns to Zomba next tour, taking over from Julien Theunnisen, who is Planning Officer, and staying on in that section with Julien when he returns. I really should have waited till after the conference to tell you, but Ron himself says it is fixed, even though it is not official yet. I was so thankful I felt no reaction at all, and then cried myself to sleep from sheer relief.

We had a lovely weekend. I took Friday morning off for shopping in Blantyre and got back to the office at 1.30 (by driving like the wind)! We took Alex, Rex and Jean Payne to the Limbe cinema on Saturday and saw an excellent film, *The Roots of Heaven* and went on to The Flamingo, the Paynes' first visit: a lovely evening which we all enjoyed tremendously. The jacaranda is in full bloom and I sat on the *khonde* all Sunday morning and feasted my eyes on it.

30th September:

I heard on Friday that I have got my passage on 25th November, a single cabin on the *City of Port Elizabeth*, which I believe is a lovely ship, with Lascar stewards – sheer heaven, so everyone says, specially if one has experienced nothing but the dreary Union Castle, as in my case. What is specially wonderful is that Alex is booked on the same ship. He booked with Ron and me when we thought we were both going in December. It will be so nice to have him to help with luggage and customs, quite apart from having a companion on the voyage. Ron's February booking on a City Line ship has fallen through, but he can go east coast on British India, which is an excellent Line, and it means he will see Tom [his guardian], after ten years, at Dar-Es-Salaam, to his great delight, so he is quite cheerful now too!

I am hardly in a fit state to write, as I have one of my colds. We went to the Police Ball on Saturday, as guests of Dennis and Bunty Moore (ex-Nigerian Police. Bunty helps Ron with his detainees' affairs). We spent a very lively hour at the house – twenty of us – and then went on to the Ball. It was a beautiful night, with a soft breeze, and we sat outside under fairy-lighted trees. The band was excellent, and most of the men *very* good dancers, so I was on my feet all evening till three and had a lovely time, but I got very hot dancing and then had to sit outside, and as the hours passed it got quite cool. Before the evening was over I suddenly realised I had a sore throat and a temperature, and that was that. Of course I could not say so and excuse myself. The worst day was yesterday, and it is now disgustingly on its way. The weather is very hot, so it increases my general discomfort. It is bad luck that I got it at this stage, when I need what is left of my energy. Ron's passport has to be renewed, so I asked Litete, our staff photographer, to take a photo of me, and of Ron. I saw them today, very much passport standard, but I think good enough to send you a copy of mine. I do *not* wear a curl in the middle

of my forehead. That was the high wind! 'Madly intellectual,' was Arthur'
comment!

Ron has decided to stay on in the house rather than go to the hostel, which he
loathed. It is a complete reprieve for me, as it spares me all the packing, but will
be hard on him and I shudder to think of him and Aflike packing all the
household stuff. However, I shall just have to shut my mind to all that – and
shut my eyes when I have to do the *un*-packing! We are giving a big Sundowner
on 9th October, so I have lots of time to plan it. I have already put sixteen
candles in jam jars to hang in the garden.

7th October:

I knew how thankful you would be to hear about Ron's posting to Zomba.
The PCs' conference is over, and they seem to have let well alone, so I think it
is safely settled. The Government has introduced a new rule – no doubt influenced by the Emergency – that no Administrative Officer can be away from the
territory for more than six months. That means instead of six months leave *plus*
travelling time, which is roughly another two months, the travelling is included
in the six months – maddening, and really the men need their leave, though I
know some of them get bored. Arthur is already bursting with plans for me on
my return, so that is all right! (The head of the Special Branch is trying to woo
me away to the Police, which I keep very quiet about, as Arthur would be
furious, to say nothing of Bryn!)

My sailing date has been put back to 21st November, which means I shall
definitely be home for Christmas. I think we disembark at Plymouth, so I shall
go up to London and stay at a hotel recommended by Arthur, very cheap, clean
and central. I leave the office on 7th November, but as Bryn is not expected to
arrive till the 8th, I have promised to go in, in the afternoons of the next week,
to see the chaps and edit the Bulletin. Arthur goes white whenever my leave is
mentioned, he really does.

The small rains came yesterday, ten days early, and everything is damp and
chill. My cold is getting better quite quickly, thank heavens.

We had a good weekend, devoted to making a fuss of Alex and his fortieth
birthday. He dined with us on Friday and on Saturday we went up to Kuchawe
for dinner and had a delightful evening. On Sunday we joined him at noon, with
Philip and Jean Richardson, Jean looking very well. He came to us for Scrabble
and supper. It was tremendously hot over the weekend, and from all the signs,
this is going to be a real snorter of a hot season. Ron seems fit and well, though
he really is very tired, mentally. I would not like to have to work on till
February, and there is no doubt that my work is already suffering, as is
Kathie's, who goes off about the same time. Allowances are made, somewhat
grudgingly, by our task master! (We all know exactly how to deal with him
now, which is going to amuse Bryn!)

16th October: [Air Letter]

There is not much news this week, so I am writing one of these. After the small rains last week the weather has settled to an absolute blaze of heat and the pen is slipping in my damp fingers now, at 4.30. My cold has cleared up at last but I have not yet recovered my spirits or energy. It really was quite dreadful this time. (I say that *every* time.)

The election results were greeted out here with tremendous relief and elation. Some of the chaps sat up all night listening to results as they came in, and everyone knew all was well on Friday morning. My party was well timed, quite undeliberately, though people said how *clever* to give an election party! (It would have been pretty flat in that case if Labour had got in!) It went with a tremendous bang. My candles in bottles gave a lovely flickering light of welcome all down the steps and round the *khonde*. I had ordered a lot of small eats from Blantyre and done quite a lot myself, and it all vanished. We had thirty guests and they nearly all stayed till 10, which is very late indeed for a Sundowner, but proof that they were enjoying it. There was not much work done in the Secretariat on Saturday morning!

We had a very quiet weekend, with no film and no outing, as we were tired. Ron strained a leg muscle at squash and is to have massage from the physiotherapist (a very horsey Irish woman). I am working very hard, as I am trying to have everything in order before I leave. Arthur has some hush-hush writing to do, unexpectedly, and of course wanted now, now, and I am having to collect masses of information and statistics for him – not a very pleasant task in this hot weather when tempers are already frayed – everyone loathes statistics and snarls slightly when asked to produce them. However, I now have a technique for dealing with slightly snarling men! I have also learned how to deal with Don Penny, our Press Officer, a very amusing, highly-strung ex-newspaper man who never stops talking and can be very entertaining for a short time.

I am now off to the library and then we are going down to spend an hour with Alex. He is feeling much better, as he is not overwhelmed at present, and can see the end approaching.

20th October:

Arthur is off to a conference in Lusaka. He left last Friday and returns this Friday. He gave me an enormous amount of work to compile and have ready for him. I am also helping Kathie and trying to get some work out of the African staff, who think they can just sink back with a sigh of relief when Arthur goes away. I really am now hanging on by the skin of my teeth, and shall be very glad to leave everything and get away. The feeling came quite suddenly. I even want to leave the office, however much I like the work.

October is the hottest month of the year here and is known in Rhodesia as 'suicide month'. It is absolutely boiling hot, and for the first time ever I am drinking gallons of water daily. It is difficult to sleep at night and I notice we all walk about the corridors slowly.

Ron would very much like you to continue sending the home papers after I leave. He has taken more interest in them this tour, as his job has demanded a certain topical background knowledge which simply did not come into field work. He is having therapy for his muscle trouble – not massage, but plates and heat to stimulate the nerves. He was told that half an hour's treatment is the equivalent of a ten mile walk, and he says he can well believe it.

We had a quiet weekend, as it was very hot and there was no good film. We had a drink at Kuchawe on Saturday evening, and it was almost as warm there as down below – astonishing. I got Monday morning off and raced over to Blantyre and back by lunch time. I ordered a cake and a record for Ron's birthday, bought odds and ends for the house, *and* a delicious cocktail dress for myself – many-petticoated black silk, with black nylon overskirt painted with pink and gold roses, a black sash held at the front with a life-size black silk rose, and a tight bodice with thin shoulder straps – the prettiest thing and not expensive. I nearly melted among the concrete buildings. I literally bumped into David Baxter, just back from leave, who engulfed me affectionately in the chemist's. They are all well and I *may* manage to see them before I go. He looked less thin and very brown, the dear man.

28th October: [Air Letter]

This will be a bit of a scribble for two reasons. First, there has just been a thunderstorm and the electricity is off, so I am writing by candlelight. Secondly, I am lying down! Over the last few days I have been developing a severe chill in my waterworks and today at lunch time, after a morning of acute pain suffered in silence in the office, I gave in and went up to the hospital and saw a very nice doctor who gave me pills and medicine and told me to go to bed for at least two days. Having said nothing in the office, there was high drama when I crawled in to tell Arthur. By this time I had gone a pale grey and he could not have been nicer, and whisked me home in his car. It is a most painful business and I am worn out and running a high temperature. However, the pills are working. It was silly to go on for so long, but one always does. If I feel better tomorrow, Jean is going to come up to the house and do some proof-reading with me!

We had a very nice long weekend with the Monday holiday. On Saturday evening we and Alex dined at Kuchawe as the guests of Tony Hingley, the charming man Alex put up some time ago. Theo and Homer (the owners) had some new records, and we enjoyed hearing them – very witty cabaret, sung at a piano by someone called Bill Williams, who discovered his talent when a POW of the Japs. After dinner we had to stop listening, as indigestion threatened! On Sunday we went to a big drinks party at the Financial Secretary's, not fun at all, just a lot of people milling around in the heat, then lunch with Alex. On Monday Barbara and Walter (Sproule) came to drinks with us and we sat out on the *khonde* with the last of the jacaranda falling round us. (The lights have just come on again!)

4th November: [Air Letter]

My 'chill' developed into a severe bout of cystitis – *what* a thing. However, as I remember you once suffered from it yourself, I will draw a veil over the agony! I really turned my face to the wall for three days – and this should be my last week in the office! Arthur is, I hear, practically hysterical, poor man. However, I am much better today and will go back tomorrow. The thought of packing is killing, but I have no doubt it will all work out once I get back some energy. My labels and ticket came today from the City Line, so I am beginning to believe I shall live and get away.

I leave Limbe at 11.45 a.m. on Wednesday 18th November, the ship at present sailing on the 21st from Beira. Bryn is expected within the next few days, and has already communicated from Cape Town. It will be interesting to see what a son and the confirmation of his post have done for him. I hope *he* will be interested to see just how hard and well Arthur and I have worked together – provided Arthur is on speaking terms with me by then!

11th November:

I feel rather odd and disembodied, as one always does at this stage. You will be glad to know I have completely recovered. The heat is tremendous, and of course I notice it more since I started preparing for my departure. I finally got up and went to the office on Friday, a bit shaky, but I was feeling so depressed at home I thought it was time I was out. I got a lovely welcome, and of course *slaved* all day – at my desk. I refused to dash about and even Arthur saw that I could not.

On Saturday evening Jean and Rex Payne took us to dinner at Kuchawe and it was wonderful to feel well and sociable again. Alex is having a hard last lap in the office and has had a bad ulcer pain for about a week. Bryn arrived back on Monday and was in the office yesterday morning. I went in to do the Bulletin in the afternoon and promised to go in again this afternoon, so I shall see him then. He, Chris and the baby are staying in the hostel and move into Alex's house when he goes.

I am going over to Blantyre on Friday to insure my luggage. I will find out from the travel agents about ports of call and dates. I have got Ron's birthday and Christmas gifts organised and just hope Aflike will produce the right parcels at the right time. Yesterday I invited myself to tea with the Wickhams to say goodbye and had a delightful time. Today Jean Payne and I are having tea together at the Club. As you know, I hate goodbyes and keep sliding out of them by telling people I shall see them again before I go. I feel at last that I have left the office work behind me and it seemed quite unreal yesterday when I went in. Everyone is complaining of the great heat and it is obviously going to be a very trying season.

I am off to make a ham and egg pie for supper. Cold food is essential in this weather and I am sick of trying to think up something new.

17th November:

As you will realise, I am in a complete daze, and highly emotional after two hours in the offices saying goodbye – I had to do it, and put it off as long as I could, as I felt so weak and unstable that I thought I might cry all over everyone. However, I pulled myself together and it went very well. The heat has been tremendous and I cannot begin to describe what packing has been like. Alex says quite seriously he would be dead without having had my help. I packed up his entire household goods and they have enough crockery to feed an army!

Last night there was a colossal thunderstorm which cleared the air for a few hours but tried the nerves dreadfully. Ron and I played three games of bad Scrabble solidly through it, as it was impossible to concentrate on anything else. Ron is subdued, working terribly hard and complaining about the heat. Lack of sleep is the worst problem – one's bed feels like an electric blanket and is always damp. I saw Bryn for a few minutes on Thursday looking very fit, and on Friday I went to Blantyre for final shopping. We had a last dinner at Kuchawe on Saturday and spent Sunday finishing up Alex's household affairs. Today after lunch I went down to the office, mainly to see Bryn, who kept me for an hour. He wants me back and said he would put in a post for me in next year's Estimates and find a place for me whatever the chaps upstairs said. Temporary European women workers are now a very tricky subject, as Africans now have their eyes on these posts. We talked shop with Arthur, made marvellous plans and I got away without shedding a tear. I said goodbye to Jean and the rest of the Department, and to some of the chaps upstairs. The Richardsons have asked us to supper tonight – Alex has been staying with them since Sunday. I have a few odds and ends to put in my suitcase tomorrow. Aflike shows signs of suppressed emotion but I am too exhausted to cope, and pretend I have not noticed! I had my hair cut and washed this morning. She says it has improved marvellously in condition. I have lost weight and look like a wizened child, but the voyage will take care of everything, heavenly thought! I shall, of course, write from the ship and ring you from London.

Chapter 23

For just over a year, I remained at home, living with my mother and sister Jess in St. Andrews. My private life was in turmoil, my marriage in crisis and my health precarious. Finally, I made the decision – and a terribly wrong decision it was to prove – to return to Ron in Nyasaland. He was some months into his fourth tour, working in Zomba in the Secretariat. My mother and I resumed our weekly correspondence.

31st January: TMV *City of Exeter*

4.30 p.m. A hurried note which I shall post at the Purser's office. Everything has gone smoothly and I got straight on board and into my lovely cabin. I have just had tea with two very pleasant people (Treasury), a Mr and Mrs Shergold, from Zomba. I have looked at the passenger list, and they are the only Nyasaland people on board, which is a relief. They get off at Cape Town, with their car. I am about to go down and see if my luggage has been delivered to my cabin. We have the Earl and Countess of Airlie on board, but I have not yet identified them.

As you will realise, I feel very odd indeed; even more so as I have just taken an Avomin, which is making my head swim. I do not know when we sail and will study the notice-board when I post this. I shall write from Cape Town. Do not worry about me. I can foresee a beneficially quiet voyage. It was lovely to find your wire, a letter from Elspeth and flowers from the aunts in my cabin.

18th February: Cape Town

We arrived here yesterday, one day late, and now expect to get to Beira on 7th March. I have already confirmed that I can stay on the ship till Friday 10th, when I catch the evening train, arriving in Limbe next day at 4.30, so I need not worry any more about that. There was a marvellous pile of family mail waiting for me yesterday, which I was thrilled to have. Also, there was a letter from the faithful Jean Payne, who says she is absolutely sure that Bryn intends taking me on in July, so that is cheering news. Ron writes that everyone is asking about me and looking forward to seeing me.

There is a good library on the ship, and I found a marvellous book which I noted when it came out some months ago – *The Leopard* by Giuseppe de Lampedusa.

We had quite a voyage to Cape Town. We were delayed a day in London by gales in the Channel and when we did sail, plunged into appalling weather. About 80% of the passengers stayed in their cabins for the first three days – gale force 9 and a roll of 45°! The captain was on the bridge for the first 36 hours and then collapsed with 'flu. The Earl of Airlie cracked two ribs and an elderly man had to have eight stitches in his head. Those of us who stayed on our feet were flying about all over the place, I indiscriminately grabbing strong men and furniture as I whizzed on my way. I found it wildly exhilarating but too dangerous for comfort. Four children had measles for the entire voyage and one went down with it quite badly just before we reached Cape Town. There was also a most unpleasant bug going the rounds, which laid me low for a night and a day with a frightful pain, running insides and awful vomiting – very exhausting. I had to stay absolutely flat on my bunk (when not rushing to the loo). The doctor visited me three times and gave me pills which worked wonders. Of course I did not have an ounce of resistance. This happened four days out of Cape Town and I am now unbelievably thin! But I am divinely brown and my hair is a lovely honey colour. I have been very, very lazy and simply lain in the sun. I have not managed to work up much of an appetite, though the food is excellent. We had a very wealthy, lively table which has now dispersed but there are still twenty-one people on board and thirty-seven more embark before we sail on Monday. I found it all a great strain and realised with rather a shock just how run down in every way I am. However, I look better and I think that by Beira I shall be very much better. It is bound to take time. At least I am gloriously, contentedly *warm*!

24th February: East London

We docked here yesterday evening and I was very happy to have your letter, the only mail I had.

I am, quite suddenly, feeling unbelievably better, though still sleeping very badly indeed. The weather is perfect and I am out in the sun with a book a great deal. When in port I sit up on the boat deck, where there is always a breeze. I have not gone ashore anywhere yet, but I may do at Durban, which I like very much. There is a marvellous Italian shoe shop which I would willingly visit again. My table companions are much less tiring than the London to Cape Town group, and are pleasant enough, but deadly dull, which is also very tiring, in a way! The Radio Officer, Mr Arthur, has been very kind and friendly (I sit at his table) and has more or less adopted me for the trip. I am now perfectly accustomed to being on my own and am quite content to keep my own company, but people are very friendly and tend to come and talk to me. I have gained no weight at all, but you would be happy to see me – mahogany and blonde and no lines left on my face. Thank God for the sun!

2nd March: Durban

I was very glad to find your letter when we arrived on Monday and delighted to have another one yesterday, answering mine from Cape Town. I now feel we are completely in touch again, and indeed we shall soon be back to our weekly routine. I am not sure if I shall write from Beira: things are complicated by currency there, and I intend to stay on the ship. It is going to be appallingly hot, I am told. If I do not write, I shall write from Zomba on Monday 13th, after I have had a day to settle in.

Yesterday morning I was persuaded by Mr Arthur to join him and his two friends on a drive about sixty miles out of Durban, through the Valley of a Thousand Hills. It was fascinating, though very hot. The splendours of the scenery, achingly familiar after my cold exile, at last impressed upon me the fact that I really and truly am back in Africa. We then went on to Pietermaritzburg, a very pretty little town with old Dutch houses and a lot of atmosphere which I would have liked more time to absorb. We got back to the ship at 4 o'clock, all soaked in sweat. It is the hottest hot season on this coast for years and the officers are dreading the time they have to spend at Beira. I am feeling very well and have put on a little weight. I am now 7st. 2lb. I shall feel it a tremendous effort to move from my little haven here and start coping with more travelling and those beastly Portuguese officials.

13th March: Zomba

The ship did not reach Beira till Tuesday, so I just had time to pack and get ready. The heat from Durban onwards was simply indescribable. When I had my hair done the day before Beira, I got it cut very short and my head felt much cooler and lighter – even so, it was soaked in sweat for the entire train journey. I went ashore at Lorenço Marques with Mr Arthur, saw over the Radio Station and (for the third time) went to the famous Polana Hotel for morning coffee. The night before I left the ship I went with his party to a Portuguese restaurant and had a delicious piri-piri chicken dinner, then on to my first nightclub, where we danced to a Portuguese singer, piano and drums – lovely. By this time I was screwed up inside with the prospect ahead and was thankful when at last I was on my own on the train, after a very friendly send-off. The journey was dirty and uncomfortable, and before Limbe I had a cold wash, all over, from the tiny basin in my minute compartment, and changed into a straight green skirt and pale yellow sleeveless blouse, so I *looked* as cool as a cucumber – and only just in time, as the train was, astonishingly, two minutes early when it arrived at Limbe. Ron was there to meet me. He is as slim as ever, brown; there are some new lines round his eyes and he looks harder. He definitely has more confidence and wider interests and leads a better life because he is out in the open more. He also gets up early and goes promptly to the office, which is a new departure with a vengeance. At present there is a great strain on both of us and we need time to adjust. On Saturday and Sunday we walked after tea and many people stopped their cars to greet me and welcome me back. Everyone says how well I look. Ron is shocked by my thinness but says that 'facially' I look very well indeed. We are in the same semi-detached house as last tour, only on the other side, and the view is familiar and lovely. As you can imagine, the house is in a perfectly awful mess and it is really *far* more difficult to get it into order than if I were starting to unpack everything from scratch. However, it is good that Ron managed even as much as he did. Nothing has been broken except the Magomero-built bookcase, and it is not seriously damaged. There was a huge bunch of roses from Jean Payne, cut from our Information flowerbed, and a note of welcome – so sweet. Alex has had malaria for two days. (He is coming in to see me after dinner tonight, as we want to meet in private before we see each other in public.) [Alex and his wife were living apart. He was back in the Secretariat and living in the Hostel.] Ron is very much occupied with stage-managing the rehearsals for the play *Black Chiffon*, and has his bridge and squash twice a week. I hope to ease myself back into Zomba society gradually and am in no hurry to meet people, but feel I should get it over. I must give myself time, I keep reminding myself.

Aflike is delighted to have me back. He has been training up his wife, Aleni, to work in the house and serve at table. She is clean, quiet and doing very well. I am a bit tied, as I have not yet got down to the Boma to renew my driving licence, so shopping is not very successful so far, done by sending a chit – usually to the wrong shop, as I am out of touch with where things are to be had.

Ron is delighted with his binoculars and has them round his neck the moment he comes into the house, and out walking we stop every four yards. (As I am short-sighted and do not possess binoculars, the boredom is *excruciating*, but of course I say nothing.) Ron varies between being quiet and natural to being white-lipped and taut, as the mood takes him – and he is now a very moody man – so that I relax a little and am suddenly thrown off balance by the change. I have had to tell him that we must take things easily or I shall simply collapse and I *think* he accepts that this is so. I am sleeping quite well, but the moment of waking up is ghastly. I feel very strange, lonely and frightened, so this letter is not very satisfactory. I also feel I am on the verge of getting control of myself, and with luck I shall suddenly find myself better able to cope, very soon. My difficulty is that sometimes I tremble all over, visibly and quite uncontrollably. It happens very suddenly, without warning, and I am so afraid of doing it in front of people – the ones I know well are the awful problem, and I dread meeting them. I am not writing in a panic – I just want you to know how I feel and share it, and then it does not seem so bad!

I am all right. I would not have written at all if not, so do not worry. I hope to be even better next time I write.

20th March:

I feel I have been here quite a long time. Alex came up and saw me after dinner on Monday and then on Wednesday last week while Ron was at the Club rehearsing. (Ron, of course, knows about this.) We are thankful to meet again, but shattered by each other's thinness. He has lost stones. We agreed the heartbreak is constant and complete. Dear Geoffrey Fricker has called in to see me, as did Jean Payne, and we had a little weep together. On Thursday evening there was a big farewell party for HE and Lady Armitage at the Club, so it was an opportunity to face the whole of Zomba at one go. I wore my new black velvet dress with your Chinese crystals (Julien Theunnisen stroked my dress with one finger and said 'Ah, you are wearing one of those delicious English dresses'! He is South African and South Africans go mad over the quality of British clothes.) Everybody was there (except Bryn and Arthur) and I met them all, so kind and welcoming. I was exhausted but cheered by the evening so much dreaded, and feel that is a big hurdle cleared.

Today, the new Speaker, Wenban-Smith, opened Leg Co, with Ron in attendance, bewigged, as Clerk. His wig arrived on Saturday. It is made of nylon and cost £26. (I spent all Saturday with him in the office, helping him prepare the Leg Co papers.) I sat in the visitors' gallery and watched, feeling homesick for the Press gallery opposite, where our office people were busy scribbling. I have not yet seen Bryn or Arthur, but met Don Penny and some of the African staff after Leg Co. *Everyone* asks me if I am going back to Information and all I can reply is, 'Yes, if there is a place for me.' I can now cope with people without too much strain. I cannot pretend that there is not a wilderness within, but at least it no longer manifests itself physically.

Aflike and his wife look after things reasonably well, but I am not reconciled to the house and the lowered standards of cleanliness and efficiency. I hope to get my driving licence this week and then I shall be mobile and do the shopping and feel more normal and independent. There is still an enormous amount to be done in the house, as I have so far concentrated on the sittingroom. *Everything* has had to be washed – curtains, carpets, rugs, cushion covers, lamp shades, bedspreads – everything that can take soap and water, in fact. There is a terrible little spare room in which I can hardly move, to clear up, containing old clothes, rags, torn linen, accumulated junk, all just thrown down. Then there are things like plugs and lamp fixtures which I do not know how to deal with, and Ron is nearly always out in the evenings, so they *stay* undone. However, patience!

28th March: [Air Letter]

This is really a fill-in, as your letter did not come yesterday, and I waited in case it came one day late, as I like to have it to answer. However, it has not yet come, so I am sending this off and will write again when I have yours.

I am settling down, in so far as I now feel I have been here for *ages*! Ron managed to spare me some time at the weekend and the house, as a result, looks more like a house and less like a bachelor's den, and I feel I can bear to touch things. The lamps are now in the right places so the lighting is pleasing, which is so important. Ron has accumulated masses of new books, most of them botanical and ornithological (and very expensive), so he is having a long bookcase made to hold them. I must say the sittingroom gives me great pleasure, which is just as well, as I live in it at present. I have my driving licence but have yet to convince Ron that I am safe driving on my own. The car was badly treated by the people who 'looked after' it for him when he was on leave, and has developed odd reactions which I am not yet familiar with. I am going to try again after tea, when I shall take him down to the Club to play squash. [That was the last time I drove the car.]

We went to a party at the Speaker's house last Thursday to meet visiting MPs, and there I came across Bryn, who said he hoped to have me back in July, but could not promise. I bumped into Arthur the day I was collecting my driving licence – 'Sweetie, you look *marvellous*. When are you coming back to help me?' There was then half an hour non-stop telling me *all* about his work, his plans for leave, and what he needed me for! And then: 'Utterly ridiculous. *Of course* Bryn can get you in – he fiddled it last time and he must just fiddle it again!' I am still occupied with the house, but it is nearly in order and then I shall *have* to find something to keep me busy. I sit out in the sun for a time each day, which keeps up my tan, behind which one can hide so much. It has been a long, wet rainy season and everyone looks pale and limp.

4th April:

Yes, I am enjoying wearing my new clothes, but at the moment the choice is limited, as I have lost weight again and everything (but *everything*!) tends to fall down or off or sideways. I am trying to eat more.

There is really little sign of the cold season yet, but because of the damp – it has rained every day since I came back – Bella is already proving invaluable. ['Bella' was a small, soft blanket my mother had crocheted in brightly coloured squares of wool during my year in St. Andrews. I still have her.] We have breakfast out on the *khonde* to combine it with birdwatching (!), and as I am in my kimono I am never warm without Bella draped round me as well. I have a great affection for 'her' and suspect she is a grown-up form of comforter, like a child's favourite toy!

I have not been out in the car again. It is difficult to pin down Ron. He is always in a hurry to be off on his own ploys or is too tired, and I cannot press the point any more. I think as always, he is so taken up with his own problems – and heaven knows he has them – that he gives not one jot of thought to me and what life is like for me, virtually a prisoner in the house. We have now faced up to the fact that this reunion has been a complete disaster – it took exactly 48 hours to find out – and can only be temporary, as we would simply destroy each other if we remained together. At present there is nothing for it but to go on, because of Government regulations about my fare, etc. I have to stay for six months before I can claim my passage home. We shall work something out for the future when the time comes. We certainly cannot afford to pay my passage now, and besides, I have plans to stay, though that is my secret. Ron is as anxious as I am that we do it decently and in a way least harmful to himself and Alex. I am telling you all this because your last letter convinced me that you wanted me to be honest and open with you.

We had a quiet Easter, which was what Ron wanted. On Friday morning we went up the mountain to walk and bird watch. We called in at Kuchawe to have a drink with Homer and Theo, who gave me a most affectionate welcome, as indeed everyone has. On Saturday we had some people here at lunch time for drinks, to whom Ron owed hospitality – he owes an enormous amount – and had a very successful gathering. I was all wound up for it, my first attempt at entertaining, but it went very easily, in an unreal kind of way. In the evening we had quite a pleasant dinner at the Speaker's.

The other day I went down to the Club at 5 o'clock, when Ron was playing squash, and there in the car park were Bryn and his son Lawrence, a wee, sturdy replica of Bryn, with his rich, glowing colouring and Chris's vague, dreamy manner. Lawrence was sitting enraptured at the wheel of a tractor parked there – bliss! Bryn's face was full of emotion when he looked at him and it made my eyes fill with tears – children are so precious, so vulnerable, and of course so are fathers.

Jean Payne is most helpful and friendly, and gives me a lift to the library when I want to go, and quite often phones me from the office, just to chat and tell me how things are going. When she first called at the house she said, 'People never take advice, so I shan't offer any, but if you ever want any, I'm here to listen to you asking' – a very profound remark. I have not known her all that long, yet she is the *only wife in Zomba* who has called on me since I came back.

11th April:

Alex phoned me this morning to tell me that he had just had a letter from his lawyer, saying that his wife has at last consulted a lawyer about getting a divorce. So we both feel that is a first step forward through the dark tunnel in which we live. He is, I think, slightly better, but he cannot break away from the terrible physical and mental exhaustion which saps him constantly and gets between him and his work. I feel it might help if he would just give in, be ill, and so have a kind of 'rest' (as I did) and begin again, but he has a horror of giving in, in case he cannot pull himself together again, and of course I understand that too. He has lost so much flesh he looks like a young man, though a big young man. He still pokes his head forward and looks at me as if I were so small he can just see me where I stand down below. I feel I would burn at the stake for him, if it would heal his suffering.,

The first night of the play was on Saturday – I go this Thursday in Geoffrey's party. Ron says the theme is too emotional for Zomba and that the audience was uncomfortable. (To me, that suggests inadequate acting, but I did not say so.) Yesterday the Armitages departed in the morning and at 5.00 p.m. Sir Glyn Jones was sworn in as the new Governor. (The king is dead, long live the king!) The ceremony was in Leg Co, before members of Leg Co, Ex Co (Executive Council), myself (!), Bryn, the CS and various others, including Peter Nicholson, as PC Southern Province. Peter told me afterwards that Margaret Baxter has had a *son*. Isn't that simply wonderful for them? After the swearing in, there was a cocktail party in one of the committee rooms, which went wonderfully well, and everyone enjoyed themselves. Ron said Sir Glyn looks like a Welsh miner. I thought he was absolutely charming. There is no doubt about it, the English just do not bother to get on with the Welsh, but I do not think the Welsh give a damn about that.

I have been trying out quite a number of new recipes, in an effort to get some more weight on both of us. Aflike, though still a tower of strength, is not what he was, I suspect simply because he is beginning to get old – and once the Africans start to age, they age quickly. I find I have far more patience than I used to have, and keep calm in domestic crises – Ron is the one who now flies up in the air. The fearful test will come when I give a dinner party and have to rely on Aleni to serve at table.

I enjoy the *London News* and home papers very much and really do read them from cover to cover, the moment they arrive. The *Spectator* has some *very* funny jokes recently – better than *Punch*.

19th April:

The rains are gradually going and there is a definite nip in the early morning air, but the days are still blazing hot when not overcast and thundery.

I have not much news for you. On Thursday evening I went to the Hostel to dine with Geoffrey, who had also invited Alex and one of the stenographers, and then we went on to the play. We had a drink before dinner in Alex's room. There is a lovely view from both back and front verandahs, but the room is like a passage, with echoing floors (one storey up), badly lit and drearily furnished. It made me feel ill to think of him living there – monstrous at his age. The evening was only just a success. I made an enormous effort and so did Alex, but as I said to him later, unhappiness, sheer, slogging unhappiness, is a bore for other people, because those who suffer from it cease to be interesting or comfortable to be with. The play had its one bad night and was not worth watching, but improved on Saturday, I was told. Afterwards, Alex went back to the Hostel and I went on with Geoffrey to a party for the cast and all the backstage helpers. I felt very out of it, as they are a very closed circle, Ron now included. Ron went off to the play on Saturday evening and Alex came up for an hour with me. He is not really getting any better in mind, and I am almost beyond myself with worry. Also, after months of respite, his ulcer is paining him again. Of course *he* worries about *me*, fighting my lone battle in this hateful house. I think I have persuaded him to seek medical help.

On Sunday morning we went to noon drinks with the Freemans. He is Director of Education, Welsh, frightfully nice and witty. They have two daughters, twelve and twenty-one, who were there on holiday and had young men coming and going. In the end we all went down to the airfield and watched one of the daughters and her young man take off in a Tiger Moth for a late lunch and afternoon tea at Cholo! It made me feel rather old, but glad to be. What a cold-blooded lot they seemed, none of them quite clean or quite polite, nice as they all were.

Yesterday Ron had to take the scenery of the play to Limbe Club and set it up there, so I went to the hairdresser's and, bliss, had my hair cut short, washed and set – a great success and I feel a different person.

Alex has lent me his typewriter since Saturday, and I practise six hours every day and am coming along nicely. [I had attended typing classes at Dundee during my year at home.] Jean is coming up in a few days to show me how Government work is 'laid out' – ghastly thought!

27th April:

The first chill of the cold season really gripped Zomba today. I am *freezing* and have been draped in Bella since 7.15 this morning. I am doing quite a bit of cooking, or rather preparing dishes to be cooked, and I must say I think I could become very interested. It is, of course, a great thing to have Aflike as assistant, and we work together very companionably.

I have been asked if I would tutor HE's son, aged thirteen in elementary Latin. I know I could, having discussed it with his former tutor, Rosemary Landreth, who only has school Latin. He broke his leg a few months ago and it was discovered to be cancerous, so it was amputated high on the hip: a dreadful tragedy. He has adapted to it amazingly well – a very likeable boy. I would enjoy it, I think. I always had a weakness for Latin!

On Sunday we went to the early cinema and saw the film of the book *I Was Monty's Double*, which was excellently done and everyone enjoyed it. We met

Alex on the way out and had a drink with him. He is obviously trying very hard
to pull himself out of his valley of despair.

Philip Richardson is going to marry again – a Colonial Office secretary called
Mary Wigley. [His wife Jean, whom I liked very much, died while I was at
home.] He met Mary when he was seconded to the Colonial Office for two years
before he and Jean came out here in 1955. I met her when she was on the staff
of the Devlin Commission. She is coming out in July.

I am now going back to my typing!

3rd May:

I am sorry my letters exude unhappiness, but I am afraid it is inevitable, if I
say anything at all – stark misery is our daily lot, at present, and there it is.

I have got a job! By a great deal of thought, effort and considerable cunning,
Geoffrey (who is Chief Establishment Officer, you may remember) and Bryn
have put their heads together and the result is, in spite of rules and regulations,
they have got me back into the Information Department – not in my old job –
but 'held against', as the official jargon has it, the stenographer's post which
will be vacant when Jean Payne goes on leave in about six weeks. I shall do the
typing, filing, telephone, Press cuttings – all that she does except shorthand –
and I hope a good deal more besides, which she does not do! As Bryn says, it
gets me in and once in, he will see what he can do about keeping me when a
stenographer is available again. The pay will be low but it is a start and I am not
grumbling one little bit. I go in on Monday, to start to take over from Jean, who
is as nervous, if not more so, than I am! I have been typing my fingers to the
bone, trying to get up some speed. So, one step further through the dark tunnel.

I also had another marvellous boost to my morale last week. Ron came in on
Friday and said Dave Davies was in Zomba, on his way to meet Iris on her
return by air on Saturday. They were staying up the mountain at Kuchawe and
invited us to dinner on Saturday night. Iris looked lovely, really stunning. She
always does when she returns from England. She said I was looking very well
and quite unchanged – *phew*!!! We had an hour on our own while the men sat
outside (arranged by Iris!) It was absolute balm on my spirit and obviously on
hers, to be together. I have told her nothing all along except that I was ill at
home, but she seems to have heard enough and guessed enough, and simply
asked me in her straightforward way, if 'things' were all right now that I was
back. With equal straightforwardness I said no, I should never have returned.
She then asked if there was any chance of Alex and me getting free and of us
finally being together, and I said, yes, there was. She was very glad for me and
said (this *astonished* me) she was not in the least surprised; she had always
thought our marriage was at great risk, because of a deep-seated incompatibil-
ity over fundamental values and the relentless pressure on me of having to
adapt myself to Ron without, in fact, giving in to him. It took my breath away.

She was so calm, unshocked and matter of fact I felt, for the first time since I came back, relaxed and almost happy, certainly a whole human being again. She has her own difficulties and was able to unburden herself to someone equally calm and unshaken by what she had to say! There is a tremendous bond between us and we give each other inner strength. I feel better just knowing she is back on the same ground as I.

Ron went off for the day on Sunday with a packed lunch and I saw Alex and was able to share with him the moral support and strength I had received from Iris.

My mind is in a bit of a whirl, for once, as I now feel there are things I should be doing in the house before starting in the office on Monday. I am having four people to dinner on Saturday, and as this is my first dinner party since I came back, I am living through every possible horror that could happen during it! We are taking them on to a film I know nothing about, with Richard Burton, called *Bramble Bush* – I said to Geoffrey, who is coming, that I am sure there will be an illegitimate baby or a kind of Moses-in-his-basket in it somewhere, simply from vague associations aroused by the title! The Freemans are coming, also Coralie Dickens, the Financial Secretary's stenographer, who is our neighbour and whom we have known since 1950. Ron tells me he owes her a lot of hospitality and I quite like her.

10th May:

It is 6 o'clock in the evening, I have just washed my hair and for the first time today have sat down in peace and quiet! I never like to write letters in the evening, as you know, but I must get this off tomorrow and I stayed late today at the office – I am not complaining – the only pleasure in life at the moment is that of having too much to do!

The rains are on their way out, and we are having the right weather for the season: beautiful, beautiful days (now that I cannot use the sunshine, of course) with Mlanje floating in white mist in the morning and cut out like black velvet on the sky in the evening. I have been too active in the office to feel cold, and I am thankful to say it is a warmer office than my little one down below, which now looks scruffy, dirty and bare. The nights are cold and I enjoy being warm under four blankets. (My writing is dreadful because my hands are shaking from too much typing practice.) I have not heard any more about tutoring HE's son, which is just as well, as I could only do it after 4 o'clock and at present, till I get accustomed to things, I am far too tired to tackle Latin myself, let alone help a young boy.

We had a very pleasant dinner party on Friday, which went smoothly, I am thankful to say. The film was badly directed but Richard Burton was excellent and the story was interesting – about a doctor who gave his best friend, who was dying of cancer, a lethal injection to put him out of his agony. Everyone had lots to say about it and they all came back here for a nightcap and stayed till after midnight!

I spent a very restless, nervous day on Sunday with the prospect of my first day in the office on Monday, but when the time came I was perfectly calm. It was a lovely day and I got a great welcome at the office, including the African staff, and all my Secretariat friends stopped their cars at lunch time when I was waiting for Ron, to call out of the window that they were glad to have me back. I felt quite overwhelmed. Taking over from Jean could not be more pleasantly done, as she is very neat and organised – all her work is pure routine which I intend to do as quickly as possible – rather a bore, but at least I can take pleasure in doing it properly. The office is next door to Bryn on one side, Kathie on the other, in a new, separate block about twenty yards above the old block, which is now occupied by Arthur and most of the African staff. Jean does not leave till the end of the month, so I have plenty of time to settle in. The typewriter is a great hulking brute compared to Alex's neat little machine, and it is taking time to get used to it. I am so nervous just now I make masses of mistakes when doing the official work, but I stay on till five every evening to practise and that work is good and my speed is increasing. It is now a matter of getting confidence and that will come – it must. Bryn has already given me other work to do and it is quite clear that once I find my feet I shall always have some of my old familiar work to turn to, whenever I have none of the secretarial work to get through. Arthur, who goes on leave soon, is in great form. On my first day he came in and asked me if I thought his ears stuck out too much (they don't) because he had just found out that the latest 'thing' in France is to get them flattened, at a cost of £5. I assured him it would be a mistake and he went off happily, saying I had saved him £5! I am finding it an enormous benefit to be among people all day, though there is a sharp reaction when day is done. Apart from the typing, it is all within my capabilities, and I am assured by Jean, and can see it myself, that that will eventually become automatic. All my difficulties over the typing come from within myself, as I knew would be the case, but I shall win that battle soon.

We are having the Speaker and his wife to dinner on Friday and to see *North-West Frontier* which Jess and I enjoyed together and which Alex and I searched for unsuccessfully all over Dundee in a bus in a snowstorm.

17th May: [Air Letter]

This is one of those weeks when suddenly I find I have not got a minute to myself – out for tea, and drinks before supper tonight, when I usually write. So here I am, writing a short letter at high speed before lunch. (I do my laundry after it!)

We had another successful dinner party last Friday – the Speaker and his wife, and Diana and Peter Youens. They all enjoyed the dinner and the film, but they stayed on for a nightcap, which I do not appreciate now, as I can hardly cope yet with late nights and the office.

I see Alex when we can. I seem to be able to endure more than he at present but, as I said, he has never given in and of course I did, and had a rest of a kind.

I continue to type my fingers to the bone after office hours and there is a definite improvement – no difficulty left except my wretched nerves!

23rd May:

I was happy to have your letter yesterday. I am wondering if it actually arrived on Saturday. Ron was at a meeting all that morning, and did not bother to collect the mail from his office before he left. I think the best arrangement for the future is for you (and everyone else I shall tell) to send your letters to the Nyasaland Information Department, Box 22. Then they will come direct to me. It relieves my mind to be independent of him.

I meant this to be a long, satisfying letter, but I suspect it will not be. It is teatime and my usual writing time, but I have one of my colds coming on and I feel miserable. We have a holiday tomorrow, so at least I need not work. The typing was going through my head and down my spine like a sledgehammer.

Alex's ulcer is giving him a bad time again. He actually went off sick this morning but was back in his office at 1.30. The heavy Hostel food does not help, but it is mainly the prolonged strain and worry. I am sometimes so terribly afraid that he will die before I can be with him.

We went to a Sundowner at GH last Thursday. It was my first this tour and a bit of an ordeal. I met Robin and Elsie Martin (Police, ex-Mlanje) and was given a very warm welcome. They are now in Zomba and hope to see something of me. It is difficult, because Ron came up against both of them at Mlanje. As I said goodnight to Lady Jones she said, 'Ah, you are the *Latin* teacher,' and I murmured feebly, 'Potential,' and slid away. I have explained to their ADC about my job, but I think they are hoping I will give in to pressure. Well, I won't. I would like to help out but I am just too tired, and it would not work. On Sunday morning Ron went up the mountain and Alex came for coffee with me. We sat out in the sun and had two peaceful hours together.

The office routine is now under control, though little fiddly things crop up every day and will no doubt continue to do so after Jean leaves. The typing quite suddenly at the end, almost, of a day shrank to something I could tackle without nervousness or a tremor in my fingers. I also know how to lay out the different Government documents: letters, drafts, minutes and forms. It is sometimes hard to concentrate, what with Bryn, Arthur and Don Penny *milling* in and out, and two phones going – Jean and I, only a foot away from each other each talking hard into one. I have actually seen her deal with both at once! I now manage to put Bryn straight through to whoever he wants or wants him, without having to play for time while I slap the switches all over the place.

Kathie came in for the first time since I came to the office. She has been in Bulawayo. I was a little wary of meeting her but she was polite and friendly. Bryn keeps a fatherly eye on me but will, I think, be more relaxed when Jean goes. She likes to be in the centre of the picture when he is around, which is all right with me.

My throat still hurts in the evening when the air gets cold, but the weather is *lovely*; warm during the day, so that I am in cottons – unheard of at the end of May!

31st May:

It is 6 o'clock, and I am sitting down to my own affairs for the first time today, having my first cigarette – I never smoke now till after dark, which reduces my consumption (of cigarettes) to a very moderate amount. I have washed my hair and made a ham and egg pie for supper, so I feel I can relax now.

My cold only lasted a week, which was wonderful. The weather is glorious, though cold at night and in the morning. We still breakfast on the *khonde*. I feast my eyes on the marvellous sight of Mlanje and Chiradzulu and count my blessings I am *here* and not away out over *there*!

Alex is thinking of moving into a flat, which would be more expensive, but possibly worth it as he loathes the Hostel so much and the food is bad for him. I think it is a good idea and am encouraging him.

Arthur went on leave a few days ago and I miss his flamboyant entrances and exits! This was Jean's last day in the office and she quite rightly left me to struggle through the typing of the Estimates – not a very professional piece of work on my part, I am afraid. Bryn is madly kind and tactful, and said I could now regard myself as a fully fledged stenographer, but really, he and I know better than that! I find myself getting involved in conversations on the telephone with friends in the Secretariat, Blantyre, even Salisbury and Lusaka, who are glad to know I am back again, when I am really trying to put them through to Bryn, who mock-grumbles audibly from next door. We have ridiculous 'intercom' conversations between the two rooms, and if the line is bad he just raises his voice and I put down the receiver and listen to instructions through the wall. I suspect we are going to have great fun together when Jean goes. I get on very well now with Don Penny, who is gradually giving me more work to do for his Press section, which is new and interesting for me. He has just had shingles, all over his brow, poor man, but did not stay off work. Arthur shrank away from him in terror when they happened to meet, as I wickedly told him it was contagious – so it is, in the early stages. ('My dear, *think* of it. Covered in that filthy muck on the ship among all those pretty women I mean to conquer'!)

Ron has taken up 'Bonsai', the growing of miniature trees, and the *khonde* is hazardous with flower pots, seedlings, piles of earth, sand and other mysteries. Aflike is not amused.

7th June:

Jean and Rex spent their last night in the Hostel, and invited me to dine with them and Alex, so we had a quiet little party. I think she felt she was deserting me! She has been very good and kind.

The office has been going as smoothly as a mill pond (touch wood) and now that Jean has gone I really get through the routine work very briskly. The typing gets easier and more accurate, though I have an occasional panic and waste an awful lot of paper. I now have a 'panic' drawer, into which the spoiled sheets are stuffed, to be used later for shopping lists and rough drafts. Kathie gives me quite a lot of Chinyanja to type – I asked her to – and the result, at first, was incredibly confusing, as of course the machine is designed to offer the easiest and speediest pattern to suit the spelling of the English language. However, it is amazing how quickly I adapt. I have spent all day working on some hush-hush election poster material – just my line and *nothing* to do with Jean's job at all! Bryn is an angel. He is in great form and delighted to be able to find me some congenial work to do. Don Penny says *one* of the ways in which I am an asset to Government is that I always smell so nice – he sniffs the air ecstatically when he comes loping, like Jacques Tati in *Monsieur Hulot's Holiday*, into my office!

Tomorrow we dine at the Speaker's with HE and Lady Jones and the Chief Justice and his wife. (The Speaker told Ron frankly he wanted us there as 'light relief'!) Sometimes these evenings turn out better than one expects, and there will be a good dinner, unplanned by me!

13th June:

I am now mistress of the telephone and know when to talk to Bryn through the inter-com and when to simply alter my voice, which immediately penetrates the wall and reaches him. The snag is that it also penetrates to Kathie on the other side and I find myself, grinning all alone, involved in a conversation with both of them. There is never a dull moment, I must say, even with Arthur away. I had a postcard from him, headed dramatically 'Off Zanzibar'! I have great fun with Don Penny too, who has realised I can be both useful and funny!

We had a very pleasant party at the Speaker's last Thursday. They had a huge fire burning, much to my relief, and I sat happy and relaxed while everyone else went crimson with heat. The present DC Zomba and his wife, Jo and Sue Maynard, were also there and are only a few years older than we, so they too helped lighten the conversation. The Speaker was in great form – no one else knew it was his birthday, so my little token present made his evening, I am glad to say, as I had gone to *endless* trouble to get it – no car and no co-operation in getting a lift – just the insistence that I get a present. I finally swallowed my pride *completely* and asked Kathie, who was going to Blantyre that day, to get me something small in leather, with the Nyasaland crest. She chose very well and at 5.30 called in to deliver it – a small bottle opener in a leather case stamped with the crest. I tied it up in bright paper and ribbon and slipped it into his hand very unobtrusively, but he was so pleased he tore it open and shouted about it to everyone! We all had a drink and at eight HE and his wife promptly appeared. We did not dine till nine, and I was starving. Ten of us sat down at the table, which looked splendid in candlelight, with everyone in evening dress. I sat between the CJ and the DC and had a great time while enjoying an excellent dinner – clear soup with a made up cream cheese floating in it, fish in a sour cream sauce, garnished with capers and grapefruit slices, pork with all the trimmings, and a lovely meringue and strawberry pudding, followed by nuts and chocolates. I talked with the CJ for the first half of the meal, about Laurens Van Der Post, and then to the DC, about Lawrence Durrell – both conversations very interesting. I find I can talk to anyone now without feeling nervous. I did not exchange more than a few words with Lady Jones, but I talked to HE for about half an hour, from coffee time till they departed. He is very Welsh, educated in England; a fierce, warm little man who gives whoever he is talking to his total attention. After they and the CJ had left, we four 'young ones' were persuaded to stay on for a nightcap and finished off the evening very pleasantly, but I was not very bright next morning in the office, as we were not in bed till after one. However, I do not have an evening like that often in Zomba nowadays and I enjoyed myself, in my present rather detached way.

Ron gave a bridge party on Saturday night – Hugh Norman-Walker and a couple I do not know at all. I left a delectable looking cold buffet for them and went out – this is quite all right; all the 'bridge widows' do this. I went to visit Alex at the Hostel, shared a sandwich supper with him in his room and went quietly to bed, coming in by the back door, as the bridge party had not broken up. Apparently the supper was a great success, especially with Hugh, which pleased me.

Things go on very happily in the office. There is a lot of hush-hush work to be typed in preparation for the Election, and it is all very interesting, seeing how it is done. Our Film Unit goes out into the villages and shows a film on how to vote. This is being done in all three provinces and a tremendous interest is being shown. The 'reaction reports' are fascinating. There are great fears and superstitions over the ballot box, which have to be overcome. I cannot write much about it, as it is all very confidential, but it is most absorbing.

There has been great excitement in the last few days over the Test Match, and I have had to listen every quarter of an hour and phone the latest score to the chaps upstairs – Greek to me, but I became knowledgeable in my precarious fashion and managed it all right. Bryn ruthlessly left me to it, as he was busy presenting his Estimates to the Finance Committee, who fight every Vote. However, he emerged from the battle triumphant and sounding very Welsh, yesterday afternoon.

The weather is lovely but getting colder all the time and I am glad of my hot coffee at elevenses.

21st June:

I owe Jess for soap, a blouse and postage, so perhaps she would let me know. There is some difficulty now over sending money out of the country, and there have been strict currency regulations introduced (on the day I arrived back) in an attempt to prevent capital from leaving the Federation during the present uneasy period, which of course has affected trade enormously, whatever they say.

I seem to have very little news for you this week, which has been very quiet. Ron went to the cinema on Saturday evening but I felt chilled and low, as if I were about to be ill with something, so I stayed in the house and went to bed early. On Sunday I had recovered and was able to go to a noon drinks party at the Youens' – very enjoyable for me, as always there. Diana still rides by on her white horse and stops to chat (my office window looks out on the road) and her bull terrier still sits under the horse for shade and grins at me.

Bryn went off on *ulendo* to the Central and Northern provinces on Saturday, so I am having a quiet week – quiet from the point of view of the work I would do for him. I have the phones going all day long and have quite a lot to do, finding the information required and phoning it back. I think everyone knows now that Jean is on leave and I am in the chair. Kathie and Don have discovered that they can say, 'Oh Ann, answer that, will you? Just say no politely . . . or . . . just say yes, but don't encourage them,' and off I go and type out a reply.

Alex is very low indeed and I think very nearly at the stage of collapse which came upon me last year. I recognise the signs only too well. I have persuaded him to make an appointment with Dr Brink, the Government psychologist, whom he consulted once before and found helpful. He really needs a complete rest physically and mentally, and I am hoping Brink will put him in hospital with the right kind of diet and give him drugs to make him quieten down and sleep. I am thankful he has agreed to seek professional help. I have felt recently that I have my back to the wall and cannot stand one more pressure. However, it is amazing how one does, especially for someone else's sake.

28th June:

The cold has suddenly struck today, and caught me in cottons! Bryn has a bad cold and now, just after tea, having frozen all day, I have a sore throat. However, it can come and go in an evening, so I hope for the best. I rushed back and looked out my blue jersey suit and my plaid skirt, which is, as I feared, unwearable – it just falls down to a ludicrous position on my hips. I may devise something with braces! Winter is 'icumen in', with a vengeance.

You ask about the Speaker. His name is Bill Wenban-Smith. He is a pet, a big, straightforward man who has been an Administrative Officer in Tanganyika for over twenty years – a typical oldfashioned DC type. He likes bird watching, walking, classical music and gets on very well with Ron. He is shy with me, but I can, if I bother, twist him round my little finger. They have *five* children, and have lived on a shoestring for years and years on frightful bush stations. Two of their children, a son and a daughter, are getting married in July and she has gone home to be there for the weddings. She is very dogmatic and domineering, with a loud county voice and an expressionless face, but I like her and know how to get on with her. They are simply delighted with the terms of his new post, which include a free, furnished house, a generous entertainment allowance and all sorts of 'super-scale' salary perks. They say frankly that it is the first time since they married that they have not had to worry over every penny, so good luck to them, I say. Their position in Zomba, which is not a friendly place, is difficult, coming so late in his career, with no old friends around them. They always give me the impression of falling over themselves with friendliness if one pays any attention to them at all!

The Budget session of Leg Co, the last session under the old constitution, starts tomorrow. Aflike has been getting out Ron's wig, starched white collar and black gown. He is up to his eyes in his work as Clerk and is having a fearful battle with the Finance people over a new system of producing *Hansard*, for which he is now responsible. They have had to introduce a new method, or rather have it ready, as under the new constitution the ministerial system will immediately create much longer sessions with more African members, all no doubt with more to say! (I am glad I am out of it.) As it is the Budget session, a tremendous number of Press releases go out from our office and I shall be roped in to help type them, so I shall not see much of the actual Council, I think. I have already typed HE's speech, which is hush-hush till after he delivers it. I had to do it by a special process on waxed paper, and was very nervous, but it went off – or rather on – like a bomb and Don Penny was delighted. This will be a most interesting session and I hope, once the Budget flap is over, to nip in when I can.

On Monday after tea, Hazel Lowe, a sweet woman whom I have scarcely spoken to since I came back, called in and asked me to go for a walk with her and then to their house for a drink. They had a horrifyingly huge fire of fir cones which I loved, as I did not have the responsibility of worrying about the chimney going on fire! Their kitten came and lay like a little dog along the arm of my chair with its chin on its paws and its tail straight out behind, purring deafeningly whenever I so much as smiled at it. It was so nice to be in a warm, happy household. They are very kind and very determined to befriend me.

Alex has not been able to see the doctor, who has been on *ulendo*, but hopes to do so tomorrow. I am seeing him for a short time this evening.

4th July:

The last week has been tragic in Zomba. The Governor's son Timothy, aged thirteen, died on Sunday evening. I told you he broke his leg and they found he had cancer of the bone, and his leg was amputated. He made a marvellous recovery in spirit, but began to fail in health and was flown to Salisbury to see a specialist. I do not know what was discovered, if anything, but they seemed cheerful about him. Then his lungs began to give trouble and he was confined to bed recently but went on with his lessons right up to the end. On Monday morning Kathie came in and said the flags at GH and the Boma were flying at half-mast. Then Bryn came in and told us. He was quite distraught, having been up to GH to help with arrangements and the Press. It is so sad for them, as he was their only son and they are middle-aged and cannot hope to have another child.

Earlier last week one of the Africans in our department – the nicest, most harmless man – who had just come back from a three months training course in England, shot himself and his wife, who was about to have twins. They found her with her youngest child still strapped to her back, unhurt, so she could not have expected what happened to her. He must have planned it carefully as their other children had been sent to relatives. He had a rather melancholy nature and his family had suffered from political persecution for some years, as his father was a Federal MP. He was not very well educated and England was too much of a strain, I think, and Bryn agrees. We all tried to help him on his return. He had been back about a month, but no one could get through to him. He began to go for long walks instead of coming to the office. It is a bitter lesson, I think – pushing the average educated African too far too quickly until he just collapses under the pressures of Western standards. I was keeping this opinion to myself, but today Bryn became a bit more forthcoming and so I told him what I thought and he agreed. He says it has happened in other territories, for example in Uganda and Kenya, only there, because they are more advanced, they more often simply have a nervous breakdown when they return to Africa from England. It has all been most upsetting, particularly for Kathie, who was sent for when they were discovered. She has always protected him in his work and helped him, and has known him since he was a child. He sent word he would be late at work, and they were not found till five in the evening, and had died in the early morning. Bryn and Kathie went at once, and of course there was a tremendous upheaval in his village. I do not think Kathie has recovered from the shock yet, though she is glad to talk about it and does so very calmly. As I say, the whole system is wrong and yet the Africans everywhere in Africa are demanding swift advancement and the colonial governments are forced to comply. I am glad to say I never had a cross word with him, and had a friendly talk with him the day before he died. It has been most upsetting, and with Leg Co in full swing, it has been hectic, with the police coming to question every-one and newspapers ringing up.

Leg Co finished today. Ron has been very overwhelmed and strained, as he had a great responsibility for the Speaker, who is new to the territory and needed support right through. I was so busy I never got a chance to go at all, but I could follow everything, as I had quite a lot of Press releases to type – nerve wracking, as I had to hurry all the time. The Speaker was so relieved on Friday at the way things were going that he asked us to go with him to the early cinema, an awful film called *The Miracle*, based, very roughly, on the Rheinhart play in which Diana Duff Cooper played the part of the Madonna. He came back for a drink and spent a happy hour browsing through our ballet books. On Saturday I had Coralie Dickens, our neighbour and Mike Leonard, the DC (just back from leave) to dine and go on to the play, *Bell, Book and Candle* – very well done. We were invited to the stage party afterwards and left it, still going strong, at 1.30. Mike is a great charmer, with a bad stammer which he manages wonderfully. He told me it greatly improves his vocabulary, as he always has to think quickly of a synonym when he gets stuck on a word! On Sunday Ron went off for the day with the Speaker to Lake Chirwa birdwatching (blasted, eternal birdwatching). I spent some hours with Alex, who at last has got a bed in the hospital, and went in on Monday morning. I may take up his mail and some books tomorrow, so I shall leave this open and let you know how he is.

Hazel and Bobby Lowe are being very kind to us both. Hazel interrupted this letter earlier and bore me off to their house for an hour. I had washed my hair and had it pinned up in a turban, and Sue, their daughter, aged seven, brought me a headscarf and asked me to do up her head in the same way. She went off to bed quite content with her straight hair well turbanned!

The Speaker gave a party for Leg Co members and wives last night, which I hoped would be cancelled because of the death of HE's son, but it was not, and turned out to be very pleasant, as everyone was rather subdued and at their best. They all seemed much more friendly, or else I now accept people far more than I did – probably the latter!

Wednesday

It is 5.30 and I have just come back from the hospital. Alex was out on the *khonde* in his dressing gown and we sat and watched the sunset glowing on Mlanje. Geoffrey joined us for a time, and drove me back. Alex has been given tranquillisers and was more calm, and more like himself. He is also being given vitamin injections which I hope will restore his energy. He will probably be in for at least a week. The doctor said he must have the constitution of a horse, because he simply did not respond at all to a normal dose of tranquillisers. (To me, that is an indication of how strung up he was.) I was dreading the visit for us both, in case it was upsetting, but it was all right.

This afternoon a strong wind began to blow from the direction of Chiperoni mountain and I have prophesised that we shall be in thick mist tomorrow. Don

Penny, a Londoner, was quite incredulous that I should even notice any change in the weather, but refused to bet on it, as he said I looked 'weather-wise'. He helps to take the place of Arthur, as he is very lively and quick-witted. I am absolutely inundated with election work – huge tables of candidates and constituencies which I have to assemble from nine different files. It means I know the details, which will no doubt be useful when the heat is on. I am going to read the latest *Spectator* now – heavenly.

13th July:

The last week has been real cold season weather and everyone is complaining. The other day Bryn took one look at me, just before coffee time, when I needed sustenance, rushed through to Kathie and said, 'Order a fan radiator for Ann, yourself and me *now*. I don't care *where* you find the money!' In her dry way, Kathie said quietly afterwards to me that they would probably arrive just in time to be used as fan coolers in the hot weather! I think my office is the least cold of them all, as it is quite small and I shut the windows as soon as possible in the morning. Don Penny's office is along the corridor at the entrance and there is so much dust raised when it is being swept out in the morning at 7.30 that he always spends the first ten minutes of the day in mine. The other morning I went into his office first thing to put a file on his desk. He rushed in, saying something which sounded like 'suffer the silly'. I looked up with raised eyebrows and he grinned and said, 'Not you, honey – silicosis'! He is a great ally of mine now. He is a typical newspaper man, hard as nails, but perceptive and kind as well – a very odd mixture. I sometimes think he should have done something else, yet he is absolutely dedicated to his job, and finds Government red tape maddening. He is terrified of files, and whenever he gets one to deal with, brings it to me for guidance. I help him willingly and am getting a finger well into the Press section pie. We are frightfully busy now, with the Election drawing near, and I have not a minute to myself, which is how I like it. I have been typing hard all day, so my hands are trembling wildly, hence the bad writing.

Alex is still in hospital. He looks better and rested, and hopes to leave over the weekend. It has been a great worry in my mind all the time and I feel ridiculously lonely with him out of circulation. He has had an amazing number of visitors, some very unexpected, casual acquaintances, which is pleasing.

Bryn wants me to stay up at the office with him and the others on the night the Election results come in. It is going to be most exciting and interesting, and there is no doubt that Dr Banda will be *in*! It will be the end of an era and bring an end to a way of life for a great many of us – in fact the end of the African Raj. I shall be able to write of all this more openly later.

We went to see *League of Gentlemen* on Friday and took the Speaker, who enjoyed himself immensely. The place was crowded out, and Bryn had to stand at the back all through, with a crowd of teenagers. He said it reminded him of his school days!

On Monday and Wednesday the Dramatic Society held auditions for *A Midsummer Night's Dream*. I went down on Monday to watch, as Ron was going anyway, and was vastly tempted to take part, especially as Hugh Norman-Walker, who is producing it, came hurrying up to me before they started and said, 'Ah, Ann, good. What's it to be, Titania or Hermia'? I said to him, 'I just do not have the stamina for that sort of thing just now,' and he picked up my hand, kissed it and rushed away. *Nice man*. It was an interesting evening, but some of those reading the parts had no idea how to speak poetry – Geoffrey was the best. He is to play Oberon.

18th July:

Today Kathie is attending the inquest on Andrew Kumbikano, our African member of staff who shot himself and his wife.

I have been up at the hospital (it is within walking distance) seeing Alex, who is *much* better. He really looks himself again and is cheerful, though naturally rather dreading emerging into the fray again.

This cold weather is exhausting despite the fact that our radiators have been going full blast. Don Penny, who has not got one, paused at my office door this morning, said, 'Look, Ann, my latest trick,' and then came in, shaking from head to foot, and announced, 'The iceman cometh!' (That is the title of an American play.) It somehow seemed terribly funny, and he got the desired reaction from me, but a baffled silence from Kathie, who was in my office. The lovely thing about Kathie is that she does not mind not knowing things and *always* asks for an explanation. Her great triumph was the day I pronounced Puisne judge exactly as it is spelt, and she was able to inform me it was, in fact, pronounced 'Puny'! Now, when I have to explain anything, I say, 'Never mind, Kathie, remember Puny!' Bryn has a bad headache today and we have been spoiling him, which he loves. He has a radiator too, and keeps his room in a much greater fug than mine, which may explain the head.

On Friday I went to Hazel's, to a birthday party she was giving for Sue, who is eight. The noise was awful and all the grown-ups had practically lost their voices by the end, but I loved it. I gave Sue a small wooden elephant's head to use as a door knocker and all the children clamoured to be given one too. It was interesting to watch them, and to see the parents come in at the end to fetch them. Bobby had a little tape recorder, and recorded the cutting of the cake, which Hazel described, and Sue singing 'Frère Jacques' in a breathless little voice. He then played it straight back for us and the children screamed with laughter. He will post it home to the grandparents – a wonderful idea.

We were all working up to fever pitch over the Election, and the place is a mass of treacherous wires, as extra telephones are being installed and Bryn now has four with which to get muddled. So much depends on our department in this particular exercise, and I think he is feeling the strain, though he never says so. I am struggling with huge maps which have to be pinned up all over our offices, and with dreadful tabulated material on large paper that I can hardly cram into the typewriter. I know the constituencies by heart and most of the candidates – African, Indian and European. I think we all wish it was really upon us now. The majority of civil servants are going to vote, which is fair enough, but I have always believed, with the old school, that civil servants should stay outside politics, though I realise one can argue it both ways. I am not on the voters' role, by choice, but I know who I would vote for in Zomba!

The weather is glorious. I sat out in the sun all Sunday morning and was actually glowing by the evening – lovely, if short-lived.

26th July:

I am a bit paralysed by the cold in the evenings. Our chimney smokes incurably, I have discovered, and so we never have a fire and I have given up asking for a radiator. My days in the office are really transformed by being warm, and I am sure it improves my work, certainly my typing.

Alex is much better and there is an improvement every time I see him. He makes his delightful jokes again, and swears to relieve tension – both good signs! It has made all the difference to me, to see him more like his old self. I was simply fading away under the strain of having him at such a low ebb.

We have had no social occasions in the last week, which I do not mind, as I have enough in the office to keep me going. Yesterday I had a lovely surprise. Bryn is away on *ulendo* so things have been quieter, and after lunch I was dealing with Press cuttings, which are a constant task I do when there is nothing else on. I looked up and saw *Iris* hurrying up the short cut to the office, looking brown and vivid and beaming at my joyful reaction. She and Dave were as usual passing through to meet Linden at the airport, out for the school holidays. I dropped everything, encouraged by Kathie, and we had nearly an hour together. We had private things to say, so I took her away from the office and we paced shamelessly round and round the Secretariat in the sun, talking ourselves hoarse, pouring out our problems. We shared the realisation that we are growing older, losing resilience and finding it more difficult to deal with what she called 'the bumps' in life. Our eyes kept filling with tears of mutual understanding and sympathy. I said I felt as if a huge weight had been lifted from me and she agreed. I went back to the office full of comfort but quivering all over, and had to pull myself together very rapidly indeed, as I had to go and have tea with Kathie, who very kindly said I could have as many of her sweet peas as I could cut. I took her at her word and returned laden, and the whole room is honey sweet with them. Iris had written to me, but her letter did not reach me. This is happening a lot and it is quite obvious that the Africans are opening mail. It is happening everywhere but is very difficult to deal with. It puts a curb on one's letter writing if one allows oneself to think about it, and Iris was rather worried, as she had said quite a lot about herself in the letter.

There is a 'flu bug going the rounds and Hazel Lowe is ill with it, so I am going to walk round tomorrow with books and some of Kathie's flowers. Last Saturday we did go out, to the Youens' for a delicious curry lunch which was so hot we were all blowing our noses. There were ten guests and I had some good talks. Bruce and Jean Wickham were there, just back from leave, and Jean and I found a secluded corner and settled down for a long talk while we ate. She is just the same, and seemed very glad to see me.

The news in Africa just now is rather grim and we wonder if there is going to be some horrible outbreak in Southern Rhodesia, though Sir Edgar Whitehead seems determined to deal with any trouble. It sounds nearly as bad as South Africa and is most depressing, but at least things seem brighter in prospect here, though I think everyone is feeling a bit tense. Secret and Most Secret files are flying about and I get plenty of exercise dashing to and fro. They should come and go in a black box, but Bryn took the keys with him (!) on *ulendo*, so I have to deliver them by hand. The Secretariat is chaotic, as arrangements for the new system go ahead. Many offices have changed hands and one finds the wrong man and phones the wrong number. Everyone is trying to be good tempered, but it is a frightful muddle at present. To make matters worse, the whole place is being rewired and there are ladders, wires and gaping holes everywhere, and one finds superstitious people standing petrified and swearing before a ladder in such a position that they have no alternative but to walk under it!

2nd August:

I am writing this at 7.00 p.m. I have had a terrific day in the office, and then walked along to visit Hazel, who is recovering from a dreadful bout of 'flu. Their son Michael, aged ten, has flown out, all by himself, for his six weeks of school holidays – a handsome boy, very shy but very poised – terrifying!

The cold weather seems to be over its peak and today has been glorious, and I feel a surge of energy and rising spirits. Alex goes from strength to strength. Geoffrey is at a conference in London, so Alex has all his work to do, and seems to be coping with it very well and with confidence. All this is an enormous relief to me.

Philip Richardson's fiancée has arrived and is doing stenographer work, for which there is a desperate demand – eleven vacancies and no UK candidates, which is not surprising considering the uneasy state of the territory. We are going to a party tomorrow to meet her, and have been invited to their wedding on 26th August. Philip has just been appointed to a new post – secretary to the Governor, which will suit him admirably.

All went well today in the office in a rather hectic atmosphere. The vultures (journalists) are gathering for the Election, and today we had Clyde Sanger of the *Guardian* and Andrew Wilson of the *Observer* snooping about, but Bryn was ready for them! Clyde Sanger used my typewriter to rattle off a quick despatch (while I hovered like an anxious hen beside my precious cabinet of secret files)! He admired the typewriter, much to my astonishment – to me that machine is just a piece of useful office equipment and, sometimes, an instrument of torture! We are all geared to such a pitch that I feel if I stuck a pin in Bryn or Don they would go off with a loud bang. The great thing is it produces a marvellous feeling of teamwork and camaraderie and we are all especially nice to each other – thank God for human contact. A second Press officer arrives on the 10th, a friend of Don's, who worked on the *Daily Sketch*. He has a young French wife, poor thing. I wonder what Zomba will do to *her*.

I am sorry about the writing. My hand is jumping all over the place.

9th August:

The blissful warm weather did not last, and Bryn and I had our radiators on all day today.

I meant to tell you before, I have managed to cut down my smoking to about five a day. Not long after I came back I was going up towards 15–20 a day and so I called a halt. I do not start now till after dark. It was a bit of an effort but it is done and I intend to stick to it through thick and thin.

Last Friday evening we went to Philip's party to meet Mary Wigley. She remembered me at once (from Devlin Commission days), saying mine was one of the few faces that immediately came back to her. She is very nice and I had a long talk with her.

There is a rather nasty lull in the office, which means I am bad-temperedly dealing with Press cuttings, in the knowledge that I shall soon be utterly swamped in them, having only just got up to date. Bryn wants me to re-do completely the filing system, which is very poor, and I shall enjoy that. I have been having bad headaches, and at last realised it was the noise of the typewriter, so I have now got it on thick baize and the relief is wonderful. Kathie thought of it, practical Kathie. Bryn has hay fever or something and I have been shooting up to the roof all day at his sudden gargantuan sneezes. He does not like to admit he has anything wrong, so I must not mention it unless he does, and he has not, so I have to remain unsympathetically silent!

Alex is well, working hard and looks his old, dear self.

I am so tired today, as indeed we all are, that I can hardly write. I have been staring out of the window for about ten minutes. There have been no social occasions since I last wrote so I can tell you about yesterday – the great day of the General Election – at once. Ron went off to Chiradzulu on Monday night to be ready on Tuesday morning – voting was from 6.30 a.m. till 5.30 p.m. Alex was in charge in Zomba and was hard at it all day. It was a lovely day and you may have heard on the News that the whole exercise was a triumph of orderliness and good behaviour, a truly marvellous performance, a *great deal* of it due to our Department's propaganda, publicity and endless explanations of *how to vote*. The whole place was very quiet, as many of the workers in the Secretariat were queuing to vote during the morning, and of course nothing was happening in our office. About 8.30, Kathie suggested we go out in her car to Kasupi to see the polling station there and visit two other small ones off the main road (where I had camped long ago)! Off we went, and it was the first time I had been out for a drive since I came back. The countryside looked absolutely beautiful and all the Africans (or nearly all) were friendly and smiling. It brought back many memories, seeing the bush again and smelling the village *bwalo* (courtyard) and the Africans, and the dusty, rustling maize. We gave a lift to several people and Kathie pumped them to such good effect that Don Penny wrote a whole Press release on the snippets of information we gave him when we got back. Bryn knew we were going and made no demur, which shows how he thought the day would go. It was crossing my mind before we left that two white women in a small car might run into trouble, but I forgot as soon as we set out. Alex, of course, nearly had a fit when I told him on the phone later. I have not yet seen him so I have not heard any details of his day.

We spent the afternoon going over and over all the arrangements and checking and double checking everything. Bryn with a phone moved in with Kathie; my office was transformed into a canteen – posters for tablecloths, and IN and OUT trays for trays to hold cups. I got an electric kettle fixed up, tins of Nescafé, crockery, and four dozen beer bottles locked in my filing cabinet! They were for the gentlemen of the Press, who were housed in the Leg Co building and forbidden to come up to our offices – results were phoned down to them or taken by messenger. About 4 o'clock I walked up to the house, had a bath and somehow filled in the time till 6, when Kathie came flying in with six dozen rolls, a pound of butter, ham and cheese, and four dozen sausage rolls which we *stuffed* into Aflike's oven. Kathie's cook, Aflike and I made the sandwiches in forty minutes flat, I ate a boiled egg in three, and Kathie took me and baskets of food to my office at 7 o'clock. The place was blazing with lights and everyone was starving, so I never stopped. Some of the African assistants are Muslim and could not, therefore, eat ham, so I made lemon curd sandwiches from two huge loaves of bread which Kathie produced as if from a hat. Bryn's office was occupied by Mr Tomkins, the Supervisor of Elections, and his assistant, with three telephones. I made endless cups of coffee and washed the cups a dozen times. At 10 o'clock I went off in a jeep and got three big pots of hot soup from a friend of Kathie's and began all over again. It was a cold night and the soup tasted like nectar. There were lulls, when no results came in, and we really had a splendid evening with all sorts of people dropping in. Kathie never moved from her phone, as she phoned every result to the Press room, GH, the CS and the Chief of Police. The Press Room was pandemonium but I never got near it. Don Penny was absolutely in his element, a bundle of nerves and energy and great fun all through. Bryn was exhausted but happy and Mr Tomkins was thrilled with it all, and produced whisky about 11 o'clock when we were all going grey and limp. I left at 11.30, but the others were there till 2.00 a.m. Ron came back from Chiradzulu at 11.45. He had to stay to count the votes, and it is a huge district – the most heavily populated in Africa.

The results are very much what was expected, with a few, a very few surprises. *The* surprise has been the marvellous efficiency of the entire operation, and I think Mr Tomkins will get an award – I think Bryn should too. [He did.] Today was spent clearing up the mess and practically spring cleaning all the offices. No work, in the ordinary sense, was done at all, but in fact we never stopped. It feels strange to think that the old order passed away in a night, and we are starting something new and not entirely pleasant or predictable, to put it mildly. As a relaxation this afternoon, for half an hour, I did some proof-reading for Kathie, which I have not had the chance to do this tour. It completely baffled her that I should enjoy it!

As I say, I am so tired I am trembling, but I would not have missed it for *anything*. I am now going to have a hot bath and unwind a bit. Don Penny's assistant, a newspaper friend from England, arrived a few days ago and was plunged *in medias res* with a vengeance! He is to start a TV service – what next? I hope you can read this scribble, which really records a piece of history!

23rd August:

The cold weather is still very much with us, and I have taken to wearing my tan suede jacket in the office and am very warm and comfortable, though it is rather bulky. Bryn said he was delighted to see me wearing 'something sensible' at last! That is his way of saying that if I do not wear warm underclothes I cannot expect to be warm! It really is bitterly cold.

Things have been quiet in the office, apart from a deluge of Press cuttings. We are getting to know our new Press Officer, Ken Robinson. He has a tiny blonde French wife and a very young baby. The wife is twenty-five and seems to take life in her stride, which is just as well. She looks about seventeen, with a lovely pink and white complexion, perfect teeth, and a mop of yellow hair which she wears hanging over her face à la Brigitte Bardot. I long to brush it back and *do* something with it. Don Penny's comment was 'terribly Left Bank', but to me it is just a waste of good looks. Alex is working well and looks well, but is very depressed and worried on my account, as I am finding life outside the office just about insupportable. However, I am trying to do something about this but will not go into detail till I know myself what the outcome is to be, which I hope will be soon.

On Saturday at lunch time we went to a very pleasant party at the DC's, Mike Leonard. I had not been there since the Watsons' day, and it was nice to enjoy that lovely view again. The countryside is looking a bit brown, but next month brings the transformation of jacaranda time. On Monday evening we went to a big Sundowner given by the new CS and his wife, Mr and Mrs Foster, from Northern Rhodesia. They are very friendly, relaxed people and will be a great asset in Zomba, I am sure. I heard Mrs Foster say to the most senior couple there, who were making a move to take their leave, thereby starting a general exodus, 'Oh , my dears, don't go yet. We are all just beginning to enjoy ourselves. Have another drink'!

My hair has desperately needed attention for some time and I said so to Kathie, who had a quiet word with Bryn and on Monday she told me to make a hair appointment and a shopping list, as she and I were going to have a day in Blantyre, today, Wednesday. It is so kind of her, as I never get to a shop. (I have only been inside our local store twice in five months, when Jean was here and took me in her car.) We left at 6.15, to avoid the traffic, which is now quite heavy. It was a lovely clear, windy morning and the countryside looked wonderful – Chiradzulu swathed in mist which was gradually lifting. I had a long, soothing time at the hairdresser's and emerged feeling a new woman. I met Kathie for coffee and then we did a lot of shopping together. I ended up buying a perfectly lovely hat for the Richardson wedding on Saturday. It is white, with a very fine straw brim and a high, high crown of swathed net with tiny bobbles on it – delicious. I shall wear my black sailcloth dress and jacket. We had a very good cold lunch at Ryall's and took our time over it. We talked about all sorts of things, our minds freed from the office atmosphere, and I think Kathie enjoyed it as much as I did. We had to go on business to the Malawi Congress Party's headquarters – the seat of Dr Banda's 'boys' as he calls them: a new building with 'Secretariat' printed on the door. Within were the most dreadful collection of Malawi spivs one could wish to see, all noisily occupied in doing absolutely nothing. The whole atmosphere made my flesh creep and gave me a sinking feeling in my stomach I have not felt for a long time. They seemed almost drunk with power and it was very alarming to witness. Kathie felt the same and was glad she had me with her. They were all deadly polite, of course, but most of them exuded antagonism if not sheer hate. I have never felt quite the sensation the experience produced in me, and I disliked it intensely. I know there must be some talented young men among them, but the general impression was ghastly. Driving back we confessed to feeling sick at heart at the deterioration, in fact the disintegration, of race relations and the thought of the mess that may yet be the fate of Nyasaland. However, I never regret an opportunity to realise exactly what is going on. We got back at 4.30 and I felt I had been away for days, which is a very good thing.

The warmer weather is on its way – utter bliss. The only snag is I am going to have trouble with my typing, I can see, as my hands always get very moist.

Saturday, the day of the wedding, was beautiful and very warm. The service was at 3 o'clock, in the English church, St. George's, a modern building and pleasant except for a hideous brick wall behind the altar. There must have been about a hundred guests, all very smart. I enjoyed the music before the service: Handel's Water Music and Kol Nidrei, which always reminds me of Daddy and Dunalastair. The reception was in the big ballroom at GH. The best speech was by the best man, Philip's son Michael, aged fifteen, who said frankly his father had written his speech for him and would we mind if he read it out! He looked so young and frail and reminded me poignantly of his mother.

Tonight we are going to a party at Bryn's, to welcome the new Press Officer and his wife. The sun has gone down and I have wrapped myself in Bella, but it is still warm, and I can feel the heat from the plain coming up on the wind.

6th September:

My affairs are coming to a head and I should be able to straighten myself out soon and tell you what is happening. The last few weeks have been rather dreadful, saved for me by the warmer weather, which has helped me enormously. Unfortunately, the cold season is having its final fling, and on Monday Zomba woke up to a real thick *chiperoni*: cold wind, pelting rain and cloud nearly down to the rooftops. Everyone went straight back into woollens again. I sunbathed on Saturday and Sunday – I even dried my hair outside – and went a marvellous dark brown in a matter of hours. Everyone noticed it and asked me if I had been weekending at the Lake! I find it a great help if I know I *look* well.

I enjoyed Bryn's party last Wednesday, thanks mainly to Don Penny, who was at his most amusing and took it upon himself to entertain me for most of the evening. The little French wife, Bernie, for whom the party was really given, had a fit of nerves at the last moment and did not come. Her husband Robbie (Keith Robinson) is fitting in very well. I have been helping him as much as I can in the office, typing out lists of people, their jobs and telephone numbers.

Bryn went off on *ulendo* to the North on Monday and does not come back till Friday, so I am catching up on my Press cuttings and doing things for Kathie, a lot of whose work is the kind I can churn out effortlessly. The first signs of the new ministerial system are beginning to manifest themselves slightly ominously! Africans with shiny briefcases frequent the corridors of the Secretariat, talking in loud, convoluted English, though I have to admit most of them speak beautifully, as far as the accent is concerned. In Bryn's absence I have already had some rather elaborate phone conversations with several. My reaction is to use Anglo-Saxon monosyllables in my quietest Scots voice! Don Penny is baffled by the fact that I am obviously at ease with the African staff and my own boys, and yet snarl over some aspects of the new set-up. He cannot get over my invariable politeness to them all. Kathie told him today he was too new to

Africa to understand that I am, in fact, more liberal in my attitude to the
Africans than he!

12th September:

The weather is back to its old self again, thank goodness, and I am therefore
back to mine! It is extraordinary how one forgets the cold *at once* and takes for
granted the smells, sights and sounds of the warmer weather. The men are into
their whites again – Bryn came bounding in in his, trying not to look selfconscious and almost succeeding. He looks much younger, as indeed most of
the men do. It is amusing to see all the chaps starting to wear shorts and open-
necked shirts at exactly the same time as the African ministers (and therefore
every clerk in the place with the money to imitate them) are appearing in
immaculate 'city suits', bowler hats and carrying the inevitable briefcase!
Either one sees the funny side or heads for high blood pressure! The pressures
are on now, the Europeans having to cope with all sorts of petty complaints and
demands – 'So-and-so has a carpet in his office. I want one.' Chiume was
shown his jolly nice house (three bedrooms, two bathrooms) and promptly said
it was too small, the furnishings (all free) were not up to standard, and of course
the whole places was hopeless *because it had no laundry*. They must be given
time to adapt themselves, I know, but the strain of all these superficial idiotisms
on top of hard work in the hot season is not going to be funny. *On top* of all that,
the Government in Britain is now drawing in its horns over a scheme for
revised salaries, inducement allowances and pensions for colonial servants
which was going to help everyone here enormously, especially if people have to
leave. So everyone is feeling let down and very demoralised. That is the
background against which we are all working so hard!

Things are very quiet indeed in our office, though hectic elsewhere. Don,
exhausted after his efforts at the Election, has gone to the Lake for a few days,
and Kathie is also on local leave for a week. She is helping her two sisters to
pack up the family house. They are both going home, having realised that they
could not endure to live here in retirement, and they are both retiring within
months of each other. Kathie goes for good at the end of her present tour. She
has saved *nothing* and says she will try to get a post as someone's companion in
a centrally heated house! I have been thinking about her a lot, as I know she was
dreading it. The house is very old fashioned and shabby, without light or
running water, so no one will be interested in buying it.

The weather was simply glorious at the weekend, and I just sat in the garden
and soaked up the sun, and got marvellously brown. We have no social occasions. The school holidays have started and everyone is much occupied with
their own affairs. I think too the men are probably having enough to cope with
in the office without being sociable as well. Just wait till the official entertaining begins and there will be some strange tales to tell, I reckon!

I will tell you next week what I have decided to do, and how things are going. You do understand, I know, that it is to save you worry that I am waiting till I have something definite to say. Think of me in the lovely sunshine.

PS. Alex moved into a flat today. The hostel food was not suiting him and that dreary room was getting him down till he could hardly bear to go back at night. This new arrangement will be much better and more comfortable for him.

19th September:

Everything is now settled and done, and I write with a calm and thankful heart.

As you know, Ron and I realised in a matter of 48 hours after my return that it was a disaster. He told me I could stay in the house for six months, to cover the liability of my passage out and make me eligible for a Government paid passage back home. I assured him I would leave at the end of six months, in fact earlier, if I could, and I have been trying. The difficulty was to find accommodation. I could not possibly afford to stay in either of the hotels, and was not entitled to a place in the Hostel as I had, officially, accommodation already, as a married woman. I had to make all my enquiries very discreetly, which took time. After I went back to the office, I told Ron I would not give up my job, as it would ruin my relationship with the department and Bryn irrevocably; that I would find a way to stay on in Zomba on my own, if allowed, as I had no intention of fading out of the scene. All this he received with lofty disdain, and I could see he never for one moment believed I would have the courage to do it. I thought and thought about it, discussed it endlessly with Alex, as he did with Geoffrey Fricker, who, unknown to me, sought Bryn's reactions. Meanwhile the domestic atmosphere deteriorated unspeakably. In the end, I wrote an official letter to Peter Youens (Deputy Chief Secretary) and told him I must leave Ron soon, but wanted to be allowed to stay on and work for Bryn. Geoffrey also saw him and filled in some detail – though all along I refused to have *anything* said or written against Ron. To cut a long story short, after weeks of waiting for the powers that be to decide my fate, I was given permission to keep my job and move into the Hostel. I told Ron at once and said I would be gone in two days.

Last Thursday I walked back to the house from the office, had tea, and packed, having done some the day before. I also phoned Bryn and told him I was moving. (I did not realise that he knew all about it. It was the only moment through the whole exercise when I broke down. He was as steady as a rock.) The biggest strain was keeping everything quiet until it was done, in case people got wind of it and started talking and damaging my chances of doing things quietly, quickly, and with decency and dignity. It was Ron's bridge evening at the Club and he knew I would be gone when he came back. I told Aflike the simple fact that I was going to live in the Hostel. He turned to stone with shock, and stood looking at me with the tears pouring down his face. We clutched each other's hands (his were like ice) and murmured stumbling words of comfort, which I cannot now remember at all. As soon as it was dark Alex came in his car and we made two journeys with my things – clothes, books, long player, records, pictures and the silver Daddy gave me. Alex lent me one of his boys and all I needed in the way of linen to settle in, and even had a sandwich supper prepared for me.

It has all gone very well. Everyone is kind, if not kinder, and the relief to my poor nervous system is unbelievable, though I have my shaky moments! I have a 'chalet' – a bed-sitter with *khonde* and a private bathroom and lavatory attached. I have found a boy, Timothy, to look after me. He cleans, does my laundry (beautifully) and brings me breakfast and afternoon tea in my room. Lunch and dinner I have in the diningroom, sharing a table with Geoffrey and John Firth (husband of Barbara, the girl with polio, who is in England). The food is excellent. I can live, with a servant, for just under £25 a month! The rest is up to me – toilet articles, cleaning materials, cigarettes, etc.

Before I left I felt hysterical and terrified, because I was afraid I had left it too late to have the strength to carry it through, and of course I only managed because of Alex's support and that of my marvellous friends and colleagues, who have just closed in quietly and surrounded me with kindness and consideration. Hazel has hovered in the background, with the offer of a spare room in her house as a last resort if I broke under the strain. Jean Payne has also been an enormous help. She and Hazel were the only women I took into my confidence, and they have both been discretion itself.

28th September:

I am sleeping well, eating well, and getting back confidence in my work, which was suffering badly. Bryn, who has a very bad cold, goes off on ten days local leave tomorrow and seems quite happy to leave me – and Kathie – in charge. He has said nothing to me about my affairs but has been indescribably kind and thoughtful, as has Kathie. Everyone is being perfectly normal and friendly.

My chalet is in fact two bed-sitters, with shared bath and lavatory. The other one is empty, which I was glad of at first, when I wanted no one about, but there is a GH stenographer moving in at the end of the month. She is a young girl and will doubtless be out a lot, but I shall not mind having someone sleeping next door to me – you know me at night in Africa! However, Geoffrey is within hailing distance, and I have a *huge* South African (who has had to be snubbed) living in the next chalet, so I am well protected. I cannot tell you what a joy it is to waken to a lovely sunny morning and feel ready for the day instead of lying screwing up my courage to face it. I have several jacaranda trees to look at from my windows at the front – and a beautiful yesterday-today-and-tomorrow just outside, scenting the air day and night.

I miss Aflike very much. He has been down three times to visit me and we have a quiet talk. He is not happy up there without me. However, I could not possibly pay him the wages he gets, and besides would not let him – Ron would be lost without him and I can manage perfectly well with Timothy (who comes from Mlanje).

I am living very quietly and peacefully and just letting myself recover. Hazel and Bobby have had me along several times, and Kathie is always inviting me 'when you feel like it', which is not yet. I appreciate her kindness and will accept, in time; but I am not yet fully in command of myself and am determined not to venture forth among people until I can trust myself *never* to be tempted into not keeping my own counsel.

I helped Alex with various things in his flat on Sunday. Philip Richardson (now on leave) has left him his beautiful Grundig radiogram with a very catholic selection of records, so we had some lovely music. Alex is working very hard and looks ridiculously younger and happier, despite the fact that his ulcer is giving him great pain. He thinks it will die down soon, as the pressures die down.

Today was the swearing in of Leg Co members and there was a great deal of noise and singing round the building. Banda brings a big African woman to his office every day – his 'nurse'! He also has a bodyguard of eight thugs who squat outside his office (Alex's comment, 'with nothing to do but pick their noses'!) all day and stare brazenly when one passes by. I said flippantly to Bryn, 'He will need a food taster one of these days,' and Bryn said actually he more or less has one, in that he insists on his kitchen staff cooking for him wherever he is! However, he seems genuinely and sensibly interested in his Ministry, and the chaps there are feeling more cheerful. I hear that the other Ministers seem to be settling down a bit and realising how much they need to depend on their European staff.

On Saturday night Hazel, Bobby, Alex and I drove to Blantyre and beyond, to the new Flamingo, which has opened recently – a Spanish style restaurant, white, with a square tower, red tiled flat roof, and a lot of iron-work on doors and windows. It has a huge verandah with ornate Spanish lamps where we sat out in the warm moonlight. We ate piri-piri chicken and danced to a small band. The people were, as Hazel said 'madly multi-racial', and there was not a single face we knew – lovely to feel anonymous and completely away from Zomba. It was Alex's first night out for sixteen months, and was like a tonic for us both, happily shared with the dear Lowes.

The odd impulse to wonder if Ron is all right comes up. I hope he is finding he has as good friends as I have. The Speaker appears to have taken him under his wing, which is good.

I am gradually settling in. I read in bed, going very early. The weather is hot, hot, and I am as usual gently blooming in it. Even I have my bath nearly cold! The jacaranda is at its very bluest, which is just before the blossoms really open out – heavenly. I miss that lovely walk up the hill among them after the office,

but I have the beautiful botanical gardens on my doorstep, so I do not grumble.
I am *all right*.

4th October:

I brought nothing but my own possessions to the Hostel, and Alex has
provided me with curtains, cushions, bed linen, towels, a tea tray, teaset, china
and cutlery – he has *masses* of everything, so it was easy to supply them. I
simply could not have made the move without his physical, material and moral
support. I think even he was surprised at how calm I was when the time came. I
have never felt so *released* in my life.

I am enjoying so much my nice room, and have now got all my books,
pictures and ornaments organised. Hazel came down to tea and drove
me all round Zomba before sunset to see the blossom. Jean Wickham called in
to say, 'You know where I am if you need me,' which was very sweet.

Bryn is on local leave till Monday, and Kathie is in Blantyre for the day, so
the office is very quiet. For the first time in my life I am using office hours in
which to write to you, and I am as jumpy as a cat with guilt!

Alex's ulcer has settled down again and he is at last free of pain and looks a
new man. He is eating and sleeping well, and feeling full of energy. He is
looking forward to being Acting Chief Establishment Officer when Geoffrey
goes on leave in a month's time. I shall miss him in the Hostel very much. This
is Alex's birthday and I phoned him this morning. He sounded very cheerful.
Tonight he is giving a small 'flat warming' party, with the Lowes and eight
other friends. Philip and Mary Richardson are coming. They should be on
leave, but Philip's son Michael developed chickenpox the day before they were
to leave, and they have had a frightful time reorganising themselves. Their
house is packed up and all their clothes await them in Brindisi, where they were
going by air from here! Michael is in hospital, his sister Jo is in quarantine in
someone's guest house, and Philip and Mary, after two days in the Hostel, are
in someone else's guest house.

Last Saturday afternoon Alex took me down to Lulat's, the Indian store
which I used to patronise so much. I had not been there this tour. They are not
open on Saturday afternoon, but they know us as good customers and opened
the door at once when we knocked! I bought blue and white striped cotton at 6*s.*
a yard to make myself a bedspread (it looks *lovely*) and some pretty golden
yellow linen to cover my two big cushions. I helped Alex choose some materials, lampshades and other things for his sittingroom, and on Sunday I went
round to the flat and helped him make it really attractive. He is simply thrilled
with the result and says it is much the nicest place he has lived in here. He told
Geoffrey that he had 'unleashed' me in the flat for a day, and the results were
unbelievable! I see him for a short time in the evening when it is possible. He
does not come to my chalet at all, ever.

I enclose a photo of Bryn, taken at Chileka when he was meeting Lord Hume, looking rather townier than usual for the occasion. Kathie and I have been going through hundreds of departmental photos and she came across this one and said, 'Your mother might like to see Bryn,' – typical Kathie thoughtfulness.

It is *boiling* hot!

10th August:

Today is very thundery and overcast and so hot I feel weighed down by it. My hands developed their usual slight heat rash and then it suddenly took off on my palms and between my fingers. I had to go up to the hospital for help. The doctor said at once it is not a heat rash but a nervous rash which must be stopped from spreading, and gave me some very effective, if painful, ointment. In the great heat I wear a pair of high, cork heeled, soft leather sandals which I can slip off under my desk. Yesterday Bryn came in and I had to get up to find a file from my cabinet. There was a long pause as I gazed at him immobilised while my feet groped all over the floor, missing the shoes. I finally said 'shoes' feebly, and dived under the desk to find them.

My chalet is a small, separate entity, with five others, set on the edge of the botanical gardens. Then there is a long, older building with bed-sittingrooms, higher up and at right angles to the chalets, and above that is the main building (which was the old Government house) which has the diningroom, kitchens and offices downstairs and a number of bedrooms and bathrooms upstairs. I am not getting much sleep these nights, as they are doing *A Midsummer Night's Dream* not fifteen yards from my room, in a perfect natural outdoor setting. I am told it is quite marvellously well done, Geoffrey being outstanding as Oberon.

At the weekend I heard that Dave Davies is coming south to be DC Zomba. Think of Iris and me, actually living on the same station!

On Saturday at lunch time I was waylaid by Hazel and swept off for a drink. Later, Alex and I drove to Limbe, saw a film (*Les Girls*, quite a good American musical with a wonderful performance by Kay Kendall) and had supper at Ryall's, a special dish called 'chicken-in-a-basket' which is exactly that – a tiny roast chicken served in a basket with chips and a hot sauce. You eat it with your fingers. Again, we were among complete strangers and felt we could be anywhere. I was back and in bed by 10.30. I forgot to say Alex's small party last Wednesday was a great success. On Sunday I made another sortie on his flat, sewing furiously to the accompaniment of Philip's lovely player. I also made him a good, bland salad lunch. I am trying to make his diet more interesting.

Kathie and I had a very quiet, easy week in the office while Bryn was away. He came back on Monday, bursting with health and looking gloriously brown. I speechlessly laid fourteen files for his attention on his desk and was then engulfed in work for the next two days as he slammed them back at me with *screeds* of notes! Arthur comes back early in the new year and will take over from Bryn, who goes on home leave shortly afterwards.

I am getting behind with my letter writing again – the heat imperceptibly deprives me of energy and will power, however much I may enjoy it. The jacaranda is glorious all over Zomba – great blue trees looming up, their petals lying almost as thickly on the ground as they cluster on the branches. I can see seven huge ones from my windows at this moment.

17th October:

I am answering your letter a day early, mainly because it is quite cool, and usually at this time in the afternoon one is paralysed with heat. Alex has lent me his fan/heater, so this room is no longer uncomfortably hot – the chalets are low lying. The heat this season is stupendous. It affects everyone's work, and we are all absentminded, and keep wandering into each other's office and then not able to remember what we have come for! I write down *everything* for myself and Bryn, and my handbag at the end of the day is full of notes written to myself!

Last week Alex was suddenly asked to go to a conference in Salisbury, leaving on Thursday morning and coming back on Saturday morning – it is only an hour by plane. On Wednesday evening I dined with Robin and Elsie Martin (ex-Mlanje), who took me on to the Police Mess to watch a quiz made up of three Police teams and an Honorary Members team. The questions were good – not too easy and not too difficult. It is a very nice Mess and quite different from the Club, as it is all Police and their guests. I felt very refreshed, and also relieved to find that I was once again free to enjoy an outing and feel blessedly up to doing so. They have asked me again, tomorrow evening, when there is a film show, which will be nice, but I must not accept too often, as it is difficult to return hospitality.

On Friday evening Sally Woods, the 'girl next door', came in for a talk before dinner and we walked up together and went on with our talk through the meal. She is twenty-seven, and is the cypher officer at GH. She was jilted twice, in England, and the emotional shock did something to her glands and from nine stones she shot up to fifteen stones and has had a battle with weight ever since. (She is now about 10½ and remarkably trim.) It was quite a story, and simply poured out. She used to share a house with a girl who has just got married, and is obviously lonely. She looks about twenty-four and has a very sweet nature. It widened my horizons to hear of someone else's problems. She also suffers from insomnia, so we were able to compare notes! Fortunately, she is not the sort of person to want to live in one's pocket, so we go on our own ways but have an occasional word together most days. She woke me up at two the other night to help her remove what she thought was a rat from her room – she was wildly upset. It was in fact a big shrew, which I managed to 'shoo' out of the door.

On Saturday I went over to Limbe for the morning to sit in at our little booth at the Commonwealth Training Week Exhibition. Mr Lipande, our executive officer, drove me over. He is about forty, with years of service, no politics and a really good civil servant of the old school. He was thrilled to be taking me over, in his Ford. It was shatteringly hot, but quite an interesting experience without much to do but hand out pamphlets and tell young Africans about jobs in Government. David Baxter was there and we fell into each other's arms. He was marvellous and kept the conversation very general, with nothing personal. At 12.45 Mr Lipande gave me a lift to the Shire Highlands Hotel, where Alex joined me from the airport, delighted with his time in Salisbury. We had a lunch which I did not notice, we were talking so much, and made our way back, visiting the Lowes *en route*. We were to have gone for a picnic with them on Sunday but all agreed it was actually too hot! Geoffrey and I had a drink with Alex before lunch on Sunday and I stayed on for lunch and we made our Christmas cards lists. I forgot to say Kathie came for tea on Thursday and first took me down to Lulat's, where I managed to find attractive Christmas cards for Alex and myself. The days are flying and I always have something on hand to do. It is quiet in the office, I think because of the great heat, but I am never idle, as I work for all of them now.
PS. I knew you would like the look of Bryn!

25th October:

I seem to have done a lot since I last wrote. On Friday evening Alex and I called in for an hour on Hazel and Bobby, and sat out on their big *khonde*, which looks straight out to Mlanje, which of course has been invisible for weeks in the heat haze, but we enjoyed what coolness there was and watched the stars coming out. They have invited us to a party on Christmas Eve – lovely. On Saturday night we took Geoffrey to the Flamingo and had a perfectly delightful evening. He fits in with us very easily and enjoys himself. It was a glorious night, with an almost full moon which shone dimly through the heat haze, which never quite goes –it is partly dust. I had a quiet day on Sunday, writing Christmas cards and letters. Monday was Federation day, and in spite of so many of all races disliking the concept, we were all thankful for the holiday. The weather is phenomenally hot and even I complain. (It is such a business finding cool enough clothes, and however fresh one is at the start of the day, one is, and looks, a limp rag by 10 o'clock.) We suddenly decided to go to Limbe to a 4.30 holiday matinee and saw a rather poor film while a tremendous thunderstorm obligingly cleared the air for the drive back. We had supper in Limbe first.

Bryn really wilts in this heat, and spends a lot of time thinking aloud in my office. Kathie and I find all the laziest jobs we can do, and spent two hours today proof-reading her Chinyanja version of the Highway Code! She feels the heat more than I do, so I have given her my office fan. I have not heard from Iris, but I believe they arrive this next weekend – dreadful time to have to pack and unpack. Alex is planning to have them for Christmas dinner and has ordered a turkey. I would like to have your recipe for stuffing to give him for it, so if you could write it out for me, I would be most grateful.

I had a talk with Bryn the other day about my future in the office. He wants me to stay on and thinks he can manage it. So that is another worry I can tick off my list!

It is nearly sunset and a small, merciful breeze is beginning to blow. How I love this time of day.

1st November:

I thought you would be interested to hear about my neighbour, Sally Woods. She has several friends of her own age who are often about the place and one of them came in at teatime the other day, having found Sally's room locked, and poured out her troubles to me. What an unhappy lot that generation is. Another girl, only twenty-four, who lives opposite – that means about fifty yards across the grass – came down also when Sally was out, with a transparent excuse about returning a book, sat down on the steps of my *khonde* and talked non-stop about herself for over an hour, while I laid aside the letter I was writing to Joan. I never, never talk of my affairs and have no desire to, but of course they all know what has happened and seem to think I would be a good person to unburden to, which I think I am, because I can listen, be sympathetic, keep it to myself and I do not change the subject onto myself! They *all* take sleeping pills and two, I know, take tranquillisers. (They keep ornate little pill boxes in their handbags!) It makes me count my blessings and be glad I had such a happy home life and such a stable background and security, for so long – and it makes me wonder what their parents are like.

The whole Service is so disheartened about the salaries revision scheme that Maudling's appointment made less of an impact than I expected. As you know, Iain Macleod was *not* popular with the chaps out here nor with the settlers. I think his policy is likely to continue, anyway, so that in this sphere the change of man may not be much felt. It will be interesting to hear impressions of him when he comes out. The fact remains Macleod is immensely able and may be the next occupant at No. 10.

Alex is well and happy. He is quite ready to take over from Geoffrey, who goes on leave next week. I shall miss Geoffrey terribly in the Hostel. We enjoy our meals together and have great fun, always. He is very thin and run down and gasping to get home to his wife and three children, all at school, whom he adores.

On Saturday Alex gave a dinner party for the Lowes, which I helped him prepare for, and then Bobby, Hazel and I went to the Club and sat together at the cinema. Alex went too and sat by himself. We saw a delightful film called *It Happened in Naples*, with Clark Gable and Sophia Loren, who made a most attractive team. On Sunday morning Alex took me up to the DC's house and we had coffee with Iris, who looks well but tired round the eyes. Dave was still at Lilongwe, handing over. Iris and Alex took to each other at once, as I knew they would. Yesterday he collected her and gave her a lift to the Hostel. She had tea with me, while we talked ourselves hoarse and felt absolutely *purged* by six o'clock! I talked a bit about what had been happening and met with complete sympathy. She has her own difficulties and talked of them for the first time ever, at great length. We agreed that it is a man's world. That realisation sometimes makes my blood run cold. Alex took us back to her house for a drink and then I went back with him and had a snack supper. I was so wrought up I burst into tears the moment we left in the car and could not face the diningroom. This happens occasionally. My outward calm is superficial and the emotional turmoil within sometimes erupts.

We have had thunder and torrential rain for the past two days, which is a great relief, especially as there is a sudden spate of work in the office, and for two days I have typed solidly from 7.30 to 3.30. Bryn was actually nervy today, because I was getting through the work more quickly than he was producing it – an unsettling turning of the tables and obviously *not* good for his morale. MEN! PS. Alex is going to try to find a job for Iris.

6th November:

Iris is coming to tea tomorrow, so I am writing a day earlier, to have plenty of time for it.

The weather alternates between *appalling* heat and very heavy rain, which brings down the temperature but is causing chills, fevers and sore throats. Poor Alex developed some raw patches on his face, ears, back and hands, which he thought were heat spots but they were diagnosed by the doctor this morning as impetigo! He may have got it handling dirty money. He was terrified, as he has never had any skin trouble before. He phoned me at once and calmed down when I said I had thought to myself it might be that and how lucky that he had gone to the doctor so soon. He was about to rush back to the flat, cover himself in ointment and boil, scald and generally disinfect the entire contents.

Geoffrey goes home tomorrow and is at this moment crashing about among his packing cases. When I have finished this letter I am going up to his room to collect his very good records, which he wants me to keep for him – lovely things, including Kol Nidrei and Max Bruch's violin concerto.

On Thursday I went up to Iris for tea. We enjoyed the wonderful view and then did what I love doing, pottered round the flower and vegetable gardens looking at the progress of the summer seedlings. I got Saturday morning off and with Iris, who was desperate to have her hair done, went to Blantyre with Alex, who had to go on business. It was a very hot day, but the journey in the early morning was beautiful and quite cool. I did lots of shopping for other people but only what I needed for myself, resisting with difficulty a very pretty Italian suit in sailcloth. We had delicious espresso coffee in the little café I used to frequent (a thousand years ago, it felt) and then a very good lunch at Ryall's. Iris loved it all, in spite of the heat, and looked so much better for the change of scene. We called in at the Lowes to deliver some shopping and found them *all* gasping in sunsuits. On Sunday evening Geoffrey and I went to Alex's for a farewell supper and we had a very happy evening *à trois*. Bryn went on *ulendo* yesterday, so things are quiet and Kathie and I are clearing up all the odd jobs.

14th November:

I am writing a day early, as Iris is coming to tea tomorrow and never leaves till after dark, when I am too tired to start a letter.

There are two small, overgrown flowerbeds in front of my chalet and I confessed to Iris that I sometimes *ached* to put in seeds so as to have something growing to watch again. She told me to have the beds dug over and has chosen some little things which she is to bring with her to put in – it is so like her. I had felt I could not do anything about it, as it was the wrong time to start seeds, but she has lots of hardy seedlings in boxes which she brought from Lilongwe. I am absolutely delighted to have a small patch of my own to browse over. The two beds are only, at most 6 feet by 4 feet each, but could look pretty and bright. The small rains are well under way and things grow as you watch. In fact the rain has been phenomenal for the time of year.

Alex's impetigo has been quite bad but is on the mend and mercifully did not go into his hair, which I dreaded for him. He has grown a beard and looks very much the big sailor, except for those desperately sensitive eyes that belie the physical toughness. Iris said he looks like a robust Christ, which is true!

Sally has taken me completely by surprise by inviting me to go in her car with two other friends to Blantyre on 5th December, her birthday, to have dinner at Giovanni's, a new restaurant which I had said I had not visited. It is so kind of her but presents one more problem of returning hospitality. Things are very quiet in the office and we are all rather sociable and leisurely, which means Bryn talks to me for *hours*!

On Thursday last week I had tea with Iris and on Saturday Dave took me up at lunch time for a drink. He looks well and is enjoying his new district. In the afternoon I read the whole of a biography of Beatrix Potter by Margaret Lane, and was completely absorbed. Why did we never have her books, I wonder? I realise now I would have loved them. I saw Alex in the evening and we spent a very aloof hour or two sitting at opposite sides of the room smoking our own cigarettes! He cheered up and we listened to several of Geoffrey's lovely records. He departed in utter chaos on Wednesday, at the end of his tether, really, and leaving Alex a hideous pile of files in the office, which at present, in his horrid state, he does not take to very kindly!

22nd November:

I am writing this just after tea and when I have finished and the sun has gone down behind the mountain I shall put in the plants Iris has given me. My little plots are all ready. Everyone in the Hostel is most intrigued.

Alex's impetigo cleared up in exactly a fortnight. It was all over his face, back, chest and upper arms, and he felt horrible, but I was so thankful his nice thick head of hair escaped. His beard was quite a sight. It came off on Sunday morning and he presented a face like a baby's, pink, soft and smooth! It has been a beastly time for him. He is enjoying the interest of his work, as he is now very much among the 'top brass' and knows what is going on, at all levels, and sits in at conferences at GH.

I have taken most of Geoffrey's records to Alex's, who has a special stand for them, but I have kept for myself the Kol Nidrei, Max Bruch, Kathleen Ferrier singing Bach and Handel, and the Trout Quintet – glorious! I have had so much pleasure already from them.

I seem to have been doing a lot of little things and enjoying myself without any marked social occasions. I had tea with Iris at the house yesterday. She is getting some tennis, which she enjoys, and of course delights in my visits and in seeing Alex, with whom she gets on very well indeed – 'such a nice, big, *kind* man, Ann', she keeps saying. I have also had tea and an evening with Hazel, whose company I really missed when we did not meet for about ten days. She is such a darling. Jean and Rex Payne and family arrived back on Monday and stayed one night in the Hostel. They all look very well and very brown. Jean *burst* into tears the moment she set eyes on me! They said how wonderfully well we both looked, and how *terrible* we had looked when they left. I have put on 4 lb. since I came to the Hostel, which is not bad. (So I now weigh 7 st. 4 lb.) I said so at lunch today, and someone said, 'And *where*, may I ask, have you *put* it?'!

I have acquired a very nice neighbour, Jean Outram, who is a temporary stenographer, having come out on holiday to visit her brother, who is one of the ADCs at Mzimba. She must be about thirty-six and is the only woman in the Hostel near me in age, so I may see something of her. We seem to have quite a lot in common. She knows St. Andrews well, as her sister went there as a student in 1948.

Today Bryn asked me to write HE's Christmas message for our vernacular/ English newspaper. It was bliss to be on my own track again, and I tossed it off in fifteen minutes. Bryn is delighted with it. He said, 'This is excellent. You've hit the nail on the head.' As you can imagine, it is not easy, in the present

political climate, to write a message which will make its appeal to everyone in
the territory.

I am reading a very interesting biography of Cheshire called *No Passing
Glory*. Arthur arrives back tonight. He is staying with Bryn and then joins me in
the Hostel – a mixed blessing?! This letter is a bit sporadic, as I have been
interrupted several times.

29th November:

I knew you would rejoice at my little garden. I have now got Jean Outram,
next door, interested, and have given her some plants, as Iris gave me too many.
I want to keep one bed free for carnations and portulaca (from Hazel).

The last two days have been hot and sunny. Today, however, the clouds are
piling up for a huge storm, without a doubt, and it is so oppressive my body
feels swollen and the veins in my hands are standing out very blue. I snatch the
sun whenever I can, and have a pale honey tan, but I am desperate for a good
long soak. It really helps me to feel well.

Iris has got the job of assistant editor of *Hansard* (which is no longer our responsibility). Alex and I are going to dine with her and Dave on Saturday. I am
giving Alex *Ring of Bright Water* for Christmas, and anticipate long thinkings
aloud about how lovely it would be to have AN OTTER!

The first session of Leg Co under the new constitution opened yesterday with
great pomp and ceremony. I watched it all from the office. I did not mind not
being there but I felt quite extraordinarily upset and depressed by the outward
show and inner chaos and falsity of hopes, promises and intentions. Kathie and
I had some strong coffee and Bryn's chocolate biscuits to 'lay the butterflies',
as Kathie put it, and we calmed down a bit. I see from *Hansard* and hear from
our Press people that so far it has gone remarkably smoothly. We have journalists from *The Times*, *Guardian*, *Observer* and others. The *Guardian*'s man,
Mr Taylor, remembered me from Emergency days, to my great surprise. I knew
his face and his paper, but I had unobtrusively to look up his name! I make it
part of my job to try to remember them all by name, and of course it is good for
public relations. I have been frantically busy, with constant interruptions, from
the moment Leg Co started.

Arthur is back, full of beans and *quite* unchanged! It is fun to have him
around, and at meals in the Hostel. He certainly enlivens the diningroom,
teasing the pretty stenographers and making them blush! Jean Payne came up
on Saturday morning to see us all. (She and Rex are horrified at the political
turn of events, as I knew they would be, and are turning their thoughts to
seeking alternatives.) Arthur made us all laugh by charging in to ask me for
matches. I said I did not carry my lighter with me, as I did not smoke in the
office. He said, 'No, no, I want a match to use as a toothpick – I am in *agony*
with a piece of bacon!' I produced a large pin and he promptly used it, threw it

out of the window, and said, 'My dears, the *relief*,' and made his exit! As far as we can see, Bryn's plan for me to edit the Annual Report has been accepted, though not officially yet. This means a return to my charge allowance, which will be welcome. I shall have to move in with Kathie, which I do not mind, though I shall miss being in charge of the telephone and all my friendly telephone conversations. We are very cramped for space. Arthur is temporarily in with Bryn – both not enjoying it!

On Saturday Alex and I went to the 4.30 cinema in Blantyre to see an unknown film called *Abandon Ship*, with Tyrone Power. It was so bad *we* had to abandon *it*! We drove to the Flamingo through the last of the sunset and watched the stars come out as we had a drink. It was early, and the little Greek proprietor was having his coffee and playing Beethoven – a lovely, peaceful time. We then went back into Blantyre and had a chicken supper at Ryall's, very quiet and pleasant. As I said to Alex, it is so *healing* to get back to the habit of happiness again. On Sunday I went to supper with Hazel and Bobby and we went on to the Police Mess, to join Robin and Elsie Martin to listen to a very good concert. The best items were the European choir singing 'As Torrents in Summer' and 'Still the Night', and two Africans, clarinet and flute, playing 'Lo, Hear the Gentle Lark' most beautifully. I had to blow my nose at the end – it took me right back to Dunalastair and Galli-Curci. The Governor was there in a party and it was quite a big social evening, which does not often come my way now. Yesterday Sally and Jean Outram brought in their tea trays to my room and we had a very pleasant tea together. This evening Jean and I are going for a drink before dinner at Alex's flat. I think they will get on well together.

6th December:

Jean (Payne) comes back to the office in the new year, so I am now worked almost off my feet, as the Annual Report work has begun, a lot of policy typing has suddenly cropped up and of course hundreds of Press cuttings as a result of the Colonial Secretary's visit. I had a very interesting if tiring experience of office work on Monday when I typed straight onto the machine Maudling's press conference held at GH. Graham Tilesley (who recorded my Chinyanja broadcast) came up to my office and played the whole tape recording to me, sentence by sentence, turning it back when I did not catch a word – all interesting, but I was worn out by the end of the day, as I then had to re-type it onto wax. Iris came to tea that day, having had a taxing day at her work, and we suddenly nearly had hysterics with mirth when I pointed out that we had been *passionately* discussing carbons, waxes, duplicating machines and type for about twenty minutes! She enjoys helping with *Hansard*, but loathes her lowly typing job. My typing is much slower than Jean Payne's but apparently I set things out very well, which I know is half the battle, when sending work out to men who have masses of files and memos to plough through. Alex sees a lot of my work and says he is always prepared to give Bryn's minutes his full attention, as they are effortless to read and have faultless punctuation.

The weather for the last week has been indescribably oppressive, with not much sun and a dreadful, breathless atmosphere. I am soaked to the skin and can literally shake off drops of perspiration when I have walked up to the office after lunch. I forgot to tell you that I had dinner at Kathie's the week before last, with the Wickhams, which was delightful. They are always just the same. I had Jean Payne down for tea last Thursday and we had a long talk. She loves being at home and really does not want in the least to go back to the office, which is a shame. On Saturday Alex and I dined with Dave and Iris and had a most enjoyable evening, talking and looking at their collection of coloured slides – wonderful ones of the Central Province and local leave at Victoria Falls. Iris is looking well although she is having a bad time. Her mother is terminally ill and there is no doubt that Iris will have to go home, to see her and to help her father through everything and get him settled. He is over eighty. I shall miss her. It is lovely to have her about, to see her every day, if only to wave to, and snatch moments on the telephone. She has a horror of being overheard and is continually breaking into her fluent French, which I manage fairly well, with some hilarious efforts on my part! On Sunday, my treat, Alex and I went over to Blantyre, on a last minute impulse, and saw the early performance of *South Pacific*, a lovely film, though the soundtrack was too loud. He had seen the show in London, and said it caught the atmosphere of the islands even better than the film.

Last night I put on my black velvet dress with your crystals, to spend Sally's birthday evening with her and two other girls. It is a long, long time since I attended a 'hen' party, and I enjoyed it, as they are all such nice girls. We drove to Blantyre in Sally's car and went to Giovanni's, which opened about two years ago. It is very well run by a Portuguese. It looked and smelt like a restaurant in London, with an attractive bar, dim lights and beautifully laid tables, each with its open spirit lamp beside it, on which delicious things were cooked for us. I had a wonderful filet mignon steak with mushrooms and asparagus, and we drank the best Portuguese wine I have ever tasted, a red one. (Sally is very interested in wines.) We all had the most fabulous peach flambé – two big peach halves, served piping hot in a wonderful orange sauce. I then treated us to brandy with our strong black coffee. We got back about 10.30 and I slept like a top and woke up thinking of good food! I gave Sally a box of Chanel No. 5 soap, which delighted her and she rushed off at once to put in among her undies! There were toothpicks provided on the table, and I wrapped up four in a tissue and today presented them to Arthur, who bridled with pleasure! Bryn is feeling the heat and is worn out with the Maudling visit, but is always cheerful and very ready to tease and laugh with me.

I am going out now to water the flowers and do some weeding. I must get the carnation cuttings from Hazel. I had a long tea and talk with her on Friday. I am sorry about my writing. I am boiling hot and a bit weary.

13th December:

I had a phone call from Iris this morning to tell me the news from home is very bad, and she has arranged to fly home just after the New Year – terrible for them all, at Christmas too.

The tall man you saw on the News meeting Maudling was Robert Foster, our new Chief Secretary, a nice big man with a very downright manner – and very downright wife! They are enormously popular and are doing Zomba's morale a lot of good.

Last Friday I had tea with Hazel and a drive round Zomba's upper slopes to see the sunset. In the evening Alex and I went to dinner with Jean and Rex, and had a very pleasant evening, hearing all about their leave. We had a quiet weekend, with dreary, wet weather which is very dismal, though it does wonders for my garden, which now has Hazel's carnations flourishing in it. A stenographer (with the extraordinary name of Babington-Tabona!) who lives two chalets down from me has a darling Pekinese who has adopted me. She comes snuffling along and sits up against me as I weed (so *hot!*) and falls over onto the plants when I move, or starts digging helpfully when I have made holes to put them in. Iris's dachshund, Mitzi, has produced three tiny puppies which Alex can carry in one hand. I am having to be very firm with us both about not having one.

In Monday afternoon I had my hair cut and washed locally, and it is marvellous to have a cool head. I then had a late tea with Iris and later Dave and Alex joined us for a drink. I was feeling very sick and shaky and had a stiff brandy. I had the next day (yesterday) off, to go to Blantyre for Christmas shopping and was determined not to be ill. There is a peculiar bug about, which the African staff call *a'nyong-nyong* (!) and I definitely have it – so have Arthur, Don Penny and three girls in the Hostel. One has a slight temperature and a constant feeling of incipient nausea – dreadful. Arthur went up to the hospital and was given pills, which he swallows audibly on every possible occasion in public. I felt shaky yesterday but had a good day. Alex took me in his car, and we offered Jean Outram a lift – she has no transport and was frantic for a day's shopping. I searched in vain for a cocktail dress and finally, in my Indian store, bought a length of fabulous heavy white slipper satin with widely spaced flowers embroidered in tiny blue and silver beads. I can get it copied from my black sailcloth dress for about a pound, so I shall have a stunning dress for £5 10*s*. We had morning coffee, lunch at Ryall's and tea at Chileka airport, where we saw Banda arriving back from Dar-es-Salaam. We went on to the Flamingo for a drink and watched the sunset. Jean was thrilled with everything. Then we went to Ryall's and had a spaghetti supper and back to Zomba. We all enjoyed the day, though I was feeling quite unwell. Today I still burn gently but feel better. It makes me a little vague and I have done several stupid things in the office. I am going to have a very early night tonight. As I write, the rain falls steadily and noisily, and the thunder is so violent it is shaking my windows!

20th December:

I have only two pages of decent writing paper left, so I must write carefully. I enclose my (HE's) Christmas message, which was accepted, unscathed, and published today.

Iris has had to put forward her flight home and now leaves on 28th December. She came to tea with me yesterday and we had a long talk. We manage to phone practically every day. How I shall miss her.

The weather has suddenly in the last few days improved again, and as usual, therefore, I with it. I am writing this sitting out on Alex's deck chair on my *khonde*, pouring with sweat and turning brown by the minute. This lovely weather is just what I need after that debilitating bug and we are all hoping it will last over Christmas. I am having supper with Alex tonight and going over all the Christmas plans and helping him with final arrangements about food. He and I are sharing a party on Boxing night, which will help me to pay off hospitality. I have been to my Indian tailor and he has almost finished my *divine* dress, which I am to collect tomorrow. Kathie has asked me to go to tea with her and help decorate her tree, which I am delighted to do. She has a lovely sensitivity in her nature. She has also asked me to a 'hen' lunch party on Saturday, but I shall have to think hard over that – I have a feeling I shall be making mince pies and stuffing from about noon onwards!

27th December:

The weather over Christmas has been radiant in the mornings and evenings, with terrific heat piling up into tremendous rain and thunder in the afternoons. On Saturday morning Arthur gave a sherry party in the office to celebrate his recent promotion to Senior Information Officer. It was great fun as we were all feeling relaxed and Christmasy. I then went on to lunch with Kathie and four of her friends, all very nice women, but lacking her sense of fun, which I find so attractive. In the evening Alex and I went to Blantyre and had our own private Christmas celebration at Giovanni's. It was a lovely moonlit night and the drive there and back was simply wonderful. I sang Christmas carols in the car and got us both into such an emotional state I had to stop! On Sunday I spent quite a day helping Alex with all his Christmas arrangements. In the evening we went to the Lowes for their party. There was a beautiful little tree shining brightly in a corner and the children's stockings hanging by the fireplace. Their parties are always marvellous. My white dress gleamed and shone – like snow and ice,

Hazel said. I tried to get a small piece of the material to send to you but these Indian tailors will hang on to the last inch of remnant and say they have used it all up. On Christmas morning Alex picked me up at 7.30 and took me to share Christmas breakfast with him. We were both glad of the company. I remained dry-eyed throughout the holiday, but not easily, and whenever I was alone I felt very vulnerable. Dave and Iris came at seven and we had a very happy evening, I am thankful to say. We had a real Christmas dinner with all the trimmings, but for Iris's sake did not have any toasts with our wine. (I made a silent toast to 'absent friends'.) We spent Monday preparing for our evening party, decorating the room with candles and flowers. We had a big order for curry puffs and sausage rolls, and I made two new dip recipes which were a great success. We had fourteen people: I asked Sally and her friend Janet (and Bryn and Chris, who were so tired they excused themselves), also Kathie and John Firth. Alex invited the Lowes and four other couples who had been good to him when he was in the Hostel. The room looked very Christmasy in candlelight and everyone seemed to enjoy themselves. Today is very quiet, and I am glad it is all safely over, though it was one of the very best Christmases I have had out here. Iris phoned this morning to say goodbye. We are having a Christmas dinner in the Hostel tomorrow night.

3rd January 1962: [Air Letter]

I am sorry this is only an air letter this week. I have suddenly been asked out to tea today and tomorrow; there is an enormous amount of work to do in the office and I am too tired to write at night, so here I am writing between lunch and 1.30!

I had a most happy New Year weekend – happier than Christmas because there was somehow less to be homesick and sad about. I could scarcely mourn the passing of such a year for me (and for you) as 1961. On Saturday evening the Paynes came to dinner at Alex's flat and we went on to quite a good film, a light comedy called *Houseboat* with Cary Grant and Sophia Loren. I sat with Jean and Rex, and Alex sat by himself. On Sunday we had a quiet day and at seven in the evening called in on Bobby and Hazel to wish them a happy time at the Zomba Club Ball. We went on to the Flamingo and had a lovely quiet evening together. The Greek proprietor knows us and gave us a table in the corner of the patio, very quiet and cool, and we had dinner there too, and did not go inside to the crowded dance floor at all. We were alone on the patio to bring in the New Year – a truly happy evening. On New Year's day we first footed the Paynes at a reasonable hour and had coffee with them. I went to bed at a ridiculously early hour and was the only one bright and fresh in the office next morning. I have moved in with Kathie and Jean is back in her old office. I plunged at once into the thick of the Annual Report. I think I have squeezed in all my news.

9th January:

Ring of Bright Water has just belatedly come for Alex, and I have been smiling over the photographs and deciding I must read it again.

In my hurried letter last week I forgot to tell you that on 28th December we had our Hostel Christmas dinner, which I dreaded, but it turned out to be very pleasant indeed, with everyone at their best. We sat at one long candlelit table and I ate everything. I had a very attentive Arthur next to me, for which I was grateful, and it was really lovely. Alex, according to him, spent a 'bitter and twisted' evening, writing letters! He is working frightfully hard but standing up to it wonderfully. Everyone is feeling very depressed about the state Nyasaland is in. It somehow brings a feeling of closing ranks and standing by each other. I am well launched on the Annual Report, though the material is only dribbling in, an indication of the onerous demands of the ministerial system on the chaps, and I hate having to nag at them. I am also engaged in writing the constitutional history of the territory, which is most absorbing. And there are always the Press cuttings, which are now so numerous they are very time consuming.

I have been seeing a lot of Jean Outram, who is feeling rather down after her Christmas in the North. We went for a long walk after tea yesterday, in the botanical gardens and then further afield. She asked me to her chalet the other evening to help her entertain some guests, and we had a very good evening, with my Black Box and some of Geoffrey's and my records.

The weather has been very wet and stormy, with brief glimpses of a very hot sun. All the plants in the garden are tall and somewhat etiolated. We had a very quiet weekend after the festivities of the week before. We have begun to play Scrabble again, and on Sunday we completed *two Times* crosswords! Sally is in bed with 'flu and I have been dashing in and out with goodies for her, holding my breath.

17th January:

I am terribly behind with my letter writing, apart from yours. I get very little time to myself just now as Jean Outram is going through a lot of difficulties and makes considerable demands on my time and energy. It worries Alex, because I get so tired, but I remember so well how lost and abandoned one can feel, so I like to offer whatever moral support I can. We have got into the habit of going for quite a long walk after tea and I take her all over Zomba to various lovely view points.

The weather is dismal – lovely sunny mornings which rapidly deteriorate into tremendous downpours that go on and on for hours, and one just cannot keep dry outside for more than a few seconds. There is a lot of illness about, especially this wretched *a' nyong-nyong*. I have had it again all day. The awful nausea makes one weak and dizzy. Alex had it for a day last week and Jean

Payne has had it. I tried to carry on today, but was simply sitting crouched at my desk, and Kathie insisted on taking me home at 9.30. I dozed all day and feel better.

Last Wednesday Alex and I had a lovely dinner with the Marwick Smiths, a very nice couple who have befriended Alex. On Thursday Hazel came down and we walked in the gardens after tea. She and Bobby called in for a drink at Alex's flat on Saturday evening. Bobby is terribly overworked and hating the frustrations of his work, poor man, preparing Development Plans for which he knows jolly well there is not the money. The things that go on now are almost unbelievable and there is a kind of despair in the general atmosphere, though people do not say much about it.

On Sunday Alex, Jean Outram and I went away for the day with John Firth, in his car, to Portuguese Mlanje. The weather was overcast as we set out and then steadily improved into brilliiant sunshine. We had coffee in Limbe, a noon drink at Mlanje Club, where I saw a few familiar faces, and got to our destination about one o'clock. We had a bottle of local wine, bread, black olives and tiny mussels as small eats, and then a delicious lunch of steak and salad heavily impregnated with garlic. By the time we finished the rain was crashing down with the peculiar violence I always connect with Mlanje district, so we drove back, stopping for tea at Cholo Club, and having a tired but happy supper of ham sandwiches at Alex's. It was a marvellous day which did us all good. We get on well together and know and sympathise with each other's difficulties.

There is a lull in the office, and I have occupied myself writing my own bits of the Annual Report and scouring the offices for photographs. I miss the car so much in the work I am on now. I used to leap into it and dash all over Zomba. I have a jeep at my disposal, but it is uncomfortable and draughty.

I heard from Dave that Iris's mother died on 30th December, the day after she got home. I am glad she got there in time, poor Iris. I am always interested to hear all the TV news – what a lot you manage to remember to tell me! Bryn has just acquired Peter Scott's *The Eye of the Wind* and will lend it to me later.

24th January:

The weather is very trying; terribly sultry and enervating, with hardly any sun, which, of course, is what is wrong with me. I *must* have my sun. I have been keeping up my walks with Jean after tea, which is good exercise but just at present I have to force myself, I am so tired. I think it may be a delayed reaction to all the stress and strain. I am also working far harder, mentally, now that I am back to my old work. The Report rolls on, and I seem to take it all far more calmly than last time. The office is very quiet indeed as Bryn and Arthur are on *ulendo* together in the North. Poor Bryn, I can imagine nothing more exhausting than *ulendo* in the North with Arthur! Bryn was forty-five on Saturday. He did not mind in the least, but Arthur who is terrified of growing old, did, and threw a terrific scene over the whole office, thereby getting all the attention which had been directed to Bryn back to himself. He will probably be ill if he finds out I will be forty next Tuesday!

On Saturday Jean Outram and John Firth joined Alex and me and we went to Blantyre to see Doris Day and Rex Harrison in *Midnight Lace*, a good thriller. We then went to Ryall's for dinner and danced for an hour. On Sunday Alex and I drove over to Chileka, had a spaghetti lunch in the restaurant and at 2.30 met Geoffrey Fricker off the plane, back for three weeks to help deal with the salaries revision battle which is raging between our chaps and the British Treasury. He has been working every day at the Colonial Office since he went home, so has had no rest or real leave, poor man. He is staying with friends, but coming on his own to dinner at Alex's flat some day next week. On Saturday this week I am giving a noon birthday party at Alex's flat. There are too many friends to take out to dinner, and yet I want to have them all, as they have been so good to me. Being on a week day I shall not celebrate much on the day, but Hazel, as always, has thought up something splendid and insisted on making me a birthday cake and having me there to eat it – so like her.

31st January:

You will be glad to hear I am feeling much better and have had no more *a'nyong-nyong*. Hazel had four days in bed with it last week and today Sally had all the symptoms plus a rash and was whisked off to hospital.

I had a great birthday. I got presents of soap and scent from Jean and Sally before I was up! I opened your parcel and was delighted with the little blue cape – ideal for the cold season and reading in bed. I was also thrilled to have the soap from Jess. I got a cable from the aunts, a card from Elspeth and from Joan. Kathie and Jean Payne gave me soap and lipstick. (The men did not know.) Hazel came for me at 3.30 and when I got there, instead of just me, she had invited Jean Outram, Jean Payne and Sally, so we had a very lively tea party. Hazel paints in oils, very well, I think, and had done a beauty for me on a small canvas, of the view from their *khonde* in the early morning, with trees silver in the sun and the plain like a sea with islands – really beautiful. In the evening Alex came for me and I had a very good dinner with him. He gave me Tweed talcum, a frilly piece of nonsense (white lace undies bought by Hazel), and a parcel ordered by catalogue has yet to come.

We had a very happy party on Saturday before lunch, and then a quiet weekend. Alex had a lot of work to do and I caught up with some letter writing, laundry and mending which I had not had the energy to do. I had a marvellous domestic Sunday morning in my room with the Black Box pounding out lovely music. On Monday I got my hair thinned, trimmed and shampooed, always a great morale booster. I dined at Alex's with Geoffrey, a very pleasant, relaxed evening.

7th February:

Sally had five days in hospital and is fully recovered. The other day after tea I was weeding and she came and talked for an hour and a half. She is so nice, never asks questions but always manages to convey that she knows I have my worries.

Yesterday and today have been days of glorious sun, and now, at four o'clock, I am in shorts and blouse, out on my *khonde* DRIPPING in the heat and going visibly brown. I did the same yesterday and already feel the better for it. We are having tremendous thunderstorms, with simultaneous lightning and thunder. Last night it went on for hours. I put on my light and read, half my attention on the livid light quivering outside. My heart was pounding.

I am now very busy in the office with the everlasting Report and three tourist pamphlets (one quite a thick book) to write 'during the lulls', as Arthur said, with his sweetest smile! I am delighted, and was not a bit put out, rather to his surprise. It is a new kind of writing for me, and a refreshing challenge.

The salaries revision has come through at last. Not being permanent and pensionable, I do not benefit all that much, but I do get over £100 a year more, and Arthur is trying to get me a charge allowance of £15 a month, so I should be earning over £800 a year by the end of the month. Alex does well, with a good increase in pension, which is the main thing for the men.

The weather has been so trying that there has not been much energy for doing anything, so social life has been quiet, but I quite enjoy that for a time. Geoffrey came to the flat one evening for a drink and is always good company. Jean (Outram) and I now do *The Times* crossword together every day and our record was its completion in 12 minutes – quite a shock! We seem to be absolutely 50/50 in our contributions, which is fun. I have had a letter from Iris, who comes back about the 24th of this month, which is lovely for me.

13th February:

Alex's birthday present arrived last week, a lovely soft white sweater, with a largish collar, buttoning up the front so that it can be worn as a cardigan or sweater. It will be wonderful in the cold weather. Geoffrey flew back to England on Friday, and came for a farewell dinner at the flat the night before – worn out and bursting to be on his way. Alex drove him to the airport, got a haircut and an afternoon's shopping. It did him good to get away. He brought me back a present of hair lacquer, which I used to scorn, but it is an absolute godsend in the damp weather and I use it a lot. One's hair goes stiff, but no one need know!

How interesting that the 'Face to Face' man last week was Roy Thomson. He has just bought up our local rag, *The Central African Times* and various other rubbishy papers belonging to the same group. I hope he pulls them together – they are awful.

I sometimes meet Bryn and Lawrence in the gardens. He is a lovely child. He is very precocious mentally, and talks in sentences. Hazel's sweet Johnnie, who is the same age, does not talk at all yet, just chuckles and gurgles disarmingly!

I am now working hard and feeling the pressure, but I have got into the swing of it. The great excitement has been Duncan Sandys's visit, only announced at the last moment. Jean (Outram) was asked on Friday to make up equal numbers at a dinner party given for him at GH on Saturday, and Sally, who is cypher officer at GH, was on call 24 hours a day for emergency cables sent and received, and was kept very busy.

The tremendous thunderstorms and cloudbursts continue, but with blazing sun in between, so I have been taking advantage of it whenever possible. We had another quiet weekend, as Alex had a lot of work to catch up on with the departure of Geoffrey.

Arthur gets a new car today – a Renault Floride, and the excitement is intense. He is his usual ebullient self. Bryn, who goes on home leave in March, is bringing back a Jaguar, so the Information Department is going to look very smart. I suggested to Arthur that as my mode of transport is my feet, I would have to buy a pair of very glamorous shoes with my pay rise! He said, 'Never mind, sweetie, just think of the *fabulous* lifts you will get'!

21st February:

The thunder and rain continue, both decreasing in intensity, and I have sunbathed every day for a week. I have a marvellous tan and am feeling better and better, which is as well, as I am working very hard indeed at present. Bryn, quite rightly, is beginning to get leave happy, and Arthur has to take on more, which means I do too! I am *so* tired in the evenings it is an effort to do anything after tea except sit in the sun and read my newspapers.

There is a great deal of 'flu about just now. Jean Outram appears about to go down with it, and Hazel has it. I walked up to visit her yesterday and found her almost speechless in bed, furious to be ill. This is her second bad bout in six months. Alex had a brief but bad attack of it on Thursday and Friday last week and is only today back in the office. He is working too hard and is very strung up over the way things are going, as indeed many of the men are.

There was a huge party on at the Hostel on Saturday to which everyone was going (and over eighty guests!) I decided I had better join in, as I had no excuse for not doing so. I like to keep myself very independent of most of the inmates. In fact, I got three invitations to join private parties, which everyone held in their rooms first. I joined Jean Outram's and had a relaxed time on her *khonde*. It was a warm, clear night with an almost full moon. She had eight guests, all of whom I know quite well, and I enjoyed it. At 10 we went up to have supper and found the main party in full swing. I stayed longer than I meant to, as Arthur and Bobby, both excellent dancers, joined up with us and kept me on the floor. When I left about one it was still at its height and beginning to get a bit rowdy.

I am trying to withdraw a little from Jean Outram, whom I find very demanding of my time and I cannot bear the feeling of my private life being invaded in any way. She really has had time to find her feet and make friends.

My writing is very bad today, as I have had a terrific day's work typing and writing.

27th February:

We are having lovely weather and there are definite signs of the approach of the cold season – the early mornings are gloriously fresh and radiant, with a hot sun and the air still cool – a perfect climate for me, but not one that lasts. I shall soon be shivering away! I am beautifully brown and relaxed.

Bryn goes on leave in the middle of next month. He and Chris go to Chipping Norton, where there is a big house converted into flats, owned by an ex-Nyasaland couple, so they know exactly what is wanted by their guests – plenty of hot water and central heating being priorities!

I was so interested to hear you had watched the 'Tonight' programme about Glenn's space flight. It made an enormous impact on people's imagination here. The exciting thing is that Bryn *saw* it! There is an American at the Consulate in Blantyre who liaised closely over timing. He phoned Bryn with exact information on time and direction and Bryn was able to phone GH and the top brass and say, 'Go out on your *khonde* in ten minutes time and you will see him come round the north shoulder of Zomba mountain,' and *bang on*, that was exactly what happened! Bryn held Lawrence up in his arms and pointed out the rocket, which was quite sizeable and gleaming in the after-glow of the sunset. The ridiculous thing is that Kathie, driving back from a tea party in broad daylight, saw him on his first orbit earlier – a flash of light streaming down the sky – and thought vaguely, 'What fun if that was Glenn,' and discovered later it was! I was shattered to have missed it, but Bryn's description helped to bring it to life for me and of course he was lyrical with excitement.

I am working like a beaver, and simply do not surface till the end of the day, but I am enjoying it all, and with more confidence and experience behind me I do much more thorough editing and save Julien Theunissen, who checks my work, an enormous amount of time. He is obviously delighted and wants me to do pamphlets on careers for the Public Service Commission. Bryn is cross and says I must not be overloaded, but I (and Alex agrees with me) consider that the more useful I make myself to *everyone* the better!

We had a wonderful day on Sunday. It was a glorious day, with clear atmosphere, high clouds and brilliant sunshine. Kathie had invited Alex and me to go (in his car) to see her old home three miles out of Blantyre. A friend lives in it at present, but they are trying to sell it and of course will lose out, because no one in their senses wants to buy a big property in Nyasaland now. It may go to a Mission. It has a lovely mature, overgrown garden with English and exotic trees, an orchard and a well. The house is L-shaped and reminded me in look and smell inside of the houses we used to stay in in the Highlands. We had lunch and tea, almost shared by a lovely golden spaniel called Pepper, who adopted me for the day, and two *huge* beasts, crosses between a great Dane and a mastiff. They adopted Alex, who looked quite like them, we all agreed!

7th March:

We have had another glorious week of sun, which I am soaking up, but the mornings have a delicious nip and in the evenings I am into sweaters already. From teatime till dark I sit out on my *khonde* with my LP records audible through the open window. I have quite a number of visitors, as everyone is out in the blessed sunshine at that time. The botanical gardens are just beyond my chalet and I am conspicuous in my yellow pants and green towelling shirt, so people stroll over when they are there walking with their children and dogs. Iris arrived back on Friday. I phoned her three times at the weekend, but their phone was out of order, so I did not see her till Monday morning, when we were both office bound. She is busy till all hours with Leg Co and we are not meeting till Friday, when I shall have tea with her.

I am working flat out and hardly see anyone in the office, but I am keeping the report material moving to the Print and am completely absorbed in it. I am determined this one will be outstanding – no more Annual Reports after Independence, so the last one may as well be special! I rather dread going on to tourist work, which I have decided is not my style, though it certainly suits Arthur. From the little I have done I find it superficial and moving towards advertising, for which I have no flair at all. However, we shall see.

Bryn gave his farewell party on Friday evening and to my surprise I enjoyed it. I got ready for it feeling cold, tired and depressed, but somehow, having to go alone and cope by myself seemed to brace me up, for once, and as soon as I walked in I knew I was all right. Kathie gave me a lift there and back. Arthur was not there as he was suffering madly from a boil in his armpit, which was making us *all* ill, I may say, as we had to listen to gruesome bulletins on its reaction to poultices. As I live in the Hostel I am the one who gets most of it – and at lunch, too! He amuses me no end and I make him laugh, so all is well. Bryn seems intrigued by the rather gay abandon of our relationship – with him I am much more relaxed, gentle and straightforward!

Sally is back from local leave in Northern Rhodesia. She is such a pet. Yesterday after tea she brought her knitting and sat beside me in the sun, not talking, but listening to my Max Bruch and Kathleen Ferrier. As cypher officer at GH she can tell me all that goes on behind the scenes. Naturally I remain dumb – all very interesting!

Tonight Alex and I are dining with Bobby and Hazel, which will be lovely. I can always relax completely with them and so can Alex. He is frightfully busy and gets desperately tired and harassed, but I can tell he is on top of his work, which is fine.

13th March:

Bryn left yesterday, highly emotional, very tired and I think very regretful at having to leave the Department at such an uneasy time. We have had a *very* edgy Acting Chief Information Office in the chair today, but I managed to make him laugh just the same. He is actually a great help to me in little things, as he has a very sharp eye for detail, which sharpens mine. My charge allowance has been confirmed, so I feel happier with some more financial backing. We continue to have glorious days and I feel very fit. (I still find sleep a problem.)

I am working very hard and enjoying it now that the Report is almost all with the Print, and rolling. Jean Payne proofreads with me and it is all going smoothly, apart from the usual bits that are always late, which I now take in my stride. Alex is very overworked, but can at least let off steam to me about it in the evenings, which makes an excellent safety valve for his nervous system. I have taken to having supper with him in the flat, and it is so lovely for me to get away from the Hostel to a more homely atmosphere.

Last week we had a very happy, peaceful evening with Bobby and Hazel, who came to the flat on Saturday before lunch for a drink. They brought Susan, their eight-year-old daughter, with them. She always makes a little posy of flowers from the garden for me. She is an absolute poppet, very sophisticated for her age. She flirts shamelessly with Alex, who of course loves it and treats her like a young lady. On Thursday I went up and had tea and a long walk with Iris. It was such a relief and happiness to see her again. Alex and I spent Saturday evening with her and Dave. She is well, physically, but very low in spirits, though she always brightens up wonderfully while we are together. She is coming to lunch with me at the Hostel tomorrow, as Dave is away all day.

Jean Outram is in bed with mild 'flu, so I am going down to her now with some books and a crossword.

21st March:

I am delighted with the Muk-Luks [American house slippers with leggings attached], as was everyone else in the office, where I opened the parcel, although Arthur *dared* me to wear them there, even under my desk on the coldest day of the year. ('My dear, I simply *must* have my staff in high heels'!)

The report on lung cancer and smoking has caused some consternation here, as nearly everyone is a heavy smoker and cigarettes are very cheap. Arthur is in a great state, as he has smoked sixty a day for years. I think it has really made a great impact – at home too.

Our lovely weather broke at last on Friday, when cyclone Kate swept the Federation – high winds and incredibly heavy rain combined to be terrifying. The main body of water just fell straight down as if from a gigantic tap, but when the wind suddenly gusted, great sheets of solid, icy rain flew in all directions. This went on for hours on end. Going to the office and back, in spite of everyone giving me lifts, I just got soaked again and again. I have had a sore throat and a temperature on and off since then, but I seem to be fit enough not to succumb. Today it has cleared. There is a splendid sunset going on now and everything smells fresh and sweet. We spent a pleasant evening with the Paynes on Friday, and played Scrabble on Saturday evening with Kathie, who had asked John Sheriff, a Hostel friend of ours, to make a fourth. On Sunday we had a drink before lunch with the Marwick Smiths. Alex continues to be snowed under at work but is coping well.

27th March:

Fine weather is now a thing of the past. We are plunged into yet another cyclone – Lucy – which hit us on Saturday. The wind has died but it has been raining *without pause* since about 2 o'clock yesterday afternoon. The clouds are down over the roof of the Hostel. It is making everyone irritable, and the constant noise of the rain on the roof gives me a dazed, headachy feeling.

I have been up to tea with Iris twice since I last wrote. She is looking and feeling better, and taking more interest in her work. We *never* have time to come to the end of what we have been saving up – or bottling up – to tell each other. It is really a great therapy for us both. On Friday Alex and I had the day in Blantyre, he on business – our first together without having someone else with us. I had my hair done, very successfully. We had an excellent lunch in Ryall's and then two hours shopping, in which I spent more doing other people's shopping than my own. It did us good to get out of Zomba. Alex really is working too hard and worrying too much, but it is difficult to do otherwise – the work *must* be done. On Saturday evening we went to the Flamingo with the Marwick Smiths – our treat. They loved it. On the way back we were caught in 'Lucy' and driving became an adventure, and quite hair-raising. I spent a very quiet day on Sunday, being very domesticated. The office is busy, but not too much so, and Arthur is not having a hard initiation, which is lucky for all of us! I am re-reading Han Suyin's *A Many Splendoured Thing* and enjoying it even more than the first time. Iris reads it about once a year! There are one or two new faces in the Hostel and I enjoy talking at lunch with them.

I am off to have a bath now, to warm myself up!

3rd April:

There is not much news, as life has been paralysed by the weather. It rained till this morning, which means nearly three weeks of it – dreadful and appallingly depressing. On Sunday morning I had *five* damp pairs of shoes to get dry and it was still pouring. Alex is going to let me have his fan/radiator, which I borrowed during the hot season, so I shall be able to dry out my room properly. I reached the stage when I was only comfortable in a hot bath – not even in bed, as it felt damp and the mosquito net smelt musty. However, today is glorious sunshine with a fresh wind, and now, at 4.30, I am out on my *khonde* in thin pants and a blouse, taking ages to write this because I keep stopping to gaze thankfully at the high blue sky.

On Friday I went to tea with Hazel and as always had such a happy time, ending up with a hilarious game of 'Happy Families' with the children. That evening Philip and Mary Richardson, just back from leave, came round to the flat for a drink before dinner. They are both looking very well, and seemed happy to see Alex and me, and perfectly ready to accept us and see something of us, which pleased me very much, for Alex's sake, as he and Philip are old friends who have much to share and remember. On Saturday I heard that Iris was recovering from a very severe 48-hour 'flu which is laying people low just now, so in the evening we crept in the car through sheets of rain to call on them and give her books and magazines. She was up, but feeling very poorly, as one does, so we stayed on quite late and cheered her up so much that she became very vivacious and bright-eyed and obviously had a temperature instead of being sub-normal as she was when we arrived! She appreciates Alex's sense of humour, so we always laugh a great deal, and of course Dave is one of the wittiest people I know.

Alex began to feel ill on Sunday, and yesterday and today he has had a fearful gastric upset, which has died down. He is very strained and overtired. I have just phoned him on Sally's phone and he is up and about, quite cheerful. I am getting down to see him for a little while and I shall see for myself how he is. Sally is so kind and always offers the use of her phone or a lift if I seem immobilised. She has decided to move into one of the new bachelor flats soon, and how I shall miss her. We fit in very well in our domestic arrangements, having baths at completely different times and not playing our LPs too loudly.

We are all happy in the office, with not too much work just at present. Arthur is in great form, though on a diet!

10th April: [Air Letter]

Iris is feeling better and had tea with me in the chalet on Friday.

We continue to have a phenomenal amount of rain, but Sunday and yesterday were both lovely days and everyone has been drying things out. On Saturday we drove to Blantyre for a change of scene and had a quiet dinner at Ryall's. We had a lovely evening, but I had had a suppressed cold for two weeks which suddenly surfaced and I began to burn and shiver. It has been dreadful till this afternoon, when I quite suddenly felt better – such a relief. We were supposed to be going to the Richardsons for a curry lunch on Sunday, but I had to opt out, I felt so wretched.

Hazel has just been down to see me, and sat out on my *khonde* while I sat inside and talked through the window, in case I infected her – she gets the same kind of hideous colds as I do!

Alex is in better form and of course as soon as I am not well he seems to forget, overcome or ignore whatever is troubling him. Sally has moved to herflat and seems to have vanished from my life, as happens in Zomba, but she wants me to go round and see it when she has settled in. Jean Outram has made some friends, which solved my problem. I still have lunch with her and pre-serve public relations. I have a new neighbour in my chalet but she is only there for a few days before moving into a flat – a big, good looking, luscious Rhodesian.

I shall do better than this next week.

18th April:

The weather is *impossible*, with sudden drops of temperature and still this relentless rain, though we do get some hours of wonderful sunshine in between. Everyone is suffering and half the people I meet greet me as huskily as I greet them. However, I have been up to my eyes in work, without a moment to feel sorry for myself. The Annual Report *and* the UNO Report are going so swiftly and smoothly I am holding my breath in expectation of a break in my good luck.

On Saturday we went with Bobby and Hazel to Blantyre to see *Butterfield 8* with Elizabeth Taylor and Lawrence Harvey – much better than I expected, and the Lowes loved it. We had a chicken supper at Ryall's, a dance or two up in the ballroom and then home by moonlight. I was desperately tired and cold-ridden, but enjoyed getting away. I lay very low on Sunday, determined to shake off my ills, and had a very early night. I felt much better on Monday and had tea with Iris that afternoon. Alex came to collect me and we stayed on for a drink. Dave enjoys Alex's company and of course Iris just loves him and gives him little affectionate pats and her dazzling smile, which please him. Last night we went to dinner at the Lowes and Alex met Elsie and Robin Martin for the first time. It was a cold, wet night and Hazel had on one of her huge log fires, which made it all very homely and relaxing.

25th April:

Jean Outram has moved into a house at Naisi, where she will stay till July, when she goes home for good. She came in to my chalet the day she left and had a long talk.

Over Easter the weather was mainly sunny, thank goodness. On Friday morning Alex worked in the office and I spent the whole morning with Iris, sitting on the *khonde* with my eyes fixed on that heavenly view, all washed clean and clear by the rain. In the evening Alex and I called in at the Marwick Smiths to wish them a happy Easter. On Saturday evening we went to the Flamingo with Jean and Rex Payne and had a very happy evening. They had not been before and were greatly taken with everything. The band was especially good and played lovely old favourites, so we danced a lot. The Paynes have a great capacity for enjoying themselves, which I appreciate very much. On Sunday, a glorious day, we took Iris and Dave to Portuguese Mlanje, which they had never visited. It was a beautiful drive, the scenery looking at its most spectacular. We had a delicious, garlic-with-everything lunch: rice and potato soup, steak, chips, asparagus and black olives, and home-made bread and cheese. For the first time in weeks I ate like a horse. The restaurant was packed with English, Rhodesian and Portuguese visitors, and there were some Portuguese soldiers with an old gramophone on which they played my Amalia Rodrigues record, creating the right atmosphere with the right voice: magic. On Monday I went to Alex's for an Easter breakfast. He gave me orange juice, a kipper, bacon and egg, brown toast, lime marmalade and coffee! And I ate it all! We had a very quiet day, playing Scrabble, doing crosswords and I reading while Alex did some work. In the evening I had a big bowl of very hot broth and retired to bed about eight. I have felt better for the rest but just cannot get myself on top and really well, which is a great bore. Everyone is feeling much the same, so I am not worried at all. Lots of people went away for Easter and there are some lovely brown, healthy faces about. Bobby, Hazel and the family went to the Lake and are not back yet, as Bobby got some local leave to add on to the long weekend. They take two rooms in a small chalet by the hotel and do their own cooking, taking a servant and all their food and bedding. Otherwise they could never afford to go away at all. Hazel takes it all in her stride, as usual, and of course the children love it.

On Tuesday morning Kathie went off to Bulawayo for a fortnight, to represent us at the Trade Fair which takes place every year. She has lots of friends there and it is really a paid holiday, as her part in our Pavilion is almost entirely decorative! She went off with a huge shopping list for herself, and clothes of Jean's and mine to put into a good dry cleaners. It is bliss to have the office to myself and I am getting through an enormous amount of work. I am longing to feel really well again so that I can settle into all the new work that will soon be coming my way.

2nd May:

The weather is *at last* settling down to cold days of brilliant sunshine – warm in the sun, freezing indoors. I am suddenly so busy that I dare not take time to go out and get warm in the sun. I have almost finished the two Reports and have been taken off tourist work (which had hardly begun) to produce an enormous publication on careers in Government Service – a lot of hack work involved but not without interest. I shall work under Ian Nance, who has been a Provincial Commissioner for years and for the first time has been brought into the Secretariat to fill a new post; I think he is scared stiff! I am feeling very much better, which is a relief, like toothache when it stops.

I had tea with Jean Payne yesterday. Her mother, who is eighty and lives with Jean's sister in Northern Rhodesia, is flying up for a visit, arriving on Friday. Jean is so excited she can hardly wait and I am so envious I could weep!

Alex sent home for three yards of navy blue Terylene to have made into trousers here. When it arrived from his tailor's it proved to be the special tailor breadth of 60 inches. So Alex has his navy blue trousers, and *I* have a neat, straight navy blue skirt and a very smart short sleeved jacket (copied from my black sailcloth jacket). I have acquired a lovely, hard-wearing suit!

Alex has taken on a new lease of life. He has managed to replace some of his inefficient staff, and now has a competent secretary and departmental assistant, which makes an enormous difference. He also feels more confident in his work and is being recognised and appreciated for his efforts, which has raised his morale. He is going to move from his flat (which has frightfully noisy, untidy neighbours) to a new house in Kalimbuka, the housing estate where he lived before. It is an attractive house of a new design and with many improvements. It has a lovely view looking towards Zomba mountain. He is also getting a new car – a Ford Consul Capri – the last one which Government will help him pay for, I imagine. It is on its way by sea now.

On Saturday evening we drove to Blantyre to see a good film, *The Sundowners*, which we both enjoyed very much. Alex was most anxious to see it and wanted me to see the Australian landscapes. What a rough life! I assured him I was sure they are nice people, but that I would have to be chained up, to be kept there! It was marvellously acted, especially by Deborah Kerr.

I have had several long phone calls with Iris, but have not seen her since Easter Sunday. She is overwhelmed in a spate of entertaining.

9th May:

I am feeling very fit and well, but the Lowes have been ill and Alex has been off since Monday, with temperature, vomiting, frightful gastric pains *and* his ulcer pain. I have had two exhausting days, walking down to see him after tea – only about a mile but it is steadily uphill all the way back and at the end of a hard day is not funny. I have therefore been fairly piano myself, as I worry about him, but I phoned this afternoon and there is a definite improvement. I am working like mad, as I am breaking new ground in working out this careers book with Ian Nance – not exciting, but there is a satisfaction in working it all out. Kathie is back from Bulawayo, with her hair much improved and a holiday look about her. She had her hair thinned and cut quite a bit and now wears it in a big French roll, which looks delightfully sophisticated and shows up her lovely Scottish bones. She brought me a present of two pairs of tiny panties of brushed nylon trimmed with lace 'for winter' wear, as she said. (Bryn would have a fit but Kathie knows me!) I am thrilled with them. Jean's mother arrived safely by air on Friday – great excitement – and is settling down happily. Kathie and I are going to tea to meet her on Monday.

The weather is really cold and we are all in winter woollies. I am into stockings and have Alex's radiator on in my room and four blankets on the bed. I have not much news for you as we have been so under the weather. We did have a drink at lunch time with Iris and Dave on Saturday, and in the evening we called in on Bobby and Hazel and found them better but very depressed, so Alex took charge and ordered them both to 'tidy up' – that meant Bobby put on a cravat and Hazel put on high heeled shoes – Alex's idea of a 'tidied up' woman! So they did so and came thankfully down to the flat and Alex, who had laid on a nice dinner for me, asked them to stay and join us. They were tremendously impressed to find themselves eating mushroom soup, roast chicken with a red wine, and strawberries and cream in a bachelor flat with very little warning. It was the first good meal they had enjoyed for days, having been so unwell, so it was all highly satisfactory and worth the trouble Alex had taken. (His head boy is very good, though not in the same league as Aflike.) On Sunday we went to Sally's for lunch. She has a delightful flat which she has made most attractive. Staying with her was her old friend Monica, with whom she shared a house till Monica married a policeman and was posted to Northern Rhodesia, and Sally moved into the Hostel. She gave us a delicious lunch. Alex was in great form, and completely charmed the two girls. He had them both twittering like plump little sparrows. Sally looks much better and happier, but is putting on weight with all the good food she is sharing with Monica, who is in the early stages of pregnancy and ravenous! She bakes her own bread and the most wonderful aroma was coming from the kitchen. If I were a bachelor girl I would revel in a place like that. Most of the girls seem to spend their time glooming over not being married. I long to tell them to enjoy each phase of life as it comes.

The next thing to look forward to socially is the Dramatic Society's production of *The Gioconda Smile*, which is on a week on Saturday. Arthur asked Alex and me but, as we never appear together in Zomba in public, Alex is not going, but to my pleasure I am. Hazel is involved behind the scenes, so Bobby will spend the evening with Alex.

I am off at a gallop to see him and get back before dark.

16th May:

We have three radiators for the offices but I have not managed to acquire one of them this season, which is why I go on and on about the cold. Arthur has one, which he hardly ever uses, as he does not feel the cold. The other two have been acquired by the African staff, and race relations being what they are now, I would rather die of cold than make a fuss. (If Bryn were here he would fix 'em in one minute flat!)

Alex is better but pretty exhausted. However, he is going to move into his house this weekend. Geoffrey comes back from leave in three weeks time, arriving on 3rd June, and I have persuaded Alex to take a fortnight's local leave from 9th June and spend a few days of it at the Lake. I am badly in need of some leave and a change of scene myself, and so is Iris, so we have a wonderful plan to join Alex at the Lake. It really would be marvellous. It is just a case of all getting permission at the same time. I think it can be done. Arthur just laughed in mock hysteria when I said some local leave was long overdue to me, as a first hint to get his reaction. However, I know he will be perfectly reasonable about it. My work with Ian Nance is at present a complete slogging bore, but may improve. It is the first time in my office life that I have been bored and felt dislike for my work. Fortunately I still have the final page proofing of the Annual Report to turn to at odd moments, so I get through the day, but it makes me tired and cross not to be properly absorbed. The only bitter consolation is that I work straight onto my typewriter, so at least I get plenty of practice.

On Friday Jean (Payne) and I had tea with Kathie and saw all her purchases from Bulawayo – quite a lot of winter clothes, which she will wear on the ship going home in October. On Monday Kathie and I went to Jean's to meet her mother, Mrs MacBrayne, a tiny, spry woman of eighty – white hair, very lively brown eyes and a flat, rather gruff west of Scotland voice. She is greatly interested in everything and Jean loves having her. On Saturday evening Dave and Iris came down for a quiet drink to see how Alex was. He went back to the office on Thursday, but took things very quietly over the weekend. Yesterday Iris came and lunched with me in the Hostel. It was over lunch that we made our heady plans for the Lake. In the afternoon (I was exhausted by evening!) I went up to Naisi and had tea with Jean Outram. She has been lent a house and a car by a teacher who has gone on leave. I had not been up to Naisi for years and felt quite sick at the sight of all those ghastly houses.

I am looking forward to my theatre night on Saturday. There have been two performances already and I have heard nothing but enthusiastic praise for the production. Alex and Bobby are going up the mountain to have dinner at Kuchawe, so that will keep them occupied for the evening.

23rd May:

The weather is cold and still rainy, which is ridiculous, but we have had some of the lovely cold season days one expects. My outing on Saturday night was pleasant, but I missed Alex very much and realised how well he looks after me, seeing me in and out of the car, helping me down steps in the dark and making sure I am warm enough! There were six of us (no one of any interest to you) and after a drink in Arthur's room we had a very good dinner in the Hostel, with good wine and a pretty table. I wore my white satin dress and my white mohair stole – a lovely soft, feminine outfit which helped my morale. The play was excellent, with first class dialogue (Aldous Huxley), and the sets and dresses were lovely. Dave and Iris were there with Ron, some rows behind, but fortunately I did not even see them till we were all going out at the end. I really enjoyed the play immensely, and the feeling of being one of a large and familiar gathering but, as I say, I did not enjoy altogether being on my own and found it had all been quite a strain, when I got back to my room and thought about it. However, Iris said I looked very calm and poised, and that my dress was 'gorgeous'. Arthur was a good host ('Here is Mrs Hitchcock, swathed in shantung'!) and we kept the conversational ball rolling between us at dinner. Alex and Bobby had a very good evening, so all was well.

Alex started to move into his house on Saturday and I helped him all day on Sunday. We are both so tired it was quite an undertaking. Over the weekend I realised just how near the end of my tether I am, and decided firmly I would ask for a little more leave and have a *whole week* at the Lake! On Monday I applied in writing and was granted it, from Monday 9th June to Wednesday 20th, and I shall, I hope, get a booking at the Lake from Tuesday to Tuesday. Alex will be there and Iris, in a mad moment, agreed she too would take the whole week. She needs it as much as I do, in a way. She is simply thrilled.

Alex's house is beginning to look very nice indeed. He has a long lounge with doors opening into a tiny diningroom. There is a smallish, modern kitchen, a minute but very well appointed bathroom (all in one), a main bedroom and a very small guest room with a wash basin, which he is using as a study. All the cupboards, shelves and wardrobes are built in, *and* there is a full length mirror which can either be fitted on a wall or inside a wardrobe door. *I* have not had a full length mirror since I came to Nyasaland! I have given him some of my pictures, as my walls here were overcrowded, and they look delightful. He is thrilled with them – my Bernard Rice's Bosnian village, grandfather's water colour of Mull and Hazel's one she did for my birthday. There is a lovely view of Zomba mountain and opposite, small hills and trees which hide Mlanje – pity. There are a lot of very well tended gardens round about, so there is a pleasant impression of clipped hedges, well kept lawns and masses of colour from bougainvillaea, hibiscus and pride of India. The Paynes are near neighbours, which is good to know, if he ever needs help in any way. I had tea with Iris yesterday and stayed till 6.30, when Alex came and picked me up. She had a lovely log fire, as did the Lowes, when we called on them on Sunday evening.

I am about to have a bath, put on slacks and go and take up curtain hems for Alex.

30th May:

I was most gratified to see the *Spectator* full of reactions to Leavis's tirade against C.P. Snow. What struck me most about it was its *bad* English and its pettiness. It fills me with horror to think that it is the performance of one of the doyens of English literature at Cambridge.

The weather is frightful again. I do not mind the odd misty day, in fact I love it, but it has been pouring with rain for the last two days. However, I have Alex's wonderful radiator in my room and never stint its use, as I do not pay for all the electricity I use – there is a fixed sum included in the rent. I borrowed Arthur's radiator 'for the morning' on Thursday and have quietly taken it over. He has not even noticed, so that's all right.

We had a pleasant holiday on Thursday, a lovely sunny day, and had a very happy time arranging books and pictures. The house looks delightful and Alex says it is by far the nicest house he has ever had. Dave and Iris came to see it in the evening, Iris bearing a glorious bouquet of peach blossom, which put the finishing touch to the sittingroom. We had a big log fire burning and it looked like a real home.

Our holiday is fixed at the Lake. Iris is coming with us and staying till the next Monday. Dave is coming to join us for a long weekend and will take her back, Alex and I returning the next day. I then have one more day and return to the office on Thursday. It is wonderful to have it all settled. It was quite a business for us all to fit in together, with permission for leave and so on. Knowing it is coming makes me realise how much I need it. I can feel myself slowing down in the office and the dullness of the work does not help, but that will pass.

On Saturday evening Alex took Kathie to the Turf Club for the BESL party, and I went up the mountain with Jean Outram, as my guest, in her car, to dine at Kuchawe. Homer and Theo gave me a great welcome and we had a magnificent dinner. Jean looked very smart and was at her best and I think enjoyed the evening as much as I did. On Sunday morning the Paynes and Jean's mother came to Alex's house for a drink before lunch and were interested in everything – the bathroom gets the most enthusiastic reaction from everyone! Hazel and Bobby have yet to see it. They have got themselves into the social swim and are coming as soon as the pace has slackened a bit.

I have moved back into Sally's room, where I began. The doors and windows are so placed that I can have the bed against the wall instead of jutting out into the room, which now looks like a sittingroom and gives me far more space.

The rain has stopped and all the birds are singing in the gardens – very homesick-making. It makes me think of Tennyson's 'Birds in the high walled garden . . .'

6th June:

BESL stands for the British Ex-Servicemen's League, a society with very strong backing here, which does a lot of good work behind the scenes. The party was held at the Turf Club, a club which opened about three years ago, at first exclusively for people interested in horses and riding, but now flourishing (especially since the old Zomba club has been threatened with multi-racialism). It is about six miles out, by the airfield.

What a pity the weather is so cold – in the south too, I hear. Hugh Norman-Walker, just home on leave, wrote to Alex on some business matter and mentioned that that day was the coldest May day on record and he was wearing gloves as he wrote!

Mr Butler made a very good impression here. Alex attended a Civil Servants' Association delegation at GH and was most impressed. Arthur said he had *never* seen anyone handle the Press with such complete calm and confidence. His wife shattered everyone at the GH Sundowner by appearing in what Iris described as 'a little brown and white cotton number', while the ladies of Zomba, as it is the cold season, flocked in stiff with brocades and furs!

The Birthday Parade went very well on Saturday morning, I heard. *Bryn* got the OBE, to our great delight, and Peter Youens, also home on leave, got the CMG. I spent the morning in my chalet washing, ironing and mending like mad. On Saturday we went over to Blantyre and saw the film *Can-Can*, with Frank Sinatra, Maurice Chevalier and Shirley MacLaine – very gay and light-hearted. We came back early, as we had to drive to Chileka on Sunday morning to meet Geoffrey, which we duly did, only to find his plane was late at Rome and missed the connection. So Alex had to go again on Monday. On Sunday evening Bobby and Hazel came for a drink and saw the house, which charmed them. On Tuesday I had a very happy tea with Iris, who has been tremendously busy with Leg Co, which lasted four horrible days. However, she is earning money for her holiday! In the evening I had a lovely dinner at Alex's with Geoffrey, who brought a breath of fresh air from home and discussed TV avidly with me. He was very surprised at how up-to-date I was. I told him that was thanks to you. He moves into the Hostel tomorrow, which is nice for me. Last night we went out to dinner with Derek and Betty Matthews, a very nice couple who have come to Zomba recently. I have worked a bit for him, and she is Alex's very competent departmental assistant. Tonight I am having dinner with Alex and Geoffrey again. I must stop and have a bath. Think of me next week at the Lake!

Chapter 24

13th June: Palm Beach

I feel I have no news for you at the moment except: blue sky, hot sun, slight breeze, cool water, warm sand equal paradise! We picked up Iris at 11 yesterday, a beautiful day, and set off in high spirits. As we drove past Kasupi, down the escarpment and crossed the ferry at Liwonde, I experienced a most extraordinary sensation. That lovely sun-drenched landscape was so familiar, but I was looking at it with different eyes – almost as if the young Ann of Kasupi days had died and I was now in another life, looking back on something that had never happened to me. It was quite soul-shaking, as I realised what a long journey I have made, emotionally.

We had a picnic lunch by the roadside and arrived here at three. The weather is absolutely perfect. It is the first time I have seen the Lake in the 'cold' season. The sky is cloudless, the light exquisitely clear, a more distilled gold than in the heat. The water is so high there are only about six feet of beach and then the rondavels, with their shaded *khondes*. The sun is divinely warm. We all have nice rooms and today Alex and I met on his *khonde* for early morning tea and watched the marvellous day begin, with nothing to do but be happy. Iris fits in very restfully. She has Mitzi, her dachshund, with her, who is great fun. She sunbathes beside us and then cools down by lying flat out just below the water line, with only her head clear of the water. Alex is brown and relaxed already and I feel as if someone had undone about a thousand knots inside me! I slept like a top last night.

19th June:

I am sorry this is a short letter, but I do not have yours to answer and there is little news. I feel I am in the middle of a lovely dream. Iris left yesterday morning and we suddenly decided to stay on till Thursday and if possible extend my leave so that I have a full fortnight and return to the office on Monday 25th. I phoned Kathie and it was all arranged in five minutes. Apparently the office is very quiet indeed and Arthur was perfectly happy to spare me till Monday. We felt a few more days, on our own, would be of great benefit, especially as the weather is quite unbelievably fair – glorious day after day exactly the same; brilliant sunshine and cold nights. I am sleeping well for the first time for many moons and Alex is a different man, completely relaxed and carefree. We are both a deep, dark brown.

We had a peaceful and happy time with Iris. Alex was wonderfully unselfish and retired some yards away with his book while we lay side by side in the sun for hours on end, talking forever. On two evenings we went out by motorboat along the shore line – very steamy and tropical, with lots of bird life, mostly fish eagles. When we turned back we faced right into the setting sun. The water was blood red flecked with gold. The hotel people say they have rarely seen such a procession of spectacular sunsets, and I know I shall never forget them. There was one special evening, about six o'clock, when the Lake was like a sheet of opalescent satin stretching away to the dim blue hills on the Portuguese side, while in the east a huge three-quarters moon glittered silver on the water and in the west a deep crimson afterglow turned it firey red. All the guests were standing about in groups, talking in low, spellbound voices.

Dave arrived on Saturday and in the evening we sat outside by the shore under the palms and watched *The Dam Busters*, an old film I have always wanted to see. A Shell Oil representative has been touring with it and obligingly showed it. On Sunday Philip and Mary Richardson came for the day and we all settled on the beach. Mary could not get over the transformation in Alex and me. We have done nothing but sunbathe, swim, do crosswords and play Scrabble in the evening; and the pattern continues. This kind of holiday is exactly what we needed. Palm Beach is very quiet now and Ted and Pixie Sweatman, the owners, are kindness itself.

26th June:

I have reached a complete deadlock in my work, having gone all out since I came back and can now do nothing until the Print produces some material for me, so having had all offers of help refused by the rest of the Department, which appears to be asleep (!) I am quite blatantly using office time in which to begin a letter to you.

The wonderful weather held at the Lake to the very last – quite unbelievably lovely, with those unforgettable sunsets to end each day, and one sunrise, on our shortest day (your longest), when I pulled aside my curtains and saw the sun come up over a black ridge of hills, flooding the water with light and already warm on my face. We left after lunch on Thursday and had a good journey back, which took exactly two and a half hours. I must say, for the first time ever, my heart sank into my boots at sight of the Hostel. It was a shattering return to reality and I woke up from my lovely dream. Philip and Mary kindly gave us dinner that night, as they thought it would help to divert us from post-holiday depression. On Friday we went to Blantyre to collect Alex's new car, only to find it was not ready – an awful disappointment for him. However, I had my hair done and we shopped, had lunch at Ryall's and went to the matinee of an Edna Ferber film called *Cimarion*, a marathon two and a half hours and very good. We then came back to the house and had supper by the fire. The weather is lovely here too, but *freezing*. On Saturday I unpacked properly and got myself settled in. In the evening we had our last holiday fling. We went to the Flamingo, where we had a lovely dinner and dance, and drove back in pure white moonlight, I singing all the French cabaret songs I could remember, which Alex loved. On Sunday morning I helped him fix a lot of household things, plugs and lamp fittings. I am more neat-handed than he, so he has taught me how to do these tasks! At noon Arthur and Derek and Betty Matthews came for drinks, all delighted with the house. Arthur was at his most amusing and had to be asked to lunch, as he stayed on till after two, when the Hostel lunch finishes! We played Scrabble in the evening in an attempt to ward off a dreadful 'Sunday night' feeling! I got a warm welcome in the office, everyone exclaiming over my tan, obvious good health and spirits. Jean is very piano, as her mother had had a bout of terrible sickness and went into hospital today. It is such a shame, as she has been so well.

Yesterday I had tea with Iris and as always we had lots to say. She is the better for her holiday and can now look forward to Linden's summer holidays visit at the end of July.

I have settled down remarkably well after the initial bump. I feel the cold dreadfully and look forward to bed at night with my nice little hot water bottle, and thank goodness I have had no difficulty in sleeping since I came back. Alex is feeling and looking a different man and has also managed to get settled back into office work without too much effort. The great thing about him is that, like me, he loves his work, even if there is far too much of it. He is hoping to get his new car on Thursday, which will be most exciting for him and add to the feeling that he is making a new start, I think, with his nice house and a good holiday behind him.

3rd July:

The lovely weather has broken at last and yesterday and today have been overcast, damp and bone-penetratingly cold.

The main item of news is that on Thursday Alex went over to Blantyre and came back with the prettiest, most graceful and elegant little car you could imagine, like a slim, white bird. It has a heater (which I confess is the most attractive thing about it, to me!), plus lots of gadgets that are fun to have, including a cigarette lighter. It has caused quite a stir because, as you know, in Africa cars are of primary importance and interest. Alex is delighted with it and looks bigger and browner than ever in it. He fills the driving seat, while I nearly vanish in the low passenger seat! It has four gears and he says is as light as air to drive.

On Saturday we had a marathon day. Before lunch we went up to have a drink with Bobby and Hazel, who were dying to have a close look at the car. You should have seen them. They were so excited they all piled in – Bobby, Hazel, Sue and Johnnie – and Shane, their big white labrador, would have followed, had I not *sat* on his back and whispered endearments into his ears! After a sandwich lunch we set off for Blantyre where we met Kathie and Lilian Jennings (her friend who lives in her old home) and saw *Ben Hur*, which is nearly four hours long. I expected to be bored and exhausted, but found it excellent as epics go – good acting, interesting story and incredible spectacle on that huge wide screen. The scenes in Rome were fascinating; and some of the places and details like the Roman standards and the clothes, rang all sorts of bells with me and set up all sorts of memories of Cicero's letters and Caesar's wars. There was a marvellous portrait, very brief, of Caesar, sick, decadent and shaky, with a terribly weak yet fierce, proud face. The figure of Jesus appeared, movingly, several times, always from the back, with long auburn hair and a rough robe, and his shadow was used to great effect. There was a long crucifix-ion scene which came off very well, its crude realities having a quite shattering effect on the imagination. The climax of the film, the chariot race, was tre-mendous, but made me feel sick, as indeed was its intention. We went on to Giovanni's and had delicious steak and a bottle of wine. Kathie and Lilian obviously loved it all, and Alex was a very good host. Norton Weir was there with a party and I had a few words with him. He is as nice as ever, and going most attractively grey. I spent Sunday morning sitting out in the sun with Iris in her garden. It is beautiful just now, full of colour and so quiet and peaceful. We talked from nine till noon! Then Jean and Rex came round to Alex's to see the car and we had a drink together. In the afternoon I made a start on his garden, putting in some plants Iris gave me – brilliant geraniums and verbena, in the zig-zag flowerbed beside the little *khonde*. In the evening we played Scrabble by the fire – a lovely day. I have been busier this week, as the Annual Report page proofs are at last pouring in from the Print. I must know it almost off by heart!

Jean's mother is making a good recovery in hospital and I shall visit her soon.

11th July:

I continue to feel very well and now sleep at night without even thinking about it – wonderful. The weather is very cold and today we are plunged in a *chiperoni*, with the mist down to our ankles and a chill, steady rain. I have been tackling my own little garden again and am delighted with a few wet days to help it on. Alex's garden is still being terraced. Iris gave me a quick growing plant with a pretty white flower, which will make a thick hedge. There are about forty cuttings along the front boundary of the garden, which is most exposed to view from the road. I am looking forward so much to getting it all gradually in order.

We have had a quiet week, as we have been concentrating on the house and garden. On Sunday afternoon we went to Limbe and saw a marvellous film I have always wanted to see – *Room at the Top*, with Lawrence Harvey and Simone Signoret. It was worth the journey just to see her. Limbe was, as always, very cold, and we came straight back for supper by the fire.

18th July:

Alex has acquired a young garden boy called Mustafa. On Saturday after lunch we worked in the garden and planned out where everything should go. The Agricultural Department provides bushes, plants, trees and grass free, so I made out a colourful plan for hibiscus, moonflower, poinsettia, bougainvillaea and morning glory. It will be a great interest to see it all work out, though of course nothing, least of all the immense expanse of grass, will grow much till the small rains in November, but the occasional *chiperoni* helps.

Arthur left on Monday for ten days in Blantyre to attend an Economic Symposium, for which he has (with me) done the publicity, so Jean and I are left to hold the fort. Don Penny returned from long leave today, and we expect a tremendous disruption when he comes in to say hello. Mr Butler's team of advisers arrived yesterday and they have been dashing about. They come into the Hostel tonight, so I shall be able to look them over at lunch tomorrow. I had tea with Iris in her garden yesterday, and then went inside and sat by the log fire till Alex came to fetch me at 6.30 from the office, poor man. On Friday I had a very happy tea with Hazel. She is as sweet as ever and always asks for news of you.

25th July:

I am writing this in bits and pieces today, beginning it just after lunch and I will finish it under the hair dryer later. The weather seems to be 'on the turn' and today is *warm*. I am washing woollens and putting them away in plastic bags, perhaps rather optimistically.

I am terribly busy. Arthur is still over in Blantyre and Jean is off. Her mother, just out of hospital, became very ill again over the weekend and cannot even be moved to hospital, so Jean is nursing her at home. Her next door neighbour is a nurse, and is helping. My career pamphlets work has suddenly raised its ugly head again, so I am up to my eyes, but happy to be so. Don Penny is back, which means a lot of fun and time-wasting, and I have had to be firm about that.

On Saturday Geoffrey invited us to lunch in his nice flat in the Hostel. There were pleasant people there, and we had a very good lunch. Betty Bathurst

Brown, who runs the Hostel and is a good friend of mine, has a golden spaniel bitch who was mated with the Inghams' red spaniel, and she has produced three perfect puppies. After much brooding, Alex has decided to have one. I am, of course, delighted. I think it will be good for him to have a puppy in his house to look after and for company. We are going up on Sunday to see them but will not take one away till about two months from now. We had a quiet weekend as there were no good films on and most of our friends had their children arriving for the school holidays. Last night we called on Iris and Dave, to see Linden, a sweet, thin, pale, very intelligent and friendly girl. She will be twelve in August, and is a confusing mixture of childishness and maturity. She is a wonderful companion for Iris, who looks years younger.

1st August:

Alex has been told there is an important constitutional change (as yet unannounced) coming up in April next year, and has been advised that his presence will be required when it happens, so he reluctantly changed his plans and thinks his long leave will now be in June 1963. It means he does a long tour, but he was told he would definitely be given another fortnight's local leave round about Christmas to help him through. I shall wait on till then also. Alex has had to go through so much alone, I do not want to ask any more of him. There are other reasons as well, of course, and these extra weeks may be very important in ensuring that our affairs will be properly settled.

Jean's mother is better and things are therefore quieter in the office, as Jean is back. On Saturday we went over to Blantyre to the afternoon cinema and saw a wonderful but desperately creepy film, *The Innocents*, with Deborah Kerr and Michael Redgrave. I saw the play in London, with Flora Robson, and have read the book, Henry James's *Turn of the Screw*. We nearly walked out but managed to see it through – and both spent an almost sleepless night, rigid with fear! I hardly stopped staring at my windows all night! I am only now not thinking of it in bed at night. We went on and had a much-needed drink at Ryall's, and a very subdued supper. It was not funny at the time. I used to have nerves of steel at *any* film, but not so now. On Sunday morning we went before lunch for drinks with the Bathurst Browns and saw the spaniel puppies, lovely wee golden bundles, still with their eyes shut. After lunch we pottered in the garden, which is beginning to look like one, with terraces completed, grass planted and Iris's hedge coming up: syringa, it is called. Yesterday I had tea with Iris and Linden. Alex came to fetch me and I sat by his lovely log fire and read *The Times* while he went off to a Sundowner at GH, from which he returned very promptly with Bobby and Hazel, who are about to go off to the Rhodesias for a fortnight's holiday with the three children.

By the most extraordinary coincidence, Tom Chalmers [Ron's guardian] is here from Dar-es-Salaam, to advise the Government on broadcasting. I see him every day as his base is Arthur's office and Jean is typing his report. He has not changed a bit – charming and madly friendly; also obviously thrilled and impressed by the light-hearted atmosphere in our Department. He is staying up at Kuchawe, but no doubt sees a lot of Ron. *What* a small world!

7th August:

I am glad Jess is pleased with the little bead bird. The African who made it we call our 'bead man'. He just turned up at the office some time before the Bulawayo Trade Fair, in which we have a pavilion, with a huge relief map of Nyasaland on the floor. Kathie is always in charge and usually takes ivory and wood carvings which she places on the map. This year she commissioned the bead man to make some items for her and he produced wonderful little models in brilliant colours – snakes, spiders, lizards, giraffes, palm trees, leopards, frogs and chameleons – all quite strikingly alive. It takes him two days to make each one. They were immensely popular at the Fair and he has had masses of orders since, which is highly satisfactory.

The warmer weather has definitely come and last Saturday I put on a cotton skirt and blouse for the office. I of course am already blooming from the change. Robbie Robinson said to me today, 'There's something special-looking about you these days. You look sort of soft and pretty!'

I had tea with Iris and Linden last Friday and we had great fun. Later Linden tactfully went out for a walk with Dave and left us to talk. That evening, after supper, Geoffrey came down for an hour. He was very depressed and we managed to cheer him up a bit. On Saturday Philip and Mary came to lunch at Alex's, and then he and I had a marvellous afternoon in the garden. There are signs of life in it now, with fairly hefty cuttings planted in brick-edged beds. On Sunday Alex worked in the morning and I did all my chores at the chalet. We had a drink with the Paynes before lunch, mainly to see Jean's mother, who has made a good recovery and flies back to Northern Rhodesia next week. They have a beautiful garden and it was pleasant to sit out and enjoy a different view. Alex again worked on Monday morning and I sat out in the sun on my *khonde* for the whole morning and got gloriously brown and glowing. We met at Geoffrey's flat for a drink before lunch, and then bore him off to Alex's for lunch with us, as he was very low. His wife has decided to come out only for the Christmas holidays for a month with the children, which means Geoffrey has to face the prospect of *another* tour in the Hostel – really dreadful for him.

Alex has heard through his lawyer that his divorce is through and will be finalised in October. It has been *such* a strain waiting for that piece of news. We just jumped into the car and drove off to Blantyre after tea and had a very early candlelit dinner at Giovanni's. I felt no great joy (how could I, with so much sadness involved?), but an *enormous* weight seemed to lift from me, and from Alex, and we could begin to feel its effects from that moment, and more and more as the hours went by and we sat and watched it happen to each other. So, one more step towards the light.

I am working very hard, mostly deadly dull stuff, but Arthur gives me some congenial jobs to do for him, when he can, bless him. (Bryn was right. I should *never* have taken on the career pamphlets for the Public Service Commission.) Tom Chalmers is still with us, and fits happily into the friendly office atmosphere. He thinks Zomba is almost too beautiful to be true and not in the least 'African'. He is right, of course, but I could take him on *ulendo* a mere ten miles away and he would have a fit!

14th August:

On Friday evening Kathie paid her first visit to Alex's house and stayed for supper and Scrabble. I had prepared, the night before, a steak and kidney pie and strawberry mousse, so we had a good supper, with Portuguese wine. She loved the house and approved of the layout of the garden, which she saw just before dark. On Saturday evening we joined Rex and Jean and went up the mountain for dinner. It was the night of the Red Cross Ball, so we knew we would have the place free of Zomba society. We dressed up to make it a real party, and I wore my French slipper satin dress. Alex loves it and says it is glamorous. We were given a great welcome at Kuchawe and a superb dinner, as always. I sunbathed all morning on Sunday and was glowing like a radiator by lunch time. In the afternoon we drove to Blantyre and saw a marvellous film, *Tunes of Glory*, with John Mills and Alec Guiness, the latter speaking with a flawless Scots accent. It was filmed on location at Stirling Castle, so the setting and atmosphere were completely authentic.

21st August:

You ask about Mr Butler's visit. He is highly thought of and gave the impression of great integrity. His assurances to the civil servants were received with belief, which is more than can be said of some of our other VIP visitors. At present he is breaking his holiday in Mull for more talks in London, as you will know, so things must be coming to a head.

I am happy in the office, with a pause in my careers pamphlets work, and busy producing another 'fact sheet' on Nyasaland. I must send you a copy to show you how far we have travelled from my weekly Bulletin days! Alex is having a bad time in the office, and I have persuaded him to leave at five, when we do some gardening before it gets dark. It is soothing to see things growing. All the bushes have taken and have little green lumps and shoots showing. We had a freak shower of rain the other night, which helped.

On Saturday afternoon we went to Blantyre and saw a very light film, *The Grass is Greener*, with Deborah Kerr and Cary Grant – lovely clothes and a beautiful stately home of England setting. We had a glorious day of sunshine on Sunday and spent it sunbathing and gardening. Yesterday I went to Linden's twelfth birthday tea. She had two friends, their mother and myself, with a marvellous sit-down tea which reminded me of our parties at Dunalastair. The cake was not big enough for candles, and Iris had made a lovely centre piece of white lilies and twelve long red candles, which were lit. There were ice cream and crackers and the children were in raptures.

Alex's puppy has his eyes open and looks delicious. He is to be called Jamie – my choice. Betty Bathurst Brown brought him in a basket to my chalet the other day, with his two sisters, to let me see them – three silky, square, heaving bundles of energy, with teeth like needles! The weather is blissfully warming up and the jacaranda is appearing on the tops of the trees already – it grows downwards in profusion. I had only one blanket last night – lovely.

28th August:

The weather is quite heavenly, and I am well, relaxed and full of energy. The heat really does transform my life. I feel steadier, more hopeful and happier than I have done for years.

On Friday I went to Blantyre with Alex. The car was in being serviced all day, so we had a hot, tiring time, walking everywhere. However, I had a very successful session with the eye specialist, a Southern Rhodesian called Rivron, very thorough and such a nice, dapper, professional man. My weak left eye has improved and my right eye remains unchanged, so he will simply put in a new left lens. It was a great relief to me, as I always worry when I start to have eye headaches.

We have heard from Bryn who, praise be, returns by sea on 13th October. On Saturday we went to the Flamingo with Philip and Mary and had a happy evening. It was a warm, moonlight night and we sat out under the stars, and danced after dinner. On Sunday we had a wonderful restful day, sunbathing and pottering in the garden. Geoffrey came for a drink at lunch time. He gets very lonely and down, and knows that he can come and be cheered up whenever he feels like it. He is such a nice man, but very shut in and far too good at pretending he is light and casual when in fact he feels things very deeply. Jean went off for a week at the Lake on Saturday, so I am very busy and enjoying it, doing her work as well as my own. Last night we went to dinner with the Richardsons to help entertain an Imperial Defence man, ex-Navy, very smooth, and a little glib about his grasp of affairs out here. Derek and Betty Matthews were there too, and we rather closed in on him and gave him quite an enlightening evening, which he was civilised enough to take in good part.

I am going to have a bath and change. Alex is picking me up just before dark and I shall plant morning glory in his garden.

5th September:

The weather is wonderful – dreamy mornings, hot days and cool evenings. It is 4.10 and I am sitting out in the sun on my *khonde*. There has been a huge forest fire raging all day on the mountain, and the air is like autumn with smoke, a lovely hazy blue floating over the mountain slopes. The jacaranda is everywhere and all the other blossom pours over every hedge, bush and tree. I am absolutely blooming myself. I sit out every teatime in the sun till it goes behind the mountain at 4.40. It will get later as the days go on – eventually 5.30.

I had tea with Hazel last Monday and heard all about their holiday. I see little of them at present, because of the school holidays, as she devotes herself to giving the children a happy time.

Our lives have been invaded by the arrival of Jamie, whom we collected on Saturday after tea. He is beautiful; a golden-fawn spaniel in miniature. Betty had tired him out and filled him with food, so he slept in my arms in the car and on my lap all evening, and did not come to till 3.00 a.m., when he let Alex know he was lonely and miserable! He is very clean and fastidious in his habits and it is taking no time at all to house-train him – thank goodness, as I could not bear to smack such a tiny, baby-faced creature – his nose is still square and his brow has a big wrinkle in it! At present Alex has to take him to the office, where he lies on Alex's feet or sleeps in his box, or goes out onto the grass, where he is admired from afar by the chaps upstairs and petted by passing stenographers, who stop to coo over him. One of our PCs looked in with haggard face yesterday (he has just acquired a pekinese puppy) and asked Alex, 'Getting much sleep?' Alex said, 'No', and was told, 'Take 'em into bed. It's the only way to get peace!' However, that is *not* the answer!

11th September:

I was interested to hear about the TV programme on the Common Market. Alex is very concerned and interested, and is if anything anti, though he agrees that the only Commonwealth ties we really want to preserve are the big three, Canada, Australia and New Zealand. As Kathie says, it will soon be a collection of dreadful little independent states interfering with things of which they are entirely ignorant, like the Afro-Asian block in the United Nations, whose presence is ludicrous but dangerous.

The weather continues to be wonderful. My own little garden is a mass of colour, and everything in Alex's is bursting with sap. The verbena cuttings I got from Iris are all in bloom and her honeysuckle is thriving. I have been so occupied with Jamie I have not had time yet to plant seed boxes but I hope to do so at the weekend. On Thursday I got the afternoon off, very unexpectedly, to go to Blantyre with Kathie to help her choose some clothes which she needs for the trip home. I had just done some good work for Arthur and she caught him in the right mood and he had said 'yes' before he knew where he was! I ordered two sandwich lunches from the Hostel and Kathie brought a thermos of iced orange juice, and we went off straight from the office and had a picnic lunch *en route*. It was a glorious day and we were lucky with our shopping, and found some lovely things for Kathie at our first attempt. I bought a basket, drinking bowl and rubber bone for the doggum, and for myself a very sophisticated cocktail dress and a pair of sky blue sailcloth jeans to replace my yellow ones which have served me well for five years. The seat simply gave, one day, all over, when I sat down rather heavily in a state of exhaustion after playing with Jamie. I had to walk down to my chalet with my handbag clutched to my rear! We had iced coffee and a roll for tea in a new café in Limbe called 'The Bamboo' and drove home in the lovely deep golden light that washes the landscape towards sunset. I think Kathie loved her day and I enjoyed it very much. I forgot to say my main purchase was a chair for Alex for his *khonde*, a black tubular frame with green plastic strips woven on the seat and back. It is very comfortable and cool, and easy to clean. That is for his birthday on 4th October. Kathie took me straight to Alex's, where I found a large man and a tiny dog chewing their nails over my late return. All my purchases for Jamie were instantly accepted and appeciated, especially the basket. We had a lovely sunny quiet weekend, not going out or seeing anybody, just pottering in the house and garden and getting Jamie settled into a routine. He is quite a handful, but so rewarding, as he learns quickly.

Kathie leaves at the end of the month and I have been collecting money for a present for her. The presentation party is to be next Friday at 3.30.

19th September:

The weather continues to be glorious. In fact it is hot enough for people to begin grumbling about it already!

The Annual Report is at last out, so I shall send you a copy by sea mail whenever the distribution to officials is complete and I get my own copy. I wonder what will be produced in its stead next year, if anything. They are quite capable of bringing in an American 'expert' with four children, free passages, house provided, car loan and so on, as is now the fashion in developing countries. We are all absolutely sick of the changing face of Nyasaland! The lowering of standards, the fear, the disintegration of good race relations and the corruption. I write very little about it, but it does go on. All the decent Europeans will be forced to go, to preserve their integrity, and only the opportunists will be left – and recruited. You would not believe the waste of money, the bungling, the personal spite and greed for power. I am a bit nervous about writing like this, but have risked it. You can imagine how Alex is feeling. He has to fight for *people* in Establishments, black and white, so his work is one of the most important outposts of integrity left. No wonder his ulcer keeps flaring up.

I had a day in Blantyre with Arthur on Monday to choose a farewell present for Kathie. He drove like the wind there and back. He is a marvellous escort and I had a great day with him. Linden and Iris came down for tea last week. They are in Salisbury now, on local leave, and Linden flies home from there. I am very tired today, so this is a bit disjointed. I shall do better next week.

26th September:

Kathie's leave date has been put off for about six weeks, as it was discovered at her retirement medical that she should have an operation, as soon as possible. It had been a bit of an anti-climax, as all the farewell parties were arranged. She had to cancel her passage, but luckily got another lovely one on the *City of Durban*, which sails in mid-November. It does mean she will see Bryn, which is nice. We carried on with all our arrangements and held her farewell party last Friday. I worked very hard all day, by myself, as Arthur kept Jean busy. I had the big empty office next to Arthur's new one cleared and cleaned, and pinned up bright tray cloths on the walls to hide marks and stains. I tied huge bows of red ribbon to cover bare light bulbs and unearthed a big Nyasaland crest for one wall. I got roses from three different sources and had six big bowls of them, and eight glue jars bearing one perfect bud each. We had seventy-six guests coming and had beer and sherry with hired glasses; and *the cake*! It was a *yard* long and weighed nearly a stone! It was a rich fruit cake, long, low and flat, with beautiful ribbons and icing, and 'Bon Voyage, Kathie' written in blue icing right along the top. I arranged for our African photographer to take a photo, which I will send you. I put the cake, with paper plates, on a side table, with twenty-four big carnations, pink to match the icing, in a black bowl behind it. It really looked like a party room and Arthur was charmed with everything, and thanked me very nicely indeed. With his permission, I fetched Kathie 15 minutes before the party was due to start, and took her in to see what we had done. As I expected, she was almost overcome with emotion and I took her into my office, sat her down and gave her a small brandy, which worked wonders, and by 3.30 she was bright-eyed and slightly flushed! Our guests, led by the Chief Secretary, began to stream in promptly at 3.30. All the chaps from upstairs and down were there and masses of stenographers. We had taken a collection from the whole of the CS's Ministry, which came to £35. We gave her a double string of lovely pearls which cost £25, and a cheque for £10, with which she intends to buy a chair for the house at home, where all the Nyasaland visitors will sit! Arthur excelled himself with an absolutely perfect speech, and Kathie very briefly replied with an equally good one, in which she said that having helped Nyasaland for years she was now going to England to help *that* undeveloped country, as she was too young yet just to retire in comfort in Scotland! She then opened her presents and cut the cake. A tremendous party ensued, everyone so affectionate and appreciative, and I think she loved every minute.

Poor Alex missed it all, as his ulcer finally caught up with him and he had to take a few days off and stayed lying low till Saturday morning, when he emerged very much more like himself. I managed to get a lift down every day, to exercise Jamie and see to things generally. We had another quiet weekend. Jamie is thriving and in high spirits. I am busy in the office and therefore happy. The weather is perfect and I am brown and relaxed. I have tea outside and stay in the sun till it vanishes behind the mountain, then I bath, change and join Alex and Jamie for a walk on the golf course – too many dogs in the botanical gardens. Alex's garden is flourishing and will really burgeon forth with the rains in November. We have lots of seeds in boxes now.

2nd October:

The weather is really hot and visibility is reduced to a small, dusty world, with the plain and Mlanje absolutely invisible. The jacaranda is fully out and Zomba wears its look of paradise. Yesterday after the office Kathie drove me right round the high road and slowly back, so that we could feast our eyes – lovely for me, and of course this will be her last sight of it, which is an almost unbearable thought. She goes into hospital on Thursday, Alex's birthday, and is operated on next day. It has been rather a weary wait for her.

We have been very quiet and domesticated again this week. We are enjoying Jamie so much. He loves us both and knows that in the evenings and at weekends he has all my attention, while Alex is obviously his master and mainstay during the night (!), in the morning and at lunch time, at all of which times, I am told, he keeps him on his toes! He has no fear and marches up to huge dogs, through their legs and out the other end before they have even begun to react. We have been busy in the garden, which is a source of great pleasure to us both. Jamie no longer goes to the office, and seems happy and settled with just the run of the house and garden.

I am busy preparing for Alex's birthday. He has asked fourteen friends for drinks in the evening and I shall do the patsy-go-lows myself. Bryn is expected within a few days. Arthur goes off on local leave, and then moves to a different Ministry. He has been offered the post of Tourist Adviser, in the Ministry of Trade and Industry, at a huge salary, and has naturally jumped at it. He will do a terrific job, I am sure. It is far more his line than the down to earthness of pure information work that is essential in our Department.

10th October:

My hairdresser has moved to Blantyre, but I have found another who is good enough. She is Afrikaans, young and pretty, with a bad limp from polio. She has overcome her disability wonderfully, especially as she is on her feet all day. She is *very* Dutch in accent. Her name is Mrs Geldenhuys.

Kathie had her operation on Friday. Jean and I have phoned every day to hear how she is. I think they have let her have too many visitors too soon. However, we dashed up in the office jeep at ten today, through a sea of jacaranda blossom, and found her well enough, though still under drugs to keep down the pain, which I gather is intense. She had managed to crawl through and have a bath yesterday. She looks suddenly older and frailer, but that may pass. Bryn arrived back on Monday evening in his beautiful new grey Jaguar (his life's ambition). They are staying with friends at Kalimbuka, and I waved to him from Alex's garden just before dark. He is coming into the office tomorrow – lovely for us all to have him back. I want to have a talk with him and try to get more work to do, and get as much varied experience as I can. In this weather I want to tackle anything! Iris came down after tea on Sunday to see the garden, and stayed on for a while. Dave has gone off on local leave but she was not able to get away from her job.

The weather is *hot* – real October weather. Alex is cheerful, despite days of ulcer pain. The burden of work in his office is responsible. He always makes an enormous effort to have a happy time with me and make the best of things, as he knows how I worry about him and how helpless I feel. Jamie is growing fast, though still really a very wee dog. He is highly strung and has to be watched and considered.

We had a lovely party on Alex's birthday. Everything went smoothly and all the small eats vanished. Alex is delighted with his nice cool chair and has been enjoying its comfort. We had another quiet weekend, and I sunbathed ruthlessly, so that I am dark, dark brown. Hazel I hardly see at present as she is busy with rehearsals for *The Yeomen of the Guard*.

17th October:

Jamie becomes more endearing and manageable daily, and we really do get far more pleasure out of life because of him. He has such a lovely nature and plenty of spirit as well. The weather is absolutely *boiling* hot, and I am blissfully happy and go through my work like a bulldozer. Bryn is back, bless him, and all is sweetness and light in the office. He has given me *masses* of interesting work (which he found in Arthur's IN tray) and I am off on all sorts of ploys which I shall mention as they take shape. He showed me over (!) his Jaguar this morning, a glorious car, and drove me down the road and back just to get the feel – sublime! He looks very well and very trim. He is greatly taken with my improved health and spirits and gazes at me with his brown eyes so friendly and pleased – such a dear man. Arthur is feeling the heat and the fact that his rather beautiful nose is slightly out of joint in favour of a bigger Welsh one. However, I think he is also feeling a little sad to be leaving us, as he does on Saturday. He has local leave and then returns to his new post. I shall miss his lightness of touch, his gaiety and good temper. I shall still be able to enjoy his company in the Hostel.

We went to Blantyre on Monday. Alex had the car serviced in the morning and I got my hair done beautifully in a new salon next to my favourite coffee shop. We did some Christmas shopping in slow stages as Blantyre was sickeningly hot. However, we had not been out of Zomba for weeks, and we both enjoyed the day. Leg Co began yesterday and ends tomorrow, an apparently uneventful session. I hope to see Iris next week, when she has recovered from coping with *Hansard*.

23rd October:

Having raved about the heat and my general good health I had to pay for it. On Wednesday there was a freak storm out of a very darkened sky. It poured with rain, the wind tore at the trees and the temperature dropped treacherously. The next two days were grey and miserable and on Saturday morning I woke up to realise I had a feverish cold which is going the rounds. I have felt really low until today, when the sun appeared again and it is as hot as ever. I spent the weekend lying down on any available horizontal surface or resisting the impulse to do so. I just felt I could not stay on my feet. In spite of this we went to dinner with Bobby and Hazel on Saturday night, to cheer ourselves up. They had also asked a rather dull couple, which was disappointing. I struggled along but after dinner when Hazel said gaily, 'Now we're *all* going to play silly games,' I suddenly broke out in an icy sweat, quite involuntarily, burned up all over, and was led out and taken back to the hostel by a very worried but relieved Alex! I hope to have tea with Hazel soon and enjoy her on my own. We had a very quiet Sunday. I got myself a good book, *Sundry Creditors* by Nigel Balchin, and just lay about all day, while Alex wrote letters in his study and Jamie sidled lovingly from one room to another to keep an eye on both! His coat is like golden silk, and he is quite slender now. He had an injection on Saturday morning for distemper and hard pad, so he was slightly feverish too! Kathie came out of hospital on Saturday and is now at her own home outside Blantyre for ten days, then comes back to friends in Zomba. I wish now she were away, as it will be a sad departure, however much she is content to go. She is looking lovely, if a little frail.

Arthur had his last day in the office on Saturday morning. Bryn was far too busy settling in to be consulted about a party, so Jean and I made some small eats and bought bottles of Babycham. We had a small gathering in Jean's office at elevenses, and I think Arthur was genuinely sad to go, though he put up a good front. Geoffrey came and had a drink with us on Saturday at lunch time, much more cheerful, as he had just organised a bedroom in the Hostel for his children at Christmas. It will be nice to have a happy family around at Christmas, which approaches with alarming speed. I have now got all my cards ready to write and send off next month. It does not seem a year since last time at all! Alex is well and absorbed in worrying about my cold!

31st October:

We have all been greatly exercised over the Cuban missile crisis, which mercifully seems to have died down. The thought of war is ghastly enough, but it seems particularly terrible when one is so far from home, family and country. It cast a dreadful shadow over everyone, as no doubt it did at home too.

After a few cool days we are back to glorious weather, but there are signs of the approaching rains – heavy thunderclouds after tea and an oppressiveness that leaves people gasping. I had tea with Iris on Wednesday, at last. It was a beautiful day and we walked all round her garden. She is delighted at my growing interest in gardening and it now forms quite a large part of our conversation. On Thursday I had tea with Hazel, which is always delightful. David and Margaret Baxter are in Zomba with their three children. David came up to the office on Friday, giving me a lovely surprise. He looks much older but is still such a likeable man. I am to go to tea with them some day soon. Margaret is in bed with malaria but getting better. On Saturday we had the unusual experience of going together to a big lunch party given by Derek and Betty Matthews, now good friends of ours. Betty very thoughtfully showed me the list of guests to see if we would fit in all right. Well, we did. It was most stimulating and enjoyable for me and it was lovely to see so many old familiar faces without feeling in any way embarrassed. I talked to everyone, non-stop. Alex went his own way and also enjoyed himself very much. We left in time to drive to Blantyre and see the 4.30 matinee of *Never on Sunday*, which neither of us much liked. I was interested to see Melina Mercouri, but it was too noisy, ebullient and shallow for me. We bumped into the Richardsons afterwards, and they asked if they could join us for dinner at Giovanni's, and of course we said yes, so bang went our tête-à-tête evening. We had quiet days on Sunday and Monday and went back to the office very brown and rested. A lot of people have been to the Lake, which is scorchingly hot in this weather, and the Hostel looks like a seaside boarding house, with scarlet faces and peeling backs. Jamie continues to enchant us. After he has dinner, about 6.45, we have the ritual of ear-washing, with an old red face flannel of Alex's, which he then fights for, all round the bathroom, growling furiously. Then he carries his brush, I his comb, onto the mat outside and I groom him, with diminishing opposition, as he realises how soothing it is, and then he is free to flit about like a golden shadow in the garden, stalking insects within the circle of light from the *khonde*. He knows that I go away at the end of an evening and jumps neatly into his basket as soon as I start collecting my things!

Today Kathie came in to say goodbye – awful, awful. My heart failed me, hers too. Bryn's office is beyond mine so she came in to me first and then went on to his. I was mopping up as quietly as possible when she walked back past my doorway, and had the sense to ignore me and walk away. [That was the last time I saw Kathie.] Bryn came in almost at once, blowing his nose, and found me shakily putting on my dark glasses. Work was out of the question and we talked for the rest of the afternoon, of Kathie, of our realisation that this was only the first of a great landslide of departures from our loved Nyasaland, and of the sadness that lies ahead for us all, after sharing so much together over the years. I have never seen Bryn so upset and I was still trembling as I walked down to the Hostel, feeling we had shared a tremendous moment of truth. *None* of us can bear to talk about it, and that was the first time Bryn and I brought it out into the open.

7th November:

My cold has gone, but I have had a few days of horrible nausea, caused by heat exhaustion, I am sure. My room at night is like an oven and it is difficult to sleep. I can take any amount of blazing, direct sunshine, but now that the thunderstorms are building up in the huge heavy clouds which cover the sun, the heat mounts to furnace pitch indoors and for most of the night, as there is no through draught and the chalet is low lying. Yesterday morning I was sick after breakfast and I felt it might happen at any time in the day. It made me realise how some women feel for most of the hot season. There is a chance of a bedroom in the Hostel itself which is cooler and more private, so I may change over. I am too exhausted to contemplate such a move just yet. Hazel thinks I am still suffering from reaction to the long months of stress and strain.

I had tea with the Baxters on Monday, and they both said I was looking better and more serene than they had ever known me. They were as kind as they could be and told me they intended to go on with their friendships with both Ron and me, without any difference, which pleased me very much. They have a *delightful* family, lively and noisy, but such nice children, with good manners and well disciplined. They all went off to the fireworks display at the Club, and I walked up to Alex's for supper in a lovely red sunset afterglow. We have had sudden showers of rain every day this week, which have lightened the atmosphere. It has been appallingly oppressive, and everyone is ailing and tired. I am very busy and enjoy every minute.

I have no news for you, as I have been lying very low. The garden is coming on in leaps and bounds: yesterday there were thirty-seven blooms on our morning glory. Arthur is back from his local leave in a game reserve in Northern Rhodesia, very brown, and bursting with tales of the animals he saw, photographed and was chased by! Jamie is full of *joie de vivre*. He had his anti-rabies injection on Saturday, which gave him stiff muscles and a temperature, but he recovered by evening and was scampering about as usual. He has a passion for bones, which he enjoys for hours lying on his special mat, which he tries to dig up in moments of frustration or boredom. Geoffrey is producing *Charlie's Aunt* for Christmas, which will be a popular choice. Iris has taken a cottage on the mountain for two weeks, as the heat was making her ill. We are hoping to go up and visit her. Peter Youens is back from leave, looking very well. Diana has stayed at home with the two girls, who are at school. There are so many separated families in Zomba, it is sad, but with children, what else can they do?

13th November:

I have not managed to get up the mountain to see Iris. It has rained every day or night, briefly but heavily, since I last wrote and the road is very bad. She is feeling the better for the cool weather, which she loves. They have taken the cottage where Ron and I spent a wet and impecunious local leave from Chiradzulu. The Baxters have been posted to Zomba, and David is in the Ministry of Education, poor man. I still have Bryn's little wireless, which he has kindly let me keep and I hear the news at 7.00 a.m. and 1 o'clock. The reception is bad now, with so much thunder about. Jamie gets covered in mud, and we have a long toilette each evening, from which he emerges looking very beautiful, I completely exhausted!

Bobby and Hazel came for a drink at lunch time on Saturday at Alex's, and we had a happy hour with them. Bobby, working himself almost to a standstill in the Ministry of Finance, looked pale and tired out, but he has a great capacity for enjoying his friends.

We had a quiet, happy weekend, gardening between downpours. I finished writing my Christmas cards while Alex went to the Remembrance Service, which was held in a violent thunderstorm. I have been doing some cooking, and getting to know the *electric stove*. I have had a lot of interruptions, as the Hostel is very full of people and lonely visitors keep dropping in.

21st November:

I am quite recovered from my low spell, and enjoying feeling really well again. I am up to my eyes in the office. Dr Banda's new tax starts in January – compulsory for everyone. It is graded and very complicated, and as Kathie is not here to translate it into Chinyanja, I have been given the desperate task of simplifying it in English, to be printed in English and the Chinyanja translation, in pamphlets for the Africans. The hours simply fly, and I emerge at the end of the day with my hair on end and my nostrils flaring, 'looking like a horse', as Elspeth used to say! Douglas Fromings, the Provincial Information Officer in Lilongwe, has come down to take Arthur's place. He is a delightful man, about fifty, an ex-missionary with a very dry sense of humour. He fits in perfectly and we are all happy together. Iris is having another week up the mountain. We have not yet visited her, as Alex dislikes the road in this weather. We have rain about every two days now, with some fairly substantial thunderstorms. I find the lightning more alarming than I used to. (I write this every year!) Iris was down at her house the other day collecting some work, and phoned me. She said the big dam on the plateau was emptied by some frightful mistake, and there are sandbanks and little pools which are attracting all sorts of rare and interesting bird life, so she practically lives there during the day. Even an otter appeared, but had to be shot, regretfully, as it was massacring the fish that are still living in isolated patches of water in hollows. The garden is lovely, with grass spreading over our stretches of hot red earth, and the morning glory and hibiscus are covered in bright flowers. Jamie is a young dog now. Alex sometimes brings him in the car when he comes to pick me up, and he sits quietly on my knee with his front paws on the door handle (locked) and his nose resting on the window ledge, his ears blowing, enjoying the delicious variety of smells offered during our drive past the Indian stores and the African hospital.

Alex, at my insistence, went for a medical and got a clean bill of health, to our intense relief, excepting, of course, the ulcer. The doctor insisted he takes an occasional tranquilliser when the office is particularly hectic, as he says Alex is in a state of hypertension. It has cheered us up. Alex dreaded that he had high blood pressure but it is perfectly normal. We have been having a quiet time, from choice. We have already received two invitations to Christmas dinner and are beginning to make a few plans ourselves. It is difficult in this heat to discuss turkey and mince pies. We are going to a house warming party at Bryn's on 1st December, which should be fun. His son Lawrence is a perfect pet – simply a replica of Bryn in miniature. When I see them together I have to resist an impulse to hug them *both*!

28th November:

The weather is dreadful: sudden tremendous downpours of rain, shattering thunder and savage lightning, usually in the early evening or in the night. During the day it is stupifyingly hot –unbelievable and beyond what *anyone* can recall in Zomba. I said to Douglas Fromings yesterday, 'I feel like melting butter,' and he said, 'That's nothing. I feel *far* more ominous than that. I feel I might burst into flame!' Everyone is limp, exhausted and slightly distrait. My memory suddenly deserts me. I dial a number and before it is answered I find in panic I have forgotten what I want to say. I have had to replace the receiver quietly after a deathly 'ush from me while an irate chap has shouted, 'Yes? Yes? Hello?' Bryn is even worse, and stands about in doorways clutching his head and muttering, 'There was something I wanted to . . .' I am very busy; my hands shake at the least exertion and I leave streaks of sweat wherever I place my hands and arms. Everyone's voice is several tones higher than normal, and tempers are easily frayed. It does not affect my temper, which is at its best in the office, but it makes me very wound up and I find I am driving myself at a ridiculous pace. It is all shared experience and less trying than it sounds, because we are all sympathetic and laugh a lot at the general lunatic atmosphere.

The only one who gets a bit nippy is Jean, who is a very methodical, tidy person and wants her routine to work like clockwork, without making any allowance for human error in those about her! My Personal Tax pamphlet has been very well received and passed by the chaps upstairs, which makes the enormous effort worthwhile. (Bryn is quietly *very* pleased.) I am about to launch into another simplification exercise – of the new constitution, which I am not looking forward to, but it is all experience and essential work at this stage. The Constitutional Conference [in London] apparently went well, though there are one or two shaky patches in the constitution for those with eyes to read between the lines.

Alex is much better, I am happy to say, standing up to the heat well and calming down under the influence of his pills, which he takes at infrequent intervals. Jamie is feeling the heat, and frequents the cool stone floor beyond the carpet. The floor is polished, and when he has obviously warmed the place he is on, we simply give him a gentle push, and he slides along to a fresh patch, rolling an eye gratefully. I occasionally take him the rounds at the Hostel, to visit a few chosen admirers. He is a deep golden brown and his coat has such a sheen it looks as if it has been oiled.

We had a lovely sociable weekend for a change. We had a drink at lunch time with Bobby and Hazel on Saturday, sitting out on their airy *khonde*, with its splendid view of Mlanje, which after the rain has emerged to dominate the landscape again. We then drove over to Blantyre after lunch and saw *The Misfits*, with Clark Gable, Marilyn Monroe and Montgomery Clift. It was very moving, though I felt it just missed its target. There were some terrible scenes of cowboys hunting down and roping wild mustangs – all part of the symbolism of the story. We had a quiet dinner at Ryall's, discussing the film and agreeing he cheated, understandably, by giving it a happy ending. It was written by Monroe's ex-husband, Arthur Miller. On Sunday morning we went to an excellent party given by Don and Molly Penny to celebrate the birth of their daughter. (They live opposite Alex.) It was a boiling hot, radiant day and everyone drank rather a lot of champagne. Bryn put in a brief appearance with Lawrence, who met Jamie for the first time and liked him. I had shut him in the kitchen but of course the boys let him out when he made a fuss and across the road he came like a bolt from the blue, dodging among the cars arriving at the party. I borrowed a piece of string and took him back to the house for safety.

5th December:

Things go on as usual, with a little more rain each week in preparation for the rains, which usually contrive to break on Christmas morning. It means the temperature drops at night, so I get a good night's sleep again. Well, I should! There have been eight burglaries in the Hostel in the last few weeks, so there is now a two-man police patrol (African) every two hours from 6.00 p.m. till 6.00 a.m. I am wakened up by them as they pound past the chalet. They then pound back half an hour later and the pattern is repeated, but it is rather reassuring.

We had a very pleasant evening at Bryn's on Saturday, leaving behind a small dog with a big bone, the only thing that consoles Jamie for our absence. Chris, as always, had laid on a wonderful buffet supper and Bryn is a very easy host. After supper they put on records and started dancing the 'Twist', which I had not seen. Chris and Don Penny were terrific and threw themselves into it with great gusto. I decided it is not for me! Douglas Fromings said in my ear at one point, 'Go to any African village and you'll see much the same thing, done better!' Anyway, the younger people had a great time. We left, feeling rather elderly, about eleven, and I think Bryn would have liked to come with us!

We both got the day off on Monday and did our Christmas shopping in Blantyre. I had my hair done and she took off three inches, a great relief in this weather. We had a successful day, though it was very hot and we were glad to leave, after an early tea in *The Bamboo*. We are booked up over the Christmas season, with our own entertaining and that of others.

We are all very busy in the office and enjoying it. I have had a lot of interruptions with this, so I hope it makes sense. Alex is well and cheerful.

12th December:

We are having wet, muggy weather without much sunshine, and there is no doubt that the rains have come early this year, without the usual flourish. I have been unable to move into the room in the Hostel as there was a sudden influx of people, but I am content to stay here. It is by far the nicest position and I have a quiet, independent neighbour. As long as I can get my outdoor rain clothes organised, I can put up with the rainy season. We have been gardening madly in the evenings, as the ground is perfect and things just grow as we watch. People actually stop and admire on their evening strolls. The temperature has fallen with the rain, and life has quickened in the office. There is a great clearing out and burning of secret files in all departments, and other work takes second place. Kathie left quite a pile and I am dealing with them – hair raising! She was in no state of mind to do any work towards the end. I sent her a long letter to Cape Town. We had a lovely visit from Bobby and Hazel the other night. She has had low fever and was not looking her usual vivid self. She has taken over the catering at the Hostel for a few weeks and it is good to have a change of food, though it is always excellent. Peaches and strawberries are in great abundance, and make a base for delicious fresh fruit salads. I at last got up to tea with Iris yesterday, and we had a long talk and a walk round that heavenly garden. Alex is well and the office is running down to the Christmas lull. Jamie is not very pleased with the wet weather and has to be persuaded to go out for essential purposes. He stays in till bursting point and starts to whine to himself.

I then throw him out gently. We have at last acquired a dress shop in Zomba and I treated myself to a dress for Christmas, in the new lurex material: gold thread, very plain, rather like a Greek tunic.

18th December:

I already have twelve Christmas cards and two parcels from home. Quite a number of people this year are sending one card to either Alex or me, and putting both our names inside. It is rather nice and comforting to see. I shall take mine down to Alex's on Christmas Eve so that we can decorate the room with both sets and have a real splash. It has been lovely this year to let myself go and send out more than I had the heart to send last year. This year I feel perfectly cheerful about Christmas.

We are working very hard in the garden, as Iris has showered us with trees, shrubs and plants. The trees are jacaranda and avocado pear. It is quite hard work after a day in the office but it is also relaxing. Iris came down after tea the other day to see how it was looking, and stayed till 7.30. Alex went off for a bit to write letters and then joined us for a drink on the *khonde*. It was a lovely balmy, sweet-smelling evening and Iris enjoyed it very much. She and Dave are coming to us for a buffet supper on Boxing night, also Chris and Bryn, and Derek and Betty Matthews. We are having Christmas lunch by ourselves and going to Jean and Rex in the evening. Geoffrey is distrait with excitement, as Paddy and the children arrive at the end of this week. Everyone is busier over Christmas plans than their work, and of course the whole place is in a state of agonised suspended animation, as there will be a great reshuffle in the New Year when all the Ministries and new appointments are announced. Bryn says it is quite likely that he may be asked to go, at once, but on the other hand, may be invited to work on under an African Minister. I hate all this uncertainty for him but it does not seem to bother him. The weather is lovely again and it is bliss to see the sun – my spirits rise with it. Alex is well, cheerful and full of plans for a happy festive season.

27th December:

We have had a wonderful Christmas, with masses of cards. I sent mine off early and got replies from lots of people I had lost touch with. Laga sent me a large card covered in writing. I got some lovely presents and was thrilled with both parcels from home. The blue bed-jacket will be a great boon in the cold weather, I promise you. *The Otter's Tale* is sheer delight and is a companion volume to *Ring of Bright Water*, which I gave Alex last year. He is thrilled with it. I got a little hide key wallet from Arthur, and a most beautiful little crystal vase from Bryn. [I still have it.] Jean gave me a pretty silk scarf, and Iris French eau de cologne. All my presents were received with great pleasure. Hazel was in raptures over earrings, which exactly matched a dress Bobby gave her for Christmas. We had a lovely time on Christmas Eve, after tea, driving round delivering our presents. The back seat of the car looked like a shop! We went out to dinner that evening with Ian and Joan Nance, our first visit and a great success. She put on a record of carols for me, as I said I had not heard any – so kind, and of course she knew I would not hear the singers at the Club. Ian is a darling, quiet, shy and terribly funny. (I worked with him when I did the wretched career pamphlets.) I went to Alex's for breakfast on Christmas morning, a lovely sunny day, as it has been right through the holiday. Jamie was delighted to have me there and never moved from my side, lying on my feet, sighing hugely with contentment. He had several extra groomings during the festivities and looked beautiful, with a bright red ribbon on his collar, which I managed to attach without· him noticing. Alex and I exchanged wonderful presents: undies, a blouse and a dressing case full of Lenthéric cosmetics for me – the most luxurious present I have ever had. I gave him an Edinburgh crystal sugar and cream set, Alexander's Memoirs and several small things I had been collecting over the months. We were invited out all over Zomba but stayed in and had our own turkey lunch. In the evening we went to Jean and Rex and had a tremendous evening. Their house was beautifully decorated. The three children were there – Lorna (nearly eleven), Bruce (twenty-two) and Vaughan (six), an amazing mixture! Boxing Day we spent getting ready for our evening party and neither of us sat down all day. The room looked very festive, with lots of flowers and all the cards festooned about the walls on red ribbon. We had several beautiful Norwegian candles and some big black ones, and I provided my Black Box and records for background music. I made two splendid puddings (both new recipes, a risk which came off) and three jellied salad shapes stuffed with goodies, to serve with rice, cold ham and turkey. Bryn and Chris, Dave and Iris, Betty and Derek and a couple from the North who were staying with them came – Iris in terrific form. Jamie behaved very well and was much admired, especially by Bryn, who could hardly keep his hands off him. I had a small, special treat to put in his dish while we were eating supper, as I did not want him sitting at people's feet yearning at their plates!

Everyone is stunned with weariness today and vaguely trying to prepare for New Year.

2nd January 1963:

We have had a most happy Christmas and New Year. On Saturday 29th we went to a big party at the Paynes, given in honour of Bruce, Jean's son, a most charming young man who lives in Northern Rhodesia. It was a pouring wet night. The rain began that morning and has hardly let up since. They had twenty-four guests, and had put up a big marquee extending beyond the *khonde*, where we all stood or sat. The sittingroom was cleared for dancing, which went on right through the evening. The party was to have been held out in the back garden, where Rex has put down a concrete dance floor, and there were fairy lights in the trees and a barbecue grill. We had the barbecue supper, supervised entirely by Rex, who is a terrifically organised man. On paper plates we were served piping hot chops, sausages and chips which we ate with our fingers. Bryn and Arthur were there, and a lot of people I do not often meet, which I always enjoy. I danced a great deal, and had a hilarious first lesson on the Twist from Arthur, who of course is marvellous at it. I came off the floor with all my muscles trembling and a wrenched spine, but he said I was 'an apt pupil'! On Sunday evening we had the Hostel dinner, to which Alex and a few other guests were invited, and had a huge Christmas dinner at a long table, about 40 of us, very gay and friendly. I woke in the night and was kept busy dashing through to the bathroom till 10 o'clock next morning, New Year's Eve. I went to the office in the afternoon, better but as weak as a kitten, and that was the end of our planned evening at the Flamingo. I went down to Alex for a light supper – a brandy and scrambled eggs – and was back and in bed by nine. It was disappointing, but there was no question of me going, and Alex was tired and did not mind a bit. I woke up on New Year's Day completely recovered. There is a lot of gastric illness about, so it was probably a bug, it was so violent and so quickly over. Alex gave a magnificent Pimm's party for twenty-six people at noon. Everyone arrived saying how jaded and exhausted they were, and in an hour they were all as bright as buttons and happy to linger on.

You ask about leave. That is still not settled, but will probably be in August. I will let you know as soon as it is final. Alex is thinking of making this his last tour in the Service. It may be better for him to settle at home and find a new job. It is all very worrying and unsettling, and of course everyone is faced with the same uncertain future.

Today the cloud is down to the Secretariat roofs and all the lights were on in the offices. I have worked very hard and start the New Year with my IN tray at a respectable level. I now share a bigger office, next to Bryn, with Douglas Fromings. Work is pouring in for me: handbooks and brochures in preparation for Independence, and the Annual Report (yes, one more!) has shrunk to a minor task to be done at odd moments! The new work is all most interesting and stimulating, but I will honour my Annual Report more than anything!

9th January:

We are having typical wet season weather, though yesterday and today have been lovely. I am snowed under with work and get very tired, but of course I thrive on it. We expect great changes when our new Minister, Chiume, gets down to things, and it is all rather a strain waiting for it, especially for Bryn, who is restless and unsettled. Douglas has taken over all the staff work, which is a great relief, as Bryn was passing a lot on to me. Douglas is such a nice man. He knows the language and the people and is marvellous with posters and pamphlets, which is not his work now, but I find him enormously helpful, as helpful as Kathie, so I am happy to work in the same office and can help him, as I know the ropes on Zomba. He has a very precise voice and manner, but we have the same sense of humour, and Bryn watches us wistfully through the glass partition between our offices, as I laugh helplessly over my desk and Douglas utters loud snorts of mirth and buries his face in his hankie.

On Friday the film *The World of Suzie Wong* was on at the Club, and Don Penny very kindly took me as his guest to the matinee at 4.30. I had a marvellous outing and talked to masses of people. The place was absolutely packed, as the film is very popular. I went back to Alex's for supper and found a very disgruntled man and hound waiting in the dark of the garden for me. Alex went on his own on Saturday evening and I had an early night, which was most welcome. I spent a lovely Sunday morning with Iris. Dave had his appendix out last week and is making a rather slow recovery. We roamed round the garden and I came away with roses and cuttings. Gardening has been a case of rushing out to plant things and then watching them being battered by the rain. Jamie is very slim and lithe now. His skin is ridiculously loose, and when he sleeps beside my chair I amuse Alex by pulling all the unfilled skin away from his body and arranging it alongside as it were. I then say, 'He is beside himself, his favourite position,' and Alex laughs, every time, and Jamie rolls an eye and grins – he really does wrinkle the skin round his mouth when he realises there is a joke about. I had a happy tea with Bobby and Hazel yesterday. They are the nicest people, so kind and affectionate. Hazel is enjoying her work at the Hostel, and giving us lovely meals, clever girl.

I have tried to write clearly as I know my writing is awful just now, with so many rough drafts scribbled in the office.

17th January:

Douglas Fromings received as a gift the coloured *Scotsman Calendar* in his mail on Monday and immediately handed it over to me to look through: beautiful, beautiful photographs of Scotland. I was homesick enough as it was, the day being your birthday, and at the end of looking at it, I was quite speechless when I handed it back to him and tried to say 'thank you'. He was so kind, gazed at me over his specs and said, 'Oh Ann, you Scots!'

Plans for leave are not definite yet. Everything is in the melting pot till 1st February, when Banda becomes Prime Minister. We cannot decide on the future till we see how fast things are going to move. Chiume takes over our Department and the Education Department, under his Ministry in February, and we shall see what happens. Bryn has a strong feeling that he will be sent on his way fairly smartly. [In fact he was asked to stay on, which he did, till he chose to resign in 1964, shortly before Independence.] He thinks there is no question of any of the rest of us having any difficulty about continuing with our jobs in the Department. It is a terrible time for *everybody*. Alex and I have the added burden of my paralysing problem, which we know will ultimately be resolved, but unfortunately the timing is not in my hands. However, we have learned to take one thing at a time and deal with it calmly.

Alex is to go to Uganda for a conference from 26th January to 1st February. I am going to stay at Kalimbuka to look after Jamie and the house. He is too young to be farmed out on anyone and not see either of us. His sister lives just up the road and her owners would happily have him, but I think it would bewilder him to come down and find all the familiar places locked and deserted. It will give me a small break from the Hostel, and I have Don Penny and Jean to give me lifts to the office and back, so it will work out very easily. It will be such a good break for Alex, who hopes to get some local leave shortly as well. He is to leave Establishments and take over Ron's job as Secretary to the Public Service Commission, a post which is to be upgraded and greatly expanded to meet the new conditions. It has given him new interest in his work, which is salutory at this stage.

We are both frantically busy in the office and tired in the evening, but as it usually pours with rain, gardening is not urgent. Today was lovely, and there is a flaming sunset on its way down the sky as I write this on the *khonde* in the last of the light, the air soft and scented. I had tea with Iris yesterday. Dave is out of hospital and is up the mountain convalescing in a cottage. She is taking me as her guest to tea at the Club tomorrow and the matinee of the latest Ingrid Bergman film *Goodbye Again*, which I am looking forward to. I miss my civilised teas at the Club. Last Saturday afternoon we drove to Blantyre to see a magnificent film *The Guns of Navarone*, and had dinner at Giovanni's; a lovely, refreshing outing.

Bryn is forty-six on Sunday!

22nd January:

We are having flat-out days in the office and a quiet social life. My tea and film with Iris fell through, as she had to go up the mountain to join Dave at the cottage for the weekend, but I went with Hazel instead and we loved the film. Alex goes off to Uganda on Saturday and returns the next Friday. He is looking forward to it and already full of ideas for his new work. I am reading Emlyn Williams's early autobiography *Georgie* and am enthralled. You would love it. He is a born writer and remembers his childhood with marvellous lucidity and manages to make it a continual excitement and stimulus to read, which is a great gift. He was a brilliant child and his academic feats at High School were stunning. There is a wonderful interlude in France for two months when he was fifteen. I had no idea that Welsh is not unlike French in some of its vocabulary, and in construction is like Latin, which he mastered in no time. He also learned Greek and Italian. I believe the book ends when he is seventeen, and I can hardly wait for the next years, which he will surely write about. Jamie is as much fun as ever. He is exactly six months old. His teeth seem to have settled down and he has stopped his wild chewing and biting. His coat is constantly changing and is going lighter again. He has a new mannerism, just developed in the last week, of nibbling delicately one's skin with his front teeth – a finger or wrist will do, but best of all, my arm!

The weather is better: plenty of rain, usually at night, and hot, sunny days. The garden is galloping ahead, but the little plants get either battered or roasted and I lose some of them. We have a group of twenty cannas, put in only a month ago, from Iris's garden, and one is already in exotic bloom, salmon-coloured. I like them at a distance, as a mass of colour. The four hibiscus bushes never stop blooming and the morning glory is a sight to behold. I see it only on Sunday mornings, in full bloom, as it takes its name from the fact that its flowers close about midday; something which only dawned on me the other day!

30th January:

Before I say anything else, I must cheer you up at once by telling you that Jean managed in the course of a conversation with Ron in his office, to bring up the subject of his affairs, with no reference to me, and he told her he had everything 'in train' since November, and he expected news from his solicitors any day, and hoped things would then be settled very quickly, and had been assured by them that they would be. I tell you this at once, as I know what a relief it will be. It has taken such a burden off my mind I feel light-headed. I managed to get word to Alex before he left for the airport, so he would be able to go away with an easier mind.

I have had a letter from Kathie, written just after Christmas. She had a streaming cold and they were snowed up. She is finding it hard to adapt herself, but she sounds cheerful and gave lots of details about the house. They have a spaniel, Pepper, whose daily walk was the only thing which persuaded any of them to venture forth, apart from shopping. They were feeding masses of birds which come every day to the garden.

I am managing very well on my own but this is one of the longest weeks I have ever known, in spite of the fact that I am run off my feet in the office and have been kept occupied in the house. Jamie did not notice Alex's absence over the weekend, as I was there all the time, but he is definitely missing him now. Every now and then he lifts up his head, listens, gazes at me and gives a little enquiring whimper. He never leaves my side in the house and garden, and sleeps by my bed. He always wakens once or twice in the night, puts his paws on the side of the bed and presses his nose against the mosquito net for reassurance. It takes me all my willpower not to have him up on the bed with me, for *my* reassurance! It is a long time since I slept alone in a house and my nerves jangle at every sound. I have tea at 5.30 in the morning, as I let Jamie out then and make his breakfast. It is lovely at that early hour and he has an ecstatic time in the garden and comes in soaked with dew and bursting with high spirits, tearing through the house and talking in gurgles of excitement to me and Lapkin, Alex's boy, who adores him. The garden/kitchen boy, Mustafa, adores him too, and keeps him entertained while I sneak off down the road to the Paynes to get a lift.

I was out to tea with Hazel yesterday and go to the Baxters tomorrow. Alex should be home at teatime on Friday. I have written masses of letters, which always makes me feel good. I am reading a book lent me by Molly Penny – *A Pride of Terrys*, by Marguerite Stein. It is fascinating. I have no room or energy to tell you about the office. It is hectic, and not made easier by Bryn at the last moment wanting a thousand and one things done before the change of Minister on Friday, all in the middle of Mr Butler's visit. However, I keep calm and just deal with them and of course it is nice that Bryn feels he can leave them to me, as he is the busiest of us all.

6th February:

Alex's main birthday present to me arrived yesterday – Lawrence Durrell's *The Alexandria Quartet*, a big volume containing the series of four novels with a common theme. I have read them all, over the last few years, but I am delighted to have them all together, as I find them fascinating and very re-readable.

Lots has been happening here. On Friday the Cabinet was sworn in at a ceremony in Leg Co. There was a vast, vast crowd of Africans thickly packed in front of the building, and we had a grandstand view from our office. All our staff went, black and white, so only Jean and I were left to hold the fort. As all the roads were closed for the morning, we took sandwiches and had lunch in the office. When the Prime Minister came out waving his wretched fly whisk, the crowd gave a deep roar, like a great animal *baying*. Then, dramatically at this historic moment, the heavens opened and down fell torrential rain. Instantly the crowd became a sea of black umbrellas, and a pathetic, brightly coloured stream of women and children began to push their way out, in search of shelter – the men had the umbrellas, *of course*. The entire ceremony was rendered a most dismal and oppressive occasion by Dr Banda, who lost the chance of a lifetime by making a political speech in the Chamber – all his speeches are abusive to the white population, and so alike one begins to feel one is listening to a slightly mad gramophone record – instead of rising to the occasion and making a dignified, statesmanlike speech which would have set the tone for the future by reassuring the expatriate community and giving the right kind of lead to the Africans. I watched the European officials driving off later and my heart sank. They all looked white and grim, and I realised a great opportunity had been missed. Bryn was almost beside himself with anger and disappointment when he came back. Well, there it is, there it is.

Alex had difficulty getting back from the airport on the crowded roads and I was at the house having tea when he arrived. Jamie went crazy with joy, yelled, rolled about, ran round in circles and finally tried to stand on his head. Alex had a very interesting and satisfactory time. He is much taken with Uganda, which is years ahead of us here. He looks well and sunburned, and is full of ideas for his new post, which will be much more difficult than the equivalent post he studied in Uganda, because Nyasaland has not followed the same historical pattern and is by far the most backward of all the territories to have been given independence. It makes one shake in one's shoes to think of the tasks ahead and the dearth of sufficiently educated and trained Africans to cope with them. I cannot think that Butler and Co. have *any* idea of what they are letting us in for, let alone the Africans, or else they have written off Nyasaland as a nuisance and a liability not to be borne by HMG. Enough.

Returning to the Hostel was not funny, but less awful than I expected. We had a lovely weekend, doing nothing but talk and be domesticated. Alex agrees I did *not* spoil Jamie – and has been spoiling him a bit ever since! Jamie knew I was going on Friday night and was most subdued. We think it does upset his equilibrium to have me coming and going, but it cannot be helped.

We had our first visit from our new Minister, Chiume, on Monday. (Jean and I were both nervous, as married European women are *not* popular in office jobs now.) Bryn was marvellous and said all the right things as he introduced him to us in turn. He told him I was in charge of all the coming publications on Independence, with about twenty-five in hand – perfectly true – and all Chiume said later was, when did I go on leave, and would I have everything well prepared by then!! (Won't I just!) I am overwhelmed with work but getting through very well, doing more than I could have believed possible. There is nothing like having a challenge. I am worn out by four o'clock, which is when I now leave, but I can see me getting tea brought up and staying longer. I do not mind in the least and will get accustomed to it.

I had tea with Iris on Monday and Alex came up to fetch me; we stayed on for a drink. Dave has recovered from his operation and looks brown and fit.
PS. I have a Vote of £4,000 all to myself to pay for my coming publications. I spent two fascinating hours with the Government Printer this morning, going over with him what I propose to do and getting it all costed – most exciting!

13th February:

It rains, rains and rains, sometimes *all* day and night, and the ground is so waterlogged the gardens look absolute swamps. Today Zomba woke to a blue sky and everyone has been more cheerful. My room was beginning to smell musty and my shoes were growing fungus. We have been lying low, socially, but on Saturday gave a dinner party, with Dave and Iris, and Ian and Joan Nance (who had us to dinner on Christmas Eve). It was a great success. Jamie gratified everyone by lying at all their feet in turn, even observing the rules of seniority, which made us all laugh when I pointed it out!

The office continues to hum with activity. Bryn is not so hard pressed, which helps me, as I sometimes have to talk things over with him to clear my mind, and he has simply not been available. Douglas is very helpful, but there is something about the way Bryn's and my mind work together that produces the mental elucidation I have to have before I start to write. I have a desk diary now and make a note of everything I have done and must do, and there is hardly space for it all. The paper work is enormous, as the Minister likes everything written down, so minutes and files pour back and forth, with awful, complicated requests which are to be carried out 'the day before yesterday', as Bryn puts it. The African staff, for the first time in their lives in our easy going Department, are feeling the crack of the whip from their black Minister, and there are protestations, scenes, even tears, all to no avail. Our hearts have hardened – we are vulnerable too and everyone absolutely *must* pull his or her weight.

I am reading John Master's latest book, *Back to the Coral Strand*. It is about the new India, and I recognise so much of what is going on and will come here. Lots of dreadful things are happening, and it depresses everyone, and at the end of an exhausting day one feels almost beaten by it all. Alex and I exchange woes and talk things over, which helps enormously. At least my work (so far) is harmless, interesting and marvellous experience, though I wish I had more training on the technical side of layout, printing and reproduction. However, the Print backs me up splendidly. I spent the whole of today studying other African countries' Independence productions and planning out the main one for Nyasaland. It is fascinating, hard work. I now have five brochures awaiting the Minister's approval. He has just had mumps, and given it to Chipembere, released from prison to become Minister of Local Government and the most fanatical of them all. You can imagine the comments!

20th February:

We have had four lovely days since Sunday, which cheers us all and helps the gardens to recover. There is a lot of illness in Zomba. Alex has had a heavy chest cold for the last few days. We are both too tired to want to do much, but on Thursday we went down to the Paynes for a drink, as it was Rex's birthday, and on Sunday evening Bobby and Hazel came down for a little while. Hazel sails home with Sue and Johnnie in about ten days and Bobby moves into the Hostel, which means someone more to talk to at lunch. There is an outbreak of measles among the children, and she is watching hers like a hawk and praying they will get away without complications. She is packing up the house and doing her job at the Hostel, and looks rather drawn, but is always her sweet self.

The office is busier than ever. I enjoy it all and am beginning to get my little office really organised and efficient. I was sharing a large office with Douglas, which was pleasant but made it difficult for either of us to work as well as we could, what with visitors, typing, phone calls and constant interruptions of every kind. So we had a partition put up and we each have our own small office, though we converse through the wall when necessary by raising our voices. I have found a European woman who is a very good artist, to do black and white drawings for my books and brochures, and have started up a small photographic section of my own, with really good black and white and coloured subjects provided by several enthusiastic amateur photographers whom I know. The African staff are not quite good enough and it takes weeks to get anything out of them. The Annual Report is pouring in (very late) and Bryn keeps giving me odd jobs, so things go at a smart pace. The good weather has put new life into me and I now wonder what I did before!

We had a quiet weekend, mainly spent in coping with Jamie, who had his second anti-rabies injection on Saturday morning. The needle must have gone straight into a muscle, as one of his hind legs went completely stiff and it was obviously agony to move at all. He yelped with pain when he tried to get up, and had to be carried out on his mat and shaken off it to get on with routine matters in the garden. He is still slightly stiff, but goes gamely about with a funny little limp. He seems to have stopped growing, and is a very small, slim dog. There are signs of wilfulness which need to be firmly dealt with, but he had no thumps this weekend as his bottom was taboo!

27th February:

We are having typical end of the wet season weather, which should last about a month more, at the most. I can smell the cold season coming, at night and in the morning. There have been some tremendous storms, with alarming lightning zipping down practically in the garden. Jamie takes it all very calmly, but is on the alert till the noise dies down. He gets close to me when the lightning is bad, because he senses my apprehension. There has been some serious flooding all over the country, which means famine later, although one must not say so now! (Banda takes offence at the use of the word 'famine' in his country.) We both got the day off on Friday and had a fine, sunny day in Blantyre, which was a great pleasure. I had my hair done, very well, and we had a good lunch at Giovanni's, the best eating place in Blantyre, and lingered over it most luxuriously. We saw quite a number of people we know. I bought a pair of winter slacks in a medium weight tweed, with a small black and white check. It was absolutely marvellous to get away just for one day, and I went back to the office next morning feeling I had had local leave, and bearing biscuits for elevenses and the usual small packet of chocolates for Bryn, which has now become a ritual I started last tour. He loves sweet things and never seems to get enough at home. We have a tacit agreement that I keep up a clandestine supply which he is not expected to share out. The minister has been away on tour (they do not 'go on *ulendo*'!) so we have had time to catch up on ourselves a bit. I stay on till 4.30 every day now, and usually end up with Bryn and Douglas perched on the table in my office, letting their hair down. We have little time to talk during the day, so I do not mind, and we exchange all the things we have heard and thought about, and it is not a waste of time. I am so lucky to have such splendid people to work with, especially these days.

We had a quiet weekend with some home cooking by me, which I enjoy and which is always greatly appreciated by my host! I spoke to Iris on the phone today and cheered her up, so she said. This rain has a bad effect on her, as she likes to spend hours a day in the garden. Tomorrow I go to Hazel for tea for the last time, which is sad. They have such a happy home and it has been a great help to have it to go to. Things in general are pretty low for us all, but Alex and I make the most of what we have besides.

6th March:

The rains are very gradually coming to an end, and we have had some lovely days with the sun still very hot. I had my farewell tea with Hazel on Thursday. We had a long talk and caught up with all our news. She is one of the sweetest women I know and I am going to miss her very much. We have a new manageress in the Hostel, who so far is doing us proud. Work is as demanding as ever but I get accustomed to the pace and I always work best under pressure. There are a lot of depressing things happening and I would like to keep a diary as a back-up to writing a book later, but keeping the diary would be risky, as it really would be dynamite! We have been very quiet. The weekend was fair and hot, and I had a marvellous lazy day on Sunday, just lying in the sun. I got beautifully brown and feel marvellous. The question of local leave has come to a head because it is now definitely settled that Alex cannot be spared till October. He will then have such a long leave due to him that with luck, and the way things are going, he will not come back. It has been a blow, but I have been prepared for it as there were signs that it was coming. As it turns out, it will be the best arrangement from our private point of view. It gives us that extra time in which to have things settled, and I have no doubt they will be. Ron goes on home leave this coming Sunday and will get things settled as quickly as possible. (He told Jean this.) It means one more jacaranda time and the best of the hot season to store away inside to help cope with the winter weather at home! I know you will be disappointed, but I feel in my bones I should stay on and see Alex through to the end of his tour, and of course Bryn will be happy, indeed thankful, to have me. Alex will be helping with the Compensation scheme for overseas civil servants, which concerns about two thousand people in Nyasaland. It will be a good task for the last one, as everyone's future in part depends on it.

13th March:

A lot of old faces are back in Zomba, as the Administration is gradually being found posts in the Secretariat because the men now have little they can do in the field. John and Dorothy Watson (John was our first DC) are here, also Mike and Joan Saunders, whose names you may remember. Our Minister left today for two months in America, so we can breathe freely for a bit and settle to routine without the constant pressure of rush jobs. On Friday I turned out a foolscap pamphlet in one day, which is no mean feat. I am up to my eyes and getting great satisfaction from all my ploys, which are going very well, touch wood. I have twenty beautiful pen and ink drawings for my publications, which I am about to send to Salisbury to be made into printing blocks. Bryn is himself again and like everyone else, looking forward to the two months' reprieve. We are all very happy together in the office and I think Arthur misses the fun. I have lunch with him nearly every day.

The weather has been wet again. It rained solidly for five hours on Sunday. Jamie gets bored and dozes in his basket, and I have to push him out the moment there is a dry blink. We have started to play Scrabble again: for a time we were too tired in the evenings.

Local leave is in complete abeyance at the moment, as Geoffrey has been put on special duties connected with Mr Butler's working party, and Alex is acting for him. However, round about Easter I hope he will get some time off. He always gets a second wind when there is an extra demand on him, but he is worryingly tired. I am sleeping badly again, but the cold weather always helps that, as there is more air in the chalet and I can get rid of the stifling mosquito net. The garden is gradually coming to, and we have managed to tidy it up and start some new growth. Our lovely morning glory was blown over and up-rooted, so we have got a new trellis up, and the seeds go in tomorrow – the ground was too soggy today.

19th March:

I had a long tea with Iris last week. At one point she said she could never decide whether it was better to have had a happy, secure family upbringing, or if life would have been easier later, when we left home, if it had not been such a shock to find out how insecure and brutal life can be. I strongly maintained our background was the best possible because it gave us inner strength to draw from, and the ability to make the best of the little things that make life bearable when it is at its worst. She came to the conclusion I was right, I am glad to say!

We are both very busy, Alex as usual plunging energetically into his work. Geoffrey is still away in Salisbury. There has been a drastic cut in our Estimates and my wings have been clipped a bit, but I have more than enough to get on with, and the new financial year begins in July, which will help.

The weather is still surprisingly wet, but there are lovely days in between and we enjoy getting into the garden and setting it to rights. Bobby Lowe came for lunch on Saturday, obviously missing Hazel and the children terribly.

26th March:

The printing blocks have come back from Salisbury very quickly, which is exciting. I have asked Chris (Jones-Walters) to do me a dozen, more delicate drawings. She is a lovely artist, and I am sure has wasted her talent over the years, but that happens to lots of the wives, as I know myself. She is drawing subjects like bees, scorpions, praying mantises and spiders.

The Secretariat is filling up with administrative officers, to serve out their time till they can leave. The result is that some of them have very little to do, but there it is. They can act for someone on leave, and of course there is a big increase in Secretariat staff under the ministerial system. A number are also working in crash training courses for Africans. For DCs who have served long and hard in the bush (e.g. Mike Saunders), it is a dreadful anticlimax, but on the other hand I think some of the wives are thankful to be in Zomba and have the chance to pull themselves together before they go home! I know I would feel that, and though some would not admit it, my guess is that is the general reaction. The atmosphere is so ghastly that everyone is longing to get out – a terribly sad ending for us all. I am frightfully lucky to have the job I have, which has not changed, merely expanded, and makes no inroads on my integrity, and *that* is becoming the crux of the matter, as far as I am concerned.

We are all more relaxed in the office. Douglas has stopped singing 'None shall sleep' all day – an ominous choice, I told him, but in my case, apt! He has a clear tenor voice and to my pleasure (I hear him through the partition) has gone on to Beethoven and hymns. He goes on leave in May and John Carver, my old friend from Mzimba days, comes in his place.

Alex is well and working hard. There is a good chance of local leave immediately after Easter, so with the Easter holiday as well he should manage about ten days. There is no chance of getting in at the Lake at Easter, but we can go after, for perhaps a week. Geoffrey is dashing to and from Salisbury and is then bound for London. He came down on Sunday morning for a drink and talked very interesting shop, non-stop, as they hardly see each other and had to catch up on developments. I sat very quietly and absorbed all the titbits! On Sunday afternoon we had a very pleasant tea with the Baxters, who have moved into a house on the terrace above Alex. The three children had all had measles, but were on the mend and very energetic. In the evening Dave and Iris came down for a visit, both in good form, and we had a very relaxed, lighthearted hour. It was a beautiful weekend and I got nicely warmed and brown. We worked like Trojans in the garden. Jamie had his first fight on Sunday morning, and came racing home, yelling with pain and fright, to show me a little nick on his face, between his eyes. It obviously gave him a splitting headache, and all through Geoffrey's visit he kept sighing, blinking and rubbing his paw over his face.

We still have torrential rain, mainly at night. The garden is lovely again. Our new morning glory is about three inches high already, and on Saturday afternoon we put in fifty yellow cannas and four poinsettias, and put up another trellis for honeysuckle. Fruit is plentiful and we eat a lot of avocado pear, guavas, grenadillas and melon. I feel we must have all we can while there is still time! I do quite a lot of cooking at the weekends and enjoy it; Alex loves it. I am reading a book by Beverly Nichols, of all people, and am delighted with it – *The Sweet and Twenties*, with lots of sketches and stories of famous personalities of the day, including Melba and Pavlova. I think you would enjoy it.

3rd April:

I have had a terrific day and am now sitting on Alex's *khonde*, having had tea, and am gradually unwinding. It has been a glorious hot day, after a night of tremendous rain. Alex works till about six every evening, so I get a lift down, change into shorts and tackle the garden. We have enough colour to attract birds, at last, and there are hosts of brilliant little sun birds swaying on the salvia and poised over the hibiscus. They bring so much life with them and twitter all the time.

I had tea with Iris on Monday. It was a beautiful golden afternoon and we went slowly round the garden, which is immense, and she has done an enormous amount to it. She has a real feeling for grouping and landscape. As she said, when she leaves she will have her interest in gardening and her interest in birds, which Africa has given her. It is marvellous that we should end up on the same station for the last lap, and it has made such a difference for both of us.

I am reading *The Mottled Lizard*, by Elspeth Huxley, an account of her childhood in Kenya, very vivid and nostalgic, and presenting the African scene at its best, as it is to me when 'recollected in tranquility', which I can now do. Iris was saying the same thing – Africa is *so* beautiful, and as our time here draws to a close, we find ourselves looking our 'last on all things lovely every hour'. I would not have dreamed a few years ago that I could ever come to that! I wish I had been fundamentally happy through it all, as I am now. It was such a battle, for so long, and my fighting spirit still surges up against the aspects I so dislike, which is right and proper.

We are dining with the Paynes at Kuchawe on Easter Saturday, which will be our first outing for ages. Bobby has moved into the Hostel and I enjoy another good companion at lunch. I had a long letter from Hazel, posted at Naples. Sue got vicious measles just after Mombasa, and Johnnie a milder dose, so poor Hazel nursed them in splendid isolation through a scorchingly hot Red Sea. However, she went ashore at Zanzibar, which was the main reason for going east coast. She sounded cheerful, but I think she has had a bad time. Sue had a temperature of 105 before the rash broke out – dreadful. The weather is really wonderful, with rain in the night and early morning, which is good for gardens. I am deeply tanned and feel very fit.

10th April:

What a turmoil dear Mr Butler has caused. I must say I cannot condone some of his ways with the Southern Rhodesians. I am staunchly British, and it makes me feel uncomfortable to hear the 'jokes' which people visiting Salisbury bring back, and it is white Rhodesians who make them up. E.g.: 'Why is the British Government like a banana? Because it is soft and yellow' – awful. It makes one wonder who is ever right. The weather is very beautiful, with glorious days and cool nights. There is a heavy dew in the morning, enough to feed the flowers.

We have good news about local leave. By great good fortune Alex has got some from Tuesday after the long Easter weekend till the next weekend, and Bryn immediately granted me the same. We have managed to get in at the Lake from Easter Monday till the next Sunday, 15th–21st April, so we have ten days holiday with only four and a half working days off. It has been a great relief, as we both need a break. We shall take Jamie, and I can hardly wait to see him take to the water. There is a chance that Dave, Iris and Linden will be there for two days, which would be delightful. They have taken a cottage on the mountain for Easter weekend and are joining us for a drink at Kuchawe on Saturday evening, when we go there with the Paynes.

I am working very hard, trying to leave everything in good order while I am away. Bryn said I looked 'wild' today, so I suspect I looked like a horse, as the family would have it! I am as brown as a berry already, having had a glorious sunny weekend. It was really hot and I was out for hours. We had a drink on Saturday evening with the Markwick Smiths, back from leave and all very well, in spite of a hard time in a freezing house in England. On Sunday evening the sunset was absolutely gorgeous and we drove up the mountain road as far as the clock and watched it behind the pines and cypresses. We then popped up to the top on the six o'clock clock and had a drink at Kuchawe with Homer and Theo Cox. It was the first time we had ever been up on our own. It has been a sad avoidance, but necessary because we knew Ron used to go bird-watching on the plateau every weekend and often ended up there for dinner or lunch, so we kept away. We drove down in misty moonlight, going very slowly so that Alex could also have a look at the incredible view below, with Zomba stretched out like a miniature Monte Carlo of twinkling lights, and Mlanje looming dimly on the horizon.

17th April: Palm Beach

Here we are at the Lake and it is heaven to be back. We had a very bad start to the holiday, as Alex had a dreadful attack of ulcer pain off and on right through the weekend, and it looked as if we might not get here at all, which was bad enough but the worry was worse, and I spent hours sitting on his *khonde* in a state of near despair, crying unstoppably behind my dark glasses and creeping in to see how he was every ten minutes. Fortunately, nobody called. It seems we are no sooner clear of one disaster area than we move into another, and I am so *tired* of coping. However, on Saturday evening we went up the mountain for dinner with the Paynes, as Alex felt better and thought the break would do him good and take him out of himself. He was very careful about what he ate and drank, and felt all right, but the pain came back in the middle of the night, and lasted till Sunday evening.

We left Zomba after lunch on Easter Monday. Alex was better and spent the morning in the office, working on something he felt he must do himself and leave completed. Jamie had the back seat of the car to himself and spent the entire journey standing at each window in turn, particularly mine, looking out with his ears flying. I kept him on his lead in case he took off. He does not appear to distinguish between the car stationary and the car moving! It was a lovely day, terribly hot, with clouds of dust. Kasupi looked hot and beautiful and I was again visited by the strange sensation I had last time – a kind of emotional *déjà vu* turned outside in. We arrived here just before sunset and were amazed to find the Lake almost up to the rondavels. It is higher than it has ever been in living memory. An unusual prevailing wind, blowing constantly, drove the waves even further and the beach was covered, the little 'sea wall' broken in places and there was a terrific amount of seepage all round. The car park looks like a swamp in the deep South, and trees and tall shrubs under which we usually sunbathe are about two feet in water. There is the path outside the rondavels, a patch of grass and then the little wall with the Lake lapping at it, about knee deep in depth. So we actually bathe on what was the beach, which means lovely smooth sand instead of the rather nasty feeling mud further out. There is no sand for small children – or dogs – to potter on. It has been a most worrying time for all the Lakeshore people, especially the hoteliers, as the water has been very destructive and they began to wonder just where and when it would stop rising and how it would affect the amenities they have to offer. They have also had a dreadful rainy season, with six weeks of not being able to get out by car, and all their supplies and guests brought by Landrover from Fort Johnston. Everyone's nerves were on edge and the intrusion of the Lake was almost the last straw. (This would make a good short story, I think!)

Jamie has been as good as gold, but has been quite dazed by the change of environment. He ignores the water and simply swam ashore and kept on walking till well inland when I carried him in yesterday. He sits on the wall and whimpers quietly when Alex swims far out and lets out a yell of distress every time he dives! It is very funny but heartrending. We brought all his food with us, and there is a great ceremony each evening, when, *each evening*, Alex cuts his thumb opening a tin of meat and bleeds, cursing, while I, in fact, get Jamie's dinner and the hound waltzes about on his hind legs and dirties my dress! There are very few other guests and as usual, we are doing absolutely nothing. The weather is perfect: hot, hot days with a breeze, warm evenings and nights cool enough to sleep well. I sleep soundly here, always, which is bliss. Alex looks marvellously well, a different man, in fact. We are perfectly happy.

24th April:

We are back in Zomba, into winter weather which came with a bang on Tuesday morning, and everyone is in thick skirts and sweaters. It is damp, dull and cold, and gets dark by 5.30. I have three blankets on my bed and am sleeping well again, thank goodness. I am a deep golden brown and still warm to the touch. I think it was a real life saving break for us both. Dave, Iris and Linden came on Thursday for two days. They were in rondavels at the opposite end from us, so we were independent of each other when we wanted to be, and they had their own table in the diningroom. The Lake continues to rise, we hear from the wireless, and all the hotels on the shore are faced with flood damage. It is of course very bad for tourism and Arthur, as Tourist Adviser, is having a bad time. Things are remarkably quiet in the office, as Bryn is in the North this week. My room looks like a new pin! Timothy washed all my curtains, blankets, rugs, cushions and bedspread.

1st May:

Alex is well and has not had a murmur from his ulcer since his return. Jamie does not like the cold and early darkness.

I am very busy rounding up the Annual Report material, which is disgracefully late – a sign of the times – and also trying to get on with the UNO Report, besides cope with the usual sudden demands for pamphlets and posters. Douglas goes on leave next week, and how we will miss him. Bryn is not in very good form, as it is demoralising for him to see the efficient little Department he has built up over the last ten years floundering in the quagmire of the new regime. He is becoming middle-aged, quite suddenly, which makes my heart ache.

The garden is thriving. It was exciting to come back from the Lake and see how things grow when we are not there to watch them! We can now have cut flowers in the house all the time. The cannas and hibiscus are tall and thick, the new morning glory is in flower, and the poinsettia bushes, planted less than a year ago, are brilliant scarlet and taller than I.

We had a very nice outing on Sunday; a curry lunch with people whom we met through Hazel, a Welsh couple, Dave and Mary Pritchard. They have a lovely house among new ones built next to the old Naisi housing estate where I began. The view is glorious and they are great gardeners. There were sixteen people there, all nice, including Bobby Lowe and Robin and Elsie Martin, back from leave and now stationed in Blantyre. We both enjoyed it immensely. Alex was given a specially made fish soufflé, as curry is one food he must not touch.

We are enjoying cosy evenings by the fire. We both feel much more steady and aloof from the awful atmosphere since we came back from the Lake. I had a farewell tea with Linden and Iris on Monday. Linden flew home on Tuesday. Iris had a bad cold and was very low.

7th May:

The cold season has set in and we have a fire every evening. Jamie still eyes the fire with misgiving. Lapkin has great difficulty when laying it as Jamie thinks it is some kind of game and backs off with the logs, ruining Lapkin's arrangement. When it was lit for the first time, Jamie tried to get into the grate to see where the smoke was going!

There is a lot of illness about and Bryn has had a very painful poisoned leg, which is most unlike him. Alex is well and cheerful and feeling the benefit of his rest, with no trouble from his ulcer. I am doing quite a lot of cooking for him, and keeping an eye on his shopping list, to see that he is not eating anything that might upset him. The cold tires me, and I feel a bit weary in the evening, but have become expert at preparing dishes quickly which can be cooked by Lapkin, who is naturally delighted with the arrangement! Geoffrey came back from Salisbury on Friday and called in the evening, to regale us with stories from the big city. We had a quiet, happy weekend, reading, talking and playing Scrabble.

Tomorrow we are going to the Club, a great event for me, taking Bobby Lowe with us, to the matinee of *Ice Cold in Alex*, which has had excellent reviews, and bringing him back for supper. He goes on leave in July and is counting the days. Hazel has bought a secondhand car, an ancient Wolseley, for £25, which goes like a bomb! Trust Hazel! On Thursday we are dining with the Accountant General and his wife. It is an invitation out of the blue, as Alex hardly knows them and I have never met them. It will be fun to meet new people.

12th May:

I have had a bit of a shock today. Alex's ulcer suddenly flared up in the last few days and he had a haemorrhage this morning and very rightly went straight into hospital. They think it has been caused by strain and exhaustion. I went up to see him after tea and he looked quite himself, and was comfortable and cheerful, drinking milk every two hours and allowed to smoke in moderation. I had had a feeling of imminent disaster for several days. I just sensed he was far from well. He will now get a good rest, be well looked after and not allowed out till he is better. He would never have given in unless this had happened. Jean rallied round, as usual, and I rushed back to the chalet, packed a case, and have come down to Alex's house to look after Jamie and keep things going. I shall lunch and tea at the Hostel and go up to see him from 4–5.30. It is a lovely walk up and only takes about seven minutes – at least that is all it took me today! I got such a fright I was in a state, but having seen him I feel better. I shall be able to see him every day. Everyone is being most kind and helpful. Thank God for my friends.

I can now go on and tell you the good news. Alex heard from his lawyer on Friday that Ron's divorce should be heard in July, so provided it is and all goes in a straightforward manner, it should be over and settled by October, at the latest. Alex has pushed his leave on into November, which means that we will probably arrive home about six weeks later than anticipated. I shall let you know as soon as we get a sailing date. I need not tell you the relief nor do I have to imagine yours. I had a tremendous reaction on Sunday, a beautiful day, which I spent *all alone*, crying weakly behind my dark glasses and praying no one would come. Alex said later he felt exactly the same when his divorce was at the same stage – a general feeling of waste, failure and sadness for others besides oneself – the old Latin philosopher's *lacrimae rerum* which I always carry within me.

On Saturday we went up the mountain at sunset and had a drink at Kuchawe by the fire. The weather has settled into the correct pattern of glorious sunshine, warm outside and cold inside, and cold at night. We had a very nice evening on Friday, with an excellent film, then Bobby back to us for supper. I have had another letter from Hazel, who is happy in Kent, in spring weather, taking the children on picnics to old childhood haunts. Rex Payne was bitten by a rabid dog last week, (which his neighbour promptly shot), so poor Rex is having that awful course of fourteen injections. All the dogs on the housing estate have had to be vaccinated, except Jamie, who had his booster only two months ago.

Chiume arrived back from two months in America yesterday, so we have been hit by a hurricane and I am launched into another pamphlet which came at me out of the blue this morning, just as I was happily settling down to produce my *magnum opus*, a Handbook on Nyasaland. However, the more work I have to do the better, so all is well with me in the office, but poor Bryn is already feeling the strain. It is time we were all away. Banda goes to London in July, so we hope we may have a definite date for Independence soon after that and are all hanging on by the skin of our teeth.

I will stop now, as I am dead tired and I think I have managed to put in all the news. We had a *delightful* evening with the Accountant General and his wife last Thursday – nice, straightforward people, very alive and stimulating. He is from Yorkshire and has lived in forty-five countries! I hope to have better news for you next week.

18th May:

Alex is making good progress. He was kept on a glass of milk every two hours till Saturday morning, when his system cleared of the remains of the haemorrhage, and he has since been eating small, light meals three times a day. Now it is just a case of resting in bed. He is much more relaxed and perfectly cheerful, and has stopped worrying about the office, which was upsetting him at first. The doctor sees him every day and the nurses are kind. He has masses of presents of fruit (which he cannot eat), flowers, books and magazines, and lots of visitors. People phone me up to enquire about him and when I go down to the Secretariat I attract groups of concerned men and women, all anxious to know how he is and all anxious to tell me that they have an aunt or cousin who has the same thing and what the treatment should be! I feel much better, having felt dreadful for the first few days: sick, shaky and very uncertain of my self control. Everyone has been most kind, and the Hostel people flock round, with offer of lifts, shopping, anything they can do to help. It has been a pleasure to find how nice people are, though I had found that out for myself already from my own experience. I think he will be kept in for another week, as he really is exhausted. I sleep in the house and Jamie is delighted to have me. Lapkin looks after me very well, and always has the fire on when I come in at 5.30. The Paynes take me to the office, I lunch and have tea at the Hostel and am up at the hospital by 4 o'clock. The weather is beautifully sunny but now really cold. Jean said it was 50 degrees on the barometer on their *khonde* this morning! The nights are glorious, with fierce bright stars and, at the moment, white moonlight.

Work in the office piles up and I have actually been bringing files home in the evening. At the weekend I worked right through at an education pamphlet and presented it to a grateful Ministry on Monday at 7.30! They made no alterations, so it was typed at once and is now in the hands of the Minister. It was quite interesting to do and I was on my mettle. I have no social news for you at all, as I have not had time for anything but visiting Alex and working. It makes the days pass remarkably quickly, and I enjoy my quiet evenings by the fire with Jamie, who is lying dreaming beside me with his head on my feet.

I am enjoying the office and have met some nice new people in the Education Department, in particular Jack Smith, who has been headmaster at what was until recently the only boys' secondary school, at Dedza in the Central Province. It is delightful coming into contact with the 'academics' and I feel very much at home with them.

Geoffrey paid a flying visit from Salisbury at the weekend, and told me Alex must stay off for as *long* as is necessary.

23rd May:

The great flap in the office has died down and I have time to take some pleasure in what I am doing. I am working quietly on my hand book and helping Bryn with some of his work.

I had a letter from Kathie the other day. She is well and enjoying the better weather. She is doing voluntary night duty at a nearby hospital. As *everyone* said, trust Kathie to do it voluntarily! She and her two sisters, all strong characters, are finding it difficult to live together, having not done so since childhood. I can well imagine!

My birthday present for Iris arrived on Monday, *The Lovely Sergeant* by Alan Burgess, a biography of Flora Sands. [Aunt Kathie's old friend who fought with the Serbs in the 1914–18 war.] I am reading through it quickly now. It is fascinating, but I do not care for his style, rather coy and ultra-feminist. It comes to life noticeably when he quotes from her diary and letters, which I wish he had used more. I wonder if she feels it has done her justice – I don't.

Alex has made an excellent recovery and left hospital this afternoon. He looks smoothed out and relaxed, with a *mane* of hair, and has lost quite a bit of weight, which was very necessary. He is to go up to outpatients on Friday, when he will discuss diet and sick leave. I am hoping he will take a fortnight off. Everyone keeps telling me – and him – that he should not try to go to the office for at least a fortnight, but he is an obstinate man. However, I mean to be just as obstinate.

The weather is cold but beautifully sunny. clear and fresh. Friday, the holiday, was a perfect day and I sat out on Alex's *khonde* from 8–1 o'clock, and got a marvellous tan which is still glowing, and I repeated the performance on Sunday. (Very amusing : Molly Penny, who lives opposite, said to Jean after the weekend, 'Your friend Ann is very lazy. She never does a thing. Just lies out in the sun!' Well, well, *well*!) I wrote letters all through the holiday, and also caught up with my newspapers. The walk up to the hospital has been good for me and I feel fit, but the grinding worry has been tiring, and the cold in the office is exhausting – the others are feeling it too. I wrapped myself in my red stole this afternoon and Bryn said, 'Oh Ann, fach, it's like Christmas!' We are all *slaving* away.

I am off to make Alex a fish soufflé – *so there*, Molly Penny!

1st June: [Air Letter]

Do not be alarmed by the air letter. It is just that I have been kept very late, which I will explain, and am so tired I know I could not manage a full letter.

Alex's ulcer has given no more trouble and we are being very careful with his diet. Today disaster struck! (I just *could not* believe it and would have liked to have hysterics if I knew how.) He trod on something sharp at the Lake, and after a few days his foot began to fester. He went up to the hospital and asked for an X-ray, which they said was not necessary. They gave him dressings and it was nearly better when he went *into* hospital. By the time he came out it was worse, and I insisted on ringing the hospital this morning. They X-rayed it, and told him he has fractured a bone in his foot, and it actually has a chip out of it. So, *it* is in plaster and *he* is on crutches. I had to go up after tea to collect his crutches and do some shopping before that, so it was dark when I got back. The great thing is we know what is wrong now, and he will have to go on resting. Sorry about this very inadequate letter. I am so tired I have a temperature!

15th June:

Bryn has gone to Blantyre, Jean and I have just had elevenses, the office is very quiet and I have jolly well settled down to write to you while I am warm, bright and not tired!

We have had a terrific number of visitors since I wrote last week: everyone calling in, in the evening, to see Alex and commiserate. It has been very pleasant, but quite tiring and a bit expensive! Dave and Iris came down on Friday and we had a birthday tea. I had ordered a special fruit cake, with marzipan and icing, which was a lovely surprise for Iris. She is delighted with the book.

Alex got the plaster off his foot after only one week and as the septic bit had not quite healed they said perhaps the bone was not fractured after all and he had better come into hospital next week (this week) and have it operated on to see if there was something in it! Can you imagine our *fury*! However, it became obvious one day later that the septic bit had cleared up, and by yesterday morning his foot was completely healed and he drove up to hospital to tell them so! He has the rest of this week off and goes back to the office on Monday, having been away just over five weeks.

24th June:

Yes, the Profumo affair is dreadful. It seems to have received complete and utter coverage at home in the papers and on TV. As you say, absorbing to watch it unfold, but shocking when one realises all the implications. I must confess it has been most interesting to read about, despite the layers of beastliness which are uncovered in the process. Poor Mr MacMillan.

I hardly dare tempt fate but am risking saying things are back to normal. Alex returned to the office yesterday, looking fit and well and about a stone lighter. He was given a great welcome and got through the day all right, but found himself very tired at the end of it. His basic trouble is exhaustion of spirit, which is not helped by the ever deteriorating atmosphere in Nyasaland, but I shall just have to do my best to keep him going and not let him be pulled down by circumstances. I *long* for the time when we get away from here. I can feel that we are both getting better every day and putting happiness and quietude between us and the past.

I got the day off on Thursday and went to Blantyre with Alex, where we had a very pleasant day which was good for us both. We did some shopping after I had my hair done. I am gradually getting together some pretty things over the months, so that I shall not suddenly find I must spend a lot of money. This is just about the time in the tour when *everything* – shoes, handbags, undies, blouses – start to go all at once and one's clothes look out of date. We had a very good lunch at Giovanni's, where we were joined by Philip Richardson, and were back by teatime.

On Sunday evening we went up the mountain on the 6 o'clock clock, coming down on the 7.30. It was a beautiful night, with a lovely lavender afterglow in the sky and a perfect new moon showing above the tall pines on the mountain road. I said, as I often do, 'Wouldn't it be exciting to see a leopard?' and two minutes later we rounded a bend, and there, braced against a huge boulder on the left-hand side of the road in the full light of our headlights, was the most splendid leopard, sitting up like a cat, ears slightly flattened and mouth slightly open, with great pale eyes looking emptily straight into ours. He got up in one marvellous movement, loped across the road (if Alex had not stopped very quickly we would have bumped him) and melted into the thick trees on the right. He seemed very pale creamy gold, with vivid black rings right up to the end of his tail. With his tail stretched he must have been at least eight feet long. What shattered me was that we had passed several Africans walking up in the dark, and the leopard had only to go a few yards down through the trees, cutting across the road's hairpin bends, to arrive at the level where we had passed them.

We had a short visit from Geoffrey on Saturday evening and heard all the behind the scenes news of the preparations for the Victoria Falls conference. Alex will be acting for Geoffrey again, from next week on.

10th July:

The conference seems to have gone off extremely well. Everyone says *the* personality of the whole occasion was Sir Roy Welensky, who made an enormous impression. Geoffrey said he really felt he was present at history in the making.

The disturbances in Nyasaland are in Blantyre and south of it, but the whole country is on a razor edge and law and order are *not* being properly maintained. It is dreadful and could be terrible, but we say little about it among ourselves, as it only causes further alarm and despondency. The atmosphere worsens daily and there is open insolence to be faced, especially towards women. I am not writing this to alarm you – if I were frightened I would not tell you at all! Leg

Co is on this week and hours of screaming hate are solemnly taken down in shorthand and on tape, and the Print works nearly all night to produce it in print next morning – absolute madness. They all scream abuse, poison and lies, and there is no one to stop them – the Speaker is ignored. Our Department is falling apart, as Chiume has axed a number of his *bêtes noires*, Don Penny included, so the Press section suffers a fearful blow. He has built it up from nothing in five years, and without his imprint it will deteriorate, to put it at its mildest. I work quietly on, minding my own business and do as well as I can. I have just been involved in an anti-rabies campaign and have produced and distributed in *two days flat* a pamphlet and poster in English and Chinyanja on the subject – this by driving everyone and using all possible charm and persuasion on the Government Printer. I liaised very successfully with the Veterinary Department. One of the officers, Dick Isaacs, works with me and we are doing a great job between us, I think. It helps to keep my mind off other things.

The weather is cold but lovely. Jamie is well, if slightly piano – like me, he does not like the cold. Alex is tired and depressed about everything, as of course all the chaps are, and each day brings out something worse. Our chief technical officer, Bill Thurlow, who does the tape recording of Leg Co, has just called in at my office. He said he was made to feel physically sick in Leg Co this morning, listening to the floods of threats and vituperation. He is a hard nut, who came here from Ghana, so he has heard it all before, but he was upset all right.

It was a beautiful sunny weekend and I got a lot of sun, so I look and feel very well though I am aware of being very strung up. Dear Bobby Lowe gave a farewell party on Thursday at the Hostel, which we attended for an hour or so, and the next night we were out to dinner, and we are going again tonight. We are being asked out more as time goes on, as everyone knows we leave in November. On Saturday evening we went up to Kuchawe for a drink. I never took my eyes off the road, but – no leopard!

Do not worry about the news from Nyasaland, and be thankful we are so near the end of it all. I shall write a better letter next week. I am tired and have not felt very cheerful.

19th July:

The time really is going very quickly. It is the hours and the days which can be so long. Alex has had several interesting days with some VIPs from the Colonial Office, which always revive him.

We have had a few pleasant social occasions, dinner parties, not with people you know. I spent Sunday morning with Iris in her marvellous garden. It was the kind of perfect day that makes Zomba look like paradise and my heart quailed at the realisation that I shall shortly be turning my back on all this beauty.

I am still very much occupied with the anti-rabies campaign. There has been a bad outbreak of rabies in Zomba, and urgent steps have been taken to tackle the problem. A three-day tie-up of dogs began two days ago, much publicised beforehand, and any dog not on a lead is shot on sight by members of the Veterinary Department from their constantly patrolling vans. After sunset the arclights on the vans comb the town and its environs for strays and the pye packs which roam after dark, especially on the outskirts. Volleys of shots punctuate the nights into the small hours. So Jamie is shut into the house and goes out only on his lead. I take him for an hour's walk after tea and he is very good, trotting along happily, occasionally sitting down to rest and lean on me. He is not an athletic doggum at all!

Quite apart from the menace of rabies, the atmosphere in Zomba hangs heavily over us all. John Carver is back and brings a little light relief in the office.

24th July:

The weather is not nearly as cold as it should be, which is delightful for me, especially as it means I do not get so tired. I am sleeping badly, which is not surprising as time goes on. I am just hoping I can break the habit before the hot season makes sleep difficult anyway. I was relying on our weekend at the Lake in August to do it for me, but Alex has decided he cannot get away, as a VIP on salaries revision has chosen to arrive that very weekend, and Alex is dealing with the whole exercise.

I have suddenly got a lot of work to do again, which is just the thing. I was told by my Veterinary friends that the anti-rabies campaign has been very successful, largely thanks to my publicity material and the timing of its distribution, which was the best they have ever had. It is nice to know, because I did it all on my own in record time, as Bryn was up to his eyes and had to leave it to me. (He is *very* pleased!) These days everyone appreciates anything done efficiently and quickly.

I had a most enjoyable weekend, beginning on Friday with the 4.30 film, to which Iris and I went together. It was Tennessee Williams's *Summer and Smoke*, with Lawrence Harvey and a wonderful actress, new to me, Geraldine Paige. It was not horrid or sordid, as his writings often are, just sad, realistic and very touching. We emerged harrowed but uplifted, like the Greeks! There was a big fire in the Club lounge and Alex was there to take us home. He bought us both a brandy, which was just the right thing, and we had a happy half hour together. On Saturday night Alex and I went to a lovely party at Naisi, at Pat Cork's house. She is the artist who did drawings for me. There was a wonderful mixture of about fifty people. Iris and Dave were there, Arthur and lots of nice people I had not seen for ages, so I roamed all evening and enjoyed myself immensely.

Jamie stood up to the three days' confinement very well and was apparently quite surprised when Alex opened the door on Friday morning and shooed him out. He has a cold in his eyes from sitting at a partially opened window gazing out, for three days. I bathe them a lot with Optrex and they are improving. I am going to settle down and read the *Observer* till Alex arrives. He works till about six every day just now, but is getting things done and therefore feels more cheerful. I am enjoying having John Carver in the office. We tease each other endlessly and laugh a lot, which is a great help these days.

31st July:

We went to the cinema at the Club on Saturday night, my first evening visit since I went into the Hostel. The place was packed and I enjoyed seeing everyone and spoke to masses of people. The film was *Only Two Can Play*, with Peter Sellers and Mai Zetterling, a Welsh comedy from the book *That Uncertain Feeling*, by Kingsley Amis, which I had read and laughed over. It was a marvellously funny film, very authentic in atmosphere, and Peter Sellers is a wonderful actor whom I have hardly ever seen, and greatly appeals to my idea of comic acting. It was filmed in Swansea, and Bryn knew every inch of the locations and was delighted with it. We had Derek Arnall to dinner and took him with us to the film. He is an old and dear friend of mine, a little man, crazy about films and photography, and a complete misfit in Government. He sold maize with us at the time of the famine and has always, since, sought me out to talk to. He likes Alex very much and he *adores* Jamie! It actually rained all day on Sunday, which was quite restful, and we had a comfortable day indoors. The garden has benefited, and we have six sweet peas in Bryn's little vase. Three bougainvillaeas and two poinsettias are in full glorious bloom, and the carnations are nearly ready to open. The whole place is pretty dried up already and the leaves have started to fall. The jacaranda trees are all a beautiful gold and in another month the leaves will be gone and that marvellous blue will be bursting out all over Zomba.

Iris, Dave and Linden (who arrived on Saturday) leave for England this Saturday, driving down to the Cape. They are not coming back. We went up to have a farewell visit last night. I had had a bad day, and was dreading it, but Iris and I behaved very well and managed to keep the tears *in* our eyes! Alex said he was proud of us both. So, another goodbye over. Alex's stenographer, a sweet Irish-Indian girl called Rose Marie Hand, had a cable yesterday to say her father had died of cancer in India. She lives in the Hostel and I had to do some coping, so I was worn out by the evening. However, it gave me a glimpse into other people's troubles, which is always salutary. As you will realise, we are waiting daily for news of our own affairs, but you cannot hurry lawyers and we must just set our teeth and hang on till we hear. I have got the morning off tomorrow, having been offered a lift to Blantyre, and I am going just to have the break. I need to have my hair thinned (as usual) and will have it washed and set. We are going to a farewell party in the evening for the Smiths. Jack Smith is the nice man in Education I have worked with on several pamphlets. He has been posted to Barotseland.

6th August:

At last I have the good news we have been waiting for so long! A letter came from our lawyer on Saturday to say that my divorce was settled on 15th July, and that on the day he was writing (30th July) he had just been informed that the finalisation was to be expedited, permission having been obtained not to wait the customary three months. He will cable us the date as soon as he knows. This means we will be able to marry within a matter of weeks, and get all our papers, passports and passages very comfortably settled without the anticipated frantic rush. I felt nothing but relief when Alex told me at his house at lunch time, and only burst into tears the very last thing that night, again out of relief. I cannot describe the pressures and strains that have simply fallen away. I had been living with nightmare visions of further delays, and all our plans and prospects in ruins round us! So, the time has come when we really can and *must* look forward, plan and think of ourselves and our future. My mind was far from office work today, as you can imagine, and I chose to do copy typing, so that my thoughts were free to roam about.

Derek Arnall came down for tea on Thursday to take photos of Jamie with me in the garden. We had *such* a time with him and were in fits of laughter by the end. It was a brilliantly hot, sunny day and Jamie was not keen to be out in the sun. Just as we got him posed he would slump down to sleep or crawl slowly into the very prickly bougainvillaea bush we were using as a background, and only a sleepy, golden eye would be visible through the leaves!

We went up to Kuchawe on Saturday evening, had a lovely dinner and enjoyed enjoying our secret! I borrowed Jean's sewing machine on Sunday and made myself a most attractive cotton dress. I just suddenly had the urge to make something. I had bought a zip and pattern in Blantyre and had some pretty material bought ages ago. I really enjoyed doing it and of course it allows one's thoughts to roam. It is many moons since I have had any desire to let them do so! Geoffrey came back from Salisbury yesterday and came for supper. We told him our news and he was simply delighted.

We are having a drink with Jean and Rex this evening, to celebrate. She, of course, wept when I told her. She has been such a discreet, faithful friend.

13th August: [Air Letter]

Sorry this is a short letter, but I am very tired and have not much news for you anyway. The weather is warming up nicely, and Mlanje has gone behind its screen of dust and heat. I shall probably not see it again, which is hard to believe. Bryn is in Salisbury, and was commissioned by Jean and me to bring back for each of us a 'shift' dress, the latest fashion to reach the Rhodesias. He thought at first we meant petticoats! One of the girls in the Hostel has made me a Chinese dress out of some gorgeous coloured silk I bought some time ago. I shall have a nice little wardrobe for the ship, but am down to rock bottom as far as warm clothes are concerned. On Saturday before lunch Geoffrey asked Alex and me to have a drink on his verandah on the second floor of the Hostel, with Sir Gordon Haddow, the salaries revision man who is Alex's special pigeon – a charming man, so quick mentally my mind was reeling by the time we left, but Alex said I kept up with him very well.

PS. Alex's best friend in the Solomons, Sir David Trench, has just been appointed the plum of Colonial Service governorships – Hong Kong!

21st August:

Alex is going to sell his china, glass and kitchen things. They are old and belong to the past, and it would be nice for us both to build up a small set of possessions of our own. Some of the stenographers who start in the Hostel decide to move into flats and are glad to buy pretty things secondhand. My neighbour in the Hostel and a friend are coming down to Alex's after tea tomorrow, and we have been looking out a selection to show them. I was afraid it might upset Alex, but no, not at all, so that is all right.

We got a day in Blantyre together on Friday and made enquiries about the car and Jamie's journey, which is gradually taking shape. On Sunday we measured him for his little travelling kennel, and he knew there was something on, which we were both very unhappy about. [It had been decided that Jamie would be flown to Scotland, and after six months quarantine, become Jess's dog, as our future was so unsettled.]

We took two couples to dinner on the mountain on Saturday, as a start in paying back hospitality for the last time. We saw *three* leopards! They were moving about at the foot of the Inn's garden as we drove up, and had only just vanished down the steep slope of the terrace as I got out of the car! They were young, much smaller than the big beauty we saw, but very impressive, with boney, chiselled profiles clear-cut against the green afterglow in the sky. It is ridiculous that I have to spend nearly fourteen years in Africa before seeing these glorious creatures. Sunday was a real hot season day and I lived on the *khonde* and was glowing nicely by the end of the day. The weather is very erratic and was quite cold again on Monday, so that we were all frozen and changed into warm clothes at lunch time.

Alex completed his task with Sir Gordon Haddow at the end of the week and saw him off with relief and regret – such an alive man. He came to the house for a drink on his last evening and Alex told him about us. He seemed very pleased with the idea! We have another dinner party for four guests at Kuchawe this Saturday and then the rest of our farewell entertainment will be done *en masse* in the house. Alex is tired but *at last* beginning to withdraw himself from his complete enslavement to the office, and I have noticed a marked rising of spirits this week, which sends mine up too. Bryn is on local leave and we are all feeling the strain: flap follows flap.

28th August: [Air Letter]

I am sorry this is a short letter this week, but I am back late, having had to stay on in the office with a sudden enormous influx of work. Bryn has had to fly to Salisbury at short notice to a conference, leaving us buried in his stuff as well. I am too tired to write a long letter, and will fit all my news in here.

Our arrangements for Jamie are coming on, and we plan to send him off about the end of September, all being well. Poor Alex got an ulcer pain on Monday and to my great relief was sensible and stayed in bed resting for two days and is now better. It is bound to come and go at this stage when he is driven so hard. He only has nine weeks to go, but to him it seems an eternity. There is such a lot to do and arrange, and we are so tired, but the final spurt will be made. We are already gradually preparing. I have all my things looked over and ready for my trunk, cases and boxes – there is not very much, apart from books! On Sunday we got out all Alex's crates from his store and went over them. I am doing most of the pricing and selling and hope to get him a reasonable sum. Jamie is thriving and beautiful.

3rd September:

I am writing this a day early, as I have the news we have all been waiting for, and I would feel better with it off my chest at once! We have not yet heard from our lawyer, who with his usual canny caution has not cabled, but has, we hope, sent off the necessary documents. On Friday Alex heard that Ron had re-married – a stenographer who was with him constantly last tour and who went home on leave with him on the same ship. There has been great speculation in Zomba as to whether they would marry, and on Friday a letter came from her to Establishments, to let them know officially and to ask about her pension. It was an odd way to hear that I was free, but not upsetting, as by now we expect anything to do with our affairs to have a peculiar twist to it! As you can imagine, we have been in a bit of a buzz ever since, but things are working out and our plans are made. Alex went to the Boma yesterday and our 'bans' go up today, and we can marry any time after 24th September. We plan to go quietly to Blantyre on Friday, 27th September to the office there, among strangers. The alternative would be the Boma, with a DC we know, which we do not want. We will then have lunch, come back to Zomba, collect Jamie and go straight up to the Lake for a long weekend. I shall leave the Hostel for good that morning and have a few weeks of married life at Kalimbuka. It has made *such* a difference to me to know that Ron is married. Until then I kept *on* thinking and worrying about him. Typically, he was all the time on the way to 'pipping me at the post' as Alex said, by doing it first! (I will never learn, will I!) Anyway the news has taken the sting out of my plans. It is a situation which requires tact and good taste, which is why we want to go to Blantyre and marry quietly with no show or fuss. I think people will appreciate why, but a wedding is a wedding and our friends want to share in our happiness. The news of Ron's marriage was Zomba-wide by the end of the weekend and my sweet little friends in the Hostel were simply bubbling over with pleasure for me at lunch time yesterday. The diningroom was in uproar. Friends like Bryn are just thankful that at last we can be happy, and the rest feel they cannot say anything personal yet, but give extra friendly smiles and waves from their cars! (Dear Jean Wickham met me in a shop on Saturday morning, kissed me and said, 'He's met his match this time,' and gave a little grim laugh!) What I am trying to tell you is that it is going to be far less of a strained emotional occasion than I thought, and I am almost free of the terrible, haunting sadness that I felt might never leave me.

Jean and Rex insisted on coming up the mountain with us for a drink to celebrate the news on Saturday evening, and we had a happy hour.

In spite of my quiet, behind-the-scenes preparations, I feel I have an awful lot to do before the 27th! Alex admitted yesterday he had too much on his mind to give his full attention to the office! We shall go to Blantyre one day next week and get the ring. I feel this letter is a bit disjointed; my mind is on ten different things at once. Bryn is back in Salisbury and I am having to help John – work comes in a deluge or not at all, at present.

11th September:

To put your mind at rest at once, the final document I was waiting for came yesterday and we really are going to be married on the morning of Friday, 27th September in Blantyre, and go up to the Lake, coming back on Wednesday and going back to the office on Thursday, 3rd October. We are off to Blantyre tomorrow to buy my ring and do some necessary shopping. I am resisting all thought of going splash on a new outfit. I have a very simple, tailored linen dress which I have only worn once and I shall wear that, with your pearl and gold necklace. The Paynes were very anxious to come as witnesses, but I know Jean would weep buckets, and I really want none of that, and have managed to explain without hurting their feelings, I hope. There are so many friends whom I have known for much longer, anyway. We meant to ask a stranger at the office in Blantyre to come in as a witness, but Geoffrey, back from Salisbury, *insists* on being with us – as a good friend of us both, as Alex's chief, and as someone who has helped us, stood by us and seen us through from the beginning. I feel very happy now; everyone is so kind and so absolutely delighted for us. We had a party of twenty-four people on Friday, consisting of Hostel friends, neighbours and office staff, and it went like a bomb, with everybody obviously though tacitly celebrating for us! We had candles everywhere and my good friend the Government Printer gave me a *car load* of roses, stocks, sweet peas and antirrhinums. The room was heavily scented and looked quite opulent with its mass of blossom. The hot season literally set in for good that day, and it was warm enough to sit out on the *khonde*, which people did. The weather is heavenly: hot, with a breeze, and the jacaranda and other blossom are like a foaming sea all over Zomba. On Saturday we went up the mountain and treated ourselves to a quiet dinner, and on Sunday evening we went to the Club with the Matthews, to see a very good performance by the Dramatic Society of Christopher Fry's *A Phoenix Too Frequent* – quite a hectic three days for us. Alex is terribly tired, but gradually relaxing, which is good to see. I feel wonderful in this weather but realise I am ready to be away – a decision or a plan, however small, requires a major effort to push it through.

18th September:

Last night I wrote to Iris and Kathie about our plans, and within the next few days I must write to Hazel and Joan. Alex and I had a successful day in Blantyre last Thursday, and got our arrangements for the 27th finalised. We will be married at 10.30 by the Administrator General (Government's Solicitor), witnessed by the Assistant Registrar General and Geoffrey. Alex has invited them to join us for champagne in a private room at Ryall's, and then we make for Zomba, change into shorts, grab the hound and go off to Palm Beach, which we should reach before sunset. We also shopped for a ring and found one which we both liked which fitted my abnormally thin finger. I had my hair done and did last minute shopping.

We had a quiet weekend. On Saturday evening we had a drink with Geoffrey on his nice cool verandah in the Hostel. There was a dance at the Club, and we saw all the Hostel girls in their party dresses tripping away to the car park with their escorts. I have some very good friends among them, and endless tales of their lives and troubles to tell you. I have been very busy clearing out my possessions and transporting them unobtrusively in Jean's car to Alex's house. All my books are there and my very few bits of glass, china and silver. I move out of the Hostel finally on my wedding morning. I hope I have told you all the things you want to know. *Everyone* is delighted for us and people are beginning to say so, which is lovely. When you write after the 27th, put Mrs A.F.S. Davidson, Box 53, Zomba, which is Alex's address.

24th September:

I thought you would be glad that we are having Geoffrey with us. I assure you we could have had *hosts* of willing friends as witnesses, and have had to be very firm indeed over several more than tentative offers! A quiet wedding is a quiet wedding, and we either have no one or everyone! Jean Kennan, who has a lovely garden, phoned me this morning and asked what colours I was wearing. She said she would like to slip down to my chalet on Friday morning after breakfast with a little buttonhole for me which I could wear or carry. I was so touched I shed a few tears, and only just managed to find my voice and say I would be delighted. I do not really know her very well, though I have known her over the years and John, her husband, started me off on the *Hansard* Index. Life is full of surprises. We are giving a party for thirty people on 4th October, Alex's birthday, and I think that will help our friends to make an occasion for celebration! By that time we shall both feel free to express our own happiness. The hot season is here and it is very hot indeed during the day. I feel the benefit of it already but by great bad luck have caught a bug which is raging in the Hostel and for a week have had a very sore throat which makes me feel sick and feverish. It is exhausting, and I have had to grit my teeth to get on with my packing and other arrangements. I have everything in very good order, I am glad to say. Nearly all my things are packed and in Alex's house, very unobtrusively managed. His sittingroom looks nicer than ever with my books in it. Jean and John Carver have been most helpful. The girls in the Hostel are excited and happy for me and make me feel ridiculously young and unsophisticated. Alex has decided to have the day off on Thursday, the day before, and take the car to Blantyre to be serviced, and I am delighted to go too, and will have my hair done. So I have my last day in the office tomorrow, and from certain whispers and furtive meetings I gather that something is being arranged – an elaborate elevenses party, I suspect!

I wish you could see Zomba just now. It is a sea of jacaranda, unbelievably beautiful. John Carver took me down to Alex's with my trunk this morning and drove me back along the top road, very slowly. The petals fall very easily and one drives under and over them in a kind of blue tunnel. My heart was in my throat and dear John got very emotional too.

1st October: Palm Beach

Here we are, on our last full day at the Lake, sitting out on our little grass plot, glowing with sunburn and shattered at the thought of having to go away from this heavenly place for the last time. We have had such a lovely, happy, peaceful time, and have been fed and looked after like royalty by the Sweatmans. There was quite a lot of people at the weekend, but now we are the only guests. The weather has been perfect and we have been out from dawn to dusk. Jamie has felt the heat a bit, as his coat is much thicker than last time, and of course this is the hottest time of the year. He still has to be persuaded to enter the water, but once in, he takes off, usually straight out to sea, as it were, with no sense of direction at all (like his mistress), so that we suddenly have to swim

madly after him and point his nose in the right direction. We have done nothing
but swim and sunbathe, and we both look transformed. We were delighted to
have your cable, and had one in Zomba from Joan, and three here from Zomba
friends. My septic throat, which was really bad, is only gradually clearing now,
but on Thursday in Blantyre I got a wonderful gargle specially made up for me
by the very good chemist whom I have known for years, and it washed out most
of the poison at once, and I knew I would be all right. In fact on Wednesday I
felt so ill I stayed in bed till lunch time, then went to the office in the afternoon.
Everything went off very well on Friday and Geoffrey said he was proud of us!
We had champagne and very good small eats in a very nice room at Ryall's,
with our three 'wedding guests', who could not have been more charming, and
then came back to Zomba, had tea, and came on here, feeling very happy with
our day. I only began to feel fit yesterday and am now absolutely fine, but I
would dearly like a week, feeling like this, to enjoy myself. This has been a
very timely break and has set us up for the last lap.

8th October:

   We have settled down to routine days again, and have just begun the heavy
packing. We are having great joy and amusement in our new life together, and
feel a contentment which carries us through everything. It is quite funny for us
both to give up our bachelor lives and start living with someone again, and we
are able to laugh at each other's efforts at polite adaptation and sudden, brief
lapses – all little things which only make life richer. I think Jamie will be flying
on 14th October. It has taken all this time to get it arranged at both ends. Alex
says I need not come to the airport, which is a great relief, though I was
prepared to do it. I think Jamie – and Alex – will be less upset without me. I will
tell you now I felt so ill the week of the wedding, Alex suggested we postpone it
till I was better, but I felt almost hysterical at the thought of *one more delay*.
Anyway, we got through! Everyone says how well, happy and young we both
look! It was sad to say goodbye to the Sweatmans and leave the Lake. As they
waved us off, Pixie picked up one of her poodles and buried her face in his coat
to hide her tears. It felt quite strange in the office next day, in spite of the warm
welcome from everyone. However, I did not have much time to feel anything,
with Alex's birthday party next day. Bryn gave me the afternoon off and I
worked steadily till six o'clock. Several of the wives coming offered me
flowers and I had masses and masses of roses, carnations and honeysuckle. By
evening the room was heady with their scent. There were candles everywhere,
and the room was cleared of furniture and looked quite excitingly festive. We
had thirty guests, all delighted to be with us. Philip Richardson unexpectedly
stepped forward, and, as Alex's oldest friend present, insisted on making a very
neat, kind speech for Alex's birthday and brought me into it at the end. I stood
beside Alex while he very briefly and charmingly replied and then we toasted

our friends. It was the real celebration of our marriage, and everyone was thrilled to wish us well: all very happy and emotional about it. Alex looked such a darling – large, brown, smooth face, eyes popping a little with emotion, and so relaxed and amusing. There was a low murmur of affection from people as he ambled forward to make his speech, which brought a lump to my throat. Everybody likes him and admires him as a colleague. Then on Saturday it was Jean's and Rex's evening, and they gave us a magnificent dinner and took us to the Club to see the Dramatic Society perform *Gaslight*, very well done. It was our first public appearance and we thoroughly enjoyed it. Sunday was a scorcher and we wore as few clothes as possible and tottered about, literally putting our house in order! This week I have started packing, and I have a few social occasions, as I am having my Hostel friends to tea in batches. I feel so well and full of energy, while people simply wilt in the heat. The maximum temperature in Zomba yesterday was 92°F.

15th October:

The heat is terrific, and it is all I can do to get on with the packing after the office. I end up shaking all over and with an upset inside from over exertion. But I have it all very well planned and will have the heavy luggage ready in lots of time to get it away by the deadline, which is the end of this month. It goes to Beira by train and the rest, which is our clothes, goes in the car with us. Jamie is a great trial to me, as he goes to sleep very quietly between my feet when I am standing still working over something, and I forget and go plunging over him and drop things. I had to get Alex to lift him out of my book box, which he settled into as soon as I had it open ready to pack, and then he lay on my carefully arranged piles of books and finally had a mock fight with our neighbour's bull terrier among them! In the heat it is difficult not to get cross, but even if I do he simply gives me a look of deep affection and tries something else. I do not think he is upset by the packing activities, just interested. This is his last week with us and he seems more endearing than ever and causes us both terrible heartache. Alex finds all his evenings filled up with writing, there is so much documentation required for our journey, with the car and Jamie to arrange for as well, and all our stops *en route* to book. I let him get on with it while I pack, and then we sit out on the *khonde* and cool down with a drink before dinner.

We have not been sociable this week, as our entertaining is now over, apart from people dropping in. The weekend was fearfully hot and we had to spend it packing. On Sunday evening we planned our route to Durban, in very easy stages (covering about half the distance per day as Ron and I did driving up from Cape Town). Alex leaves his office on 2nd November, I on the 8th. I shall have worked exactly two and a half years this tour, which gives me about £200 paid leave. We move into the Hostel transit room on the 11th and on the 13th we leave Zomba, stay our last night in Nyasaland at Mwanza Inn, and on 14th

November we are over the border. We have two nights in Salisbury, one in Bulawayo, one in Louis Tricard, one in Pretoria, one in Ladfontein, and on the 20th we arrive in Durban and stay in a hotel by the sea about ten miles out of town, until the ship sails on the 27th. We have decided against any touring or sight-seeing. We just want to be together and enjoy a holiday. This journey has been planned in easy stages to spare Alex worry and fatigue. He is the better of his break at the Lake, but he is absolutely exhausted, mentally and physically, although he is more like his old self already, looks *years* younger and is fundamentally at peace with himself.

Do not worry about the long journey to Durban. After we leave Nyasaland the roads are splendid, and we shall do our daily stint mostly in one long morning, except between Mwanza and Salisbury, when we leave at dawn, take breakfast with us, and get to Salisbury in the early evening.

23rd October:

It was confirmed today that we sail on the *City of York* on 27th November from Durban.

Jamie saw more of the packing than I intended, as his departure was delayed, but he seemed to find it all interesting until just the last few days when tea chests and trunks were everywhere and he began to feel there was no floor space for him – I found him more than once curled up on the dressing table! He left on Monday and arrives at his Kennels today. I will not go into detail about Monday. There was a lot of crying going on behind dark glasses – still is! The house is so still and quiet without him, and he was so much a part of our life that each phase of the day seems all wrong without him. Kind Bryn asked me on Tuesday how our day had gone on Monday, and I could only just answer 'Well, it's over.' Jamie had a beautifully made box to travel in, far more comfortable and ventilated than two others we saw at the terminal. He was quite used to it, as we kept it in the corner of the sittingroom and he wandered in and out of it and sometimes slept in it. With him he had his rug, an old espadrille of mine, a box of food, his stainless steel food and water bowls, and his lead. I must stop writing about him or I shall be off again!

It is quite incredibly hot and even I keep on saying so, which is unusual. Packing has been a real ordeal, but it is almost done now and I have managed to space it out very well. On Saturday evening we went to Sally Wood's house warming party. (She lived next to me in the Hostel for my first year, went on leave, is back and in a flat.) It was a lovely party with delicious food and lots of young people, whom I always enjoy. We went on to the Club to see Vivien Leigh in *The Roman Spring of Mrs. Stone*, a rather awful film which left a bad taste, but she was marvellous, as always, and so beautiful still. Last night we dined with John Carver and tomorrow we dine with the Marwick Smiths. *Everyone* is saying, 'You must come and have a meal with us before you go'!

29th October:

Everyone is asking us to go and see them, or is calling in, and it is all a bit much as we are too tired to enjoy it. We had a cable on Thursday from the Kennels to say Jamie arrived safely. We are gradually recovering from the awful wrench of parting and the worry of wondering if he would survive that marathon journey. We do not lack the company of dogs, as all Jamie's friends visit us, looking for him!

Alex has handed in his resignation, along with 20% of the Service and that is only the beginning of the landslide. It is a relief, even though it leaves the future unsettled, but we have been preparing ourselves for that for months, and have plans. We are both up to our eyes in the office. There has been a complete revolution in arrangements in mine, and the Information Department as we all know it is coming to an end. The Minister has moved into Bryn's office and he may be seconded elsewhere till he finally departs next May. I have had two interviews with Chiume, who, contrary to Bryn's idea, was unaware of my imminent departure and is full of plans for me to work for him! So I am working for them both and am just about at a standstill when I get home, but I enjoy it and will willingly slave away for one more week. Jean is very depressed and would like to go with Bryn if he leaves and work for him – all very unsettling and sad. John and I share an office and have crazy fun to relieve the tension.

We have had some heavy showers of rain, which have cooled things down and put an end to the jacaranda. It has eased the packing, but I love the blazing blue succession of days, which is over now, and the thunder clouds are beginning to pile up oppressively. The heavy packing is completed and we will take it over to Limbe next Monday.

We had a pleasant dinner with the Marwick Smiths on Thursday, and on Friday went to the afternoon cinema to see *Guns of Darkness* with the evergreen David Niven and Leslie Caron. It was a second-rate film, but we enjoyed the outing. The novelty of being able to go to the Club together has not yet worn off! We had a quiet weekend, with three couples calling in for a last visit. John Carver called in on Saturday evening on his way to a party with his pretty girl whom I think he will very soon get engaged to, although he is now rather a confirmed bachelor of 35! She is 23, delightful and a strong character. They have already been engaged and he broke it off, but I think she will win! We were out for dinner last night and go again tonight. We are very tired and have reached the stage when we cannot remember being otherwise, and of course we are looking forward to being away. I feel numb rather than sad, although saying goodbye to people hurts very badly – I hate it. We have managed to sell everything and now have one big item left, the fridge, which I think Arthur is going to buy.

5th November:

We are bearing Jamie's absence better and can talk about him now. I can still get touched on the raw. On Sunday I whisked open the little cupboard where I kept his brush, comb and anti-flea powder, and got a definite whiff of him and some golden down floated out: I promptly burst into tears!

Things are moving here. By the end of the weekend we had our nine heavy boxes all done up and labelled. On Friday afternoon we went to the Club and saw *The Road to Hong Kong*, with Bing and Bob still being very funny. We have had a lot of people calling in, and I have reached the stage when I wish it were all over. There are so many dear people I must still face goodbyes with. We are the first couple to go since the Compensation Scheme came into effect on 1st November, and I think our imminent departure is bringing home to people what an enormous exodus is on its way. I cannot walk through the Secretariat without men dashing out of their offices to ask if they will be seeing us to say goodbye, and I dread Tuesday, when I must go right through the Secretariat from top to bottom and pay my final visit to everyone. Jean and Bruce Wickham came for a drink last night. It was lovely to see them and we had a long talk. They leave next May, as do the Baxters and a host of others. The office is hectic and I never have a moment to brood, which is just as well. We move out of the house on Monday and have two nights in the Hostel, so I shall see all my friends there again. We are taking Jean and Rex up to Kuchawe on Monday for a farewell dinner. We went to Limbe yesterday and got our luggage straight through Customs and left it at the station. I paid a last visit to Boutique Meganne, my dress shop where I have been such a good customer since 1957, when I started working and had money to buy my clothes. I also had my hair thinned and cut. The heat is tremendous, and more trying now, as it is very sultry and thundery, and we get the occasional downpour which only makes the atmosphere steamier than ever. This is Alex's fourth hot season and he is feeling it more than he ever has. He was to stop work on Saturday but has to go on for a few more days, there are so many vital details concerning everyone's future to be dealt with. We are both exhausted, but basically perfectly happy!

12th November:

Your air letter reached me at lunch time and I am sitting in the Secretariat car park in the car, (3.00 p.m.) scribbling a hasty letter while Alex makes his farewell rounds. I am happy we have heard from you again before we leave tomorrow. At the last moment I decided I could not face going back to the Hostel and saying any more goodbyes. Alex agreed at once and rang up Kuchawe, where we have had such lovely times, and Homer and Theo were happy to have us. (John Carver actually broke down and wept when I said goodbye to him and that just finished me for any more.) We went up on the 6 o'clock clock yesterday and the Paynes joined us for dinner on the 7 o'clock. We had a very pleasant last evening and Jean and I managed not to disgrace ourselves. She is wildly upset at our going, and is already hating the office without me. My last day there was such a strain I asked Bryn if I could stay away in the afternoon, and he instantly agreed. I could see that he was hating every minute too. [It was to be twenty-six years before Bryn and I met again.] I spent nearly all morning saying goodbyes in the Secretariat and then had to face our little farewell party – only Europeans, as the African staff is too frightened or too uninterested nowadays to join in. We had a slightly inhibited celebration, as Chiume's office is only a matter of feet away. I was presented with two huge luxurious bath towels and a trolley set – Jean's choice, as she thought I would welcome household goods. They are lovely, but I am sorry it is not something that would last for always.

The last week has been quite wild, with so many people calling in and inviting us out. Once I left the office the pace quickened at home and Alex can hardly believe that the house has been emptied so thoroughly. It has been marvellous to see him getting more relaxed in spite of his exhaustion, and last night we lay in bed grinning at each other like children. We had *three* blankets on the bed and my nose was cold when I woke this morning. We drove down at 7.30 through swirling mist with Zomba invisible below us. We spent two hours in the Bank sorting out our affairs. It is bliss to have Alex to help me as he is extremely methodical and businesslike. I have managed to save as much as I meant to, and between us we can enjoy a really good trip without feeling we are being too extravagant. The rest goes home to my bank. I wrote to the manager and received a very nice letter back. Geoffrey is coming up to have a farewell drink with us this evening, and then we shall have a quiet dinner and go to bed.

This letter is a little vague, as I feel very much between two worlds. I cannot wait to get right away and start building up a new life with Alex. I refuse to believe there is not some small corner of the earth where we can put down roots, far from the erstwhile paradise from which the almost indecent rush of recent political events in Africa has banished us and our kind forever. Nevertheless, I know that when I go tomorrow, I shall carry within me a deep sense of desolation, which I suspect will never quite leave me. [It never has.]